C++:
The Complete Reference,
Fourth Edition

About the Author

Herbert Schildt is the world's leading programming author. He is an authority on the C, C++, Java, and C# languages, and is a master Windows programmer. His programming books have sold more than 3 million copies worldwide and have been translated into all major foreign languages. He is the author of numerous bestsellers, including C++: The *Complete Reference, C#: The Complete Reference, Java 2: The Complete Reference, C: The Complete Reference, C++ from the Ground Up, C++: A Beginner's Guide, C#: A Beginner's Guide,* and *Java 2: A Beginner's Guide*. Schildt holds a master's degree in computer science from the University of Illinois. He can be reached at his consulting office at (217) 586-4683.

C++:
The Complete Reference,
Fourth Edition

Herbert Schildt

McGraw-Hill/Osborne

New York   Chicago   San Francisco
Lisbon   London   Madrid   Mexico City
Milan   New Delhi   San Juan
Seoul   Singapore   Sydney   Toronto

The McGraw·Hill Companies

McGraw-Hill/Osborne
2600 Tenth Street
Berkeley, California 94710
U.S.A.

To arrange bulk purchase discounts for sales promotions, premiums, or fund-raisers, please contact **McGraw-Hill/**Osborne at the above address. For information on translations or book distributors outside the U.S.A., please see the International Contact Information page immediately following the index of this book.

C++: The Complete Reference, Fourth Edition

90 DOC DOC 019

ISBN 0-07-222680-3

Publisher
Brandon A. Nordin

Vice President & Associate Publisher
Scott Rogers

Acquisitions Editor
Lisa McClain

Senior Project Editor
LeeAnn Pickrell

Acquisitions Coordinator
Athena Honore

Indexer
Sheryl Schildt

Computer Designers
Lucie Ericksen, Melinda Moore Lytle

Illustrators
Michael Mueller, Lyssa Wald

Series Design
Peter F. Hancik

This book was composed with Corel VENTURA™ Publ

Information has been obtained by **McGraw-Hill**/Osborne from sources believe[d] to be reliable. However, because of the possibility of human or mechanical error by our sources, **McGraw-Hill**/Osborn[e] guarantee the accuracy, adequacy, or completeness of any information and is no[t] the results obtained from the use of such information.

Contents at a Glance

Part V	Applying C++

Contents

Part I

The Foundation of C++: The C Subset

Part II

C++

Part III

The Standard Function Library

Part IV

The Standard C++ Class Library

Part V

Applying C++

Introduction

If there is one language that defines modern programming, it is C++. Its syntax, style, and philosophy have set the standard by which all other languages are judged. Furthermore, C++ is the universal language of programming. When an algorithm or technique is described, it is usually done so using the C++ syntax. The long-term success of C++ has also left a lasting impression on computer language development. For example, both Java and C# are descended from C++. Frankly, to be a professional programmer implies proficiency in C++. It is the one language that no programmer can afford to ignore.

This is the fourth edition of *C++: The Complete Reference*. It fully describes and demonstrates the keywords, syntax, functions, classes, and features that define the C++ language. More specifically, this book fully describes Standard C++. This is the version of C++ defined by the ANSI/ISO Standard for C++ and it is the version of C++ that is supported by all major compilers, including Microsoft's Visual C++ and Borland's C++ Builder. Thus, the information in this book is applicable to all modern programming environments.

In the time that has passed since the previous edition of this book, there have been no changes to the C++ language. There have, however, been big changes to the computing environment. For example, a new standard for C, called C99, was created, Java became the dominant language for Web programming, the .NET Framework was released, and C# was invented. Through all the changes of the past few years, one thing has remained constant: the staying power of C++. C++ has been, is, and will remain the preeminent language for the development of high-performance software well into the foreseeable future.

What's New in the Fourth Edition

The overall structure and organization of the fourth edition is similar to the third edition. Thus, if you have been using the third edition, you will feel right at home with the fourth edition. Most of the changes to the fourth edition involve updating and expanding the coverage throughout. In some cases, additional details were added. In other cases, the presentation of a topic was improved. In still other situations, descriptions were modernized to reflect the current programming environment. Several new sections were also added. In Part One, the relationship of C++ to the new C standard, called C99, is noted where appropriate.

Two appendices were also added. The first described the extended keywords defined by Microsoft that are used for creating managed code for the .NET Framework. The second shows off an area of personal interest: robotics. Robotics has long been a hobby of mine and I thought that many readers would find my experimental robot to be of interest. Most of the software that drives it is, of course, written in C++!

Finally, all code examples were retested against the current crop of compilers, including Microsoft's Visual Studio .NET and Borland's C++ Builder.

What's Inside

This books covers in detail all aspects of the C++ language, including its foundation, C. The book is divided into these five parts:

- The C Subset—The foundation of C++
- The C++ language
- The Standard Function Library
- The Standard Class Library
- Sample C++ applications

Part One provides a comprehensive discussion of the C subset of C++. As most readers will know, C is the foundation upon which C++ was built. It is the C subset that defines the bedrock features of C++, including such things as **for** loops and **if** statements. It also defines the essential nature of C++'s block structure, pointers, and functions. Since many readers are already familiar with and proficient in C, discussing the C subset separately in Part One prevents the knowledgeable C programmer from having to "wade through" reams of information he or she already knows. Instead, the experienced C programmer can simply turn to the sections of this book that cover the C++-specific features.

Part Two discusses in detail the features that move beyond the C foundation and define the C++ language These include its object-oriented features such as classes, constructors, destructors, RTTI, and templates. Thus, Part Two covers those constructs that "make C++, C++."

Part Three describes the standard function library and Part Four examines the standard class library, including the STL (Standard Template Library). Part Five shows two practical examples of applying C++ and object-oriented programming.

A Book for All Programmers

This C++ reference is designed for all C++ programmers, regardless of their experience level. It does assume, however, a reader able to create at least a simple program. If you are just learning C++, this book will make an excellent companion to any C++ tutorial and serve as a source of answers to your specific questions. Experienced C++ pros will find the in-depth coverage of C++'s more advanced features especially useful.

If You're Using Windows

If your computer uses Windows, then you have chosen the right language. C++ is completely at home with Windows programming. However, none of the programs in this book are Windows programs. Instead, they are console-based programs. The reason for this is easy to understand: Windows programs are, by their nature, large and complex. The overhead required to create even a minimal Windows skeletal program is 50 to 70 lines of code. To write Windows programs that demonstrate the features of C++ would require hundreds of lines of code each. Put simply, Windows is not an appropriate environment in which to discuss the features of a programming language. However, you can still use a Windows-based compiler to compile the programs in this book because the compiler will automatically create a console session in which to execute your program.

Don't Forget: Code on the Web

Remember, the source code for all of the programs in this book is available free-of-charge on the Web at **www.osborne.com**. Downloading this code prevents you from having to type in the examples.

For Further Study

C++: The Complete Reference is your gateway to the Herb Schildt series of programming books. Here are some others that you will find of interest.

To learn more about C++, try

C++: A Beginner's Guide

C++ from the Ground Up

Teach Yourself C++

STL Programming from the Ground Up

C++ Programmer's Reference

To learn about Java programming, we recommend the following:

Java 2: A Beginner's Guide

Java 2: The Complete Reference

Java 2 Programmer's Reference

To learn about C#, Herb offers these books:

C#: A Beginner's Guide

C#: The Complete Reference

To learn about Windows programming we suggest the following Schildt books:

Windows 98 Programming from the Ground Up

Windows 2000 Programming from the Ground Up

MFC Programming from the Ground Up

The Windows Programming Annotated Archives

If you want to learn about the C language, which is the foundation of all modern programming, then the following titles will be of interest.

C: The Complete Reference
Teach Yourself C

When you need solid answers, fast, turn to Herbert Schildt, the recognized authority on programming.

The Complete Reference

C++

Part I

The Foundation of C++:
The C Subset

This book divides its description of the C++ language into two parts.
Part One discusses the C-like features of C++. This is commonly
referred to as the *C subset* of C++. Part Two describes those features
specific to C++. Together, these parts describe the entire C++ language.

As you may know, C++ was built upon the foundation of C. In fact, C++ includes the entire C language, and (with minor exceptions) all C programs are also C++ programs. When C++ was invented, the C language was used as the starting point. To C were added several new features and extensions designed to support object oriented programming (OOP). However, the C-like aspects of C++ were never abandoned, and the 1989 ANSI/ISO C Standard is a *base document* for the International Standard for C++. Thus, an understanding of C++ implies an understanding of C.

In a book such as this *Complete Reference*, dividing the C++ language into two pieces— the C foundation and the C++-specific features—achieves three major benefits:

- The dividing line between C and C++ is clearly delineated.
- Readers already familiar with C can easily find the C++-specific information.
- It provides a convenient place in which to discuss those features of C++ that relate mostly to the C subset.

Understanding the dividing line between C and C++ is important because both are widely used languages, and it is very likely that you will be called upon to write or maintain both C and C++ code. When working on C code, you need to know where C ends and C++ begins. Many C++ programmers will, from time to time, be required to write code that is limited to the "C subset." This will be especially true for embedded systems programming and the maintenance of existing applications. Knowing the difference between C and C++ is simply part of being a top-notch professional C++ programmer.

A clear understanding of C is also valuable when converting C code into C++. To do this in a professional manner, a solid knowledge of C is required. For example, without a thorough understanding of the C I/O system, it is not possible to convert an I/O-intensive C program into C++ in an efficient manner.

Many readers already know C. Covering the C-like features of C++ in their own section makes it easier for the experienced C programmer to find information about C++ quickly and easily, without having to "wade through" reams of information that he or she already knows. Of course, throughout Part One, any minor differences between C and C++ are noted. Also, separating the C foundation from the more advanced, object-oriented features of C++ makes it possible to tightly focus on those advanced features because all of the basics have already been discussed.

Although C++ contains the entire C language, not all of the features provided by the C language are commonly used when writing "C++-style" programs. For example, the C I/O system is still available to the C++ programmer even though C++ defines its own, object-oriented version. The preprocessor is another example. The preprocessor is very important to C, but less so to C++. Discussing several of the "C-only" features in Part I prevents them from cluttering up the remainder of the book.

Remember: The C subset described in Part One constitutes the core of C++ and the foundation upon which C++'s object-oriented features are built. All the features described here are part of C++ and available for your use.

 Part I of this book is excerpted from my book C: The Complete Reference (McGraw-Hill/Osborne). If you are particularly interested in C, you will find this book helpful.

The
Complete
Reference

Chapter 1

An Overview of C

To understand C++ is to understand the forces that drove its creation, the ideas that shaped it, and the legacy it inherits. Thus, the story of C++ begins with C. This chapter presents an overview of the C programming language, its origins, its uses, and its underlying philosophy. Because C++ is built upon C, this chapter provides an important historical perspective on the roots of C++. Much of what "makes C++, C++" had its genesis in the C language.

The Origins and History of C

C was invented and first implemented by Dennis Ritchie on a DEC PDP-11 that used the UNIX operating system. C is the result of a development process that started with an older language called BCPL. BCPL was developed by Martin Richards, and it influenced a language called B, which was invented by Ken Thompson. B led to the development of C in the 1970s.

For many years, the de facto standard for C was the version supplied with the UNIX operating system. It was first described in *The C Programming Language* by Brian Kernighan and Dennis Ritchie (Englewood Cliffs, N.J.: Prentice-Hall, 1978). In the summer of 1983 a committee was established to create an ANSI (American National Standards Institute) standard that would define the C language. The standardization process took six years (much longer than anyone reasonably expected at the time).

The ANSI C standard was finally adopted in December of 1989, with the first copies becoming available in early 1990. The standard was also adopted by ISO (International Standards Organization) and the resulting standard was typically referred to as ANSI/ISO Standard C. In 1995, Amendment 1 to the C standard was adopted, which, among other things, added several new library functions. The 1989 standard for C, along with Amendment 1, became the *base document* for Standard C++, defining the *C subset* of C++. The version of C defined by the 1989 standard is commonly referred to as C89.

After 1989, C++ took center stage, and during the 1990s the development of a standard for C++ consumed most programmers' attention, with a standard for C++ being adopted by the end of 1998. However, work on C continued along quietly. The end result was the 1999 standard for C, usually referred to as C99. In general, C99 retained nearly all of the features of C89 and did not alter the main aspects of the language. Thus, the C language described by C99 is essentially the same as the one described by C89. The C99 standardization committee focused on two main areas: the addition of several numeric libraries and the development of some special-use, but highly innovative, new features, such as variable- length arrays and the **restrict** pointer qualifier. In a few cases, features originally from C++, such as single-line comments, were also incorporated into C99. Because the standard for C++ was finalized before C99 was created, none of the C99 innovations are found in Standard C++.

C89 vs. C99

Although the innovations in C99 are important from a computer science point of view, they are currently of little practical consequence because, at the time of this writing, no widely-used compiler implements C99. Rather, it is C89 that defines the version of C that most programmers think of as "C" and that all mainstream compilers recognize. Furthermore, it is C89 that forms the C subset of C++. Although several of the new features added by C99 will eventually find their way into the next standard for C++, currently these new features are incompatible with C++.

Because C89 is the standard that forms the C subset of C++, and because it is the version of C that the vast majority of C programmers currently know, it is the version of C discussed in Part I. Thus, when the term *C* is used, take it to mean the C defined by C89. However, important differences between C89 and C99 that relate specifically to C++ are noted, such as when C99 adds a feature that improves compatibility with C++.

C Is a Middle-Level Language

C is often called a *middle-level* computer language. This does not mean that C is less powerful, harder to use, or less developed than a high-level language such as BASIC or Pascal; nor does it imply that C has the cumbersome nature of assembly language (and its associated troubles). Rather, C is thought of as a middle-level language because it combines the best elements of high-level languages with the control and flexibility of assembly language. Table 1-1 shows how C fits into the spectrum of computer languages.

As a middle-level language, C allows the manipulation of bits, bytes, and addresses—the basic elements with which the computer functions. Despite this fact, C code is also

Highest level	Ada
	Modula-2
	Pascal
	COBOL
	FORTRAN
	BASIC
Middle level	Java
	C#
	C++
	C
	Forth
	Macro-assembler
Lowest level	Assembler

Table 1-1. *C's Place in the World of Languages*

portable. *Portability* means that it is easy to adapt software written for one type of computer or operating system to another. For example, if you can easily convert a program written for UNIX so that it runs under Windows, that program is portable.

All high-level programming languages support the concept of data types. A *data type* defines a set of values that a variable can store along with a set of operations that can be performed on that variable. Common data types are integer, character, and real. Although C has five basic built-in data types, it is not a strongly typed language, as are Pascal and Ada. C permits almost all type conversions. For example, you may freely intermix character and integer types in an expression.

Unlike a high-level language, C performs almost no run-time error checking. For example, no check is performed to ensure that array boundaries are not overrun. These types of checks are the responsibility of the programmer.

In the same vein, C does not demand strict type compatibility between a parameter and an argument. As you may know from your other programming experience, a high-level computer language will typically require that the type of an argument be (more or less) exactly the same type as the parameter that will receive the argument. However, such is not the case for C. Instead, C allows an argument to be of any type so long as it can be reasonably converted into the type of the parameter. Further, C provides all of the automatic conversions to accomplish this.

C is special in that it allows the direct manipulation of bits, bytes, words, and pointers. This makes it well suited for system-level programming, where these operations are common.

Another important aspect of C is that it has only a few keywords, which are the commands that make up the C language. For example, C89 defines only 32 keywords, with C99 adding just another 5. Some computer languages have several times more. For comparison, most versions of BASIC have well over 100 keywords!

C Is a Structured Language

In your previous programming experience, you may have heard the term *block-structured* applied to a computer language. Although the term block-structured language does not strictly apply to C, C is commonly referred to simply as a *structured* language. It has many similarities to other structured languages, such as ALGOL, Pascal, and Modula-2.

Note *The reason that C (and C++) is not, technically, a block-structured language is that block-structured languages permit procedures or functions to be declared inside other procedures or functions. However, since C does not allow the creation of functions within functions, it cannot formally be called block-structured.*

The distinguishing feature of a structured language is *compartmentalization* of code and data. This is the ability of a language to section off and hide from the rest of the program all information and instructions necessary to perform a specific task. One way that you achieve compartmentalization is by using subroutines that employ local (temporary) variables. By using local variables, you can write subroutines so that the events that occur within them cause no side effects in other parts of the program.

This capability makes it easier for programs to share sections of code. If you develop compartmentalized functions, you only need to know what a function does, not how it does it. Remember, excessive use of global variables (variables known throughout the entire program) may allow bugs to creep into a program by allowing unwanted side effects. (Anyone who has programmed in standard BASIC is well aware of this problem.)

Note   *The concept of compartmentalization is greatly expanded by C++. Specifically, in C++, one part of your program may tightly control which other parts of your program are allowed access.*

A structured language allows you a variety of programming possibilities. It directly supports several loop constructs, such as **while**, **do-while**, and **for**. In a structured language, the use of **goto** is either prohibited or discouraged and is not the common form of program control (as is the case in standard BASIC and traditional FORTRAN, for example). A structured language allows you to place statements anywhere on a line and does not require a strict field concept (as some older FORTRANs do).

Here are some examples of structured and nonstructured languages:

Nonstructured	Structured
FORTRAN	Pascal
BASIC	Ada
COBOL	Java
	C#
	C++
	C
	Modula-2

Structured languages tend to be modern. In fact, a mark of an old computer language is that it is nonstructured. Today, few programmers would consider using a nonstructured language for serious, new programs.

Note   *New versions of many older languages have attempted to add structured elements. BASIC is an example—in particular Visual Basic by Microsoft. However, the shortcomings of these languages can never be fully mitigated because they were not designed with structured features from the beginning.*

C's main structural component is the function—C's stand-alone subroutine. In C, functions are the building blocks in which all program activity occurs. They allow you to define and code separately the separate tasks in a program, thus allowing your programs to be modular. After you have created a function, you can rely on it to work properly in various situations without creating side effects in other parts of the program. Being able to create stand-alone functions is extremely critical in larger projects where one programmer's code must not accidentally affect another's code.

Another way to structure and compartmentalize code in C is through the use of code blocks. A *code block* is a logically connected group of program statements that is treated as a unit. In C, you create a code block by placing a sequence of statements between opening and closing curly braces. In this example,

```
if (x < 10)  {
  printf("Too low, try again.\n");
  scanf("%d", &x);
}
```

the two statements after the **if** and between the curly braces are both executed if **x** is less than 10. These two statements together with the braces represent a code block. They are a logical unit: one of the statements cannot execute without the other executing also. Code blocks allow many algorithms to be implemented with clarity, elegance, and efficiency. Moreover, they help the programmer better conceptualize the true nature of the algorithm being implemented.

C Is a Programmer's Language

Surprisingly, not all computer programming languages are for programmers. Consider the classic examples of nonprogrammer languages, COBOL and BASIC. COBOL was designed not to better the programmer's lot, not to improve the reliability of the code produced, and not even to improve the speed with which code can be written. Rather, COBOL was designed, in part, to enable nonprogrammers to read and presumably (however unlikely) to understand the program. BASIC was created essentially to allow nonprogrammers to program a computer to solve relatively simple problems.

In contrast, C was created, influenced, and field-tested by working programmers. The end result is that C gives the programmer what the programmer wants: few restrictions, few complaints, block structures, stand-alone functions, and a compact set of keywords. By using C, you can nearly achieve the efficiency of assembly code combined with the structure of ALGOL or Modula-2. It is no wonder that C and C++ are easily two of the most popular languages among topflight professional programmers.

The fact that you can often use C in place of assembly language is a major factor in its popularity among programmers. Assembly language uses a symbolic representation of the actual binary code that the computer executes directly. Each assembly-language operation maps into a single task for the computer to perform. Although assembly language gives programmers the potential to accomplish tasks with maximum flexibility and efficiency, it is notoriously difficult to work with when developing and debugging a program. Furthermore, since assembly language is unstructured, the final program tends to be spaghetti code—a tangled mess of jumps, calls, and indexes. This lack of structure makes assembly-language programs difficult to read, enhance, and maintain.

Perhaps more important, assembly-language routines are not portable between machines with different central processing units (CPUs).

Initially, C was used for systems programming. A *systems program* forms a portion of the operating system of the computer or its support utilities. For example, the following are usually called systems programs:

- Operating systems
- Interpreters
- Editors
- Compilers
- File utilities
- Performance enhancers
- Real-time executives
- Device drivers

As C grew in popularity, many programmers began to use it to program all tasks because of its portability and efficiency—and because they liked it! At the time of its creation, C was a much longed-for, dramatic improvement in programming languages. Of course, C++ has carried on this tradition.

With the advent of C++, some thought that C as a distinct language would die out. Such has not been the case. First, not all programs require the application of the object-oriented programming features provided by C++. For example, applications such as embedded systems are still typically programmed in C. Second, much of the world still runs on C code, and those programs will continue to be enhanced and maintained. While C's greatest legacy is as the foundation for C++, C will continue to be a vibrant, widely used language for many years to come.

The Form of a C Program

Table 1-2 lists the 32 keywords that, combined with the formal C syntax, form C89, the C subset of C++. All are, of course, also keywords in C++.

In addition, many compilers have added several keywords that better exploit their operating environment. For example, several compilers include keywords to manage the memory organization of the 8086 family of processors, to support inter-language programming, and to access interrupts. Here is a list of some commonly used extended keywords:

asm	_cs	_ds	_es
_ss	cdecl	far	huge
interrupt	near	pascal	

auto	double	int	struct
break	else	long	switch
case	enum	register	typedef
char	extern	return	union
const	float	short	unsigned
continue	for	signed	void
default	goto	sizeof	volatile
do	if	static	while

Table 1-2.   *The 32 Keywords Defined by the C Subset of C++*

Your compiler may also support other extensions that help it take better advantage of its specific environment.

Notice that all of the keywords are lowercase. C/C++ is *case-sensitive*. Thus, in a C/C++ program, uppercase and lowercase are different. This means that **else** is a keyword, while **ELSE** is not. You may not use a keyword for any other purpose in a program— that is, you may not use it as a variable or function name.

All C programs consist of one or more functions. The only function that must be present is called **main( )**, which is the first function called when program execution begins. In well-written C code, **main( )** contains what is, in essence, an outline of what the program does. The outline is composed of function calls. Although **main( )** is not a keyword, treat it as if it were. For example, don't try to use **main** as the name of a variable because you will probably confuse the compiler.

The general form of a C program is illustrated in Figure 1-1, where **f1( )** through **fN( )** represent user-defined functions.

The Library and Linking

Technically speaking, you can create a useful, functional C or C++ program that consists solely of the statements that you actually created. However, this is quite rare because neither C nor C++ provides any keywords that perform such things as I/O operations, high-level mathematical computations, or character handling. As a result, most programs include calls to various functions contained in the *standard library*.

All C++ compilers come with a standard library of functions that perform most commonly needed tasks. Standard C++ specifies a minimal set of functions that will be supported by all compilers. However, your compiler will probably contain many other functions. For example, the standard library does not define any graphics functions, but your compiler will probably include some.

```
global declarations

return-type main (parameter list)

{

 statement sequence

}

return-type f1 (parameter list)

{

 statement sequence

}

return-type f2 (parameter list)

{

 statement sequence

}

.

.

.

return-type fN(parameter list)

{

 statement sequence

}
```

Figure 1-1.   *The general form of a C program*

The C++ standard library can be divided into two halves: the standard function library and the class library. The standard function library is inherited from the C language. C++ supports the entire function library defined by C89. Thus, all of the standard C functions are available for use in C++ programs that you write.

In addition to the standard function library, C++ also defines its own class library. The class library provides object-oriented routines that your programs may use. It also defines the Standard Template Library (STL), which offers off-the-shelf solutions to a variety of programming problems. Both the class library and the STL are discussed later in this book. In Part One, only the standard function library is used, since it is the only one that is also defined by C.

The standard function library contains most of the general-purpose functions that you will use. When you call a library function, the compiler "remembers" its name. Later, the linker combines the code you wrote with the object code for the library function, which is found in the standard library. This process is called *linking*. Some compilers have their own linker, while others use the standard linker supplied by your operating system.

The functions in the library are in *relocatable* format. This means that the memory addresses for the various machine-code instructions have not been absolutely defined— only offset information has been kept. When your program links with the functions in the standard library, these memory offsets are used to create the actual addresses used. Several technical manuals and books explain this process in more detail. However, you do not need any further explanation of the actual relocation process to program in C++.

Many of the functions that you will need as you write programs are in the standard library. They act as building blocks that you combine. If you write a function that you will use again and again, you can place it into a library, too.

Separate Compilation

Most short programs are completely contained within one source file. However, as a program's length grows, so does its compile time (and long compile times make for short tempers). Hence, C/C++ allows a program to be contained in multiple files and lets you compile each file separately. Once you have compiled all files, they are linked, along with any library routines, to form the complete object code. The advantage of separate compilation is that if you change the code of one file, you do not need to recompile the entire program. On all but the most simple projects, this saves a substantial amount of time. The user documentation to your C/C++ compiler will contain instructions for compiling multiple-file programs.

Understanding the .C and .CPP File Extensions

The programs in Part One of this book are, of course, valid C++ programs and can be compiled using any modern C++ compiler. They are also valid C programs and can be compiled using a C compiler. Thus, if you are called upon to write C programs, the programs shown in Part One qualify as examples. Traditionally, C programs use the file extension **.C** and C++ programs use the extension **.CPP**. A C++ compiler uses the file extension to determine what type of program it is compiling. This is important because the compiler assumes that any program using the **.C** extension is a C program and that any file using **.CPP** is a C++ program. Unless explicitly noted otherwise, you may use either extension for the programs in Part One. However, the programs in the rest of this book will require **.CPP**.

One last point: Although C is a subset of C++, there are a few minor differences between the two languages and in a few cases, you may need to compile a C program *as a C program* (using the **.C** extension). Any instances of this will be noted.

The
Complete
Reference

Chapter 2

Expressions

This chapter examines the most fundamental element of the C (as well as the C++) language: the expression. As you will see, expressions in C/C++ are substantially more general and more powerful than in most other computer languages. Expressions are formed from these atomic elements: data and operators. Data may be represented either by variables or by constants. Like most other computer languages, C/C++ supports a number of different types of data. It also provides a wide variety of operators.

The Five Basic Data Types

There are five atomic data types in the C subset: character, integer, floating-point, double floating-point, and valueless (**char**, **int**, **float**, **double**, and **void**, respectively). As you will see, all other data types in C are based upon one of these types. The size and range of these data types may vary between processor types and compilers. However, in all cases a character is 1 byte. The size of an integer is usually the same as the word length of the execution environment of the program. For most 16-bit environments, such as DOS or Windows 3.1, an integer is 16 bits. For most 32-bit environments, such as Windows 2000, an integer is 32 bits. However, you cannot make assumptions about the size of an integer if you want your programs to be portable to the widest range of environments. It is important to understand that both C and C++ only stipulate the *minimal range* of each data type, not its size in bytes.

Note   *To the five basic data types defined by C, C++ adds two more: **bool** and **wchar_t**. These are discussed in Part Two.*

The exact format of floating-point values will depend upon how they are implemented. Integers will generally correspond to the natural size of a word on the host computer. Values of type **char** are generally used to hold values defined by the ASCII character set. Values outside that range may be handled differently by different compilers.

The range of **float** and **double** will depend upon the method used to represent the floating-point numbers. Whatever the method, the range is quite large. Standard C specifies that the minimum range for a floating-point value is 1E−37 to 1E+37. The minimum number of digits of precision for each floating-point type is shown in Table 2-1.

Note   *Standard C++ does not specify a minimum size or range for the basic types. Instead, it simply states that they must meet certain requirements. For example, Standard C++ states that an **int** will "have the natural size suggested by the architecture of the execution environment." In all cases, this will meet or exceed the minimum ranges specified by Standard C. Each C++ compiler specifies the size and range of the basic types in the header **<climits>**.*

Type	Typical Size in Bits	Minimal Range
char	8	−127 to 127
unsigned char	8	0 to 255
signed char	8	−127 to 127
int	16 or 32	−32,767 to 32,767
unsigned int	16 or 32	0 to 65,535
signed int	16 or 32	same as **int**
short int	16	−32,767 to 32,767
unsigned short int	16	0 to 65,535
signed short int	16	same as **short int**
long int	32	−2,147,483,647 to 2,147,483,647
signed long int	32	same as **long int**
unsigned long int	32	0 to 4,294,967,295
float	32	Six digits of precision
double	64	Ten digits of precision
long double	80	Ten digits of precision

Table 2-1.   *All Data Types Defined by the ANSI/ISO C Standard*

The type **void** either explicitly declares a function as returning no value or creates generic pointers. Both of these uses are discussed in subsequent chapters.

Modifying the Basic Types

Except for type **void**, the basic data types may have various modifiers preceding them. You use a *modifier* to alter the meaning of the base type to fit various situations more precisely. The list of modifiers is shown here:

    signed
    unsigned
    long
    short

You can apply the modifiers **signed**, **short**, **long**, and **unsigned** to integer base types. You can apply **unsigned** and **signed** to characters. You may also apply **long** to **double**. Table 2-1 shows all valid data type combinations, along with their minimal ranges and approximate bit widths. (These values also apply to a typical C++ implementation.) Remember, the table shows the *minimum range* that these types will have as specified by Standard C/C++, not their typical range. For example, on computers that use two's complement arithmetic (which is nearly all), an integer will have a range of at least 32,767 to –32,768.

The use of **signed** on integers is allowed, but redundant because the default integer declaration assumes a signed number. The most important use of **signed** is to modify **char** in implementations in which **char** is unsigned by default.

The difference between signed and unsigned integers is in the way that the high-order bit of the integer is interpreted. If you specify a signed integer, the compiler generates code that assumes that the high-order bit of an integer is to be used as a *sign flag*. If the sign flag is 0, the number is positive; if it is 1, the number is negative.

In general, negative numbers are represented using the *two's complement* approach, which reverses all bits in the number (except the sign flag), adds 1 to this number, and sets the sign flag to 1.

Signed integers are important for a great many algorithms, but they only have half the absolute magnitude of their unsigned relatives. For example, here is 32,767:

    0 1 1 1 1 1 1 1 1 1 1 1 1 1 1 1

If the high-order bit were set to 1, the number would be interpreted as –1. However, if you declare this to be an **unsigned int**, the number becomes 65,535 when the high-order bit is set to 1.

When a type modifier is used by itself (that is, when it does not precede a basic type), then **int** is assumed. Thus, the following sets of type specifiers are equivalent:

Specifier	Same As
signed	signed int
unsigned	unsigned int
long	long int
short	short int

Although the **int** is implied, many programmers specify the **int** anyway.

Identifier Names

In C/C++, the names of variables, functions, labels, and various other user-defined objects are called *identifiers*. These identifiers can vary from one to several characters.

The first character must be a letter or an underscore, and subsequent characters must be either letters, digits, or underscores. Here are some correct and incorrect identifier names:

Correct	Incorrect
Count	1count
test23	hi!there
high_balance	high...balance

In C, identifiers may be of any length. However, not all characters will necessarily be significant. If the identifier will be involved in an external link process, then at least the first six characters will be significant. These identifiers, called *external names*, include function names and global variables that are shared between files. If the identifier is not used in an external link process, then at least the first 31 characters will be significant. This type of identifier is called an *internal name* and includes the names of local variables, for example. In C++, there is no limit to the length of an identifier, and at least the first 1,024 characters are significant. This difference may be important if you are converting a program from C to C++.

In an identifier, upper- and lowercase are treated as distinct. Hence, **count**, **Count**, and **COUNT** are three separate identifiers.

An identifier cannot be the same as a C or C++ keyword, and should not have the same name as functions that are in the C or C++ library.

Variables

As you probably know, a *variable* is a named location in memory that is used to hold a value that may be modified by the program. All variables must be declared before they can be used. The general form of a declaration is

type variable_list;

Here, *type* must be a valid data type plus any modifiers, and *variable_list* may consist of one or more identifier names separated by commas. Here are some declarations:

```
int i,j,l;
short int si;
unsigned int ui;
double balance, profit, loss;
```

Remember, in C/C++ the name of a variable has nothing to do with its type.

Where Variables Are Declared

Variables will be declared in three basic places: inside functions, in the definition of function parameters, and outside of all functions. These are local variables, formal parameters, and global variables.

Local Variables

Variables that are declared inside a function are called *local variables*. In some C/C++ literature, these variables are referred to as *automatic* variables. This book uses the more common term, local variable. Local variables may be referenced only by statements that are inside the block in which the variables are declared. In other words, local variables are not known outside their own code block. Remember, a block of code begins with an opening curly brace and terminates with a closing curly brace.

Local variables exist only while the block of code in which they are declared is executing. That is, a local variable is created upon entry into its block and destroyed upon exit.

The most common code block in which local variables are declared is the function. For example, consider the following two functions:

```
void func1(void)
{
  int x;

  x = 10;
}

void func2(void)
{
  int x;

  x = -199;
}
```

The integer variable **x** is declared twice, once in **func1( )** and once in **func2( )**. The **x** in **func1( )** has no bearing on or relationship to the **x** in **func2( )**. This is because each **x** is known only to the code within the block in which it is declared.

The C language contains the keyword **auto**, which you can use to declare local variables. However, since all nonglobal variables are, by default, assumed to be **auto**, this keyword is virtually never used. Hence, the examples in this book will not use it. (It has been said that **auto** was included in C to provide for source-level compatibility with its predecessor B. Further, **auto** is supported in C++ to provide compatibility with C.)

For reasons of convenience and tradition, most programmers declare all the variables used by a function immediately after the function's opening curly braceand before any other statements. However, you may declare local variables within any code block. The block defined by a function is simply a special case. For example,

```
void f(void)
{
  int t;

  scanf("%d%*c", &t);

  if(t==1) {
    char s[80];   /* this is created only upon
                     entry into this block */
    printf("Enter name:");
    gets(s);
    /* do something ... */
  }
}
```

Here, the local variable **s** is created upon entry into the **if** code block and destroyed upon exit. Furthermore, **s** is known only within the **if** block and may not be referenced elsewhere—even in other parts of the function that contains it.

Declaring variables within the block of code that uses them helps prevent unwanted side effects. Since a variable does not exist outside the block in which it is declared, it cannot be accidentally altered.

There is an important difference between C (as defined by C89) and C++ as to where you can declare local variables. In C, you must declare all local variables at the start of a block, prior to any "action" statements. For example, in C89 the following function is in error.

```
/* For C89, this function is in error,
   but it is perfectly acceptable for C++.
*/
void f(void)
{
  int i;

  i = 10;

  int j;  /* this line will cause an error */
```

```
   j = 20;
}
```

However, in C++, this function is perfectly valid because you can declare local variables at any point within a block, prior to their first use. (The topic of C++ variable declaration is discussed in depth in Part Two.) As a point of interest, C99 allows you to define variables at any point within a block.

Because local variables are created and destroyed with each entry and exit from the block in which they are declared, their content is lost once the block is left. This is especially important to remember when calling a function. When a function is called, its local variables are created, and upon its return they are destroyed. This means that local variables cannot retain their values between calls. (However, you can direct the compiler to retain their values by using the **static** modifier.)

Unless otherwise specified, local variables are stored on the stack. The fact that the stack is a dynamic and changing region of memory explains why local variables cannot, in general, hold their values between function calls.

You can initialize a local variable to some known value. This value will be assigned to the variable each time the block of code in which it is declared is entered. For example, the following program prints the number 10 ten times:

```
#include <stdio.h>

void f(void);

int main(void)
{
  int i;

  for(i=0; i<10; i++)  f();

  return 0;
}

void f(void)
{
  int j = 10;

  printf("%d ", j);

  j++;  /* this line has no lasting effect */
}
```

Formal Parameters

If a function is to use arguments, it must declare variables that will accept the values
of the arguments. These variables are called the *formal parameters* of the function. They
behave like any other local variables inside the function. As shown in the following
program fragment, their declarations occur after the function name and inside
parentheses:

```
/* Return 1 if c is part of string s; 0 otherwise */
int is_in(char *s, char c)
{
  while(*s)
    if(*s==c) return 1;
    else s++;

  return 0;
}
```

The function **is_in( )** has two parameters: **s** and **c**. This function returns 1 if the character
specified in **c** is contained within the string **s**; 0 if it is not.

You must specify the type of the formal parameters by declaring them as just shown.
Then you may use them inside the function as normal local variables. Keep in mind that,
as local variables, they are also dynamic and are destroyed upon exit from the function.

As with local variables, you may make assignments to a function's formal parameters
or use them in any allowable expression. Even though these variables receive the value of
the arguments passed to the function, you can use them like any other local variable.

Global Variables

Unlike local variables, *global variables* are known throughout the program and may be
used by any piece of code. Also, they will hold their value throughout the program's
execution. You create global variables by declaring them outside of any function. Any
expression may access them, regardless of what block of code that expression is in.

In the following program, the variable **count** has been declared outside of all functions.
Although its declaration occurs before the **main( )** function, you could have placed it
anywhere before its first use as long as it was not in a function. However, it is usually
best to declare global variables at the top of the program.

```
#include <stdio.h>
int count;  /* count is global */

void func1(void);
```

```
void func2(void);

int main(void)
{
  count = 100;
  func1();

  return 0;
}

void func1(void)
{
  int temp;

  temp = count;
  func2();
  printf("count is %d", count); /* will print 100 */
}

void func2(void)
{
  int count;

  for(count=1; count<10; count++)
    putchar('.');
}
```

Look closely at this program. Notice that although neither **main( )** nor **func1( )** has declared the variable **count**, both may use it. **func2( )**, however, has declared a local variable called **count**. When **func2( )** refers to **count**, it refers to only its local variable, not the global one. If a global variable and a local variable have the same name, all references to that variable name inside the code block in which the local variable is declared will refer to that local variable and have no effect on the global variable. This can be convenient, but forgetting it can cause your program to act strangely, even though it looks correct.

Storage for global variables is in a fixed region of memory set aside for this purpose by the compiler. Global variables are helpful when many functions in your program use the same data. You should avoid using unnecessary global variables, however. They take up memory the entire time your program is executing, not just when they are needed. In addition, using a global where a local variable would do makes a function less general because it relies on something that must be defined outside itself. Finally, using a large number of global variables can lead to program errors because of unknown and unwanted side effects. A major problem in developing large programs is the accidental changing of a variable's value because it was used elsewhere in the program. This can happen in C/C++ if you use too many global variables in your programs.

The const and volatile Qualifiers

There are two qualifiers that control how variables may be accessed or modified: **const** and **volatile**. They must precede the type modifiers and the type names that they qualify. These qualifiers are formally referred to as the *cv-qualifiers*.

const

Variables of type **const** may not be changed by your program. (A **const** variable can be given an initial value, however.) The compiler is free to place variables of this type into read-only memory (ROM). For example,

```
const int a=10;
```

creates an integer variable called **a** with an initial value of 10 that your program may not modify. However, you can use the variable **a** in other types of expressions. A **const** variable will receive its value either from an explicit initialization or by some hardware-dependent means.

The **const** qualifier can be used to protect the objects pointed to by the arguments to a function from being modified by that function. That is, when a pointer is passed to a function, that function can modify the actual variable pointed to by the pointer. However, if the pointer is specified as **const** in the parameter declaration, the function code won't be able to modify what it points to. For example, the **sp_to_dash( )** function in the following program prints a dash for each space in its string argument. That is, the string "this is a test" will be printed as "this-is-a-test". The use of **const** in the parameter declaration ensures that the code inside the function cannot modify the object pointed to by the parameter.

```
#include <stdio.h>

void sp_to_dash(const char *str);

int main(void)
{
  sp_to_dash("this is a test");

  return 0;
}
```

```
void sp_to_dash(const char *str)
{
  while(*str) {
    if(*str== ' ') printf("%c", '-');
    else printf("%c", *str);
    str++;
  }
}
```

If you had written **sp_to_dash( )** in such a way that the string would be modified, it would not compile. For example, if you had coded **sp_to_dash( )** as follows, you would receive a compile-time error:

```
/* This is wrong. */
void sp_to_dash(const char *str)
{
  while(*str) {
    if(*str==' ' ) *str = '-'; /* can't do this; str is const */
    printf("%c", *str);
    str++;
  }
}
```

Many functions in the standard library use **const** in their parameter declarations. For example, the **strlen( )** function has this prototype:

size_t strlen(const char *str);

Specifying *str* as **const** ensures that **strlen( )** will not modify the string pointed to by *str*. In general, when a standard library function has no need to modify an object pointed to by a calling argument, it is declared as **const.**

You can also use **const** to verify that your program does not modify a variable. Remember, a variable of type **const** can be modified by something outside your program. For example, a hardware device may set its value. However, by declaring a variable as **const**, you can prove that any changes to that variable occur because of external events.

volatile

The modifier **volatile** tells the compiler that a variable's value may be changed in ways not explicitly specified by the program. For example, a global variable's address may be passed to the operating system's clock routine and used to hold the real time of the system. In this situation, the contents of the variable are altered without any explicit assignment statements in the program. This is important because most C/C++ compilers automatically optimize certain expressions by assuming that a variable's content is unchanging if it does not occur on the left side of an assignment statement; thus, it might not be reexamined each time it is referenced. Also, some compilers change the order of evaluation of an expression during the compilation process. The **volatile** modifier prevents these changes.

You can use **const** and **volatile** together. For example, if 0x30 is assumed to be the value of a port that is changed by external conditions only, the following declaration would prevent any possibility of accidental side effects:

```
const volatile char *port = (const volatile char *) 0x30;
```

Storage Class Specifiers

There are four storage class specifiers supported by C:

    extern
    static
    register
    auto

These specifiers tell the compiler how to store the subsequent variable. The general form of a declaration that uses one is shown here.

    storage_specifier type var_name;

Notice that the storage specifier precedes the rest of the variable declaration.

 *C++ adds another storage-class specifier called **mutable**, which is described in Part Two.*

extern

Before examining **extern**, a brief description of C/C++ linkage is in order. C and C++ define three categories of linkage: external, internal, and none. In general, functions and global variables have external linkage. This means that they are available to all files that comprise a program. Global objects declared as **static** (described in the next section) have internal linkage. These are known only within the file in which they are declared. Local variables have no linkage and are therefore known only within their own block.

The principal use of **extern** is to specify that an object is declared with external linkage elsewhere in the program. To understand why this is important it is necessary to understand the difference between a *declaration* and a *definition*. A declaration declares the name and type of an object. A definition causes storage to be allocated for the object. While there can be many declarations of the same object, there can be *only one* definition for the object.

In most cases, variable declarations are also definitions. However, by preceding a variable name with the **extern** specifier, you can declare a variable without defining it. Thus, when you need to refer to a variable that is defined in another part of your program, you can declare that variable using **extern**.

Here is an example that uses **extern**. Notice that the global variables **first** and **last** are declared *after* **main( )**.

```
#include <stdio.h>

int main(void)
{
  extern int first, last; /* use global vars */

  printf("%d %d", first, last);

  return 0;
}

/* global definition of first and last */
int first = 10, last = 20;
```

This programs outputs **10 20** because the global variables **first** and **last** used by the **printf( )** statement are initialized to these values. Because the **extern** declaration in **main( )** tells the compiler that **first** and **last** are declared elsewhere (in this case, later in the same file), the program can be compiled without error even though **first** and **last** are used prior to their definition.

It is important to understand that the **extern** variable declarations as shown in the preceding program are necessary only because **first** and **last** had not yet been declared prior to their use in **main( )**. Had their declarations occurred prior to **main( )**, then there would have been no need for the **extern** statement. Remember, if the compiler finds a variable that has not been declared within the current block, the compiler checks if it matches any of the variables declared within enclosing blocks. If it does not, the compiler then checks the previously declared global variables. If a match is found, the compiler assumes that that is the variable being referenced. The **extern** specifier is needed when you want to use a variable that is declared later in the file.

As mentioned, **extern** allows you to declare a variable without defining it. However, if you give that variable an initialization, then the **extern** declaration becomes a definition. This is important because an object can have multiple declarations, but only one definition.

There is an important use of **extern** that relates to mutiple-file programs. In C/C++, a program can be spread across two or more files, compiled separately, and then linked together. When this is the case, there must be some way of telling all the files about the global variables required by the program. The best (and most portable) way to do this is to declare all of your global variables in one file and use **extern** declarations in the other, as in Figure 2-1.

In File Two, the global variable list was copied from File One and the **extern** specifier was added to the declarations. The **extern** specifier tells the compiler that the variable types and names that follow it have been defined elsewhere. In other words, **extern** lets the compiler know what the types and names are for these global variables without actually creating storage for them again. When the linker links the two modules, all references to the external variables are resolved.

In real world, multi-file programs, **extern** declarations are normally contained in a header file that is simply included with each source code file. This is both easier and less error prone than manually duplicating **extern** declarations in each file.

In C++, the **extern** specifier has another use, which is described in Part Two.

Note   *extern can also be applied to a function declaration, but doing so is redundant.*

```
File One                        File Two

int x, y;                       extern int x, y;

char ch;                        extern char ch;

int main(void)                  void func22(void)

{                               {

 /* ... */                       x = y / 10;

}                               }


void func1(void)                void func23(void)

{                               {

 x = 123;                        y = 10;

}                               }
```

Figure 2-1.   *Using global variables in separately compiled modules*

static Variables

static variables are permanent variables within their own function or file. Unlike global variables, they are not known outside their function or file, but they maintain their values between calls. This feature makes them useful when you write generalized functions and function libraries that other programmers may use. **static** has different effects upon local variables and global variables.

static Local Variables

When you apply the **static** modifier to a local variable, the compiler creates permanent storage for it, much as it creates storage for a global variable. The key difference between a **static** local variable and a global variable is that the **static** local variable remains known only to the block in which it is declared. In simple terms, a **static** local variable is a local variable that retains its value between function calls.

static local variables are very important to the creation of stand-alone functions because several types of routines must preserve a value between calls. If **static** variables were not allowed, globals would have to be used, opening the door to possible side effects. An example of a function that benefits from a **static** local variable is a number-series generator that produces a new value based on the previous one. You could use a global variable to hold this value. However, each time the function is used in a program, you would have to declare that global variable and make sure that it did not conflict with any other global variables already in place. The better solution is to declare the variable that holds the generated number to be **static**, as in this program fragment:

```
int series(void)
{
  static int series_num;

  series_num = series_num+23;
  return series_num;
}
```

In this example, the variable **series_num** stays in existence between function calls, instead of coming and going the way a normal local variable would. This means that each call to **series( )** can produce a new member in the series based on the preceding number without declaring that variable globally.

You can give a **static** local variable an initialization value. This value is assigned only once, at program start-up—not each time the block of code is entered, as with normal local variables. For example, this version of **series( )** initializes **series_num** to 100:

```
int series(void)
{
```

```
static int series_num = 100;

series_num = series_num+23;
return series_num;
}
```

As the function now stands, the series will always begin with the same value—in this case, 123. While this might be acceptable for some applications, most series generators need to let the user specify the starting point. One way to give **series_num** a user-specified value is to make it a global variable and then let the user set its value. However, not defining **series_num** as global was the point of making it **static**. This leads to the second use of **static.**

static Global Variables

Applying the specifier **static** to a global variable instructs the compiler to create a global variable that is known only to the file in which you declared it. This means that even though the variable is global, routines in other files may have no knowledge of it or alter its contents directly, keeping it free from side effects. For the few situations where a local **static** variable cannot do the job, you can create a small file that contains only the functions that need the global **static** variable, separately compile that file, and use it without fear of side effects.

To illustrate a global **static** variable, the series generator example from the previous section is recoded so that a seed value initializes the series through a call to a second function called **series_start( )**. The entire file containing **series( )**, **series_start( )**, and **series_num** is shown here:

```
/* This must all be in one file - preferably by itself. */

static int series_num;
void series_start(int seed);
int series(void);

int series(void)
{
  series_num = series_num+23;
  return series_num;
}

/* initialize series_num */
void series_start(int seed)
{
  series_num = seed;
}
```

Calling **series_start( )** with some known integer value initializes the series generator. After that, calls to **series( )** generate the next element in the series.

To review: The names of local **static** variables are known only to the block of code in which they are declared; the names of global **static** variables are known only to the file in which they reside. If you place the **series( )** and **series_start( )** functions in a library, you can use the functions but cannot reference the variable **series_num**, which is hidden from the rest of the code in your program. In fact, you can even declare and use another variable called **series_num** in your program (in another file, of course). In essence, the **static** modifier permits variables that are known only to the functions that need them, without unwanted side effects.

static variables enable you to hide portions of your program from other portions. This can be a tremendous advantage when you are trying to manage a very large and complex program.

 *In C++, the preceding use of **static** is still supported, but deprecated. This means that it is not recommended for new code. Instead, you should use a namespace, which is described in Part Two.*

register Variables

The **register** storage specifier originally applied only to variables of type **int, char**, or pointer types. However, **register**'s definition has been broadened so that it applies to any type of variable.

Originally, the **register** specifier requested that the compiler keep the value of a variable in a register of the CPU rather than in memory, where normal variables are stored. This meant that operations on a **register** variable could occur much faster than on a normal variable because the **register** variable was actually held in the CPU and did not require a memory access to determine or modify its value.

Today, the definition of **register** has been greatly expanded and it now may be applied to any type of variable. Standard C simply states "that access to the object be as fast as possible." (Standard C++ states that **register** is a "hint to the implementation that the object so declared will be heavily used.") In practice, characters and integers are still stored in registers in the CPU. Larger objects like arrays obviously cannot be stored in a register, but they may still receive preferential treatment by the compiler. Depending upon the implementation of the C/C++ compiler and its operating environment, **register** variables may be handled in any way deemed fit by the compiler's implementor. In fact, it is technically permissible for a compiler to ignore the **register** specifier altogether and treat variables modified by it as if they weren't, but this is seldom done in practice.

You can only apply the **register** specifier to local variables and to the formal parameters in a function. Global **register** variables are not allowed. Here is an example that uses **register** variables. This function computes the result of M^e for integers:

```
int int_pwr(register int m,  register int e)
{
  register int temp;

  temp = 1;

  for(; e; e--) temp = temp * m;
  return temp;
}
```

In this example, **e**, **m**, and **temp** are declared as **register** variables because they are all used within the loop. The fact that **register** variables are optimized for speed makes them ideal for control of or use in loops. Generally, **register** variables are used where they will do the most good, which are often places where many references will be made to the same variable. This is important because you can declare any number of variables as being of type **register**, but not all will receive the same access speed optimization.

The number of **register** variables optimized for speed within any one code block is determined by both the environment and the specific implementation of C/C++. You don't have to worry about declaring too many **register** variables because the compiler automatically transforms **register** variables into nonregister variables when the limit is reached. (This ensures portability of code across a broad line of processors.)

Usually at least two **register** variables of type **char** or **int** can actually be held in the registers of the CPU. Because environments vary widely, consult your compiler's documentation to determine if you can apply any other types of optimization options.

In C, you cannot find the address of a **register** variable using the & operator (discussed later in this chapter). This makes sense because a **register** variable might be stored in a register of the CPU, which is not usually addressable. But this restriction does not apply to C++. However, taking the address of a **register** variable in C++ may prevent it from being fully optimized.

Although the description of **register** has been broadened beyond its traditional meaning, in practice it still generally has a significant effect only with integer and character types. Thus, you should probably not count on substantial speed improvements for other variable types.

Variable Initializations

You can give variables a value as you declare them by placing an equal sign and a value after the variable name. The general form of initialization is

type variable_name = value;

Some examples are

```
char ch = 'a';
int first = 0;
float balance = 123.23;
```

Global and **static** local variables are initialized only at the start of the program. Local variables (excluding **static** local variables) are initialized each time the block in which they are declared is entered. Local variables that are not initialized have unknown values before the first assignment is made to them. Uninitialized global and **static** local variables are automatically set to zero.

Constants

Constants refer to fixed values that the program cannot alter. Constants can be of any of the basic data types. The way each constant is represented depends upon its type. Constants are also called *literals*.

Character constants are enclosed between single quotes. For example 'a' and '%' are both character constants. Both C and C++ define wide characters (used mostly in non-English language environments), which are 16 bits long. To specify a wide character constant, precede the character with an **L**. For example,

```
wchar_t wc;
wc = L'A';
```

Here, **wc** is assigned the wide-character constant equivalent of A. The type of wide characters is **wchar_t**. In C, this type is defined in a header file and is not a built-in type. In C++, **wchar_t** is built in.

Integer constants are specified as numbers without fractional components. For example, 10 and –100 are integer constants. Floating-point constants require the decimal point followed by the number's fractional component. For example, 11.123 is a floating-point constant. C/C++ also allows you to use scientific notation for floating-point numbers.

There are two floating-point types: **float** and **double**. There are also several variations of the basic types that you can generate using the type modifiers. By default, the compiler fits a numeric constant into the smallest compatible data type that will hold it. Therefore, assuming 16-bit integers, 10 is **int** by default, but 103,000 is a **long**. Even though the value 10 could fit into a character type, the compiler will not cross type boundaries. The only exception to the smallest type rule are floating-point constants, which are assumed to be **double**s.

For most programs you will write, the compiler defaults are adequate. However, you can specify precisely the type of numeric constant you want by using a suffix. For floating-point types, if you follow the number with an F, the number is treated

as a **float**. If you follow it with an L, the number becomes a **long double**. For integer
types, the U suffix stands for **unsigned** and the L for **long**. Here are some examples:

Data type	Constant examples
int	1 123 21000 −234
long int	35000L −34L
unsigned int	10000U 987U 40000U
float	123.23F 4.34e−3F
double	123.23 1.0 −0.9876324
long double	1001.2L

Hexadecimal and Octal Constants

It is sometimes easier to use a number system based on 8 or 16 rather than 10 (our
standard decimal system). The number system based on 8 is called *octal* and uses the
digits 0 through 7. In octal, the number 10 is the same as 8 in decimal. The base 16 number
system is called *hexadecimal* and uses the digits 0 through 9 plus the letters A through F,
which stand for 10, 11, 12, 13, 14, and 15, respectively. For example, the hexadecimal
number 10 is 16 in decimal. Because these two number systems are used frequently,
C/C++ allows you to specify integer constants in hexadecimal or octal instead of
decimal. A hexadecimal constant must consist of a 0x followed by the constant in
hexadecimal form. An octal constant begins with a 0. Here are some examples:

```
int hex = 0x80;   /* 128 in decimal */
int oct = 012;    /* 10 in decimal */
```

String Constants

C/C++ supports one other type of constant: the string. A *string* is a set of characters
enclosed in double quotes. For example, "this is a test" is a string. You have seen examples
of strings in some of the **printf( )** statements in the sample programs. Although C
allows you to define string constants, it does not formally have a string data type.
(C++ *does* define a string class, however.)

You must not confuse strings with characters. A single character constant is enclosed
in single quotes, as in 'a'. However, "a" is a string containing only one letter.

Backslash Character Constants

Enclosing character constants in single quotes works for most printing characters. A
few, however, such as the carriage return, are impossible to enter into a string from the
keyboard. For this reason, C/C++ include the special *backslash character constants* shown

in Table 2-2 so that you may easily enter these special characters as constants. These are also referred to as *escape sequences*. You should use the backslash codes instead of their ASCII equivalents to help ensure portability.

For example, the following program outputs a new line and a tab and then prints the string **This is a test**.

```
#include <stdio.h>

int main(void)
{
  printf("\n\tThis is a test.");

  return 0;
}
```

Code	Meaning
\b	Backspace
\f	Form feed
\n	New line
\r	Carriage return
\t	Horizontal tab
\"	Double quote
\'	Single quote
\0	Null
\\	Backslash
\v	Vertical tab
\a	Alert
\?	Question mark
\N	Octal constant (where N is an octal constant)
\xN	Hexadecimal constant (where N is a hexadecimal constant)

Table 2-2. *Backslash Codes*

Operators

C/C++ is rich in built-in operators. In fact, it places more significance on operators than do most other computer languages. There are four main classes of operators: *arithmetic*, *relational*, *logical*, and *bitwise*. In addition, there are some special operators for particular tasks.

The Assignment Operator

You can use the assignment operator within any valid expression. This is not the case with many computer languages (including Pascal, BASIC, and FORTRAN), which treat the assignment operator as a special case statement. The general form of the assignment operator is

   variable_name = expression;

where an expression may be as simple as a single constant or as complex as you require. C/C++ uses a single equal sign to indicate assignment (unlike Pascal or Modula-2, which use the := construct). The *target*, or left part, of the assignment must be a variable or a pointer, not a function or a constant.

   Frequently in literature on C/C++ and in compiler error messages you will see these two terms: lvalue and rvalue. Simply put, an *lvalue* is any object that can occur on the left side of an assignment statement. For all practical purposes, "lvalue" means "variable." The term *rvalue* refers to expressions on the right side of an assignment and simply means the value of an expression.

Type Conversion in Assignments

When variables of one type are mixed with variables of another type, a *type conversion* will occur. In an assignment statement, the type conversion rule is easy: The value of the right side (expression side) of the assignment is converted to the type of the left side (target variable), as illustrated here:

```
int x;
char ch;
float  f;

void func(void)
{
  ch = x;     /* line 1 */
  x = f;      /* line 2 */
  f = ch;     /* line 3 */
  f = x;      /* line 4 */
}
```

In line 1, the left high-order bits of the integer variable **x** are lopped off, leaving **ch** with the lower 8 bits. If **x** were between 255 and 0, **ch** and **x** would have identical values. Otherwise, the value of **ch** would reflect only the lower-order bits of **x**. In line 2, **x** will receive the nonfractional part of **f**. In line 3, **f** will convert the 8-bit integer value stored in **ch** to the same value in the floating-point format. This also happens in line 4, except that **f** will convert an integer value into floating-point format.

When converting from integers to characters and long integers to integers, the appropriate amount of high-order bits will be removed. In many 16-bit environments, this means that 8 bits will be lost when going from an integer to a character and 16 bits will be lost when going from a long integer to an integer. For 32-bit environments, 24 bits will be lost when converting from an integer to a character and 16 bits will be lost when converting from an integer to a short integer.

Table 2-3 summarizes the assignment type conversions. Remember that the conversion of an **int** to a **float**, or a **float** to a **double**, and so on, does not add any precision or accuracy. These kinds of conversions only change the form in which the value is represented. In addition, some compilers always treat a **char** variable as positive, no matter what value it has, when converting it to an **int** or **float**. Other compilers treat **char** variable values greater than 127 as negative numbers when converting. Generally

Target Type	Expression Type	Possible Info Loss
signed char	char	If value > 127, target is negative
char	short int	High-order 8 bits
char	int (16 bits)	High-order 8 bits
char	int (32 bits)	High-order 24 bits
char	long int	High-order 24 bits
short int	int (16 bits)	None
short int	int (32 bits)	High-order 16 bits
int (16 bits)	long int	High-order 16 bits
int (32 bits)	long int	None
int	float	Fractional part and possibly more
float	double	Precision, result rounded
double	long double	Precision, result rounded

Table 2-3.   *The Outcome of Common Type Conversions*

speaking, you should use **char** variables for characters, and use **int**s, **short int**s, or **signed char**s when needed to avoid possible portability problems.

To use Table 2-3 to make a conversion not shown, simply convert one type at a time until you finish. For example, to convert from **double** to **int**, first convert from **double** to **float** and then from **float** to **int**.

Multiple Assignments

C/C++ allows you to assign many variables the same value by using multiple assignments in a single statement. For example, this program fragment assigns **x**, **y**, and **z** the value 0:

```
x = y = z = 0;
```

In professional programs, variables are frequently assigned common values using this method.

Arithmetic Operators

Table 2-4 lists C/C++'s arithmetic operators. The operators **+**, **−**, *****, and **/** work as they do in most other computer languages. You can apply them to almost any built-in data type. When you apply **/** to an integer or character, any remainder will be truncated. For example, 5/2 will equal 2 in integer division.

The modulus operator **%** also works in C/C++ as it does in other languages, yielding the remainder of an integer division. However, you cannot use it on floating-point types. The following code fragment illustrates **%**:

```
int x, y;

x = 5;
y = 2;

printf("%d ", x/y);    /* will display 2 */
printf("%d ", x%y);    /* will display 1, the remainder of
                          the integer division */

x = 1;
y = 2;

printf("%d %d", x/y, x%y); /*  will display 0 1 */
```

The last line prints a 0 and a 1 because 1/2 in integer division is 0 with a remainder of 1.

The unary minus multiplies its operand by −1. That is, any number preceded by a minus sign switches its sign.

Operator	Action
–	Subtraction, also unary minus
+	Addition
*	Multiplication
/	Division
%	Modulus
– –	Decrement
++	Increment

Table 2-4.   *Arithmetic Operators*

Increment and Decrement

C/C++ includes two useful operators not found in some other computer languages. These are the increment and decrement operators, **++** and **– –**. The operator **++** adds 1 to its operand, and **– –** subtracts 1. In other words:

```
x = x+1;
```

is the same as

```
++x;
```

and

```
x = x-1;
```

is the same as

```
x--;
```

Both the increment and decrement operators may either precede (prefix) or follow (postfix) the operand. For example,

```
x = x+1;
```

can be written

```
++x;
```

or

```
x++;
```

There is, however, a difference between the prefix and postfix forms when you use these operators in an expression. When an increment or decrement operator precedes its operand, the increment or decrement operation is performed before obtaining the value of the operand for use in the expression. If the operator follows its operand, the value of the operand is obtained before incrementing or decrementing it. For instance,

```
x = 10;
y = ++x;
```

sets **y** to 11. However, if you write the code as

```
x = 10;
y = x++;
```

y is set to 10. Either way, **x** is set to 11; the difference is in when it happens.

Most C/C++ compilers produce very fast, efficient object code for increment and decrement operations—code that is better than that generated by using the equivalent assignment statement. For this reason, you should use the increment and decrement operators when you can.

Here is the precedence of the arithmetic operators:

highest	++ −−
	− (unary minus)
	* / %
lowest	+ −

Operators on the same level of precedence are evaluated by the compiler from left to right. Of course, you can use parentheses to alter the order of evaluation. C/C++ treats parentheses in the same way as virtually all other computer languages. Parentheses force an operation, or set of operations, to have a higher level of precedence.

Relational and Logical Operators

In the term *relational operator*, relational refers to the relationships that values can have with one another. In the term *logical operator*, logical refers to the ways these relationships can be connected. Because the relational and logical operators often work together, they are discussed together here.

The idea of true and false underlies the concepts of relational and logical operators. In C, true is any value other than zero. False is zero. Expressions that use relational or logical operators return 0 for false and 1 for true.

C++ fully supports the zero/non-zero concept of true and false. However, it also defines the **bool** data type and the Boolean constants **true** and **false**. In C++, a 0 value is automatically converted into **false,** and a non-zero value is automatically converted into **true**. The reverse also applies: **true** converts to 1 and **false** converts to 0. In C++, the outcome of a relational or logical operation is **true** or **false**. But since this automatically converts into 1 or 0, the distinction between C and C++ on this issue is mostly academic.

Table 2-5 shows the relational and logical operators. The truth table for the logical operators is shown here using 1's and 0's.

p	q	p && q	p || q	!p
0	0	0	0	1
0	1	0	1	1
1	1	1	1	0
1	0	0	1	0

Both the relational and logical operators are lower in precedence than the arithmetic operators. That is, an expression like 10 > 1+12 is evaluated as if it were written 10 > (1+12). Of course, the result is false.

You can combine several operations together into one expression, as shown here:

10>5 && !(10<9) || 3<=4

In this case, the result is true.

Although neither C nor C++ contain an exclusive OR (XOR) logical operator, you can easily create a function that performs this task using the other logical operators. The outcome of an XOR operation is true if and only if one operand (but not both) is

Relational Operators

Operator	Action
>	Greater than
>=	Greater than or equal
<	Less than
<=	Less than or equal
= =	Equal
!=	Not equal

Logical Operators

Operator	Action
&&	AND
||	OR
!	NOT

Table 2-5.   *Relational and Logical Operators*

true. The following program contains the function **xor( )**, which returns the outcome of an exclusive OR operation performed on its two arguments:

```
#include <stdio.h>

int xor(int a, int b);

int main(void)
{
  printf("%d", xor(1, 0));
  printf("%d", xor(1, 1));
  printf("%d", xor(0, 1));
  printf("%d", xor(0, 0));

  return 0;
}
```

```
/* Perform a logical XOR operation using the
   two arguments. */
int xor(int a, int b)
{
  return (a || b) && !(a && b);
}
```

The following table shows the relative precedence of the relational and logical operators:

Highest	!
	> >= < <=
	== !=
	&&
Lowest	||

As with arithmetic expressions, you can use parentheses to alter the natural order of evaluation in a relational and/or logical expression. For example,

!0 && 0 || 0

is false. However, when you add parentheses to the same expression, as shown here, the result is true:

!(0 && 0) || 0

Remember, all relational and logical expressions produce either a true or false result. Therefore, the following program fragment is not only correct, but will print the number 1.

```
int x;

x = 100;
printf("%d", x>10);
```

Bitwise Operators

Unlike many other languages, C/C++ supports a full complement of bitwise operators. Since C was designed to take the place of assembly language for most programming tasks, it needed to be able to support many operations that can be done in assembler, including operations on bits. *Bitwise operation* refers to testing, setting, or shifting the actual bits in a byte or word, which correspond to the **char** and **int** data types and variants. You cannot use bitwise operations on **float**, **double**, **long double**, **void**, **bool**, or other, more complex types. Table 2-6 lists the operators that apply to bitwise operations. These operations are applied to the individual bits of the operands.

The bitwise AND, OR, and NOT (one's complement) are governed by the same truth table as their logical equivalents, except that they work bit by bit. The exclusive OR has the truth table shown here:

p	q	p ^q
0	0	0
1	0	1
1	1	0
0	1	1

As the table indicates, the outcome of an XOR is true only if exactly one of the operands is true; otherwise, it is false.

Bitwise operations most often find application in device drivers—such as modem programs, disk file routines, and printer routines — because the bitwise operations can be used to mask off certain bits, such as parity. (The parity bit confirms that the rest of the bits in the byte are unchanged. It is usually the high-order bit in each byte.)

Operator	Action
&	AND
|	OR
^	Exclusive OR (XOR)
~	One's complement (NOT)
>>	Shift right
<<	Shift left

Table 2-6.   *Bitwise Operators*

Think of the bitwise AND as a way to clear a bit. That is, any bit that is 0 in either operand causes the corresponding bit in the outcome to be set to 0. For example, the following function reads a character from the modem port and resets the parity bit to 0:

```
char get_char_from_modem(void)
{
  char ch;

  ch = read_modem(); /* get a character from the
                        modem port */
  return(ch & 127);
}
```

Parity is often indicated by the eighth bit, which is set to 0 by ANDing it with a byte that has bits 1 through 7 set to 1 and bit 8 set to 0. The expression **ch & 127** means to AND together the bits in **ch** with the bits that make up the number 127. The net result is that the eighth bit of **ch** is set to 0. In the following example, assume that **ch** had received the character "A" and had the parity bit set:

```
Parity bit
↓
1 1 0 0 0 0 0 1    ch containing an "A" with parity set
0 1 1 1 1 1 1 1    127 in binary
&_____     bitwise AND
0 1 0 0 0 0 0 1    "A" without parity
```

The bitwise OR, as the reverse of AND, can be used to set a bit. Any bit that is set to 1 in either operand causes the corresponding bit in the outcome to be set to 1. For example, the following is 128 | 3:

```
1 0 0 0 0 0 0 0    128 in binary
0 0 0 0 0 0 1 1    3 in binary
|_____     bitwise OR
1 0 0 0 0 0 1 1    result
```

An exclusive OR, usually abbreviated XOR, will set a bit on if and only if the bits being compared are different. For example, 127 ^120 is

```
  01111111    127 in binary
  01111000    120 in binary
^_____   bitwise XOR
  00000111    result
```

Remember, relational and logical operators always produce a result that is either true or false, whereas the similar bitwise operations may produce any arbitrary value in accordance with the specific operation. In other words, bitwise operations may produce values other than 0 or 1, while logical operators will always evaluate to 0 or 1.

The bit-shift operators, >> and <<, move all bits in a value to the right or left as specified. The general form of the shift-right statement is

value >> number of bit positions

The general form of the shift-left statement is

value << number of bit positions

As bits are shifted off one end, 0's are brought in the other end. (In the case of a signed, negative integer, a right shift will cause a 1 to be brought in so that the sign bit is preserved.) Remember, a shift is not a rotate. That is, the bits shifted off one end do not come back around to the other. The bits shifted off are lost.

Bit-shift operations can be very useful when you are decoding input from an external device, like a D/A converter, and reading status information. The bitwise shift operators can also quickly multiply and divide integers. A shift right effectively divides a number by 2 and a shift left multiplies it by 2, as shown in Table 2-7. The following program illustrates the shift operators:

```c
/* A bit shift example. */
#include <stdio.h>

int main(void)
{
  unsigned int i;
  int j;

  i = 1;
```

```
/* left shifts */
for(j=0; j<4; j++) {
  i = i << 1;  /* left shift i by 1, which
                  is same as a multiply by 2 */
  printf("Left shift %d: %d\n", j, i);
}

/* right shifts */
for(j=0; j<4; j++) {
  i = i >> 1;  /* right shift i by 1, which
                  is same as a division by 2 */
  printf("Right shift %d: %d\n", j, i);
}

return 0;
}
```

The one's complement operator, ~, reverses the state of each bit in its operand. That is, all 1's are set to 0, and all 0's are set to 1.

The bitwise operators are often used in cipher routines. If you want to make a disk file appear unreadable, perform some bitwise manipulations on it. One of the simplest

unsigned char x;	x as each statement executes	value of x
x = 7;	0 0 0 0 0 1 1 1	7
x = x<<1;	0 0 0 0 1 1 1 0	14
x = x<<3;	0 1 1 1 0 0 0 0	112
x = x<<2;	1 1 0 0 0 0 0 0	192
x = x>>1;	0 1 1 0 0 0 0 0	96
x = x>>2;	0 0 0 1 1 0 0 0	24

*Each left shift multiplies by 2. Notice that information has been lost after x<<2 because a bit was shifted off the end.

**Each right shift divides by 2. Notice that subsequent divisions do not bring back any lost bits.

Table 2-7. *Multiplication and Division with Shift Operators*

methods is to complement each byte by using the one's complement to reverse each bit in the byte, as is shown here:

```
Original byte              0 0 1 0 1 1 0 0  ◄
After 1st complement       1 1 0 1 0 0 1 1         ─► Same
After 2nd complement       0 0 1 0 1 1 0 0  ◄
```

Notice that a sequence of two complements in a row always produces the original number. Thus, the first complement represents the coded version of that byte. The second complement decodes the byte to its original value.

You could use the **encode( )** function shown here to encode a character.

```
/* A simple cipher function. */
char encode(char ch)
{
  return(~ch); /* complement it */
}
```

Of course, a file encoded using **encode( )** would be very easy to crack!

The ? Operator

C/C++ contains a very powerful and convenient operator that replaces certain statements of the if-then-else form. The ternary operator **?** takes the general form

Exp1 ? Exp2 : Exp3;

where *Exp1*, *Exp2*, and *Exp3* are expressions. Notice the use and placement of the colon.

The **?** operator works like this: *Exp1* is evaluated. If it is true, *Exp2* is evaluated and becomes the value of the expression. If *Exp1* is false, *Exp3* is evaluated and its value becomes the value of the expression. For example, in

```
x = 10;

y = x>9 ? 100 : 200;
```

y is assigned the value 100. If **x** had been less than 9, **y** would have received the value 200. The same code written using the **if-else** statement is

```
x = 10;
```

```
if(x>9) y = 100;
else y = 200;
```

The **?** operator will be discussed more fully in Chapter 3 in relationship to the other conditional statements.

The & and * Pointer Operators

A *pointer* is the memory address of some object. A *pointer variable* is a variable that is specifically declared to hold a pointer to an object of its specified type. Knowing a variable's address can be of great help in certain types of routines. However, pointers have three main functions in C/C++. They can provide a fast means of referencing array elements. They allow functions to modify their calling parameters. Lastly, they support linked lists and other dynamic data structures. Chapter 5 is devoted exclusively to pointers. However, this chapter briefly covers the two operators that are used to manipulate pointers.

The first pointer operator is **&**, a unary operator that returns the memory address of its operand. (Remember, a unary operator only requires one operand.) For example,

```
m = &count;
```

places into **m** the memory address of the variable **count**. This address is the computer's internal location of the variable. It has nothing to do with the value of **count**. You can think of **&** as meaning "the address of." Therefore, the preceding assignment statement means "**m** receives the address of **count**."

To better understand this assignment, assume that the variable **count** is at memory location 2000. Also assume that **count** has a value of 100. Then, after the previous assignment, **m** will have the value 2000.

The second pointer operator is ***** , which is the complement of **&**. The ***** is a unary operator that returns the value of the variable located at the address that follows it. For example, if **m** contains the memory address of the variable **count**,

```
q = *m;
```

places the value of **count** into **q**. Now **q** has the value 100 because 100 is stored at location 2000, the memory address that was stored in **m**. Think of ***** as meaning "at address." In this case, you could read the statement as "**q** receives the value at address **m**."

Unfortunately, the multiplication symbol and the "at address" symbol are the same, and the symbol for the bitwise AND and the "address of" symbol are the same.

These operators have no relationship to each other. Both **&** and * have a higher precedence than all other arithmetic operators except the unary minus, with which they share equal precedence.

Variables that will hold memory addresses (i.e., pointers), must be declared by putting * in front of the variable name. This indicates to the compiler that it will hold a pointer. For example, to declare **ch** as a pointer to a character, write

```
char *ch;
```

Here, **ch** is not a character but a pointer to a character—there is a big difference. The type of data that a pointer points to, in this case **char**, is called the *base type* of the pointer. However, the pointer variable itself is a variable that holds the address to an object of the base type. Thus, a character pointer (or any pointer) is of sufficient size to hold any address as defined by the architecture of the computer. However, as a rule, a pointer should only point to data that is of that pointer's base type.

You can mix both pointer and nonpointer variables in the same declaration statement. For example,

```
int x, *y, count;
```

declares **x** and **count** as integer types and **y** as a pointer to an integer type.

The following program uses * and **&** operators to put the value 10 into a variable called **target**. As expected, this program displays the value 10 on the screen.

```
#include <stdio.h>

int main(void)
{
  int target, source;
  int *m;

  source = 10;
  m = &source;
  target = *m;

  printf("%d", target);

  return 0;
}
```

The Compile-Time Operator sizeof

sizeof is a unary compile-time operator that returns the length, in bytes, of the variable or parenthesized type-specifier that it precedes. For example, assuming that integers are 4 bytes and **double**s are 8 bytes,

```
double f;

printf("%d ", sizeof f);
printf("%d", sizeof(int));
```

will display **8 4**.

Remember, to compute the size of a type, you must enclose the type name in parentheses. This is not necessary for variable names, although there is no harm done if you do so.

C/C++ defines (using **typedef**) a special type called **size_t**, which corresponds loosely to an unsigned integer. Technically, the value returned by **sizeof** is of type **size_t**. For all practical purposes, however, you can think of it (and use it) as if it were an unsigned integer value.

sizeof primarily helps to generate portable code that depends upon the size of the built-in data types. For example, imagine a database program that needs to store six integer values per record. If you want to port the database program to a variety of computers, you must not assume the size of an integer, but must determine its actual length using **sizeof**. This being the case, you could use the following routine to write a record to a disk file:

```
/* Write 6 integers to a disk file. */
void put_rec(int rec[6], FILE *fp)
{
  int len;

  len = fwrite(rec, sizeof(int)*6, 1, fp);
  if(len != 1) printf("Write Error");
}
```

Coded as shown, **put_rec( )** compiles and runs correctly in any environment, including those that use 16- and 32-bit integers.

One final point: **sizeof** is evaluated at compile time, and the value it produces is treated as a constant within your program.

The Comma Operator

The comma operator strings together several expressions. The left side of the comma operator is always evaluated as **void**. This means that the expression on the right side becomes the value of the total comma-separated expression. For example,

```
x = (y=3, y+1);
```

first assigns **y** the value 3 and then assigns **x** the value 4. The parentheses are necessary because the comma operator has a lower precedence than the assignment operator.

Essentially, the comma causes a sequence of operations. When you use it on the right side of an assignment statement, the value assigned is the value of the last expression of the comma-separated list.

The comma operator has somewhat the same meaning as the word "and" in normal English as used in the phrase "do this and this and this."

The Dot (.) and Arrow (−>) Operators

In C, the **.** (dot) and the **−>**(arrow) operators access individual elements of structures and unions. *Structures* and *unions* are compound (also called *aggregate*) data types that may be referenced under a single name (see Chapter 7). In C++, the dot and arrow operators are also used to access the members of a class.

The dot operator is used when working with a structure or union directly. The arrow operator is used when a pointer to a structure or union is used. For example, given the fragment

```
struct employee
{
  char name[80];
  int age;
  float wage;
} emp;

struct employee *p = &emp; /* address of emp into p */
```

you would write the following code to assign the value 123.23 to the **wage** member of structure variable **emp**:

```
emp.wage = 123.23;
```

However, the same assignment using a pointer to **emp** would be

```
p->wage = 123.23;
```

The [ ] and ( ) Operators

Parentheses are operators that increase the precedence of the operations inside them. Square brackets perform array indexing (arrays are discussed fully in Chapter 4). Given an array, the expression within square brackets provides an index into that array. For example,

```
#include <stdio.h>
char s[80];

int main(void)
{
  s[3] = 'X';
  printf("%c", s[3]);

  return 0;
}
```

first assigns the value **'X'** to the fourth element (remember, all arrays begin at 0) of array **s**, and then prints that element.

Precedence Summary

Table 2-8 lists the precedence of all operators defined by C. Note that all operators, except the unary operators and **?**, associate from left to right. The unary operators (*****, **&**, **−**) and **?** associate from right to left.

Note *C++ defines a few additional operators, which are discussed at length in Part Two.*

Expressions

Operators, constants, and variables are the constituents of expressions. An *expression* in C/C++ is any valid combination of these elements. Because most expressions tend to follow the general rules of algebra, they are often taken for granted. However, a few aspects of expressions relate specifically to C and C++.

Order of Evaluation

Neither C nor C++ specifies the order in which the subexpressions of an expression are evaluated. This leaves the compiler free to rearrange an expression to produce more optimal code. However, it also means that your code should never rely upon the order in which subexpressions are evaluated. For example, the expression

```
x = f1() + f2();
```

does not ensure that **f1( )** will be called before **f2( )**.

Highest	( ) [ ] –> .
	! ~ ++ –– (type) * & sizeof
	* / %
	+ –
	<< >>
	< <= > >=
	== !=
	&
	^
	|
	&&
	||
Highest	
	?:
	= += –= *= /= etc.
Lowest	,

Table 2-8. *The Precedence of C Operators*

Type Conversion in Expressions

When constants and variables of different types are mixed in an expression, they are all converted to the same type. The compiler converts all operands up to the type of the largest operand, which is called *type promotion*. First, all **char** and **short int** values are automatically elevated to **int**. (This process is called *integral promotion*.) Once this step has been completed, all other conversions are done operation by operation, as described in the following type conversion algorithm:

IF an operand is a **long double**
THEN the second is converted to **long double**
ELSE IF an operand is a **double**
THEN the second is converted to **double**

ELSE IF an operand is a **float**
THEN the second is converted to **float**
ELSE IF an operand is an **unsigned long**
THEN the second is converted to **unsigned long**
ELSE IF an operand is **long**
THEN the second is converted to **long**
ELSE IF an operand is **unsigned int**
THEN the second is converted to **unsigned int**

There is one additional special case: If one operand is **long** and the other is **unsigned int**, and if the value of the **unsigned int** cannot be represented by a **long**, both operands are converted to **unsigned long**.

Once these conversion rules have been applied, each pair of operands is of the same type and the result of each operation is the same as the type of both operands.

For example, consider the type conversions that occur in Figure 2-2. First, the character **ch** is converted to an integer. Then the outcome of **ch/i** is converted to a **double** because **f*d** is **double**. The outcome of **f+i** is **float**, because **f** is a **float**. The final result is **double**.

Casts

You can force an expression to be of a specific type by using a *cast*. The general form of a cast is

(type) expression

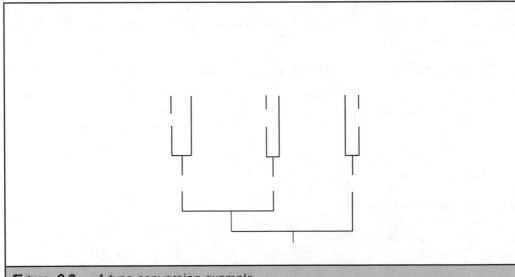

Figure 2-2.   *A type conversion example*

where *type* is a valid data type. For example, to make sure that the expression **x/2** evaluates to type **float**, write

```
(float) x/2
```

Casts are technically operators. As an operator, a cast is unary and has the same precedence as any other unary operator.

Although casts are not usually used a great deal in programming, they can be very helpful when needed. For example, suppose you wish to use an integer for loop control, yet to perform computation on it requires a fractional part, as in the following program:

```
#include <stdio.h>

int main(void) /* print i and i/2 with fractions */
{
  int i;

  for(i=1; i<=100; ++i)
    printf("%d / 2 is: %f\n", i, (float) i /2);

  return 0;
}
```

Without the cast **(float)**, only an integer division would have been performed. The cast ensures that the fractional part of the answer is displayed.

 *C++ adds four more casting operators, such as **const_cast** and **static_cast**. These operators are discussed in Part Two.*

Spacing and Parentheses

You can add tabs and spaces to expressions to make them easier to read. For example, the following two expressions are the same:

```
x=10/y~(127/x);
```

```
x = 10 / y ~(127/x);
```

Redundant or additional parentheses do not cause errors or slow down the execution of an expression. You should use parentheses to clarify the exact order of evaluation, both for yourself and for others. For example, which of the following two expressions is easier to read?

```
x = y/3-34*temp+127;

x = (y/3) - (34*temp) + 127;
```

Compound Assignments

There is a variation on the assignment statement, called *compound assignment*, that simplifies the coding of a certain type of assignment operation. For example,

```
x = x+10;
```

can be written as

```
x += 10;
```

The operator **+=** tells the compiler to assign to **x** the value of **x** plus 10.

Compound assignment operators exist for all the binary operators (those that require two operands). In general, statements like:

var = var operator expression

can be rewritten as

var operator = expression

For another example,

```
x = x-100;
```

is the same as

```
x -= 100;
```

Compound assignment is widely used in professionally written C/C++ programs; you should become familiar with it. Compound assignment is also commonly referred to as *shorthand assignment* because it is more compact.

Chapter 3

Statements

This chapter discusses the statement. In the most general sense, a *statement* is a part of your program that can be executed. That is, a statement specifies an action. C and C++ categorize statements into these groups:

- Selection
- Iteration
- Jump
- Label
- Expression
- Block

Included in the selection statements are **if** and **switch**. (The term *conditional statement* is often used in place of "selection statement.") The iteration statements are **while, for,** and **do-while**. These are also commonly called *loop statements*. The jump statements are **break, continue, goto**, and **return**. The label statements include the **case** and **default** statements (discussed along with the **switch** statement) and the label statement (discussed with **goto**). Expression statements are statements composed of a valid expression. Block statements are simply blocks of code. (Remember, a block begins with a { and ends with a }.) Block statements are also referred to as *compound statements*.

Note   *C++ adds two additional statement types: the **try** block (used by exception handling) and the declaration statement. These are discussed in Part Two.*

Since many statements rely upon the outcome of some conditional test, let's begin by reviewing the concepts of true and false.

True and False in C and C++

Many C/C++ statements rely upon a conditional expression that determines what course of action is to be taken. A conditional expression evaluates to either a true or false value. In C, a true value is any nonzero value, including negative numbers. A false value is 0. This approach to true and false allows a wide range of routines to be coded extremely efficiently.

C++ fully supports the zero/nonzero definition of true and false just described. But C++ also defines a Boolean data type called **bool,** which can have only the values **true** and **false**. As explained in Chapter 2, in C++, a 0 value is automatically converted into **false** and a nonzero value is automatically converted into **true**. The reverse also applies: **true** converts to 1 and **false** converts to 0. In C++, the expression that controls a conditional statement is technically of type **bool**. But since any nonzero value converts to **true** and any zero value converts to **false**, there is no practical difference between C and C++ on this point.

C99 has added a Boolean type called _Bool, but it is incompatible with C++. See Part Two for a discussion on how to achieve compatibility between C99's _Bool and C++'s bool types.

Selection Statements

C/C++ supports two types of selection statements: **if** and **switch**. In addition, the **?** operator is an alternative to **if** in certain circumstances.

if

The general form of the **if** statement is

> if (*expression*) *statement*;
> else *statement*;

where a *statement* may consist of a single statement, a block of statements, or nothing (in the case of empty statements). The **else** clause is optional.

If *expression* evaluates to true (anything other than 0), the statement or block that forms the target of **if** is executed; otherwise, the statement or block that is the target of **else** will be executed, if it exists. Remember, only the code associated with **if** or the code associated with **else** executes, never both.

In C, the conditional statement controlling **if** must produce a scalar result. A *scalar* is either an integer, character, pointer, or floating-point type. In C++, it may also be of type **bool**. It is rare to use a floating-point number to control a conditional statement because this slows execution time considerably. (It takes several instructions to perform a floating-point operation. It takes relatively few instructions to perform an integer or character operation.)

The following program contains an example of **if**. The program plays a very simple version of the "guess the magic number" game. It prints the message ** **Right** ** when the player guesses the magic number. It generates the magic number using the standard random number generator **rand( )**, which returns an arbitrary number between 0 and **RAND_MAX** (which defines an integer value that is 32,767 or larger). **rand( )** requires the header file **stdlib.h**. (A C++ program may also use the new-style header **<cstdlib>**.)

```
/* Magic number program #1. */
#include <stdio.h>
#include <stdlib.h>

int main(void)
{
  int magic; /* magic number */
```

```
    int guess; /* user's guess */

    magic = rand(); /* generate the magic number */

    printf("Guess the magic number: ");
    scanf("%d", &guess);

    if(guess == magic) printf("** Right **");

    return 0;
}
```

Taking the magic number program further, the next version illustrates the use of the **else** statement to print a message in response to the wrong number.

```
/* Magic number program #2. */
#include <stdio.h>
#include <stdlib.h>

int main(void)
{
  int magic; /* magic number */
  int guess; /* user's guess */

  magic = rand(); /* generate the magic number */

  printf("Guess the magic number: ");
  scanf("%d", &guess);

  if(guess == magic) printf("** Right **");
  else printf("Wrong");

  return 0;
}
```

Nested ifs

A nested **if** is an **if** that is the target of another **if** or **else**. Nested **if**s are very common in programming. In a nested **if**, an **else** statement always refers to the nearest **if** statement that is within the same block as the **else** and that is not already associated with an **else**. For example,

```
if(i)
{
  if(j) statement 1;
  if(k) statement 2; /* this if */
  else  statement 3; /* is associated with this else */
}
else statement 4; /* associated with if(i) */
```

As noted, the final **else** is not associated with **if(j)** because it is not in the same block. Rather, the final **else** is associated with **if(i)**. Also, the inner **else** is associated with **if(k)**, which is the nearest **if**.

The C language guarantees at least 15 levels of nesting. In practice, most compilers allow substantially more. More importantly, Standard C++ suggests that at least 256 levels of nested **if**s be allowed in a C++ program. However, nesting beyond a few levels is seldom necessary, and excessive nesting can quickly confuse the meaning of an algorithm.

You can use a nested **if** to further improve the magic number program by providing the player with feedback about a wrong guess.

```
/* Magic number program #3. */
#include <stdio.h>
#include <stdlib.h>

int main(void)
{
  int magic; /* magic number */
  int guess; /* user's guess */

  magic = rand(); /* get a random number */

  printf("Guess the magic number: ");
  scanf("%d", &guess);

  if (guess == magic) {
    printf("** Right **");
    printf(" %d is the magic number\n", magic);
  }
  else {
    printf("Wrong, ");
    if(guess > magic) printf("too high\n");
    else printf("too low\n");
  }
```

```
   return 0;
}
```

The if-else-if Ladder

A common programming construct is the *if-else-if ladder,* sometimes called the *if-else-if staircase* because of its appearance. Its general form is

```
if (expression) statement;
else
  if (expression) statement;
  else
    if (expression) statement;
    .
    .
    .
    else statement;
```

The conditions are evaluated from the top downward. As soon as a true condition is found, the statement associated with it is executed and the rest of the ladder is bypassed. If none of the conditions are true, the final **else** is executed. That is, if all other conditional tests fail, the last **else** statement is performed. If the final **else** is not present, no action takes place if all other conditions are false.

Although the indentation of the preceding if-else-if ladder is technically correct, it can lead to overly deep indentation. For this reason, the if-else-if ladder is generally indented like this:

```
if (expression)
  statement;
else if (expression)
  statement;
else if (expression)
  statement;
.

.

.
else
  statement;
```

Using an if-else-if ladder, the magic number program becomes

```
/* Magic number program #4. */
#include <stdio.h>
```

```
#include <stdlib.h>

int main(void)
{
  int magic; /* magic number */
  int guess; /* user's guess */

  magic = rand(); /* generate the magic number */

  printf("Guess the magic number: ");
  scanf("%d", &guess);

  if(guess == magic) {
    printf("** Right ** ");
    printf("%d is the magic number", magic);
  }
  else if(guess > magic)
    printf("Wrong, too high");
  else printf("Wrong, too low");

  return 0;
}
```

The ? Alternative

You can use the **?** operator to replace **if-else** statements of the general form:

> if(*condition*) *expression*;
> else *expression*;

However, the target of both **if** and **else** must be a single expression—not another statement.

The **?** is called a *ternary operator* because it requires three operands. It takes the general form

> *Exp1* ? *Exp2* : *Exp3*

where *Exp1*, *Exp2*, and *Exp3* are expressions. Notice the use and placement of the colon.

The value of a **?** expression is determined as follows: *Exp1* is evaluated. If it is true, *Exp2* is evaluated and becomes the value of the entire **?** expression. If *Exp1* is false, then *Exp3* is evaluated and its value becomes the value of the expression. For example, consider

```
x = 10;
y = x>9 ? 100 : 200;
```

In this example, **y** is assigned the value 100. If **x** had been less than 9, **y** would have received the value 200. The same code written with the **if-else** statement would be

```
x = 10;
if(x>9) y = 100;
else y = 200;
```

The following program uses the **?** operator to square an integer value entered by the user. However, this program preserves the sign (10 squared is 100 and −10 squared is −100).

```c
#include <stdio.h>

int main(void)
{
  int isqrd, i;

  printf("Enter a number: ");
  scanf("%d", &i);

  isqrd = i>0 ? i*i : -(i*i);

  printf("%d squared is %d", i, isqrd);

  return 0;
}
```

The use of the **?** operator to replace **if-else** statements is not restricted to assignments only. Remember, all functions (except those declared as **void**) return a value. Thus, you can use one or more function calls in a **?** expression. When the function's name is encountered, the function is executed so that its return value may be determined. Therefore, you can execute one or more function calls using the **?** operator by placing the calls in the expressions that form the **?**'s operands. Here is an example.

```c
#include <stdio.h>

int f1(int n);
int f2(void);
```

THE FOUNDATION OF C++:
THE C SUBSET

```c
int main(void)
{
  int t;

  printf("Enter a number: ");
  scanf("%d", &t);

  /* print proper message */
  t ? f1(t) + f2() : printf("zero entered.\n");

  return 0;
}

int f1(int n)
{
  printf("%d ", n);
  return 0;
}

int f2(void)
{
  printf("entered.\n");
  return 0;
}
```

Entering a 0 in this example calls the **printf( )** function and displays the message **zero entered**. If you enter any other number, both **f1( )** and **f2( )** execute. Note that the value of the **?** expression is discarded in this example. You don't need to assign it to anything.

A word of warning: Some C++ compilers rearrange the order of evaluation of an expression in an attempt to optimize the object code. This could cause functions that form the operands of the **?** operator to execute in an unintended sequence.

Using the **?** operator, you can rewrite the magic number program yet again.

```c
/* Magic number program #5. */
#include <stdio.h>
#include <stdlib.h>

int main(void)
{
  int magic;
  int guess;
```

```
    magic = rand(); /* generate the magic number */

    printf("Guess the magic number: ");
    scanf("%d", &guess);

    if(guess == magic) {
      printf("** Right ** ");
      printf("%d is the magic number", magic);
    }
    else
      guess > magic ? printf("High") : printf("Low");

    return 0;
  }
```

Here, the **?** operator displays the proper message based on the outcome of the test **guess > magic**.

The Conditional Expression

Sometimes newcomers to C/C++ are confused by the fact that you can use any valid expression to control the **if** or the **?** operator. That is, you are not restricted to expressions involving the relational and logical operators (as is the case in languages like BASIC or Pascal). The expression must simply evaluate to either a true or false (zero or nonzero) value. For example, the following program reads two integers from the keyboard and displays the quotient. It uses an **if** statement, controlled by the second number, to avoid a divide-by-zero error.

```
/* Divide the first number by the second. */

#include <stdio.h>

int main(void)
{
  int a, b;

  printf("Enter two numbers: ");
  scanf("%d%d", &a, &b);

  if(b) printf("%d\n", a/b);
  else printf("Cannot divide by zero.\n");

  return 0;
}
```

This approach works because if **b** is 0, the condition controlling the **if** is false and the **else** executes. Otherwise, the condition is true (nonzero) and the division takes place.

One other point: Writing the **if** statement as shown here

```
if(b != 0) printf("%d\n", a/b);
```

is redundant, potentially inefficient, and is considered bad style. Since the value of **b** alone is sufficient to control the **if**, there is no need to test it against 0.

switch

C/C++ has a built-in multiple-branch selection statement, called **switch**, which successively tests the value of an expression against a list of integer or character constants. When a match is found, the statements associated with that constant are executed. The general form of the **switch** statement is

```
switch (expression) {
  case constant1:
    statement sequence
    break;
  case constant2:
    statement sequence
    break;
  case constant3:
    statement sequence
    break;
  .
  .
  .
  default
    statement sequence
}
```

The *expression* must evaluate to a character or integer value. Floating-point expressions, for example, are not allowed. The value of *expression* is tested, in order, against the values of the constants specified in the **case** statements. When a match is found, the statement sequence associated with that **case** is executed until the **break** statement or the end of the **switch** statement is reached. The **default** statement is executed if no matches are found. The **default** is optional and, if it is not present, no action takes place if all matches fail.

In C, a **switch** can have at least 257 **case** statements. Standard C++ recommends that *at least* 16,384 **case** statements be supported! In practice, you will want to limit the number of **case** statements to a smaller amount for efficiency. Although **case** is a label statement, it cannot exist by itself, outside of a **switch**.

The **break** statement is one of C/C++'s jump statements. You can use it in loops as well as in the **switch** statement (see the section "Iteration Statements"). When **break** is encountered in a **switch**, program execution "jumps" to the line of code following the **switch** statement.

There are three important things to know about the **switch** statement:

■ The **switch** differs from the **if** in that **switch** can only test for equality, whereas **if** can evaluate any type of relational or logical expression.

■ No two **case** constants in the same **switch** can have identical values. Of course, a **switch** statement enclosed by an outer **switch** may have **case** constants that are the same.

■ If character constants are used in the **switch** statement, they are automatically converted to integers.

The **switch** statement is often used to process keyboard commands, such as menu selection. As shown here, the function **menu( )** displays a menu for a spelling-checker program and calls the proper procedures:

```
void menu(void)
{
  char ch;

  printf("1. Check Spelling\n");
  printf("2. Correct Spelling Errors\n");
  printf("3. Display Spelling Errors\n");
  printf("Strike Any Other Key to Skip\n");
  printf("      Enter your choice: ");

  ch = getchar(); /* read the selection from
                     the keyboard */

  switch(ch) {
    case '1':
      check_spelling();
      break;
    case '2':
      correct_errors();
      break;
    case '3':
      display_errors();
      break;
    default :
```

```
      printf("No option selected");
   }
}
```

Technically, the **break** statements inside the **switch** statement are optional. They terminate the statement sequence associated with each constant. If the **break** statement is omitted, execution will continue on into the next **case**'s statements until either a **break** or the end of the **switch** is reached. For example, the following function uses the "drop through" nature of the **case**s to simplify the code for a device-driver input handler:

```
/* Process a value */
void inp_handler(int i)
{
  int flag;

  flag = -1;

  switch(i) {
    case 1:  /* These cases have common */
    case 2:  /* statement sequences. */
    case 3:
      flag = 0;
      break;
    case 4:
      flag = 1;
    case 5:
      error(flag);
      break;
    default:
      process(i);
  }
}
```

This example illustrates two aspects of **switch**. First, you can have **case** statements that have no statement sequence associated with them. When this occurs, execution simply drops through to the next **case**. In this example, the first three **case**s all execute the same statements, which are

```
flag = 0;
break;
```

Second, execution of one statement sequence continues into the next **case** if no **break** statement is present. If **i** matches 4, **flag** is set to 1 and, because there is no **break** statement at the end of that **case**, execution continues and the call to **error(flag)** is executed. If **i** had matched 5, **error(flag)** would have been called with a flag value of –1 (rather than 1).

The fact that **case**s can run together when no **break** is present prevents the unnecessary duplication of statements, resulting in more efficient code.

Nested switch Statements

You can have a **switch** as part of the statement sequence of an outer **switch**. Even if the **case** constants of the inner and outer **switch** contain common values, no conflicts arise. For example, the following code fragment is perfectly acceptable:

```
switch(x) {
  case 1:
    switch(y) {
      case 0: printf("Divide by zero error.\n");
              break;
      case 1: process(x,y);
    }
    break;
  case 2:
    .
    .
    .
```

Iteration Statements

In C/C++, and all other modern programming languages, iteration statements (also called *loops*) allow a set of instructions to be executed repeatedly until a certain condition is reached. This condition may be predefined (as in the **for** loop), or open-ended (as in the **while** and **do-while** loops).

The for Loop

The general design of the **for** loop is reflected in some form or another in all procedural programming languages. However, in C/C++, it provides unexpected flexibility and power.

The general form of the **for** statement is

for(*initialization*; *condition*; *increment*) *statement*;

The **for** loop allows many variations, but its most common form works like this. The *initialization* is an assignment statement that is used to set the loop control variable. The *condition* is a relational expression that determines when the loop exits. The *increment* defines how the loop control variable changes each time the loop is repeated. You must separate these three major sections by semicolons. The **for** loop continues to execute as long as the condition is true. Once the condition becomes false, program execution resumes on the statement following the **for**.

In the following program, a **for** loop is used to print the numbers 1 through 100 on the screen:

```
#include <stdio.h>

int main(void)
{
  int x;

  for(x=1; x <= 100; x++) printf("%d ", x);

  return 0;
}
```

In the loop, **x** is initially set to 1 and then compared with 100. Since **x** is less than 100, **printf( )** is called and the loop iterates. This causes **x** to be increased by 1 and again tested to see if it is still less than or equal to 100. If it is, **printf( )** is called. This process repeats until **x** is greater than 100, at which point the loop terminates. In this example, **x** is the loop control variable, which is changed and checked each time the loop repeats.

The following example is a **for** loop that iterates multiple statements:

```
for(x=100; x != 65; x -= 5) {
  z = x*x;
  printf("The square of %d, %f", x, z);
}
```

Both the squaring of **x** and the call to **printf( )** are executed until **x** equals 65. Note that the loop is *negative running*: **x** is initialized to 100 and 5 is subtracted from it each time the loop repeats.

In **for** loops, the conditional test is always performed at the top of the loop. This means that the code inside the loop may not be executed at all if the condition is false to begin with. For example, in

```
x = 10;
for(y=10; y!=x; ++y) printf("%d", y);
printf("%d", y);   /* this is the only printf()
                      statement that will execute */
```

the loop will never execute because **x** and **y** are equal when the loop is entered. Because this causes the conditional expression to evaluate to false, neither the body of the loop nor the increment portion of the loop executes. Hence, **y** still has the value 10, and the only output produced by the fragment is the number 10 printed once on the screen.

for Loop Variations

The previous discussion described the most common form of the **for** loop. However, several variations of the **for** are allowed that increase its power, flexibility, and applicability to certain programming situations.

One of the most common variations uses the comma operator to allow two or more variables to control the loop. (Remember, you use the comma operator to string together a number of expressions in a "do this and this" fashion. See Chapter 2.) For example, the variables **x** and **y** control the following loop, and both are initialized inside the **for** statement:

```
for(x=0, y=0; x+y<10; ++x) {
  y = getchar();
  y = y - '0'; /* subtract the ASCII code for 0
                 from y */
  .
  .
  .
}
```

Commas separate the two initialization statements. Each time the loop repeats, **x** is incremented and **y**'s value is set by keyboard input. Both **x** and **y** must be at the correct value for the loop to terminate. Even though **y**'s value is set by keyboard input, **y** must be initialized to 0 so that its value is defined before the first evaluation of the conditional expression. (If **y** were not defined, it could by chance contain the value 10, making the conditional test false and preventing the loop from executing.)

The **converge( )** function, shown next, demonstrates multiple loop control variables in action. The **converge( )** function copies the contents of one string into another by moving characters from both ends, converging in the middle.

```
/* Demonstrate multiple loop control variables. */
#include <stdio.h>
#include <string.h>

void converge(char *targ, char *src);

int main(void)
{
```

```
    char target[80] = "XXXXXXXXXXXXXXXXXXXXXXXXXXXXXX";

    converge(target, "This is a test of converge().");
    printf("Final string: %s\n", target);

    return 0;
}

/* This function copies one string into another.
   It copies characters to both the ends,
   converging at the middle. */
void converge(char *targ, char *src)
{
  int i, j;

  printf("%s\n", targ);
  for(i=0, j=strlen(src); i<=j; i++, j--) {
    targ[i] = src[i];
    targ[j] = src[j];
    printf("%s\n", targ);
  }
}
```

Here is the output produced by the program.

```
XXXXXXXXXXXXXXXXXXXXXXXXXXXXXX
TXXXXXXXXXXXXXXXXXXXXXXXXXXXXX
ThXXXXXXXXXXXXXXXXXXXXXXXXXXXX.
ThiXXXXXXXXXXXXXXXXXXXXXXXXXX).
ThisXXXXXXXXXXXXXXXXXXXXXXXX().
This XXXXXXXXXXXXXXXXXXXXXe().
This iXXXXXXXXXXXXXXXXXXge().
This isXXXXXXXXXXXXXXXXrge().
This is XXXXXXXXXXXXXXerge().
This is aXXXXXXXXXXXXverge().
This is a XXXXXXXXXXnverge().
This is a tXXXXXXXXonverge().
This is a teXXXXXXconverge().
This is a tesXXXX converge().
This is a testXXf converge().
This is a test of converge().
Final string: This is a test of converge().
```

In **converge( )**, the **for** loop uses two loop control variables, **i** and **j**, to index the string from opposite ends. As the loop iterates, **i** is increased and **j** is decreased. The loop stops when **i** is greater than **j**, thus ensuring that all characters are copied.

The conditional expression does not have to involve testing the loop control variable against some target value. In fact, the condition may be any relational or logical statement. This means that you can test for several possible terminating conditions.

For example, you could use the following function to log a user onto a remote system. The user has three tries to enter the password. The loop terminates when the three tries are used up or the user enters the correct password.

```
void sign_on(void)
{
  char str[20] = "";
  int x;

  for(x=0; x<3 && strcmp(str, "password"); ++x) {
    printf("Enter password please:");
    gets(str);
  }

  if(x==3) return;
  /* else log user in ... */
}
```

This function uses **strcmp( )**, the standard library function that compares two strings and returns 0 if they match.

Remember, each of the three sections of the **for** loop may consist of any valid expression. The expressions need not actually have anything to do with what the sections are generally used for. With this in mind, consider the following example:

```
#include <stdio.h>

int sqrnum(int num);
int readnum(void);
int prompt(void);

int main(void)
{
  int t;
```

```
   for(prompt(); t=readnum(); prompt())
     sqrnum(t);

   return 0;
}

int prompt(void)
{
  printf("Enter a number: ");
  return 0;
}

int readnum(void)
{
  int t;

  scanf("%d", &t);
  return t;
}

int sqrnum(int num)
{
  printf("%d\n", num*num);
  return num*num;
}
```

Look closely at the **for** loop in **main( )**. Notice that each part of the **for** loop is composed of function calls that prompt the user and read a number entered from the keyboard. If the number entered is 0, the loop terminates because the conditional expression will be false. Otherwise, the number is squared. Thus, this **for** loop uses the initialization and increment portions in a nontraditional but completely valid sense.

Another interesting trait of the **for** loop is that pieces of the loop definition need not be there. In fact, there need not be an expression present for any of the sections— the expressions are optional. For example, this loop will run until the user enters **123**:

```
for(x=0; x!=123; ) scanf("%d", &x);
```

Notice that the increment portion of the **for** definition is blank. This means that each time the loop repeats, x is tested to see if it equals 123, but no further action takes place. If you type **123** at the keyboard, however, the loop condition becomes false and the loop terminates.

The initialization of the loop control variable can occur outside the **for** statement. This most frequently happens when the initial condition of the loop control variable must be computed by some complex means as in this example:

```
gets(s);  /* read a string into s */
if(*s) x = strlen(s); /* get the string's length */
else x = 10;

for( ; x<10; ) {
  printf("%d", x);
  ++x;
}
```

The initialization section has been left blank and **x** is initialized before the loop is entered.

The Infinite Loop

Although you can use any loop statement to create an infinite loop, **for** is traditionally used for this purpose. Since none of the three expressions that form the **for** loop are required, you can make an endless loop by leaving the conditional expression empty:

```
for( ; ; ) printf("This loop will run forever.\n");
```

When the conditional expression is absent, it is assumed to be true. You may have an initialization and increment expression, but C++ programmers more commonly use the **for(;;)** construct to signify an infinite loop.

Actually, the **for(;;)** construct does not guarantee an infinite loop because a **break** statement, encountered anywhere inside the body of a loop, causes immediate termination. (**break** is discussed in detail later in this chapter.) Program control then resumes at the code following the loop, as shown here:

```
ch = '\0';

for( ; ; ) {
  ch = getchar(); /* get a character */
  if(ch=='A') break; /* exit the loop */
}

printf("you typed an A");
```

This loop will run until the user types an **A** at the keyboard.

for Loops with No Bodies

A statement may be empty. This means that the body of the **for** loop (or any other loop) may also be empty. You can use this fact to improve the efficiency of certain algorithms and to create time delay loops.

Removing spaces from an input stream is a common programming task. For example, a database program may allow a query such as "show all balances less than 400." The database needs to have each word fed to it separately, without leading spaces. That is, the database input processor recognizes "**show**" but not " **show**". The following loop shows one way to accomplish this. It advances past leading spaces in the string pointed to by **str**.

```
for( ; *str == ' '; str++) ;
```

As you can see, this loop has no body—and no need for one either.

Time delay loops are often used in programs. The following code shows how to create one by using **for**:

```
for(t=0; t<SOME_VALUE; t++) ;
```

The while Loop

The second loop available in C/C++ is the **while** loop. Its general form is

while(*condition*) *statement*;

where *statement* is either an empty statement, a single statement, or a block of statements. The *condition* may be any expression, and true is any nonzero value. The loop iterates while the condition is true. When the condition becomes false, program control passes to the line of code immediately following the loop.

The following example shows a keyboard input routine that simply loops until the user types **A**:

```
char wait_for_char(void)
{
  char ch;

  ch = '\0';  /* initialize ch */
  while(ch != 'A') ch = getchar();
  return ch;
}
```

First, **ch** is initialized to null. As a local variable, its value is not known when
wait_for_char( ) is executed. The **while** loop then checks to see if **ch** is not equal to **A**.
Because **ch** was initialized to null, the test is true and the loop begins. Each time you
press a key, the condition is tested again. Once you enter an **A**, the condition becomes
false because **ch** equals **A**, and the loop terminates.

Like **for** loops, **while** loops check the test condition at the top of the loop, which
means that the body of the loop will not execute if the condition is false to begin with.
This feature may eliminate the need to perform a separate conditional test before the
loop. The **pad( )** function provides a good illustration of this. It adds spaces to the end
of a string to fill the string to a predefined length. If the string is already at the desired
length, no spaces are added.

```c
#include <stdio.h>
#include <string.h>

void pad(char *s, int length);

int main(void)
{
  char str[80];

  strcpy(str, "this is a test");
  pad(str, 40);
  printf("%d", strlen(str));

  return 0;
}

/* Add spaces to the end of a string. */
void pad(char *s, int length)
{
  int l;

  l = strlen(s); /* find out how long it is */

  while(l<length) {
    s[l] = ' '; /* insert a space */
    l++;
  }
  s[l]= '\0'; /* strings need to be
                 terminated in a null */
}
```

The two arguments of **pad( )** are **s**, a pointer to the string to lengthen, and **length**, the number of characters that **s** should have. If the length of string **s** is already equal to or greater than **length**, the code inside the **while** loop does not execute. If **s** is shorter than **length**, **pad( )** adds the required number of spaces. The **strlen( )** function, part of the standard library, returns the length of the string.

If several separate conditions need to terminate a **while** loop, a single variable commonly forms the conditional expression. The value of this variable is set at various points throughout the loop. In this example,

```
void func1(void)
{
  int working;

  working = 1; /* i.e., true */

  while(working) {
    working = process1();
    if(working)
      working = process2();
    if(working)
      working = process3();
  }
}
```

any of the three routines may return false and cause the loop to exit.

There need not be any statements in the body of the **while** loop. For example,

```
while((ch=getchar()) != 'A') ;
```

will simply loop until the user types **A**. If you feel uncomfortable putting the assignment inside the **while** conditional expression, remember that the equal sign is just an operator that evaluates to the value of the right-hand operand.

The do-while Loop

Unlike **for** and **while** loops, which test the loop condition at the top of the loop, the **do-while** loop checks its condition at the bottom of the loop. This means that a **do-while** loop always executes at least once. The general form of the **do-while** loop is

```
do {
  statement;
} while(condition);
```

Although the curly braces are not necessary when only one statement is present, they are usually used to avoid confusion (to you, not the compiler) with the **while**. The **do-while** loop iterates until *condition* becomes false.

The following **do-while** loop will read numbers from the keyboard until it finds a number less than or equal to 100.

```
do {
  scanf("%d", &num);
} while(num > 100);
```

Perhaps the most common use of the **do-while** loop is in a menu selection function. When the user enters a valid response, it is returned as the value of the function. Invalid responses cause a reprompt. The following code shows an improved version of the spelling-checker menu developed earlier in this chapter:

```
void menu(void)
{
  char ch;

  printf("1. Check Spelling\n");
  printf("2. Correct Spelling Errors\n");
  printf("3. Display Spelling Errors\n");
  printf("      Enter your choice: ");

  do {
    ch = getchar(); /* read the selection from
                       the keyboard */
    switch(ch) {
      case '1':
        check_spelling();
        break;
      case '2':
        correct_errors();
        break;
      case '3':
        display_errors();
        break;
    }
  } while(ch!='1' && ch!='2' && ch!='3');
}
```

Here, the **do-while** loop is a good choice because you will always want a menu function to display the menu at least once. After the options have been displayed, the program will loop until a valid option is selected.

Declaring Variables within Selection and Iteration Statements

In C++ (but not C89), it is possible to declare a variable within the conditional expression of an **if** or **switch**, within the conditional expression of a **while** loop, or within the initialization portion of a **for** loop. A variable declared in one of these places has its scope limited to the block of code controlled by that statement. For example, a variable declared within a **for** loop will be local to that loop.

Here is an example that declares a variable within the initialization portion of a **for** loop:

```
/* i is local to for loop; j is known outside loop. */
int j;
for(int i = 0; i<10; i++)
  j = i * i;

/* i = 10; // *** Error *** -- i not known here! */
```

Here, **i** is declared within the initialization portion of the **for** and is used to control the loop. Outside the loop, **i** is unknown.

Since often a loop control variable in a **for** is needed only by that loop, the declaration of the variable in the initialization portion of the **for** is becoming common practice. Remember, however, that this is not supported by C89. (This restriction was removed from C by C99.)

> **Tip** *Whether a variable declared within the initialization portion of a **for** loop is local to that loop has changed over time. Originally, the variable was available after the **for**. However, Standard C++ restricts the variable to the scope of the **for** loop as just described.*

If your compiler fully complies with Standard C++, then you can also declare a variable within any conditional expression, such as those used by the **if** or a **while**. For example, this fragment,

```
if(int x = 20) {
  x = x - y;
```

```
    if(x>10) y = 0;
}
```

declares **x** and assigns it the value 20. Since this is a true value, the target of the **if**
executes. Variables declared within a conditional statement have their scope limited
to the block of code controlled by that statement. Thus, in this case, **x** is not known
outside the **if**. Frankly, not all programmers believe that declaring variables within
conditional statements is good practice, and this technique will not be used in
this book.

Jump Statements

C/C++ has four statements that perform an unconditional branch: **return**, **goto**, **break**,
and **continue**. Of these, you may use **return** and **goto** anywhere in your program. You
may use the **break** and **continue** statements in conjunction with any of the loop
statements. As discussed earlier in this chapter, you can also use **break** with **switch**.

The return Statement

The **return** statement is used to return from a function. It is categorized as a jump
statement because it causes execution to return (jump back) to the point at which the
call to the function was made. A **return** may or may not have a value associated with
it. If **return** has a value associated with it, that value becomes the return value of the
function. In C89, a non-**void** function does not technically have to return a value. If no
return value is specified, a garbage value is returned. However, in C++ (and in C99),
a non-**void** function *must* return a value. That is, in C++, if a function is specified as
returning a value, any **return** statement within it must have a value associated with it.
(Even in C89, if a function is declared as returning a value, it is good practice to
actually return one!)

The general form of the **return** statement is

return *expression*;

The *expression* is present only if the function is declared as returning a value. In this
case, the value of *expression* will become the return value of the function.

You can use as many **return** statements as you like within a function. However,
the function will stop executing as soon as it encounters the first **return**. The } that ends
a function also causes the function to return. It is the same as a **return** without any
specified value. If this occurs within a non-**void** function, then the return value of the
function is undefined.

A function declared as **void** may not contain a **return** statement that specifies a
value. Since a **void** function has no return value, it makes sense that no **return**
statement within a **void** function can return a value.

See Chapter 6 for more information on **return**.

The goto Statement

Since C/C++ has a rich set of control structures and allows additional control using **break** and **continue**, there is little need for **goto**. Most programmers' chief concern about the **goto** is its tendency to render programs unreadable. Nevertheless, although the **goto** statement fell out of favor some years ago, it occasionally has its uses. There are no programming situations that require **goto**. Rather, it is a convenience, which, if used wisely, can be a benefit in a narrow set of programming situations, such as jumping out of a set of deeply nested loops. The **goto** is not used outside of this section.

The **goto** statement requires a label for operation. (A *label* is a valid identifier followed by a colon.) Furthermore, the label must be in the same function as the **goto** that uses it—you cannot jump between functions. The general form of the **goto** statement is

    goto *label*;
    .
    .
    .
    label:

where *label* is any valid label either before or after **goto**. For example, you could create a loop from 1 to 100 using the **goto** and a label, as shown here:

```
x = 1;
loop1:
  x++;
  if(x<100) goto loop1;
```

The break Statement

The **break** statement has two uses. You can use it to terminate a **case** in the **switch** statement (covered in the section on **switch** earlier in this chapter). You can also use it to force immediate termination of a loop, bypassing the normal loop conditional test.

When the **break** statement is encountered inside a loop, the loop is immediately terminated and program control resumes at the next statement following the loop. For example,

```
#include <stdio.h>

int main(void)
{
  int t;
```

```
for(t=0; t<100; t++) {
  printf("%d ", t);
  if(t==10) break;
}

return 0;
}
```

prints the numbers 0 through 10 on the screen. Then the loop terminates because **break** causes immediate exit from the loop, overriding the conditional test **t<100**.

Programmers often use the **break** statement in loops in which a special condition can cause immediate termination. For example, here a keypress can stop the execution of the **look_up( )** function:

```
void look_up(char *name)
{
  do {
    /* look up names ... */
    if(kbhit()) break;
  } while(!found);
  /* process match */
}
```

The **kbhit( )** function returns 0 if you do not press a key. Otherwise, it returns a nonzero value. Because of the wide differences between computing environments, neither Standard C nor Standard C++ defines **kbhit( )**, but you will almost certainly have it (or one with a slightly different name) supplied with your compiler.

A **break** causes an exit from only the innermost loop. For example,

```
for(t=0; t<100; ++t) {
  count = 1;
  for(;;) {
    printf("%d ", count);
    count++;
    if(count==10) break;
  }
}
```

prints the numbers 1 through 10 on the screen 100 times. Each time execution encounters **break**, control is passed back to the outer **for** loop.

A **break** used in a **switch** statement will affect only that **switch**. It does not affect any loop the **switch** happens to be in.

The exit( ) Function

Although **exit( )** is not a program control statement, a short digression that discusses it is in order at this time. Just as you can break out of a loop, you can break out of a program by using the standard library function **exit( )**. This function causes immediate termination of the entire program, forcing a return to the operating system. In effect, the **exit( )** function acts as if it were breaking out of the entire program.

The general form of the **exit( )** function is

void exit(int *return_code*);

The value of *return_code* is returned to the calling process, which is usually the operating system. Zero is generally used as a return code to indicate normal program termination. Other arguments are used to indicate some sort of error. You can also use the macros **EXIT_SUCCESS** and **EXIT_FAILURE** for the *return_code*. The **exit( )** function requires the header **stdlib.h**. A C++ program may also use the C++-style header **<cstdlib>**.

Programmers frequently use **exit( )** when a mandatory condition for program execution is not satisfied. For example, imagine a virtual reality computer game that requires a special graphics adapter. The **main( )** function of this game might look like this:

```
#include <stdlib.h>

int main(void)
{
    if(!virtual_graphics()) exit(1);
    play();
    /* ... */
}
/* .... */
```

where **virtual_graphics( )** is a user-defined function that returns true if the virtual-reality graphics adapter is present. If the adapter is not in the system, **virtual_graphics( )** returns false and the program terminates.

As another example, this version of **menu( )** uses **exit( )** to quit the program and return to the operating system:

```
void menu(void)
{
```

```
    char ch;

    printf("1. Check Spelling\n");
    printf("2. Correct Spelling Errors\n");
    printf("3. Display Spelling Errors\n");
    printf("4. Quit\n");
    printf("        Enter your choice: ");

    do {
      ch = getchar(); /* read the selection from
                          the keyboard */
        switch(ch) {
          case '1':
            check_spelling();
            break;
          case '2':
            correct_errors();
            break;
          case '3':
            display_errors();
            break;
          case '4':
            exit(0); /* return to OS */
        }
    } while(ch!='1' && ch!='2' && ch!='3');
}
```

The continue Statement

The **continue** statement works somewhat like the **break** statement. Instead of forcing
termination, however, **continue** forces the next iteration of the loop to take place,
skipping any code in between. For the **for** loop, **continue** causes the conditional test
and increment portions of the loop to execute. For the **while** and **do-while** loops,
program control passes to the conditional tests. For example, the following program
counts the number of spaces contained in the string entered by the user:

```
/* Count spaces */
#include <stdio.h>

int main(void)
{
```

```
  char s[80], *str;
  int space;

  printf("Enter a string: ");
  gets(s);
  str = s;

  for(space=0; *str; str++) {
    if(*str != ' ') continue;
    space++;
  }
  printf("%d spaces\n", space);

  return 0;
}
```

Each character is tested to see if it is a space. If it is not, the **continue** statement forces the **for** to iterate again. If the character *is* a space, **space** is incremented.

The following example shows how you can use **continue** to expedite the exit from a loop by forcing the conditional test to be performed sooner:

```
void code(void)
{
  char done, ch;

  done = 0;
  while(!done) {
    ch = getchar();
    if(ch=='$') {
      done = 1;
      continue;
    }
    putchar(ch+1); /* shift the alphabet one
                      position higher */
  }
}
```

This function codes a message by shifting all characters you type one letter higher. For example, an **A** becomes a **B**. The function will terminate when you type a **$**. After a **$** has been input, no further output will occur because the conditional test, brought into effect by **continue**, will find **done** to be true and will cause the loop to exit.

Expression Statements

Chapter 2 covered expressions thoroughly. However, a few special points are mentioned here. Remember, an expression statement is simply a valid expression followed by a semicolon, as in

```
func();  /* a function call */
a = b+c; /* an assignment statement */
b+f();   /* a valid, but strange statement */
;        /* an empty statement */
```

The first expression statement executes a function call. The second is an assignment. The third expression, though strange, is still evaluated by the C++ compiler and the function **f( )** is called. The final example shows that a statement can be empty (sometimes called a *null statement*).

Block Statements

Block statements are simply groups of related statements that are treated as a unit. The statements that make up a block are logically bound together. Block statements are also called *compound statements*. A block is begun with a { and terminated by its matching }. Programmers use block statements most commonly to create a multistatement target for some other statement, such as **if**. However, you may place a block statement anywhere you would put any other statement. For example, this is perfectly valid (although unusual) C/C++ code:

```
#include <stdio.h>

int main(void)
{
  int i;

  {  /* a block statement */
    i = 120;
    printf("%d", i);
  }

  return 0;
}
```

Chapter 4

Arrays and
Null-Terminated Strings

n *array* is a collection of variables of the same type that are referred to through a common name. A specific element in an array is accessed by an index. In C/C++, all arrays consist of contiguous memory locations. The lowest address corresponds to the first element and the highest address to the last element. Arrays may have from one to several dimensions. The most common array is the *null-terminated string*, which is simply an array of characters terminated by a null.

Arrays and pointers are closely related; a discussion of one usually refers to the other. This chapter focuses on arrays, while Chapter 5 looks closely at pointers. You should read both to understand fully these important constructs.

Single-Dimension Arrays

The general form for declaring a single-dimension array is

   type var_name[size];

Like other variables, arrays must be explicitly declared so that the compiler may allocate space for them in memory. Here, *type* declares the base type of the array, which is the type of each element in the array, and *size* defines how many elements the array will hold. For example, to declare a 100-element array called **balance** of type **double**, use this statement:

```
double balance[100];
```

An element is accessed by indexing the array name. This is done by placing the index of the element within square brackets after the name of the array. For example,

```
balance[3] = 12.23;
```

assigns element number 3 in **balance** the value 12.23.

In C/C++, all arrays have 0 as the index of their first element. Therefore, when you write

```
char p[10];
```

you are declaring a character array that has ten elements, **p[0]** through **p[9]**. For example, the following program loads an integer array with the numbers 0 through 99:

```
#include <stdio.h>

int main(void)
{
```

```
int x[100]; /* this declares a 100-integer array */
int t;

/* load x with values 0 through 99 */
for(t=0; t<100; ++t) x[t] = t;

/* display contents of x */
for(t=0; t<100; ++t) printf("%d ", x[t]);

return 0;
}
```

The amount of storage required to hold an array is directly related to its type and size. For a single-dimension array, the total size in bytes is computed as shown here:

total bytes = sizeof(base type) x size of array

C/C++ has no bounds checking on arrays. You could overwrite either end of an array and write into some other variable's data or even into the program's code. As the programmer, it is your job to provide bounds checking where needed. For example, this code will compile without error, but is incorrect because the **for** loop will cause the array **count** to be overrun.

```
int count[10], i;

/* this causes count to be overrun */
for(i=0; i<100; i++) count[i] = i;
```

Single-dimension arrays are essentially lists of information of the same type that are stored in contiguous memory locations in index order. For example, Figure 4-1 shows how array **a** appears in memory if it starts at memory location 1000 and is declared as shown here:

```
char a[7];
```

Element	a[0]	a[1]	a[2]	a[3]	a[4]	a[5]	a[6]
Address	1000	1001	1002	1003	1004	1005	1006

Figure 4-1.   *A seven-element character array beginning at location 1000*

Generating a Pointer to an Array

You can generate a pointer to the first element of an array by simply specifying the array name, without any index. For example, given

```
int sample[10];
```

you can generate a pointer to the first element by using the name **sample**. Thus, the following program fragment assigns **p** the address of the first element of **sample**:

```
int *p;
int sample[10];

p = sample;
```

You can also specify the address of the first element of an array using the **&** operator. For example, **sample** and **&sample[0]** both produce the same results. However, in professionally written C/C++ code, you will almost never see **&sample[0]**.

Passing Single-Dimension Arrays to Functions

In C/C++, you cannot pass an entire array as an argument to a function. You can, however, pass to the function a pointer to an array by specifying the array's name without an index. For example, the following program fragment passes the address of **i** to **func1( )**:

```
int main(void)
{
  int i[10];

  func1(i);
  .
  .
  .
}
```

If a function receives a single-dimension array, you may declare its formal parameter in one of three ways: as a pointer, as a sized array, or as an unsized array. For example, to receive **i**, a function called **func1( )** can be declared as

```
void func1(int *x) /* pointer */
{
```

```
      .
      .
      .
}
```

or

```
void func1(int x[10]) /* sized array */
{

   .
   .
   .

}
```

or finally as

```
void func1(int x[]) /* unsized array */
{

   .
   .
   .

}
```

All three declaration methods produce similar results because each tells the compiler that an integer pointer is going to be received. The first declaration actually uses a pointer. The second employs the standard array declaration. In the final version, a modified version of an array declaration simply specifies that an array of type **int** of some length is to be received. As you can see, the length of the array doesn't matter as far as the function is concerned because C/C++ performs no bounds checking. In fact, as far as the compiler is concerned,

```
void func1(int x[32])
{

   .
   .
   .

}
```

also works because the compiler generates code that instructs **func1( )** to receive a pointer—it does not actually create a 32-element array.

Null-Terminated Strings

By far the most common use of the one-dimensional array is as a character string. C++ supports two types of strings. The first is the *null-terminated string*, which is a null-terminated character array. (A null is zero.) Thus a null-terminated string contains the characters that comprise the string followed by a null. This is the only type of string defined by C, and it is still the most widely used. Sometimes null-terminated strings are called *C-strings*. C++ also defines a string class, called **string**, which provides an object-oriented approach to string handling. It is described later in this book. Here, null-terminated strings are examined.

When declaring a character array that will hold a null-terminated string, you need to declare it to be one character longer than the largest string that it is to hold. For example, to declare an array **str** that can hold a 10-character string, you would write

```
char str[11];
```

This makes room for the null at the end of the string.

When you use a quoted string constant in your program, you are also creating a null-terminated string. A *string constant* is a list of characters enclosed in double quotes. For example,

"hello there"

You do not need to add the null to the end of string constants manually—the compiler does this for you automatically.

C/C++ supports a wide range of functions that manipulate null-terminated strings. The most common are

Name	Function
strcpy(*s1*, *s2*)	Copies *s2* into *s1*.
strcat(*s1*, *s2*)	Concatenates *s2* onto the end of *s1*.
strlen(*s1*)	Returns the length of *s1*.
strcmp(*s1*, *s2*)	Returns 0 if *s1* and *s2* are the same; less than 0 if *s1*<*s2*; greater than 0 if *s1*>*s2*.
strchr(*s1*, *ch*)	Returns a pointer to the first occurrence of *ch* in *s1*.
strstr(*s1*, *s2*)	Returns a pointer to the first occurrence of *s2* in *s1*.

These functions use the standard header file **string.h**. (C++ programs can also use the C++-style header **<cstring>**.) The following program illustrates the use of these string functions:

```
#include <stdio.h>
#include <string.h>

int main(void)
{
  char s1[80], s2[80];

  gets(s1);
  gets(s2);

  printf("lengths: %d %d\n", strlen(s1), strlen(s2));

  if(!strcmp(s1, s2)) printf("The strings are equal\n");

  strcat(s1, s2);
  printf("%s\n", s1);

  strcpy(s1, "This is a test.\n");
  printf(s1);
  if(strchr("hello", 'e')) printf("e is in hello\n");
  if(strstr("hi there", "hi")) printf("found hi");

  return 0;
}
```

If you run this program and enter the strings "**hello**" and "**hello**", the output is

```
lengths: 5 5
The strings are equal
hellohello
This is a test.
e is in hello
found hi
```

Remember, **strcmp( )** returns false if the strings are equal. Be sure to use the logical operator **!** to reverse the condition, as just shown, if you are testing for equality.

Although C++ defines a string class, null-terminated strings are still widely used in existing programs. They will probably stay in wide use because they offer a high level of efficiency and afford the programmer detailed control of string operations. However, for many simple string-handling chores, C++'s string class provides a convenient alternative.

Two-Dimensional Arrays

C/C++ supports multidimensional arrays. The simplest form of the multidimensional array is the two-dimensional array. A two-dimensional array is, essentially, an array of one-dimensional arrays. To declare a two-dimensional integer array **d** of size 10,20, you would write

```
int d[10][20];
```

Pay careful attention to the declaration. Some other computer languages use commas to separate the array dimensions; C/C++, in contrast, places each dimension in its own set of brackets.

Similarly, to access point 1,2 of array **d**, you would use

```
d[1][2]
```

The following example loads a two-dimensional array with the numbers 1 through 12 and prints them row by row.

```c
#include <stdio.h>

int main(void)
{
  int t, i, num[3][4];

  for(t=0; t<3; ++t)
    for(i=0; i<4; ++i)
      num[t][i] = (t*4)+i+1;

  /* now print them out */
  for(t=0; t<3; ++t) {
    for(i=0; i<4; ++i)
      printf("%3d ", num[t][i]);
    printf("\n");
  }

  return 0;
}
```

In this example, **num[0][0]** has the value 1, **num[0][1]** the value 2, **num[0][2]** the value 3, and so on. The value of **num[2][3]** will be 12. You can visualize the **num** array as shown here:

num [t] [i]

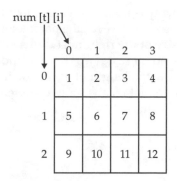

Two-dimensional arrays are stored in a row-column matrix, where the first index indicates the row and the second indicates the column. This means that the rightmost index changes faster than the leftmost when accessing the elements in the array in the order in which they are actually stored in memory. See Figure 4-2 for a graphic representation of a two-dimensional array in memory.

In the case of a two-dimensional array, the following formula yields the number of bytes of memory needed to hold it:

bytes = size of 1st index x size of 2nd index x sizeof(base type)

Therefore, assuming 4-byte integers, an integer array with dimensions 10,5 would have

10 x 5 x 4

or 200 bytes allocated.

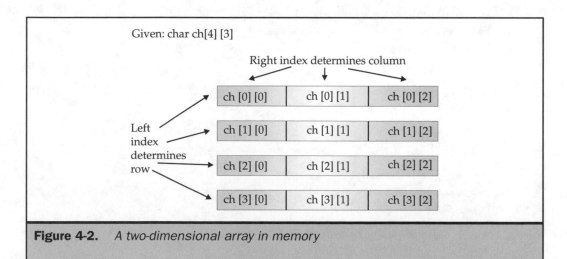

Figure 4-2.   *A two-dimensional array in memory*

When a two-dimensional array is used as an argument to a function, only a pointer to the first element is actually passed. However, the parameter receiving a two-dimensional array must define at least the size of the rightmost dimension. (You can specify the left dimension if you like, but it is not necessary.) The rightmost dimension is needed because the compiler must know the length of each row if it is to index the array correctly. For example, a function that receives a two-dimensional integer array with dimensions 10,10 is declared like this:

```
void func1(int x[][10])
{
        .
        .
        .
}
```

The compiler needs to know the size of the right dimension in order to correctly execute expressions such as

```
x[2][4]
```

inside the function. If the length of the rows is not known, the compiler cannot determine where the third row begins.

The following short program uses a two-dimensional array to store the numeric grade for each student in a teacher's classes. The program assumes that the teacher has three classes and a maximum of 30 students per class. Notice the way the array **grade** is accessed by each of the functions.

```
/* A simple student grades database. */
#include <stdio.h>
#include <ctype.h>
#include <stdlib.h>

#define CLASSES  3
#define GRADES   30

int grade[CLASSES][GRADES];

void enter_grades(void);
int get_grade(int num);
void disp_grades(int g[][GRADES]);
```

```
int main(void)
{
  char ch, str[80];

  for(;;) {
    do {
      printf("(E)nter grades\n");
      printf("(R)eport grades\n");
      printf("(Q)uit\n");
      gets(str);
      ch = toupper(*str);
    } while(ch!='E' && ch!='R' && ch!='Q');

    switch(ch) {
      case 'E':
        enter_grades();
        break;
      case 'R':
        disp_grades(grade);
        break;
      case 'Q':
        exit(0);
    }
  }

  return 0;
}

/* Enter the student's grades. */
void enter_grades(void)
{
  int t, i;

  for(t=0; t<CLASSES; t++) {
    printf("Class # %d:\n", t+1);
    for(i=0; i<GRADES; ++i)
      grade[t][i] = get_grade(i);
  }
}

/* Read a grade. */
int get_grade(int num)
```

```
{
  char s[80];

  printf("Enter grade for student # %d:\n", num+1);
  gets(s);
  return(atoi(s));
}

/* Display grades. */
void disp_grades(int g[][GRADES])
{
  int t, i;

  for(t=0; t<CLASSES; ++t) {
    printf("Class # %d:\n", t+1);
    for(i=0; i<GRADES; ++i)
      printf("Student #%d is %d\n", i+1, g[t][i]);
  }
}
```

Arrays of Strings

It is not uncommon in programming to use an array of strings. For example, the input processor to a database may verify user commands against an array of valid commands. To create an array of null-terminated strings, use a two-dimensional character array. The size of the left index determines the number of strings and the size of the right index specifies the maximum length of each string. The following code declares an array of 30 strings, each with a maximum length of 79 characters, plus the null terminator.

```
char str_array[30][80];
```

It is easy to access an individual string: You simply specify only the left index. For example, the following statement calls **gets( )** with the third string in **str_array**.

```
gets(str_array[2]);
```

The preceding statement is functionally equivalent to

```
gets(&str_array[2][0]);
```

but the first of the two forms is much more common in professionally written C/C++ code.

To better understand how string arrays work, study the following short program, which uses a string array as the basis for a very simple text editor:

```c
/* A very simple text editor. */
#include <stdio.h>

#define MAX 100
#define LEN 80

char text[MAX][LEN];

int main(void)
{
  register int t, i, j;

  printf("Enter an empty line to quit.\n");

  for(t=0; t<MAX; t++) {
    printf("%d: ", t);
    gets(text[t]);
    if(!*text[t]) break; /* quit on blank line */
  }

  for(i=0; i<t; i++) {
    for(j=0; text[i][j]; j++) putchar(text[i][j]);
    putchar('\n');
  }

  return 0;
}
```

This program inputs lines of text until a blank line is entered. Then it redisplays each line one character at a time.

Multidimensional Arrays

C/C++ allows arrays of more than two dimensions. The exact limit, if any, is determined by your compiler. The general form of a multidimensional array declaration is

type name[*Size1*][*Size2*][*Size3*]. . .[*SizeN*];

Arrays of more than three dimensions are not often used because of the amount of memory they require. For example, a four-dimensional character array with dimensions 10,6,9,4 requires

```
10 * 6 * 9 * 4
```

or 2,160 bytes. If the array held 2-byte integers, 4,320 bytes would be needed. If the array held **double**s (assuming 8 bytes per **double**), 17,280 bytes would be required. The storage required increases exponentially with the number of dimensions. For example, if a fifth dimension of size 10 was added to the preceding array, then 172, 800 bytes would be required.

In multidimensional arrays, it takes the computer time to compute each index. This means that accessing an element in a multidimensional array can be slower than accessing an element in a single-dimension array.

When passing multidimensional arrays into functions, you must declare all but the leftmost dimension. For example, if you declare array **m** as

```
int m[4][3][6][5];
```

a function, **func1( )**, that receives **m**, would look like this:

```
void func1(int d[][3][6][5])
{
    .
    .
    .
}
```

Of course, you can include the first dimension if you like.

Indexing Pointers

In C/C++, pointers and arrays are closely related. As you know, an array name without an index is a pointer to the first element in the array. For example, consider the following array.

```
char p[10];
```

The following statements are identical:

```
p
&p[0]
```

Put another way,

```
p == &p[0]
```

evaluates to true because the address of the first element of an array is the same as the address of the array.

As stated, an array name without an index generates a pointer. Conversely, a pointer can be indexed as if it were declared to be an array. For example, consider this program fragment:

```
int *p, i[10];
p = i;
p[5] = 100;  /* assign using index */
*(p+5) = 100; /* assign using pointer arithmetic */
```

Both assignment statements place the value 100 in the sixth element of **i**. The first statement indexes **p**; the second uses pointer arithmetic. Either way, the result is the same. (Chapter 5 discusses pointers and pointer arithmetic.)

This same concept also applies to arrays of two or more dimensions. For example, assuming that **a** is a 10-by-10 integer array, these two statements are equivalent:

```
a
&a[0][0]
```

Furthermore, the 0,4 element of **a** may be referenced two ways: either by array indexing, **a[0][4]**, or by the pointer, ***((int *)a+4)**. Similarly, element 1,2 is either **a[1][2]** or ***((int *)a+12)**. In general, for any two-dimensional array

a[j][k] is equivalent to *((*base-type* *)a+(j**row length*)+k)

The cast of the pointer to the array into a pointer of its base type is necessary in order for the pointer arithmetic to operate properly. Pointers are sometimes used to access arrays because pointer arithmetic is often faster than array indexing.

A two-dimensional array can be reduced to a pointer to an array of one-dimensional arrays. Therefore, using a separate pointer variable is one easy way to use pointers to access elements within a row of a two-dimensional array. The following function illustrates this technique. It will print the contents of the specified row for the global integer array **num**:

```
int num[10][10];
```

```
        .
        .
        .
void  pr_row(int j)
{
  int *p, t;

  p = (int *) &num[j][0]; /* get address of first
                               element in row j */

  for(t=0; t<10; ++t) printf("%d ", *(p+t));
}
```

You can generalize this routine by making the calling arguments be the row, the row length, and a pointer to the first array element, as shown here:

```
void pr_row(int j, int row_dimension, int *p)
{
  int t;

  p = p + (j * row_dimension);

  for(t=0; t<row_dimension; ++t)
    printf("%d ", *(p+t));
}
        .
        .
        .
void f(void)
{
  int num[10][10];

  pr_row(0, 10, (int *) num); /* print first row */
}
```

Arrays of greater than two dimensions may be reduced in a similar way. For example, a three-dimensional array can be reduced to a pointer to a two-dimensional array, which can be reduced to a pointer to a single-dimension array. Generally, an n-dimensional array can be reduced to a pointer and an (n-1)-dimensional array. This new array can be reduced again with the same method. The process ends when a single-dimension array is produced.

Array Initialization

C/C++ allows the initialization of arrays at the time of their declaration. The general form of array initialization is similar to that of other variables, as shown here:

type_specifier array_name[size1]. . .[sizeN] = { value_list };

The *value_list* is a comma-separated list of values whose type is compatible with *type_specifier*. The first value is placed in the first position of the array, the second value in the second position, and so on. Note that a semicolon follows the }.

In the following example, a 10-element integer array is initialized with the numbers 1 through 10:

```
int i[10] = {1, 2, 3, 4, 5, 6, 7, 8, 9, 10};
```

This means that **i[0]** will have the value 1 and **i[9]** will have the value 10.

Character arrays that hold strings allow a shorthand initialization that takes the form:

char *array_name[size]* = "*string*";

For example, this code fragment initializes **str** to the phrase "I like C++".

```
char str[11] = "I like C++";
```

This is the same as writing

```
char str[11] = {'I', ' ', 'l', 'i', 'k', 'e',' ', 'C',
                '+', '+', '\0'};
```

Because null-terminated strings end with a null, you must make sure that the array you declare is long enough to include the null. This is why **str** is 11 characters long even though "I like C++" is only 10. When you use the string constant, the compiler automatically supplies the null terminator.

Multidimensional arrays are initialized the same as single-dimension ones. For example, the following initializes **sqrs** with the numbers 1 through 10 and their squares.

```
int sqrs[10][2] = {
  1, 1,
```

```
        2, 4,
        3, 9,
        4, 16,
        5, 25,
        6, 36,
        7, 49,
        8, 64,
        9, 81,
        10, 100
};
```

When initializing a multidimensional array, you may add braces around the initializers for each dimension. This is called *subaggregate grouping*. For example, here is another way to write the preceding declaration.

```
int sqrs[10][2] = {
    {1, 1},
    {2, 4},
    {3, 9},
    {4, 16},
    {5, 25},
    {6, 36},
    {7, 49},
    {8, 64},
    {9, 81},
    {10, 100}
};
```

When using subaggregate grouping, if you don't supply enough initializers for a given group, the remaining members will be set to zero automatically.

Unsized Array Initializations

Imagine that you are using array initialization to build a table of error messages, as shown here:

```
char e1[12] = "Read error\n";
char e2[13] = "Write error\n";
char e3[18] = "Cannot open file\n";
```

As you might guess, it is tedious to count the characters in each message manually to determine the correct array dimension. Fortunately, you can let the compiler automatically calculate the dimensions of the arrays. If, in an array initialization statement, the size of the array is not specified, the C/C++ compiler automatically creates an array big enough to hold all the initializers present. This is called an *unsized array*. Using this approach, the message table becomes

```
char e1[] = "Read error\n";
char e2[] = "Write error\n";
char e3[] = "Cannot open file\n";
```

Given these initializations, this statement

```
printf("%s has length %d\n",  e2,  sizeof e2);
```

will print

```
Write error has length 13
```

Besides being less tedious, unsized array initialization allows you to change any of the messages without fear of using incorrect array dimensions.

Unsized array initializations are not restricted to one-dimensional arrays. For multidimensional arrays, you must specify all but the leftmost dimension. (The other dimensions are needed to allow the compiler to index the array properly.) In this way, you may build tables of varying lengths and the compiler automatically allocates enough storage for them. For example, the declaration of **sqrs** as an unsized array is shown here:

```
int sqrs[][2] = {
  {1, 1},
  {2, 4},
  {3, 9},
  {4, 16},
  {5, 25},
  {6, 36},
  {7, 49},
  {8, 64},
  {9, 81},
  {10, 100}
};
```

The advantage of this declaration over the sized version is that you may lengthen or shorten the table without changing the array dimensions.

A Tic-Tac-Toe Example

The longer example that follows illustrates many of the ways that you can manipulate arrays with C/C++. This section develops a simple tic-tac-toe program. Two-dimensional arrays are commonly used to simulate board game matrices.

The computer plays a very simple game. When it is the computer's turn, it uses **get_computer_move( )** to scan the matrix, looking for an unoccupied cell. When it finds one, it puts an **O** there. If it cannot find an empty location, it reports a draw game and exits. The **get_player_move( )** function asks you where you want to place an **X**. The upper-left corner is location 1,1; the lower-right corner is 3,3.

The matrix array is initialized to contain spaces. Each move made by the player or the computer changes a space into either an X or an O. This makes it easy to display the matrix on the screen.

Each time a move has been made, the program calls the **check( )** function. This function returns a space if there is no winner yet, an X if you have won, or an O if the computer has won. It scans the rows, the columns, and then the diagonals, looking for one that contains either all X's or all O's.

The **disp_matrix( )** function displays the current state of the game. Notice how initializing the matrix with spaces simplified this function.

The routines in this example all access the **matrix** array differently. Study them to make sure that you understand each array operation.

```
/* A simple Tic Tac Toe game. */
#include <stdio.h>
#include <stdlib.h>

char matrix[3][3];   /* the tic tac toe matrix */

char check(void);
void init_matrix(void);
void get_player_move(void);
void get_computer_move(void);
void disp_matrix(void);

int main(void)
{
  char done;

  printf("This is the game of Tic Tac Toe.\n");
  printf("You will be playing against the computer.\n");

  done = ' ';
```

```
    init_matrix();
    do{
      disp_matrix();
      get_player_move();
      done = check(); /* see if winner */
      if(done!= ' ') break; /* winner!*/
      get_computer_move();
      done = check(); /* see if winner */
    } while(done== ' ');
    if(done=='X') printf("You won!\n");
    else printf("I won!!!!\n");
    disp_matrix(); /* show final positions */

    return 0;
}

/* Initialize the matrix. */
void init_matrix(void)
{
  int i, j;

  for(i=0; i<3; i++)
    for(j=0; j<3; j++) matrix[i][j] =  ' ';
}

/* Get a player's move. */
void get_player_move(void)
{
  int x, y;

  printf("Enter X,Y coordinates for your move: ");
  scanf("%d%*c%d", &x, &y);

  x--; y--;

  if(matrix[x][y]!= ' '){
    printf("Invalid move, try again.\n");
    get_player_move();
  }
  else matrix[x][y] = 'X';
}
```

```c
/* Get a move from the computer. */
void get_computer_move(void)
{
  int i, j;
  for(i=0; i<3; i++){
    for(j=0; j<3; j++)
      if(matrix[i][j]==' ') break;
    if(matrix[i][j]==' ') break;
  }

  if(i*j==9)  {
    printf("draw\n");
    exit(0);
  }
  else
    matrix[i][j] = 'O';
}

/* Display the matrix on the screen. */
void disp_matrix(void)
{
  int t;

  for(t=0; t<3; t++) {
    printf(" %c | %c | %c ",matrix[t][0],
            matrix[t][1], matrix [t][2]);
    if(t!=2) printf("\n---|---|---\n");
  }
  printf("\n");
}

/* See if there is a winner. */
char check(void)
{
  int i;

  for(i=0; i<3; i++)  /* check rows */
    if(matrix[i][0]==matrix[i][1] &&
       matrix[i][0]==matrix[i][2]) return matrix[i][0];

  for(i=0; i<3; i++)  /* check columns */
    if(matrix[0][i]==matrix[1][i] &&
```

```
        matrix[0][i]==matrix[2][i]) return matrix[0][i];

  /* test diagonals */
  if(matrix[0][0]==matrix[1][1] &&
     matrix[1][1]==matrix[2][2])
       return matrix[0][0];

  if(matrix[0][2]==matrix[1][1] &&
     matrix[1][1]==matrix[2][0])
       return matrix[0][2];

  return ' ';
}
```

Chapter 5

Pointers

The correct understanding and use of pointers is critical to successful C/C++ programming. There are three reasons for this: First, pointers provide the means by which functions can modify their calling arguments. Second, pointers support dynamic allocation. Third, pointers can improve the efficiency of certain routines. Also, as you will see in Part Two, pointers take on additional roles in C++.

Pointers are one of the strongest but also one of the most dangerous features in C/C++. For example, uninitialized pointers (or pointers containing invalid values) can cause your system to crash. Perhaps worse, it is easy to use pointers incorrectly, causing bugs that are very difficult to find.

Because of both their importance and their potential for abuse, this chapter examines the subject of pointers in detail.

What Are Pointers?

A *pointer* is a variable that holds a memory address. This address is the location of another object (typically another variable) in memory. For example, if one variable contains the address of another variable, the first variable is said to *point to* the second. Figure 5-1 illustrates this situation.

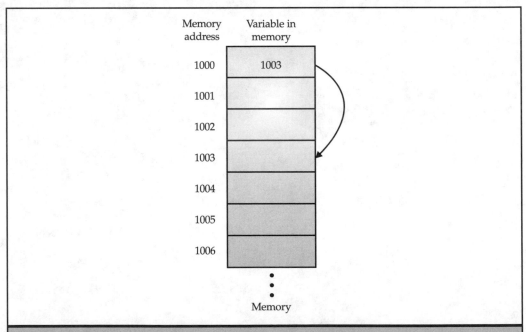

Figure 5-1. *One variable points to another*

Pointer Variables

If a variable is going to hold a pointer, it must be declared as such. A pointer declaration consists of a base type, an *, and the variable name. The general form for declaring a pointer variable is

type *name;

where *type* is the base type of the pointer and may be any valid type. The name of the pointer variable is specified by *name.*

The base type of the pointer defines what type of variables the pointer can point to. Technically, any type of pointer can point anywhere in memory. However, all pointer arithmetic is done relative to its base type, so it is important to declare the pointer correctly. (Pointer arithmetic is discussed later in this chapter.)

The Pointer Operators

The pointer operators were discussed in Chapter 2. We will take a closer look at them here, beginning with a review of their basic operation. There are two special pointer operators: * and &. The & is a unary operator that returns the memory address of its operand. (Remember, a unary operator only requires one operand.) For example,

```
m = &count;
```

places into **m** the memory address of the variable **count**. This address is the computer's internal location of the variable. It has nothing to do with the value of **count**. You can think of & as returning "the address of." Therefore, the preceding assignment statement means "m receives the address of **count**."

To understand the above assignment better, assume that the variable **count** uses memory location 2000 to store its value. Also assume that **count** has a value of 100. Then, after the preceding assignment, **m** will have the value 2000.

The second pointer operator, *, is the complement of &. It is a unary operator that returns the value located at the address that follows. For example, if **m** contains the memory address of the variable **count**,

```
q = *m;
```

places the value of **count** into **q**. Thus, **q** will have the value 100 because 100 is stored at location 2000, which is the memory address that was stored in **m**. You can think of * as "at address." In this case, the preceding statement means "q receives the value at address **m**."

Both **&** and ***** have a higher precedence than all other arithmetic operators except the unary minus, with which they are equal.

You must make sure that your pointer variables always point to the correct type of data. For example, when you declare a pointer to be of type **int**, the compiler assumes that any address that it holds points to an integer variable—whether it actually does or not. Because you can assign any address you want to a pointer variable, the following program compiles without error, but does not produce the desired result:

```
#include <stdio.h>

int main(void)
{
  double x = 100.1, y;
  int  *p;

  /* The next statement causes p (which is an
     integer pointer) to point to a double. */
  p = (int *)&x;

  /* The next statement does not operate as
     expected. */
  y = *p;


  printf("%f", y); /* won't output 100.1 */
  return 0;
}
```

This will not assign the value of **x** to **y**. Because **p** is declared as an integer pointer, only 4 bytes of information (assuming 4-byte integers) will be transferred to **y**, not the 8 bytes that normally make up a **double**.

 In C++, it is illegal to convert one type of pointer into another without the use of an explicit type cast. In C, casts should be used for most pointer conversions.

Pointer Expressions

In general, expressions involving pointers conform to the same rules as other expressions. This section examines a few special aspects of pointer expressions.

Pointer Assignments

As with any variable, you may use a pointer on the right-hand side of an assignment statement to assign its value to another pointer. For example,

```
#include <stdio.h>

int main(void)
{
  int x;
  int *p1, *p2;

  p1 = &x;
  p2 = p1;

  printf(" %p", p2); /* print the address of x, not x's value! */

  return 0;
}
```

Both **p1** and **p2** now point to **x**. The address of **x** is displayed by using the **%p printf( )** format specifier, which causes **printf( )** to display an address in the format used by the host computer.

Pointer Arithmetic

There are only two arithmetic operations that you may use on pointers: addition and subtraction. To understand what occurs in pointer arithmetic, let **p1** be an integer pointer with a current value of 2000. Also, assume integers are 2 bytes long. After the expression

```
p1++;
```

p1 contains 2002, not 2001. The reason for this is that each time **p1** is incremented, it will point to the next integer. The same is true of decrements. For example, assuming that **p1** has the value 2000, the expression

```
p1--;
```

causes **p1** to have the value 1998.

Generalizing from the preceding example, the following rules govern pointer arithmetic. Each time a pointer is incremented, it points to the memory location of the next element of its base type. Each time it is decremented, it points to the location of the previous element. When applied to character pointers, this will appear as "normal" arithmetic because characters are always 1 byte long. All other pointers will increase or decrease by the length of the data type they point to. This approach ensures that a pointer is always pointing to an appropriate element of its base type. Figure 5-2 illustrates this concept.

You are not limited to the increment and decrement operators. For example, you may add or subtract integers to or from pointers. The expression

```
p1 = p1 + 12;
```

makes **p1** point to the twelfth element of **p1**'s type beyond the one it currently points to.

Besides addition and subtraction of a pointer and an integer, only one other arithmetic operation is allowed: You may subtract one pointer from another in order to find the number of objects of their base type that separate the two. All other arithmetic operations are prohibited. Specifically, you may not multiply or divide pointers; you may not add two pointers; you may not apply the bitwise operators to them; and you may not add or subtract type **float** or **double** to or from pointers.

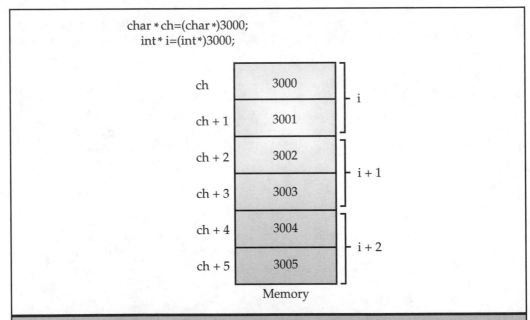

Figure 5-2.   *All pointer arithmetic is relative to its base type (assume 2-byte integers)*

Pointer Comparisons

You can compare two pointers in a relational expression. For instance, given two pointers **p** and **q**, the following statement is perfectly valid:

```
if(p<q) printf("p points to lower memory than q\n");
```

Generally, pointer comparisons are used when two or more pointers point to a common object, such as an array. As an example, a pair of stack routines are developed that store and retrieve integer values. A stack is a list that uses first-in, last-out accessing. It is often compared to a stack of plates on a table—the first one set down is the last one to be used. Stacks are used frequently in compilers, interpreters, spreadsheets, and other system-related software. To create a stack, you need two functions: **push( )** and **pop( )**. The **push( )** function places values on the stack and **pop( )** takes them off. These routines are shown here with a simple **main( )** function to drive them. The program puts the values you enter into the stack. If you enter **0**, a value is popped from the stack. To stop the program, enter **–1**.

```c
#include <stdio.h>
#include <stdlib.h>

#define SIZE 50

void push(int i);
int pop(void);

int  *tos, *p1, stack[SIZE];

int main(void)
{
  int value;

  tos = stack; /* tos points to the top of stack */
  p1 = stack; /* initialize p1 */

  do {
    printf("Enter value: ");
    scanf("%d", &value);
    if(value!=0) push(value);
    else printf("value on top is %d\n", pop());
  } while(value!=-1);
```

```
    return 0;
}

void push(int i)
{
  p1++;
  if(p1==(tos+SIZE)) {
    printf("Stack Overflow.\n");
    exit(1);
  }
  *p1 = i;
}

int pop(void)
{
  if(p1==tos) {
    printf("Stack Underflow.\n");
    exit(1);
  }
  p1--;
  return *(p1+1);
}
```

You can see that memory for the stack is provided by the array **stack**. The pointer
p1 is set to point to the first element in **stack**. The **p1** variable accesses the stack. The
variable **tos** holds the memory address of the top of the stack. It is used to prevent
stack overflows and underflows. Once the stack has been initialized, **push( )** and
pop( ) may be used. Both the **push( )** and **pop( )** functions perform a relational test
on the pointer **p1** to detect limit errors. In **push( )**, **p1** is tested against the end of
stack by adding **SIZE** (the size of the stack) to **tos**. This prevents an overflow. In
pop( ), **p1** is checked against **tos** to be sure that a stack underflow has not occurred.

In **pop( )**, the parentheses are necessary in the return statement. Without them, the
statement would look like this:

```
return *p1 +1;
```

which would return the value at location **p1** plus one, not the value of the location **p1+1**.

Pointers and Arrays

There is a close relationship between pointers and arrays. Consider this program fragment:

```
char str[80], *p1;
p1 = str;
```

Here, **p1** has been set to the address of the first array element in **str**. To access the fifth element in **str**, you could write

```
str[4]
```

or

```
*(p1+4)
```

Both statements will return the fifth element. Remember, arrays start at 0. To access the fifth element, you must use 4 to index **str**. You also add 4 to the pointer **p1** to access the fifth element because **p1** currently points to the first element of **str**. (Recall that an array name without an index returns the starting address of the array, which is the address of the first element.)

The preceding example can be generalized. In essence, C/C++ provides two methods of accessing array elements: pointer arithmetic and array indexing. Although the standard array-indexing notation is sometimes easier to understand, pointer arithmetic can be faster. Since speed is often a consideration in programming, C/C++ programmers commonly use pointers to access array elements.

These two versions of **putstr( )**—one with array indexing and one with pointers— illustrate how you can use pointers in place of array indexing. The **putstr( )** function writes a string to the standard output device one character at a time.

```
/* Index s as an array. */
void putstr(char *s)
{
  register int t;

  for(t=0; s[t]; ++t) putchar(s[t]);
}
```

```
/* Access s as a pointer. */
void putstr(char *s)
{
  while(*s) putchar(*s++);
}
```

Most professional C/C++ programmers would find the second version easier to
read and understand. In fact, the pointer version is the way routines of this sort
are commonly written in C/C++.

Arrays of Pointers

Pointers may be arrayed like any other data type. The declaration for an **int** pointer
array of size 10 is

```
int *x[10];
```

To assign the address of an integer variable called **var** to the third element of the
pointer array, write

```
x[2] = &var;
```

To find the value of **var**, write

```
*x[2]
```

If you want to pass an array of pointers into a function, you can use the same
method that you use to pass other arrays—simply call the function with the array
name without any indexes. For example, a function that can receive array **x** looks
like this:

```
void display_array(int *q[])
{
  int t;

  for(t=0; t<10; t++)
    printf("%d ", *q[t]);
}
```

Remember, **q** is not a pointer to integers, but rather a pointer to an array of pointers to integers. Therefore you need to declare the parameter **q** as an array of integer pointers, as just shown. You cannot declare **q** simply as an integer pointer because that is not what it is.

Pointer arrays are often used to hold pointers to strings. You can create a function that outputs an error message given its code number, as shown here:

```
void syntax_error(int num)
{
  static char *err[] = {
    "Cannot Open File\n",
    "Read Error\n",
    "Write Error\n",
    "Media Failure\n"
  };

  printf("%s", err[num]);
}
```

The array **err** holds pointers to each string. As you can see, **printf( )** inside **syntax_error( )** is called with a character pointer that points to one of the various error messages indexed by the error number passed to the function. For example, if **num** is passed a 2, the message **Write Error** is displayed.

As a point of interest, note that the command line argument **argv** is an array of character pointers. (See Chapter 6.)

Multiple Indirection

You can have a pointer point to another pointer that points to the target value. This situation is called *multiple indirection*, or *pointers to pointers*. Pointers to pointers can be confusing. Figure 5-3 helps clarify the concept of multiple indirection. As you can see, the value of a normal pointer is the address of the object that contains the value desired. In the case of a pointer to a pointer, the first pointer contains the address of the second pointer, which points to the object that contains the value desired.

Multiple indirection can be carried on to whatever extent rquired, but more than a pointer to a pointer is rarely needed. In fact, excessive indirection is difficult to follow and prone to conceptual errors.

Note   *Do not confuse multiple indirection with high-level data structures, such as linked lists, that use pointers. These are two fundamentally different concepts.*

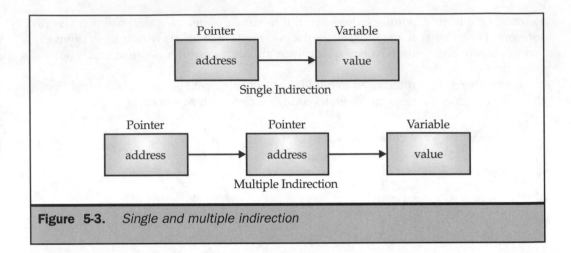

Figure 5-3. *Single and multiple indirection*

A variable that is a pointer to a pointer must be declared as such. You do this by placing an additional asterisk in front of the variable name. For example, the following declaration tells the compiler that **newbalance** is a pointer to a pointer of type **float**:

```
float **newbalance;
```

You should understand that **newbalance** is not a pointer to a floating-point number but rather a pointer to a **float** pointer.

To access the target value indirectly pointed to by a pointer to a pointer, you must apply the asterisk operator twice, as in this example:

```
#include <stdio.h>

int main(void)
{
  int x, *p, **q;

  x = 10;
  p = &x;
  q = &p;

  printf("%d", **q); /* print the value of x */

  return 0;
}
```

Here, **p** is declared as a pointer to an integer and **q** as a pointer to a pointer to an integer. The call to **printf( )** prints the number **10** on the screen.

Initializing Pointers

After a nonstatic local pointer is declared but before it has been assigned a value, it contains an unknown value. (Global and **static** local pointers are automatically initialized to null.) Should you try to use the pointer before giving it a valid value, you will probably crash your program—and possibly your computer's operating system as well—a very nasty type of error!

There is an important convention that most C/C++ programmers follow when working with pointers: A pointer that does not currently point to a valid memory location is given the value null (which is zero). By convention, any pointer that is null implies that it points to nothing and should not be used. However, just because a pointer has a null value does not make it "safe." The use of null is simply a convention that programmers follow. It is not a rule enforced by the C or C++ languages. For example, if you use a null pointer on the left side of an assignment statement, you still run the risk of crashing your program or operating system.

Because a null pointer is assumed to be unused, you can use the null pointer to make many of your pointer routines easier to code and more efficient. For example, you could use a null pointer to mark the end of a pointer array. A routine that accesses that array knows that it has reached the end when it encounters the null value. The **search( )** function shown here illustrates this type of approach.

```
/* look up a name */
int search(char *p[], char *name)
{
  register int t;

  for(t=0; p[t]; ++t)
    if(!strcmp(p[t], name)) return t;

    return -1; /* not found */
}
```

The **for** loop inside **search( )** runs until either a match is found or a null pointer is encountered. Assuming the end of the array is marked with a null, the condition controlling the loop fails when it is reached.

C/C++ programmers commonly initialize strings. You saw an example of this in the **syntax_error( )** function in the section "Arrays of Pointers." Another variation on the initialization theme is the following type of string declaration:

```
char *p = "hello world";
```

As you can see, the pointer **p** is not an array. The reason this sort of initialization works is because of the way the compiler operates. All C/C++ compilers create what is called a *string table*, which is used to store the string constants used by the program. Therefore, the preceding declaration statement places the address of **hello world**, as stored in the string table, into the pointer **p**. Throughout a program, **p** can be used like any other string (except that it should not be altered). For example, the following program is perfectly valid:

```
#include <stdio.h>
#include <string.h>

char *p = "hello world";

int main(void)
{
  register int t;

  /* print the string forward and backwards */
  printf(p);
  for(t=strlen(p)-1; t>-1; t--) printf("%c", p[t]);

  return 0;
}
```

In Standard C++, the type of a string literal is technically **const char ***. But C++ provides an automatic conversion to **char ***. Thus, the preceding program is still valid. However, this automatic conversion is a deprecated feature, which means that you should not rely upon it for new code. For new programs, you should assume that string literals are indeed constants and the declaration of **p** in the preceding program should be written like this.

```
const char *p = "hello world";
```

Pointers to Functions

A particularly confusing yet powerful feature of C++ is the *function pointer*. Even though a function is not a variable, it still has a physical location in memory that can be assigned to a pointer. This address is the entry point of the function and it is the address used when the function is called. Once a pointer points to a function, the function can be called through that pointer. Function pointers also allow functions to be passed as arguments to other functions.

You obtain the address of a function by using the function's name without any parentheses or arguments. (This is similar to the way an array's address is obtained when only the array name, without indexes, is used.) To see how this is done, study the following program, paying close attention to the declarations:

```
#include <stdio.h>
#include <string.h>

void check(char *a, char *b,
           int (*cmp)(const char *, const char *));

int main(void)
{
  char s1[80], s2[80];
  int (*p)(const char *, const char *);

  p = strcmp;

  gets(s1);
  gets(s2);

  check(s1, s2, p);

  return 0;
}

void check(char *a, char *b,
           int (*cmp)(const char *, const char *))
{
  printf("Testing for equality.\n");
  if(!(*cmp)(a, b)) printf("Equal");
  else printf("Not Equal");
}
```

When the **check( )** function is called, two character pointers and one function pointer are passed as parameters. Inside the function **check( )**, the arguments are declared as character pointers and a function pointer. Notice how the function pointer is declared. You must use a similar form when declaring other function pointers, although the return type and parameters of the function may differ. The parentheses around the ***cmp** are necessary for the compiler to interpret this statement correctly.

Inside **check( )**, the expression

```
(*cmp)(a, b)
```

calls **strcmp( )**, which is pointed to by **cmp**, with the arguments **a** and **b**. The parentheses around ***cmp** are necessary. This is one way to call a function through a pointer. A second, simpler syntax, as shown here, may also be used.

```
cmp(a, b);
```

The reason that you will frequently see the first style is that it tips off anyone reading your code that a function is being called through a pointer. (That is, that **cmp** is a function pointer, not the name of a function.) Other than that, the two expressions are equivalent.

Note that you can call **check( )** by using **strcmp( )** directly, as shown here:

```
check(s1, s2, strcmp);
```

This eliminates the need for an additional pointer variable.

You may wonder why anyone would write a program in this way. Obviously, nothing is gained and significant confusion is introduced in the previous example. However, at times it is advantageous to pass functions as parameters or to create an array of functions. For example, when a compiler or interpreter is written, the parser (the part that evaluates expressions) often calls various support functions, such as those that compute mathematical operations (sine, cosine, tangent, etc.), perform I/O, or access system resources. Instead of having a large **switch** statement with all of these functions listed in it, an array of function pointers can be created. In this approach, the proper function is selected by its index. You can get the flavor of this type of usage by studying the expanded version of the previous example. In this program, **check( )** can be made to check for either alphabetical equality or numeric equality by simply calling it with a different comparison function.

```
#include <stdio.h>
#include <ctype.h>
#include <stdlib.h>
#include <string.h>

void check(char *a, char *b,
           int (*cmp)(const char *, const char *));
int numcmp(const char *a, const char *b);

int main(void)
{
  char s1[80], s2[80];
```

```
      gets(s1);
      gets(s2);

      if(isalpha(*s1))
             check(s1, s2, strcmp);
      else
             check(s1, s2, numcmp);

      return 0;
}

void check(char *a, char *b,
           int (*cmp)(const char *, const char *))
{
  printf("Testing for equality.\n");
  if(!(*cmp)(a, b)) printf("Equal");
  else printf("Not Equal");
}

int numcmp(const char *a, const char *b)
{
  if(atoi(a)==atoi(b)) return 0;
  else return 1;
}
```

In this program, if you enter a letter, **strcmp( )** is passed to **check( )**. Otherwise, **numcmp( )** is used. Since **check( )** calls the function that it is passed, it can use different comparison functions in different cases.

C's Dynamic Allocation Functions

Pointers provide necessary support for C/C++'s dynamic allocation system. *Dynamic allocation* is the means by which a program can obtain memory while it is running. As you know, global variables are allocated storage at compile time. Local variables use the stack. However, neither global nor local variables can be added during program execution. Yet there will be times when the storage needs of a program cannot be known ahead of time. For example, a program might use a dynamic data structure, such as a linked list or binary tree. Such structures are inherently dynamic in nature, growing or shrinking as needed. To implement such a data structure requires that a program be able to allocate and free memory.

C++ actually supports two complete dynamic allocation systems: the one defined by C and the one specific to C++. The system specific to C++ contains several improvements over that used by C, and this approach is discussed in Part Two. Here, C's dynamic allocation functions are described.

Memory allocated by C's dynamic allocation functions is obtained from the *heap*—the region of free memory that lies between your program and its permanent storage area and the stack. Although the size of the heap is unknown, it generally contains a fairly large amount of free memory.

The core of C's allocation system consists of the functions **malloc( )** and **free( )**. (Most compilers supply several other dynamic allocation functions, but these two are the most important.) These functions work together using the free memory region to establish and maintain a list of available storage. The **malloc( )** function allocates memory and the **free( )** function releases it. That is, each time a **malloc( )** memory request is made, a portion of the remaining free memory is allocated. Each time a **free( )** memory release call is made, memory is returned to the system. Any program that uses these functions should include the header file **stdlib.h**. (A C++ program may also use the C++-style header **<cstdlib>**.)

The **malloc( )** function has this prototype:

void *malloc(size_t *number_of_bytes*);

Here, *number_of_bytes* is the number of bytes of memory you wish to allocate. (The type **size_t** is defined in **stdlib.h** as, more or less, an **unsigned** integer.) The **malloc( )** function returns a pointer of type **void ***, which means that you can assign it to any type of pointer. After a successful call, **malloc( )** returns a pointer to the first byte of the region of memory allocated from the heap. If there is not enough available memory to satisfy the **malloc( )** request, an allocation failure occurs and **malloc( )** returns a null.

The code fragment shown here allocates 1,000 bytes of contiguous memory:

```
char *p;
p = malloc(1000); /* get 1000 bytes */
```

After the assignment, **p** points to the start of 1,000 bytes of free memory.

In the preceding example, notice that no type cast is used to assign the return value of **malloc( )** to **p**. In C, a **void *** pointer is automatically converted to the type of the pointer on the left side of an assignment. However, it is important to understand that this automatic conversion *does not* occur in C++. In C++, an explicit type cast is needed when a **void *** pointer is assigned to another type of pointer. Thus, in C++, the preceding assignment must be written like this:

```
p = (char *) malloc(1000);
```

As a general rule, in C++ you must use a type cast when assigning (or otherwise converting) one type of pointer to another. This is one of the few fundamental differences between C and C++.

The next example allocates space for 50 integers. Notice the use of **sizeof** to ensure portability.

```
int *p;
p = (int *) malloc(50*sizeof(int));
```

Since the heap is not infinite, whenever you allocate memory, you must check the value returned by **malloc( )** to make sure that it is not null before using the pointer. Using a null pointer will almost certainly crash your program. The proper way to allocate memory and test for a valid pointer is illustrated in this code fragment:

```
p = (int *) malloc(100);
if(!p) {
  printf("Out of memory.\n");
  exit(1);
}
```

Of course, you can substitute some other sort of error handler in place of the call to **exit( )**. Just make sure that you do not use the pointer **p** if it is null.

The **free( )** function is the opposite of **malloc( )** in that it returns previously allocated memory to the system. Once the memory has been freed, it may be reused by a subsequent call to **malloc( )**. The function **free( )** has this prototype:

void free(void *p);

Here, *p* is a pointer to memory that was previously allocated using **malloc( )**. It is critical that you *never* call **free( )** with an invalid argument; otherwise, you will destroy the free list.

Problems with Pointers

Nothing will get you into more trouble than a wild pointer! Pointers are a mixed blessing. They give you tremendous power and are necessary for many programs. At the same time, when a pointer accidentally contains a wrong value, it can be the most difficult bug to find.

An erroneous pointer is difficult to find because the pointer itself is not the problem. The problem is that each time you perform an operation using the bad pointer, you are reading or writing to some unknown piece of memory. If you read from it, the worst that can happen is that you get garbage. However, if you write to it, you might be writing over other pieces of your code or data. This may not show up until later in the execution of your program, and may lead you to look for the bug in the wrong place. There may be little or no evidence to suggest that the pointer is the original cause of the problem. This type of bug causes programmers to lose sleep time and time again.

Because pointer errors are such nightmares, you should do your best never to generate one. To help you avoid them, a few of the more common errors are discussed here. The classic example of a pointer error is the *uninitialized pointer*. Consider this program.

```
/* This program is wrong. */
int main(void)
{
  int x, *p;

  x = 10;
  *p = x;

  return 0;
}
```

This program assigns the value 10 to some unknown memory location. Here is why: Since the pointer **p** has never been given a value, it contains an unknown value when the assignment ***p = x** takes place. This causes the value of **x** to be written to some unknown memory location. This type of problem often goes unnoticed when your program is small because the odds are in favor of **p** containing a "safe" address—one that is not in your code, data area, or operating system. However, as your program grows, the probability increases of **p** pointing to something vital. Eventually, your program stops working. The solution is to always make sure that a pointer is pointing at something valid before it is used.

A second common error is caused by a simple misunderstanding of how to use a pointer. Consider the following:

```
/* This program is wrong. */
#include <stdio.h>

int main(void)
{
```

```
    int x, *p;

    x = 10;
    p = x;

    printf("%d", *p);

    return 0;
}
```

The call to **printf( )** does not print the value of **x**, which is 10, on the screen. It prints some unknown value because the assignment

```
    p = x;
```

is wrong. That statement assigns the value 10 to the pointer **p**. However, **p** is supposed to contain an address, not a value. To correct the program, write

```
    p = &x;
```

Another error that sometimes occurs is caused by incorrect assumptions about the placement of variables in memory. You can never know where your data will be placed in memory, or if it will be placed there the same way again, or whether each compiler will treat it in the same way. For these reasons, making any comparisons between pointers that do not point to a common object may yield unexpected results. For example,

```
    char s[80], y[80];
    char *p1, *p2;

    p1 = s;
    p2 = y;
    if(p1 < p2) . . .
```

is generally an invalid concept. (In very unusual situations, you might use something like this to determine the relative position of the variables. But this would be rare.)

A related error results when you assume that two adjacent arrays may be indexed as one by simply incrementing a pointer across the array boundaries. For example,

```
    int first[10], second[10];
    int *p, t;
```

```
p = first;
for(t=0; t<20; ++t)  *p++ = t;
```

This is not a good way to initialize the arrays **first** and **second** with the numbers 0 through 19. Even though it may work on some compilers under certain circumstances, it assumes that both arrays will be placed back to back in memory with **first** first. This may not always be the case.

The next program illustrates a very dangerous type of bug. See if you can find it.

```
/* This program has a bug. */
#include <string.h>
#include <stdio.h>

int main(void)
{
  char *p1;
  char s[80];

  p1 = s;
  do {
    gets(s);  /* read a string */

    /* print the decimal equivalent of each
       character */
    while(*p1) printf(" %d", *p1++);

  } while(strcmp(s, "done"));

  return 0;
}
```

This program uses **p1** to print the ASCII values associated with the characters contained in **s**. The problem is that **p1** is assigned the address of **s** only once. The first time through the loop, **p1** points to the first character in **s**. However, the second time through, it continues where it left off because it is not reset to the start of **s**. This next character may be part of the second string, another variable, or a piece of the program! The proper way to write this program is

```
/* This program is now correct. */
#include <string.h>
```

```
#include <stdio.h>

int main(void)
{
  char *p1;
  char s[80];

  do {
    p1 = s;
    gets(s);  /* read a string */

    /* print the decimal equivalent of each
       character */
    while(*p1) printf(" %d", *p1++);

  } while(strcmp(s, "done"));

  return 0;
}
```

Here, each time the loop iterates, **p1** is set to the start of the string. In general, you should remember to reinitialize a pointer if it is to be reused.

The fact that handling pointers incorrectly can cause tricky bugs is no reason to avoid using them. Just be careful, and make sure that you know where each pointer is pointing before you use it.

The Complete Reference

Chapter 6

Functions

F unctions are the building blocks of C and C++ and the place where all program activity occurs. This chapter examines their C-like features, including passing arguments, returning values, prototypes, and recursion. Part Two discusses the C++-specific features of functions, such as function overloading and reference parameters.

The General Form of a Function

The general form of a function is

    ret-type function-name(parameter list)
    {
      body of the function
    }

The *ret-type* specifies the type of data that the function returns. A function may return any type of data except an array. The *parameter list* is a comma-separated list of variable names and their associated types that receive the values of the arguments when the function is called. A function may be without parameters, in which case the parameter list is empty. However, even if there are no parameters, the parentheses are still required.

In variable declarations, you can declare many variables to be of a common type by using a comma-separated list of variable names. In contrast, all function parameters must be declared individually, each including both the type and name. That is, the parameter declaration list for a function takes this general form:

    f(type varname1, type varname2, . . . , type varnameN)

For example, here are correct and incorrect function parameter declarations:

```
f(int i, int k, int j) /* correct */
f(int i, k, float j)   /* incorrect */
```

Scope Rules of Functions

The *scope rules* of a language are the rules that govern whether a piece of code knows about or has access to another piece of code or data.

Each function is a discrete block of code. A function's code is private to that function and cannot be accessed by any statement in any other function except through a call to that function. (For instance, you cannot use **goto** to jump into the middle of another function.) The code that constitutes the body of a function is hidden from the rest of the program and, unless it uses global variables or data, it can neither affect nor be affected by other parts of the program. Stated another way, the code and data that are defined within one function cannot interact with the code or data defined in another function because the two functions have a different scope.

Variables that are defined within a function are called *local* variables. A local variable comes into existence when the function is entered and is destroyed upon exit. That is, local variables cannot hold their value between function calls. The only exception to this rule is when the variable is declared with the **static** storage class specifier. This causes the compiler to treat the variable as if it were a global variable for storage purposes, but limits its scope to within the function. (Chapter 2 covers global and local variables in depth.)

In C (and C++) you cannot define a function within a function. This is why neither C nor C++ are technically block-structured languages.

Function Arguments

If a function is to use arguments, it must declare variables that accept the values of the arguments. These variables are called the *formal parameters* of the function. They behave like other local variables inside the function and are created upon entry into the function and destroyed upon exit. As shown in the following function, the parameter declarations occur after the function name:

```
/* Return 1 if c is part of string s; 0 otherwise. */
int is_in(char *s,  char c)
{
  while(*s)
    if(*s==c) return 1;
    else s++;
  return 0;
}
```

The function **is_in( )** has two parameters: **s** and **c**. This function returns 1 if the character **c** is part of the string **s**; otherwise, it returns 0.

As with local variables, you may make assignments to a function's formal parameters or use them in an expression. Even though these variables perform the special task of receiving the value of the arguments passed to the function, you can use them as you do any other local variable.

Call by Value, Call by Reference

In a computer language, there are two ways that arguments can be passed to a subroutine. The first is known as *call by value*. This method copies the *value of* an argument into the formal parameter of the subroutine. In this case, changes made to the parameter have no effect on the argument.

Call by reference is the second way of passing arguments to a subroutine. In this method, the *address* of an argument is copied into the parameter. Inside the subroutine, the address is used to access the actual argument used in the call. This means that changes made to the parameter affect the argument.

By default, C/C++ uses call by value to pass arguments. In general, this means that code within a function cannot alter the arguments used to call the function. Consider the following program:

```
#include <stdio.h>

int sqr(int x);

int main(void)
{
  int t=10;

  printf("%d %d", sqr(t), t);

  return 0;
}

int sqr(int x)
{
  x = x*x;
  return(x);
}
```

In this example, the value of the argument to **sqr( )**, 10, is copied into the parameter x. When the assignment x = x*x takes place, only the local variable x is modified. The variable **t**, used to call **sqr( )**, still has the value 10. Hence, the output is **100 10**.

Remember that it is a copy of the value of the argument that is passed into the function. What occurs inside the function has no effect on the variable used in the call.

Creating a Call by Reference

Even though C/C++ uses call by value for passing parameters, you can create a call by reference by passing a pointer to an argument, instead of the argument itself. Since the address of the argument is passed to the function, code within the function can change the value of the argument outside the function.

Pointers are passed to functions just like any other value. Of course, you need to declare the parameters as pointer types. For example, the function **swap( )**, which exchanges the values of the two integer variables pointed to by its arguments, shows how.

```
void swap(int *x, int *y)
{
  int temp;

  temp = *x;   /* save the value at address x */
  *x = *y;     /* put y into x */
  *y = temp;   /* put x into y */
}
```

swap( ) is able to exchange the values of the two variables pointed to by **x** and **y** because their addresses (not their values) are passed. Thus, within the function, the contents of the variables can be accessed using standard pointer operations, and the contents of the variables used to call the function are swapped.

Remember that **swap( )** (or any other function that uses pointer parameters) must be called with the *addresses of the arguments*. The following fragment shows the correct way to call **swap( )**:

```
void swap(int *x, int *y);

int main(void)
{
  int i, j;

  i = 10;
  j = 20;
  printf("%d %d", i, j);
  swap(&i, &j); /* pass the addresses of i and j */
  printf("%d %d", i, j);
  return 0;
}
```

In this example, the variable **i** is assigned the value 10 and **j** is assigned the value 20. Then **swap( )** is called with the addresses of **i** and **j**. (The unary operator **&** is used to produce the address of the variables.) Therefore, the addresses of **i** and **j**, not their values, are passed into the function **swap( )**. After **swap( )** returns, the values of **i** and **j** will be exchanged.

Note   *C++ allows you to fully automate a call by reference through the use of reference parameters. This feature is described in Part Two.*

Calling Functions with Arrays

Arrays are covered in detail in Chapter 4. However, this section discusses passing arrays as arguments to functions because it is an exception to the normal call-by-value parameter passing.

When an array is used as a function argument, its address is passed to a function. This is an exception to the call-by-value parameter passing convention. In this case, the code inside the function is operating on, and potentially altering, the actual contents of the array used to call the function. For example, consider the function **print_upper( )**, which prints its string argument in uppercase:

```c
#include <stdio.h>
#include <ctype.h>

void print_upper(char *string);

int main(void)
{
  char s[80];

  gets(s);
  print_upper(s);
  printf("\ns is now uppercase: %s", s);
  return 0;
}

/* Print a string in uppercase. */
void print_upper(char *string)
{
  register int t;

  for(t=0; string[t]; ++t)  {
    string[t] = toupper(string[t]);
    putchar(string[t]);
  }
}
```

After the call to **print_upper( )**, the contents of array **s** in **main( )** have also been changed to uppercase. If this is not what you want, you could write the program like this:

```c
#include <stdio.h>
#include <ctype.h>
```

```
void print_upper(char *string);

int main(void)
{
  char s[80];

  gets(s);
  print_upper(s);
  printf("\ns is unchanged: %s", s);

  return 0;
}

void print_upper(char *string)
{
  register int t;

  for(t=0; string[t]; ++t)
    putchar(toupper(string[t]));
}
```

In this version, the contents of array **s** remain unchanged because its values are not altered inside **print_upper( )**.

The standard library function **gets( )** is a classic example of passing arrays into functions. Although the **gets( )** in your standard library is more sophisticated, the following simpler version, called **xgets( )**, will give you an idea of how it works.

```
/* A simple version of the standard
   gets() library function. */
char *xgets(char *s)
{
  char ch, *p;
  int t;

  p = s;  /* gets() returns a pointer to s */

  for(t=0; t<80; ++t){
    ch = getchar();

    switch(ch) {
```

```
      case '\n':
        s[t] = '\0'; /* terminate the string */
        return p;
      case '\b':
        if(t>0) t--;
        break;
      default:
        s[t] = ch;
    }
  }
  s[79] = '\0';
  return p;
}
```

The **xgets( )** function must be called with a character pointer. This, of course, can be the name of a character array, which by definition is a character pointer. Upon entry, **xgets( )** establishes a **for** loop from 0 to 79. This prevents larger strings from being entered at the keyboard. If more than 80 characters are entered, the function returns. (The real **gets( )** function does not have this restriction.) Because C/C++ has no built-in bounds checking, you should make sure that any array used to call **xgets( )** can accept at least 80 characters. As you type characters on the keyboard, they are placed in the string. If you type a backspace, the counter **t** is reduced by 1, effectively removing the previous character from the array. When you press ENTER, a null is placed at the end of the string, signaling its termination. Because the actual array used to call **xgets( )** is modified, upon return it contains the characters that you type.

argc and argv—Arguments to main( )

Sometimes it is useful to pass information into a program when you run it. Generally, you pass information into the **main( )** function via command line arguments. A *command line argument* is the information that follows the program's name on the command line of the operating system. For example, when you compile a program, you might type something like the following after the command prompt:

cc *program_name*

where *program_name* is a command line argument that specifies the name of the program you wish to compile.

There are two special built-in arguments, **argv** and **argc**, that are used to receive command line arguments. The **argc** parameter holds the number of arguments on the command line and is an integer. It is always at least 1 because the name of the program qualifies as the first argument. The **argv** parameter is a pointer to an array of character pointers. Each element in this array points to a command line argument. All command line arguments are strings—any numbers will have to be converted by the program into the proper internal format. For example, this simple program prints **Hello** and your name on the screen if you type it directly after the program name.

```
#include <stdio.h>
#include <stdlib.h>

int main(int argc, char *argv[])
{
  if(argc!=2) {
    printf("You forgot to type your name.\n");
    exit(1);
  }
  printf("Hello %s", argv[1]);

  return 0;
}
```

If you called this program **name** and your name were Tom, you would type **name Tom** to run the program. The output from the program would be **Hello Tom**.

In many environments, each command line argument must be separated by a space or a tab. Commas, semicolons, and the like are not considered separators. For example,

```
run Spot, run
```

is made up of three strings, while

```
Herb,Rick,Fred
```

is a single string since commas are not generally legal separators.

Some environments allow you to enclose within double quotes a string containing spaces. This causes the entire string to be treated as a single argument. Check your operating system documentation for details on the definition of command line parameters for your system.

You must declare **argv** properly. The most common method is

```
char *argv[];
```

The empty brackets indicate that the array is of undetermined length. You can now access the individual arguments by indexing **argv**. For example, **argv[0]** points to the first string, which is always the program's name; **argv[1]** points to the first argument, and so on.

Another short example using command line arguments is the program called **countdown**, shown here. It counts down from a starting value (which is specified on the command line) and beeps when it reaches 0. Notice that the first argument containing the number is converted into an integer by the standard function **atoi( )**.If the string "display" is the second command line argument, the countdown will also be displayed on the screen.

```c
/* Countdown program. */
#include <stdio.h>
#include <stdlib.h>
#include <ctype.h>
#include <string.h>

int main(int argc, char *argv[])
{
  int disp, count;

  if(argc<2) {
    printf("You must enter the length of the count\n");
    printf("on the command line.  Try again.\n");
    exit(1);
  }

  if(argc==3 && !strcmp(argv[2], "display")) disp = 1;
  else disp = 0;

  for(count=atoi(argv[1]); count; --count)
    if(disp) printf("%d\n", count);

  putchar('\a');  /* this will ring the bell */
  printf("Done");

  return 0;
}
```

Notice that if no command line arguments have been specified, an error message is printed. A program with command line arguments often issues instructions if the user attempts to run the program without entering the proper information.

To access an individual character in one of the command line arguments, add a second index to **argv**. For example, the next program displays all of the arguments with which it was called, one character at a time:

```c
#include <stdio.h>

int main(int argc, char *argv[])
{
  int t, i;

  for(t=0; t<argc; ++t) {
    i = 0;

    while(argv[t][i]) {
      putchar(argv[t][i]);
      ++i;
    }
    printf("\n");
  }

  return 0;
}
```

Remember, the first index accesses the string, and the second index accesses the individual characters of the string.

Normally, you use **argc** and **argv** to get initial commands into your program. In theory, you can have up to 32,767 arguments, but most operating systems do not allow more than a few. You typically use these arguments to indicate a filename or an option. Using command line arguments gives your program a professional appearance and facilitates its use in batch files.

When a program does not require command line parameters, it is common practice to explicitly declare **main( )** as having no parameters. For C programs this is accomplished by using the **void** keyword in its parameter list. (This is the approach used by the programs in Part One of this book.) However, for C++ programs you may simply specify an empty parameter list. In C++, the use of **void** to indicate an empty parameter list is allowed, but redundant.

The names **argc** and **argv** are traditional but arbitrary. You may name these two parameters to **main( )** anything you like. Also, some compilers may support additional arguments to **main( )**, so be sure to check your user's manual.

The return Statement

The **return** statement itself is described in Chapter 3. As explained, it has two important uses. First, it causes an immediate exit from the function that it is in. That is, it causes program execution to return to the calling code. Second, it may be used to return a value. This section examines how the **return** statement is used.

Returning from a Function

There are two ways that a function terminates execution and returns to the caller. The first occurs when the last statement in the function has executed and, conceptually, the function's ending curly brace (}) is encountered. (Of course, the curly brace isn't actually present in the object code, but you can think of it in this way.) For example, the **pr_reverse( )** function in this program simply prints the string "I like C++" backwards on the screen and then returns.

```
#include <string.h>
#include <stdio.h>

void pr_reverse(char *s);

int main(void)
{
  pr_reverse("I like C++");

  return 0;
}

void pr_reverse(char *s)
{
  register int t;

  for(t=strlen(s)-1; t>=0; t--) putchar(s[t]);
}
```

Once the string has been displayed, there is nothing left for **pr_reverse( )** to do, so it returns to the place from which it was called.

Actually, not many functions use this default method of terminating their execution. Most functions rely on the **return** statement to stop execution either because a value must be returned or to make a function's code simpler and more efficient.

A function may contain several **return** statements. For example, the **find_substr( )** function in the following program returns the starting position of a substring within a string, or returns −1 if no match is found.

```
#include <stdio.h>

int find_substr(char *s1, char *s2);

int main(void)
{
```

```
    if(find_substr("C++ is fun", "is") != -1)
      printf("substring is found");

    return 0;
}

/* Return index of first match of s2 in s1. */
int find_substr(char *s1, char *s2)
{
  register int t;
  char *p, *p2;

  for(t=0; s1[t]; t++) {
    p = &s1[t];
    p2 = s2;

    while(*p2 && *p2==*p) {
      p++;
      p2++;
    }
    if(!*p2) return t; /* 1st return */
  }
  return -1; /* 2nd return */
}
```

Returning Values

All functions, except those of type **void**, return a value. This value is specified by the
return statement. In C89, if a non-**void** function does not explicitly return a value via
a **return** statement, then a garbage value is returned. In C++ (and C99), a non-**void**
function *must* contain a **return** statement that returns a value. That is, in C++, if a function
is specified as returning a value, any **return** statement within it must have a value
associated with it. However, if execution reaches the end of a non-**void** function, then
a garbage value is returned. Although this condition is not a syntax error, it is still a
fundamental flaw and should be avoided.

As long as a function is not declared as **void**, you may use it as an operand in an
expression. Therefore, each of the following expressions is valid:

```
x = power(y);
if(max(x,y) > 100) printf("greater");
for(ch=getchar(); isdigit(ch); ) ... ;
```

As a general rule, a function cannot be the target of an assignment. A statement such as

```
swap(x,y) = 100; /* incorrect statement */
```

is wrong. The C/C++ compiler will flag it as an error and will not compile a program that contains it. (As is discussed in Part Two, C++ allows some interesting exceptions to this general rule, enabling some types of functions to occur on the left side of an assignment.)

When you write programs, your functions generally will be of three types. The first type is simply computational. These functions are specifically designed to perform operations on their arguments and return a value based on that operation. A computational function is a "pure" function. Examples are the standard library functions **sqrt( )** and **sin( )**, which compute the square root and sine of their arguments.

The second type of function manipulates information and returns a value that simply indicates the success or failure of that manipulation. An example is the library function **fclose( )**, which is used to close a file. If the close operation is successful, the function returns 0; if the operation is unsuccessful, it returns **EOF**.

The last type of function has no explicit return value. In essence, the function is strictly procedural and produces no value. An example is **exit( )**, which terminates a program. All functions that do not return values should be declared as returning type **void**. By declaring a function as **void**, you keep it from being used in an expression, thus preventing accidental misuse.

Sometimes, functions that really don't produce an interesting result return something anyway. For example, **printf( )** returns the number of characters written. Yet it would be unusual to find a program that actually checked this. In other words, although all functions, except those of type **void**, return values, you don't have to use the return value for anything. A common question concerning function return values is, "Don't I have to assign this value to some variable since a value is being returned?" The answer is no. If there is no assignment specified, the return value is simply discarded. Consider the following program, which uses the function **mul( )**:

```
#include <stdio.h>

int mul(int a, int b);

int main(void)
{
  int x, y, z;

  x = 10;   y = 20;
```

```
   z = mul(x, y);              /* 1 */
   printf("%d", mul(x,y));     /* 2 */
   mul(x, y);                  /* 3 */

   return 0;
}

int mul(int a, int b)
{
  return a*b;
}
```

In line 1, the return value of **mul( )** is assigned to **z**. In line 2, the return value is not actually assigned, but it is used by the **printf( )** function. Finally, in line 3, the return value is lost because it is neither assigned to another variable nor used as part of an expression.

Returning Pointers

Although functions that return pointers are handled just like any other type of function, a few important concepts need to be discussed.

Pointers to variables are neither integers nor unsigned integers. They are the memory addresses of a certain type of data. The reason for this distinction is because pointer arithmetic is relative to the base type. For example, if an integer pointer is incremented, it will contain a value that is 4 greater than its previous value (assuming 4-byte integers). In general, each time a pointer is incremented (or decremented), it points to the next (or previous) item of its type. Since the length of different data types may differ, the compiler must know what type of data the pointer is pointing to. For this reason, a function that returns a pointer must declare explicitly what type of pointer it is returning. For example, you should not use a return type of **int *** to return a **char *** pointer!

To return a pointer, a function must be declared as having a pointer return type. For example, this function returns a pointer to the first occurrence of the character **c** in string **s**:

```
/* Return pointer of first occurrence of c in s. */
char *match(char c, char *s)
{
  while(c!=*s && *s) s++;
  return(s);
}
```

If no match is found, a pointer to the null terminator is returned. Here is a short program that uses **match( )**:

```
#include <stdio.h>

char *match(char c, char *s);   /* prototype */

int main(void)
{
  char s[80], *p, ch;

  gets(s);
  ch = getchar();
  p = match(ch, s);

  if(*p)  /* there is a match */
    printf("%s ", p);
  else
    printf("No match found.");

  return 0;
}
```

This program reads a string and then a character. If the character is in the string, the program prints the string from the point of match. Otherwise, it prints **No match found**.

Functions of Type void

One of **void**'s uses is to explicitly declare functions that do not return values. This prevents their use in any expression and helps avert accidental misuse. For example, the function **print_vertical( )** prints its string argument vertically down the side of the screen. Since it returns no value, it is declared as **void**.

```
void print_vertical(char *str)
{
  while(*str)
    printf("%c\n", *str++);
}
```

Here is an example that uses **print_vertical( )**.

```
#include <stdio.h>
```

```
void print_vertical(char *str);   /* prototype */

int main(int argc, char *argv[])
{
  if(argc > 1) print_vertical(argv[1]);

  return 0;
}

void print_vertical(char *str)
{
  while(*str)
    printf("%c\n", *str++);
}
```

One last point: Early versions of C did not define the **void** keyword. Thus, in early C programs, functions that did not return values simply defaulted to type **int**. Therefore, don't be surprised to see many examples of this in older code.

What Does main( ) Return?

The **main( )** function returns an integer to the calling process, which is generally the operating system. Returning a value from **main( )** is the equivalent of calling **exit( )** with the same value. If **main( )** does not explicitly return a value, the value passed to the calling process is technically undefined. In practice, most C/C++ compilers automatically return 0, but do not rely on this if portability is a concern.

Recursion

In C/C++, a function can call itself. A function is said to be *recursive* if a statement in the body of the function calls itself. Recursion is the process of defining something in terms of itself, and is sometimes called *circular definition*.

A simple example of a recursive function is **factr( )**, which computes the factorial of an integer. The factorial of a number **n** is the product of all the whole numbers between 1 and **n**. For example, 3 factorial is 1 x 2 x 3, or 6. Both **factr( )** and its iterative equivalent are shown here:

```
/* recursive */
int factr(int n) {
  int answer;

  if(n==1) return(1);
```

```
    answer = factr(n-1)*n; /* recursive call */
    return(answer);
}

/* non-recursive */
int fact(int n) {
  int t, answer;

  answer = 1;

  for(t=1; t<=n; t++)
    answer=answer*(t);

  return(answer);
}
```

The nonrecursive version of **fact( )** should be clear. It uses a loop that runs from 1 to **n** and progressively multiplies each number by the moving product.

The operation of the recursive **factr( )** is a little more complex. When **factr( )** is called with an argument of 1, the function returns 1. Otherwise, it returns the product of **factr(n–1)*n**. To evaluate this expression, **factr( )** is called with **n–1**. This happens until **n** equals 1 and the calls to the function begin returning.

Computing the factorial of 2, the first call to **factr( )** causes a second, recursive call with the argument of 1. This call returns 1, which is then multiplied by 2 (the original **n** value). The answer is then 2. Try working through the computation of 3 factorial on your own. (You might want to insert **printf( )** statements into **factr( )** to see the level of each call and what the intermediate answers are.)

When a function calls itself, a new set of local variables and parameters are allocated storage on the stack, and the function code is executed from the top with these new variables. A recursive call does not make a new copy of the function. Only the values being operated upon are new. As each recursive call returns, the old local variables and parameters are removed from the stack and execution resumes at the point of the function call inside the function. Recursive functions could be said to "telescope" out and back.

Often, recursive routines do not significantly reduce code size or improve memory utilization over their iterative counterparts. Also, the recursive versions of most routines may execute a bit slower than their iterative equivalents because of the overhead of the repeated function calls. In fact, many recursive calls to a function could cause a stack overrun. Because storage for function parameters and local variables is on the stack and each new call creates a new copy of these variables, the stack could be exhausted. However, you probably will not have to worry about this unless a recursive function runs wild.

The main advantage to recursive functions is that you can use them to create clearer and simpler versions of several algorithms. For example, the Quicksort algorithm is difficult to implement in an iterative way. Also, some problems, especially ones related to artificial intelligence, lend themselves to recursive solutions. Finally, some people seem to think recursively more easily than iteratively.

When writing recursive functions, you must have a conditional statement, such as an **if**, somewhere to force the function to return without the recursive call being executed. If you don't, the function will never return once you call it. Omitting the conditional statement is a common error when writing recursive functions. Use **printf( )** liberally during program development so that you can watch what is going on and abort execution if you see a mistake.

Function Prototypes

In C++ all functions must be declared before they are used. This is normally accomplished using a *function prototype*. Function prototypes were not part of the original C language. They were, however, added when C was standardized. While prototypes are not technically required by Standard C, their use is strongly encouraged. Prototypes have always been *required* by C++. In this book, all examples include full function prototypes. Prototypes enable both C and C++ to provide stronger type checking, somewhat like that provided by languages such as Pascal. When you use prototypes, the compiler can find and report any illegal type conversions between the type of arguments used to call a function and the type definition of its parameters. The compiler will also catch differences between the number of arguments used to call a function and the number of parameters in the function.

The general form of a function prototype is

type func_name(type parm_name1, type parm_name2,. . .,
            type parm_nameN);

The use of parameter names is optional. However, they enable the compiler to identify any type mismatches by name when an error occurs, so it is a good idea to include them.

The following program illustrates the value of function prototypes. It produces an error message because it contains an attempt to call **sqr_it( )** with an integer argument instead of the integer pointer required. (It is illegal to convert an integer into a pointer.)

```
/* This program uses a function prototype to
   enforce strong type checking. */

void sqr_it(int *i); /* prototype */

int main(void)
{
```

```
    int x;

    x = 10;
    sqr_it(x);   /* type mismatch */

    return 0;
}

void sqr_it(int *i)
{
    *i = *i * *i;
}
```

A function's definition can also serve as its prototype if the definition occurs prior to the function's first use in the program. For example, this is a valid program.

```
#include <stdio.h>

/* This definition will also serve
   as a prototype within this program. */
void f(int a, int b)
{
    printf("%d ", a % b);
}

int main(void)
{
    f(10,3);

    return 0;
}
```

In this example, since **f( )** is defined prior to its use in **main( ),** no separate prototype is required. While it is possible for a function's definition to serve as its prototype in small programs, it is seldom possible in large ones—especially when several files are used. The programs in this book include a separate prototype for each function because that is the way C/C++ code is normally written in practice.

The only function that does not require a prototype is **main( ),** since it is the first function called when your program begins.

Because of the need for compatibility with the original version of C, there is a small but important difference between how C and C++ handle the prototyping of a function that has no parameters. In C++, an empty parameter list is simply indicated in the prototype by the absence of any parameters. For example,

```
int f(); /* C++ prototype for a function with no parameters */
```

However, in C this prototype means something different. For historical reasons, an empty parameter list simply says that *no parameter information* is given. As far as the compiler is concerned, the function could have several parameters or no parameters. In C, when a function has no parameters, its prototype uses **void** inside the parameter list. For example, here is **f( )**'s prototype as it would appear in a C program.

```
float f(void);
```

This tells the compiler that the function has no parameters, and any call to that function that has parameters is an error. In C++, the use of **void** inside an empty parameter list is still allowed, but is redundant.

In C++, f( ) and f(void) are equivalent.

Function prototypes help you trap bugs before they occur. In addition, they help verify that your program is working correctly by not allowing functions to be called with mismatched arguments.

One last point: Since early versions of C did not support the full prototype syntax, prototypes are technically optional in C. This is necessary to support pre-prototype C code. If you are porting older C code to C++, you may need to add full function prototypes before it will compile. Remember: Although prototypes are optional in C, they are required by C++. This means that every function in a C++ program must be fully prototyped.

Standard Library Function Prototypes

Any standard library function used by your program must be prototyped. To accomplish this, you must include the appropriate *header* for each library function. All necessary headers are provided by the C/C++ compiler. In C, the library headers are (usually) files that use the .H extension. In C++, headers may be either separate files or built into the compiler itself. In either case, a header contains two main elements: any definitions used by the library functions and the prototypes for the library functions. For example, **stdio.h** is included in almost all programs in this part of the book because it contains the prototype for **printf( )**. The headers for the standard library are described in Part Three.

Declaring Variable-Length Parameter Lists

You can specify a function that has a variable number of parameters. The most common example is **printf( )**. To tell the compiler that an unknown number of arguments may be passed to a function, you must end the declaration of its parameters using three periods. For example, this prototype specifies that **func( )** will have at least two integer parameters and an unknown number (including 0) of parameters after that.

```
int func(int a, int b, ...);
```

This form of declaration is also used by a function's definition.

Any function that uses a variable number of parameters must have at least one actual parameter. For example, this is incorrect:

```
int func(...); /* illegal */
```

Old-Style Versus Modern Function Parameter Declarations

Early versions of C used a different parameter declaration method than does either Standard C or Standard C++. This early approach is sometimes called the *classic* form. This book uses a declaration approach called the *modern* form. Standard C supports both forms, but strongly recommends the modern form. Standard C++ only supports the modern parameter declaration method. However, you should know the old-style form because many older C programs still use it.

The old-style function parameter declaration consists of two parts: a parameter list, which goes inside the parentheses that follow the function name, and the actual parameter declarations, which go between the closing parentheses and the function's opening curly brace. The general form of the old-style parameter definition is

```
type func_name(parm1, parm2, . . .parmN)
type parm1;
type parm2;
  .
  .
  .
type parmN;
{
function code
}
```

For example, this modern declaration:

```
float f(int a, int b, char ch)
{
  /* ... */
}
```

will look like this in its old-style form:

```
float f(a, b, ch)
int a, b;
char ch;
{
  /* ... */
}
```

Notice that the old-style form allows the declaration of more than one parameter in a list after the type name.

 The old-style form of parameter declaration is designated as obsolete by the C language and is not supported by C++.

The
Complete
Reference

Chapter 7

Structures, Unions, Enumerations, and User-Defined Types

The C language gives you five ways to create a custom data type:

1. The *structure*, which is a grouping of variables under one name and is called an *aggregate* data type. (The terms *compound* or *conglomerate* are also commonly used.)

2. The *bit-field*, which is a variation on the structure and allows easy access to individual bits.

3. The *union*, which enables the same piece of memory to be defined as two or more different types of variables.

4. The *enumeration*, which is a list of named integer constants.

5. The **typedef** keyword, which defines a new name for an existing type.

C++ supports all of the above and adds classes, which are described in Part Two. The other methods of creating custom data types are described here.

 In C++, structures and unions have both object-oriented and non-object-oriented attributes. This chapter discusses only their C-like, non-object-oriented features. Their object-oriented qualities are described later in this book.

Structures

A structure is a collection of variables referenced under one name, providing a convenient means of keeping related information together. A *structure declaration* forms a template that may be used to create structure objects (that is, instances of a structure). The variables that make up the structure are called *members*. (Structure members are also commonly referred to as *elements* or *fields*.)

Generally, all of the members of a structure are logically related. For example, the name and address information in a mailing list would normally be represented in a structure. The following code fragment shows how to declare a structure that defines the name and address fields. The keyword **struct** tells the compiler that a structure is being declared.

```
struct addr
{
  char name[30];
  char street[40];
  char city[20];
  char state[3];
  unsigned long int zip;
};
```

Notice that the declaration is terminated by a semicolon. This is because a structure declaration is a statement. The type name of the structure is **addr**. As such, **addr** identifies this particular data structure and is its type specifier.

At this point, *no variable has actually been created*. Only the form of the data has been defined. When you define a structure, you are defining a compound variable type, not a variable. Not until you declare a variable of that type does one actually exist. In C, to declare a variable (i.e., a physical object) of type **addr**, write

```
struct addr addr_info;
```

This declares a variable of type **addr** called **addr_info**. In C++, you may use this shorter form.

```
addr addr_info;
```

As you can see, the keyword **struct** is not needed. In C++, once a structure has been declared, you may declare variables of its type using only its type name, without preceding it with the keyword **struct**. The reason for this difference is that in C, a structure's name does not define a complete type name. In fact, Standard C refers to a structure's name as a *tag*. In C, you must precede the tag with the keyword **struct** when declaring variables. However, in C++, a structure's name is a complete type name and may be used by itself to define variables. Keep in mind, however, that it is still perfectly legal to use the C-style declaration in a C++ program. Since the programs in Part One of this book are valid for both C and C++, they will use the C declaration method. Just remember that C++ allows the shorter form.

When a structure variable (such as **addr_info**) is declared, the compiler automatically allocates sufficient memory to accommodate all of its members. Figure 7-1 shows how **addr_info** appears in memory assuming 1-byte characters and 4-byte long integers.

You may also declare one or more structure variables when you declare a structure. For example,

```
struct addr {
  char name[30];
  char street[40];
  char city[20];
  char state[3];
  unsigned long int zip;
} addr_info, binfo, cinfo;
```

defines a structure type called **addr** and declares variables **addr_info**, **binfo**, and **cinfo** of that type. It is important to understand that each structure object contains its own

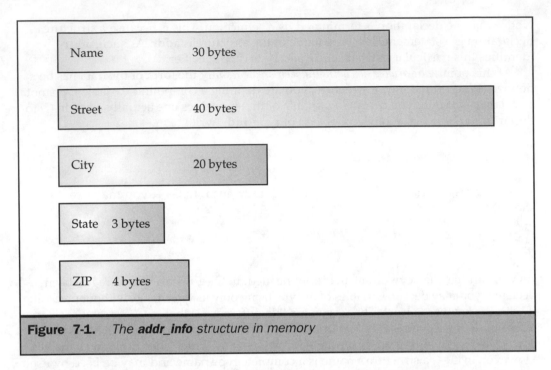

Figure 7-1. *The **addr_info** structure in memory*

copies of the structure's members. For example, the **zip** field of **binfo** is separate from the **zip** field of **cinfo**. Thus, changes to **zip** in **binfo** do not affect the **zip** in **cinfo**.

If you only need one structure variable, the structure type name is not needed. That means that

```
struct {
  char name[30];
  char street[40];
  char city[20];
  char state[3];
  unsigned long int zip;
} addr_info;
```

declares one variable named **addr_info** as defined by the structure preceding it.

The general form of a structure declaration is

struct *struct-type-name* {
  type member-name;
  type member-name;
  type member-name;
  .
  .

        .
        } *structure-variables*;

where either *struct-type-name* or *structure-variables* may be omitted, but not both.

Accessing Structure Members

Individual members of a structure are accessed through the use of the . operator (usually called the *dot operator*). For example, the following code assigns the ZIP code 12345 to the **zip** field of the structure variable **addr_info** declared earlier:

```
addr_info.zip = 12345;
```

The structure variable name followed by a period and the member name references that individual member. The general form for accessing a member of a structure is

   structure-name.member-name

Therefore, to print the ZIP code on the screen, write

```
printf("%lu", addr_info.zip);
```

This prints the ZIP code contained in the **zip** member of the structure variable **addr_info**.
   In the same fashion, the character array **addr_info.name** can be used to call **gets( )**, as shown here:

```
gets(addr_info.name);
```

This passes a character pointer to the start of **name**.
   Since **name** is a character array, you can access the individual characters of **addr_info.name** by indexing **name**. For example, you can print the contents of **addr_info.name** one character at a time by using the following code:

```
register int t;

for(t=0; addr_info.name[t]; ++t)
  putchar(addr_info.name[t]);
```

Structure Assignments

The information contained in one structure may be assigned to another structure of the same type using a single assignment statement. That is, you do not need to assign the value of each member separately. The following program illustrates structure assignments:

```
#include <stdio.h>

int main(void)
{
  struct {
    int a;
    int b;
  } x, y;

  x.a = 10;

  y = x;   /* assign one structure to another */

  printf("%d", y.a);

  return 0;
}
```

After the assignment, **y.a** will contain the value 10.

Arrays of Structures

Perhaps the most common usage of structures is in arrays of structures. To declare an array of structures, you must first define a structure and then declare an array variable of that type. For example, to declare a 100-element array of structures of type **addr**, defined earlier, write

```
struct addr addr_info[100];
```

This creates 100 sets of variables that are organized as defined in the structure **addr**.

To access a specific structure, index the structure name. For example, to print the ZIP code of structure 3, write

```
printf("%lu", addr_info[2].zip);
```

Like all array variables, arrays of structures begin indexing at 0.

Passing Structures to Functions

This section discusses passing structures and their members to functions.

Passing Structure Members to Functions

When you pass a member of a structure to a function, you are actually passing the value of that member to the function. Therefore, you are passing a simple variable (unless, of course, that element is compound, such as an array). For example, consider this structure:

```
struct fred
{
  char x;
  int y;
  float z;
  char s[10];
} mike;
```

Here are examples of each member being passed to a function:

```
func(mike.x);     /* passes character value of x */
func2(mike.y);    /* passes integer value of y */
func3(mike.z);    /* passes float value of z */
func4(mike.s);    /* passes address of string s */
func(mike.s[2]);  /* passes character value of s[2] */
```

If you wish to pass the *address* of an individual structure member, put the **&** operator before the structure name. For example, to pass the address of the members of the structure **mike**, write

```
func(&mike.x);     /* passes address of character x */
func2(&mike.y);    /* passes address of integer y */
func3(&mike.z);    /* passes address of float z */
func4(mike.s);     /* passes address of string s */
func(&mike.s[2]);  /* passes address of character s[2] */
```

Note that the **&** operator precedes the structure name, not the individual member name. Note also that **s** already signifies an address, so no **&** is required.

Passing Entire Structures to Functions

When a structure is used as an argument to a function, the entire structure is passed using the standard call-by-value method. Of course, this means that any changes made to the contents of the structure inside the function to which it is passed do not affect the structure used as an argument.

When using a structure as a parameter, remember that the type of the argument must match the type of the parameter. For example, in the following program both the argument **arg** and the parameter **parm** are declared as the same type of structure.

```
#include <stdio.h>

/* Define a structure type. */
struct struct_type {
  int a, b;
  char ch;
} ;

void f1(struct struct_type parm);

int main(void)
{
  struct struct_type arg;

  arg.a = 1000;

  f1(arg);

  return 0;
}

void f1(struct struct_type parm)
{
  printf("%d", parm.a);
}
```

As this program illustrates, if you will be declaring parameters that are structures, you must make the declaration of the structure type global so that all parts of your program can use it. For example, had **struct_type** been declared inside **main( )** (for example), then it would not have been visible to **f1( ).**

As just stated, when passing structures, the type of the argument must match the type of the parameter. It is not sufficient for them to simply be physically similar; their type names must match. For example, the following version of the preceding program is incorrect and will not compile because the type name of the argument used to call **f1( )** differs from the type name of its parameter.

```
/* This program is incorrect and will not compile. */
#include <stdio.h>

/* Define a structure type. */
struct struct_type {
  int a, b;
  char ch;
} ;

/* Define a structure similar to struct_type,
   but with a different name. */
struct struct_type2 {
  int a, b;
  char ch;
} ;

void f1(struct struct_type2 parm);

int main(void)
{
  struct struct_type arg;

  arg.a = 1000;

  f1(arg); /* type mismatch */

  return 0;
}

void f1(struct struct_type2 parm)
{
  printf("%d", parm.a);
}
```

Structure Pointers

C/C++ allows pointers to structures just as it allows pointers to any other type of variable. However, there are some special aspects to structure pointers that you should know.

Declaring a Structure Pointer

Like other pointers, structure pointers are declared by placing * in front of a structure variable's name. For example, assuming the previously defined structure **addr**, the following declares **addr_pointer** as a pointer to data of that type:

```
struct addr *addr_pointer;
```

Remember, in C++ it is not necessary to precede this declaration with the keyword **struct**.

Using Structure Pointers

There are two primary uses for structure pointers: to pass a structure to a function using call by reference, and to create linked lists and other dynamic data structures that rely on dynamic allocation. This chapter covers the first use.

There is one major drawback to passing all but the simplest structures to functions: the overhead needed to push the structure onto the stack when the function call is executed. (Recall that arguments are passed to functions on the stack.) For simple structures with few members, this overhead is not too great. If the structure contains many members, however, or if some of its members are arrays, run-time performance may degrade to unacceptable levels. The solution to this problem is to pass only a pointer to the structure.

When a pointer to a structure is passed to a function, only the address of the structure is pushed on the stack. This makes for very fast function calls. A second advantage, in some cases, is when a function needs to reference the actual structure used as the argument, instead of a copy. By passing a pointer, the function can modify the contents of the structure used in the call.

To find the address of a structure, place the **&** operator before the structure's name. For example, given the following fragment:

```
struct bal {
  float balance;
  char name[80];
} person;

struct bal *p;  /* declare a structure pointer */
```

then

```
p = &person;
```

places the address of the structure **person** into the pointer **p**.

To access the members of a structure using a pointer to that structure, you must use the –> operator. For example, this references the **balance** field:

```
p->balance
```

The –> is usually called the *arrow operator*, and consists of the minus sign followed by a greater-than sign. The arrow is used in place of the dot operator when you are accessing a structure member through a pointer to the structure.

To see how a structure pointer can be used, examine this simple program, which prints the hours, minutes, and seconds on your screen using a software timer.

```c
/* Display a software timer. */
#include <stdio.h>

#define DELAY 128000

struct my_time {
  int hours;
  int minutes;
  int seconds;
} ;

void display(struct my_time *t);
void update(struct my_time *t);
void delay(void);

int main(void)
{
  struct my_time systime;

  systime.hours = 0;
  systime.minutes = 0;
  systime.seconds = 0;

  for(;;) {
    update(&systime);
    display(&systime);
  }

  return 0;
}
```

```
void update(struct my_time *t)
{
  t->seconds++;
  if(t->seconds==60) {
    t->seconds = 0;
    t->minutes++;
  }

  if(t->minutes==60) {
    t->minutes = 0;
    t->hours++;
  }

  if(t->hours==24) t->hours = 0;
  delay();
}

void display(struct my_time *t)
{
  printf("%02d:", t->hours);
  printf("%02d:", t->minutes);
  printf("%02d\n", t->seconds);
}

void delay(void)
{
  long int t;

  /* change this as needed */
  for(t=1; t<DELAY; ++t) ;
}
```

The timing of this program is adjusted by changing the definition of **DELAY**.

As you can see, a global structure called **my_time** is defined but no variable is declared. Inside **main( )**, the structure **systime** is declared and initialized to 00:00:00. This means that **systime** is known directly only to the **main( )** function.

The functions **update( )** (which changes the time) and **display( )** (which prints the time) are passed the address of **systime**. In both functions, their arguments are declared as a pointer to a **my_time** structure.

Inside **update( )** and **display( )**, each member of **systime** is accessed via a pointer. Because **update( )** receives a pointer to the **systime** structure, it can update its value.

For example, to set the hours back to 0 when 24:00:00 is reached, **update( )** contains this line of code:

```
if(t->hours==24) t->hours = 0;
```

This tells the compiler to take the address in **t** (which points to **systime** in **main( )**) and use it to reset **hours** to zero.

Remember, use the dot operator to access structure elements when operating on the structure itself. When you have a pointer to a structure, use the arrow operator.

Arrays and Structures Within Structures

A member of a structure may be either a simple or aggregate type. A simple member is one that is of any of the built-in data types, such as integer or character. You have already seen one type of aggregate element: the character arrays used in **addr**. Other aggregate data types include one-dimensional and multidimensional arrays of the other data types, and structures.

A member of a structure that is an array is treated as you might expect from the earlier examples. For example, consider this structure:

```
struct x {
  int a[10][10]; /* 10 x 10 array of ints */
  float b;
} y;
```

To reference integer 3,7 in **a** of structure **y**, write

```
y.a[3][7]
```

When a structure is a member of another structure, it is called a *nested structure*. For example, the structure **address** is nested inside **emp** in this example:

```
struct emp {
  struct addr address; /* nested structure */
  float wage;
} worker;
```

Here, structure **emp** has been defined as having two members. The first is a structure of type **addr**, which contains an employee's address. The other is **wage**, which holds the employee's wage. The following code fragment assigns 93456 to the **zip** element of **address**.

```
worker.address.zip = 93456;
```

As you can see, the members of each structure are referenced from outermost to innermost. C guarantees that structures can be nested to at least 15 levels. Standard C++ suggests that at least 256 levels of nesting be allowed.

Bit-Fields

Unlike some other computer languages, C/C++ has a built-in feature called a *bit-field* that allows you to access a single bit. Bit-fields can be useful for a number of reasons, such as:

■ If storage is limited, you can store several Boolean (true/false) variables in one byte.

■ Certain devices transmit status information encoded into one or more bits within a byte.

■ Certain encryption routines need to access the bits within a byte.

Although these tasks can be performed using the bitwise operators, a bit-field can add more clarity (and possibly efficiency) to your code.

To access individual bits, C/C++ uses a method based on the structure. In fact, a bit-field is really just a special type of structure member that defines how long, in bits, the field is to be. The general form of a bit-field definition is

```
struct struct-type-name {
  type name1 : length;
  type name2 : length;
  .
  .
  .
  type nameN : length;
} variable_list;
```

Here, *type* is the type of the bit-field and *length* is the number of bits in the field. A bit-field must be declared as an integral or enumeration type. Bit-fields of length 1 should be declared as **unsigned**, because a single bit cannot have a sign.

Bit-fields are frequently used when analyzing input from a hardware device. For example, the status port of a serial communications adapter might return a status byte organized like this:

Bit	Meaning When Set
0	Change in clear-to-send line
1	Change in data-set-ready
2	Trailing edge detected
3	Change in receive line
4	Clear-to-send
5	Data-set-ready
6	Telephone ringing
7	Received signal

You can represent the information in a status byte using the following bit-field:

```
struct status_type {
  unsigned delta_cts: 1;
  unsigned delta_dsr: 1;
  unsigned tr_edge:   1;
  unsigned delta_rec: 1;
  unsigned cts:       1;
  unsigned dsr:       1;
  unsigned ring:      1;
  unsigned rec_line:  1;
} status;
```

You might use a routine similar to that shown here to enable a program to determine when it can send or receive data.

```
status = get_port_status();
if(status.cts) printf("clear to send");
if(status.dsr) printf("data ready");
```

To assign a value to a bit-field, simply use the form you would use for any other type of structure element. For example, this code fragment clears the **ring** field:

```
status.ring = 0;
```

As you can see from this example, each bit-field is accessed with the dot operator. However, if the structure is referenced through a pointer, you must use the –> operator.

You do not have to name each bit-field. This makes it easy to reach the bit you want, bypassing unused ones. For example, if you only care about the **cts** and **dsr** bits, you could declare the **status_type** structure like this:

```
struct status_type {
  unsigned :    4;
  unsigned cts: 1;
  unsigned dsr: 1;
} status;
```

Also, notice that the bits after **dsr** do not need to be specified if they are not used.

It is valid to mix normal structure members with bit-fields. For example,

```
struct emp {
  struct addr address;
  float pay;
  unsigned lay_off:    1; /* lay off or active */
  unsigned hourly:     1; /* hourly pay or wage */
  unsigned deductions: 3; /* IRS deductions */
};
```

defines an employee record that uses only 1 byte to hold three pieces of information: the employee's status, whether the employee is salaried, and the number of deductions. Without the bit-field, this information would have taken 3 bytes.

Bit-fields have certain restrictions. You cannot take the address of a bit-field. Bit-fields cannot be arrayed. They cannot be declared as **static**. You cannot know, from machine to machine, whether the fields will run from right to left or from left to right; this implies that any code using bit-fields may have some machine dependencies. Other restrictions may be imposed by various specific implementations.

Unions

A *union* is a memory location that is shared by two or more different types of variables. A union provides a way of interpreting the same bit pattern in two or more different ways. Declaring a **union** is similar to declaring a structure. Its general form is

    union *union-type-name* {
      type member-name;

```
        type member-name;
        type member-name;
        .
        .
        .
    } union-variables;
```

For example:

```
union u_type {
  int i;
  char ch;
};
```

This declaration does not create any variables. You may declare a variable either by placing its name at the end of the declaration or by using a separate declaration statement. In C, to declare a **union** variable called **cnvt** of type **u_type** using the definition just given, write

```
union u_type cnvt;
```

When declaring **union** variables in C++, you need use only the type name— you don't need to precede it with the keyword **union**. For example, this is how **cnvt** is declared in C++:

```
u_type cnvt;
```

In C++, preceding this declaration with the keyword **union** is allowed, but redundant. In C++, the name of a **union** defines a complete type name. In C, a union name is its tag and it must be preceded by the keyword **union**. (This is similar to the situation with structures described earlier.) However, since the programs in this chapter are valid for both C and C++, the C-style declaration form will be used.

In **cnvt**, both integer **i** and character **ch** share the same memory location. Of course, **i** occupies 2 bytes (assuming 2-byte integers) and **ch** uses only 1. Figure 7-2 shows how **i** and **ch** share the same address. At any point in your program, you can refer to the data stored in a **cnvt** as either an integer or a character.

When a **union** variable is declared, the compiler automatically allocates enough storage to hold the largest member of the **union**. For example (assuming 2-byte integers), **cnvt** is 2 bytes long so that it can hold **i,** even though **ch** requires only 1 byte.

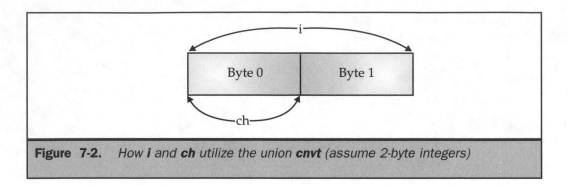

Figure 7-2.   *How **i** and **ch** utilize the union **cnvt** (assume 2-byte integers)*

To access a member of a **union**, use the same syntax that you would use for structures: the dot and arrow operators. If you are operating on the **union** directly, use the dot operator. If the **union** is accessed through a pointer, use the arrow operator. For example, to assign the integer 10 to element **i** of **cnvt**, write

```
cnvt.i = 10;
```

In the next example, a pointer to **cnvt** is passed to a function:

```
void func1(union u_type *un)
{
  un->i = 10; /* assign 10 to cnvt through
               a pointer */
}
```

Unions are used frequently when specialized type conversions are needed because you can refer to the data held in the **union** in fundamentally different ways. For example, you may use a **union** to manipulate the bytes that comprise a **double** in order to alter its precision or to perform some unusual type of rounding.

To get an idea of the usefulness of a **union** when nonstandard type conversions are needed, consider the problem of writing a short integer to a disk file. The C/C++ standard library defines no function specifically designed to write a short integer to a file. While you can write any type of data to a file using **fwrite( )**, using **fwrite( )** incurs excessive overhead for such a simple operation. However, using a **union** you can easily create a function called **putw( )**, which writes the binary representation of a short integer to a file one byte at a time. (This example assumes that short integers are 2 bytes long.) To see how, first create a **union** consisting of one short integer and a 2-byte character array:

```
union pw {
  short int i;
```

```
     char ch[2];
};
```

Now, you can use **pw** to create the version of **putw( )** shown in the following program.

```
#include <stdio.h>

union pw {
  short int i;
  char ch[2];
};

int putw(short int num, FILE *fp);

int main(void)
{
  FILE *fp;

  fp = fopen("test.tmp", "wb+");

  putw(1000, fp);   /* write the value 1000 as an integer */
  fclose(fp);

  return 0;
}

int putw(short int num, FILE *fp)
{
  union pw word;

  word.i = num;

  putc(word.ch[0], fp); /* write first half */
  return putc(word.ch[1], fp); /* write second half */
}
```

Although **putw( )** is called with a short integer, it can still use the standard function **putc( )** to write each byte in the integer to a disk file one byte at a time.

Note   *C++ supports a special type of union called an anonymous union which is discussed in Part Two of this book.*

Enumerations

An *enumeration* is a set of named integer constants that specify all the legal values a variable of that type may have. Enumerations are common in everyday life. For example, an enumeration of the coins used in the United States is

penny, nickel, dime, quarter, half-dollar, dollar

Enumerations are defined much like structures; the keyword **enum** signals the start of an enumeration type. The general form for enumerations is

enum *enum-type-name* { *enumeration list* } *variable_list*;

Here, both the type name and the variable list are optional. (But at least one must be present.) The following code fragment defines an enumeration called **coin**:

```
enum coin { penny, nickel, dime, quarter,
          half_dollar, dollar};
```

The enumeration type name can be used to declare variables of its type. In C, the following declares **money** to be a variable of type **coin**.

```
enum coin money;
```

In C++, the variable **money** may be declared using this shorter form:

```
coin money;
```

In C++, an enumeration name specifies a complete type. In C, an enumeration name is its tag and it requires the keyword **enum** to complete it. (This is similar to the situation as it applies to structures and unions, described earlier.)

Given these declarations, the following types of statements are perfectly valid:

```
money = dime;
if(money==quarter) printf("Money is a quarter.\n");
```

The key point to understand about an enumeration is that each of the symbols stands for an integer value. As such, they may be used anywhere that an integer may be used. Each symbol is given a value one greater than the symbol that precedes it. The value of the first enumeration symbol is 0. Therefore,

```
printf("%d %d", penny, dime);
```

displays **0 2** on the screen.

You can specify the value of one or more of the symbols by using an initializer. Do this by following the symbol with an equal sign and an integer value. Symbols that appear after initializers are assigned values greater than the previous initialization value. For example, the following code assigns the value of 100 to **quarter**:

```
enum coin { penny, nickel, dime, quarter=100,
            half_dollar, dollar};
```

Now, the values of these symbols are

penny	0
nickel	1
dime	2
quarter	100
half_dollar	101
dollar	102

One common but erroneous assumption about enumerations is that the symbols can be input and output directly. This is not the case. For example, the following code fragment will not perform as desired:

```
/* this will not work */
money = dollar;
printf("%s", money);
```

Remember, **dollar** is simply a name for an integer; it is not a string. For the same reason, you cannot use this code to achieve the desired results:

```
/* this code is wrong */
strcpy(money, "dime");
```

That is, a string that contains the name of a symbol is not automatically converted to that symbol.

Actually, creating code to input and output enumeration symbols is quite tedious (unless you are willing to settle for their integer values). For example, you need the following code to display, in words, the kind of coins that **money** contains:

```
switch(money) {
  case penny: printf("penny");
    break;
  case nickel: printf("nickel");
    break;
  case dime: printf("dime");
    break;
  case quarter: printf("quarter");
    break;
  case half_dollar: printf("half_dollar");
    break;
  case dollar: printf("dollar");
}
```

Sometimes you can declare an array of strings and use the enumeration value as an index to translate that value into its corresponding string. For example, this code also outputs the proper string:

```
char name[][12]={
  "penny",
  "nickel",
  "dime",
  "quarter",
  "half_dollar",
  "dollar"
};
printf("%s", name[money]);
```

Of course, this only works if no symbol is initialized, because the string array must be indexed starting at 0 in strictly ascending order using increments of 1.

Since enumeration values must be converted manually to their human-readable string values for I/O operations, they are most useful in routines that do not make such conversions. An enumeration is often used to define a compiler's symbol table, for example. Enumerations are also used to help prove the validity of a program by providing a compile-time redundancy check confirming that a variable is assigned only valid values.

Using sizeof to Ensure Portability

You have seen that structures and unions can be used to create variables of different sizes, and that the actual size of these variables may change from machine to machine. The **sizeof** operator computes the size of any variable or type and can help eliminate machine-dependent code from your programs. This operator is especially useful where structures or unions are concerned.

For the following discussion, assume an implementation, common to many C/C++ compilers, that has the sizes for data types shown here:

Type	Size in Bytes
char	1
int	4
double	8

Therefore, the following code will print the numbers 1, 4, and 8 on the screen:

```
char ch;
int i;
double f;

printf("%d", sizeof(ch));
printf("%d", sizeof(i));
printf("%d", sizeof(f));
```

The size of a structure is equal to *or greater than* the sum of the sizes of its members. For example,

```
struct s {
  char ch;
  int i;
  double f;
} s_var;
```

Here, **sizeof(s_var)** is at least 13 (8 + 4 + 1). However, the size of **s_var** might be greater because the compiler is allowed to pad a structure in order to achieve word or paragraph alignment. (A paragraph is 16 bytes.) Since the size of a structure may be greater than the sum of the sizes of its members, you should always use **sizeof** when you need to know the size of a structure.

Since **sizeof** is a compile-time operator, all the information necessary to compute the size of any variable is known at compile time. This is especially meaningful for **union**s, because the size of a **union** is always equal to the size of its largest member. For example, consider

```
union u {
  char ch;
  int i;
  double f;
} u_var;
```

Here, the **sizeof(u_var)** is 8. At run time, it does not matter what **u_var** is actually holding. All that matters is the size of its largest member, because any **union** must be as large as its largest element.

typedef

You can define new data type names by using the keyword **typedef**. You are not actually *creating* a new data type, but rather defining a new name for an existing type. This process can help make machine-dependent programs more portable. If you define your own type name for each machine-dependent data type used by your program, then only the **typedef** statements have to be changed when compiling for a new environment. **typedef** also can aid in self-documenting your code by allowing descriptive names for the standard data types. The general form of the **typedef** statement is

typedef *type newname*;

where *type* is any valid data type and *newname* is the new name for this type. The new name you define is in addition to, not a replacement for, the existing type name.

For example, you could create a new name for **float** by using

```
typedef float balance;
```

This statement tells the compiler to recognize **balance** as another name for **float**. Next, you could create a **float** variable using **balance**:

```
balance over_due;
```

Here, **over_due** is a floating-point variable of type **balance**, which is another word for **float**.

Now that **balance** has been defined, it can be used in another **typedef**. For example,

```
typedef balance overdraft;
```

tells the compiler to recognize **overdraft** as another name for **balance**, which is another name for **float**.

Using **typedef** can make your code easier to read and easier to port to a new machine, but you are not creating a new physical type.

Chapter 8

C-Style Console I/O

C++ supports two complete I/O systems. The first it inherits from C. The second is the object-oriented I/O system defined by C++. This and the next chapter discuss the C-like I/O system. (Part Two examines C++ I/O.) While you will probably want to use the C++ I/O system for most new projects, C-style I/O is still quite common, and knowledge of its features is fundamental to a complete understanding of C++.

In C, input and output are accomplished through library functions. There are both console and file I/O functions. Technically, there is little distinction between console I/O and file I/O, but conceptually they are in very different worlds. This chapter examines in detail the console I/O functions. The next chapter presents the file I/O system and describes how the two systems relate.

With one exception, this chapter covers only console I/O functions defined by Standard C++. Standard C++ does not define any functions that perform various screen control operations (such as cursor positioning) or that display graphics, because these operations vary widely between machines. Nor does it define any functions that write to a window or dialog box under Windows. Instead, the console I/O functions perform only TTY-based output. However, most compilers include in their libraries screen control and graphics functions that apply to the specific environment in which the compiler is designed to run. And, of course, you may use C++ to write Windows programs, but keep in mind that the C++ language does not directly define functions that perform these tasks.

The Standard C I/O functions all use the header file **stdio.h**. C++ programs can also use the C++-style header **<cstdio>**.

This chapter refers to the console I/O functions as performing input from the keyboard and output to the screen. However, these functions actually have the standard input and standard output of the system as the target and/or source of their I/O operations. Furthermore, standard input and standard output may be redirected to other devices. These concepts are covered in Chapter 9.

An Important Application Note

Part One of this book uses the C-like I/O system because it is the only style of I/O that is defined for the C subset of C++. As explained, C++ also defines its own object-oriented I/O system. For most C++ applications, you will want to use the C++-specific I/O system, not the C I/O system described in this chapter. However, an understanding of C-based I/O is important for the following reasons:

- At some point in your career you may be called upon to write code that is restricted to the C subset. In this case, you will need to use the C-like I/O functions.

- For the foreseeable future, C and C++ will coexist. Also, many programs will be hybrids of both C and C++ code. Further, it will be common for C programs to be "upgraded" into C++ programs. Thus, knowledge of both the C and the C++

I/O system will be necessary. For example, in order to change the C-style I/O functions into their C++ object-oriented equivalents, you will need to know how both the C and C++ I/O systems operate.

■ An understanding of the basic principles behind the C-like I/O system is crucial to an understanding of the C++ object-oriented I/O system. (Both share the same general concepts.)

■ In certain situations (for example, in very short programs), it may be easier to use C's non-object-oriented approach to I/O than it is to use the object-oriented I/O defined by C++.

In addition, there is an unwritten rule that any C++ programmer must also be a C programmer. If you don't know how to use the C I/O system, you will be limiting your professional horizons.

Reading and Writing Characters

The simplest of the console I/O functions are **getchar( )**, which reads a character from the keyboard, and **putchar( )**, which prints a character to the screen. The **getchar( )** function waits until a key is pressed and then returns its value. The key pressed is also automatically echoed to the screen. The **putchar( )** function writes a character to the screen at the current cursor position. The prototypes for **getchar( )** and **putchar( )** are shown here:

```
int getchar(void);
int putchar(int c);
```

As its prototype shows, the **getchar( )** function is declared as returning an integer. However, you can assign this value to a **char** variable, as is usually done, because the character is contained in the low-order byte. (The high-order byte is normally zero.) **getchar( )** returns **EOF** if an error occurs.

In the case of **putchar( ),** even though it is declared as taking an integer parameter, you will generally call it using a character argument. Only the low-order byte of its parameter is actually output to the screen. The **putchar( )** function returns the character written, or **EOF** if an error occurs. (The **EOF** macro is defined in **stdio.h** and is generally equal to –1.)

The following program illustrates **getchar( )** and **putchar( ).** It inputs characters from the keyboard and displays them in reverse case—that is, it prints uppercase as lowercase and lowercase as uppercase. To stop the program, enter a period.

```
#include <stdio.h>
#include <ctype.h>
```

```
int main(void)
{
  char ch;

  printf("Enter some text (type a period to quit).\n");
  do {
    ch = getchar();

    if(islower(ch)) ch = toupper(ch);
    else ch = tolower(ch);

    putchar(ch);
  } while (ch != '.');

  return 0;
}
```

A Problem with getchar( )

There are some potential problems with **getchar( )**. Normally, **getchar( )** is implemented in such a way that it buffers input until ENTER is pressed. This is called *line-buffered* input; you have to press ENTER before anything you typed is actually sent to your program. Also, since **getchar( )** inputs only one character each time it is called, line-buffering may leave one or more characters waiting in the input queue, which is annoying in interactive environments. Even though Standard C/C++ specify that **getchar( )** can be implemented as an interactive function, it seldom is. Therefore, if the preceding program did not behave as you expected, you now know why.

Alternatives to getchar( )

getchar( ) might not be implemented by your compiler in such a way that it is useful in an interactive environment. If this is the case, you might want to use a different function to read characters from the keyboard. Standard C++ does not define any function that is guaranteed to provide interactive input, but virtually all C++ compilers do. Although these functions are not defined by Standard C++, they are commonly used since **getchar( )** does not fill the needs of most programmers.

Two of the most common alternative functions, **getch( )** and **getche( )**, have these prototypes:

```
int getch(void);
int getche(void);
```

For most compilers, the prototypes for these functions are found in the header file **conio.h**. For some compilers, these functions have a leading underscore. For example, in Microsoft's Visual C++, they are called **_getch( )** and **_getche( )**.

The **getch( )** function waits for a keypress, after which it returns immediately. It does not echo the character to the screen. The **getche( )** function is the same as **getch( )**, but the key is echoed. You will frequently see **getche( )** or **getch( )** used instead of **getchar( )** when a character needs to be read from the keyboard in an interactive program. However, if your compiler does not support these alternative functions, or if **getchar( )** is implemented as an interactive function by your compiler, you should substitute **getchar( )** when necessary.

For example, the previous program is shown here using **getch( )** instead of **getchar( )**:

```c
#include <stdio.h>
#include <conio.h>
#include <ctype.h>

int main(void)
{
  char ch;

  printf("Enter some text (type a period to quit).\n");
  do {
    ch = getch();

    if(islower(ch)) ch = toupper(ch);
    else ch = tolower(ch);

    putchar(ch);
  } while (ch != '.');

  return 0;
}
```

When you run this version of the program, each time you press a key, it is immediately transmitted to the program and displayed in reverse case. Input is no longer line-buffered. While the code in this book will not make further use of **getch( )** or **getche( )**, they may be useful in the programs that you write.

Note *At the time of this writing, when using Microsoft's Visual C++ compiler, _getche( ) and _getch( ) are not compatible with the standard C/C++ input functions, such as scanf( ) or gets( ). Instead, you must use special versions of the standard functions, such as cscanf( ) or cgets( ). You will need to examine the Visual C++ documentation for details.*

Reading and Writing Strings

The next step up in console I/O, in terms of complexity and power, are the functions **gets( )** and **puts( )**. They enable you to read and write strings of characters.

The **gets( )** function reads a string of characters entered at the keyboard and places them at the address pointed to by its argument. You may type characters at the keyboard until you press ENTER. The carriage return does not become part of the string; instead, a null terminator is placed at the end and **gets( )** returns. In fact, you cannot use **gets( )** to return a carriage return (although **getchar( )** can do so). You can correct typing mistakes by using the backspace key before pressing ENTER. The prototype for **gets( )** is

    char *gets(char *str);

where *str* is a character array that receives the characters input by the user. **gets( )** also returns *str*. The following program reads a string into the array **str** and prints its length:

```
#include <stdio.h>
#include <string.h>

int main(void)
{
  char str[80];

  gets(str);
  printf("Length is %d", strlen(str));

  return 0;
}
```

You need to be careful when using **gets( )** because it performs no boundary checks on the array that is receiving input. Thus, it is possible for the user to enter more characters than the array can hold. While **gets( )** is fine for sample programs and simple utilities that only you will use, you will want to avoid its use in commercial code. One alternative is the **fgets( )** function described in the next chapter, which allows you to prevent an array overrun.

The **puts( )** function writes its string argument to the screen followed by a newline. Its prototype is:

    int puts(const char *str);

puts( ) recognizes the same backslash codes as **printf( )**, such as '\t' for tab. A call to **puts( )** requires far less overhead than the same call to **printf( )** because **puts( )**

can only output a string of characters—it cannot output numbers or do format conversions. Therefore, **puts( )** takes up less space and runs faster than **printf( )**. For this reason, the **puts( )** function is often used when it is important to have highly optimized code. The **puts( )** function returns **EOF** if an error occurs. Otherwise, it returns a nonnegative value. However, when writing to the console, you can usually assume that no error will occur, so the return value of **puts( )** is seldom monitored. The following statement displays **hello**:

```
puts("hello");
```

Table 8-1 summarizes the basic console I/O functions.

The following program, a simple computerized dictionary, demonstrates several of the basic console I/O functions. It prompts the user to enter a word and then checks to see if the word matches one in its built-in database. If a match is found, the program prints the word's meaning. Pay special attention to the indirection used in this program. If you have any trouble understanding it, remember that the **dic** array is an array of pointers to strings. Notice that the list must be terminated by two nulls.

Function	Operation
getchar( )	Reads a character from the keyboard; waits for carriage return.
getche( )	Reads a character with echo; does not wait for carriage return; not defined by Standard C/C++, but a common extension.
getch( )	Reads a character without echo; does not wait for carriage return; not defined by Standard C/C++, but a common extension.
putchar( )	Writes a character to the screen.
gets( )	Reads a string from the keyboard.
puts( )	Writes a string to the screen.

Table 8-1. *The Basic I/O Functions*

```c
/* A simple dictionary. */
#include <stdio.h>
#include <string.h>
#include <ctype.h>

/* list of words and meanings */
char  *dic[][40] = {
  "atlas", "A volume of maps.",
  "car", "A motorized vehicle.",
  "telephone", "A communication device.",
  "airplane", "A flying machine.",
  "", ""   /* null terminate the list */
};

int main(void)
{
  char word[80], ch;
  char **p;

  do {
    puts("\nEnter word: ");
    scanf("%s", word);

    p = (char **)dic;

    /* find matching word and print its meaning */
    do {
      if(!strcmp(*p, word)) {
        puts("Meaning:");
        puts(*(p+1));
        break;
      }
      if(!strcmp(*p, word)) break;
      p = p + 2;  /* advance through the list */
    } while(*p);
    if(!*p) puts("Word not in dictionary.");
    printf("Another? (y/n): ");
    scanf(" %c%*c", &ch);
  } while(toupper(ch) != 'N');

  return 0;
}
```

Formatted Console I/O

The functions **printf( )** and **scanf( )** perform formatted output and input—that is, they can read and write data in various formats that are under your control. The **printf( )** function writes data to the console. The **scanf( )** function, its complement, reads data from the keyboard. Both functions can operate on any of the built-in data types, including characters, strings, and numbers.

printf( )

The prototype for **printf( )** is

   int printf(const char *control_string, ...);

The **printf( )** function returns the number of characters written or a negative value if an error occurs.

The *control_string* consists of two types of items. The first type is composed of characters that will be printed on the screen. The second type contains format specifiers that define the way the subsequent arguments are displayed. A format specifier begins with a percent sign and is followed by the format code. There must be exactly the same number of arguments as there are format specifiers, and the format specifiers and the arguments are matched in order from left to right. For example, this **printf( )** call

```
printf("I like %c%s", 'C', "++ very much!");
```

displays

```
I like C++ very much!
```

The **printf( )** function accepts a wide variety of format specifiers, as shown in Table 8-2.

Code	Format
%c	Character
%d	Signed decimal integers

Table 8-2. *printf( ) Format Specifiers*

Code	Format
%i	Signed decimal integers
%e	Scientific notation (lowercase e)
%E	Scientific notation (uppercase E)
%f	Decimal floating point
%g	Uses %e or %f, whichever is shorter
%G	Uses %E or %F, whichever is shorter
%o	Unsigned octal
%s	String of characters
%u	Unsigned decimal integers
%x	Unsigned hexadecimal (lowercase letters)
%X	Unsigned hexadecimal (uppercase letters)
%p	Displays a pointer
%n	The associated argument must be a pointer to an integer. This specifier causes the number of characters written so far to be put into that integer.
%%	Prints a % sign

Table 8-2.   *printf( ) Format Specifiers* (continued)

Printing Characters

To print an individual character, use **%c**. This causes its matching argument to be output, unmodified, to the screen.

To print a string, use **%s**.

Printing Numbers

You may use either **%d** or **%i** to indicate a signed decimal number. These format specifiers are equivalent; both are supported for historical reasons.

To output an unsigned value, use **%u**.

The **%f** format specifier displays numbers in floating point.

The **%e** and **%E** specifiers tell **printf( )** to display a **double** argument in scientific notation. Numbers represented in scientific notation take this general form:

x.dddddE+/−yy

If you want to display the letter "E" in uppercase, use the **%E** format; otherwise use **%e**.

You can tell **printf( )** to use either **%f** or **%e** by using the **%g** or **%G** format specifiers. This causes **printf( )** to select the format specifier that produces the shortest output. Where applicable, use **%G** if you want "E" shown in uppercase; otherwise, use **%g**. The following program demonstrates the effect of the **%g** format specifier:

```
#include <stdio.h>

int main(void)
{
  double f;

  for(f=1.0; f<1.0e+10; f=f*10)
    printf("%g ", f);

  return 0;
}
```

It produces the following output.

```
1 10 100 1000 10000 100000 1e+006 1e+007 1e+008 1e+009
```

You can display unsigned integers in octal or hexadecimal format using **%o** and **%x**, respectively. Since the hexadecimal number system uses the letters A through F to represent the numbers 10 through 15, you can display these letters in either upper- or lowercase. For uppercase, use the **%X** format specifier; for lowercase, use **%x**, as shown here:

```
#include <stdio.h>

int main(void)
{
  unsigned num;

  for(num=0; num<255; num++) {
    printf("%o ", num);
    printf("%x ", num);
```

```
    printf("%X\n", num);
  }

  return 0;
}
```

Displaying an Address

If you wish to display an address, use **%p**. This format specifier causes **printf( )** to display a machine address in a format compatible with the type of addressing used by the computer. The next program displays the address of **sample**:

```
#include <stdio.h>

int sample;

int main(void)
{
  printf("%p", &sample);

  return 0;
}
```

The %n Specifier

The **%n** format specifier is different from the others. Instead of telling **printf( )** to display something, it causes **printf( )** to load the variable pointed to by its corresponding argument with a value equal to the number of characters that have been output. In other words, the value that corresponds to the **%n** format specifier must be a pointer to a variable. After the call to **printf( )** has returned, this variable will hold the number of characters output, up to the point at which the **%n** was encountered. Examine this program to understand this somewhat unusual format code.

```
#include <stdio.h>

int main(void)
{
  int count;

  printf("this%n is a test\n", &count);
  printf("%d", count);
```

```
    return 0;
}
```

This program displays **this is a test** followed by the number 4. The **%n** format specifier is used primarily to enable your program to perform dynamic formatting.

Format Modifiers

Many format specifiers may take modifiers that alter their meaning slightly. For example, you can specify a minimum field width, the number of decimal places, and left justification. The format modifier goes between the percent sign and the format code. These modifiers are discussed next.

The Minimum Field Width Specifier

An integer placed between the % sign and the format code acts as a *minimum field width specifier*. This pads the output with spaces to ensure that it reaches a certain minimum length. If the string or number is longer than that minimum, it will still be printed in full. The default padding is done with spaces. If you wish to pad with 0's, place a 0 before the field width specifier. For example, **%05d** will pad a number of less than five digits with 0's so that its total length is five. The following program demonstrates the minimum field width specifier:

```c
#include <stdio.h>

int main(void)
{
  double item;

  item = 10.12304;

  printf("%f\n", item);
  printf("%10f\n", item);
  printf("%012f\n", item);

  return 0;
}
```

This program produces the following output:

```
10.123040
 10.123040
00010.123040
```

The minimum field width modifier is most commonly used to produce tables in which the columns line up. For example, the next program produces a table of squares and cubes for the numbers between 1 and 19:

```c
#include <stdio.h>

int main(void)
{
  int i;

  /* display a table of squares and cubes */
  for(i=1; i<20; i++)
    printf("%8d %8d %8d\n", i, i*i, i*i*i);

  return 0;
}
```

A sample of its output is shown here:

```
   1        1        1
   2        4        8
   3        9       27
   4       16       64
   5       25      125
   6       36      216
   7       49      343
   8       64      512
   9       81      729
  10      100     1000
  11      121     1331
  12      144     1728
  13      169     2197
  14      196     2744
  15      225     3375
  16      256     4096
  17      289     4913
  18      324     5832
  19      361     6859
```

The Precision Specifier

The *precision specifier* follows the minimum field width specifier (if there is one). It consists of a period followed by an integer. Its exact meaning depends upon the type of data it is applied to.

When you apply the precision specifier to floating-point data using the **%f**, **%e**, or **%E** specifiers, it determines the number of decimal places displayed. For example, **%10.4f** displays a number at least ten characters wide with four decimal places.

When the precision specifier is applied to **%g** or **%G**, it specifies the number of significant digits.

Applied to strings, the precision specifier specifies the maximum field length. For example, **%5.7s** displays a string at least five and not exceeding seven characters long. If the string is longer than the maximum field width, the end characters will be truncated.

When applied to integer types, the precision specifier determines the minimum number of digits that will appear for each number. Leading zeros are added to achieve the required number of digits.

The following program illustrates the precision specifier:

```
#include <stdio.h>

int main(void)
{
  printf("%.4f\n", 123.1234567);
  printf("%3.8d\n", 1000);
  printf("%10.15s\n", "This is a simple test.");

  return 0;
}
```

It produces the following output:

```
123.1235
00001000
This is a simpl
```

Justifying Output

By default, all output is right-justified. That is, if the field width is larger than the data printed, the data will be placed on the right edge of the field. You can force output to be left-justified by placing a minus sign directly after the %. For example, **%−10.2f** left-justifies a floating-point number with two decimal places in a 10-character field.

The following program illustrates left justification:

```
#include <stdio.h>

int main(void)
{
  printf("right-justified:%8d\n", 100);
  printf("left-justified:%-8d\n", 100);
```

```
    return 0;
}
```

Handling Other Data Types

There are two format modifiers that allow **printf( )** to display **short** and **long** integers. These modifiers may be applied to the **d, i, o, u,** and **x** type specifiers. The **l** (*ell*) modifier tells **printf( )** that a **long** data type follows. For example, **%ld** means that a **long int** is to be displayed. The **h** modifier instructs **printf( )** to display a **short** integer. For instance, **%hu** indicates that the data is of type **short unsigned int**.

The **l** and **h** modifiers can also be applied to the **n** specifier, to indicate that the corresponding argument is a pointer to a long or short integer, respectively.

If your compiler fully complies with Standard C++, then you can use the **l** modifier with the **c** format to indicate a wide-character. You can also use the **l** modifier with the **s** format to indicate a wide-character string.

The **L** modifier may prefix the floating-point specifiers **e, f,** and **g,** and indicates that a **long double** follows.

The * and # Modifiers

The **printf( )** function supports two additional modifiers to some of its format specifiers: * and #.

Preceding **g, G, f, E,** or **e** specifiers with a # ensures that there will be a decimal point even if there are no decimal digits. If you precede the **x** or **X** format specifier with a #, the hexadecimal number will be printed with a **0x** prefix. Preceding the **o** specifier with # causes the number to be printed with a leading zero. You cannot apply # to any other format specifiers.

Instead of constants, the minimum field width and precision specifiers may be provided by arguments to **printf( )**. To accomplish this, use an * as a placeholder. When the format string is scanned, **printf( )** will match the * to an argument in the order in which they occur. For example, in Figure 8-1, the minimum field width is 10, the precision is 4, and the value to be displayed is **123.3**.

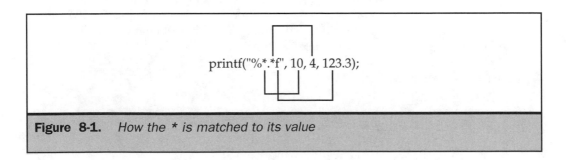

Figure 8-1. *How the * is matched to its value*

The following program illustrates both # and *:

```
#include <stdio.h>

int main(void)
{
  printf("%x %#x\n", 10, 10);
  printf("%*.*f", 10, 4, 1234.34);

  return 0;
}
```

scanf( )

scanf( ) is the general-purpose console input routine. It can read all the built-in data types and automatically convert numbers into the proper internal format. It is much like the reverse of **printf( )**. The prototype for **scanf( )** is

int scanf(const char *control_string, ...);

The **scanf( )** function returns the number of data items successfully assigned a value. If an error occurs, **scanf( )** returns **EOF**. The *control_string* determines how values are read into the variables pointed to in the argument list.

The control string consists of three classifications of characters:

- Format specifiers
- White-space characters
- Non-white-space characters

Let's take a look at each of these now.

Format Specifiers

The input format specifiers are preceded by a % sign and tell **scanf( )** what type of data is to be read next. These codes are listed in Table 8-3. The format specifiers are matched, in order from left to right, with the arguments in the argument list. Let's look at some examples.

Inputting Numbers

To read an integer, use either the **%d** or **%i** specifier. To read a floating-point number represented in either standard or scientific notation, use **%e**, **%f**, or **%g**.

You can use **scanf( )** to read integers in either octal or hexadecimal form by using the **%o** and **%x** format commands, respectively. The **%x** may be in either upper- or lowercase.

Code	Meaning
%c	Read a single character.
%d	Read a decimal integer.
%i	Read an integer in either decimal, octal, or hexadecimal format.
%e	Read a floating-point number.
%f	Read a floating-point number.
%g	Read a floating-point number.
%o	Read an octal number.
%s	Read a string.
%x	Read a hexadecimal number.
%p	Read a pointer.
%n	Receives an integer value equal to the number of characters read so far.
%u	Read an unsigned decimal integer.
%[ ]	Scan for a set of characters.
%%	Read a percent sign.

Table 8-3.   *scanf( ) Format Specifiers*

Either way, you may enter the letters "A" through "F" in either case when entering hexadecimal numbers. The following program reads an octal and hexadecimal number:

```
#include <stdio.h>

int main(void)
{
  int i, j;

  scanf("%o%x", &i, &j);
  printf("%o %x", i, j);

  return 0;
}
```

The **scanf( )** function stops reading a number when the first nonnumeric character is encountered.

Inputting Unsigned Integers

To input an unsigned integer, use the **%u** format specifier. For example,

```
unsigned num;
scanf("%u", &num);
```

reads an unsigned number and puts its value into **num**.

Reading Individual Characters Using scanf( )

As explained earlier in this chapter, you can read individual characters using **getchar( )** or a derivative function. You can also use **scanf( )** for this purpose if you use the **%c** format specifier. However, like most implementations of **getchar( )**, **scanf( )** will generally line-buffer input when the **%c** specifier is used. This makes it somewhat troublesome in an interactive environment.

Although spaces, tabs, and newlines are used as field separators when reading other types of data, when reading a single character, white-space characters are read like any other character. For example, with an input stream of "**x y**," this code fragment

```
scanf("%c%c%c", &a, &b, &c);
```

returns with the character **x** in **a**, a space in **b**, and the character **y** in **c**.

Reading Strings

The **scanf( )** function can be used to read a string from the input stream using the **%s** format specifier. Using **%s** causes **scanf( )** to read characters until it encounters a white-space character. The characters that are read are put into the character array pointed to by the corresponding argument and the result is null terminated. As it applies to **scanf( )**, a white-space character is either a space, a newline, a tab, a vertical tab, or a form feed. Unlike **gets( )**, which reads a string until a carriage return is typed, **scanf( )** reads a string until the first white space is entered. This means that you cannot use **scanf( )** to read a string like "this is a test" because the first space terminates the reading process. To see the effect of the **%s** specifier, try this program using the string "hello there".

```
#include <stdio.h>

int main(void)
```

```
{
  char str[80];

  printf("Enter a string: ");
  scanf("%s", str);
  printf("Here's your string: %s", str);

  return 0;
}
```

The program responds with only the "hello" portion of the string.

Inputting an Address

To input a memory address, use the **%p** format specifier. This specifier causes **scanf( )** to read an address in the format defined by the architecture of the CPU. For example, this program inputs an address and then displays what is at that memory address:

```
#include <stdio.h>

int main(void)
{
  char *p;

  printf("Enter an address: ");
  scanf("%p", &p);
  printf("Value at location %p is %c\n", p, *p);

  return 0;
}
```

The %n Specifier

The **%n** specifier instructs **scanf( )** to assign the number of characters read from the input stream at the point at which the **%n** was encountered to the variable pointed to by the corresponding argument.

Using a Scanset

The **scanf( )** function supports a general-purpose format specifier called a scanset. A *scanset* defines a set of characters. When **scanf( )** processes a scanset, it will input characters as long as those characters are part of the set defined by the scanset. The characters read will be assigned to the character array that is pointed to by the scanset's corresponding argument. You define a scanset by putting the characters to scan for inside square brackets. The beginning square bracket must be prefixed by a percent sign. For example, the following scanset tells **scanf( )** to read only the characters X, Y, and Z.

```
%[XYZ]
```

When you use a scanset, **scanf( )** continues to read characters, putting them into the corresponding character array until it encounters a character that is not in the scanset. Upon return from **scanf( )**, this array will contain a null-terminated string that consists of the characters that have been read. To see how this works, try this program:

```
#include <stdio.h>

int main(void)
{
  int i;
  char str[80], str2[80];

  scanf("%d%[abcdefg]%s", &i, str, str2);
  printf("%d %s %s", i, str, str2);

  return 0;
}
```

Enter **123abcdtye** followed by ENTER. The program will then display **123 abcd tye**. Because the "t" is not part of the scanset, **scanf( )** stops reading characters into **str** when it encounters the "t." The remaining characters are put into **str2**.

You can specify an inverted set if the first character in the set is a ^. The ^ instructs **scanf( )** to accept any character that is *not* defined by the scanset.

In most implementations you can specify a range using a hyphen. For example, this tells **scanf( )** to accept the characters A through Z:

```
%[A-Z]
```

One important point to remember is that the scanset is case sensitive. If you want to scan for both upper- and lowercase letters, you must specify them individually.

Discarding Unwanted White Space

A white-space character in the control string causes **scanf( )** to skip over one or more leading white-space characters in the input stream. A white-space character is either a space, a tab, vertical tab, form feed, or a newline. In essence, one white-space character in the control string causes **scanf( )** to read, but not store, any number (including zero) of white-space characters up to the first non-white-space character.

Non-White-Space Characters in the Control String

A non-white-space character in the control string causes **scanf( )** to read and discard matching characters in the input stream. For example, **"%d,%d"** causes **scanf( )** to read an integer, read and discard a comma, and then read another integer. If the specified character is not found, **scanf( )** terminates. If you wish to read and discard a percent sign, use %% in the control string.

You Must Pass scanf( ) Addresses

All the variables used to receive values through **scanf( )** must be passed by their addresses. This means that all arguments must be pointers to the variables used as arguments. Recall that this is one way of creating a call by reference, and it allows a function to alter the contents of an argument. For example, to read an integer into the variable **count**, you would use the following **scanf( )** call:

```
scanf("%d", &count);
```

Strings will be read into character arrays, and the array name, without any index, is the address of the first element of the array. So, to read a string into the character array **str**, you would use

```
scanf("%s", str);
```

In this case, **str** is already a pointer and need not be preceded by the & operator.

Format Modifiers

As with **printf( )**, **scanf( )** allows a number of its format specifiers to be modified.
   The format specifiers can include a maximum field length modifier. This is an integer, placed between the % and the format specifier, that limits the number of characters read for that field. For example, to read no more than 20 characters into **str**, write

```
scanf("%20s", str);
```

If the input stream is greater than 20 characters, a subsequent call to input begins where this call leaves off. For example, if you enter

ABCDEFGHIJKLMNOPQRSTUVWXYZ

as the response to the **scanf( )** call in this example, only the first 20 characters, or up to the "T," are placed into **str** because of the maximum field width specifier. This means that the remaining characters, UVWXYZ, have not yet been used. If another **scanf( )** call is made, such as

```
scanf("%s", str);
```

the letters UVWXYZ are placed into **str**. Input for a field may terminate before the maximum field length is reached if a white space is encountered. In this case, **scanf( )** moves on to the next field.

To read a long integer, put an **l** (*ell*) in front of the format specifier. To read a short integer, put an **h** in front of the format specifier. These modifiers can be used with the **d**, **i**, **o**, **u**, **x**, and **n** format codes.

By default, the **f**, **e**, and **g** specifiers instruct **scanf( )** to assign data to a **float**. If you put an **l** (*ell*) in front of one of these specifiers, **scanf( )** assigns the data to a **double**. Using an **L** tells **scanf( )** that the variable receiving the data is a **long double**.

Suppressing Input

You can tell **scanf( )** to read a field but not assign it to any variable by preceding that field's format code with an *. For example, given

```
scanf("%d%*c%d", &x, &y);
```

you could enter the coordinate pair **10,10**. The comma would be correctly read, but not assigned to anything. Assignment suppression is especially useful when you need to process only a part of what is being entered.

The Complete Reference

Chapter 9

File I/O

T his chapter describes the C file system. As explained in Chapter 8, C++ supports two complete I/O systems: the one inherited from C and the object-oriented system defined by C++. This chapter covers the C file system. (The C++ file system is discussed in Part Two.) While most new code will use the C++ file system, knowledge of the C file system is still important for the reasons given in the preceding chapter.

C Versus C++ File I/O

There is sometimes confusion over how C's file system relates to C++. First, C++ supports the entire Standard C file system. Thus, if you will be porting C code to C++, you will not have to change all of your I/O routines right away. Second, C++ defines its own, object-oriented I/O system, which includes both I/O functions and I/O operators. The C++ I/O system completely duplicates the functionality of the C I/O system and renders the C file system redundant. While you will usually want to use the C++ I/O system, you are free to use the C file system if you like. Of course, most C++ programmers elect to use the C++ I/O system for reasons that are made clear in Part Two of this book.

Streams and Files

Before beginning our discussion of the C file system, it is necessary to know the difference between the terms *streams* and *files*. The C I/O system supplies a consistent interface to the programmer independent of the actual device being accessed. That is, the C I/O system provides a level of abstraction between the programmer and the device. This abstraction is called a *stream* and the actual device is called a *file*. It is important to understand how streams and files interact.

  The concept of streams and files is also important to the C++ I/O system discussed in Part Two.

Streams

The C file system is designed to work with a wide variety of devices, including terminals, disk drives, and tape drives. Even though each device is very different, the file system transforms each into a logical device called a stream. All streams behave similarly. Because streams are largely device independent, the same function that can write to a disk file can also be used to write to another type of device, such as the console. There are two types of streams: text and binary.

Text Streams

A *text stream* is a sequence of characters. Standard C allows (but does not require) a text stream to be organized into lines terminated by a newline character. However, the newline character is optional on the last line. (Actually, most C/C++ compilers do not terminate text streams with newline characters.) In a text stream, certain character translations may occur as required by the host environment. For example, a newline may be converted to a carriage return/linefeed pair. Therefore, there may not be a one-to-one relationship between the characters that are written (or read) and those on the external device. Also, because of possible translations, the number of characters written (or read) may not be the same as those on the external device.

Binary Streams

A *binary stream* is a sequence of bytes that have a one-to-one correspondence to those in the external device—that is, no character translations occur. Also, the number of bytes written (or read) is the same as the number on the external device. However, an implementation-defined number of null bytes may be appended to a binary stream. These null bytes might be used to pad the information so that it fills a sector on a disk, for example.

Files

In C/C++, a *file* may be anything from a disk file to a terminal or printer. You associate a stream with a specific file by performing an open operation. Once a file is open, information may be exchanged between it and your program.

Not all files have the same capabilities. For example, a disk file can support random access while some printers cannot. This brings up an important point about the C I/O system: All streams are the same but all files are not.

If the file can support *position requests*, opening that file also initializes the *file position indicator* to the start of the file. As each character is read from or written to the file, the position indicator is incremented, ensuring progression through the file.

You disassociate a file from a specific stream with a close operation. If you close a file opened for output, the contents, if any, of its associated stream are written to the external device. This process is generally referred to as *flushing* the stream, and guarantees that no information is accidentally left in the disk buffer. All files are closed automatically when your program terminates normally, either by **main( )** returning to the operating system or by a call to **exit( )**. Files are not closed when a program terminates abnormally, such as when it crashes or when it calls **abort( )**.

Each stream that is associated with a file has a file control structure of type **FILE**. Never modify this file control block.

If you are new to programming, the separation of streams and files may seem unnecessary or contrived. Just remember that its main purpose is to provide a consistent interface. You need only think in terms of streams and use only one file system to accomplish all I/O operations. The I/O system automatically converts the raw input or output from each device into an easily managed stream.

File System Basics

The C file system is composed of several interrelated functions. The most common of these are shown in Table 9-1. They require the header **stdio.h**. C++ programs may also use the C++-style header **<cstdio>**.

Name	Function
fopen( )	Opens a file.
fclose( )	Closes a file.
putc( )	Writes a character to a file.
fputc( )	Same as **putc( )**.
getc( )	Reads a character from a file.
fgetc( )	Same as **getc( )**.
fgets( )	Reads a string from a file.
fputs( )	Writes a string to a file.
fseek( )	Seeks to a specified byte in a file.
ftell( )	Returns the current file position.
fprintf( )	Is to a file what **printf( )** is to the console.
fscanf( )	Is to a file what **scanf( )** is to the console.
feof( )	Returns true if end-of-file is reached.
ferror( )	Returns true if an error has occurred.
rewind( )	Resets the file position indicator to the beginning of the file.
remove( )	Erases a file.
fflush( )	Flushes a file.

Table 9-1. *Commonly Used C File-System Functions*

THE FOUNDATION OF C++:
THE C SUBSET

The header file **stdio.h** and **<cstdio>** header provide the prototypes for the I/O functions and define these three types: **size_t**, **fpos_t**, and **FILE**. The **size_t** type is some variety of unsigned integer, as is **fpos_t**. The **FILE** type is discussed in the next section.

Also defined in **stdio.h** and **<cstdio>** are several macros. The ones relevant to this chapter are **NULL**, **EOF**, **FOPEN_MAX**, **SEEK_SET**, **SEEK_CUR**, and **SEEK_END**. The **NULL** macro defines a null pointer. The **EOF** macro is generally defined as –1 and is the value returned when an input function tries to read past the end of the file. **FOPEN_MAX** defines an integer value that determines the number of files that may be open at any one time. The other macros are used with **fseek( )**, which is the function that performs random access on a file.

The File Pointer

The file pointer is the common thread that unites the C I/O system. A *file pointer* is a pointer to a structure of type **FILE**. It points to information that defines various things about the file, including its name, status, and the current position of the file. In essence, the file pointer identifies a specific file and is used by the associated stream to direct the operation of the I/O functions. In order to read or write files, your program needs to use file pointers. To obtain a file pointer variable, use a statement like this:

```
FILE *fp;
```

Opening a File

The **fopen( )** function opens a stream for use and links a file with that stream. Then it returns the file pointer associated with that file. Most often (and for the rest of this discussion), the file is a disk file. The **fopen( )** function has this prototype:

FILE *fopen(const char *filename, const char *mode);

where *filename* is a pointer to a string of characters that make up a valid filename and may include a path specification. The string pointed to by *mode* determines how the file will be opened. Table 9-2 shows the legal values for *mode*. Strings like "r+b" may also be represented as "rb+."

Mode	Meaning
r	Open a text file for reading.
w	Create a text file for writing.
a	Append to a text file.

Table 9-2. *The Legal Values for Mode*

Mode	Meaning
rb	Open a binary file for reading.
wb	Create a binary file for writing.
ab	Append to a binary file.
r+	Open a text file for read/write.
w+	Create a text file for read/write.
a+	Append or create a text file for read/write.
r+b	Open a binary file for read/write.
w+b	Create a binary file for read/write.
a+b	Append or create a binary file for read/write.

Table 9-2. *The Legal Values for Mode* (continued)

As stated, the **fopen( )** function returns a file pointer. Your program should never alter the value of this pointer. If an error occurs when it is trying to open the file, **fopen( )** returns a null pointer.

The following code uses **fopen( )** to open a file named TEST for output.

```
FILE *fp;
fp = fopen("test", "w");
```

While technically correct, you will usually see the preceding code written like this:

```
FILE *fp;

if ((fp = fopen("test","w"))==NULL) {
  printf("Cannot open file.\n");
  exit(1);
}
```

This method will detect any error in opening a file, such as a write-protected or a full disk, before your program attempts to write to it. In general, you will always want to confirm that **fopen( )** succeeded before attempting any other operations on the file.

Although most of the file modes are self-explanatory, a few comments are in order. If, when opening a file for read-only operations, the file does not exist, **fopen( )** will fail. When opening a file using append mode, if the file does not exist, it will be created. Further, when a file is opened for append, all new data written to the file will be written to the end of the file. The original contents will remain unchanged. If, when a file is opened for writing, the file does not exist, it will be created. If it does exist, the contents of the original file will be destroyed and a new file created. The difference between modes **r+** and **w+** is that **r+** will not create a file if it does not exist; however, **w+** will. Further, if the file already exists, opening it with **w+** destroys its contents; opening it with **r+** does not.

As Table 9-2 shows, a file may be opened in either text or binary mode. In most implementations, in text mode, carriage return/linefeed sequences are translated to newline characters on input. On output, the reverse occurs: newlines are translated to carriage return/linefeeds. No such translations occur on binary files.

The number of files that may be open at any one time is specified by **FOPEN_MAX**. This value will usually be at least 8, but you must check your compiler's documentation for its exact value.

Closing a File

The **fclose( )** function closes a stream that was opened by a call to **fopen( )**. It writes any data still remaining in the disk buffer to the file and does a formal operating-system-level close on the file. Failure to close a stream invites all kinds of trouble, including lost data, destroyed files, and possible intermittent errors in your program. **fclose( )** also frees the file control block associated with the stream, making it available for reuse. There is an operating-system limit to the number of open files you may have at any one time, so you may have to close one file before opening another.

The **fclose( )** function has this prototype:

```
int fclose(FILE *fp);
```

where *fp* is the file pointer returned by the call to **fopen( )**. A return value of zero signifies a successful close operation. The function returns **EOF** if an error occurs. You can use the standard function **ferror( )** (discussed shortly) to determine and report any problems. Generally, **fclose( )** will fail only when a disk has been prematurely removed from the drive or there is no more space on the disk.

Writing a Character

The C I/O system defines two equivalent functions that output a character: **putc( )** and **fputc( )**. (Actually, **putc( )** is usually implemented as a macro.) There are two identical functions simply to preserve compatibility with older versions of C. This book uses **putc( )**, but you can use **fputc( )** if you like.

The **putc( )** function writes characters to a file that was previously opened for writing using the **fopen( )** function. The prototype of this function is

int putc(int *ch*, FILE **fp*);

where *fp* is the file pointer returned by **fopen( )** and *ch* is the character to be output. The file pointer tells **putc( )** which file to write to. Although *ch* is defined as an **int,** only the low-order byte is written.

If a **putc( )** operation is successful, it returns the character written. Otherwise, it returns **EOF.**

Reading a Character

There are also two equivalent functions that input a character: **getc( )** and **fgetc( )**. Both are defined to preserve compatibility with older versions of C. This book uses **getc( )** (which is usually implemented as a macro), but you can use **fgetc( )** if you like.

The **getc( )** function reads characters from a file opened in read mode by **fopen( )**. The prototype of **getc( )** is

int getc(FILE **fp*);

where *fp* is a file pointer of type **FILE** returned by **fopen( )**. **getc( )** returns an integer, but the character is contained in the low-order byte. Unless an error occurs, the high-order byte is zero.

The **getc( )** function returns an **EOF** when the end of the file has been reached. Therefore, to read to the end of a text file, you could use the following code:

```
do {
  ch = getc(fp);
} while(ch!=EOF);
```

However, **getc( )** also returns **EOF** if an error occurs. You can use **ferror( )** to determine precisely what has occurred.

Using fopen( ), getc( ), putc( ), and fclose( )

The functions **fopen( )**, **getc( )**, **putc( )**, and **fclose( )** constitute the minimal set of file routines. The following program, KTOD, is a simple example of using **putc( )**, **fopen( )**, and **fclose( )**. It reads characters from the keyboard and writes them to a disk file until the user types a dollar sign. The filename is specified from the command line. For example, if you call this program KTOD, typing **KTOD TEST** allows you to enter lines of text into the file called TEST.

```
/* KTOD: A key to disk program. */
#include <stdio.h>
#include <stdlib.h>

int main(int argc, char *argv[])
{
  FILE *fp;
  char ch;

  if(argc!=2) {
    printf("You forgot to enter the filename.\n");
    exit(1);
  }

  if((fp=fopen(argv[1], "w"))==NULL) {
    printf("Cannot open file.\n");
    exit(1);
  }

  do {
    ch = getchar();
    putc(ch, fp);
  } while (ch != '$');

  fclose(fp);

  return 0;
}
```

The complementary program DTOS reads any text file and displays the contents on the screen. It demonstrates **getc( )**.

```
/* DTOS: A program that reads files and displays them
         on the screen. */
#include <stdio.h>
#include <stdlib.h>

int main(int argc, char *argv[])
{
  FILE *fp;
  char ch;
```

```
    if(argc!=2) {
      printf("You forgot to enter the filename.\n");
      exit(1);
    }

    if((fp=fopen(argv[1], "r"))==NULL) {
      printf("Cannot open file.\n");
      exit(1);
    }

    ch = getc(fp);    /* read one character */

    while (ch!=EOF) {
      putchar(ch);   /* print on screen */
      ch = getc(fp);
    }

    fclose(fp);

    return 0;
}
```

To try these two programs, first use KTOD to create a text file. Then read its contents using DTOS.

Using feof( )

As just described, **getc( )** returns **EOF** when the end of the file has been encountered. However, testing the value returned by **getc( )** may not be the best way to determine when you have arrived at the end of a file. First, the file system can operate on both text and binary files. When a file is opened for binary input, an integer value that will test equal to **EOF** may be read. This would cause the input routine to indicate an end-of-file condition even though the physical end of the file had not been reached. Second, **getc( )** returns **EOF** when it fails and when it reaches the end of the file. Using only the return value of **getc( )**, it is impossible to know which occurred. To solve these problems, the C file system includes the function **feof( )**, which determines when the end of the file has been encountered. The **feof( )** function has this prototype:

int feof(FILE *fp);

feof( ) returns true if the end of the file has been reached; otherwise, it returns 0. Therefore, the following routine reads a binary file until the end of the file is encountered:

```
while(!feof(fp)) ch = getc(fp);
```

Of course, you can apply this method to text files as well as binary files.

The following program, which copies text or binary files, contains an example of
feof( ). The files are opened in binary mode and **feof( )** checks for the end of the file.

```
/* Copy a file. */
#include <stdio.h>
#include <stdlib.h>

int main(int argc, char *argv[])
{
  FILE *in, *out;
  char ch;

  if(argc!=3) {
    printf("You forgot to enter a filename.\n");
    exit(1);
  }

  if((in=fopen(argv[1], "rb"))==NULL) {
    printf("Cannot open source file.\n");
    exit(1);
  }
  if((out=fopen(argv[2], "wb")) == NULL) {
    printf("Cannot open destination file.\n");
    exit(1);
  }

  /* This code actually copies the file. */
  while(!feof(in)) {
    ch = getc(in);
    if(!feof(in)) putc(ch, out);
  }

  fclose(in);
  fclose(out);

  return 0;
}
```

Working with Strings: fputs( ) and fgets( )

In addition to **getc( )** and **putc( )**, the C file system supports the related functions **fgets( )** and **fputs( )**, which read and write character strings from and to a disk file. These functions work just like **putc( )** and **getc( )**, but instead of reading or writing a single character, they read or write strings. They have the following prototypes:

int fputs(const char *str*, FILE *fp*);
char *fgets(char *str*, int *length*, FILE *fp*);

The **fputs( )** function writes the string pointed to by *str* to the specified stream. It returns **EOF** if an error occurs.

The **fgets( )** function reads a string from the specified stream until either a newline character is read or *length* −1 characters have been read. If a newline is read, it will be part of the string (unlike the **gets( )** function). The resultant string will be null terminated. The function returns *str* if successful and a null pointer if an error occurs.

The following program demonstrates **fputs( )**. It reads strings from the keyboard and writes them to the file called TEST. To terminate the program, enter a blank line. Since **gets( )** does not store the newline character, one is added before each string is written to the file so that the file can be read more easily.

```c
#include <stdio.h>
#include <stdlib.h>
#include <string.h>

int main(void)
{
  char str[80];
  FILE *fp;

  if((fp = fopen("TEST", "w"))==NULL) {
    printf("Cannot open file.\n");
    exit(1);
  }

  do {
    printf("Enter a string (CR to quit):\n");
    gets(str);
    strcat(str, "\n");  /* add a newline */
    fputs(str, fp);
  } while(*str!='\n');

  return 0;
}
```

rewind( )

The **rewind( )** function resets the file position indicator to the beginning of the file specified as its argument. That is, it "rewinds" the file. Its prototype is

    void rewind(FILE *fp);

where *fp* is a valid file pointer.

To see an example of **rewind( )**, you can modify the program from the previous section so that it displays the contents of the file just created. To accomplish this, the program rewinds the file after input is complete and then uses **fgets( )** to read back the file. Notice that the file must now be opened in read/write mode using "**w+**" for the mode parameter.

```
#include <stdio.h>
#include <stdlib.h>
#include <string.h>

int main(void)
{
  char str[80];
  FILE *fp;

  if((fp = fopen("TEST", "w+"))==NULL) {
    printf("Cannot open file.\n");
    exit(1);
  }

  do {
    printf("Enter a string (CR to quit):\n");
    gets(str);
    strcat(str, "\n");  /* add a newline */
    fputs(str, fp);
  } while(*str!='\n');

  /* now, read and display the file */
  rewind(fp);  /* reset file position indicator to
                  start of the file. */
  while(!feof(fp)) {
    fgets(str, 79, fp);
    printf(str);
  }
```

```
    return 0;
}
```

ferror( )

The **ferror( )** function determines whether a file operation has produced an error. The **ferror( )** function has this prototype:

int ferror(FILE *fp);

where fp is a valid file pointer. It returns true if an error has occurred during the last file operation; otherwise, it returns false. Because each file operation sets the error condition, **ferror( )** should be called immediately after each file operation; otherwise, an error may be lost.

The following program illustrates **ferror( )** by removing tabs from a file and substituting the appropriate number of spaces. The tab size is defined by **TAB_SIZE**. Notice how **ferror( )** is called after each file operation. To use the program, specify the names of the input and output files on the command line.

```c
/* The program substitutes spaces for tabs
   in a text file and supplies error checking. */

#include <stdio.h>
#include <stdlib.h>

#define TAB_SIZE 8
#define IN 0
#define OUT 1

void err(int e);

int main(int argc, char *argv[])
{
  FILE *in, *out;
  int tab, i;
  char ch;

  if(argc!=3) {
    printf("usage: detab <in> <out>\n");
    exit(1);
  }

  if((in = fopen(argv[1], "rb"))==NULL) {
```

```
      printf("Cannot open %s.\n", argv[1]);
      exit(1);
  }

  if((out = fopen(argv[2], "wb"))==NULL) {
    printf("Cannot open %s.\n", argv[1]);
    exit(1);
  }

  tab = 0;
  do {
    ch = getc(in);
    if(ferror(in)) err(IN);

    /* if tab found, output appropriate number of spaces */
    if(ch=='\t') {
      for(i=tab; i<8; i++) {
        putc(' ', out);
        if(ferror(out)) err(OUT);
      }
      tab = 0;
    }
    else {
      putc(ch, out);
      if(ferror(out)) err(OUT);
      tab++;
      if(tab==TAB_SIZE) tab = 0;
      if(ch=='\n' || ch=='\r') tab = 0;
    }
  } while(!feof(in));
  fclose(in);
  fclose(out);

  return 0;
}

void err(int e)
{
  if(e==IN) printf("Error on input.\n");
  else printf("Error on output.\n");
  exit(1);
}
```

Erasing Files

The **remove( )** function erases the specified file. Its prototype is

> int remove(const char *filename);

It returns zero if successful; otherwise, it returns a nonzero value.

The following program erases the file specified on the command line. However, it first gives you a chance to change your mind. A utility like this might be useful to new computer users.

```c
/* Double check before erasing. */
#include <stdio.h>
#include <stdlib.h>
#include <ctype.h>

int main(int argc, char *argv[])
{
  char str[80];

  if(argc!=2) {
    printf("usage: xerase <filename>\n");
    exit(1);
  }

  printf("Erase %s? (Y/N): ", argv[1]);
  gets(str);

  if(toupper(*str)=='Y')
    if(remove(argv[1])) {
      printf("Cannot erase file.\n");
      exit(1);
    }
  return 0;
}
```

Flushing a Stream

If you wish to flush the contents of an output stream, use the **fflush( )** function, whose prototype is shown here:

> int fflush(FILE *fp);

This function writes the contents of any buffered data to the file associated with *fp*. If you call **fflush( )** with *fp* being null, all files opened for output are flushed.

The **fflush( )** function returns 0 if successful; otherwise, it returns **EOF**.

fread( ) and fwrite( )

To read and write data types that are longer than one byte, the C file system provides two functions: **fread( )** and **fwrite( )**. These functions allow the reading and writing of blocks of any type of data. Their prototypes are

size_t fread(void *buffer*, size_t *num_bytes*, size_t *count*, FILE *fp*);
size_t fwrite(const void *buffer*, size_t *num_bytes*, size_t *count*, FILE *fp*);

For **fread( )**, *buffer* is a pointer to a region of memory that will receive the data from the file. For **fwrite( )**, *buffer* is a pointer to the information that will be written to the file. The value of *count* determines how many items are read or written, with each item being *num_bytes* bytes in length. (Remember, the type **size_t** is defined as some type of unsigned integer.) Finally, *fp* is a file pointer to a previously opened stream.

The **fread( )** function returns the number of items read. This value may be less than *count* if the end of the file is reached or an error occurs. The **fwrite( )** function returns the number of items written. This value will equal *count* unless an error occurs.

Using fread( ) and fwrite( )

As long as the file has been opened for binary data, **fread( )** and **fwrite( )** can read and write any type of information. For example, the following program writes and then reads back a **double**, an **int**, and a **long** to and from a disk file. Notice how it uses **sizeof** to determine the length of each data type.

```c
/* Write some non-character data to a disk file
   and read it back.  */
#include <stdio.h>
#include <stdlib.h>

int main(void)
{
  FILE *fp;
  double d = 12.23;
  int i = 101;
  long l = 123023L;
```

THE FOUNDATION OF C++: THE C SUBSET

```
if((fp=fopen("test", "wb+"))==NULL) {
  printf("Cannot open file.\n");
  exit(1);
}

fwrite(&d, sizeof(double), 1, fp);
fwrite(&i, sizeof(int), 1, fp);
fwrite(&l, sizeof(long), 1, fp);

rewind(fp);

fread(&d, sizeof(double), 1, fp);
fread(&i, sizeof(int), 1, fp);
fread(&l, sizeof(long), 1, fp);

printf("%f %d %ld", d, i, l);

fclose(fp);

return 0;
}
```

As this program illustrates, the buffer can be (and often is) merely the memory used to hold a variable. In this simple program, the return values of **fread( )** and **fwrite( )** are ignored. In the real world, however, you should check their return values for errors.

One of the most useful applications of **fread( )** and **fwrite( )** involves reading and writing user-defined data types, especially structures. For example, given this structure:

```
struct struct_type {
  float balance;
  char name[80];
} cust;
```

the following statement writes the contents of **cust** to the file pointed to by **fp**.

```
fwrite(&cust, sizeof(struct struct_type), 1, fp);
```

fseek( ) and Random-Access I/O

You can perform random-access read and write operations using the C I/O system with the help of **fseek( )**, which sets the file position indicator. Its prototype is shown here:

int fseek(FILE *fp, long int *numbytes*, int *origin*);

Here, *fp* is a file pointer returned by a call to **fopen( )**. *numbytes* is the number of bytes from *origin* that will become the new current position, and *origin* is one of the following macros:

Origin	Macro Name
Beginning of file	SEEK_SET
Current position	SEEK_CUR
End of file	SEEK_END

Therefore, to seek *numbytes* from the start of the file, *origin* should be **SEEK_SET**. To seek from the current position, use **SEEK_CUR;** and to seek from the end of the file, use **SEEK_END**. The **fseek( )** function returns 0 when successful and a nonzero value if an error occurs.

The following program illustrates **fseek( )**. It seeks to and displays the specified byte in the specified file. Specify the filename and then the byte to seek to on the command line.

```
#include <stdio.h>
#include <stdlib.h>

int main(int argc, char *argv[])
{
  FILE *fp;

  if(argc!=3) {
    printf("Usage: SEEK filename byte\n");
    exit(1);
  }

  if((fp = fopen(argv[1], "rb"))==NULL) {
    printf("Cannot open file.\n");
```

```
    exit(1);
}

if(fseek(fp, atol(argv[2]), SEEK_SET)) {
  printf("Seek error.\n");
  exit(1);
}

printf("Byte at %ld is %c.\n", atol(argv[2]), getc(fp));
fclose(fp);

return 0;
}
```

You can use **fseek( )** to seek in multiples of any type of data by simply multiplying the size of the data by the number of the item you want to reach. For example, assume that you have a mailing list that consists of structures of type **list_type.** To seek to the tenth address in the file that holds the addresses, use this statement:

```
fseek(fp, 9*sizeof(struct list_type), SEEK_SET);
```

You can determine the current location of a file using **ftell( ).** Its prototype is

long int ftell(FILE *fp);

It returns the location of the current position of the file associated with fp. If a failure occurs, it returns –1.

In general, you will want to use random access only on binary files. The reason for this is simple. Because text files may have character translations performed on them, there may not be a direct correspondence between what is in the file and the byte to which it would appear that you want to seek. The only time you should use **fseek( )** with a text file is when seeking to a position previously determined by **ftell( ),** using **SEEK_SET** as the origin.

Remember one important point: Even a file that contains only text can be opened as a binary file, if you like. There is no inherent restriction about random access on files containing text. The restriction applies only to files opened as text files.

fprintf( ) and fscanf( )

In addition to the basic I/O functions already discussed, the C I/O system includes **fprintf( )** and **fscanf( ).** These functions behave exactly like **printf( )** and **scanf( )** except that they operate with files. The prototypes of **fprintf( )** and **fscanf( )** are

int fprintf(FILE *fp*, const char *control_string*,. . .);
int fscanf(FILE *fp*, const char *control_string*,. . .);

where *fp* is a file pointer returned by a call to **fopen( )**. **fprintf( )** and **fscanf( )** direct their I/O operations to the file pointed to by *fp*.

As an example, the following program reads a string and an integer from the keyboard and writes them to a disk file called TEST. The program then reads the file and displays the information on the screen. After running this program, examine the TEST file. As you will see, it contains human-readable text.

```c
/* fscanf() - fprintf() example */
#include <stdio.h>
#include <io.h>
#include <stdlib.h>

int main(void)
{
  FILE *fp;
  char s[80];
  int t;

  if((fp=fopen("test", "w")) == NULL) {
    printf("Cannot open file.\n");
    exit(1);
  }

  printf("Enter a string and a number: ");
  fscanf(stdin, "%s%d", s, &t); /* read from keyboard */

  fprintf(fp, "%s %d", s, t); /* write to file */
  fclose(fp);

  if((fp=fopen("test","r")) == NULL) {
    printf("Cannot open file.\n");
    exit(1);
  }

  fscanf(fp, "%s%d", s, &t); /* read from file */
  fprintf(stdout, "%s %d", s, t); /* print on screen */

  return 0;
}
```

A word of warning: Although **fprintf( )** and **fscanf( )** often are the easiest way to write and read assorted data to disk files, they are not always the most efficient. Because formatted ASCII data is being written as it would appear on the screen (instead of in binary), extra overhead is incurred with each call. So, if speed or file size is a concern, you should probably use **fread( )** and **fwrite( )**.

The Standard Streams

As it relates to the C file system, when a program starts execution, three streams are opened automatically. They are **stdin** (standard input), **stdout** (standard output), and **stderr** (standard error). Normally, these streams refer to the console, but they may be redirected by the operating system to some other device in environments that support redirectable I/O. (Redirectable I/O is supported by Windows, DOS, Unix, and OS/2, for example.)

Because the standard streams are file pointers, they may be used by the C I/O system to perform I/O operations on the console. For example, **putchar( )** could be defined like this:

```
int putchar(char c)
{
  return putc(c, stdout);
}
```

In general, **stdin** is used to read from the console, and **stdout** and **stderr** are used to write to the console.

You may use **stdin**, **stdout**, and **stderr** as file pointers in any function that uses a variable of type **FILE ***. For example, you could use **fgets( )** to input a string from the console using a call like this:

```
char str[255];
fgets(str, 80, stdin);
```

In fact, using **fgets( )** in this manner can be quite useful. As mentioned earlier in this book, when using **gets( )** it is possible to overrun the array that is being used to receive the characters entered by the user because **gets( )** provides no bounds checking. When used with **stdin**, the **fgets( )** function offers a useful alternative because it can limit the number of characters read and thus prevent array overruns. The only trouble is that **fgets( )** does not remove the newline character and **gets( )** does, so you will have to manually remove it, as shown in the following program.

```
#include <stdio.h>
#include <string.h>

int main(void)
{
  char str[80];
  int i;

  printf("Enter a string: ");
  fgets(str, 10, stdin);

  /* remove newline, if present */
  i = strlen(str)-1;
  if(str[i]=='\n') str[i] = '\0';

  printf("This is your string: %s", str);

  return 0;
}
```

Keep in mind that **stdin**, **stdout**, and **stderr** are not variables in the normal sense and may not be assigned a value using **fopen( )**. Also, just as these file pointers are created automatically at the start of your program, they are closed automatically at the end; you should not try to close them.

The Console I/O Connection

There is actually little distinction between console I/O and file I/O. The console I/O functions described in Chapter 8 actually direct their I/O operations to either **stdin** or **stdout**. In essence, the console I/O functions are simply special versions of their parallel file functions. The reason they exist is as a convenience to you, the programmer.

As described in the previous section, you can perform console I/O using any of the file system functions. However, what might surprise you is that you can perform disk file I/O using console I/O functions, such as **printf( )**! This is because all of the console I/O functions operate on **stdin** and **stdout**. In environments that allow redirection of I/O, this means that **stdin** and **stdout** could refer to a device other than the keyboard and screen. For example, consider this program:

```
#include <stdio.h>
```

```
int main(void)
{
  char str[80];

  printf("Enter a string: ");
  gets(str);
  printf(str);

  return 0;
}
```

Assume that this program is called TEST. If you execute TEST normally, it displays its prompt on the screen, reads a string from the keyboard, and displays that string on the display. However, in an environment that supports I/O redirection, either **stdin**, **stdout**, or both could be redirected to a file. For example, in a DOS or Windows environment, executing TEST like this:

```
TEST > OUTPUT
```

causes the output of TEST to be written to a file called OUTPUT. Executing TEST like this:

```
TEST < INPUT > OUTPUT
```

directs **stdin** to the file called INPUT and sends output to the file called OUTPUT.
When a program terminates, any redirected streams are reset to their default status.

Using freopen( ) to Redirect the Standard Streams

You can redirect the standard streams by using the **freopen( )** function. This function associates an existing stream with a new file. Thus, you can use it to associate a standard stream with a new file. Its prototype is

FILE *freopen(const char *filename, const char *mode, FILE *stream);

where filename is a pointer to the filename you wish associated with the stream pointed to by stream. The file is opened using the value of mode, which may have the same values as those used with **fopen( )**. **freopen( )** returns stream if successful or **NULL** on failure.

The following program uses **freopen( )** to redirect **stdout** to a file called OUTPUT:

```
#include <stdio.h>

int main(void)
{
  char str[80];

  freopen("OUTPUT", "w", stdout);

  printf("Enter a string: ");
  gets(str);
  printf(str);

  return 0;
}
```

In general, redirecting the standard streams by using **freopen( )** is useful in special situations, such as debugging. However, performing disk I/O using redirected **stdin** and **stdout** is not as efficient as using functions like **fread( )** or **fwrite( )**.

Chapter 10

The Preprocessor
and Comments

Y ou can include various instructions to the compiler in the source code of a
C/C++ program. These are called *preprocessor directives*, and although not
actually part of the C or C++ language per se, they expand the scope of the
programming environment. This chapter also examines comments.

The Preprocessor

Before beginning, it is important to put the preprocessor in historical perspective.
As it relates to C++, the preprocessor is largely a holdover from C. Moreover, the
C++ preprocessor is virtually identical to the one defined by C. The main difference
between C and C++ in this regard is the degree to which each relies upon the
preprocessor. In C, each preprocessor directive is necessary. In C++, some features
have been rendered redundant by newer and better C++ language elements. In fact,
one of the long-term design goals of C++ is the elimination of the preprocessor
altogether. But for now and well into the foreseeable future, the preprocessor will
still be widely used.

The preprocessor contains the following directives:

#define	#elif	#else	#endif
#error	#if	#ifdef	#ifndef
#include	#line	#pragma	#undef

As you can see, all preprocessor directives begin with a # sign. In addition, each
preprocessing directive must be on its own line. For example,

```
#include <stdio.h>  #include <stdlib.h>
```

will not work.

#define

The **#define** directive defines an identifier and a character sequence (i.e., a set of
characters) that will be substituted for the identifier each time it is encountered in the
source file. The identifier is referred to as a *macro name* and the replacement process as
macro replacement. The general form of the directive is

#define *macro-name char-sequence*

Notice that there is no semicolon in this statement. There may be any number of spaces
between the identifier and the character sequence, but once the character sequence
begins, it is terminated only by a newline.

For example, if you wish to use the word **LEFT** for the value 1 and the word **RIGHT** for the value 0, you could declare these two #**define** directives:

```
#define LEFT 1
#define RIGHT 0
```

This causes the compiler to substitute a 1 or a 0 each time **LEFT** or **RIGHT** is encountered in your source file. For example, the following prints **0 1 2** on the screen:

```
printf("%d %d %d", RIGHT, LEFT, LEFT+1);
```

Once a macro name has been defined, it may be used as part of the definition of other macro names. For example, this code defines the values of **ONE**, **TWO**, and **THREE**:

```
#define ONE     1
#define TWO     ONE+ONE
#define THREE   ONE+TWO
```

Macro substitution is simply the replacement of an identifier by the character sequence associated with it. Therefore, if you wish to define a standard error message, you might write something like this:

```
#define E_MS "standard error on input\n"
/* ... */
printf(E_MS);
```

The compiler will actually substitute the string "standard error on input\n" when the identifier **E_MS** is encountered. To the compiler, the **printf( )** statement will actually appear to be

```
printf("standard error on input\n");
```

No text substitutions occur if the identifier is within a quoted string. For example,

```
#define XYZ this is a test

printf("XYZ");
```

does not print **this is a test**, but rather **XYZ**.

If the character sequence is longer than one line, you may continue it on the next by placing a backslash at the end of the line, as shown here:

```
#define LONG_STRING "this is a very long \
string that is used as an example"
```

C/C++ programmers commonly use uppercase letters for defined identifiers. This convention helps anyone reading the program know at a glance that a macro replacement will take place. Also, it is usually best to put all **#defines** at the start of the file or in a separate header file rather than sprinkling them throughout the program.

Macros are most frequently used to define names for "magic numbers" that occur in a program. For example, you may have a program that defines an array and has several routines that access that array. Instead of "hard-coding" the array's size with a constant, you can define the size using a **#define** statement and then use that macro name whenever the array size is needed. In this way, if you need to change the size of the array, you will only need to change the **#define** statement and then recompile your program. For example,

```
#define MAX_SIZE 100
/* ... */
float balance[MAX_SIZE];
/* ... */
for(i=0; i<MAX_SIZE; i++) printf("%f", balance[i]);
/* ... */
for(i=0; i<MAX_SIZE; i++) x =+ balance[i];
```

Since **MAX_SIZE** defines the size of the array **balance,** if the size of **balance** needs to be changed in the future, you need only change the definition of **MAX_SIZE.** All subsequent references to it will be automatically updated when you recompile your program.

C++ provides a better way of defining constants, which uses the ***const*** *keyword. This is described in Part Two.*

Defining Function-like Macros

The **#define** directive has another powerful feature: the macro name can have arguments. Each time the macro name is encountered, the arguments used in its definition are replaced by the actual arguments found in the program. This form of a macro is called a *function-like macro.* For example,

```
#include <stdio.h>

#define ABS(a)  (a)<0 ? -(a) : (a)

int main(void)
{
  printf("abs of -1 and 1: %d %d", ABS(-1), ABS(1));

  return 0;
}
```

When this program is compiled, **a** in the macro definition will be substituted with the values –1 and 1. The parentheses that enclose **a** ensure proper substitution in all cases. For example, if the parentheses around **a** were removed, this expression

```
ABS(10-20)
```

would be converted to

```
10-20<0 ? -10-20 : 10-20
```

after macro replacement and would yield the wrong result.

The use of a function-like macro in place of real functions has one major benefit: It increases the execution speed of the code because there is no function call overhead. However, if the size of the function-like macro is very large, this increased speed may be paid for with an increase in the size of the program because of duplicated code.

Note   *Although parameterized macros are a valuable feature, C++ has a better way of creating inline code, which uses the **inline** keyword.*

#error

The **#error** directive forces the compiler to stop compilation. It is used primarily for debugging. The general form of the **#error** directive is

#error *error-message*

The *error-message* is not between double quotes. When the **#error** directive is encountered, the error message is displayed, possibly along with other information defined by the compiler.

#include

The **#include** directive instructs the compiler to read another source file in addition to the one that contains the **#include** directive. The name of the additional source file must be enclosed between double quotes or angle brackets. For example,

```
#include "stdio.h"
#include <stdio.h>
```

both instruct the compiler to read and compile the header for the C I/O system library functions.

Include files can have **#include** directives in them. This is referred to as *nested includes*. The number of levels of nesting allowed varies between compilers. However, Standard C stipulates that at least eight nested inclusions will be available. Standard C++ recommends that at least 256 levels of nesting be supported.

Whether the filename is enclosed by quotes or by angle brackets determines how the search for the specified file is conducted. If the filename is enclosed in angle brackets, the file is searched for in a manner defined by the creator of the compiler. Often, this means searching some special directory set aside for include files. If the filename is enclosed in quotes, the file is looked for in another implementation-defined manner. For many compilers, this means searching the current working directory. If the file is not found, the search is repeated as if the filename had been enclosed in angle brackets.

Typically, most programmers use angle brackets to include the standard header files. The use of quotes is generally reserved for including files specifically related to the program at hand. However, there is no hard and fast rule that demands this usage.

In addition to *files*, a C++ program can use the **#include** directive to include a C++ *header*. C++ defines a set of standard headers that provide the information necessary to the various C++ libraries. A header is a standard identifier that might, but need not, map to a filename. Thus, a header is simply an abstraction that guarantees that the appropriate information required by your program is included. Various issues associated with headers are described in Part Two.

Conditional Compilation Directives

There are several directives that allow you to selectively compile portions of your program's source code. This process is called *conditional compilation* and is used widely by commercial software houses that provide and maintain many customized versions of one program.

#if, #else, #elif, and #endif

Perhaps the most commonly used conditional compilation directives are the **#if**, **#else**, **#elif**, and **#endif**. These directives allow you to conditionally include portions of code based upon the outcome of a constant expression.

The general form of **#if** is

```
#if constant-expression
    statement sequence
#endif
```

If the constant expression following **#if** is true, the code that is between it and **#endif** is compiled. Otherwise, the intervening code is skipped. The **#endif** directive marks the end of an **#if** block. For example,

```
/* Simple #if example. */
#include <stdio.h>

#define MAX 100

int main(void)
{
#if MAX>99
  printf("Compiled for array greater than 99.\n");
#endif

  return 0;
}
```

This program displays the message on the screen because **MAX** is greater than 99. This example illustrates an important point. The expression that follows the **#if** is evaluated at compile time. Therefore, it must contain only previously defined identifiers and constants—no variables may be used.

The **#else** directive works much like the **else** that is part of the C++ language: it establishes an alternative if **#if** fails. The previous example can be expanded as shown here:

```
/* Simple #if/#else example. */
#include <stdio.h>
```

```
#define MAX 10

int main(void)
{
#if MAX>99
  printf("Compiled for array greater than 99.\n");
#else
  printf("Compiled for small array.\n");
#endif

  return 0;
}
```

In this case, **MAX** is defined to be less than 99, so the **#if** portion of the code is not compiled. The **#else** alternative is compiled, however, and the message **Compiled for small array** is displayed.

Notice that **#else** is used to mark both the end of the **#if** block and the beginning of the **#else** block. This is necessary because there can only be one **#endif** associated with any **#if**.

The **#elif** directive means "else if" and establishes an if-else-if chain for multiple compilation options. **#elif** is followed by a constant expression. If the expression is true, that block of code is compiled and no other **#elif** expressions are tested. Otherwise, the next block in the series is checked. The general form for **#elif** is

```
#if expression
   statement sequence
#elif expression 1
   statement sequence
#elif expression 2
   statement sequence
#elif expression 3
   statement sequence
#elif expression 4
   .
   .
   .
#elif expression N
   statement sequence
#endif
```

For example, the following fragment uses the value of **ACTIVE_COUNTRY** to define the currency sign:

```
#define US 0
#define ENGLAND 1
#define JAPAN 2

#define ACTIVE_COUNTRY US

#if ACTIVE_COUNTRY == US
  char currency[] = "dollar";
#elif ACTIVE_COUNTRY == ENGLAND
  char currency[] = "pound";
#else
  char currency[] = "yen";
#endif
```

Standard C states that **#if**s and **#elif**s may be nested at least eight levels. Standard C++ suggests that at least 256 levels of nesting be allowed. When nested, each **#endif**, **#else**, or **#elif** associates with the nearest **#if** or **#elif**. For example, the following is perfectly valid:

```
#if MAX>100
  #if SERIAL_VERSION
    int port=198;
  #elif
    int port=200;
  #endif
#else
  char out_buffer[100];
#endif
```

#ifdef and #ifndef

Another method of conditional compilation uses the directives **#ifdef** and **#ifndef**, which mean "if defined" and "if not defined," respectively. The general form of **#ifdef** is

```
#ifdef macro-name
  statement sequence
#endif
```

If *macro-name* has been previously defined in a **#define** statement, the block of code will be compiled.

The general form of **#ifndef** is

```
#ifndef macro-name
  statement sequence
#endif
```

If *macro-name* is currently undefined by a **#define** statement, the block of code is compiled.

Both **#ifdef** and **#ifndef** may use an **#else** or **#elif** statement. For example,

```
#include <stdio.h>

#define TED 10

int main(void)
{
#ifdef TED
  printf("Hi Ted\n");
#else
  printf("Hi anyone\n");
#endif
#ifndef RALPH
  printf("RALPH not defined\n");
#endif

  return 0;
}
```

will print **Hi Ted** and **RALPH not defined**. However, if **TED** were not defined, **Hi anyone** would be displayed, followed by **RALPH not defined**.

You may nest **#ifdef**s and **#ifndef**s to at least eight levels in Standard C. Standard C++ suggests that at least 256 levels of nesting be supported.

#undef

The **#undef** directive removes a previously defined definition of the macro name that follows it. That is, it "undefines" a macro. The general form for **#undef** is

```
#undef macro-name
```

For example,

```
#define LEN 100
#define WIDTH 100

char array[LEN][WIDTH];

#undef LEN
#undef WIDTH
/* at this point both LEN and WIDTH are undefined */
```

Both **LEN** and **WIDTH** are defined until the **#undef** statements are encountered.

#undef is used principally to allow macro names to be localized to only those sections of code that need them.

Using defined

In addition to **#ifdef**, there is a second way to determine if a macro name is defined. You can use the **#if** directive in conjunction with the **defined** compile-time operator. The **defined** operator has this general form:

defined *macro-name*

If *macro-name* is currently defined, then the expression is true. Otherwise, it is false. For example, to determine if the macro **MYFILE** is defined, you can use either of these two preprocessing commands:

```
#if defined MYFILE
```

or

```
#ifdef MYFILE
```

You may also precede **defined** with the ! to reverse the condition. For example, the following fragment is compiled only if **DEBUG** is not defined.

```
#if !defined DEBUG
  printf("Final version!\n");
#endif
```

One reason for using **defined** is that it allows the existence of a macro name to be determined by a **#elif** statement.

#line

The **#line** directive changes the contents of _ _**LINE**_ _ and _ _**FILE**_ _, which are predefined identifiers in the compiler. The _ _**LINE**_ _ identifier contains the line number of the currently compiled line of code. The _ _**FILE**_ _ identifier is a string that contains the name of the source file being compiled. The general form for **#line** is

   #line *number* "*filename*"

where *number* is any positive integer and becomes the new value of _ _**LINE**_ _, and the optional *filename* is any valid file identifier, which becomes the new value of _ _**FILE**_ _. **#line** is primarily used for debugging and special applications.

For example, the following code specifies that the line count will begin with 100. The **printf( )** statement displays the number 102 because it is the third line in the program after the **#line 100** statement.

```
#include <stdio.h>

#line 100                   /* reset the line counter */
int main(void)              /* line 100 */
{                           /* line 101 */
  printf("%d\n",__LINE__);  /* line 102 */

  return 0;
}
```

#pragma

#pragma is an implementation-defined directive that allows various instructions to be given to the compiler. For example, a compiler may have an option that supports program execution tracing. A trace option would then be specified by a **#pragma** statement. You must check the compiler's documentation for details and options.

The # and ## Preprocessor Operators

There are two preprocessor operators: # and ##. These operators are used with the **#define** statement.

The # operator, which is generally called the *stringize* operator, turns the argument it precedes into a quoted string. For example, consider this program.

```
#include <stdio.h>

#define mkstr(s)   # s

int main(void)
{
  printf(mkstr(I like C++));

  return 0;
}
```

The preprocessor turns the line

```
printf(mkstr(I like C++));
```

into

```
printf("I like C++");
```

The ## operator, called the *pasting* operator, concatenates two tokens. For example,

```
#include <stdio.h>

#define concat(a, b)   a ## b

int main(void)
{
  int xy = 10;

  printf("%d", concat(x, y));

  return 0;
}
```

The preprocessor transforms

```
printf("%d", concat(x, y));
```

into

```
printf("%d", xy);
```

If these operators seem strange to you, keep in mind that they are not needed or used in most programs. They exist primarily to allow the preprocessor to handle some special cases.

Predefined Macro Names

C++ specifies six built-in predefined macro names. They are

> _ _LINE_ _
> _ _FILE_ _
> _ _DATE_ _
> _ _TIME_ _
> _ _STDC_ _
> _ _cplusplus

The C language defines the first five of these. Each will be described here, in turn.

The _ _**LINE**_ _ and _ _**FILE**_ _ macros were described in the discussion of **#line**. Briefly, they contain the current line number and filename of the program when it is being compiled.

The _ _**DATE**_ _ macro contains a string of the form *month/day/year* that is the date of the translation of the source file into object code.

The _ _**TIME**_ _ macro contains the time at which the program was compiled. The time is represented in a string having the form *hour:minute:second*.

The meaning of _ _**STDC**_ _ is implementation-defined. Generally, if _ _**STDC**_ _ is defined, the compiler will accept only standard C/C++ code that does not contain any nonstandard extensions.

A compiler conforming to Standard C++ will define _ _**cplusplus** as a value containing at least six digits. Nonconforming compilers will use a value with five or less digits.

Comments

C89 defines only one style of comment, which begins with the character pair **/*** and ends with ***/**. There must be no spaces between the asterisk and the slash. The compiler ignores any text between the beginning and ending comment symbols. For example, this program prints only **hello** on the screen:

```
#include <stdio.h>

int main(void)
{
  printf("hello");
  /* printf("there"); */

  return 0;
}
```

This style of comment is commonly called a *multiline comment* because the text of the comment may extend over two or more lines. For example,

```
/* this is a
multi-line
comment */
```

Comments may be placed anywhere in a program, as long as they do not appear in the middle of a keyword or identifier. For example, this comment is valid:

```
x = 10+ /* add the numbers */5;
```

while

```
swi/*this will not work*/tch(c) { ...
```

is incorrect because a keyword cannot contain a comment. However, you should not generally place comments in the middle of expressions because it obscures their meaning.

Multiline comments may not be nested. That is, one comment may not contain another comment. For example, this code fragment causes a compile-time error:

```
/* this is an outer comment
  x = y/a;
  /* this is an inner comment - and causes an error */
*/
```

Single-Line Comments

C++ (and C99) supports two types of comments. The first is the multiline comment. The second is the *single-line comment*. Single-line comments begin with a **//** and end at the end of the line. For example,

```
// this is a single-line comment
```

Single line comments are especially useful when short, line-by-line descriptions are needed. Although they are not technically supported by C89, many C compilers will accept them anyway, and single-line comments were added to C by C99. One last point: a single-line comment can be nested within a multiline comment.

You should include comments whenever they are needed to explain the operation of the code. All but the most obvious functions should have a comment at the top that states what the function does, how it is called, and what it returns.

The
Complete
Reference

Part II

C++

Part One examined the C subset of C++. Part Two describes those features of the language specific to C++. That is, it discusses those features of C++ that it does not have in common with C. Because many of the C++ features are designed to support object-oriented programming (OOP), Part Two also provides a discussion of its theory and merits. We will begin with an overview of C++.

Chapter 11

An Overview of C++

This chapter provides an overview of the key concepts embodied in C++. C++ is an object-oriented programming language, and its object-oriented features are highly interrelated. In several instances, this interrelatedness makes it difficult to describe one feature of C++ without implicitly involving several others. Moreover, the object-oriented features of C++ are, in many places, so intertwined that discussion of one feature *implies* prior knowledge of another. To address this problem, this chapter presents a quick overview of the most important aspects of C++, including its history, its key features, and the difference between traditional and Standard C++. The remaining chapters examine C++ in detail.

The Origins of C++

C++ began as an expanded version of C. The C++ extensions were first invented by Bjarne Stroustrup in 1979 at Bell Laboratories in Murray Hill, New Jersey. He initially called the new language "C with Classes." However, in 1983 the name was changed to C++.

Although C was one of the most liked and widely used professional programming languages in the world, the invention of C++ was necessitated by one major programming factor: increasing complexity. Over the years, computer programs have become larger and more complex. Even though C is an excellent programming language, it has its limits. In C, once a program exceeds from 25,000 to 100,000 lines of code, it becomes so complex that it is difficult to grasp as a totality. The purpose of C++ is to allow this barrier to be broken. The essence of C++ is to allow the programmer to comprehend and manage larger, more complex programs.

Most additions made by Stroustrup to C support object-oriented programming, sometimes referred to as OOP. (See the next section for a brief explanation of object-oriented programming.) Stroustrup states that some of C++'s object-oriented features were inspired by another object-oriented language called Simula67. Therefore, C++ represents the blending of two powerful programming methods.

Since C++ was first invented, it has undergone three major revisions, with each adding to and altering the language. The first revision was in 1985 and the second in 1990. The third occurred during the standardization of C++. Several years ago, work began on a standard for C++. Toward that end, a joint ANSI (American National Standards Institute) and ISO (International Standards Organization) standardization committee was formed. The first draft of the proposed standard was created on January 25, 1994. In that draft, the ANSI/ISO C++ committee (of which I was a member) kept the features first defined by Stroustrup and added some new ones as well. But in general, this initial draft reflected the state of C++ at the time.

Soon after the completion of the first draft of the C++ standard, an event occurred that caused the language to be greatly expanded: the creation of the Standard Template Library (STL) by Alexander Stepanov. The STL is a set of generic routines that you can use to manipulate data. It is both powerful and elegant, but also quite large. Subsequent to the first draft, the committee voted to include the STL in the specification for C++. The addition of the STL expanded the scope of C++ well beyond its original definition. While important, the inclusion of the STL, among other things, slowed the standardization of C++.

It is fair to say that the standardization of C++ took far longer than anyone had expected when it began. In the process, many new features were added to the language and many small changes were made. In fact, the version of C++ defined by the C++ committee is much larger and more complex than Stroustrup's original design. The final draft was passed out of committee on November 14, 1997 and an ANSI/ISO standard for C++ became a reality in 1998. This specification for C++ is commonly referred to as *Standard C++*.

The material in this book describes Standard C++, including all of its newest features. This is the version of C++ created by the ANSI/ISO standardization committee, and it is the one that is currently accepted by all major compilers.

What Is Object-Oriented Programming?

Since object-oriented programming (OOP) drove the creation of C++, it is necessary to understand its foundational principles. OOP is a powerful way to approach the job of programming. Programming methodologies have changed dramatically since the invention of the computer, primarily to accommodate the increasing complexity of programs. For example, when computers were first invented, programming was done by toggling in the binary machine instructions using the computer's front panel. As long as programs were just a few hundred instructions long, this approach worked. As programs grew, assembly language was invented so that a programmer could deal with larger, increasingly complex programs, using symbolic representations of the machine instructions. As programs continued to grow, high-level languages were introduced that gave the programmer more tools with which to handle complexity. The first widespread language was, of course, FORTRAN. Although FORTRAN was a very impressive first step, it is hardly a language that encourages clear, easy-to-understand programs.

The 1960s gave birth to structured programming. This is the method encouraged by languages such as C and Pascal. The use of structured languages made it possible to write moderately complex programs fairly easily. Structured languages are characterized by their support for stand-alone subroutines, local variables, rich control constructs, and their lack of reliance upon the GOTO. Although structured languages are a powerful tool, they reach their limit when a project becomes too large.

Consider this: At each milestone in the development of programming, techniques and tools were created to allow the programmer to deal with increasingly greater complexity. Each step of the way, the new approach took the best elements of the previous methods and moved forward. Prior to the invention of OOP, many projects were nearing (or exceeding) the point where the structured approach no longer worked. Object-oriented methods were created to help programmers break through these barriers.

Object-oriented programming took the best ideas of structured programming and combined them with several new concepts. The result was a different way of organizing a program. In the most general sense, a program can be organized in one of two ways: around its code (what is happening) or around its data (who is being affected). Using only structured programming techniques, programs are typically organized around code. This approach can be thought of as "code acting on data." For example, a program written in a structured language such as C is defined by its functions, any of which may operate on any type of data used by the program.

Object-oriented programs work the other way around. They are organized around data, with the key principle being "data controlling access to code." In an object-oriented language, you define the data and the routines that are permitted to act on that data. Thus, a data type defines precisely what sort of operations can be applied to that data.

To support the principles of object-oriented programming, all OOP languages have three traits in common: encapsulation, polymorphism, and inheritance. Let's examine each.

Encapsulation

Encapsulation is the mechanism that binds together code and the data it manipulates, and keeps both safe from outside interference and misuse. In an object-oriented language, code and data may be combined in such a way that a self-contained "black box" is created. When code and data are linked together in this fashion, an *object* is created. In other words, an object is the device that supports encapsulation.

Within an object, code, data, or both may be *private* to that object or *public*. Private code or data is known to and accessible only by another part of the object. That is, private code or data may not be accessed by a piece of the program that exists outside the object. When code or data is public, other parts of your program may access it even though it is defined within an object. Typically, the public parts of an object are used to provide a controlled interface to the private elements of the object.

For all intents and purposes, an object is a variable of a user-defined type. It may seem strange that an object that links both code and data can be thought of as a variable. However, in object-oriented programming, this is precisely the case. Each time you define a new type of object, you are creating a new data type. Each specific instance of this data type is a compound variable.

Polymorphism

Object-oriented programming languages support *polymorphism*, which is characterized by the phrase "one interface, multiple methods." In simple terms, polymorphism is the attribute that allows one interface to control access to a general class of actions. The specific action selected is determined by the exact nature of the situation. A real-world example of polymorphism is a thermostat. No matter what type of furnace your house has (gas, oil, electric, etc.), the thermostat works the same way. In this case, the thermostat (which is the interface) is the same no matter what type of furnace (method) you have. For example, if you want a 70-degree temperature, you set the thermostat to 70 degrees. It doesn't matter what type of furnace actually provides the heat.

This same principle can also apply to programming. For example, you might have a program that defines three different types of stacks. One stack is used for integer values, one for character values, and one for floating-point values. Because of polymorphism, you can define one set of names, **push( )** and **pop( )**, that can be used for all three stacks. In your program you will create three specific versions of these functions, one for each type of stack, but names of the functions will be the same. The compiler will automatically select the right function based upon the data being stored. Thus, the interface to a stack—the functions **push( )** and **pop( )**—are the same no matter which type of stack is being used. The individual versions of these functions define the specific implementations (methods) for each type of data.

Polymorphism helps reduce complexity by allowing the same interface to be used to access a general class of actions. It is the compiler's job to select the *specific action* (i.e., method) as it applies to each situation. You, the programmer, don't need to do this selection manually. You need only remember and utilize the *general interface*.

The first object-oriented programming languages were interpreters, so polymorphism was, of course, supported at run time. However, C++ is a compiled language. Therefore, in C++, both run-time and compile-time polymorphism are supported.

Inheritance

Inheritance is the process by which one object can acquire the properties of another object. This is important because it supports the concept of *classification*. If you think about it, most knowledge is made manageable by hierarchical classifications. For example, a Red Delicious apple is part of the classification *apple*, which in turn is part of the *fruit* class, which is under the larger class *food*. Without the use of classifications, each object would have to define explicitly all of its characteristics. However, through the use of classifications, an object need only define those qualities that make it unique within its class. It is the inheritance mechanism that makes it possible for one object to be a specific instance of a more general case. As you will see, inheritance is an important aspect of object-oriented programming.

Some C++ Fundamentals

In Part One, the C subset of C++ was described and C programs were used to demonstrate those features. From this point forward, all examples will be "C++

programs." That is, they will be making use of features unique to C++. For ease of discussion, we will refer to these C++-specific features simply as "C++ features" from now on.

If you come from a C background, or if you have been studying the C subset programs in Part One, be aware that C++ programs differ from C programs in some important respects. Most of the differences have to do with taking advantage of C++'s object-oriented capabilities. But C++ programs differ from C programs in other ways, including how I/O is performed and what headers are included. Also, most C++ programs share a set of common traits that clearly identify them *as* C++ programs. Before moving on to C++'s object-oriented constructs, an understanding of the fundamental elements of a C++ program is required.

This section describes several issues relating to nearly all C++ programs. Along the way, some important differences with C and earlier versions of C++ are pointed out.

A Sample C++ Program

Let's start with the short sample C++ program shown here.

```
#include <iostream>
using namespace std;

int main()
{
  int i;

  cout << "This is output.\n";  // this is a single line comment
  /* you can still use C style comments */

  // input a number using >>
  cout << "Enter a number: ";
  cin >> i;

  // now, output a number using <<
  cout << i << " squared is " << i*i << "\n";

  return 0;
}
```

As you can see, this program looks much different from the C subset programs found in Part One. A line-by-line commentary will be useful. To begin, the header **<iostream>** is included. This header supports C++-style I/O operations. (**<iostream>** is to C++ what **stdio.h** is to C.) Notice one other thing: there is no **.h** extension to the name **iostream**. The reason is that **<iostream>** is one of the modern-style headers defined by Standard C++. Modern C++ headers do not use the **.h** extension.

The next line in the program is

```
using namespace std;
```

This tells the compiler to use the **std** namespace. Namespaces are a recent addition to C++. A namespace creates a declarative region in which various program elements can be placed. Namespaces help in the organization of large programs. The **using** statement informs the compiler that you want to use the **std** namespace. This is the namespace in which the entire Standard C++ library is declared. By using the **std** namespace you simplify access to the standard library. The programs in Part One, which use only the C subset, don't need a namespace statement because the C library functions are also available in the default, global namespace.

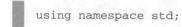

Since both new-style headers and namespaces are recent additions to C++, you may encounter older code that does not use them. Also, if you are using an older compiler, it may not support them. Instructions for using an older compiler are found later in this chapter.

Now examine the following line.

```
int main()
```

Notice that the parameter list in **main( )** is empty. In C++, this indicates that **main( )** has no parameters. This differs from C. In C, a function that has no parameters must use **void** in its parameter list, as shown here:

```
int main(void)
```

This was the way **main( )** was declared in the programs in Part One. However, in C++, the use of **void** is redundant and unnecessary. As a general rule, in C++ when a function takes no parameters, its parameter list is simply empty; the use of **void** is not required.

The next line contains two C++ features.

```
cout << "This is output.\n";  // this is a single line comment
```

First, the statement

```
cout << "This is output.\n";
```

causes **This is output**. to be displayed on the screen, followed by a carriage return-linefeed combination. In C++, the << has an expanded role. It is still the left shift operator, but when it is used as shown in this example, it is also an *output operator*. The word **cout** is an identifier that is linked to the screen. (Actually, like C, C++ supports I/O redirection, but for the sake of discussion, assume that **cout** refers to the screen.) You can use **cout** and the << to output any of the built-in data types, as well as strings of characters.

Note that you can still use **printf( )** or any other of C's I/O functions in a C++ program. However, most programmers feel that using << is more in the spirit of C++. Further, while using **printf( )** to output a string is virtually equivalent to using << in this case, the C++ I/O system can be expanded to perform operations on objects that you define (something that you cannot do using **printf( )**).

What follows the output expression is a C++ *single-line comment*. As mentioned in Chapter 10, C++ defines two types of comments. First, you may use a multiline comment, which works the same in C++ as in C. You can also define a single-line comment by using //; whatever follows such a comment is ignored by the compiler until the end of the line is reached. In general, C++ programmers use multiline comments when a longer comment is being created and use single-line comments when only a short remark is needed.

Next, the program prompts the user for a number. The number is read from the keyboard with this statement:

```
cin >> i;
```

In C++, the >> operator still retains its right shift meaning. However, when used as shown, it also is C++'s *input operator*. This statement causes **i** to be given a value read from the keyboard. The identifier **cin** refers to the standard input device, which is usually the keyboard. In general, you can use **cin >>** to input a variable of any of the basic data types plus strings.

Note *The line of code just described is not misprinted. Specifically, there is not supposed to be an & in front of the **i**. When inputting information using a C-based function like **scanf( )**, you have to explicitly pass a pointer to the variable that will receive the information. This means preceding the variable name with the "address of" operator, &. However, because of the way the >> operator is implemented in C++, you do not need (in fact, must not use) the &. The reason for this is explained in Chapter 13.*

Although it is not illustrated by the example, you are free to use any of the C-based input functions, such as **scanf( )**, instead of using **>>**. However, as with **cout**, most programmers feel that **cin >>** is more in the spirit of C++.

Another interesting line in the program is shown here:

```
cout << i << "squared is " << i*i << "\n";
```

Assuming that **i** has the value 10, this statement causes the phrase **10 squared is 100** to be displayed, followed by a carriage return-linefeed. As this line illustrates, you can run together several << output operations.

The program ends with this statement:

```
return 0;
```

This causes zero to be returned to the calling process (which is usually the operating system). This works the same in C++ as it does in C. Returning zero indicates that the program terminated normally. Abnormal program termination should be signaled by returning a nonzero value. You may also use the values **EXIT_SUCCESS** and **EXIT_FAILURE** if you like.

A Closer Look at the I/O Operators

As stated, when used for I/O, the << and >> operators are capable of handling any of C++'s built-in data types. For example, this program inputs a **float**, a **double**, and a string and then outputs them:

```
#include <iostream>
using namespace std;

int main()
{
  float f;
  char str[80];
  double d;

  cout << "Enter two floating point numbers: ";
  cin >> f >> d;

  cout << "Enter a string: ";
  cin >> str;

  cout << f << " " << d << " " << str;

  return 0;
}
```

When you run this program, try entering **This is a test.** when prompted for the string. When the program redisplays the information you entered, only the word "This" will be displayed. The rest of the string is not shown because the >> operator stops reading input when the first white-space character is encountered. Thus, "is a test" is never read by the program. This program also illustrates that you can string together several input operations in a single statement.

The C++ I/O operators recognize the entire set of backslash character constants described in Chapter 2. For example, it is perfectly acceptable to write

```
cout << "A\tB\tC";
```

This statement outputs the letters A, B, and C, separated by tabs.

Declaring Local Variables

If you come from a C background, you need to be aware of an important difference between C and C++ regarding when local variables can be declared. In C89, you must declare all local variables used within a block at the start of that block. You cannot declare a variable in a block after an "action" statement has occurred. For example, in C89, this fragment is incorrect:

```
/* Incorrect in C89. OK in C++. */
int f()
{
  int i;
  i = 10;

  int j;  /* won't compile as a C program */
  j = i*2;

  return j;
}
```

In a C89 program, this function is in error because the assignment intervenes between the declaration of **i** and that of **j**. However, when compiling it as a C++ program, this fragment is perfectly acceptable. In C++ (and C99) you may declare local variables at any point within a block—not just at the beginning.

Here is another example. This version of the program from the preceding section declares **str** just before it is needed.

```
#include <iostream>
using namespace std;

int main()
{
  float f;
```

```
    double d;
    cout << "Enter two floating point numbers: ";
    cin >> f >> d;

    cout << "Enter a string: ";
    char str[80];  // str declared here, just before 1st use
    cin >> str;

    cout << f << " " << d << " " << str;

    return 0;
}
```

Whether you declare all variables at the start of a block or at the point of first use is completely up to you. Since much of the philosophy behind C++ is the encapsulation of code and data, it makes sense that you can declare variables close to where they are used instead of just at the beginning of the block. In the preceding example, the declarations are separated simply for illustration, but it is easy to imagine more complex examples in which this feature of C++ is more valuable.

Declaring variables close to where they are used can help you avoid accidental side effects. However, the greatest benefit of declaring variables at the point of first use is gained in large functions. Frankly, in short functions (like many of the examples in this book), there is little reason not to simply declare variables at the start of a function. For this reason, this book will declare variables at the point of first use only when it seems warranted by the size or complexity of a function.

There is some debate as to the general wisdom of localizing the declaration of variables. Opponents suggest that sprinkling declarations throughout a block makes it harder, not easier, for someone reading the code to find quickly the declarations of all variables used in that block, making the program harder to maintain. For this reason, some C++ programmers do not make significant use of this feature. This book will not take a stand either way on this issue. However, when applied properly, especially in large functions, declaring variables at the point of their first use can help you create bug-free programs more easily.

No Default to int

A few years ago, there was a change to C++ that may affect older C++ code as well as C code being ported to C++. Both C89 and the original specification for C++ state that when no explicit type is specified in a declaration, type **int** is assumed. However, the "default-to-int" rule was dropped from C++ during standardization. C99 also drops this rule. However, there is still a large body of C and older C++ code that uses this rule.

The most common use of the "default-to-int" rule is with function return types. It was common practice to not specify **int** explicitly when a function returned an integer result. For example, in C89 and older C++ code the following function is valid.

```
func(int i)
{
   return i*i;
}
```

In Standard C++, this function must have the return type of **int** specified, as shown here.

```
int func(int i)
{
   return i*i;
}
```

As a practical matter, nearly all C++ compilers still support the "default-to-int" rule for compatibility with older code. However, you should not use this feature for new code because it is no longer allowed.

The bool Data Type

C++ defines a built-in Boolean type called **bool**. Objects of type **bool** can store only the values **true** or **false**, which are keywords defined by C++. As explained in Part One, automatic conversions take place which allow **bool** values to be converted to integers, and vice versa. Specifically, any non-zero value is converted to **true** and zero is converted to **false**. The reverse also occurs; **true** is converted to 1 and **false** is converted to zero. Thus, the fundamental concept of zero being false and non-zero being true is still fully entrenched in the C++ language.

Note	*Although C89 (the C subset of C++) does not define a Boolean type, C99 adds to the C language a type called __Bool, which is capable of storing the values 1 and 0 (i.e., true/false). Unlike C++, C99 does not define **true** and **false** as keywords. Thus, __Bool as defined by C99 is incompatible with **bool** as defined by C++.*

*The reason that C99 specifies __Bool rather than **bool** as a keyword is that many preexisting C programs have aleady defined their own custom versions of **bool**. By defining the Boolean type as __Bool, C99 avoids breaking this preexisting code. However, it is possible to achieve compatibility between C++ and C99 on this point because C99 adds the header **<stdbool.h>** which defines the macros **bool**, **true**, and **false**. By including this header, you can create code that is compatible with both C99 and C++.*

Old-Style vs. Modern C++

As explained, C++ underwent a rather extensive evolutionary process during its development and standardization. As a result, there are really two versions of C++. The first is the traditional version that is based upon Bjarne Stroustrup's original designs. The second is Standard C++, which was created by Stroustrup and the ANSI/ISO standardization committee. While these two versions of C++ are very similar at their core, Standard C++ contains several enhancements not found in traditional C++. Thus, Standard C++ is essentially a superset of traditional C++.

This book describes Standard C++. This is the version of C++ defined by the ANSI/ISO standardization committee and the one implemented by all modern C++ compilers. The code in this book reflects the contemporary coding style and practices as encouraged by Standard C++. However, if you are using an older compiler, it may not accept all of the programs in this book. Here's why. During the process of standardization, the ANSI/ISO committee added many new features to the language. As these features were defined, they were implemented by compiler developers. Of course, there is always a lag time between when a new feature is added to the language and when it is available in commercial compilers. Since features were added to C++ over a period of years, an older compiler might not support one or more of them. This is important because two recent additions to the C++ language affect every program that you will write—even the simplest. If you are using an older compiler that does not accept these new features, don't worry. There is an easy work-around, which is described here.

The key differences between old-style and modern code involve two features: new-style headers and the **namespace** statement. To understand the differences, we will begin by looking at two versions of a minimal, do-nothing C++ program. The first version shown here reflects the way C++ programs were written using old-style coding.

```
/*
   An old-style C++ program.
*/

#include <iostream.h>

int main()
{
  return 0;
}
```

Pay special attention to the **#include** statement. It includes the file **iostream.h**, not the header **<iostream>**. Also notice that no **namespace** statement is present.

Here is the second version of the skeleton, which uses the modern style.

```
/*
   A modern-style C++ program that uses
   the new-style headers and a namespace.
*/
#include <iostream>
using namespace std;

int main()
{
  return 0;
}
```

This version uses the C++-style header and specifies a namespace. Both of these features were mentioned in passing earlier. Let's look closely at them now.

The New C++ Headers

As you know, when you use a library function in a program, you must include its header. This is done using the **#include** statement. For example, in C, to include the header for the I/O functions, you include **stdio.h** with a statement like this:

```
#include <stdio.h>
```

Here, **stdio.h** is the name of the file used by the I/O functions, and the preceding statement causes that file to be included in your program. The key point is that this **#include** statement normally *includes a file*.

When C++ was first invented and for several years after that, it used the same style of headers as did C. That is, it used *header files*. In fact, Standard C++ still supports C-style headers for header files that you create and for backward compatibility. However, Standard C++ created a new kind of header that is used by the Standard C++ library. The new-style headers *do not* specify filenames. Instead, they simply specify standard identifiers that may be mapped to files by the compiler, although they need not be. The new-style C++ headers are an abstraction that simply guarantee that the appropriate prototypes and definitions required by the C++ library have been declared.

Since the new-style headers are not filenames, they do not have a **.h** extension. They consist solely of the header name contained between angle brackets. For example, here are some of the new-style headers supported by Standard C++.

<iostream>   <fstream>   <vector>   <string>

The new-style headers are included using the **#include** statement. The only difference is that the new-style headers do not necessarily represent filenames.

Because C++ includes the entire C function library, it still supports the standard C-style header files associated with that library. That is, header files such as **stdio.h** or **ctype.h** are still available. However, Standard C++ also defines new-style headers that you can use in place of these header files. The C++ versions of the C standard headers simply add a "c" prefix to the filename and drop the **.h**. For example, the C++ new-style header for **math.h** is **<cmath>**. The one for **string.h** is **<cstring>**. Although it is currently permissible to include a C-style header file when using C library functions, this approach is deprecated by Standard C++ (that is, it is not recommended). For this reason, from this point forward, this book will use new-style C++ headers in all **#include** statements. If your compiler does not support new-style headers for the C function library, then simply substitute the old-style, C-like headers.

Since the new-style header is a relatively recent addition to C++, you will still find many, many older programs that don't use it. These programs employ C-style headers, in which a filename is specified. As the old-style skeletal program shows, the traditional way to include the I/O header is as shown here.

```
#include <iostream.h>
```

This causes the file **iostream.h** to be included in your program. In general, an old-style header file will use the same name as its corresponding new-style header with a **.h** appended.

As of this writing, all C++ compilers support the old-style headers. However, the old-style headers have been declared obsolete and their use in new programs is not recommended. This is why they are not used in this book.

  While still common in existing C++ code, old-style headers are obsolete.

Namespaces

When you include a new-style header in your program, the contents of that header are contained in the **std** namespace. A *namespace* is simply a declarative region. The purpose of a namespace is to localize the names of identifiers to avoid name collisions. Elements declared in one namespace are separate from elements declared in another. Originally, the names of the C++ library functions, etc., were simply put into the global namespace (as they are in C). However, with the advent of the new-style headers, the contents of these headers were placed in the **std** namespace. We will look closely at namespaces later in this book. For now, you won't need to worry about them because the statement

```
using namespace std;
```

brings the **std** namespace into visibility (i.e., it puts **std** into the global namespace). After this statement has been compiled, there is no difference between working with an old-style header and a new-style one.

One other point: for the sake of compatibility, when a C++ program includes a C header, such as **stdio.h**, its contents are put into the global namespace. This allows a C++ compiler to compile C-subset programs.

Working with an Old Compiler

As explained, both namespaces and the new-style headers are fairly recent additions to the C++ language, added during standardization. While all new C++ compilers support these features, older compilers may not. When this is the case, your compiler will report one or more errors when it tries to compile the first two lines of the sample programs in this book. If this is the case, there is an easy work-around: simply use an old-style header and delete the **namespace** statement. That is, just replace

```
#include <iostream>
using namespace std;
```

with

```
#include <iostream.h>
```

This change transforms a modern program into an old-style one. Since the old-style header reads all of its contents into the global namespace, there is no need for a **namespace** statement.

One other point: for now and for the next few years, you will see many C++ programs that use the old-style headers and do not include a **using** statement. Your C++ compiler will be able to compile them just fine. However, for new programs, you should use the modern style because it is the only style of program that complies with the C++ Standard. While old-style programs will continue to be supported for many years, they are technically noncompliant.

Introducing C++ Classes

This section introduces C++'s most important feature: the class. In C++, to create an object, you first must define its general form by using the keyword **class**. A **class** is similar syntactically to a structure. Here is an example. The following class defines a type called **stack**, which will be used to create a stack:

```
#define SIZE 100
```

```
// This creates the class stack.
class stack {
  int stck[SIZE];
  int tos;
public:
  void init();
  void push(int i);
  int pop();
};
```

A **class** may contain private as well as public parts. By default, all items defined in a **class** are private. For example, the variables **stck** and **tos** are private. This means that they cannot be accessed by any function that is not a member of the **class**. This is one way that encapsulation is achieved—access to certain items of data may be tightly controlled by keeping them private. Although it is not shown in this example, you can also define private functions, which then may be called only by other members of the **class**.

To make parts of a **class** public (that is, accessible to other parts of your program), you must declare them after the **public** keyword. All variables or functions defined after **public** can be accessed by all other functions in the program. Essentially, the rest of your program accesses an object through its public functions. Although you can have public variables, good practice dictates that you should try to limit their use. Instead, you should make all data private and control access to it through public functions. One other point: Notice that the **public** keyword is followed by a colon.

The functions **init( )**, **push( )**, and **pop( )** are called *member functions* because they are part of the class **stack**. The variables **stck** and **tos** are called *member variables* (or *data members*). Remember, an object forms a bond between code and data. Only member functions have access to the private members of their class. Thus, only **init( )**, **push( )**, and **pop( )** may access **stck** and **tos**.

Once you have defined a **class**, you can create an object of that type by using the class name. In essence, the class name becomes a new data type specifier. For example, this creates an object called **mystack** of type **stack**:

```
stack mystack;
```

When you declare an object of a class, you are creating an *instance* of that class. In this case, **mystack** is an instance of **stack**. You may also create objects when the **class** is defined by putting their names after the closing curly brace, in exactly the same way as you would with a structure.

To review: In C++, **class** creates a new data type that may be used to create objects of that type. Therefore, an object is an instance of a class in just the same way that some other variable is an instance of the **int** data type, for example. Put differently, a class is a logical abstraction, while an object is real. (That is, an object exists inside the memory of the computer.)

The general form of a simple **class** declaration is

```
class class-name {
    private data and functions
public:
    public data and functions
} object name list;
```

Of course, the *object name list* may be empty.

Inside the declaration of **stack**, member functions were identified using their prototypes. In C++, all functions must be prototyped. Prototypes are not optional. The prototype for a member function within a class definition serves as that function's prototype in general.

When it comes time to actually code a function that is the member of a class, you must tell the compiler which class the function belongs to by qualifying its name with the name of the class of which it is a member. For example, here is one way to code the **push( )** function:

```
void stack::push(int i)
{
  if(tos==SIZE) {
    cout << "Stack is full.\n";
    return;
  }
  stck[tos] = i;
  tos++;
}
```

The **::** is called the *scope resolution operator*. Essentially, it tells the compiler that this version of **push( )** belongs to the **stack** class or, put differently, that this **push( )** is in **stack**'s scope. In C++, several different classes can use the same function name. The compiler knows which function belongs to which class because of the scope resolution operator.

When you refer to a member of a class from a piece of code that is not part of the class, you must always do so in conjunction with an object of that class. To do so, use the object's name, followed by the dot operator, followed by the name of the member. This rule applies whether you are accessing a data member or a function member. For example, this calls **init( )** for object **stack1**.

```
stack stack1, stack2;

stack1.init();
```

This fragment creates two objects, **stack1** and **stack2**, and initializes **stack1**. Understand that **stack1** and **stack2** are two separate objects. This means, for example, that initializing **stack1** does *not* cause **stack2** to be initialized as well. The only relationship **stack1** has with **stack2** is that they are objects of the same type.

Within a class, one member function can call another member function or refer to a data member directly, without using the dot operator. It is only when a member is referred to by code that does not belong to the class that the object name and the dot operator must be used.

The program shown here puts together all the pieces and missing details and illustrates the **stack** class:

```cpp
#include <iostream>
using namespace std;

#define SIZE 100

// This creates the class stack.
class stack {
  int stck[SIZE];
  int tos;
public:
  void init();
  void push(int i);
  int pop();
};

void stack::init()
{
  tos = 0;
}

void stack::push(int i)
{
  if(tos==SIZE) {
    cout << "Stack is full.\n";
    return;
  }
  stck[tos] = i;
  tos++;
}

int stack::pop()
{
  if(tos==0) {
```

```
      cout << "Stack underflow.\n";
      return 0;
    }
    tos--;
    return stck[tos];
}

int main()
{
  stack stack1, stack2;  // create two stack objects

  stack1.init();
  stack2.init();

  stack1.push(1);
  stack2.push(2);

  stack1.push(3);
  stack2.push(4);

  cout << stack1.pop() << " ";
  cout << stack1.pop() << " ";
  cout << stack2.pop() << " ";
  cout << stack2.pop() << "\n";

  return 0;
}
```

The output from this program is shown here.

```
3 1 4 2
```

One last point: Recall that the private members of an object are accessible only by functions that are members of that object. For example, a statement like

```
stack1.tos = 0; // Error, tos is private.
```

could not be in the **main( )** function of the previous program because **tos** is private.

Function Overloading

One way that C++ achieves polymorphism is through the use of function overloading. In C++, two or more functions can share the same name as long as their parameter declarations are different. In this situation, the functions that share the same name are said to be *overloaded*, and the process is referred to as *function overloading*.

To see why function overloading is important, first consider three functions defined by the C subset: **abs( )**, **labs( )**, and **fabs( )**. The **abs( )** function returns the absolute value of an integer, **labs( )** returns the absolute value of a **long**, and **fabs( )** returns the absolute value of a **double**. Although these functions perform almost identical actions, in C three slightly different names must be used to represent these essentially similar tasks. This makes the situation more complex, conceptually, than it actually is. Even though the underlying concept of each function is the same, the programmer has to remember three things, not just one. However, in C++, you can use just one name for all three functions, as this program illustrates:

```
#include <iostream>
using namespace std;

// abs is overloaded three ways
int abs(int i);
double abs(double d);
long abs(long l);

int main()
{
  cout << abs(-10) << "\n";

  cout << abs(-11.0) << "\n";

  cout << abs(-9L) << "\n";

  return 0;
}

int abs(int i)
{
  cout << "Using integer abs()\n";
```

```
   return i<0 ? -i : i;
}

double abs(double d)
{
  cout << "Using double abs()\n";

  return d<0.0 ? -d : d;
}

long abs(long l)
{
  cout << "Using long abs()\n";

  return l<0 ? -l : l;
}
```

The output from this program is shown here.

```
Using integer abs()
10
Using double abs()
11
Using long abs()
9
```

This program creates three similar but different functions called **abs( )**, each of which returns the absolute value of its argument. The compiler knows which function to call in each situation because of the type of the argument. The value of overloaded functions is that they allow related sets of functions to be accessed with a common name. Thus, the name **abs( )** represents the *general action* that is being performed. It is left to the compiler to choose the right *specific method* for a particular circumstance. You need only remember the general action being performed. Due to polymorphism, three things to remember have been reduced to one. This example is fairly trivial, but if you expand the concept, you can see how polymorphism can help you manage very complex programs.

In general, to overload a function, simply declare different versions of it. The compiler takes care of the rest. You must observe one important restriction when overloading a function: the type and/or number of the parameters of each overloaded function must differ. It is not sufficient for two functions to differ only in their return types. They must differ in the types or number of their parameters. (Return types do not provide sufficient information in all cases for the compiler to decide which function to use.) Of course, overloaded functions *may* differ in their return types, too.

Here is another example that uses overloaded functions:

```cpp
#include <iostream>
#include <cstdio>
#include <cstring>
using namespace std;

void stradd(char *s1, char *s2);
void stradd(char *s1, int i);

int main()
{
  char str[80];

  strcpy(str, "Hello ");
  stradd(str, "there");
  cout << str << "\n";

  stradd(str, 100);
  cout << str << "\n";

  return 0;
}

// concatenate two strings
void stradd(char *s1, char *s2)
{
  strcat(s1, s2);
}

// concatenate a string with a "stringized" integer
void stradd(char *s1, int i)
{
  char temp[80];

  sprintf(temp, "%d", i);
  strcat(s1, temp);
}
```

In this program, the function **stradd( )** is overloaded. One version concatenates two strings (just like **strcat( )** does). The other version "stringizes" an integer and then appends that to a string. Here, overloading is used to create one interface that appends either a string or an integer to another string.

You can use the same name to overload unrelated functions, but you should not. For example, you could use the name **sqr( )** to create functions that return the *square* of an **int** and the *square root* of a **double**. However, these two operations are fundamentally different; applying function overloading in this manner defeats its purpose (and, in fact, is considered bad programming style). In practice, you should overload only closely related operations.

Operator Overloading

Polymorphism is also achieved in C++ through operator overloading. As you know, in C++, it is possible to use the << and >> operators to perform console I/O operations. They can perform these extra operations because in the **<iostream>** header, these operators are overloaded. When an operator is overloaded, it takes on an additional meaning relative to a certain class. However, it still retains all of its old meanings.

In general, you can overload most of C++'s operators by defining what they mean relative to a specific class. For example, think back to the **stack** class developed earlier in this chapter. It is possible to overload the + operator relative to objects of type **stack** so that it appends the contents of one stack to the contents of another. However, the + still retains its original meaning relative to other types of data.

Because operator overloading is, in practice, somewhat more complex than function overloading, examples are deferred until Chapter 14.

Inheritance

As stated earlier in this chapter, inheritance is one of the major traits of an object-oriented programming language. In C++, inheritance is supported by allowing one class to incorporate another class into its declaration. Inheritance allows a hierarchy of classes to be built, moving from most general to most specific. The process involves first defining a *base class*, which defines those qualities common to all objects to be derived from the base. The base class represents the most general description. The classes derived from the base are usually referred to as *derived classes*. A derived class includes all features of the generic base class and then adds qualities specific to the derived class. To demonstrate how this works, the next example creates classes that categorize different types of buildings.

To begin, the **building** class is declared, as shown here. It will serve as the base for two derived classes.

```
class building {
  int rooms;
  int floors;
  int area;
```

```
public:
  void set_rooms(int num);
  int get_rooms();
  void set_floors(int num);
  int get_floors();
  void set_area(int num);
  int get_area();
};
```

Because (for the sake of this example) all buildings have three common features—one or more rooms, one or more floors, and a total area—the **building** class embodies these components into its declaration. The member functions beginning with **set** set the values of the private data. The functions starting with get return those values.

You can now use this broad definition of a building to create derived classes that describe specific types of buildings. For example, here is a derived class called **house:**

```
// house is derived from building
class house : public building {
  int bedrooms;
  int baths;
public:
  void set_bedrooms(int num);
  int get_bedrooms();
  void set_baths(int num);
  int get_baths();
};
```

Notice how **building** is inherited. The general form for inheritance is

class *derived-class : access base-class* {
    // body of new class
}

Here, *access* is optional. However, if present, it must be **public**, **private**, or **protected**. (These options are further examined in Chapter 12.) For now, all inherited classes will use **public**. Using **public** means that all of the public members of the base class will become public members of the derived class. Therefore, the public members of the class **building** become public members of the derived class **house** and are available to the member functions of **house** just as if they had been declared inside **house**. However, **house**'s member functions *do not* have access to the private elements of **building**. This is an important point. Even though **house** inherits **building**, it has access only to the public members of **building**. In this way, inheritance does not circumvent the principles of encapsulation necessary to OOP.

 A derived class has direct access to both its own members and the public members of the base class.

Here is a program illustrating inheritance. It creates two derived classes of **building** using inheritance; one is **house**, the other, **school**.

```cpp
#include <iostream>
using namespace std;

class building {
  int rooms;
  int floors;
  int area;
public:
  void set_rooms(int num);
  int get_rooms();
  void set_floors(int num);
  int get_floors();
  void set_area(int num);
  int get_area();
};

// house is derived from building
class house : public building {
  int bedrooms;
  int baths;
public:
  void set_bedrooms(int num);
  int get_bedrooms();
  void set_baths(int num);
  int get_baths();
};

// school is also derived from building
class school : public building {
  int classrooms;
  int offices;
public:
  void set_classrooms(int num);
```

```
  int get_classrooms();
  void set_offices(int num);
  int get_offices();
};

void building::set_rooms(int num)
{
  rooms = num;
}

void building::set_floors(int num)
{
  floors = num;
}

void building::set_area(int num)
{
  area = num;
}

int building::get_rooms()
{
  return rooms;
}

int building::get_floors()
{
  return floors;
}

int building::get_area()
{
  return area;
}

void house::set_bedrooms(int num)
{
  bedrooms = num;
}

void house::set_baths(int num)
{
```

```
    baths = num;
}

int house::get_bedrooms()
{
  return bedrooms;
}

int house::get_baths()
{
  return baths;
}

void school::set_classrooms(int num)
{
  classrooms = num;
}

void school::set_offices(int num)
{
  offices = num;
}

int school::get_classrooms()
{
  return classrooms;
}

int school::get_offices()
{
  return offices;
}

int main()
{
  house h;
  school s;

  h.set_rooms(12);
  h.set_floors(3);
  h.set_area(4500);
  h.set_bedrooms(5);
```

```
    h.set_baths(3);

    cout << "house has " << h.get_bedrooms();
    cout << " bedrooms\n";

    s.set_rooms(200);
    s.set_classrooms(180);
    s.set_offices(5);
    s.set_area(25000);

    cout << "school has " << s.get_classrooms();
    cout << " classrooms\n";
    cout << "Its area is " << s.get_area();

    return 0;
}
```

The output produced by this program is shown here.

```
house has 5 bedrooms
school has 180 classrooms
Its area is 25000
```

As this program shows, the major advantage of inheritance is that you can create a general classification that can be incorporated into more specific ones. In this way, each object can precisely represent its own subclass.

When writing about C++, the terms *base* and *derived* are generally used to describe the inheritance relationship. However, the terms *parent* and *child* are also used. You may also see the terms *superclass* and *subclass*.

Aside from providing the advantages of hierarchical classification, inheritance also provides support for run-time polymorphism through the mechanism of **virtual** functions. (Refer to Chapter 16 for details.)

Constructors and Destructors

It is very common for some part of an object to require initialization before it can be used. For example, think back to the **stack** class developed earlier in this chapter. Before the stack could be used, **tos** had to be set to zero. This was performed by using the function **init( )**. Because the requirement for initialization is so common, C++ allows objects to initialize themselves when they are created. This automatic initialization is performed through the use of a constructor function.

A *constructor* is a special function that is a member of a class and has the same name as that class. For example, here is how the **stack** class looks when converted to use a constructor for initialization:

```
// This creates the class stack.
class stack {
  int stck[SIZE];
  int tos;
public:
  stack();  // constructor
  void push(int i);
  int pop();
};
```

Notice that the constructor **stack( )** has no return type specified. In C++, constructors cannot return values and, thus, have no return type.

The **stack( )** constructor is coded like this:

```
// stack's constructor
stack::stack()
{
  tos = 0;
  cout << "Stack Initialized\n";
}
```

Keep in mind that the message **Stack Initialized** is output as a way to illustrate the constructor. In actual practice, most constructors will not output or input anything. They will simply perform various initializations.

An object's constructor is automatically called when the object is created. This means that it is called when the object's declaration is executed. If you are accustomed to thinking of a declaration statement as being passive, this is not the case for C++. In C++, a declaration statement is a statement that is executed. This distinction is not just academic. The code executed to construct an object may be quite significant. An object's constructor is called once for global or **static** local objects. For local objects, the constructor is called each time the object declaration is encountered.

The complement of the constructor is the *destructor*. In many circumstances, an object will need to perform some action or actions when it is destroyed. Local objects are created when their block is entered, and destroyed when the block is left. Global objects are destroyed when the program terminates. When an object is destroyed, its destructor (if it has one) is automatically called. There are many reasons why a destructor may be needed. For example, an object may need to deallocate memory that it had previously allocated or it may need to close a file that it had opened. In C++, it is the destructor that handles deactivation events. The destructor has the same name as the constructor, but it is preceded by a ~. For example, here is the **stack** class and its constructor and destructor. (Keep in mind that the **stack** class does not require a destructor; the one shown here is just for illustration.)

```
// This creates the class stack.
class stack {
  int stck[SIZE];
  int tos;
public:
  stack();  // constructor
  ~stack(); // destructor
  void push(int i);
  int pop();
};

// stack's constructor
stack::stack()
{
  tos = 0;
  cout << "Stack Initialized\n";
}

// stack's destructor
stack::~stack()
{
  cout << "Stack Destroyed\n";
}
```

Notice that, like constructors, destructors do not have return values.

To see how constructors and destructors work, here is a new version of the **stack** program examined earlier in this chapter. Observe that **init( )** is no longer needed.

```
// Using a constructor and destructor.
#include <iostream>
using namespace std;

#define SIZE 100

// This creates the class stack.
class stack {
  int stck[SIZE];
  int tos;
public:
```

```cpp
  stack();    // constructor
  ~stack();   // destructor
  void push(int i);
  int pop();
};

// stack's constructor
stack::stack()
{
  tos = 0;
  cout << "Stack Initialized\n";
}

// stack's destructor
stack::~stack()
{
  cout << "Stack Destroyed\n";
}

void stack::push(int i)
{
  if(tos==SIZE) {
    cout << "Stack is full.\n";
    return;
  }
  stck[tos] = i;
  tos++;
}

int stack::pop()
{
  if(tos==0) {
    cout << "Stack underflow.\n";
    return 0;
  }
  tos--;
  return stck[tos];
}

int main()
{
  stack a, b;  // create two stack objects
```

```
    a.push(1);
    b.push(2);

    a.push(3);
    b.push(4);

    cout << a.pop() << " ";
    cout << a.pop() << " ";
    cout << b.pop() << " ";
    cout << b.pop() << "\n";

    return 0;
}
```

This program displays the following:

```
Stack Initialized
Stack Initialized
3 1 4 2
Stack Destroyed
Stack Destroyed
```

The C++ Keywords

There are 63 keywords currently defined for Standard C++. These are shown in Table 11-1. Together with the formal C++ syntax, they form the C++ programming language. Also, early versions of C++ defined the **overload** keyword, but it is obsolete. Keep in mind that C++ is a case-sensitive language and it requires that all keywords be in lowercase.

asm	auto	bool	break
case	catch	char	class
const	const_cast	continue	default
delete	do	double	dynamic_cast
else	enum	explicit	export

Table 11-1.   *The C++ keywords*

extern	false	float	for
friend	goto	if	inline
int	long	mutable	namespace
new	operator	private	protected
public	register	reinterpret_cast	return
short	signed	sizeof	static
static_cast	struct	switch	template
this	throw	true	try
typedef	typeid	typename	union
unsigned	using	virtual	void
volatile	wchar_t	while	

Table 11-1.   *The C++ keywords* (continued)

The General Form of a C++ Program

Although individual styles will differ, most C++ programs will have this general form:

```
#includes
base-class declarations
derived class declarations
nonmember function prototypes
int main( )
{
    //...
}
nonmember function definitions
```

In most large projects, all **class** declarations will be put into a header file and included with each module. But the general organization of a program remains the same.

The remaining chapters in this section examine in greater detail the features discussed in this chapter, as well as all other aspects of C++.

The Complete Reference

Chapter 12

Classes and Objects

In C++, the class forms the basis for object-oriented programming. The class is used to define the nature of an object, and it is C++'s basic unit of encapsulation. This chapter examines classes and objects in detail.

Classes

Classes are created using the keyword **class**. A class declaration defines a new type that links code and data. This new type is then used to declare objects of that class. Thus, a class is a logical abstraction, but an object has physical existence. In other words, an object is an *instance* of a class.

A class declaration is similar syntactically to a structure. In Chapter 11, a simplified general form of a class declaration was shown. Here is the entire general form of a **class** declaration that does not inherit any other class.

```
class class-name {
    private data and functions
access-specifier:
    data and functions
access-specifier:
    data and functions
// ...
access-specifier:
    data and functions
} object-list;
```

The *object-list* is optional. If present, it declares objects of the class. Here, *access-specifier* is one of these three C++ keywords:

public

private

protected

By default, functions and data declared within a class are private to that class and may be accessed only by other members of the class. The **public** access specifier allows functions or data to be accessible to other parts of your program. The **protected** access specifier is needed only when inheritance is involved (see Chapter 15). Once an access specifier has been used, it remains in effect until either another access specifier is encountered or the end of the class declaration is reached.

You may change access specifications as often as you like within a **class** declaration. For example, you may switch to **public** for some declarations and then switch back to **private** again. The class declaration in the following example illustrates this feature:

```cpp
#include <iostream>
#include <cstring>
using namespace std;

class employee {
  char name[80]; // private by default
public:
  void putname(char *n); // these are public
  void getname(char *n);
private:
  double wage; // now, private again
public:
  void putwage(double w); // back to public
  double getwage();
};

void employee::putname(char *n)
{
  strcpy(name, n);
}

void employee::getname(char *n)
{
  strcpy(n, name);
}

void employee::putwage(double w)
{
  wage = w;
}

double employee::getwage()
{
  return wage;
}

int main()
{
  employee ted;
  char name[80];

  ted.putname("Ted Jones");
  ted.putwage(75000);
```

```
    ted.getname(name);
    cout << name << " makes $";
    cout << ted.getwage() << " per year.";

    return 0;
}
```

Here, **employee** is a simple class that is used to store an employee's name and wage. Notice that the **public** access specifier is used twice.

Although you may use the access specifiers as often as you like within a class declaration, the only advantage of doing so is that by visually grouping various parts of a class, you may make it easier for someone else reading the program to understand it. However, to the compiler, using multiple access specifiers makes no difference. Actually, most programmers find it easier to have only one **private, protected,** and **public** section within each class. For example, most programmers would code the **employee** class as shown here, with all private elements grouped together and all public elements grouped together:

```
class employee {
  char name[80];
  double wage;
public:
  void putname(char *n);
  void getname(char *n);
  void putwage(double w);
  double getwage();
};
```

Functions that are declared within a class are called *member functions*. Member functions may access any element of the class of which they are a part. This includes all **private** elements. Variables that are elements of a class are called *member variables* or *data members*. (The term *instance variable* is also used.) Collectively, any element of a class can be referred to as a member of that class.

There are a few restrictions that apply to class members. A non-**static** member variable cannot have an initializer. No member can be an object of the class that is being declared. (Although a member can be a pointer to the class that is being declared.) No member can be declared as **auto, extern,** or **register**.

In general, you should make all data members of a class private to that class. This is part of the way that encapsulation is achieved. However, there may be situations in which you will need to make one or more variables public. (For example, a heavily

used variable may need to be accessible globally in order to achieve faster run times.)
When a variable is public, it may be accessed directly by any other part of your
program. The syntax for accessing a public data member is the same as for calling a
member function: Specify the object's name, the dot operator, and the variable name.
This simple program illustrates the use of a public variable:

```cpp
#include <iostream>
using namespace std;

class myclass {
public:
  int i, j, k; // accessible to entire program
};

int main()
{
  myclass a, b;

  a.i = 100; // access to i, j, and k is OK
  a.j = 4;
  a.k = a.i * a.j;

  b.k = 12; // remember, a.k and b.k are different
  cout << a.k << " " << b.k;

  return 0;
}
```

Structures and Classes Are Related

Structures are part of the C subset and were inherited from the C language. As you
have seen, a **class** is syntactically similar to a **struct**. But the relationship between a
class and a **struct** is closer than you may at first think. In C++, the role of the structure
was expanded, making it an alternative way to specify a class. In fact, the only difference
between a **class** and a **struct** is that by default all members are public in a **struct** and
private in a **class**. In all other respects, structures and classes are equivalent. That is,
in C++, a *structure defines a class type*. For example, consider this short program, which
uses a structure to declare a class that controls access to a string:

```cpp
// Using a structure to define a class.
#include <iostream>
#include <cstring>
```

```
using namespace std;

struct mystr {
  void buildstr(char *s); // public
  void showstr();
private: // now go private
  char str[255];
} ;

void mystr::buildstr(char *s)
{
  if(!*s) *str = '\0'; // initialize string
  else strcat(str, s);
}

void mystr::showstr()
{
  cout << str << "\n";
}

int main()
{
  mystr s;

  s.buildstr(""); // init
  s.buildstr("Hello ");
  s.buildstr("there!");

  s.showstr();

  return 0;
}
```

This program displays the string **Hello there!**.

The class **mystr** could be rewritten by using **class** as shown here:

```
class mystr {
  char str[255];
public:
  void buildstr(char *s); // public
  void showstr();
} ;
```

You might wonder why C++ contains the two virtually equivalent keywords **struct** and **class**. This seeming redundancy is justified for several reasons. First, there is no fundamental reason not to increase the capabilities of a structure. In C, structures already provide a means of grouping data. Therefore, it is a small step to allow them to include member functions. Second, because structures and classes are related, it may be easier to port existing C programs to C++. Finally, although **struct** and **class** are virtually equivalent today, providing two different keywords allows the definition of a **class** to be free to evolve. In order for C++ to remain compatible with C, the definition of **struct** must always be tied to its C definition.

Although you can use a **struct** where you use a **class**, most programmers don't. Usually it is best to use a **class** when you want a class, and a **struct** when you want a C-like structure. This is the style that this book will follow. Sometimes the acronym *POD* is used to describe a C-style structure—one that does not contain member functions, constructors, or destructors. It stands for Plain Old Data.

 In C++, a structure declaration defines a class type.

Unions and Classes Are Related

Like a structure, a **union** may also be used to define a class. In C++, **union**s may contain both member functions and variables. They may also include constructors and destructors. A **union** in C++ retains all of its C-like features, the most important being that all data elements share the same location in memory. Like the structure, **union** members are public by default and are fully compatible with C. In the next example, a **union** is used to swap the bytes that make up an **unsigned short** integer. (This example assumes that short integers are 2 bytes long.)

```
#include <iostream>
using namespace std;

union swap_byte {
  void swap();
  void set_byte(unsigned short i);
  void show_word();

  unsigned short u;
  unsigned char c[2];
};

void swap_byte::swap()
{
```

```
    unsigned char t;

    t = c[0];
    c[0] = c[1];
    c[1] = t;
}

void swap_byte::show_word()
{
    cout << u;
}

void swap_byte::set_byte(unsigned short i)
{
    u = i;
}

int main()
{
    swap_byte b;

    b.set_byte(49034);
    b.swap();
    b.show_word();

    return 0;
}
```

Like a structure, a **union** declaration in C++ defines a special type of class. This means that the principle of encapsulation is preserved.

There are several restrictions that must be observed when you use C++ unions. First, a **union** cannot inherit any other classes of any type. Further, a **union** cannot be a base class. A **union** cannot have virtual member functions. (Virtual functions are discussed in Chapter 17.) No **static** variables can be members of a **union**. A reference member cannot be used. A **union** cannot have as a member any object that overloads the = operator. Finally, no object can be a member of a **union** if the object has an explicit constructor or destructor function.

As with **struct**, the term POD is also commonly applied to unions that do not contain member functions, constructors, or destructors.

Anonymous Unions

There is a special type of **union** in C++ called an *anonymous union*. An anonymous union does not include a type name, and no objects of the union can be declared.

Instead, an anonymous union tells the compiler that its member variables are to share the same location. However, the variables themselves are referred to directly, without the normal dot operator syntax. For example, consider this program:

```
#include <iostream>
#include <cstring>
using namespace std;

int main()
{
  // define anonymous union
  union {
    long l;
    double d;
    char s[4];
  } ;

  // now, reference union elements directly
  l = 100000;
  cout << l << " ";
  d = 123.2342;
  cout << d << " ";
  strcpy(s, "hi");
  cout << s;

  return 0;
}
```

As you can see, the elements of the union are referenced as if they had been declared as normal local variables. In fact, relative to your program, that is exactly how you will use them. Further, even though they are defined within a **union** declaration, they are at the same scope level as any other local variable within the same block. This implies that the names of the members of an anonymous union must not conflict with other identifiers known within the same scope.

All restrictions involving **union**s apply to anonymous ones, with these additions. First, the only elements contained within an anonymous union must be data. No member functions are allowed. Anonymous unions cannot contain **private** or **protected** elements. Finally, global anonymous unions must be specified as **static**.

Friend Functions

It is possible to grant a nonmember function access to the private members of a class by using a **friend**. A **friend** function has access to all **private** and **protected** members of the class for which it is a **friend**. To declare a **friend** function, include its prototype within the class, preceding it with the keyword **friend**. Consider this program:

```cpp
#include <iostream>
using namespace std;

class myclass {
  int a, b;
public:
  friend int sum(myclass x);
  void set_ab(int i, int j);
};

void myclass::set_ab(int i, int j)
{
  a = i;
  b = j;
}

// Note: sum() is not a member function of any class.
int sum(myclass x)
{
  /* Because sum() is a friend of myclass, it can
     directly access a and b. */

  return x.a + x.b;
}

int main()
{
  myclass n;

  n.set_ab(3, 4);

  cout << sum(n);

  return 0;
}
```

In this example, the **sum( )** function is not a member of **myclass**. However, it still has full access to its private members. Also, notice that **sum( )** is called without the use of the dot operator. Because it is not a member function, it does not need to be (indeed, it may not be) qualified with an object's name.

Although there is nothing gained by making **sum( )** a **friend** rather than a member function of **myclass**, there are some circumstances in which **friend** functions are quite valuable. First, friends can be useful when you are overloading certain types of operators (see Chapter 14). Second, **friend** functions make the creation of some types of I/O functions easier (see Chapter 18). The third reason that **friend** functions may be desirable is that in some cases, two or more classes may contain members that are interrelated relative to other parts of your program. Let's examine this third usage now.

To begin, imagine two different classes, each of which displays a pop-up message on the screen when error conditions occur. Other parts of your program may wish to know if a pop-up message is currently being displayed before writing to the screen so that no message is accidentally overwritten. Although you can create member functions in each class that return a value indicating whether a message is active, this means additional overhead when the condition is checked (that is, two function calls, not just one). If the condition needs to be checked frequently, this additional overhead may not be acceptable. However, using a function that is a **friend** of each class, it is possible to check the status of each object by calling only this one function. Thus, in situations like this, a **friend** function allows you to generate more efficient code. The following program illustrates this concept:

```
#include <iostream>
using namespace std;

const int IDLE = 0;
const int INUSE = 1;

class C2;  // forward declaration

class C1 {
  int status;  // IDLE if off, INUSE if on screen
  // ...
public:
  void set_status(int state);
  friend int idle(C1 a, C2 b);
};

class C2 {
  int status; // IDLE if off, INUSE if on screen
  // ...
public:
  void set_status(int state);
  friend int idle(C1 a, C2 b);
};
```

C++

```
void C1::set_status(int state)
{
  status = state;
}

void C2::set_status(int state)
{
  status = state;
}

int idle(C1 a, C2 b)
{
  if(a.status || b.status) return 0;
  else return 1;
}

int main()
{
  C1 x;
  C2 y;

  x.set_status(IDLE);
  y.set_status(IDLE);

  if(idle(x, y)) cout << "Screen can be used.\n";
  else cout << "In use.\n";

  x.set_status(INUSE);

  if(idle(x, y)) cout << "Screen can be used.\n";
  else cout << "In use.\n";

  return 0;
}
```

Notice that this program uses a *forward declaration* (also called a *forward reference*) for the class **C2**. This is necessary because the declaration of **idle( )** inside **C1** refers to **C2** before it is declared. To create a forward declaration to a class, simply use the form shown in this program.

A **friend** of one class may be a member of another. For example, here is the preceding program rewritten so that **idle( )** is a member of **C1**:

```cpp
#include <iostream>
using namespace std;

const int IDLE = 0;
const int INUSE = 1;

class C2;   // forward declaration

class C1 {
  int status;  // IDLE if off, INUSE if on screen
  // ...
public:
  void set_status(int state);
  int idle(C2 b);   // now a member of C1
};

class C2 {
  int status;  // IDLE if off, INUSE if on screen
  // ...
public:
  void set_status(int state);
  friend int C1::idle(C2 b);
};

void C1::set_status(int state)
{
  status = state;
}

void C2::set_status(int state)
{
  status = state;
}

// idle() is member of C1, but friend of C2
int C1::idle(C2 b)
{
  if(status || b.status) return 0;
  else return 1;
}

int main()
{
```

```
   C1 x;
   C2 y;

   x.set_status(IDLE);
   y.set_status(IDLE);

   if(x.idle(y)) cout << "Screen can be used.\n";
   else cout << "In use.\n";
   x.set_status(INUSE);

   if(x.idle(y)) cout << "Screen can be used.\n";
   else cout << "In use.\n";

   return 0;
 }
```

Because **idle( )** is a member of **C1**, it can access the **status** variable of objects of type
C1 directly. Thus, only objects of type **C2** need be passed to **idle( )**.

There are two important restrictions that apply to **friend** functions. First, a derived
class does not inherit **friend** functions. Second, **friend** functions may not have a
storage-class specifier. That is, they may not be declared as **static** or **extern**.

Friend Classes

It is possible for one class to be a **friend** of another class. When this is the case, the
friend class and all of its member functions have access to the private members
defined within the other class. For example,

```
// Using a friend class.
#include <iostream>
using namespace std;

class TwoValues {
  int a;
  int b;
public:
  TwoValues(int i, int j) { a = i; b = j; }
  friend class Min;
};

class Min {
```

```
public:
  int min(TwoValues x);
};

int Min::min(TwoValues x)
{
  return x.a < x.b ? x.a : x.b;
}

int main()
{
  TwoValues ob(10, 20);
  Min m;

  cout << m.min(ob);

  return 0;
}
```

In this example, class **Min** has access to the private variables **a** and **b** declared within the **TwoValues** class.

It is critical to understand that when one class is a **friend** of another, it only has access to names defined within the other class. It does not inherit the other class. Specifically, the members of the first class do not become members of the **friend** class.

Friend classes are seldom used. They are supported to allow certain special case situations to be handled.

Inline Functions

There is an important feature in C++, called an *inline function,* that is commonly used with classes. Since the rest of this chapter (and the rest of the book) will make heavy use of it, inline functions are examined here.

In C++, you can create short functions that are not actually called; rather, their code is expanded in line at the point of each invocation. This process is similar to using a function-like macro. To cause a function to be expanded in line rather than called, precede its definition with the **inline** keyword. For example, in this program, the function **max( )** is expanded in line instead of called:

```
#include <iostream>
using namespace std;
```

```
inline int max(int a, int b)
{
  return a>b ? a : b;
}

int main()
{
  cout << max(10, 20);
  cout << " " << max(99, 88);

  return 0;
}
```

As far as the compiler is concerned, the preceding program is equivalent to this one:

```
#include <iostream>
using namespace std;

int main()
{

  cout << (10>20 ? 10 : 20);
  cout << " " << (99>88 ? 99 : 88);

  return 0;
}
```

The reason that **inline** functions are an important addition to C++ is that they allow you to create very efficient code. Since classes typically require several frequently executed interface functions (which provide access to private data), the efficiency of these functions is of critical concern. As you probably know, each time a function is called, a significant amount of overhead is generated by the calling and return mechanism. Typically, arguments are pushed onto the stack and various registers are saved when a function is called, and then restored when the function returns. The trouble is that these instructions take time. However, when a function is expanded in line, none of those operations occur. Although expanding function calls in line can produce faster run times, it can also result in larger code size because of duplicated code. For this reason, it is best to **inline** only very small functions. Further, it is also a good idea to **inline** only those functions that will have significant impact on the performance of your program.

Like the **register** specifier, **inline** is actually just a *request*, not a command, to the compiler. The compiler can choose to ignore it. Also, some compilers may not inline all types of functions. For example, it is common for a compiler not to inline a recursive function. You will need to check your compiler's documentation for any restrictions to **inline.** Remember, if a function cannot be inlined, it will simply be called as a normal function.

Inline functions may be class member functions. For example, this is a perfectly valid C++ program:

```
#include <iostream>
using namespace std;

class myclass {
  int a, b;
public:
  void init(int i, int j);
  void show();
};

// Create an inline function.
inline void myclass::init(int i, int j)
{
  a = i;
  b = j;
}

// Create another inline function.
inline void myclass::show()
{
  cout << a << " " << b << "\n";
}

int main()
{
  myclass x;

  x.init(10, 20);
  x.show();

  return 0;
}
```

Note   *The **inline** keyword is not part of the C subset of C++. Thus, it is not defined by C89. However, it has been added by C99.*

Defining Inline Functions Within a Class

It is possible to define short functions completely within a class declaration. When a function is defined inside a class declaration, it is automatically made into an **inline** function (if possible). It is not necessary (but not an error) to precede its declaration with the **inline** keyword. For example, the preceding program is rewritten here with the definitions of **init( )** and **show( )** contained within the declaration of **myclass**:

```
#include <iostream>
using namespace std;

class myclass {
  int a, b;
public:
  // automatic inline
  void init(int i, int j) { a=i; b=j; }
  void show() { cout << a << " " << b << "\n"; }
};

int main()
{
  myclass x;

  x.init(10, 20);
  x.show();

  return 0;
}
```

Notice the format of the function code within **myclass**. Because inline functions are often short, this style of coding within a class is fairly typical. However, you are free to use any format you like. For example, this is a perfectly valid way to rewrite the **myclass** declaration:

```
#include <iostream>
using namespace std;

class myclass {
  int a, b;
public:
  // automatic inline
  void init(int i, int j)
  {
    a = i;
```

```
    b = j;
  }

  void show()
  {
    cout << a << " " << b << "\n";
  }
};
```

Technically, the inlining of the **show( )** function is of limited value because (in general) the amount of time the I/O statement will take far exceeds the overhead of a function call. However, it is extremely common to see all short member functions defined inside their class in C++ programs. (In fact, it is rare to see short member functions defined outside their class declarations in professionally written C++ code.)

Constructor and destructor functions may also be inlined, either by default, if defined within their class, or explicitly.

Parameterized Constructors

It is possible to pass arguments to constructors. Typically, these arguments help initialize an object when it is created. To create a parameterized constructor, simply add parameters to it the way you would to any other function. When you define the constructor's body, use the parameters to initialize the object. For example, here is a simple class that includes a parameterized constructor:

```
#include <iostream>
using namespace std;

class myclass {
  int a, b;
public:
  myclass(int i, int j) {a=i; b=j;}
  void show() {cout << a << " " << b;}
};

int main()
{
  myclass ob(3, 5);

  ob.show();

  return 0;
}
```

Notice that in the definition of **myclass( )**, the parameters **i** and **j** are used to give initial values to **a** and **b**.

The program illustrates the most common way to specify arguments when you declare an object that uses a parameterized constructor. Specifically, this statement

```
myclass ob(3, 4);
```

causes an object called **ob** to be created and passes the arguments **3** and **4** to the **i** and **j** parameters of **myclass( )**. You may also pass arguments using this type of declaration statement:

```
myclass ob = myclass(3, 4);
```

However, the first method is the one generally used, and this is the approach taken by most of the examples in this book. Actually, there is a small technical difference between the two types of declarations that relates to copy constructors. (Copy constructors are discussed in Chapter 14.)

Here is another example that uses a parameterized constructor. It creates a class that stores information about library books.

```
#include <iostream>
#include <cstring>
using namespace std;

const int IN = 1;
const int CHECKED_OUT = 0;

class book {
  char author[40];
  char title[40];
  int status;
public:
  book(char *n, char *t, int s);
  int get_status() {return status;}
  void set_status(int s) {status = s;}
  void show();
};

book::book(char *n, char *t, int s)
{
  strcpy(author, n);
```

```
   strcpy(title, t);
   status = s;
}

void book::show()
{
  cout << title << " by " << author;
  cout << " is ";
  if(status==IN) cout << "in.\n";
  else cout << "out.\n";
}

int main()
{
  book b1("Twain", "Tom Sawyer", IN);
  book b2("Melville", "Moby Dick", CHECKED_OUT);

  b1.show();
  b2.show();

  return 0;
}
```

Parameterized constructors are very useful because they allow you to avoid having to make an additional function call simply to initialize one or more variables in an object. Each function call you can avoid makes your program more efficient. Also, notice that the short **get_status( )** and **set_status( )** functions are defined in line, within the **book** class. This is a common practice when writing C++ programs.

Constructors with One Parameter: A Special Case

If a constructor only has one parameter, there is a third way to pass an initial value to that constructor. For example, consider the following short program.

```
#include <iostream>
using namespace std;

class X {
  int a;
public:
```

```
   X(int j) { a = j; }
   int geta() { return a; }
};

int main()
{
  X ob = 99; // passes 99 to j

  cout << ob.geta(); // outputs 99

  return 0;
}
```

Here, the constructor for **X** takes one parameter. Pay special attention to how **ob** is declared in **main( )**. In this form of initialization, 99 is automatically passed to the **j** parameter in the **X( )** constructor. That is, the declaration statement is handled by the compiler as if it were written like this:

```
X ob = X(99);
```

In general, any time you have a constructor that requires only one argument, you can use either *ob*(*i*) or *ob* = *i* to initialize an object. The reason for this is that whenever you create a constructor that takes one argument, you are also implicitly creating a conversion from the type of that argument to the type of the class.

Remember that the alternative shown here applies only to constructors that have exactly one parameter.

Static Class Members

Both function and data members of a class can be made **static**. This section explains the consequences of each.

Static Data Members

When you precede a member variable's declaration with **static**, you are telling the compiler that only one copy of that variable will exist and that all objects of the class will share that variable. Unlike regular data members, individual copies of a **static** member variable are not made for each object. No matter how many objects of a class are created, only one copy of a **static** data member exists. Thus, all objects of that class use that same variable. All **static** variables are initialized to zero before the first object is created.

When you declare a **static** data member within a class, you are *not* defining it. (That is, you are not allocating storage for it.) Instead, you must provide a global definition for it elsewhere, outside the class. This is done by redeclaring the **static** variable using the scope resolution operator to identify the class to which it belongs. This causes storage for the variable to be allocated. (Remember, a class declaration is simply a logical construct that does not have physical reality.)

To understand the usage and effect of a **static** data member, consider this program:

```
#include <iostream>
using namespace std;

class shared {
  static int a;
  int b;
public:
  void set(int i, int j) {a=i; b=j;}
  void show();
} ;

int shared::a; // define a

void shared::show()
{
  cout << "This is static a: " << a;
  cout << "\nThis is non-static b: " << b;
  cout << "\n";
}

int main()
{
  shared x, y;

  x.set(1, 1); // set a to 1
  x.show();

  y.set(2, 2); // change a to 2
  y.show();

  x.show(); /* Here, a has been changed for both x and y
               because a is shared by both objects. */

  return 0;
}
```

This program displays the following output when run.

```
This is static a: 1
This is non-static b: 1
This is static a: 2
This is non-static b: 2
This is static a: 2
This is non-static b: 1
```

Notice that the integer **a** is declared both inside **shared** and outside of it. As mentioned earlier, this is necessary because the declaration of **a** inside **shared** does not allocate storage.

Note *As a convenience, older versions of C++ did not require the second declaration of a* ***static*** *member variable. However, this convenience gave rise to serious inconsistencies and it was eliminated several years ago. However, you may still find older C++ code that does not redeclare* ***static*** *member variables. In these cases, you will need to add the required definitions.*

A **static** member variable exists *before* any object of its class is created. For example, in the following short program, **a** is both **public** and **static**. Thus it may be directly accessed in **main( )**. Further, since **a** exists before an object of **shared** is created, **a** can be given a value at any time. As this program illustrates, the value of **a** is unchanged by the creation of object **x**. For this reason, both output statements display the same value: 99.

```cpp
#include <iostream>
using namespace std;

class shared {
public:
  static int a;
} ;

int shared::a; // define a

int main()
{
  // initialize a before creating any objects
  shared::a = 99;

  cout << "This is initial value of a: " << shared::a;
```

```
  cout << "\n";

  shared x;

  cout << "This is x.a: " << x.a;

  return 0;
}
```

Notice how **a** is referred to through the use of the class name and the scope resolution operator. In general, to refer to a **static** member independently of an object, you must qualify it by using the name of the class of which it is a member.

One use of a **static** member variable is to provide access control to some shared resource used by all objects of a class. For example, you might create several objects, each of which needs to write to a specific disk file. Clearly, however, only one object can be allowed to write to the file at a time. In this case, you will want to declare a **static** variable that indicates when the file is in use and when it is free. Each object then interrogates this variable before writing to the file. The following program shows how you might use a **static** variable of this type to control access to a scarce resource:

```
#include <iostream>
using namespace std;

class cl {
  static int resource;
public:
  int get_resource();
  void free_resource() {resource = 0;}
};

int cl::resource; // define resource

int cl::get_resource()
{
  if(resource) return 0; // resource already in use
  else {
    resource = 1;
    return 1;  // resource allocated to this object
  }
}
```

```
int main()
{
  cl ob1, ob2;

  if(ob1.get_resource()) cout << "ob1 has resource\n";

  if(!ob2.get_resource()) cout << "ob2 denied resource\n";

  ob1.free_resource();   // let someone else use it

  if(ob2.get_resource())
    cout << "ob2 can now use resource\n";

  return 0;
}
```

Another interesting use of a **static** member variable is to keep track of the number of objects of a particular class type that are in existence. For example,

```
#include <iostream>
using namespace std;

class Counter {
public:
  static int count;
  Counter() { count++; }
  ~Counter() { count--; }
};
int Counter::count;

void f();

int main(void)
{
  Counter o1;
  cout << "Objects in existence: ";
  cout << Counter::count << "\n";

  Counter o2;
  cout << "Objects in existence: ";
  cout << Counter::count << "\n";
```

```
  f();
  cout << "Objects in existence: ";
  cout << Counter::count << "\n";

  return 0;
}

void f()
{
  Counter temp;
  cout << "Objects in existence: ";
  cout << Counter::count << "\n";
  // temp is destroyed when f() returns
}
```

This program produces the following output.

```
Objects in existence: 1
Objects in existence: 2
Objects in existence: 3
Objects in existence: 2
```

As you can see, the **static** member variable **count** is incremented whenever an object is created and decremented when an object is destroyed. This way, it keeps track of how many objects of type **Counter** are currently in existence.

By using **static** member variables, you should be able to virtually eliminate any need for global variables. The trouble with global variables relative to OOP is that they almost always violate the principle of encapsulation.

Static Member Functions

Member functions may also be declared as **static**. There are several restrictions placed on **static** member functions. They may only directly refer to other **static** members of the class. (Of course, global functions and data may be accessed by **static** member functions.) A **static** member function does not have a **this** pointer. (See Chapter 13 for information on **this**.) There cannot be a **static** and a non-**static** version of the same function. A **static** member function may not be virtual. Finally, they cannot be declared as **const** or **volatile**.

Following is a slightly reworked version of the shared-resource program from the previous section. Notice that **get_resource( )** is now declared as **static**. As the program illustrates, **get_resource( )** may be called either by itself, independently of any object, by using the class name and the scope resolution operator, or in connection with an object.

```
#include <iostream>
using namespace std;

class cl {
  static int resource;
public:
  static int get_resource();
  void free_resource() { resource = 0; }
};

int cl::resource; // define resource

int cl::get_resource()
{
  if(resource) return 0; // resource already in use
  else {
    resource = 1;
    return 1;  // resource allocated to this object
  }
}

int main()
{
  cl ob1, ob2;

  /* get_resource() is static so may be called independent
     of any object. */
  if(cl::get_resource()) cout << "ob1 has resource\n";

  if(!cl::get_resource()) cout << "ob2 denied resource\n";

  ob1.free_resource();

  if(ob2.get_resource()) // can still call using object syntax
    cout << "ob2 can now use resource\n";

  return 0;
}
```

Actually, **static** member functions have limited applications, but one good use
for them is to "preinitialize" private **static** data before any object is actually created. For
example, this is a perfectly valid C++ program:

```
#include <iostream>
using namespace std;

class static_type {
  static int i;
public:
  static void init(int x) {i = x;}
  void show() {cout << i;}
};

int static_type::i; // define i

int main()
{
  // init static data before object creation
  static_type::init(100);

  static_type x;
  x.show(); // displays 100

  return 0;
}
```

When Constructors and Destructors Are Executed

As a general rule, an object's constructor is called when the object comes into existence, and an object's destructor is called when the object is destroyed. Precisely when these events occur is discussed here.

A local object's constructor is executed when the object's declaration statement is encountered. The destructors for local objects are executed in the reverse order of the constructor functions.

Global objects have their constructors execute *before* **main( )** begins execution. Global constructors are executed in order of their declaration, within the same file. You cannot know the order of execution of global constructors spread among several files. Global destructors execute in reverse order *after* **main( )** has terminated.

This program illustrates when constructors and destructors are executed:

```
#include <iostream>
using namespace std;
```

```
class myclass {
public:
  int who;
  myclass(int id);
  ~myclass();
} glob_ob1(1), glob_ob2(2);

myclass::myclass(int id)
{
  cout << "Initializing " << id << "\n";
  who = id;
}

myclass::~myclass()
{
  cout << "Destructing " << who << "\n";
}

int main()
{
  myclass local_ob1(3);

  cout << "This will not be first line displayed.\n";

  myclass local_ob2(4);

  return 0;
}
```

It displays this output:

```
Initializing 1
Initializing 2
Initializing 3
This will not be first line displayed.
Initializing 4
Destructing 4
Destructing 3
Destructing 2
Destructing 1
```

One thing: Because of differences between compilers and execution environments, you may or may not see the last two lines of output.

The Scope Resolution Operator

As you know, the **::** operator links a class name with a member name in order to tell the compiler what class the member belongs to. However, the scope resolution operator has another related use: it can allow access to a name in an enclosing scope that is "hidden" by a local declaration of the same name. For example, consider this fragment:

```
int i;  // global i

void f()
{
  int i; // local i

  i = 10; // uses local i
  .
  .
  .
}
```

As the comment suggests, the assignment **i = 10** refers to the local **i**. But what if function **f( )** needs to access the global version of **i**? It may do so by preceding the **i** with the **::** operator, as shown here.

```
int i;  // global i

void f()
{
  int i; // local i

  ::i = 10; // now refers to global i
  .
  .
  .
}
```

Nested Classes

It is possible to define one class within another. Doing so creates a *nested* class. Since a **class** declaration does, in fact, define a scope, a nested class is valid only within the scope of the enclosing class. Frankly, nested classes are seldom used. Because of C++'s flexible and powerful inheritance mechanism, the need for nested classes is virtually nonexistent.

Local Classes

A class may be defined within a function. For example, this is a valid C++ program:

```
#include <iostream>
using namespace std;

void f();

int main()
{
  f();
  // myclass not known here
  return 0;
}

void f()
{
  class myclass {
    int i;
  public:
    void put_i(int n) { i=n; }
    int get_i() { return i; }
  } ob;

  ob.put_i(10);
  cout << ob.get_i();
}
```

When a class is declared within a function, it is known only to that function and unknown outside of it.

Several restrictions apply to local classes. First, all member functions must be defined within the class declaration. The local class may not use or access local variables of the function in which it is declared (except that a local class has access to **static** local variables declared within the function or those declared as **extern**). It may access type names and enumerators defined by the enclosing function, however. No **static** variables may be declared inside a local class. Because of these restrictions, local classes are not common in C++ programming.

Passing Objects to Functions

Objects may be passed to functions in just the same way that any other type of variable can. Objects are passed to functions through the use of the standard call-by-value mechanism. Although the passing of objects is straightforward, some rather

unexpected events occur that relate to constructors and destructors. To understand
why, consider this short program.

```cpp
// Passing an object to a function.
#include <iostream>
using namespace std;

class myclass {
  int i;
public:
  myclass(int n);
  ~myclass();
  void set_i(int n) { i=n; }
  int get_i() { return i; }
};

myclass::myclass(int n)
{
  i = n;
  cout << "Constructing " << i << "\n";
}

myclass::~myclass()
{
  cout << "Destroying " << i << "\n";
}

void f(myclass ob);

int main()
{
  myclass o(1);

  f(o);
  cout << "This is i in main: ";
  cout << o.get_i() << "\n";

  return 0;
}

void f(myclass ob)
{
  ob.set_i(2);
```

```
    cout << "This is local i: " << ob.get_i();
    cout << "\n";
}
```

This program produces this output:

```
Constructing 1
This is local i: 2
Destroying 2
This is i in main: 1
Destroying 1
```

As the output shows, there is one call to the constructor, which occurs when **o** is created in **main( )**, but there are *two* calls to the destructor. Let's see why this is the case.

When an object is passed to a function, a copy of that object is made (and this copy becomes the parameter in the function). This means that a new object comes into existence. When the function terminates, the copy of the argument (i.e., the parameter) is destroyed. This raises two fundamental questions: First, is the object's constructor called when the copy is made? Second, is the object's destructor called when the copy is destroyed? The answers may, at first, surprise you.

When a copy of an argument is made during a function call, the normal constructor is *not* called. Instead, the object's *copy constructor* is called. A copy constructor defines how a copy of an object is made. As explained in Chapter 14, you can explicitly define a copy constructor for a class that you create . However, if a class does not explicitly define a copy constructor, as is the case here, then C++ provides one by default. The default copy constructor creates a bitwise (that is, identical) copy of the object. The reason a bitwise copy is made is easy to understand if you think about it. Since a normal constructor is used to initialize some aspect of an object, it must not be called to make a copy of an already existing object. Such a call would alter the contents of the object. When passing an object to a function, you want to use the current state of the object, not its initial state.

However, when the function terminates and the copy of the object used as an argument is destroyed, the destructor *is* called. This is necessary because the object has gone out of scope. This is why the preceding program had two calls to the destructor. The first was when the parameter to **f( )** went out-of-scope. The second is when **o** inside **main( )** was destroyed when the program ended.

To summarize: When a copy of an object is created to be used as an argument to a function, the normal constructor is not called. Instead, the default copy constructor makes a bit-by-bit identical copy. However, when the copy is destroyed (usually by going out of scope when the function returns), the destructor is called.

Because the default copy constructor creates an exact duplicate of the original, it can, at times, be a source of trouble. Even though objects are passed to functions by means of the normal call-by-value parameter passing mechanism which, in theory, protects and insulates the calling argument, it is still possible for a side effect to occur that may affect, or even damage, the object used as an argument. For example, if an object used as an argument allocates memory and frees that memory when it is destroyed, then its local copy inside the function will free the same memory when its destructor is called. This will leave the original object damaged and effectively useless. To prevent this type of problem you will need to define the copy operation by creating a copy constructor for the class, as explained in Chapter 14.

Returning Objects

A function may return an object to the caller. For example, this is a valid C++ program:

```
// Returning objects from a function.
#include <iostream>
using namespace std;

class myclass {
  int i;
public:
  void set_i(int n) { i=n; }
  int get_i() { return i; }
};

myclass f();  // return object of type myclass

int main()
{
  myclass o;

  o = f();

  cout << o.get_i() << "\n";

  return 0;
}

myclass f()
{
  myclass x;

  x.set_i(1);
  return x;
}
```

When an object is returned by a function, a temporary object is automatically created that holds the return value. It is this object that is actually returned by the function. After the value has been returned, this object is destroyed. The destruction of this temporary object may cause unexpected side effects in some situations. For example, if the object returned by the function has a destructor that frees dynamically allocated memory, that memory will be freed even though the object that is receiving the return value is still using it. There are ways to overcome this problem that involve overloading the assignment operator (see Chapter 15) and defining a copy constructor (see Chapter 14).

Object Assignment

Assuming that both objects are of the same type, you can assign one object to another. This causes the data of the object on the right side to be copied into the data of the object on the left. For example, this program displays **99**:

```
// Assigning objects.
#include <iostream>
using namespace std;

class myclass {
  int i;
public:
  void set_i(int n) { i=n; }
  int get_i() { return i; }
};

int main()
{
  myclass ob1, ob2;

  ob1.set_i(99);
  ob2 = ob1; // assign data from ob1 to ob2

  cout << "This is ob2's i: " << ob2.get_i();

  return 0;
}
```

By default, all data from one object is assigned to the other by use of a bit-by-bit copy. However, it is possible to overload the assignment operator and define some other assignment procedure (see Chapter 15).

The Complete
Reference

C++

Chapter 13

Arrays, Pointers, References, and the Dynamic Allocation Operators

In Part One, pointers and arrays were examined as they relate to C++'s built-in types. Here, they are discussed relative to objects. This chapter also looks at a feature related to the pointer called a *reference*. The chapter concludes with an examination of C++'s dynamic allocation operators.

Arrays of Objects

In C++, it is possible to have arrays of objects. The syntax for declaring and using an object array is exactly the same as it is for any other type of array. For example, this program uses a three-element array of objects:

```cpp
#include <iostream>
using namespace std;

class cl {
  int i;
public:
  void set_i(int j) { i=j; }
  int get_i() { return i; }
};

int main()
{
  cl ob[3];
  int i;

  for(i=0; i<3; i++) ob[i].set_i(i+1);

  for(i=0; i<3; i++)
    cout << ob[i].get_i() << "\n";

  return 0;
}
```

This program displays the numbers **1**, **2**, and **3** on the screen.

If a class defines a parameterized constructor, you may initialize each object in an array by specifying an initialization list, just like you do for other types of arrays. However, the exact form of the initialization list will be decided by the number of parameters required by the object's constructors. For objects whose constructors have only one parameter, you can simply specify a list of initial values, using the normal array-initialization syntax. As each element in the array is created, a value from the

list is passed to the constructor's parameter. For example, here is a slightly different
version of the preceding program that uses an initialization:

```
#include <iostream>
using namespace std;

class cl {
  int i;
public:
  cl(int j) { i=j; } // constructor
  int get_i() { return i; }
};

int main()
{
  cl ob[3] = {1, 2, 3}; // initializers
  int i;

  for(i=0; i<3; i++)
    cout << ob[i].get_i() << "\n";

  return 0;
}
```

As before, this program displays the numbers **1**, **2**, and **3** on the screen.

Actually, the initialization syntax shown in the preceding program is shorthand for
this longer form:

```
cl ob[3] = { cl(1), cl(2), cl(3) };
```

Here, the constructor for **cl** is invoked explicitly. Of course, the short form used in the
program is more common. The short form works because of the automatic conversion
that applies to constructors taking only one argument (see Chapter 12). Thus, the short
form can only be used to initialize object arrays whose constructors only require one
argument.

If an object's constructor requires two or more arguments, you will have to use the
longer initialization form. For example,

```
#include <iostream>
using namespace std;
```

```
class cl {
  int h;
  int i;
public:
  cl(int j, int k) { h=j; i=k; } // constructor with 2 parameters
  int get_i() {return i;}
  int get_h() {return h;}
};

int main()
{
  cl ob[3] = {
    cl(1, 2), // initialize
    cl(3, 4),
    cl(5, 6)
  };

  int i;

  for(i=0; i<3; i++) {
    cout << ob[i].get_h();
    cout << ", ";
    cout << ob[i].get_i() << "\n";
  }

  return 0;
}
```

Here, **cl**'s constructor has two parameters and, therefore, requires two arguments. This means that the shorthand initialization format cannot be used and the long form, shown in the example, must be employed.

Creating Initialized vs. Uninitialized Arrays

A special case situation occurs if you intend to create both initialized and uninitialized arrays of objects. Consider the following **class.**

```
class cl {
  int i;
public:
  cl(int j) { i=j; }
```

```
   int get_i() { return i; }
};
```

Here, the constructor defined by **cl** requires one parameter. This implies that any array declared of this type must be initialized. That is, it precludes this array declaration:

```
cl a[9]; // error, constructor requires initializers
```

The reason that this statement isn't valid (as **cl** is currently defined) is that it implies that **cl** has a parameterless constructor because no initializers are specified. However, as it stands, **cl** does not have a parameterless constructor. Because there is no valid constructor that corresponds to this declaration, the compiler will report an error. To solve this problem, you need to overload the constructor, adding one that takes no parameters, as shown next. In this way, arrays that are initialized and those that are not are both allowed.

```
class cl {
  int i;
public:
  cl() { i=0; } // called for non-initialized arrays
  cl(int j) { i=j; } // called for initialized arrays
  int get_i() { return i; }
};
```

Given this **class**, both of the following statements are permissible:

```
cl a1[3] = {3, 5, 6}; // initialized
```

```
cl a2[34]; // uninitialized
```

Pointers to Objects

Just as you can have pointers to other types of variables, you can have pointers to objects. When accessing members of a class given a pointer to an object, use the arrow (–>) operator instead of the dot operator. The next program illustrates how to access an object given a pointer to it:

```
#include <iostream>
using namespace std;
```

```
class cl {
  int i;
public:
  cl(int j) { i=j; }
  int get_i() { return i; }
};

int main()
{
  cl ob(88), *p;

  p = &ob; // get address of ob

  cout << p->get_i(); // use -> to call get_i()

  return 0;
}
```

As you know, when a pointer is incremented, it points to the next element of its type. For example, an integer pointer will point to the next integer. In general, all pointer arithmetic is relative to the base type of the pointer. (That is, it is relative to the type of data that the pointer is declared as pointing to.) The same is true of pointers to objects. For example, this program uses a pointer to access all three elements of array **ob** after being assigned **ob**'s starting address:

```
#include <iostream>
using namespace std;

class cl {
  int i;
public:
  cl() { i=0; }
  cl(int j) { i=j; }
  int get_i() { return i; }
};

int main()
{
  cl ob[3] = {1, 2, 3};
```

```
    cl *p;
    int i;

    p = ob; // get start of array
    for(i=0; i<3; i++) {
      cout << p->get_i() << "\n";
      p++; // point to next object
    }

    return 0;
}
```

You can assign the address of a public member of an object to a pointer and then access that member by using the pointer. For example, this is a valid C++ program that displays the number **1** on the screen:

```
#include <iostream>
using namespace std;

class cl {
public:
  int i;
  cl(int j) { i=j; }
};

int main()
{
  cl ob(1);
  int *p;

  p = &ob.i; // get address of ob.i

  cout << *p; // access ob.i via p

  return 0;
}
```

Because **p** is pointing to an integer, it is declared as an integer pointer. It is irrelevant that **i** is a member of **ob** in this situation.

Type Checking C++ Pointers

There is one important thing to understand about pointers in C++: You may assign one pointer to another only if the two pointer types are compatible. For example, given:

```
int *pi;
float *pf;
```

in C++, the following assignment is illegal:

```
pi = pf; // error -- type mismatch
```

Of course, you can override any type incompatibilities using a cast, but doing so bypasses C++'s type-checking mechanism.

The this Pointer

When a member function is called, it is automatically passed an implicit argument that is a pointer to the invoking object (that is, the object on which the function is called). This pointer is called **this**. To understand **this**, first consider a program that creates a class called **pwr** that computes the result of a number raised to some power:

```cpp
#include <iostream>
using namespace std;

class pwr {
  double b;
  int e;
  double val;
public:
  pwr(double base, int exp);
  double get_pwr() { return val; }
};

pwr::pwr(double base, int exp)
{
  b = base;
  e = exp;
  val = 1;
  if(exp==0) return;
  for( ; exp>0; exp--) val = val * b;
```

```
}

int main()
{
  pwr x(4.0, 2), y(2.5, 1), z(5.7, 0);

  cout << x.get_pwr() << " ";
  cout << y.get_pwr() << " ";
  cout << z.get_pwr() << "\n";

  return 0;
}
```

Within a member function, the members of a class can be accessed directly, without any object or class qualification. Thus, inside **pwr( )**, the statement

```
b = base;
```

means that the copy of **b** associated with the invoking object will be assigned the value contained in **base**. However, the same statement can also be written like this:

```
this->b = base;
```

The **this** pointer points to the object that invoked **pwr( )**. Thus, **this –>b** refers to that object's copy of **b**. For example, if **pwr( )** had been invoked by **x** (as in **x(4.0, 2)**), then **this** in the preceding statement would have been pointing to **x**. Writing the statement without using **this** is really just shorthand.

Here is the entire **pwr( )** constructor written using the **this** pointer:

```
pwr::pwr(double base, int exp)
{
  this->b = base;
  this->e = exp;
  this->val = 1;
  if(exp==0) return;
  for( ; exp>0; exp--)
    this->val = this->val * this->b;
}
```

Actually, no C++ programmer would write **pwr( )** as just shown because nothing is gained, and the standard form is easier. However, the **this** pointer is very important when operators are overloaded and whenever a member function must utilize a pointer to the object that invoked it.

Remember that the **this** pointer is automatically passed to all member functions. Therefore, **get_pwr( )** could also be rewritten as shown here:

```
double get_pwr() { return this->val; }
```

In this case, if **get_pwr( )** is invoked like this:

```
y.get_pwr();
```

then **this** will point to object **y**.

Two final points about **this**. First, **friend** functions are not members of a class and, therefore, are not passed a **this** pointer. Second, **static** member functions do not have a **this** pointer.

Pointers to Derived Types

In general, a pointer of one type cannot point to an object of a different type. However, there is an important exception to this rule that relates only to derived classes. To begin, assume two classes called **B** and **D**. Further, assume that **D** is derived from the base class **B**. In this situation, a pointer of type **B *** may also point to an object of type **D**. More generally, a base class pointer can also be used as a pointer to an object of any class derived from that base.

Although a base class pointer can be used to point to a derived object, the opposite is not true. A pointer of type **D *** may not point to an object of type **B**. Further, although you can use a base pointer to point to a derived object, you can access only the members of the derived type that were inherited from the base. That is, you won't be able to access any members added by the derived class. (You can cast a base pointer into a derived pointer and gain full access to the entire derived class, however.)

Here is a short program that illustrates the use of a base pointer to access derived objects.

```
#include <iostream>
using namespace std;

class base {
  int i;
public:
  void set_i(int num) { i=num; }
  int get_i() { return i; }
```

```
};
class derived: public base {
  int j;
public:
  void set_j(int num) { j=num; }
  int get_j() { return j; }
};

int main()
{
  base *bp;
  derived d;

  bp = &d; // base pointer points to derived object

  // access derived object using base pointer
  bp->set_i(10);
  cout << bp->get_i() << " ";

/* The following won't work. You can't access elements of
   a derived class using a base class pointer.

  bp->set_j(88); // error
  cout << bp->get_j(); // error

*/
  return 0;
}
```

As you can see, a base pointer is used to access an object of a derived class.

Although you must be careful, it is possible to cast a base pointer into a pointer of the derived type to access a member of the derived class through the base pointer. For example, this is valid C++ code:

```
// access now allowed because of cast
((derived *)bp)->set_j(88);
cout << ((derived *)bp)->get_j();
```

It is important to remember that pointer arithmetic is relative to the base type of the pointer. For this reason, when a base pointer is pointing to a derived object, incrementing the pointer does not cause it to point to the next object of the derived type. Instead, it will point to what it thinks is the next object of the base type. This, of course, usually spells trouble. For example, this program, while syntactically correct, contains this error.

```
// This program contains an error.
#include <iostream>
using namespace std;

class base {
  int i;
public:
  void set_i(int num) { i=num; }
  int get_i() { return i; }
};

class derived: public base {
  int j;
public:
  void set_j(int num) {j=num;}
  int get_j() {return j;}
};

int main()
{
  base *bp;
  derived d[2];

  bp = d;

  d[0].set_i(1);
  d[1].set_i(2);

  cout << bp->get_i() << " ";
  bp++; // relative to base, not derived
  cout << bp->get_i(); // garbage value displayed

  return 0;
}
```

The use of base pointers to derived types is most useful when creating run-time polymorphism through the mechanism of virtual functions (see Chapter 17).

Pointers to Class Members

C++ allows you to generate a special type of pointer that "points" generically to a member of a class, not to a specific instance of that member in an object. This sort of pointer is called a *pointer to a class member* or a *pointer-to-member*, for short. A pointer to a member is not the same as a normal C++ pointer. Instead, a pointer to a member provides only an offset into an object of the member's class at which that member can be found. Since member pointers are not true pointers, the **.** and **–>** cannot be applied to them. To access a member of a class given a pointer to it, you must use the special pointer-to-member operators **.*** and **–>***. Their job is to allow you to access a member of a class given a pointer to that member.

Here is an example:

```
#include <iostream>
using namespace std;

class cl {
public:
  cl(int i) { val=i; }
  int val;
  int double_val() { return val+val; }
};

int main()
{
  int cl::*data; // data member pointer
  int (cl::*func)(); // function member pointer
  cl ob1(1), ob2(2); // create objects

  data = &cl::val; // get offset of val
  func = &cl::double_val; // get offset of double_val()

  cout << "Here are values: ";
  cout << ob1.*data << " " << ob2.*data << "\n";

  cout << "Here they are doubled: ";
  cout << (ob1.*func)() << " ";
  cout << (ob2.*func)() << "\n";

  return 0;
}
```

In **main( )**, this program creates two member pointers: **data** and **func**. Note carefully the syntax of each declaration. When declaring pointers to members, you must specify the class and use the scope resolution operator. The program also creates objects of **cl** called **ob1** and **ob2**. As the program illustrates, member pointers may point to either functions or data. Next, the program obtains the addresses of **val** and **double_val( )**. As stated earlier, these "addresses" are really just offsets into an object of type **cl**, at which point **val** and **double_val( )** will be found. Next, to display the values of each object's **val**, each is accessed through **data**. Finally, the program uses **func** to call the **double_val( )** function. The extra parentheses are necessary in order to correctly associate the .* operator.

When you are accessing a member of an object by using an object or a reference (discussed later in this chapter), you must use the .* operator. However, if you are using a pointer to the object, you need to use the –>* operator, as illustrated in this version of the preceding program:

```cpp
#include <iostream>
using namespace std;

class cl {
public:
  cl(int i) { val=i; }
  int val;
  int double_val() { return val+val; }
};

int main()
{
  int cl::*data; // data member pointer
  int (cl::*func)(); // function member pointer
  cl ob1(1), ob2(2); // create objects
  cl *p1, *p2;

  p1 = &ob1; // access objects through a pointer
  p2 = &ob2;

  data = &cl::val; // get offset of val
  func = &cl::double_val; // get offset of double_val()

  cout << "Here are values: ";
  cout << p1->*data << " " << p2->*data << "\n";

  cout << "Here they are doubled: ";
```

```
    cout << (p1->*func)() << " ";
    cout << (p2->*func)() << "\n";

    return 0;
}
```

In this version, **p1** and **p2** are pointers to objects of type **cl**. Therefore, the **–>*** operator is used to access **val** and **double_val( )**.

Remember, pointers to members are different from pointers to specific instances of elements of an object. Consider this fragment (assume that **cl** is declared as shown in the preceding programs):

```
int cl::*d;
int *p;
cl o;

p = &o.val // this is address of a specific val

d = &cl::val // this is offset of generic val
```

Here, **p** is a pointer to an integer inside a *specific* object. However, **d** is simply an offset that indicates where **val** will be found in any object of type **cl**.

In general, pointer-to-member operators are applied in special-case situations. They are not typically used in day-to-day programming.

References

C++ contains a feature that is related to the pointer called a *reference*. A reference is essentially an implicit pointer. There are three ways that a reference can be used: as a function parameter, as a function return value, or as a stand-alone reference. Each is examined here.

Reference Parameters

Probably the most important use for a reference is to allow you to create functions that automatically use call-by-reference parameter passing. As explained in Chapter 6, arguments can be passed to functions in one of two ways: using call-by-value or call-by-reference. When using call-by-value, a copy of the argument is passed to the function. Call-by-reference passes the address of the argument to the function. By default, C++ uses call-by-value, but it provides two ways to achieve call-by-reference parameter passing. First, you can explicitly pass a pointer to the argument. Second, you can use a reference parameter. For most circumstances the best way is to use a reference parameter.

To fully understand what a reference parameter is and why it is valuable, we will begin by reviewing how a call-by-reference can be generated using a pointer parameter. The following program manually creates a call-by-reference parameter using a pointer in the function called **neg( )**, which reverses the sign of the integer variable pointed to by its argument.

```
// Manually create a call-by-reference using a pointer.
#include <iostream>
using namespace std;

void neg(int *i);

int main()
{
  int x;

  x = 10;
  cout << x << " negated is ";

  neg(&x);
  cout << x << "\n";

  return 0;
}

void neg(int *i)
{
  *i = -*i;
}
```

In this program, **neg( )** takes as a parameter a pointer to the integer whose sign it will reverse. Therefore, **neg( )** must be explicitly called with the address of **x**. Further, inside **neg( )** the * operator must be used to access the variable pointed to by **i**. This is how you generate a "manual" call-by-reference in C++, and it is the only way to obtain a call-by-reference using the C subset. Fortunately, in C++ you can automate this feature by using a reference parameter.

To create a reference parameter, precede the parameter's name with an **&**. For example, here is how to declare **neg( )** with **i** declared as a reference parameter:

```
void neg(int &i);
```

For all practical purposes, this causes **i** to become another name for whatever argument **neg( )** is called with. Any operations that are applied to **i** actually affect the calling argument. In technical terms, **i** is an implicit pointer that automatically refers to the argument used in the call to **neg( )**. Once **i** has been made into a reference, it is no longer necessary (or even legal) to apply the * operator. Instead, each time **i** is used, it is implicitly a reference to the argument and any changes made to **i** affect the argument. Further, when calling **neg( )**, it is no longer necessary (or legal) to precede the argument's name with the **&** operator. Instead, the compiler does this automatically. Here is the reference version of the preceding program:

```cpp
// Use a reference parameter.
#include <iostream>
using namespace std;

void neg(int &i); // i now a reference

int main()
{
  int x;

  x = 10;
  cout << x << " negated is ";

  neg(x); // no longer need the & operator
  cout << x << "\n";

  return 0;
}

void neg(int &i)
{
  i = -i; // i is now a reference, don't need *
}
```

To review: When you create a reference parameter, it automatically refers to (implicitly points to) the argument used to call the function. Therefore, in the preceding program, the statement

```cpp
i = -i ;
```

actually operates on **x,** not on a copy of **x**. There is no need to apply the **&** operator to an argument. Also, inside the function, the reference parameter is used directly without the need to apply the * operator. In general, when you assign a value to a reference, you are actually assigning that value to the variable that the reference points to.

Inside the function, it is not possible to change what the reference parameter is pointing to. That is, a statement like

```
i++:
```

inside **neg( )** increments the value of the variable used in the call. It does not cause **i** to point to some new location.

Here is another example. This program uses reference parameters to swap the values of the variables it is called with. The **swap( )** function is the classic example of call-by-reference parameter passing.

```cpp
#include <iostream>
using namespace std;

void swap(int &i, int &j);

int main()
{
  int a, b, c, d;

  a = 1;
  b = 2;
  c = 3;
  d = 4;

  cout << "a and b: " << a << " " << b << "\n";
  swap(a, b); // no & operator needed
  cout << "a and b: " << a << " " << b << "\n";

  cout << "c and d: " << c << " " << d << "\n";
  swap(c, d);
  cout << "c and d: " << c << " " << d << "\n";

  return 0;
}

void swap(int &i, int &j)
{
  int t;

  t = i; // no * operator needed
```

```
   i = j;
   j = t;
}
```

This program displays the following:

```
a and b: 1 2
a and b: 2 1
c and d: 3 4
c and d: 4 3
```

Passing References to Objects

In Chapter 12 it was explained that when an object is passed as an argument to a function, a copy of that object is made. When the function terminates, the copy's destructor is called. However, when you pass by reference, no copy of the object is made. This means that no object used as a parameter is destroyed when the function terminates, and the parameter's destructor is not called. For example, try this program:

```cpp
#include <iostream>
using namespace std;

class cl {
  int id;
public:
  int i;
  cl(int i);
  ~cl();
  void neg(cl &o) { o.i = -o.i; } // no temporary created
};

cl::cl(int num)
{
  cout << "Constructing " << num << "\n";
  id = num;
}

cl::~cl()
{
  cout << "Destructing " << id << "\n";
}
```

```
int main()
{
  cl o(1);

  o.i = 10;
  o.neg(o);

  cout << o.i << "\n";

  return 0;
}
```

Here is the output of this program:

```
Constructing 1
-10
Destructing 1
```

As you can see, only one call is made to **cl**'s destructor. Had **o** been passed by value, a second object would have been created inside **neg( )**, and the destructor would have been called a second time when that object was destroyed at the time **neg( )** terminated.

As the code inside **neg( )** illustrates, when you access a member of a class through a reference, you use the dot operator. The arrow operator is reserved for use with pointers only.

When passing parameters by reference, remember that changes to the object inside the function affect the calling object.

One other point: Passing all but the smallest objects by reference is faster than passing them by value. Arguments are usually passed on the stack. Thus, large objects take a considerable number of CPU cycles to push onto and pop from the stack.

Returning References

A function may return a reference. This has the rather startling effect of allowing a function to be used on the left side of an assignment statement! For example, consider this simple program:

```
#include <iostream>
using namespace std;

char &replace(int i); // return a reference
```

```
char s[80] = "Hello There";

int main()
{

  replace(5) = 'X'; // assign X to space after Hello

  cout << s;

  return 0;
}

char &replace(int i)
{
  return s[i];
}
```

This program replaces the space between **Hello** and **There** with an **X**. That is, the program displays **HelloXthere**. Take a look at how this is accomplished. First, **replace( )** is declared as returning a reference to a character. As **replace( )** is coded, it returns a reference to the element of **s** that is specified by its argument **i**. The reference returned by **replace( )** is then used in **main( )** to assign to that element the character **X**.

One thing you must be careful about when returning references is that the object being referred to does not go out of scope after the function terminates.

Independent References

By far the most common uses for references are to pass an argument using call-by-reference and to act as a return value from a function. However, you can declare a reference that is simply a variable. This type of reference is called an *independent reference*.

When you create an independent reference, all you are creating is another name for an object. All independent references must be initialized when they are created. The reason for this is easy to understand. Aside from initialization, you cannot change what object a reference variable points to. Therefore, it must be initialized when it is declared. (In C++, initialization is a wholly separate operation from assignment.)

The following program illustrates an independent reference:

```
#include <iostream>
using namespace std;
```

```
int main()
{
  int a;
  int &ref = a; // independent reference

  a = 10;
  cout << a << " " << ref << "\n";

  ref = 100;
  cout << a << " " << ref << "\n";

  int b = 19;
  ref = b; // this puts b's value into a
  cout << a << " " << ref << "\n";

  ref--; // this decrements a
         // it does not affect what ref refers to

  cout << a << " " << ref << "\n";

  return 0;
}
```

The program displays this output:

```
10 10
100 100
19 19
18 18
```

Actually, independent references are of little real value because each one is, literally, just another name for another variable. Having two names to describe the same object is likely to confuse, not organize, your program.

References to Derived Types

Similar to the situation as described for pointers earlier, a base class reference can be used to refer to an object of a derived class. The most common application of this is found in function parameters. A base class reference parameter can receive objects of the base class as well as any other type derived from that base.

Restrictions to References

There are a number of restrictions that apply to references. You cannot reference another reference. Put differently, you cannot obtain the address of a reference. You cannot create arrays of references. You cannot create a pointer to a reference. You cannot reference a bit-field.

A reference variable must be initialized when it is declared unless it is a member of a class, a function parameter, or a return value. Null references are prohibited.

A Matter of Style

When declaring pointer and reference variables, some C++ programmers use a unique coding style that associates the * or the & with the type name and not the variable. For example, here are two functionally equivalent declarations:

```
int& p; // & associated with type
int &p; // & associated with variable
```

Associating the * or & with the type name reflects the desire of some programmers for C++ to contain a separate pointer type. However, the trouble with associating the & or * with the type name rather than the variable is that, according to the formal C++ syntax, neither the & nor the * is distributive over a list of variables. Thus, misleading declarations are easily created. For example, the following declaration creates *one, not two*, integer pointers.

```
int* a, b;
```

Here, **b** is declared as an integer (not an integer pointer) because, as specified by the C++ syntax, when used in a declaration, the * (or &) is linked to the individual variable that it precedes, not to the type that it follows. The trouble with this declaration is that the visual message suggests that both **a** and **b** are pointer types, even though, in fact, only **a** is a pointer. This visual confusion not only misleads novice C++ programmers, but occasionally old pros, too.

It is important to understand that, as far as the C++ compiler is concerned, it doesn't matter whether you write **int *p** or **int* p.** Thus, if you prefer to associate the * or & with the type rather than the variable, feel free to do so. However, to avoid confusion, this book will continue to associate the * and the & with the variables that they modify rather than their types.

C++'s Dynamic Allocation Operators

C++ provides two dynamic allocation operators: **new** and **delete**. These operators are used to allocate and free memory at run time. Dynamic allocation is an important part of almost all real-world programs. As explained in Part One, C++ also supports dynamic memory allocation functions, called **malloc( )** and **free( )**. These are included for the sake of compatibility with C. However, for C++ code, you should use the **new** and **delete** operators because they have several advantages.

The **new** operator allocates memory and returns a pointer to the start of it. The **delete** operator frees memory previously allocated using **new**. The general forms of **new** and **delete** are shown here:

p_var = new *type*;
delete *p_var*;

Here, *p_var* is a pointer variable that receives a pointer to memory that is large enough to hold an item of type *type*.

Since the heap is finite, it can become exhausted. If there is insufficient available memory to fill an allocation request, then **new** will fail and a **bad_alloc** exception will be generated. This exception is defined in the header **<new>**. Your program should handle this exception and take appropriate action if a failure occurs. (Exception handling is described in Chapter 19.) If this exception is not handled by your program, then your program will be terminated.

The actions of **new** on failure as just described are specified by Standard C++. The trouble is that not all compilers, especially older ones, will have implemented **new** in compliance with Standard C++. When C++ was first invented, **new** returned null on failure. Later, this was changed such that **new** caused an exception on failure. Finally, it was decided that a **new** failure will generate an exception by default, but that a null pointer could be returned instead, as an option. Thus, **new** has been implemented differently, at different times, by compiler manufacturers. Although all compilers will eventually implement **new** in compliance with Standard C++, currently the only way to know the precise action of **new** on failure is to check your compiler's documentation.

Since Standard C++ specifies that **new** generates an exception on failure, this is the way the code in this book is written. If your compiler handles an allocation failure differently, you will need to make the appropriate changes.

Here is a program that allocates memory to hold an integer:

```
#include <iostream>
#include <new>
using namespace std;

int main()
{
  int *p;

  try {
```

```
    p = new int; // allocate space for an int
} catch (bad_alloc xa) {
  cout << "Allocation Failure\n";
  return 1;
}

*p = 100;

cout << "At " << p << " ";
cout << "is the value " << *p << "\n";

delete p;

return 0;
}
```

This program assigns to **p** an address in the heap that is large enough to hold an integer. It then assigns that memory the value 100 and displays the contents of the memory on the screen. Finally, it frees the dynamically allocated memory. Remember, if your compiler implements **new** such that it returns null on failure, you must change the preceding program appropriately.

The **delete** operator must be used only with a valid pointer previously allocated by using **new**. Using any other type of pointer with **delete** is undefined and will almost certainly cause serious problems, such as a system crash.

Although **new** and **delete** perform functions similar to **malloc( )** and **free( )**, they have several advantages. First, **new** automatically allocates enough memory to hold an object of the specified type. You do not need to use the **sizeof** operator. Because the size is computed automatically, it eliminates any possibility for error in this regard. Second, **new** automatically returns a pointer of the specified type. You don't need to use an explicit type cast as you do when allocating memory by using **malloc( )**. Finally, both **new** and **delete** can be overloaded, allowing you to create customized allocation systems.

Although there is no formal rule that states this, it is best not to mix **new** and **delete** with **malloc( )** and **free( )** in the same program. There is no guarantee that they are mutually compatible.

Initializing Allocated Memory

You can initialize allocated memory to some known value by putting an initializer after the type name in the **new** statement. Here is the general form of **new** when an initialization is included:

   p_var = new *var_type (initializer);*

Of course, the type of the initializer must be compatible with the type of data for which memory is being allocated.

This program gives the allocated integer an initial value of 87:

```
#include <iostream>
#include <new>
using namespace std;

int main()
{
  int *p;

  try {
    p = new int (87); // initialize to 87
  } catch (bad_alloc xa) {
    cout << "Allocation Failure\n";
    return 1;
  }

  cout << "At " << p << " ";
  cout << "is the value " << *p << "\n";

  delete p;

  return 0;
}
```

Allocating Arrays

You can allocate arrays using **new** by using this general form:

p_var = new *array_type [size]*;

Here, *size* specifies the number of elements in the array.

To free an array, use this form of **delete:**

delete [ ] *p_var*;

Here, the [ ] informs **delete** that an array is being released.

For example, the next program allocates a 10-element integer array.

```
#include <iostream>
#include <new>
using namespace std;

int main()
{
  int *p, i;

  try {
    p = new int [10]; // allocate 10 integer array
  } catch (bad_alloc xa) {
    cout << "Allocation Failure\n";
    return 1;
  }

  for(i=0; i<10; i++ )
    p[i] = i;

  for(i=0; i<10; i++)
    cout << p[i] << " ";

  delete [] p; // release the array

  return 0;
}
```

Notice the **delete** statement. As just mentioned, when an array allocated by **new** is released, **delete** must be made aware that an array is being freed by using the [ ]. (As you will see in the next section, this is especially important when you are allocating arrays of objects.)

One restriction applies to allocating arrays: They may not be given initial values. That is, you may not specify an initializer when allocating arrays.

Allocating Objects

You can allocate objects dynamically by using **new**. When you do this, an object is created and a pointer is returned to it. The dynamically created object acts just like any other object. When it is created, its constructor (if it has one) is called. When the object is freed, its destructor is executed.

Here is a short program that creates a class called **balance** that links a person's name with his or her account balance. Inside **main( )**, an object of type **balance** is created dynamically.

```cpp
#include <iostream>
#include <new>
#include <cstring>
using namespace std;

class balance {
  double cur_bal;
  char name[80];
public:
  void set(double n, char *s) {
    cur_bal = n;
    strcpy(name, s);
  }

  void get_bal(double &n, char *s) {
    n = cur_bal;
    strcpy(s, name);
  }
};

int main()
{
  balance *p;
  char s[80];
  double n;

  try {
    p = new balance;
  } catch (bad_alloc xa) {
    cout << "Allocation Failure\n";
    return 1;
  }

  p->set(12387.87, "Ralph Wilson");

  p->get_bal(n, s);

  cout << s << "'s balance is: " << n;
```

```
    cout << "\n";

    delete p;

    return 0;
}
```

Because **p** contains a pointer to an object, the arrow operator is used to access members of the object.

As stated, dynamically allocated objects may have constructors and destructors. Also, the constructors can be parameterized. Examine this version of the previous program:

```
#include <iostream>
#include <new>
#include <cstring>
using namespace std;

class balance {
  double cur_bal;
  char name[80];
public:
  balance(double n, char *s) {
    cur_bal = n;
    strcpy(name, s);
  }
  ~balance() {
    cout << "Destructing ";
    cout << name << "\n";
  }
  void get_bal(double &n, char *s) {
    n = cur_bal;
    strcpy(s, name);
  }
};

int main()
{
  balance *p;
  char s[80];
  double n;
```

```
// this version uses an initializer
try {
  p = new balance (12387.87, "Ralph Wilson");
} catch (bad_alloc xa) {
  cout << "Allocation Failure\n";
  return 1;
}

p->get_bal(n, s);

cout << s << "'s balance is: " << n;
cout << "\n";

delete p;

return 0;
}
```

Notice that the parameters to the object's constructor are specified after the type name, just as in other sorts of initializations.

You can allocate arrays of objects, but there is one catch. Since no array allocated by **new** can have an initializer, you must make sure that if the class contains constructors, one will be parameterless. If you don't, the C++ compiler will not find a matching constructor when you attempt to allocate the array and will not compile your program.

In this version of the preceding program, an array of **balance** objects is allocated, and the parameterless constructor is called.

```
#include <iostream>
#include <new>
#include <cstring>
using namespace std;

class balance {
  double cur_bal;
  char name[80];
public:
  balance(double n, char *s) {
    cur_bal = n;
    strcpy(name, s);
  }
  balance() {} // parameterless constructor
```

```
  ~balance() {
    cout << "Destructing ";
    cout << name << "\n";
  }
  void set(double n, char *s) {
    cur_bal = n;
    strcpy(name, s);
  }
  void get_bal(double &n, char *s) {
    n = cur_bal;
    strcpy(s, name);
  }
};

int main()
{
  balance *p;
  char s[80];
  double n;
  int i;

  try {
    p = new balance [3]; // allocate entire array
  } catch (bad_alloc xa) {
    cout << "Allocation Failure\n";
    return 1;
  }

  // note use of dot, not arrow operators
  p[0].set(12387.87, "Ralph Wilson");
  p[1].set(144.00, "A. C. Conners");
  p[2].set(-11.23, "I. M. Overdrawn");

  for(i=0; i<3; i++) {
    p[i].get_bal(n, s);

    cout << s << "'s balance is: " << n;
    cout << "\n";
  }

  delete [] p;
  return 0;
}
```

C++

The output from this program is shown here.

```
Ralph Wilson's balance is: 12387.9
A. C. Conners's balance is: 144
I. M. Overdrawn's balance is: -11.23
Destructing I. M. Overdrawn
Destructing A. C. Conners
Destructing Ralph Wilson
```

One reason that you need to use the **delete [ ]** form when deleting an array of dynamically allocated objects is so that the destructor can be called for each object in the array.

The nothrow Alternative

In Standard C++ it is possible to have **new** return **null** instead of throwing an exception when an allocation failure occurs. This form of **new** is most useful when you are compiling older code with a modern C++ compiler. It is also valuable when you are replacing calls to **malloc( )** with **new**. (This is common when updating C code to C++.) This form of **new** is shown here:

p_var = new(nothrow) *type*;

Here, *p_var* is a pointer variable of *type*. The **nothrow** form of **new** works like the original version of **new** from years ago. Since it returns null on failure, it can be "dropped into" older code without having to add exception handling. However, for new code, exceptions provide a better alternative. To use the **nothrow** option, you must include the header **<new>**.

The following program shows how to use the **new(nothrow)** alternative.

```cpp
// Demonstrate nothrow version of new.
#include <iostream>
#include <new>
using namespace std;

int main()
{
  int *p, i;

  p = new(nothrow) int[32]; // use nothrow option
  if(!p) {
    cout << "Allocation failure.\n";
```

```
      return 1;
  }

  for(i=0; i<32; i++) p[i] = i;

  for(i=0; i<32; i++) cout << p[i] << " ";

  delete [] p; // free the memory

  return 0;
}
```

As this program demonstrates, when using the **nothrow** approach, you must check the pointer returned by **new** after each allocation request.

The Placement Form of new

There is a special form of **new**, called the *placement form*, that can be used to specify an alternative method of allocating memory. It is primarily useful when overloading the **new** operator for special circumstances. Here is its general form:

> *p_var* = new (*arg-list*) *type*;

Here, *arg-list* is a comma-separated list of values passed to an overloaded form of **new**.

Chapter 14

Function Overloading, Copy Constructors, and Default Arguments

This chapter examines function overloading, copy constructors, and default arguments. Function overloading is one of the defining aspects of the C++ programming language. Not only does it provide support for compile-time polymorphism, it also adds flexibility and convenience. Some of the most commonly overloaded functions are constructors. Perhaps the most important form of an overloaded constructor is the copy constructor. Closely related to function overloading are default arguments. Default arguments can sometimes provide an alternative to function overloading.

Function Overloading

Function overloading is the process of using the same name for two or more functions. The secret to overloading is that each redefinition of the function must use either different types of parameters or a different number of parameters. It is only through these differences that the compiler knows which function to call in any given situation. For example, this program overloads **myfunc( )** by using different types of parameters.

```
#include <iostream>
using namespace std;

int myfunc(int i); // these differ in types of parameters
double myfunc(double i);

int main()
{

  cout << myfunc(10) << " "; // calls myfunc(int i)
  cout << myfunc(5.4); // calls myfunc(double i)

  return 0;
}

double myfunc(double i)
{
  return i;
}

int myfunc(int i)
{
  return i;
}
```

The next program overloads **myfunc( )** using a different number of parameters:

```
#include <iostream>
using namespace std;

int myfunc(int i); // these differ in number of parameters
int myfunc(int i, int j);

int main()
{
  cout << myfunc(10) << " "; // calls myfunc(int i)
  cout << myfunc(4, 5); // calls myfunc(int i, int j)

  return 0;
}

int myfunc(int i)
{
  return i;
}

int myfunc(int i, int j)
{
  return i*j;
}
```

As mentioned, the key point about function overloading is that the functions must differ in regard to the types and/or number of parameters. Two functions differing only in their return types cannot be overloaded. For example, this is an invalid attempt to overload **myfunc( )**:

```
int myfunc(int i);   // Error: differing return types are
float myfunc(int i); // insufficient when overloading.
```

Sometimes, two function declarations will appear to differ, when in fact they do not. For example, consider the following declarations.

```
void f(int *p);
void f(int p[]); // error, *p is same as p[]
```

Remember, to the compiler ***p** is the same as **p[ ]**. Therefore, although the two prototypes appear to differ in the types of their parameter, in actuality they do not.

Overloading Constructors

Constructors can be overloaded; in fact, overloaded constructors are very common. There are three main reasons why you will want to overload a constructor: to gain flexibility, to allow both initialized and uninitialized objects to be created, and to define copy constructors. In this section, the first two of these are examined. The following section describes the copy constructor.

Overloading a Constructor to Gain Flexibility

Many times you will create a class for which there are two or more possible ways to construct an object. In these cases, you will want to provide an overloaded constructor for each way. This is a self-enforcing rule because if you attempt to create an object for which there is no matching constructor, a compile-time error results.

By providing a constructor for each way that a user of your class may plausibly want to construct an object, you increase the flexibility of your class. The user is free to choose the best way to construct an object given the specific circumstance. Consider this program that creates a class called **date**, which holds a calendar date. Notice that the constructor is overloaded two ways:

```
#include <iostream>
#include <cstdio>
using namespace std;

class date {
  int day, month, year;
public:
  date(char *d);
  date(int m, int d, int y);
  void show_date();
};

// Initialize using string.
date::date(char *d)
{
  sscanf(d, "%d%*c%d%*c%d", &month, &day, &year);
}

// Initialize using integers.
date::date(int m, int d, int y)
{
```

```
    day = d;
    month = m;
    year = y;
}

void date::show_date()
{
    cout << month << "/" << day;
    cout << "/" << year << "\n";
}

int main()
{
    date ob1(12, 4, 2003), ob2("10/22/2003");

    ob1.show_date();
    ob2.show_date();

    return 0;
}
```

In this program, you can initialize an object of type **date**, either by specifying the date using three integers to represent the month, day, and year, or by using a string that contains the date in this general form:

mm/dd/yyyy

Since both are common ways to represent a date, it makes sense that **date** allow both when constructing an object.

As the **date** class illustrates, perhaps the most common reason to overload a constructor is to allow an object to be created by using the most appropriate and natural means for each particular circumstance. For example, in the following **main( )**, the user is prompted for the date, which is input to array **s**. This string can then be used directly to create **d**. There is no need for it to be converted to any other form. However, if **date( )** were not overloaded to accept the string form, you would have to manually convert it into three integers.

```
int main()
{
    char s[80];
```

```
cout << "Enter new date: ";
cin >> s;

date d(s);
d.show_date();

return 0;
}
```

In another situation, initializing an object of type **date** by using three integers may be more convenient. For example, if the date is generated by some sort of computational method, then creating a **date** object using **date(int, int, int)** is the most natural and appropriate constructor to employ. The point here is that by overloading **date**'s constructor, you have made it more flexible and easier to use. This increased flexibility and ease of use are especially important if you are creating class libraries that will be used by other programmers.

Allowing Both Initialized and Uninitialized Objects

Another common reason constructors are overloaded is to allow both initialized and uninitialized objects (or, more precisely, default initialized objects) to be created. This is especially important if you want to be able to create dynamic arrays of objects of some class, since it is not possible to initialize a dynamically allocated array. To allow uninitialized arrays of objects along with initialized objects, you must include a constructor that supports initialization and one that does not.

For example, the following program declares two arrays of type **powers**; one is initialized and the other is not. It also dynamically allocates an array.

```
#include <iostream>
#include <new>
using namespace std;

class powers {
  int x;
public:
  // overload constructor two ways
  powers() { x = 0; } // no initializer
  powers(int n) { x = n; } // initializer

  int getx() { return x; }
  void setx(int i) { x = i; }
```

```
};

int main()
{
  powers ofTwo[] = {1, 2, 4, 8, 16}; // initialized
  powers ofThree[5]; // uninitialized
  powers *p;
  int i;

  // show powers of two
  cout << "Powers of two: ";
  for(i=0; i<5; i++) {
    cout << ofTwo[i].getx() << " ";
  }
  cout << "\n\n";

  // set powers of three
  ofThree[0].setx(1);
  ofThree[1].setx(3);
  ofThree[2].setx(9);
  ofThree[3].setx(27);
  ofThree[4].setx(81);

  // show powers of three
  cout << "Powers of three: ";
  for(i=0; i<5; i++) {
    cout << ofThree[i].getx() << " ";
  }
  cout << "\n\n";

  // dynamically allocate an array
  try {
    p = new powers[5]; // no initialization
  } catch (bad_alloc xa) {
      cout << "Allocation Failure\n";
      return 1;
  }

  // initialize dynamic array with powers of two
  for(i=0; i<5; i++) {
    p[i].setx(ofTwo[i].getx());
```

```
   }

   // show powers of two
   cout << "Powers of two: ";
   for(i=0; i<5; i++) {
     cout << p[i].getx() << " ";
   }
   cout << "\n\n";

   delete [] p;
   return 0;
}
```

In this example, both constructors are necessary. The default constructor is used to construct the uninitialized **ofThree** array and the dynamically allocated array. The parameterized constructor is called to create the objects for the **ofTwo** array.

Copy Constructors

One of the more important forms of an overloaded constructor is the *copy constructor*. Defining a copy constructor can help you prevent problems that might occur when one object is used to initialize another.

Let's begin by restating the problem that the copy constructor is designed to solve. By default, when one object is used to initialize another, C++ performs a bitwise copy. That is, an identical copy of the initializing object is created in the target object. Although this is perfectly adequate for many cases—and generally exactly what you want to happen—there are situations in which a bitwise copy should not be used. One of the most common is when an object allocates memory when it is created. For example, assume a class called *MyClass* that allocates memory for each object when it is created, and an object *A* of that class. This means that *A* has already allocated its memory. Further, assume that *A* is used to initialize *B*, as shown here:

MyClass B = A;

If a bitwise copy is performed, then *B* will be an exact copy of *A*. This means that *B* will be using the same piece of allocated memory that *A* is using, instead of allocating its own. Clearly, this is not the desired outcome. For example, if *MyClass* includes a destructor that frees the memory, then the same piece of memory will be freed twice when *A* and *B* are destroyed!

The same type of problem can occur in two additional ways: first, when a copy of an object is made when it is passed as an argument to a function; second, when a temporary object is created as a return value from a function. Remember, temporary objects are automatically created to hold the return value of a function and they may also be created in certain other circumstances.

To solve the type of problem just described, C++ allows you to create a copy constructor, which the compiler uses when one object initializes another. Thus, your copy constructor bypasses the default bitwise copy. The most common general form of a copy constructor is

```
classname (const classname &o) {
   // body of constructor
}
```

Here, *o* is a reference to the object on the right side of the initialization. It is permissible for a copy constructor to have additional parameters as long as they have default arguments defined for them. However, in all cases the first parameter must be a reference to the object doing the initializing.

It is important to understand that C++ defines two distinct types of situations in which the value of one object is given to another. The first is assignment. The second is initialization, which can occur any of three ways:

- When one object explicitly initializes another, such as in a declaration
- When a copy of an object is made to be passed to a function
- When a temporary object is generated (most commonly, as a return value)

The copy constructor applies only to initializations. For example, assuming a class called **myclass**, and that **y** is an object of type **myclass**, each of the following statements involves initialization.

```
myclass x = y; // y explicitly initializing x
func(y);       // y passed as a parameter
y = func();    // y receiving a temporary, return object
```

Following is an example where an explicit copy constructor is needed. This program creates a very limited "safe" integer array type that prevents array boundaries from being overrun. (Chapter 15 shows a better way to create a safe array that uses overloaded operators.) Storage for each array is allocated by the use of **new**, and a pointer to the memory is maintained within each array object.

```
/* This program creates a "safe" array class.  Since space
   for the array is allocated using new, a copy constructor
   is provided to allocate memory when one array object is
   used to initialize another.
*/
```

```cpp
#include <iostream>
#include <new>
#include <cstdlib>
using namespace std;

class array {
  int *p;
  int size;
public:
  array(int sz) {
    try {
      p = new int[sz];
    } catch (bad_alloc xa) {
      cout << "Allocation Failure\n";
      exit(EXIT_FAILURE);
    }
    size = sz;
  }
  ~array() { delete [] p; }

  // copy constructor
  array(const array &a);

  void put(int i, int j) {
    if(i>=0 && i<size) p[i] = j;
  }
  int get(int i) {
    return p[i];
  }
};

// Copy Constructor
array::array(const array &a) {
  int i;

  try {
    p = new int[a.size];
  } catch (bad_alloc xa) {
    cout << "Allocation Failure\n";
    exit(EXIT_FAILURE);
  }
  for(i=0; i<a.size; i++) p[i] = a.p[i];
}
```

```
int main()
{
   array num(10);
   int i;

   for(i=0; i<10; i++) num.put(i, i);
   for(i=9; i>=0; i--) cout << num.get(i);
   cout << "\n";

   // create another array and initialize with num
   array x(num); // invokes copy constructor
   for(i=0; i<10; i++) cout << x.get(i);

   return 0;
}
```

Let's look closely at what happens when **num** is used to initialize **x** in the statement

```
array x(num); // invokes copy constructor
```

The copy constructor is called, memory for the new array is allocated and stored in **x.p**, and the contents of **num** are copied to **x**'s array. In this way, **x** and **num** have arrays that contain the same values, but each array is separate and distinct. (That is, **num.p** and **x.p** do not point to the same piece of memory.) If the copy constructor had not been created, the default bitwise initialization would have resulted in **x** and **num** sharing the same memory for their arrays. (That is, **num.p** and **x.p** would have indeed pointed to the same location.)

Remember that the copy constructor is called only for initializations. For example, this sequence does not call the copy constructor defined in the preceding program:

```
array a(10);
// ...
array b(10);

b = a; // does not call copy constructor
```

In this case, **b = a** performs the assignment operation. If = is not overloaded (as it is not here), a bitwise copy will be made. Therefore, in some cases, you may need to overload the = operator as well as create a copy constructor to avoid certain types of problems (see Chapter 15).

Finding the Address of an Overloaded Function

As explained in Chapter 5, you can obtain the address of a function. One reason to do so is to assign the address of the function to a pointer and then call that function through that pointer. If the function is not overloaded, this process is straightforward. However, for overloaded functions, the process requires a little more subtlety. To understand why, first consider this statement, which assigns the address of some function called **myfunc( )** to a pointer called **p**:

```
p = myfunc;
```

If **myfunc( )** is not overloaded, there is one and only one function called **myfunc( )**, and the compiler has no difficulty assigning its address to **p**. However, if **myfunc( )** is overloaded, how does the compiler know which version's address to assign to **p**? The answer is that it depends upon how **p** is declared. For example, consider this program:

```
#include <iostream>
using namespace std;

int myfunc(int a);
int myfunc(int a, int b);

int main()
{
  int (*fp)(int a); // pointer to int f(int)

  fp = myfunc; // points to myfunc(int)

  cout << fp(5);

  return 0;
}

int myfunc(int a)
{
  return a;
}

int myfunc(int a, int b)
{
  return a*b;
}
```

Here, there are two versions of **myfunc( )**. Both return **int**, but one takes a single integer argument; the other requires two integer arguments. In the program, **fp** is declared as a pointer to a function that returns an integer and that takes one integer argument. When **fp** is assigned the address of **myfunc( )**, C++ uses this information to select the **myfunc(int a)** version of **myfunc( )**. Had **fp** been declared like this:

```
int (*fp)(int a, int b);
```

then **fp** would have been assigned the address of the **myfunc(int a, int b)** version of **myfunc( )**.

In general, when you assign the address of an overloaded function to a function pointer, it is the declaration of the pointer that determines which function's address is obtained. Further, the declaration of the function pointer must exactly match one and only one of the overloaded function's declarations.

The overload Anachronism

When C++ was created, the keyword **overload** was required to create an overloaded function. It is obsolete and no longer used or supported. Indeed, it is not even a reserved word in Standard C++. However, because you might encounter older programs, and for its historical interest, it is a good idea to know how **overload** was used. Here is its general form:

overload *func-name*;

Here, *func-name* is the name of the function that you will be overloading. This statement must precede the overloaded declarations. For example, this tells an old-style compiler that you will be overloading a function called **test( )**:

```
overload test;
```

Default Function Arguments

C++ allows a function to assign a parameter a default value when no argument corresponding to that parameter is specified in a call to that function. The default value is specified in a manner syntactically similar to a variable initialization. For example, this declares **myfunc( )** as taking one **double** argument with a default value of 0.0:

```
void myfunc(double d = 0.0)
{
  // ...
}
```

Now, **myfunc( )** can be called one of two ways, as the following examples show:

```
myfunc(198.234); // pass an explicit value
myfunc();        // let function use default
```

The first call passes the value 198.234 to **d**. The second call automatically gives **d** the default value zero.

One reason that default arguments are included in C++ is because they provide another method for the programmer to manage greater complexity. To handle the widest variety of situations, quite frequently a function contains more parameters than are required for its most common usage. Thus, when the default arguments apply, you need specify only the arguments that are meaningful to the exact situation, not all those needed by the most general case. For example, many of the C++ I/O functions make use of default arguments for just this reason.

A simple illustration of how useful a default function argument can be is shown by the **clrscr( )** function in the following program. The **clrscr( )** function clears the screen by outputting a series of linefeeds (not the most efficient way, but sufficient for this example). Because a very common video mode displays 25 lines of text, the default argument of 25 is provided. However, because some video modes display more or less than 25 lines, you can override the default argument by specifying one explicitly.

```cpp
#include <iostream>
using namespace std;

void clrscr(int size=25);

int main()
{
  register int i;

  for(i=0; i<30; i++ ) cout << i << endl;
  cin.get();
  clrscr(); // clears 25 lines

  for(i=0; i<30; i++ ) cout << i << endl;
  cin.get();
  clrscr(10); // clears 10 lines

  return 0;
}

void clrscr(int size)
```

```
{
  for(; size; size--) cout << endl;
}
```

As this program illustrates, when the default value is appropriate to the situation, no argument need be specified when **clrscr( )** is called. However, it is still possible to override the default and give **size** a different value when needed.

A default argument can also be used as a flag telling the function to reuse a previous argument. To illustrate this usage, a function called **iputs( )** is developed here that automatically indents a string by a specified amount. To begin, here is a version of this function that does not use a default argument:

```
void iputs(char *str, int indent)
{
  if(indent < 0) indent = 0;

  for( ; indent; indent--) cout << " ";

  cout << str << "\n";
}
```

This version of **iputs( )** is called with the string to output as the first argument and the amount to indent as the second. Although there is nothing wrong with writing **iputs( )** this way, you can improve its usability by providing a default argument for the **indent** parameter that tells **iputs( )** to indent to the previously specified level. It is quite common to display a block of text with each line indented the same amount. In this situation, instead of having to supply the same **indent** argument over and over, you can give **indent** a default value that tells **iputs( )** to indent to the level of the previous call. This approach is illustrated in the following program:

```
#include <iostream>
using namespace std;

/* Default indent to -1.  This value tells the function
   to reuse the previous value. */
void iputs(char *str, int indent = -1);

int main()
{
  iputs("Hello there", 10);
  iputs("This will be indented 10 spaces by default");
```

```
    iputs("This will be indented 5 spaces", 5);
    iputs("This is not indented", 0);

    return 0;
}

void iputs(char *str, int indent)
{
    static i = 0; // holds previous indent value

    if(indent >= 0)
      i = indent;
    else  // reuse old indent value
      indent = i;

    for( ; indent; indent--) cout << " ";

    cout << str << "\n";
}
```

This program displays this output:

```
        Hello there
        This will be indented 10 spaces by default
    This will be indented 5 spaces
This is not indented
```

When you are creating functions that have default arguments, it is important to remember that the default values must be specified only once, and this must be the first time the function is declared within the file. In the preceding example, the default argument was specified in **iputs( )**'s prototype. If you try to specify new (or even the same) default values in **iputs( )**'s definition, the compiler will display an error and not compile your program. Even though default arguments for the same function cannot be redefined, you can specify different default arguments for each version of an overloaded function.

All parameters that take default values must appear to the right of those that do not. For example, it is incorrect to define **iputs( )** like this:

```
// wrong!
void iputs(int indent = -1, char *str);
```

Once you begin to define parameters that take default values, you cannot specify a nondefaulting parameter. That is, a declaration like this is also wrong and will not compile:

```
int myfunc(float f, char *str, int i=10, int j);
```

Because **i** has been given a default value, **j** must be given one too.

You can also use default parameters in an object's constructor. For example, the **cube** class shown here maintains the integer dimensions of a cube. Its constructor defaults all dimensions to zero if no other arguments are supplied, as shown here:

```
#include <iostream>
using namespace std;

class cube {
  int x, y, z;
public:
  cube(int i=0, int j=0, int k=0) {
    x=i;
    y=j;
    z=k;
  }

  int volume() {
    return x*y*z;
  }
};

int main()
{
  cube a(2,3,4), b;

  cout << a.volume() << endl;
  cout << b.volume();

  return 0;
}
```

There are two advantages to including default arguments, when appropriate, in a constructor. First, they prevent you from having to provide an overloaded constructor that takes no parameters. For example, if the parameters to **cube( )** were not given

defaults, the second constructor shown here would be needed to handle the declaration
of **b** (which specified no arguments).

```
cube() {x=0; y=0; z=0}
```

Second, defaulting common initial values is more convenient than specifying them
each time an object is declared.

Default Arguments vs. Overloading

In some situations, default arguments can be used as a shorthand form of function
overloading. The **cube** class's constructor just shown is one example. Let's look at
another. Imagine that you want to create two customized versions of the standard
strcat( ) function. The first version will operate like **strcat( )** and concatenate the entire
contents of one string to the end of another. The second version takes a third argument
that specifies the number of characters to concatenate. That is, the second version
will only concatenate a specified number of characters from one string to the end of
another. Thus, assuming that you call your customized functions **mystrcat( )**, they
will have the following prototypes:

```
void mystrcat(char *s1, char *s2, int len);
void mystrcat(char *s1, char *s2);
```

The first version will copy **len** characters from **s2** to the end of **s1**. The second version
will copy the entire string pointed to by **s2** onto the end of the string pointed to by **s1**
and operates like **strcat( )**.

While it would not be wrong to implement two versions of **mystrcat( )** to create the
two versions that you desire, there is an easier way. Using a default argument, you can
create only one version of **mystrcat( )** that performs both functions. The following
program demonstrates this.

```cpp
// A customized version of strcat().
#include <iostream>
#include <cstring>
using namespace std;

void mystrcat(char *s1, char *s2, int len = -1);

int main()
{
  char str1[80] = "This is a test";
  char str2[80] = "0123456789";
```

```
    mystrcat(str1, str2, 5); // concatenate 5 chars
    cout << str1 << '\n';

    strcpy(str1, "This is a test"); // reset str1

    mystrcat(str1, str2); // concatenate entire string
    cout << str1 << '\n';

    return 0;
}

// A custom version of strcat().
void mystrcat(char *s1, char *s2, int len)
{
  // find end of s1
  while(*s1) s1++;

  if(len == -1) len = strlen(s2);

  while(*s2 && len) {
    *s1 = *s2; // copy chars
    s1++;
    s2++;
    len--;
  }

  *s1 = '\0'; // null terminate s1
}
```

Here, **mystrcat( )** concatenates up to **len** characters from the string pointed to by **s2** onto the end of the string pointed to by **s1**. However, if **len** is –1, as it will be when it is allowed to default, **mystrcat( )** concatenates the entire string pointed to by **s2** onto **s1**. (Thus, when **len** is –1, the function operates like the standard **strcat( )** function.) By using a default argument for **len**, it is possible to combine both operations into one function. In this way, default arguments sometimes provide an alternative to function overloading.

Using Default Arguments Correctly

Although default arguments can be a very powerful tool when used correctly, they can also be misused. The point of default arguments is to allow a function to perform its job in an efficient, easy-to-use manner while still allowing considerable flexibility. Toward this end, all default arguments should reflect the way a function is generally used, or a reasonable alternate usage. When there is no single value that can be meaningfully associated with a parameter, there is no reason to declare a default argument. In fact, declaring default arguments when there is insufficient basis for doing so destructures your code, because they are liable to mislead and confuse anyone reading your program.

One other important guideline you should follow when using default arguments is this: No default argument should cause a harmful or destructive action. That is, the accidental use of a default argument should not cause a catastrophe.

Function Overloading and Ambiguity

You can create a situation in which the compiler is unable to choose between two (or more) overloaded functions. When this happens, the situation is said to be *ambiguous*. Ambiguous statements are errors, and programs containing ambiguity will not compile.

By far the main cause of ambiguity involves C++'s automatic type conversions. As you know, C++ automatically attempts to convert the arguments used to call a function into the type of arguments expected by the function. For example, consider this fragment:

```
int myfunc(double d);
// ...
cout << myfunc('c'); // not an error, conversion applied
```

As the comment indicates, this is not an error because C++ automatically converts the character **c** into its **double** equivalent. In C++, very few type conversions of this sort are actually disallowed. Although automatic type conversions are convenient, they are also a prime cause of ambiguity. For example, consider the following program:

```
#include <iostream>
using namespace std;

float myfunc(float i);
double myfunc(double i);

int main()
{
  cout << myfunc(10.1) << " "; // unambiguous, calls myfunc(double)
  cout << myfunc(10); // ambiguous

  return 0;
}
```

```
float myfunc(float i)
{
  return i;
}

double myfunc(double i)
{
  return -i;
}
```

Here, **myfunc( )** is overloaded so that it can take arguments of either type **float** or type **double**. In the unambiguous line, **myfunc(double)** is called because, unless explicitly specified as **float**, all floating-point constants in C++ are automatically of type **double**. Hence, that call is unambiguous. However, when **myfunc( )** is called by using the integer 10, ambiguity is introduced because the compiler has no way of knowing whether it should be converted to a **float** or to a **double**. This causes an error message to be displayed, and the program will not compile.

As the preceding example illustrates, it is not the overloading of **myfunc( )** relative to **double** and **float** that causes the ambiguity. Rather, it is the specific call to **myfunc( )** using an indeterminate type of argument that causes the confusion. Put differently, the error is not caused by the overloading of **myfunc( )**, but by the specific invocation.

Here is another example of ambiguity caused by C++'s automatic type conversions:

```
#include <iostream>
using namespace std;

char myfunc(unsigned char ch);
char myfunc(char ch);

int main()
{
  cout << myfunc('c'); // this calls myfunc(char)
  cout << myfunc(88) << " "; // ambiguous

  return 0;
}

char myfunc(unsigned char ch)
{
  return ch-1;
```

```
}

char myfunc(char ch)
{
  return ch+1;
}
```

In C++, **unsigned char** and **char** are *not* inherently ambiguous. However, when
myfunc( ) is called by using the integer 88, the compiler does not know which function
to call. That is, should 88 be converted into a **char** or an **unsigned char**?

Another way you can cause ambiguity is by using default arguments in overloaded
functions. To see how, examine this program:

```
#include <iostream>
using namespace std;

int myfunc(int i);
int myfunc(int i, int j=1);

int main()
{
  cout << myfunc(4, 5) << " "; // unambiguous
  cout << myfunc(10); // ambiguous

  return 0;
}

int myfunc(int i)
{
  return i;
}

int myfunc(int i, int j)
{
  return i*j;
}
```

Here, in the first call to **myfunc( ),** two arguments are specified; therefore, no
ambiguity is introduced and **myfunc(int i, int j)** is called. However, when the second
call to **myfunc( )** is made, ambiguity occurs because the compiler does not know whether
to call the version of **myfunc( )** that takes one argument or to apply the default to the
version that takes two arguments.

Some types of overloaded functions are simply inherently ambiguous even if, at first, they may not seem so. For example, consider this program.

```
// This program contains an error.
#include <iostream>
using namespace std;

void f(int x);
void f(int &x); // error

int main()
{
  int a=10;

  f(a); // error, which f()?

  return 0;
}

void f(int x)
{
  cout << "In f(int)\n";
}

void f(int &x)
{
  cout << "In f(int &)\n";
}
```

As the comments in the program describe, two functions cannot be overloaded when the only difference is that one takes a reference parameter and the other takes a normal, call-by-value parameter. In this situation, the compiler has no way of knowing which version of the function is intended when it is called. Remember, there is no syntactical difference in the way that an argument is specified when it will be received by a reference parameter or by a value parameter.

The Complete Reference

C++

Chapter 15

Operator Overloading

losely related to function overloading is operator overloading. In C++, you can overload most operators so that they perform special operations relative to classes that you create. For example, a class that maintains a stack might overload + to perform a push operation and – – to perform a pop. When an operator is overloaded, none of its original meanings are lost. Instead, the type of objects it can be applied to is expanded.

The ability to overload operators is one of C++'s most powerful features. It allows the full integration of new class types into the programming environment. After overloading the appropriate operators, you can use objects in expressions in just the same way that you use C++'s built-in data types. Operator overloading also forms the basis of C++'s approach to I/O.

You overload operators by creating operator functions. An *operator function* defines the operations that the overloaded operator will perform relative to the class upon which it will work. An operator function is created using the keyword **operator**. Operator functions can be either members or nonmembers of a class. Nonmember operator functions are almost always friend functions of the class, however. The way operator functions are written differs between member and nonmember functions. Therefore, each will be examined separately, beginning with member operator functions.

Creating a Member Operator Function

A member operator function takes this general form:

*ret-type class-name::*operator#*(arg-list)*
{
  // operations
}

Often, operator functions return an object of the class they operate on, but *ret-type* can be any valid type. The # is a placeholder. When you create an operator function, substitute the operator for the #. For example, if you are overloading the / operator, use **operator/.** When you are overloading a unary operator, *arg-list* will be empty. When you are overloading binary operators, *arg-list* will contain one parameter. (The reasons for this seemingly unusual situation will be made clear in a moment.)

Here is a simple first example of operator overloading. This program creates a class called **loc**, which stores longitude and latitude values. It overloads the + operator relative to this class. Examine this program carefully, paying special attention to the definition of **operator+( ):**

```cpp
#include <iostream>
using namespace std;

class loc {
  int longitude, latitude;
public:
  loc() {}
  loc(int lg, int lt) {
    longitude = lg;
    latitude = lt;
  }

  void show() {
    cout << longitude << " ";
    cout << latitude << "\n";
  }

  loc operator+(loc op2);
};

// Overload + for loc.
loc loc::operator+(loc op2)
{
  loc temp;

  temp.longitude = op2.longitude + longitude;
  temp.latitude = op2.latitude + latitude;

  return temp;
}

int main()
{
  loc ob1(10, 20), ob2( 5, 30);

  ob1.show(); // displays 10 20
  ob2.show(); // displays 5 30

  ob1 = ob1 + ob2;
  ob1.show(); // displays 15 50

  return 0;
}
```

As you can see, **operator+( )** has only one parameter even though it overloads the binary + operator. (You might expect two parameters corresponding to the two operands of a binary operator.) The reason that **operator+( )** takes only one parameter is that the operand on the left side of the + is passed implicitly to the function through the **this** pointer. The operand on the right is passed in the parameter **op2**. The fact that the left operand is passed using **this** also implies one important point: When binary operators are overloaded, it is the object on the left that generates the call to the operator function.

As mentioned, it is common for an overloaded operator function to return an object of the class it operates upon. By doing so, it allows the operator to be used in larger expressions. For example, if the **operator+( )** function returned some other type, this expression would not have been valid:

```
ob1 = ob1 + ob2;
```

In order for the sum of **ob1** and **ob2** to be assigned to **ob1**, the outcome of that operation must be an object of type **loc**.

Further, having **operator+( )** return an object of type **loc** makes possible the following statement:

```
(ob1+ob2).show(); // displays outcome of ob1+ob2
```

In this situation, **ob1+ob2** generates a temporary object that ceases to exist after the call to **show( )** terminates.

It is important to understand that an operator function can return any type and that the type returned depends solely upon your specific application. It is just that, often, an operator function will return an object of the class upon which it operates.

One last point about the **operator+( )** function: It does not modify either operand. Because the traditional use of the + operator does not modify either operand, it makes sense for the overloaded version not to do so either. (For example, 5+7 yields 12, but neither 5 nor 7 is changed.) Although you are free to perform any operation you want inside an operator function, it is usually best to stay within the context of the normal use of the operator.

The next program adds three additional overloaded operators to the **loc** class: the **–**, the **=**, and the unary **++**. Pay special attention to how these functions are defined.

```
#include <iostream>
using namespace std;

class loc {
  int longitude, latitude;
```

```
public:
  loc() {} // needed to construct temporaries
  loc(int lg, int lt) {
    longitude = lg;
    latitude = lt;
  }

  void show() {
    cout << longitude << " ";
    cout << latitude << "\n";
  }

  loc operator+(loc op2);
  loc operator-(loc op2);
  loc operator=(loc op2);
  loc operator++();
};

// Overload + for loc.
loc loc::operator+(loc op2)
{
  loc temp;

  temp.longitude = op2.longitude + longitude;
  temp.latitude = op2.latitude + latitude;

  return temp;
}

// Overload - for loc.
loc loc::operator-(loc op2)
{
  loc temp;

  // notice order of operands
  temp.longitude = longitude - op2.longitude;
  temp.latitude = latitude - op2.latitude;

  return temp;
}

// Overload asignment for loc.
```

```
loc loc::operator=(loc op2)
{
  longitude = op2.longitude;
  latitude = op2.latitude;

  return *this; // i.e., return object that generated call
}

// Overload prefix ++ for loc.
loc loc::operator++()
{
  longitude++;
  latitude++;

  return *this;
}

int main()
{
  loc ob1(10, 20), ob2( 5, 30), ob3(90, 90);

  ob1.show();
  ob2.show();

  ++ob1;
  ob1.show(); // displays 11 21

  ob2 = ++ob1;
  ob1.show(); // displays 12 22
  ob2.show(); // displays 12 22

  ob1 = ob2 = ob3; // multiple assignment
  ob1.show(); // displays 90 90
  ob2.show(); // displays 90 90

  return 0;
}
```

First, examine the **operator–( )** function. Notice the order of the operands in the subtraction. In keeping with the meaning of subtraction, the operand on the right side of the minus sign is subtracted from the operand on the left. Because it is the object on the left that generates the call to the **operator–( )** function, **op2**'s data must be subtracted from the data pointed to by **this**. It is important to remember which operand generates the call to the function.

In C++, if the = is not overloaded, a default assignment operation is created automatically for any class you define. The default assignment is simply a member-by-member, bitwise copy. By overloading the =, you can define explicitly what the assignment does relative to a class. In this example, the overloaded = does exactly the same thing as the default, but in other situations, it could perform other operations. Notice that the **operator=( )** function returns ***this**, which is the object that generated the call. This arrangement is necessary if you want to be able to use multiple assignment operations such as this:

```
ob1 = ob2 = ob3; // multiple assignment
```

Now, look at the definition of **operator++( )**. As you can see, it takes no parameters. Since **++** is a unary operator, its only operand is implicitly passed by using the **this** pointer.

Notice that both **operator=( )** and **operator++( )** alter the value of an operand. In the case of assignment, the operand on the left (the one generating the call to the **operator=( )** function) is assigned a new value. In the case of the **++**, the operand is incremented. As stated previously, although you are free to make these operators do anything you please, it is almost always wisest to stay consistent with their original meanings.

Creating Prefix and Postfix Forms of the Increment and Decrement Operators

In the preceding program, only the prefix form of the increment operator was overloaded. However, Standard C++ allows you to explicitly create separate prefix and postfix versions of the increment or decrement operators. To accomplish this, you must define two versions of the **operator++( )** function. One is defined as shown in the foregoing program. The other is declared like this:

```
loc operator++(int x);
```

If the **++** precedes its operand, the **operator++( )** function is called. If the **++** follows its operand, the **operator++(int x)** is called and **x** has the value zero.

The preceding example can be generalized. Here are the general forms for the prefix and postfix **++** and **– –** operator functions.

```
// Prefix increment
type operator++( ) {
  // body of prefix operator
}
```

```
// Postfix increment
type operator++(int x) {
  // body of postfix operator
}


// Prefix decrement
type operator– –( ) {
  // body of prefix operator
}


// Postfix decrement
type operator– –(int x) {
  // body of postfix operator
}
```

Note *You should be careful when working with older C++ programs where the increment and decrement operators are concerned. In older versions of C++, it was not possible to specify separate prefix and postfix versions of an overloaded ++ or – –. The prefix form was used for both.*

Overloading the Shorthand Operators

You can overload any of C++'s "shorthand" operators, such as **+=, –=,** and the like. For example, this function overloads **+=** relative to **loc**:

```
loc loc::operator+=(loc op2)
{
  longitude = op2.longitude + longitude;
  latitude = op2.latitude + latitude;

  return *this;
}
```

When overloading one of these operators, keep in mind that you are simply combining an assignment with another type of operation.

Operator Overloading Restrictions

There are some restrictions that apply to operator overloading. You cannot alter the precedence of an operator. You cannot change the number of operands that an operator takes. (You can choose to ignore an operand, however.) Except for the function call operator (described later), operator functions cannot have default arguments. Finally, these operators cannot be overloaded:

. :: .* ?

As stated, technically you are free to perform any activity inside an operator function. For example, if you want to overload the + operator in such a way that it writes **I like C++** 10 times to a disk file, you can do so. However, when you stray significantly from the normal meaning of an operator, you run the risk of dangerously destructuring your program. When someone reading your program sees a statement like **Ob1+Ob2**, he or she expects something resembling addition to be taking place— not a disk access, for example. Therefore, before decoupling an overloaded operator from its normal meaning, be sure that you have sufficient reason to do so. One good example where decoupling is successful is found in the way C++ overloads the << and >> operators for I/O. Although the I/O operations have no relationship to bit shifting, these operators provide a visual "clue" as to their meaning relative to both I/O and bit shifting, and this decoupling works. In general, however, it is best to stay within the context of the expected meaning of an operator when overloading it.

Except for the = operator, operator functions are inherited by a derived class. However, a derived class is free to overload any operator (including those overloaded by the base class) it chooses relative to itself.

Operator Overloading Using a Friend Function

You can overload an operator for a class by using a nonmember function, which is usually a friend of the class. Since a **friend** function is not a member of the class, it does not have a **this** pointer. Therefore, an overloaded friend operator function is passed the operands explicitly. This means that a friend function that overloads a binary operator has two parameters, and a friend function that overloads a unary operator has one parameter. When overloading a binary operator using a friend function, the left operand is passed in the first parameter and the right operand is passed in the second parameter.

In this program, the **operator+( )** function is made into a friend:

```
#include <iostream>
using namespace std;

class loc {
  int longitude, latitude;
public:
```

```cpp
  loc() {} // needed to construct temporaries
  loc(int lg, int lt) {
    longitude = lg;
    latitude = lt;
  }

  void show() {
    cout << longitude << " ";
    cout << latitude << "\n";
  }

  friend loc operator+(loc op1, loc op2); // now a friend
  loc operator-(loc op2);
  loc operator=(loc op2);
  loc operator++();
};

// Now, + is overloaded using friend function.
loc operator+(loc op1, loc op2)
{
  loc temp;

  temp.longitude = op1.longitude + op2.longitude;
  temp.latitude = op1.latitude + op2.latitude;

  return temp;
}

// Overload - for loc.
loc loc::operator-(loc op2)
{
  loc temp;

  // notice order of operands
  temp.longitude = longitude - op2.longitude;
  temp.latitude = latitude - op2.latitude;

  return temp;
}

// Overload assignment for loc.
```

```
loc loc::operator=(loc op2)
{
  longitude = op2.longitude;
  latitude = op2.latitude;

  return *this; // i.e., return object that generated call
}

// Overload ++ for loc.
loc loc::operator++()
{
  longitude++;
  latitude++;

  return *this;
}

int main()
{
  loc ob1(10, 20), ob2( 5, 30);

  ob1 = ob1 + ob2;
  ob1.show();

  return 0;
}
```

There are some restrictions that apply to friend operator functions. First, you may not overload the =, ( ), [ ], or –> operators by using a friend function. Second, as explained in the next section, when overloading the increment or decrement operators, you will need to use a reference parameter when using a friend function.

Using a Friend to Overload ++ or ––

If you want to use a friend function to overload the increment or decrement operators, you must pass the operand as a reference parameter. This is because friend functions do not have **this** pointers. Assuming that you stay true to the original meaning of the ++ and – – operators, these operations imply the modification of the operand they operate upon. However, if you overload these operators by using a friend, then the operand is passed by value as a parameter. This means that a friend operator function has no way to modify the operand. Since the friend operator function is not passed a **this** pointer to the operand, but rather a copy of the operand, no changes made to that parameter affect the operand that generated the call. However, you can remedy this situation by specifying the parameter to the friend operator function as a reference parameter. This causes any changes made to the parameter inside the function to affect the operand that generated the call. For example, this program uses friend functions to overload the prefix versions of **++** and **– –** operators relative to the **loc** class:

```cpp
#include <iostream>
using namespace std;

class loc {
  int longitude, latitude;
public:
  loc() {}
  loc(int lg, int lt) {
    longitude = lg;
    latitude = lt;
  }

  void show() {
    cout << longitude << " ";
    cout << latitude << "\n";
  }

  loc operator=(loc op2);
  friend loc operator++(loc &op);
  friend loc operator--(loc &op);
};

// Overload assignment for loc.
loc loc::operator=(loc op2)
{
  longitude = op2.longitude;
  latitude = op2.latitude;

  return *this; // i.e., return object that generated call
}

// Now a friend; use a reference parameter.
loc operator++(loc &op)
{
```

```
    op.longitude++;
    op.latitude++;

    return op;
}

// Make op-- a friend; use reference.
loc operator--(loc &op)
{
    op.longitude--;
    op.latitude--;

    return op;
}

int main()
{
    loc ob1(10, 20), ob2;

    ob1.show();
    ++ob1;
    ob1.show(); // displays 11 21

    ob2 =  ++ob1;
    ob2.show(); // displays 12 22

    --ob2;
    ob2.show(); // displays 11 21

    return 0;
}
```

If you want to overload the postfix versions of the increment and decrement operators using a friend, simply specify a second, dummy integer parameter. For example, this shows the prototype for the **friend,** postfix version of the increment operator relative to **loc.**

```
// friend, postfix version of ++
friend loc operator++(loc &op, int x);
```

Friend Operator Functions Add Flexibility

In many cases, whether you overload an operator by using a friend or a member function makes no functional difference. In those cases, it is usually best to overload by using member functions. However, there is one situation in which overloading by using a friend increases the flexibility of an overloaded operator. Let's examine this case now.

As you know, when you overload a binary operator by using a member function, the object on the left side of the operator generates the call to the operator function. Further, a pointer to that object is passed in the **this** pointer. Now, assume some class that defines a member **operator+( )** function that adds an object of the class to an integer. Given an object of that class called **Ob**, the following expression is valid:

Ob + 100 // valid

In this case, **Ob** generates the call to the overloaded + function, and the addition is performed. But what happens if the expression is written like this?

100 + Ob // invalid

In this case, it is the integer that appears on the left. Since an integer is a built-in type, no operation between an integer and an object of **Ob**'s type is defined. Therefore, the compiler will not compile this expression. As you can imagine, in some applications, having to always position the object on the left could be a significant burden and cause of frustration.

The solution to the preceding problem is to overload addition using a friend, not a member, function. When this is done, both arguments are explicitly passed to the operator function. Therefore, to allow both *object+integer* and *integer+object*, simply overload the function twice—one version for each situation. Thus, when you overload an operator by using two **friend** functions, the object may appear on either the left or right side of the operator.

This program illustrates how **friend** functions are used to define an operation that involves an object and built-in type:

```
#include <iostream>
using namespace std;

class loc {
  int longitude, latitude;
public:
```

```cpp
  loc() {}
  loc(int lg, int lt) {
    longitude = lg;
    latitude = lt;
  }

  void show() {
    cout << longitude << " ";
    cout << latitude << "\n";
  }

  friend loc operator+(loc op1, int op2);
  friend loc operator+(int op1, loc op2);
};

// + is overloaded for loc + int.
loc operator+(loc op1, int op2)
{
  loc temp;

  temp.longitude = op1.longitude + op2;
  temp.latitude = op1.latitude + op2;

  return temp;
}
// + is overloaded for int + loc.
loc operator+(int op1, loc op2)
{
  loc temp;

  temp.longitude = op1 + op2.longitude;
  temp.latitude = op1 + op2.latitude;

  return temp;
}

int main()
{
  loc ob1(10, 20), ob2( 5, 30), ob3(7, 14);

  ob1.show();
```

C++

```
    ob2.show();
    ob3.show();

    ob1 = ob2 + 10; // both of these
    ob3 = 10 + ob2; // are valid

    ob1.show();
    ob3.show();

    return 0;
}
```

Overloading new and delete

It is possible to overload **new** and **delete**. You might choose to do this if you want
to use some special allocation method. For example, you may want allocation routines
that automatically begin using a disk file as virtual memory when the heap has been
exhausted. Whatever the reason, it is a very simple matter to overload these operators.

The skeletons for the functions that overload **new** and **delete** are shown here:

```
// Allocate an object.
void *operator new(size_t size)
{
  /* Perform allocation.  Throw bad_alloc on failure.
     Constructor called automatically. */
  return pointer_to_memory;
}

// Delete an object.
void operator delete(void *p)
{
  /* Free memory pointed to by p.
     Destructor called automatically. */
}
```

The type **size_t** is a defined type capable of containing the largest single piece
of memory that can be allocated. (**size_t** is essentially an unsigned integer.) The
parameter **size** will contain the number of bytes needed to hold the object being
allocated. This is the amount of memory that your version of **new** must allocate. The
overloaded **new** function must return a pointer to the memory that it allocates, or
throw a **bad_alloc** exception if an allocation error occurs. Beyond these constraints,
the overloaded **new** function can do anything else you require. When you allocate an

object using **new** (whether your own version or not), the object's constructor is automatically called.

The **delete** function receives a pointer to the region of memory to be freed. It then releases the previously allocated memory back to the system. When an object is deleted, its destructor is automatically called.

The **new** and **delete** operators may be overloaded globally so that all uses of these operators call your custom versions. They may also be overloaded relative to one or more classes. Lets begin with an example of overloading **new** and **delete** relative to a class. For the sake of simplicity, no new allocation scheme will be used. Instead, the overloaded operators will simply invoke the standard library functions **malloc( )** and **free( ).** (In your own application, you may, of course, implement any alternative allocation scheme you like.)

To overload the **new** and **delete** operators for a class, simply make the overloaded operator functions class members. For example, here the **new** and **delete** operators are overloaded for the **loc** class:

```
#include <iostream>
#include <cstdlib>
#include <new>
using namespace std;

class loc {
  int longitude, latitude;
public:
  loc() {}
  loc(int lg, int lt) {
    longitude = lg;
    latitude = lt;
  }

  void show() {
    cout << longitude << " ";
    cout << latitude << "\n";
  }

  void *operator new(size_t size);
  void operator delete(void *p);
};

// new overloaded relative to loc.
void *loc::operator new(size_t size)
{
  void *p;
```

```
    cout << "In overloaded new.\n";
    p = malloc(size);
    if(!p) {
      bad_alloc ba;
      throw ba;
    }
    return p;
}

// delete overloaded relative to loc.
void loc::operator delete(void *p)
{
  cout << "In overloaded delete.\n";
  free(p);
}

int main()
{
  loc *p1, *p2;

  try {
    p1 = new loc (10, 20);
  } catch (bad_alloc xa) {
    cout << "Allocation error for p1.\n";
    return 1;
  }

  try {
    p2 = new loc (-10, -20);
  } catch (bad_alloc xa) {
    cout << "Allocation error for p2.\n";
    return 1;;
  }

  p1->show();
  p2->show();

  delete p1;
  delete p2;

  return 0;
}
```

Output from this program is shown here.

```
In overloaded new.
In overloaded new.
10 20
-10 -20
In overloaded delete.
In overloaded delete.
```

When **new** and **delete** are for a specific class, the use of these operators on any other type of data causes the original **new** or **delete** to be employed. The overloaded operators are only applied to the types for which they are defined. This means that if you add this line to the **main( )**, the default **new** will be executed:

```
int *f = new float; // uses default new
```

You can overload **new** and **delete** globally by overloading these operators outside of any class declaration. When **new** and **delete** are overloaded globally, C++'s default **new** and **delete** are ignored and the new operators are used for all allocation requests. Of course, if you have defined any versions of **new** and **delete** relative to one or more classes, then the class-specific versions are used when allocating objects of the class for which they are defined. In other words, when **new** or **delete** are encountered, the compiler first checks to see whether they are defined relative to the class they are operating on. If so, those specific versions are used. If not, C++ uses the globally defined **new** and **delete**. If these have been overloaded, the overloaded versions are used.

To see an example of overloading **new** and **delete** globally, examine this program:

```
#include <iostream>
#include <cstdlib>
#include <new>
using namespace std;

class loc {
int longitude, latitude;
public:
  loc() {}
  loc(int lg, int lt) {
    longitude = lg;
    latitude = lt;
  }
```

C++

```
   void show() {
     cout << longitude << " ";
     cout << latitude << "\n";
   }
};

// Global new
void *operator new(size_t size)
{
  void *p;

  p = malloc(size);
  if(!p) {
    bad_alloc ba;
    throw ba;
  }
  return p;
}

// Global delete
void operator delete(void *p)
{
  free(p);
}

int main()
{
  loc *p1, *p2;
  float *f;

  try {
    p1 = new loc (10, 20);
  } catch (bad_alloc xa) {
    cout << "Allocation error for p1.\n";
    return 1;;
  }

  try {
    p2 = new loc (-10, -20);
  } catch (bad_alloc xa) {
    cout << "Allocation error for p2.\n";
    return 1;;
```

```
  }

  try {
    f = new float; // uses overloaded new, too
  } catch (bad_alloc xa) {
    cout << "Allocation error for f.\n";
    return 1;;
  }

  *f = 10.10F;
  cout << *f << "\n";

  p1->show();
  p2->show();

  delete p1;
  delete p2;
  delete f;

  return 0;
}
```

Run this program to prove to yourself that the built-in **new** and **delete** operators have indeed been overloaded.

Overloading new and delete for Arrays

If you want to be able to allocate arrays of objects using your own allocation system, you will need to overload **new** and **delete** a second time. To allocate and free arrays, you must use these forms of **new** and **delete**.

```
// Allocate an array of objects.
void *operator new[](size_t size)
{
  /* Perform allocation.  Throw bad_alloc on failure.
     Constructor for each element called automatically. */
  return pointer_to_memory;
}

// Delete an array of objects.
void operator delete[](void *p)
```

```
{
  /* Free memory pointed to by p.
     Destructor for each element called automatically.
  */
}
```

When allocating an array, the constructor for each object in the array is automatically called. When freeing an array, each object's destructor is automatically called. You do not have to provide explicit code to accomplish these actions.

The following program allocates and frees an object and an array of objects of type **loc.**

```
#include <iostream>
#include <cstdlib>
#include <new>
using namespace std;

class loc {
  int longitude, latitude;
public:
  loc() {longitude = latitude = 0;}
  loc(int lg, int lt) {
    longitude = lg;
    latitude = lt;
  }

  void show() {
    cout << longitude << " ";
    cout << latitude << "\n";
  }

  void *operator new(size_t size);
  void operator delete(void *p);

  void *operator new[](size_t size);
  void operator delete[](void *p);
};

// new overloaded relative to loc.
void *loc::operator new(size_t size)
{
```

```
void *p;

  cout << "In overloaded new.\n";
  p = malloc(size);
  if(!p) {
    bad_alloc ba;
    throw ba;
  }
  return p;
}

// delete overloaded relative to loc.
void loc::operator delete(void *p)
{
  cout << "In overloaded delete.\n";
  free(p);
}

// new overloaded for loc arrays.
void *loc::operator new[](size_t size)
{
  void *p;

  cout << "Using overload new[].\n";
  p = malloc(size);
  if(!p) {
    bad_alloc ba;
    throw ba;
  }
  return p;
}

// delete overloaded for loc arrays.
void loc::operator delete[](void *p)
{
  cout << "Freeing array using overloaded delete[]\n";
  free(p);
}

int main()
{
  loc *p1, *p2;
```

```
    int i;

    try {
      p1 = new loc (10, 20); // allocate an object
    } catch (bad_alloc xa) {
      cout << "Allocation error for p1.\n";
      return 1;;
    }

    try {
      p2 = new loc [10]; // allocate an array
    } catch (bad_alloc xa) {
      cout << "Allocation error for p2.\n";
      return 1;;
    }

    p1->show();

    for(i=0; i<10; i++)
      p2[i].show();

    delete p1; // free an object
    delete [] p2; // free an array

    return 0;
  }
```

Overloading the nothrow Version of new and delete

You can also create overloaded **nothrow** versions of **new** and **delete**. To do so, use
these skeletons.

```
// Nothrow version of new.
void *operator new(size_t size, const nothrow_t &n)
{
  // Perform allocation.
  if(success) return pointer_to_memory;
  else return 0;
}


// Nothrow version of new for arrays.
```

```
void *operator new[](size_t size, const nothrow_t &n)
{
  // Perform allocation.
  if(success) return pointer_to_memory;
  else return 0;
}

void operator delete(void *p, const nothrow_t &n)
{
  // free memory
}

void operator delete[](void *p, const nothrow_t &n)
{
  // free memory
}
```

The type **nothrow_t** is defined in **<new>**. This is the type of the **nothrow** object. The **nothrow_t** parameter is unused.

Overloading Some Special Operators

C++ defines array subscripting, function calling, and class member access as operations. The operators that perform these functions are the **[ ]**, **( )**, and **–>**, respectively. These rather exotic operators may be overloaded in C++, opening up some very interesting uses.

One important restriction applies to overloading these three operators: They must be nonstatic member functions. They cannot be **friend**s.

Overloading [ ]

In C++, the **[ ]** is considered a binary operator when you are overloading it. Therefore, the general form of a member **operator[ ]( )** function is as shown here:

type class-name::operator[](int *i*)
{
  // . . .
}

Technically, the parameter does not have to be of type **int**, but an **operator[ ]( )** function is typically used to provide array subscripting, and as such, an integer value is generally used.

Given an object called **O**, the expression

```
O[3]
```

translates into this call to the **operator[ ]( )** function:

```
O.operator[](3)
```

That is, the value of the expression within the subscripting operators is passed to the **operator[ ]( )** function in its explicit parameter. The **this** pointer will point to **O**, the object that generated the call.

In the following program, **atype** declares an array of three integers. Its constructor initializes each member of the array to the specified values. The overloaded **operator[ ]( )** function returns the value of the array as indexed by the value of its parameter.

```cpp
#include <iostream>
using namespace std;

class atype {
  int a[3];
public:
  atype(int i, int j, int k) {
    a[0] = i;
    a[1] = j;
    a[2] = k;
  }
  int operator[](int i) { return a[i]; }
};

int main()
{
  atype ob(1, 2, 3);

  cout << ob[1]; // displays 2

  return 0;
}
```

You can design the **operator[ ]( )** function in such a way that the [ ] can be used on both the left and right sides of an assignment statement. To do this, simply specify the return value of **operator[ ]( )** as a reference. The following program makes this change and shows its use:

```cpp
#include <iostream>
using namespace std;

class atype {
  int a[3];
public:
  atype(int i, int j, int k) {
    a[0] = i;
    a[1] = j;
    a[2] = k;
  }
  int &operator[](int i) { return a[i]; }
};

int main()
{
  atype ob(1, 2, 3);

  cout << ob[1]; // displays 2
  cout << " ";

  ob[1] = 25; // [] on left of =

  cout << ob[1]; // now displays 25

  return 0;
}
```

Because **operator[ ]( )** now returns a reference to the array element indexed by **i**, it can be used on the left side of an assignment to modify an element of the array. (Of course, it may still be used on the right side as well.)

One advantage of being able to overload the [ ] operator is that it allows a means of implementing safe array indexing in C++. As you know, in C++, it is possible to overrun (or underrun) an array boundary at run time without generating a run-time error message. However, if you create a class that contains the array, and allow access to that array only through the overloaded [ ] subscripting operator, then you can intercept an out-of-range index. For example, this program adds a range check to the preceding program and proves that it works:

```cpp
// A safe array example.
#include <iostream>
#include <cstdlib>
using namespace std;

class atype {
  int a[3];
public:
  atype(int i, int j, int k) {
    a[0] = i;
    a[1] = j;
    a[2] = k;
  }
  int &operator[](int i);
};

// Provide range checking for atype.
int &atype::operator[](int i)
{
  if(i<0 || i> 2) {
    cout << "Boundary Error\n";
    exit(1);
  }
  return a[i];
}

int main()
{
  atype ob(1, 2, 3);

  cout << ob[1]; // displays 2
  cout << " ";

  ob[1] = 25; // [] appears on left
  cout << ob[1]; // displays 25

  ob[3] = 44; // generates runtime error, 3 out-of-range

  return 0;
}
```

In this program, when the statement

```
ob[3] = 44;
```

executes, the boundary error is intercepted by **operator[]( )**, and the program is terminated before any damage can be done. (In actual practice, some sort of error-handling function would be called to deal with the out-of-range condition; the program would not have to terminate.)

Overloading ( )

When you overload the **( )** function call operator, you are not, per se, creating a new way to call a function. Rather, you are creating an operator function that can be passed an arbitrary number of parameters. Let's begin with an example. Given the overloaded operator function declaration

```
double operator()(int a, float f, char *s);
```

and an object **O** of its class, then the statement

```
O(10, 23.34, "hi");
```

translates into this call to the **operator( )** function.

```
O.operator()(10, 23.34, "hi");
```

In general, when you overload the **( )** operator, you define the parameters that you want to pass to that function. When you use the **( )** operator in your program, the arguments you specify are copied to those parameters. As always, the object that generates the call (**O** in this example) is pointed to by the **this** pointer.

Here is an example of overloading **( )** for the **loc** class. It assigns the value of its two arguments to the longitude and latitude of the object to which it is applied.

```
#include <iostream>
using namespace std;

class loc {
  int longitude, latitude;
public:
```

```cpp
  loc() {}
  loc(int lg, int lt) {
    longitude = lg;
    latitude = lt;
  }

  void show() {
    cout << longitude << " ";
    cout << latitude << "\n";
  }

  loc operator+(loc op2);
  loc operator()(int i, int j);
};

// Overload ( ) for loc.
loc loc::operator()(int i, int j)
{
  longitude = i;
  latitude = j;

  return *this;
}

// Overload + for loc.
loc loc::operator+(loc op2)
{
  loc temp;

  temp.longitude = op2.longitude + longitude;
  temp.latitude = op2.latitude + latitude;
  return temp;
}

int main()
{
  loc ob1(10, 20), ob2(1, 1);

  ob1.show();
  ob1(7, 8); // can be executed by itself
  ob1.show();
```

```
   ob1 = ob2 + ob1(10, 10); // can be used in expressions
   ob1.show();

   return 0;
}
```

The output produced by the program is shown here.

```
10 20
7 8
11 11
```

Remember, when overloading ( ), you can use any type of parameters and return any type of value. These types will be dictated by the demands of your programs. You can also specify default arguments.

Overloading –>

The –> pointer operator, also called the *class member access* operator, is considered a unary operator when overloading. Its general usage is shown here:

object->element;

Here, *object* is the object that activates the call. The **operator–>( )** function must return a pointer to an object of the class that **operator–>( )** operates upon. The *element* must be some member accessible within the object.

The following program illustrates overloading the –> by showing the equivalence between **ob.i** and **ob–>i** when **operator–>( )** returns the **this** pointer:

```
#include <iostream>
using namespace std;

class myclass {
public:
  int i;
  myclass *operator->() {return this;}
};

int main()
{
  myclass ob;
```

```
    ob->i = 10; // same as ob.i

    cout << ob.i << " " << ob->i;

    return 0;
}
```

An **operator–>( )** function must be a member of the class upon which it works.

Overloading the Comma Operator

You can overload C++'s comma operator. The comma is a binary operator, and like all overloaded operators, you can make an overloaded comma perform any operation you want. However, if you want the overloaded comma to perform in a fashion similar to its normal operation, then your version must discard the values of all operands except the rightmost. The rightmost value becomes the result of the comma operation. This is the way the comma works by default in C++.

Here is a program that illustrates the effect of overloading the comma operator.

```
#include <iostream>
using namespace std;

class loc {
  int longitude, latitude;
public:
  loc() {}
  loc(int lg, int lt) {
    longitude = lg;
    latitude = lt;
  }

  void show() {
    cout << longitude << " ";
    cout << latitude << "\n";
  }

  loc operator+(loc op2);
  loc operator,(loc op2);
```

```
};

// overload comma for loc
loc loc::operator,(loc op2)
{
  loc temp;

  temp.longitude = op2.longitude;
  temp.latitude = op2.latitude;
  cout << op2.longitude << " " << op2.latitude << "\n";

  return temp;
}

// Overload + for loc
loc loc::operator+(loc op2)
{
  loc temp;

  temp.longitude = op2.longitude + longitude;
  temp.latitude = op2.latitude + latitude;

  return temp;
}

int main()
{
  loc ob1(10, 20), ob2( 5, 30), ob3(1, 1);

  ob1.show();
  ob2.show();
  ob3.show();
  cout << "\n";

  ob1 = (ob1, ob2+ob2, ob3);

  ob1.show(); // displays 1 1, the value of ob3

  return 0;
}
```

This program displays the following output:

```
10 20
5 30
1 1

10 60
1 1
1 1
```

Notice that although the values of the left-hand operands are discarded, each expression is still evaluated by the compiler so that any desired side effects will be performed.

Remember, the left-hand operand is passed via **this**, and its value is discarded by the **operator,( )** function. The value of the right-hand operation is returned by the function. This causes the overloaded comma to behave similarly to its default operation. If you want the overloaded comma to do something else, you will have to change these two features.

Chapter 16

Inheritance

Inheritance is one of the cornerstones of OOP because it allows the creation of hierarchical classifications. Using inheritance, you can create a general class that defines traits common to a set of related items. This class may then be inherited by other, more specific classes, each adding only those things that are unique to the inheriting class.

In keeping with standard C++ terminology, a class that is inherited is referred to as a *base class*. The class that does the inheriting is called the *derived class*. Further, a derived class can be used as a base class for another derived class. In this way, multiple inheritance is achieved.

C++'s support of inheritance is both rich and flexible. Inheritance was introduced in Chapter 11. It is examined in detail here.

Base-Class Access Control

When a class inherits another, the members of the base class become members of the derived class. Class inheritance uses this general form:

```
class derived-class-name : access base-class-name {
  // body of class
};
```

The access status of the base-class members inside the derived class is determined by *access*. The base-class access specifier must be either **public**, **private**, or **protected**. If no access specifier is present, the access specifier is **private** by default if the derived class is a **class**. If the derived class is a **struct**, then **public** is the default in the absence of an explicit access specifier. Let's examine the ramifications of using **public** or **private** access. (The **protected** specifier is examined in the next section.)

When the access specifier for a base class is **public**, all public members of the base become public members of the derived class, and all protected members of the base become protected members of the derived class. In all cases, the base's private elements remain private to the base and are not accessible by members of the derived class. For example, as illustrated in this program, objects of type **derived** can directly access the public members of **base**:

```cpp
#include <iostream>
using namespace std;

class base {
  int i, j;
public:
  void set(int a, int b) { i=a; j=b; }
```

```
  void show() { cout << i << " " << j << "\n"; }
};

class derived : public base {
  int k;
public:
  derived(int x) { k=x; }
  void showk() { cout << k << "\n"; }
};

int main()
{
  derived ob(3);

  ob.set(1, 2); // access member of base
  ob.show(); // access member of base

  ob.showk(); // uses member of derived class

  return 0;
}
```

When the base class is inherited by using the **private** access specifier, all public and protected members of the base class become private members of the derived class. For example, the following program will not even compile because both **set( )** and **show( )** are now private elements of **derived**:

```
// This program won't compile.
#include <iostream>
using namespace std;

class base {
  int i, j;
public:
  void set(int a, int b) { i=a; j=b; }
  void show() { cout << i << " " << j << "\n";}
};

// Public elements of base are private in derived.
class derived : private base {
  int k;
```

```
public:
  derived(int x) { k=x; }
  void showk() { cout << k << "\n"; }
};

int main()
{
  derived ob(3);

  ob.set(1, 2); // error, can't access set()
  ob.show(); // error, can't access show()

  return 0;
}
```

Remember *When a base class' access specifier is **private**, public and protected members of the base become private members of the derived class. This means that they are still accessible by members of the derived class but cannot be accessed by parts of your program that are not members of either the base or derived class.*

Inheritance and protected Members

The **protected** keyword is included in C++ to provide greater flexibility in the inheritance mechanism. When a member of a class is declared as **protected**, that member is not accessible by other, nonmember elements of the program. With one important exception, access to a protected member is the same as access to a private member—it can be accessed only by other members of its class. The sole exception to this is when a protected member is inherited. In this case, a protected member differs substantially from a private one.

As explained in the preceding section, a private member of a base class is not accessible by other parts of your program, including any derived class. However, protected members behave differently. If the base class is inherited as **public**, then the base class' protected members become protected members of the derived class and are, therefore, accessible by the derived class. By using **protected**, you can create class members that are private to their class but that can still be inherited and accessed by a derived class. Here is an example:

```
#include <iostream>
using namespace std;

class base {
```

```
protected:
  int i, j; // private to base, but accessible by derived
public:
  void set(int a, int b) { i=a; j=b; }
  void show() { cout << i << " " << j << "\n"; }
};

class derived : public base {
  int k;
public:
  // derived may access base's i and j
  void setk() { k=i*j; }

  void showk() { cout << k << "\n"; }
};

int main()
{
  derived ob;

  ob.set(2, 3); // OK, known to derived
  ob.show(); // OK, known to derived

  ob.setk();
  ob.showk();

  return 0;
}
```

In this example, because **base** is inherited by **derived** as **public** and because **i** and **j** are declared as **protected, derived**'s function **setk( )** may access them. If **i** and **j** had been declared as **private** by **base**, then **derived** would not have access to them, and the program would not compile.

When a derived class is used as a base class for another derived class, any protected member of the initial base class that is inherited (as public) by the first derived class may also be inherited as protected again by a second derived class. For example, this program is correct, and **derived2** does indeed have access to **i** and **j**.

```
#include <iostream>
using namespace std;

class base {
```

```
protected:
  int i, j;
public:
  void set(int a, int b) { i=a; j=b; }
  void show() { cout << i << " " << j << "\n"; }
};

// i and j inherited as protected.
class derived1 : public base {
  int k;
public:
  void setk() { k = i*j; } // legal
  void showk() { cout << k << "\n"; }
};

// i and j inherited indirectly through derived1.
class derived2 : public derived1 {
  int m;
public:
  void setm() { m = i-j; } // legal
  void showm() { cout << m << "\n"; }
};

int main()
{
  derived1 ob1;
  derived2 ob2;

  ob1.set(2, 3);
  ob1.show();
  ob1.setk();
  ob1.showk();

  ob2.set(3, 4);
  ob2.show();
  ob2.setk();
  ob2.setm();
  ob2.showk();
  ob2.showm();

  return 0;
}
```

If, however, **base** were inherited as **private**, then all members of **base** would become private members of **derived1**, which means that they would not be accessible by **derived2**. (However, **i** and **j** would still be accessible by **derived1**.) This situation is illustrated by the following program, which is in error (and won't compile). The comments describe each error:

```
// This program won't compile.
#include <iostream>
using namespace std;

class base {
protected:
  int i, j;
public:
  void set(int a, int b) { i=a; j=b; }
  void show() { cout << i << " " << j << "\n"; }
};

// Now, all elements of base are private in derived1.
class derived1 : private base {
  int k;
public:
  // this is legal because i and j are private to derived1
  void setk() { k = i*j; } // OK
  void showk() { cout << k << "\n"; }
};

// Access to i, j, set(), and show() not inherited.
class derived2 : public derived1 {
  int m;
public:
  // illegal because i and j are private to derived1
  void setm() { m = i-j; } // Error
  void showm() { cout << m << "\n"; }
};

int main()
{
  derived1 ob1;
  derived2 ob2;

  ob1.set(1, 2); // error, can't use set()
```

```
  ob1.show(); // error, can't use show()

  ob2.set(3, 4); // error, can't use set()
  ob2.show(); // error, can't use show()

  return 0;
}
```

Note *Even though **base** is inherited as **private** by **derived1**, **derived1** still has access to base's **public** and **protected** elements. However, it cannot pass along this privilege.*

Protected Base-Class Inheritance

It is possible to inherit a base class as **protected**. When this is done, all public and protected members of the base class become protected members of the derived class. For example,

```
#include <iostream>
using namespace std;

class base {
protected:
  int i, j; // private to base, but accessible by derived
public:
  void setij(int a, int b) { i=a; j=b; }
  void showij() { cout << i << " " << j << "\n"; }
};

// Inherit base as protected.
class derived : protected base{
  int k;
public:
  // derived may access base's i and j and setij().
  void setk() { setij(10, 12); k = i*j; }

  // may access showij() here
  void showall() { cout << k << " "; showij(); }
};

int main()
```

```
{
  derived ob;

//  ob.setij(2, 3); // illegal, setij() is
//                   protected member of derived

  ob.setk(); // OK, public member of derived
  ob.showall(); // OK, public member of derived

// ob.showij(); // illegal, showij() is protected
//              member of derived

  return 0;
}
```

As you can see by reading the comments, even though **setij( )** and **showij( )** are public members of **base**, they become protected members of **derived** when it is inherited using the **protected** access specifier. This means that they will not be accessible inside **main( )**.

Inheriting Multiple Base Classes

It is possible for a derived class to inherit two or more base classes. For example, in this short example, **derived** inherits both **base1** and **base2**.

```
// An example of multiple base classes.

#include <iostream>
using namespace std;

class base1 {
protected:
  int x;
public:
  void showx() { cout << x << "\n"; }
};

class base2 {
protected:
  int y;
public:
```

```
    void showy() {cout << y << "\n";}
};

// Inherit multiple base classes.
class derived: public base1, public base2 {
public:
  void set(int i, int j) { x=i; y=j; }
};

int main()
{
  derived ob;

  ob.set(10, 20); // provided by derived
  ob.showx(); // from base1
  ob.showy(); // from base2

  return 0;
}
```

As the example illustrates, to inherit more than one base class, use a comma-separated list. Further, be sure to use an access-specifier for each base inherited.

Constructors, Destructors, and Inheritance

There are two major questions that arise relative to constructors and destructors when inheritance is involved. First, when are base-class and derived-class constructors and destructors called? Second, how can parameters be passed to base-class constructors? This section examines these two important topics.

When Constructors and Destructors Are Executed

It is possible for a base class, a derived class, or both to contain constructors and/or destructors. It is important to understand the order in which these functions are executed when an object of a derived class comes into existence and when it goes out of existence. To begin, examine this short program:

```
#include <iostream>
using namespace std;
```

```
class base {
public:
  base() { cout << "Constructing base\n"; }
  ~base() { cout << "Destructing base\n"; }
};

class derived: public base {
public:
  derived() { cout << "Constructing derived\n"; }
  ~derived() { cout << "Destructing derived\n"; }
};

int main()
{
  derived ob;

  // do nothing but construct and destruct ob

  return 0;
}
```

As the comment in **main( )** indicates, this program simply constructs and then destroys an object called **ob** that is of class **derived**. When executed, this program displays

```
Constructing base
Constructing derived
Destructing derived
Destructing base
```

As you can see, first **base**'s constructor is executed followed by **derived**'s. Next (because **ob** is immediately destroyed in this program), **derived**'s destructor is called, followed by **base**'s.

The results of the foregoing experiment can be generalized. When an object of a derived class is created, the base class' constructor will be called first, followed by the derived class' constructor. When a derived object is destroyed, its destructor is called first, followed by the base class' destructor. Put differently, constructors are executed in their order of derivation. Destructors are executed in reverse order of derivation.

If you think about it, it makes sense that constructors are executed in order of derivation. Because a base class has no knowledge of any derived class, any initialization it needs to perform is separate from and possibly prerequisite to any initialization performed by the derived class. Therefore, it must be executed first.

Likewise, it is quite sensible that destructors be executed in reverse order of derivation. Because the base class underlies the derived class, the destruction of the base object implies the destruction of the derived object. Therefore, the derived destructor must be called before the object is fully destroyed.

In cases of multiple inheritance (that is, where a derived class becomes the base class for another derived class), the general rule applies: Constructors are called in order of derivation, destructors in reverse order. For example, this program

```cpp
#include <iostream>
using namespace std;

class base {
public:
  base() { cout << "Constructing base\n"; }
  ~base() { cout << "Destructing base\n"; }
};

class derived1 : public base {
public:
  derived1() { cout << "Constructing derived1\n"; }
  ~derived1() { cout << "Destructing derived1\n"; }
};

class derived2: public derived1 {
public:
  derived2() { cout << "Constructing derived2\n"; }
  ~derived2() { cout << "Destructing derived2\n"; }
};

int main()
{
  derived2 ob;

  // construct and destruct ob

  return 0;
}
```

displays this output:

```
Constructing base
Constructing derived1
Constructing derived2
Destructing derived2
Destructing derived1
Destructing base
```

The same general rule applies in situations involving multiple base classes. For example, this program

```cpp
#include <iostream>
using namespace std;

class base1 {
public:
  base1() { cout << "Constructing base1\n"; }
  ~base1() { cout << "Destructing base1\n"; }
};

class base2 {
public:
  base2() { cout << "Constructing base2\n"; }
  ~base2() { cout << "Destructing base2\n"; }
};

class derived: public base1, public base2 {
public:
  derived() { cout << "Constructing derived\n"; }
  ~derived() { cout << "Destructing derived\n"; }
};

int main()
{
  derived ob;

  // construct and destruct ob

  return 0;
}
```

produces this output:

```
Constructing base1
Constructing base2
Constructing derived
Destructing derived
Destructing base2
Destructing base1
```

As you can see, constructors are called in order of derivation, left to right, as specified in **derived**'s inheritance list. Destructors are called in reverse order, right to left. This means that had **base2** been specified before **base1** in **derived**'s list, as shown here:

```
class derived: public base2, public base1 {
```

then the output of this program would have looked like this:

```
Constructing base2
Constructing base1
Constructing derived
Destructing derived
Destructing base1
Destructing base2
```

Passing Parameters to Base-Class Constructors

So far, none of the preceding examples have included constructors that require arguments. In cases where only the derived class' constructor requires one or more parameters, you simply use the standard parameterized constructor syntax (see Chapter 12). However, how do you pass arguments to a constructor in a base class? The answer is to use an expanded form of the derived class's constructor declaration that passes along arguments to one or more base-class constructors. The general form of this expanded derived-class constructor declaration is shown here:

```
derived-constructor(arg-list) : base1(arg-list),
                               base2(arg-list),
                               // ...
                               baseN(arg-list)
{
    // body of derived constructor
}
```

Here, *base1* through *baseN* are the names of the base classes inherited by the derived class. Notice that a colon separates the derived class' constructor declaration from the base-class specifications, and that the base-class specifications are separated from each other by commas, in the case of multiple base classes. Consider this program:

```
#include <iostream>
using namespace std;

class base {
protected:
  int i;
public:
  base(int x) { i=x; cout << "Constructing base\n"; }
  ~base() { cout << "Destructing base\n"; }
};

class derived: public base {
  int j;
public:
  // derived uses x; y is passed along to base.
  derived(int x, int y): base(y)
    { j=x; cout << "Constructing derived\n"; }

  ~derived() { cout << "Destructing derived\n"; }
  void show() { cout << i << " " << j << "\n"; }
};

int main()
{
  derived ob(3, 4);

  ob.show(); // displays 4 3

  return 0;
}
```

Here, **derived**'s constructor is declared as taking two parameters, **x** and **y**. However, **derived( )** uses only **x**; **y** is passed along to **base( )**. In general, the derived class' constructor must declare both the parameter(s) that it requires as well as any required by the base class. As the example illustrates, any parameters required by the base class are passed to it in the base class' argument list specified after the colon.

Here is an example that uses multiple base classes:

```cpp
#include <iostream>
using namespace std;

class base1 {
protected:
  int i;
public:
  base1(int x) { i=x; cout << "Constructing base1\n"; }
  ~base1() { cout << "Destructing base1\n"; }
};

class base2 {
protected:
  int k;
public:
  base2(int x) { k=x; cout << "Constructing base2\n"; }
  ~base2() { cout << "Destructing base1\n"; }
};

class derived: public base1, public base2 {
  int j;
public:
  derived(int x, int y, int z): base1(y), base2(z)
    { j=x; cout << "Constructing derived\n"; }

  ~derived() { cout << "Destructing derived\n"; }
  void show() { cout << i << " " << j << " " << k << "\n"; }
};

int main()
{
  derived ob(3, 4, 5);

  ob.show(); // displays 4 3 5

  return 0;
}
```

It is important to understand that arguments to a base-class constructor are passed via arguments to the derived class' constructor. Therefore, even if a derived class' constructor does not use any arguments, it will still need to declare one if the base class requires it. In this situation, the arguments passed to the derived class are simply passed along to the base. For example, in this program, the derived class' constructor takes no arguments, but **base1( )** and **base2( )** do:

```cpp
#include <iostream>
using namespace std;

class base1 {
protected:
  int i;
public:
  base1(int x) { i=x; cout << "Constructing base1\n"; }
  ~base1() { cout << "Destructing base1\n"; }
};

class base2 {
protected:
  int k;
public:
  base2(int x) { k=x; cout << "Constructing base2\n"; }
  ~base2() { cout << "Destructing base2\n"; }
};

class derived: public base1, public base2 {
public:
  /* Derived constructor uses no parameter,
     but still must be declared as taking them to
     pass them along to base classes.
  */

  derived(int x, int y): base1(x), base2(y)
    { cout << "Constructing derived\n"; }

  ~derived() { cout << "Destructing derived\n"; }
  void show() { cout << i << " " << k << "\n"; }
};

int main()
{
  derived ob(3, 4);

  ob.show(); // displays 3 4
```

```
      return 0;
}
```

A derived class' constructor is free to make use of any and all parameters that it is declared as taking, even if one or more are passed along to a base class. Put differently, passing an argument along to a base class does not preclude its use by the derived class as well. For example, this fragment is perfectly valid:

```
class derived: public base {
  int j;
public:
  // derived uses both x and y and then passes them to base.
  derived(int x, int y): base(x, y)
    { j = x*y; cout << "Constructing derived\n"; }
```

One final point to keep in mind when passing arguments to base-class constructors: The argument can consist of any expression valid at the time. This includes function calls and variables. This is in keeping with the fact that C++ allows dynamic initialization.

Granting Access

When a base class is inherited as **private**, all public and protected members of that class become private members of the derived class. However, in certain circumstances, you may want to restore one or more inherited members to their original access specification. For example, you might want to grant certain public members of the base class public status in the derived class even though the base class is inherited as **private**. In Standard C++, you have two ways to accomplish this. First, you can use a **using** statement, which is the preferred way. The **using** statement is designed primarily to support namespaces and is discussed in Chapter 23. The second way to restore an inherited member's access specification is to employ an *access declaration* within the derived class. Access declarations are currently supported by Standard C++, but they are deprecated. This means that they should not be used for new code. Since there are still many, many existing programs that use access declarations, they will be examined here.

An access declaration takes this general form:

base-class::member;

The access declaration is put under the appropriate access heading in the derived class' declaration. Notice that no type declaration is required (or, indeed, allowed) in an access declaration.

To see how an access declaration works, let's begin with this short fragment:

```
class base {
public:
  int j; // public in base
};

// Inherit base as private.
class derived: private base {
public:

  // here is access declaration
  base::j; // make j public again
  .
  .
  .
};
```

Because **base** is inherited as **private** by **derived**, the public member **j** is made a private member of **derived**. However, by including

```
base::j;
```

as the access declaration under **derived**'s **public** heading, **j** is restored to its public status.

You can use an access declaration to restore the access rights of public and protected members. However, you cannot use an access declaration to raise or lower a member's access status. For example, a member declared as private in a base class cannot be made public by a derived class. (If C++ allowed this to occur, it would destroy its encapsulation mechanism!)

The following program illustrates the access declaration; notice how it uses access declarations to restore **j**, **seti( )**, and **geti( )** to **public** status.

```
#include <iostream>
using namespace std;

class base {
  int i; // private to base
```

```
public:
  int j, k;
  void seti(int x) { i = x; }
  int geti() { return i; }
};

// Inherit base as private.
class derived: private base {
public:
  /* The next three statements override
     base's inheritance as private and restore j,
     seti(), and geti() to public access. */
  base::j; // make j public again - but not k
  base::seti; // make seti() public
  base::geti; // make geti() public

// base::i; // illegal, you cannot elevate access

  int a; // public
};

int main()
{
  derived ob;

//ob.i = 10; // illegal because i is private in derived

  ob.j = 20; // legal because j is made public in derived
//ob.k = 30; // illegal because k is private in derived

  ob.a = 40; // legal because a is public in derived
  ob.seti(10);

  cout << ob.geti() << " " << ob.j << " " << ob.a;

  return 0;
}
```

Access declarations are supported in C++ to accommodate those situations in which most of an inherited class is intended to be made private, but a few members are to retain their public or protected status.

*While Standard C++ still supports access declarations, they are deprecated. This means that they are allowed for now, but they might not be supported in the future. Instead, the standard suggests achieving the same effect by applying the **using** keyword.*

Virtual Base Classes

An element of ambiguity can be introduced into a C++ program when multiple base classes are inherited. For example, consider this incorrect program:

```
// This program contains an error and will not compile.
#include <iostream>
using namespace std;

class base {
public:
  int i;
};

// derived1 inherits base.
class derived1 :  public base {
public:
  int j;
};

// derived2 inherits base.
class derived2 : public base {
public:
  int k;
};

/* derived3 inherits both derived1 and derived2.
   This means that there are two copies of base
   in derived3! */
class derived3 : public derived1, public derived2 {
public:
  int sum;
};

int main()
{
```

```
    derived3 ob;

    ob.i = 10; // this is ambiguous, which i???
    ob.j = 20;
    ob.k = 30;

    // i ambiguous here, too
    ob.sum = ob.i + ob.j + ob.k;

    // also ambiguous, which i?
    cout << ob.i << " ";

    cout << ob.j << " " << ob.k << " ";
    cout << ob.sum;

    return 0;
}
```

As the comments in the program indicate, both **derived1** and **derived2** inherit **base**. However, **derived3** inherits both **derived1** and **derived2**. This means that there are two copies of **base** present in an object of type **derived3**. Therefore, in an expression like

```
    ob.i = 10;
```

which **i** is being referred to, the one in **derived1** or the one in **derived2?** Because there are two copies of **base** present in object **ob**, there are two **ob.i**s! As you can see, the statement is inherently ambiguous.

There are two ways to remedy the preceding program. The first is to apply the scope resolution operator to **i** and manually select one **i**. For example, this version of the program does compile and run as expected:

```
// This program uses explicit scope resolution to select i.
#include <iostream>
using namespace std;

class base {
public:
  int i;
};


// derived1 inherits base.
```

```
class derived1 :  public base {
public:
  int j;
};

// derived2 inherits base.
class derived2 : public base {
public:
  int k;
};

/* derived3 inherits both derived1 and derived2.
   This means that there are two copies of base
   in derived3! */
class derived3 : public derived1, public derived2 {
public:
  int sum;
};

int main()
{
  derived3 ob;

  ob.derived1::i = 10; // scope resolved, use derived1's i
  ob.j = 20;
  ob.k = 30;

  // scope resolved
  ob.sum = ob.derived1::i + ob.j + ob.k;

  // also resolved here
  cout << ob.derived1::i << " ";

  cout << ob.j << " " << ob.k << " ";
  cout << ob.sum;

  return 0;
}
```

As you can see, because the **::** was applied, the program has manually selected **derived1**'s version of **base**. However, this solution raises a deeper issue: What if only one copy of **base** is actually required? Is there some way to prevent two copies from being included in **derived3**? The answer, as you probably have guessed, is yes. This solution is achieved using **virtual** base classes.

When two or more objects are derived from a common base class, you can prevent multiple copies of the base class from being present in an object derived from those objects by declaring the base class as **virtual** when it is inherited. You accomplish this by preceding the base class' name with the keyword **virtual** when it is inherited. For example, here is another version of the example program in which **derived3** contains only one copy of **base**:

```
// This program uses virtual base classes.
#include <iostream>
using namespace std;

class base {
public:
  int i;
};

// derived1 inherits base as virtual.
class derived1 : virtual public base {
public:
  int j;
};

// derived2 inherits base as virtual.
class derived2 : virtual public base {
public:
  int k;
};

/* derived3 inherits both derived1 and derived2.
   This time, there is only one copy of base class. */
class derived3 : public derived1, public derived2 {
public:
  int sum;
};

int main()
{
  derived3 ob;

  ob.i = 10; // now unambiguous
```

```
   ob.j = 20;
   ob.k = 30;

   // unambiguous
   ob.sum = ob.i + ob.j + ob.k;

   // unambiguous
   cout << ob.i << " ";

   cout << ob.j << " " << ob.k << " ";
   cout << ob.sum;

   return 0;
}
```

As you can see, the keyword **virtual** precedes the rest of the inherited **class'** specification. Now that both **derived1** and **derived2** have inherited **base** as **virtual**, any multiple inheritance involving them will cause only one copy of **base** to be present. Therefore, in **derived3**, there is only one copy of **base** and **ob.i = 10** is perfectly valid and unambiguous.

One further point to keep in mind: Even though both **derived1** and **derived2** specify **base** as **virtual**, **base** is still present in objects of either type. For example, the following sequence is perfectly valid:

```
// define a class of type derived1
derived1 myclass;

myclass.i = 88;
```

The only difference between a normal base class and a **virtual** one is what occurs when an object inherits the base more than once. If **virtual** base classes are used, then only one base class is present in the object. Otherwise, multiple copies will be found.

C++

The
Complete
Reference

C++

Chapter 17

Virtual Functions
and Polymorphism

Polymorphism is supported by C++ both at compile time and at run time. As discussed in earlier chapters, compile-time polymorphism is achieved by overloading functions and operators. Run-time polymorphism is accomplished by using inheritance and virtual functions, and these are the topics of this chapter.

Virtual Functions

A *virtual function* is a member function that is declared within a base class and redefined by a derived class. To create a virtual function, precede the function's declaration in the base class with the keyword **virtual**. When a class containing a virtual function is inherited, the derived class redefines the virtual function to fit its own needs. In essence, virtual functions implement the "one interface, multiple methods" philosophy that underlies polymorphism. The virtual function within the base class defines the *form* of the *interface* to that function. Each redefinition of the virtual function by a derived class implements its operation as it relates specifically to the derived class. That is, the redefinition creates a *specific method*.

When accessed "normally," virtual functions behave just like any other type of class member function. However, what makes virtual functions important and capable of supporting run-time polymorphism is how they behave when accessed via a pointer. As discussed in Chapter 13, a base-class pointer can be used to point to an object of any class derived from that base. When a base pointer points to a derived object that contains a virtual function, C++ determines which version of that function to call based upon *the type of object pointed to* by the pointer. And this determination is made *at run time*. Thus, when different objects are pointed to, different versions of the virtual function are executed. The same effect applies to base-class references.

To begin, examine this short example:

```cpp
#include <iostream>
using namespace std;

class base {
public:
  virtual void vfunc() {
    cout << "This is base's vfunc().\n";
  }
};

class derived1 : public base {
public:
  void vfunc() {
    cout << "This is derived1's vfunc().\n";
  }
```

```
};

class derived2 : public base {
public:
  void vfunc() {
    cout << "This is derived2's vfunc().\n";
  }
};

int main()
{
  base *p, b;
  derived1 d1;
  derived2 d2;

  // point to base
  p = &b;
  p->vfunc(); // access base's vfunc()

  // point to derived1
  p = &d1;
  p->vfunc(); // access derived1's vfunc()

  // point to derived2
  p = &d2;
  p->vfunc(); // access derived2's vfunc()

  return 0;
}
```

This program displays the following:

```
This is base's vfunc().
This is derived1's vfunc().
This is derived2's vfunc().
```

As the program illustrates, inside **base**, the virtual function **vfunc( )** is declared. Notice that the keyword **virtual** precedes the rest of the function declaration. When **vfunc( )** is redefined by **derived1** and **derived2**, the keyword **virtual** is not needed. (However, it is not an error to include it when redefining a virtual function inside a derived class; it's just not needed.)

In this program, **base** is inherited by both **derived1** and **derived2**. Inside each class definition, **vfunc( )** is redefined relative to that class. Inside **main( )**, four variables are declared:

Name	Type
p	base class pointer
b	object of base
d1	object of derived1
d2	object of derived2

Next, **p** is assigned the address of **b,** and **vfunc( )** is called via **p**. Since **p** is pointing to an object of type **base**, that version of **vfunc( )** is executed. Next, **p** is set to the address of **d1**, and again **vfunc( )** is called by using **p**. This time **p** points to an object of type **derived1**. This causes **derived1::vfunc( )** to be executed. Finally, **p** is assigned the address of **d2**, and **p–>vfunc( )** causes the version of **vfunc( )** redefined inside **derived2** to be executed. The key point here is that the kind of object to which **p** points determines which version of **vfunc( )** is executed. Further, this determination is made at run time, and this process forms the basis for run-time polymorphism.

Although you can call a virtual function in the "normal" manner by using an object's name and the dot operator, it is only when access is through a base-class pointer (or reference) that run-time polymorphism is achieved. For example, assuming the preceding example, this is syntactically valid:

```
d2.vfunc(); // calls derived2's vfunc()
```

Although calling a virtual function in this manner is not wrong, it simply does not take advantage of the virtual nature of **vfunc( )**.

At first glance, the redefinition of a virtual function by a derived class appears similar to function overloading. However, this is not the case, and the term *overloading* is not applied to virtual function redefinition because several differences exist. Perhaps the most important is that the prototype for a redefined virtual function must match exactly the prototype specified in the base class. This differs from overloading a normal function, in which return types and the number and type of parameters may differ. (In fact, when you overload a function, either the number or the type of the parameters *must* differ! It is through these differences that C++ can select the correct version of an overloaded function.) However, when a virtual function is redefined, all aspects of its prototype must be the same. If you change the prototype when you attempt to redefine a virtual function, the function will simply be considered overloaded by the C++ compiler, and its virtual nature will be lost. Another important restriction is that virtual functions must be nonstatic members of the classes of which they are part. They cannot be **friend**s. Finally, constructor functions cannot be virtual, but destructor functions can.

Because of the restrictions and differences between function overloading and virtual function redefinition, the term *overriding* is used to describe virtual function redefinition by a derived class.

Calling a Virtual Function
Through a Base Class Reference

In the preceding example, a virtual function was called through a base-class pointer, but the polymorphic nature of a virtual function is also available when called through a base-class reference. As explained in Chapter 13, a reference is an implicit pointer. Thus, a base-class reference can be used to refer to an object of the base class or any object derived from that base. When a virtual function is called through a base-class reference, the version of the function executed is determined by the object being referred to at the time of the call.

The most common situation in which a virtual function is invoked through a base class reference is when the reference is a function parameter. For example, consider the following variation on the preceding program.

```
/* Here, a base class reference is used to access
   a virtual function. */
#include <iostream>
using namespace std;

class base {
public:
  virtual void vfunc() {
    cout << "This is base's vfunc().\n";
  }
};

class derived1 : public base {
public:
  void vfunc() {
    cout << "This is derived1's vfunc().\n";
  }
};

class derived2 : public base {
public:
```

```
    void vfunc() {
      cout << "This is derived2's vfunc().\n";
    }
};

// Use a base class reference parameter.
void f(base &r) {
  r.vfunc();
}

int main()
{
  base b;
  derived1 d1;
  derived2 d2;

  f(b); // pass a base object to f()
  f(d1); // pass a derived1 object to f()
  f(d2); // pass a derived2 object to f()

  return 0;
}
```

This program produces the same output as its preceding version. In this example, the
function **f( )** defines a reference parameter of type **base**. Inside **main( )**, the function
is called using objects of type **base**, **derived1**, and **derived2**. Inside **f( )**, the specific
version of **vfunc( )** that is called is determined by the type of object being referenced
when the function is called.

For the sake of simplicity, the rest of the examples in this chapter will call virtual
functions through base-class pointers, but the effects are same for base-class references.

The Virtual Attribute Is Inherited

When a virtual function is inherited, its virtual nature is also inherited. This means that
when a derived class that has inherited a virtual function is itself used as a base class
for another derived class, the virtual function can still be overridden. Put differently, no
matter how many times a virtual function is inherited, it remains virtual. For example,
consider this program:

```
#include <iostream>
using namespace std;
```

```cpp
class base {
public:
  virtual void vfunc() {
    cout << "This is base's vfunc().\n";
  }
};

class derived1 : public base {
public:
  void vfunc() {
    cout << "This is derived1's vfunc().\n";
  }
};

/* derived2 inherits virtual function vfunc()
   from derived1. */
class derived2 : public derived1 {
public:
  // vfunc() is still virtual
  void vfunc() {
    cout << "This is derived2's vfunc().\n";
  }
};

int main()
{
  base *p, b;
  derived1 d1;
  derived2 d2;

  // point to base
  p = &b;
  p->vfunc(); // access base's vfunc()

  // point to derived1
  p = &d1;
  p->vfunc(); // access derived1's vfunc()

  // point to derived2
  p = &d2;
  p->vfunc(); // access derived2's vfunc()
```

C++

```
    return 0;
}
```

As expected, the preceding program displays this output:

```
This is base's vfunc().
This is derived1's vfunc().
This is derived2's vfunc().
```

In this case, **derived2** inherits **derived1** rather than **base**, but **vfunc( )** is still virtual.

Virtual Functions Are Hierarchical

As explained, when a function is declared as **virtual** by a base class, it may be overridden by a derived class. However, the function does not have to be overridden. When a derived class fails to override a virtual function, then when an object of that derived class accesses that function, the function defined by the base class is used. For example, consider this program in which **derived2** does not override **vfunc( )**:

```
#include <iostream>
using namespace std;

class base {
public:
  virtual void vfunc() {
    cout << "This is base's vfunc().\n";
  }
};

class derived1 : public base {
public:
  void vfunc() {
    cout << "This is derived1's vfunc().\n";
  }
};

class derived2 : public base {
```

```
public:
// vfunc() not overridden by derived2, base's is used
};

int main()
{
  base *p, b;
  derived1 d1;
  derived2 d2;

  // point to base
  p = &b;
  p->vfunc(); // access base's vfunc()

  // point to derived1
  p = &d1;
  p->vfunc(); // access derived1's vfunc()

  // point to derived2
  p = &d2;
  p->vfunc(); // use base's vfunc()

  return 0;
}
```

The program produces this output:

```
This is base's vfunc().
This is derived1's vfunc().
This is base's vfunc().
```

Because **derived2** does not override **vfunc( )**, the function defined by **base** is used when **vfunc( )** is referenced relative to objects of type **derived2**.

The preceding program illustrates a special case of a more general rule. Because inheritance is hierarchical in C++, it makes sense that virtual functions are also hierarchical. This means that when a derived class fails to override a virtual function, the first redefinition found in reverse order of derivation is used. For example, in the following program, **derived2** is derived from **derived1**, which is derived from **base**. However, **derived2** does not override **vfunc( )**. This means that, relative to **derived2**, the closest version of **vfunc( )** is in **derived1**. Therefore, it is **derived1::vfunc( )** that is used when an object of **derived2** attempts to call **vfunc( )**.

```cpp
#include <iostream>
using namespace std;

class base {
public:
  virtual void vfunc() {
    cout << "This is base's vfunc().\n";
  }
};

class derived1 : public base {
public:
  void vfunc() {
    cout << "This is derived1's vfunc().\n";
  }
};

class derived2 : public derived1 {
public:
/* vfunc() not overridden by derived2.
   In this case, since derived2 is derived from
   derived1, derived1's vfunc() is used.
*/
};

int main()
{
  base *p, b;
  derived1 d1;
  derived2 d2;

  // point to base
  p = &b;
  p->vfunc(); // access base's vfunc()

  // point to derived1
  p = &d1;
  p->vfunc(); // access derived1's vfunc()
```

```
    // point to derived2
    p = &d2;
    p->vfunc(); // use derived1's vfunc()

    return 0;
}
```

The program displays the following:

```
This is base's vfunc().
This is derived1's vfunc().
This is derived1's vfunc().
```

Pure Virtual Functions

As the examples in the preceding section illustrate, when a virtual function is not redefined by a derived class, the version defined in the base class will be used. However, in many situations there can be no meaningful definition of a virtual function within a base class. For example, a base class may not be able to define an object sufficiently to allow a base-class virtual function to be created. Further, in some situations you will want to ensure that all derived classes override a virtual function. To handle these two cases, C++ supports the pure virtual function.

A *pure virtual function* is a virtual function that has no definition within the base class. To declare a pure virtual function, use this general form:

virtual *type func-name(parameter-list)* = 0;

When a virtual function is made pure, any derived class must provide its own definition. If the derived class fails to override the pure virtual function, a compile-time error will result.

The following program contains a simple example of a pure virtual function. The base class, **number**, contains an integer called **val**, the function **setval( )**, and the pure virtual function **show( )**. The derived classes **hextype**, **dectype**, and **octtype** inherit **number** and redefine **show( )** so that it outputs the value of **val** in each respective number base (that is, hexadecimal, decimal, or octal).

```
#include <iostream>
using namespace std;

class number {
```

```cpp
protected:
  int val;
public:
  void setval(int i) { val = i; }

  // show() is a pure virtual function
  virtual void show() = 0;
};

class hextype : public number {
public:
  void show() {
    cout << hex << val << "\n";
  }
};

class dectype : public number {
public:
  void show() {
    cout << val << "\n";
  }
};

class octtype : public number {
public:
  void show() {
    cout << oct << val << "\n";
  }
};

int main()
{
  dectype d;
  hextype h;
  octtype o;

  d.setval(20);
  d.show(); // displays 20 - decimal

  h.setval(20);
  h.show(); // displays 14 - hexadecimal
```

```
o.setval(20);
o.show();  // displays 24 - octal

return 0;
}
```

Although this example is quite simple, it illustrates how a base class may not be able to meaningfully define a virtual function. In this case, **number** simply provides the common interface for the derived types to use. There is no reason to define **show( )** inside **number** since the base of the number is undefined. Of course, you can always create a placeholder definition of a virtual function. However, making **show( )** pure also ensures that all derived classes will indeed redefine it to meet their own needs.

Keep in mind that when a virtual function is declared as pure, all derived classes must override it. If a derived class fails to do this, a compile-time error will result.

Abstract Classes

A class that contains at least one pure virtual function is said to be *abstract*. Because an abstract class contains one or more functions for which there is no definition (that is, a pure virtual function), no objects of an abstract class may be created. Instead, an abstract class constitutes an incomplete type that is used as a foundation for derived classes.

Although you cannot create objects of an abstract class, you can create pointers and references to an abstract class. This allows abstract classes to support run-time polymorphism, which relies upon base-class pointers and references to select the proper virtual function.

Using Virtual Functions

One of the central aspects of object-oriented programming is the principle of "one interface, multiple methods." This means that a general class of actions can be defined, the interface to which is constant, with each derivation defining its own specific operations. In concrete C++ terms, a base class can be used to define the nature of the interface to a general class. Each derived class then implements the specific operations as they relate to the type of data used by the derived type.

One of the most powerful and flexible ways to implement the "one interface, multiple methods" approach is to use virtual functions, abstract classes, and run-time polymorphism. Using these features, you create a class hierarchy that moves from general to specific (base to derived). Following this philosophy, you define all common features and interfaces in a base class. In cases where certain actions can be implemented only by the derived class, use a virtual function. In essence, in the base

C++

class you create and define everything you can that relates to the general case. The derived class fills in the specific details.

Following is a simple example that illustrates the value of the "one interface, multiple methods" philosophy. A class hierarchy is created that performs conversions from one system of units to another. (For example, liters to gallons.) The base class **convert** declares two variables, **val1** and **val2**, which hold the initial and converted values, respectively. It also defines the functions **getinit( )** and **getconv( )**, which return the initial value and the converted value. These elements of **convert** are fixed and applicable to all derived classes that will inherit **convert**. However, the function that will actually perform the conversion, **compute( )**, is a pure virtual function that must be defined by the classes derived from **convert**. The specific nature of **compute( )** will be determined by what type of conversion is taking place.

```cpp
// Virtual function practical example.
#include <iostream>
using namespace std;

class convert {
protected:
  double val1;  // initial value
  double val2;  // converted value
public:
  convert(double i) {
    val1 = i;
  }
  double getconv() { return val2; }
  double getinit() { return val1; }

  virtual void compute() = 0;
};

// Liters to gallons.
class l_to_g : public convert {
public:
  l_to_g(double i) : convert(i) { }
  void compute() {
    val2 = val1 / 3.7854;
  }
};

// Fahrenheit to Celsius
class f_to_c : public convert {
```

```
public:
  f_to_c(double i) : convert(i) { }
  void compute() {
    val2 = (val1-32) / 1.8;
  }
};

int main()
{
  convert *p;  // pointer to base class

  l_to_g lgob(4);
  f_to_c fcob(70);

  // use virtual function mechanism to convert
  p = &lgob;
  cout << p->getinit() << " liters is ";
  p->compute();
  cout << p->getconv() << " gallons\n";  // l_to_g

  p = &fcob;
  cout << p->getinit() << " in Fahrenheit is ";
  p->compute();
  cout << p->getconv() << " Celsius\n";  // f_to_c

  return 0;
}
```

The preceding program creates two derived classes from **convert**, called **l_to_g** and **f_to_c**. These classes perform the conversions of liters to gallons and Fahrenheit to Celsius, respectively. Each derived class overrides **compute( )** in its own way to perform the desired conversion. However, even though the actual conversion (that is, method) differs between **l_to_g** and **f_to_c**, the interface remains constant.

One of the benefits of derived classes and virtual functions is that handling a new case is a very easy matter. For example, assuming the preceding program, you can add a conversion from feet to meters by including this class:

```
// Feet to meters
class f_to_m : public convert {
public:
  f_to_m(double i) : convert(i) { }
```

```
void compute() {
  val2 = val1 / 3.28;
  }
};
```

An important use of abstract classes and virtual functions is in *class libraries*. You can create a generic, extensible class library that will be used by other programmers. Another programmer will inherit your general class, which defines the interface and all elements common to all classes derived from it, and will add those functions specific to the derived class. By creating class libraries, you are able to create and control the interface of a general class while still letting other programmers adapt it to their specific needs.

One final point: The base class **convert** is an example of an abstract class. The virtual function **compute( )** is not defined within **convert** because no meaningful definition can be provided. The class **convert** simply does not contain sufficient information for **compute( )** to be defined. It is only when **convert** is inherited by a derived class that a complete type is created.

Early vs. Late Binding

Before concluding this chapter on virtual functions and run-time polymorphism, there are two terms that need to be defined because they are used frequently in discussions of C++ and object-oriented programming: *early binding* and *late binding*.

Early binding refers to events that occur at compile time. In essence, early binding occurs when all information needed to call a function is known at compile time. (Put differently, early binding means that an object and a function call are bound during compilation.) Examples of early binding include normal function calls (including standard library functions), overloaded function calls, and overloaded operators. The main advantage to early binding is efficiency. Because all information necessary to call a function is determined at compile time, these types of function calls are very fast.

The opposite of early binding is *late binding*. As it relates to C++, late binding refers to function calls that are not resolved until run time. Virtual functions are used to achieve late binding. As you know, when access is via a base pointer or reference, the virtual function actually called is determined by the type of object pointed to by the pointer. Because in most cases this cannot be determined at compile time, the object and the function are not linked until run time. The main advantage to late binding is flexibility. Unlike early binding, late binding allows you to create programs that can respond to events occurring while the program executes without having to create a large amount of "contingency code." Keep in mind that because a function call is not resolved until run time, late binding can make for somewhat slower execution times.

Chapter 18

Templates

The template is one of C++'s most sophisticated and high-powered features. Although not part of the original specification for C++, it was added several years ago and is supported by all modern C++ compilers. Using templates, it is possible to create generic functions and classes. In a generic function or class, the type of data upon which the function or class operates is specified as a parameter. Thus, you can use one function or class with several different types of data without having to explicitly recode specific versions for each data type. Both generic functions and generic classes are discussed in this chapter.

Generic Functions

A generic function defines a general set of operations that will be applied to various types of data. The type of data that the function will operate upon is passed to it as a parameter. Through a generic function, a single general procedure can be applied to a wide range of data. As you probably know, many algorithms are logically the same no matter what type of data is being operated upon. For example, the Quicksort sorting algorithm is the same whether it is applied to an array of integers or an array of floats. It is just that the type of the data being sorted is different. By creating a generic function, you can define the nature of the algorithm, independent of any data. Once you have done this, the compiler will automatically generate the correct code for the type of data that is actually used when you execute the function. In essence, when you create a generic function you are creating a function that can automatically overload itself.

A generic function is created using the keyword **template**. The normal meaning of the word "template" accurately reflects its use in C++. It is used to create a template (or framework) that describes what a function will do, leaving it to the compiler to fill in the details as needed. The general form of a template function definition is shown here:

```
template <class Ttype> ret-type func-name(parameter list)
{
    // body of function
}
```

Here, *Ttype* is a placeholder name for a data type used by the function. This name may be used within the function definition. However, it is only a placeholder that the compiler will automatically replace with an actual data type when it creates a specific version of the function. Although the use of the keyword **class** to specify a generic type in a **template** declaration is traditional, you may also use the keyword **typename**.

The following example creates a generic function that swaps the values of the two variables with which it is called. Because the general process of exchanging two values is independent of the type of the variables, it is a good candidate for being made into a generic function.

```
// Function template example.
#include <iostream>
using namespace std;

// This is a function template.
template <class X> void swapargs(X &a, X &b)
{
  X temp;

  temp = a;
  a = b;
  b = temp;
}

int main()
{
  int i=10, j=20;
  double x=10.1, y=23.3;
  char a='x', b='z';

  cout << "Original i, j: " << i << ' ' << j << '\n';
  cout << "Original x, y: " << x << ' ' << y << '\n';
  cout << "Original a, b: " << a << ' ' << b << '\n';

  swapargs(i, j); // swap integers
  swapargs(x, y); // swap floats
  swapargs(a, b); // swap chars

  cout << "Swapped i, j: " << i << ' ' << j << '\n';
  cout << "Swapped x, y: " << x << ' ' << y << '\n';
  cout << "Swapped a, b: " << a << ' ' << b << '\n';

  return 0;
}
```

Let's look closely at this program. The line:

```
template <class X> void swapargs(X &a, X &b)
```

tells the compiler two things: that a template is being created and that a generic
definition is beginning. Here, **X** is a generic type that is used as a placeholder. After the
template portion, the function **swapargs( )** is declared, using **X** as the data type of the
values that will be swapped. In **main( )**, the **swapargs( )** function is called using three

different types of data: **int**s, **double**s, and **char**s. Because **swapargs( )** is a generic function, the compiler automatically creates three versions of **swapargs( )**: one that will exchange integer values, one that will exchange floating-point values, and one that will swap characters.

Here are some important terms related to templates. First, a generic function (that is, a function definition preceded by a **template** statement) is also called a *template function*. Both terms will be used interchangeably in this book. When the compiler creates a specific version of this function, it is said to have created a *specialization*. This is also called a *generated function*. The act of generating a function is referred to as *instantiating* it. Put differently, a generated function is a specific instance of a template function.

Since C++ does not recognize end-of-line as a statement terminator, the **template** clause of a generic function definition does not have to be on the same line as the function's name. The following example shows another common way to format the **swapargs( )** function.

```
template <class X>
void swapargs(X &a, X &b)
{
  X temp;

  temp = a;
  a = b;
  b = temp;
}
```

If you use this form, it is important to understand that no other statements can occur between the **template** statement and the start of the generic function definition. For example, the fragment shown next will not compile.

```
// This will not compile.
template <class X>
int i; // this is an error
void swapargs(X &a, X &b)
{
  X temp;

  temp = a;
  a = b;
  b = temp;
}
```

As the comments imply, the **template** specification must directly precede the function definition.

A Function with Two Generic Types

You can define more than one generic data type in the **template** statement by using a comma-separated list. For example, this program creates a template function that has two generic types.

```
#include <iostream>
using namespace std;

template <class type1, class type2>
void myfunc(type1 x, type2 y)
{
  cout << x << ' ' << y << '\n';
}

int main()
{
  myfunc(10, "I like C++");

  myfunc(98.6, 19L);

  return 0;
}
```

In this example, the placeholder types **type1** and **type2** are replaced by the compiler with the data types **int** and **char ***, and **double** and **long**, respectively, when the compiler generates the specific instances of **myfunc( )** within **main( )**.

 When you create a template function, you are, in essence, allowing the compiler to generate as many different versions of that function as are necessary for handling the various ways that your program calls the function.

Explicitly Overloading a Generic Function

Even though a generic function overloads itself as needed, you can explicitly overload one, too. This is formally called *explicit specialization*. If you overload a generic function, that overloaded function overrides (or "hides") the generic function relative to that specific version. For example, consider the following revised version of the argument-swapping example shown earlier.

```
// Overriding a template function.
#include <iostream>
using namespace std;
```

```cpp
template <class X> void swapargs(X &a, X &b)
{
  X temp;

  temp = a;
  a = b;
  b = temp;
  cout << "Inside template swapargs.\n";
}

// This overrides the generic version of swapargs() for ints.
void swapargs(int &a, int &b)
{
  int temp;

  temp = a;
  a = b;
  b = temp;
  cout << "Inside swapargs int specialization.\n";
}

int main()
{
  int i=10, j=20;
  double x=10.1, y=23.3;
  char a='x', b='z';

  cout << "Original i, j: " << i << ' ' << j << '\n';
  cout << "Original x, y: " << x << ' ' << y << '\n';
  cout << "Original a, b: " << a << ' ' << b << '\n';

  swapargs(i, j); // calls explicitly overloaded swapargs()
  swapargs(x, y); // calls generic swapargs()
  swapargs(a, b); // calls generic swapargs()

  cout << "Swapped i, j: " << i << ' ' << j << '\n';
  cout << "Swapped x, y: " << x << ' ' << y << '\n';
  cout << "Swapped a, b: " << a << ' ' << b << '\n';

  return 0;
}
```

This program displays the following output.

```
Original i, j: 10 20
Original x, y: 10.1 23.3
Original a, b: x z
Inside swapargs int specialization.
Inside template swapargs.
Inside template swapargs.
Swapped i, j: 20 10
Swapped x, y: 23.3 10.1
Swapped a, b: z x
```

As the comments inside the program indicate, when **swapargs(i, j)** is called, it invokes the explicitly overloaded version of **swapargs( )** defined in the program. Thus, the compiler does not generate this version of the generic **swapargs( )** function, because the generic function is overridden by the explicit overloading.

Recently, a new-style syntax was introduced to denote the explicit specialization of a function. This new method uses the **template** keyword. For example, using the new-style specialization syntax, the overloaded **swapargs( )** function from the preceding program looks like this.

```
// Use new-style specialization syntax.
template<> void swapargs<int>(int &a, int &b)
{
  int temp;

  temp = a;
  a = b;
  b = temp;
  cout << "Inside swapargs int specialization.\n";
}
```

As you can see, the new-style syntax uses the **template<>** construct to indicate specialization. The type of data for which the specialization is being created is placed inside the angle brackets following the function name. This same syntax is used to specialize any type of generic function. While there is no advantage to using one specialization syntax over the other at this time, the new-style is probably a better approach for the long term.

Explicit specialization of a template allows you to tailor a version of a generic function to accommodate a unique situation—perhaps to take advantage of some performance boost that applies to only one type of data, for example. However, as a general rule, if you need to have different versions of a function for different data types, you should use overloaded functions rather than templates.

Overloading a Function Template

In addition to creating explicit, overloaded versions of a generic function, you can also overload the **template** specification itself. To do so, simply create another version of the template that differs from any others in its parameter list. For example:

```
// Overload a function template declaration.
#include <iostream>
using namespace std;

// First version of f() template.
template <class X> void f(X a)
{
  cout << "Inside f(X a)\n";
}

// Second version of f() template.
template <class X, class Y> void f(X a, Y b)
{
  cout << "Inside f(X a, Y b)\n";
}

int main()
{
  f(10);     // calls f(X)
  f(10, 20); // calls f(X, Y)

  return 0;
}
```

Here, the template for **f( )** is overloaded to accept either one or two parameters.

Using Standard Parameters with Template Functions

You can mix standard parameters with generic type parameters in a template function. These nongeneric parameters work just like they do with any other function. For example:

```
// Using standard parameters in a template function.
#include <iostream>
using namespace std;
```

```
const int TABWIDTH = 8;

// Display data at specified tab position.
template<class X> void tabOut(X data, int tab)
{
  for(; tab; tab--)
    for(int i=0; i<TABWIDTH; i++) cout << ' ';

    cout << data << "\n";
}

int main()
{
  tabOut("This is a test", 0);
  tabOut(100, 1);
  tabOut('X', 2);
  tabOut(10/3, 3);

  return 0;
}
```

Here is the output produced by this program.

```
This is a test
        100
                X
                        3
```

In the program, the function **tabOut( )** displays its first argument at the tab position requested by its second argument. Since the first argument is a generic type, **tabOut( )** can be used to display any type of data. The **tab** parameter is a standard, call-by-value parameter. The mixing of generic and nongeneric parameters causes no trouble and is, indeed, both common and useful.

Generic Function Restrictions

Generic functions are similar to overloaded functions except that they are more restrictive. When functions are overloaded, you may have different actions performed within the body of each function. But a generic function must perform the same general action for all versions—only the type of data can differ. Consider the overloaded functions in the following example program. These functions could *not* be replaced by a generic function because they do not do the same thing.

```cpp
#include <iostream>
#include <cmath>
using namespace std;

void myfunc(int i)
{
  cout << "value is: " << i << "\n";
}

void myfunc(double d)
{
  double intpart;
  double fracpart;

  fracpart = modf(d, &intpart);
  cout << "Fractional part: " << fracpart;
  cout << "\n";
  cout << "Integer part: " << intpart;
}

int main()
{
  myfunc(1);
  myfunc(12.2);

  return 0;
}
```

Applying Generic Functions

Generic functions are one of C++'s most useful features. They can be applied to all types of situations. As mentioned earlier, whenever you have a function that defines a generalizable algorithm, you can make it into a template function. Once you have done so, you may use it with any type of data without having to recode it. Before moving on to generic classes, two examples of applying generic functions will be given. They illustrate how easy it is to take advantage of this powerful C++ feature.

A Generic Sort

Sorting is exactly the type of operation for which generic functions were designed.
Within wide latitude, a sorting algorithm is the same no matter what type of data is
being sorted. The following program illustrates this by creating a generic bubble sort.
While the bubble sort is a rather poor sorting algorithm, its operation is clear and
uncluttered and it makes an easy-to-understand example. The **bubble( )** function
will sort any type of array. It is called with a pointer to the first element in the array
and the number of elements in the array.

```cpp
// A Generic bubble sort.
#include <iostream>
using namespace std;

template <class X> void bubble(
  X *items,  // pointer to array to be sorted
  int count) // number of items in array
{
  register int a, b;
  X t;

  for(a=1; a<count; a++)
    for(b=count-1; b>=a; b--)
      if(items[b-1] > items[b]) {
        // exchange elements
        t = items[b-1];
        items[b-1] = items[b];
        items[b] = t;
      }
}

int main()
{
  int iarray[7] = {7, 5, 4, 3, 9, 8, 6};
  double darray[5] = {4.3, 2.5, -0.9, 100.2, 3.0};

  int i;

  cout << "Here is unsorted integer array: ";
  for(i=0;  i<7; i++)
```

C++

```
      cout << iarray[i] << ' ';
   cout << endl;

   cout << "Here is unsorted double array: ";
   for(i=0;  i<5; i++)
     cout << darray[i] << ' ';
   cout << endl;

   bubble(iarray, 7);
   bubble(darray, 5);

   cout << "Here is sorted integer array: ";
   for(i=0;  i<7; i++)
     cout << iarray[i] << ' ';
   cout << endl;

   cout << "Here is sorted double array: ";
   for(i=0;  i<5; i++)
     cout << darray[i] << ' ';
   cout << endl;

   return 0;
}
```

The output produced by the program is shown here.

```
Here is unsorted integer array: 7 5 4 3 9 8 6
Here is unsorted double array: 4.3 2.5 -0.9 100.2 3
Here is sorted integer array: 3 4 5 6 7 8 9
Here is sorted double array: -0.9 2.5 3 4.3 100.2
```

As you can see, the preceding program creates two arrays: one integer and one **double**. It then sorts each. Because **bubble( )** is a template function, it is automatically over-loaded to accommodate the two different types of data. You might want to try using **bubble( )** to sort other types of data, including classes that you create. In each case, the compiler will create the right version of the function for you.

Compacting an Array

Another function that benefits from being made into a template is called **compact( )**. This function compacts the elements in an array. It is not uncommon to want to remove elements from the middle of an array and then move the remaining elements down so that all unused elements are at the end. This sort of operation is the same for all types of arrays because it is independent of the type data actually being operated upon. The generic **compact( )** function shown in the following program is called with a pointer to the first element in the array, the number of elements in the array, and the starting and ending indexes of the elements to be removed. The function then removes those elements and compacts the array. For the purposes of illustration, it also zeroes the unused elements at the end of the array that have been freed by the compaction.

```cpp
// A Generic array compaction function.
#include <iostream>
using namespace std;

template <class X> void compact(
  X *items,   // pointer to array to be compacted
  int count, // number of items in array
  int start, // starting index of compacted region
  int end)    // ending index of compacted region
{
  register int i;

  for(i=end+1; i<count; i++, start++)
    items[start] = items[i];

  /* For the sake of illustration, the remainder of
     the array will be zeroed. */
  for( ; start<count; start++) items[start] = (X) 0;
}

int main()
{
  int nums[7] = {0, 1, 2, 3, 4, 5, 6};
  char str[18] = "Generic Functions";

  int i;

  cout << "Here is uncompacted integer array: ";
  for(i=0;  i<7; i++)
    cout << nums[i] << ' ';
  cout << endl;

  cout << "Here is uncompacted string: ";
  for(i=0;  i<18; i++)
```

```
      cout << str[i] << ' ';
   cout << endl;

   compact(nums, 7, 2, 4);
   compact(str, 18, 6, 10);

   cout << "Here is compacted integer array: ";
   for(i=0;  i<7; i++)
     cout << nums[i] << ' ';
   cout << endl;

   cout << "Here is compacted string: ";
   for(i=0;  i<18; i++)
     cout << str[i] << ' ';
   cout << endl;

   return 0;
}
```

This program compacts two different types of arrays. One is an integer array, and the other is a string. However, the **compact( )** function will work for any type of array. The output from this program in shown here.

```
Here is uncompacted integer array: 0 1 2 3 4 5 6
Here is uncompacted string: G e n e r i c   F u n c t i o n s
Here is compacted integer array: 0 1 5 6 0 0 0
Here is compacted string: G e n e r i c t i o n s
```

As the preceding examples illustrate, once you begin to think in terms of templates, many uses will naturally suggest themselves. As long as the underlying logic of a function is independent of the data, it can be made into a generic function.

Generic Classes

In addition to generic functions, you can also define a generic class. When you do this, you create a class that defines all the algorithms used by that class; however, the actual type of the data being manipulated will be specified as a parameter when objects of that class are created.

Generic classes are useful when a class uses logic that can be generalized. For example, the same algorithms that maintain a queue of integers will also work for a queue of characters, and the same mechanism that maintains a linked list of mailing addresses will also maintain a linked list of auto part information. When you create a generic class, it can perform the operation you define, such as maintaining a queue or a linked list, for any type of data. The compiler will automatically generate the correct type of object, based upon the type you specify when the object is created.

The general form of a generic class declaration is shown here:

template <class *Ttype*> class *class-name* {

   .

   .

   .

}

Here, *Ttype* is the placeholder type name, which will be specified when a class is instantiated. If necessary, you can define more than one generic data type using a comma-separated list.

Once you have created a generic class, you create a specific instance of that class using the following general form:

class-name <*type*> *ob*;

Here, *type* is the type name of the data that the class will be operating upon. Member functions of a generic class are themselves automatically generic. You need not use **template** to explicitly specify them as such.

In the following program, the **stack** class (first introduced in Chapter 11) is reworked into a generic class. Thus, it can be used to store objects of any type. In this example, a character stack and a floating-point stack are created, but any data type can be used.

```
// This function demonstrates a generic stack.
#include <iostream>
using namespace std;

const int SIZE = 10;

// Create a generic stack class
template <class StackType> class stack {
  StackType stck[SIZE]; // holds the stack
  int tos; // index of top-of-stack

public:
  stack() { tos = 0; } // initialize stack
  void push(StackType ob); // push object on stack
```

```
    StackType pop(); // pop object from stack
};

// Push an object.
template <class StackType> void stack<StackType>::push(StackType ob)
{
  if(tos==SIZE) {
    cout << "Stack is full.\n";
    return;
  }
  stck[tos] = ob;
  tos++;
}
// Pop an object.
template <class StackType> StackType stack<StackType>::pop()
{
  if(tos==0) {
    cout << "Stack is empty.\n";
    return 0; // return null on empty stack
  }
  tos--;
  return stck[tos];
}

int main()
{
  // Demonstrate character stacks.
  stack<char> s1, s2;  // create two character stacks
  int i;

  s1.push('a');
  s2.push('x');
  s1.push('b');
  s2.push('y');
  s1.push('c');
  s2.push('z');

  for(i=0; i<3; i++) cout << "Pop s1: " << s1.pop() << "\n";
  for(i=0; i<3; i++) cout << "Pop s2: " << s2.pop() << "\n";

  // demonstrate double stacks
  stack<double> ds1, ds2;  // create two double stacks
```

```
    ds1.push(1.1);
    ds2.push(2.2);
    ds1.push(3.3);
    ds2.push(4.4);
    ds1.push(5.5);
    ds2.push(6.6);

    for(i=0; i<3; i++) cout << "Pop ds1: " << ds1.pop() << "\n";
    for(i=0; i<3; i++) cout << "Pop ds2: " << ds2.pop() << "\n";

    return 0;
}
```

As you can see, the declaration of a generic class is similar to that of a generic function. The actual type of data stored by the stack is generic in the class declaration. It is not until an object of the stack is declared that the actual data type is determined. When a specific instance of **stack** is declared, the compiler automatically generates all the functions and variables necessary for handling the actual data. In this example, two different types of stacks are declared. Two are integer stacks. Two are stacks of **double**s. Pay special attention to these declarations:

```
stack<char> s1, s2;   // create two character stacks
stack<double> ds1, ds2;  // create two double stacks
```

Notice how the desired data type is passed inside the angle brackets. By changing the type of data specified when **stack** objects are created, you can change the type of data stored in that stack. For example, by using the following declaration, you can create another stack that stores character pointers.

```
stack<char *> chrptrQ;
```

You can also create stacks to store data types that you create. For example, if you want to use the following structure to store address information,

```
struct addr {
  char name[40];
  char street[40];
  char city[30];
  char state[3];
```

```
    char zip[12];
};
```

then to use **stack** to generate a stack that will store objects of type **addr**, use a declaration like this:

```
stack<addr> obj;
```

As the **stack** class illustrates, generic functions and classes are powerful tools that you can use to maximize your programming efforts, because they allow you to define the general form of an object that can then be used with any type of data. You are saved from the tedium of creating separate implementations for each data type with which you want the algorithm to work. The compiler automatically creates the specific versions of the class for you.

An Example with Two Generic Data Types

A template class can have more than one generic data type. Simply declare all the data types required by the class in a comma-separated list within the **template** specification. For example, the following short example creates a class that uses two generic data types.

```
/* This example uses two generic data types in a
   class definition.
*/
#include <iostream>
using namespace std;

template <class Type1, class Type2> class myclass
{
  Type1 i;
  Type2 j;
public:
  myclass(Type1 a, Type2 b) { i = a; j = b; }
  void show() { cout << i << ' ' << j << '\n'; }
};

int main()
{
  myclass<int, double> ob1(10, 0.23);
  myclass<char, char *> ob2('X', "Templates add power.");
```

```
    ob1.show(); // show int, double
    ob2.show(); // show char, char *

    return 0;
}
```

This program produces the following output:

```
10 0.23
X Templates add power.
```

The program declares two types of objects. **ob1** uses **int** and **double** data. **ob2** uses a character and a character pointer. For both cases, the compiler automatically generates the appropriate data and functions to accommodate the way the objects are created.

Applying Template Classes: A Generic Array Class

To illustrate the practical benefits of template classes, let's look at one way in which they are commonly applied. As you saw in Chapter 15, you can overload the [ ] operator. Doing so allows you to create your own array implementations, including "safe arrays" that provide run-time boundary checking. As you know, in C++, it is possible to overrun (or underrun) an array boundary at run time without generating a run-time error message. However, if you create a class that contains the array, and allow access to that array only through the overloaded [ ] subscripting operator, then you can intercept an out-of-range index.

By combining operator overloading with a template class, it is possible to create a generic safe-array type that can be used for creating safe arrays of any data type. This type of array is shown in the following program:

```
// A generic safe array example.
#include <iostream>
#include <cstdlib>
using namespace std;

const int SIZE = 10;

template <class AType> class atype {
  AType a[SIZE];
public:
  atype() {
```

```
      register int i;
      for(i=0; i<SIZE; i++) a[i] = i;
  }
  AType &operator[](int i);
};

// Provide range checking for atype.
template <class AType> AType &atype<AType>::operator[](int i)
{
  if(i<0 || i> SIZE-1) {
    cout << "\nIndex value of ";
    cout << i << " is out-of-bounds.\n";
    exit(1);
  }
  return a[i];
}

int main()
{
  atype<int> intob; // integer array
  atype<double> doubleob; // double array

  int i;

  cout << "Integer array: ";
  for(i=0; i<SIZE; i++) intob[i] = i;
  for(i=0; i<SIZE; i++) cout << intob[i] << "  ";
  cout << '\n';

  cout << "Double array: ";
  for(i=0; i<SIZE; i++) doubleob[i] = (double) i/3;
  for(i=0; i<SIZE; i++) cout << doubleob[i] << "  ";
  cout << '\n';

  intob[12] = 100; // generates runtime error

  return 0;
}
```

This program implements a generic safe-array type and then demonstrates its use by creating an array of **int**s and an array of **double**s. You should try creating other types of arrays. As this example shows, part of the power of generic classes is that they allow you to write the code once, debug it, and then apply it to any type of data without having to re-engineer it for each specific application.

Using Non-Type Arguments with Generic Classes

In the template specification for a generic class, you may also specify non-type arguments. That is, in a template specification you can specify what you would normally think of as a standard argument, such as an integer or a pointer. The syntax to accomplish this is essentially the same as for normal function parameters: simply include the type and name of the argument. For example, here is a better way to implement the safe-array class presented in the preceding section. It allows you to specify the size of the array.

```cpp
// Demonstrate non-type template arguments.
#include <iostream>
#include <cstdlib>
using namespace std;

// Here, int size is a non-type argument.
template <class AType, int size> class atype {
  AType a[size]; // length of array is passed in size
public:
  atype() {
    register int i;
    for(i=0; i<size; i++) a[i] = i;
  }
  AType &operator[](int i);
};

// Provide range checking for atype.
template <class AType, int size>
AType &atype<AType, size>::operator[](int i)
{
  if(i<0 || i> size-1) {
    cout << "\nIndex value of ";
    cout << i << " is out-of-bounds.\n";
    exit(1);
  }
  return a[i];
}

int main()
{
```

```
atype<int, 10> intob;        // integer array of size 10
atype<double, 15> doubleob; // double array of size 15

int i;

cout << "Integer array: ";
for(i=0; i<10; i++) intob[i] = i;
for(i=0; i<10; i++) cout << intob[i] << "  ";
cout << '\n';

cout << "Double array: ";
for(i=0; i<15; i++) doubleob[i] = (double) i/3;
for(i=0; i<15; i++) cout << doubleob[i] << "  ";
cout << '\n';

intob[12] = 100; // generates runtime error

return 0;
}
```

Look carefully at the template specification for **atype**. Note that **size** is declared as an **int**. This parameter is then used within **atype** to declare the size of the array **a**. Even though **size** is depicted as a "variable" in the source code, its value is known at compile time. This allows it to be used to set the size of the array. **size** is also used in the bounds checking within the **operator[ ]( )** function. Within **main( )**, notice how the integer and floating-point arrays are created. The second parameter specifies the size of each array.

Non-type parameters are restricted to integers, pointers, or references. Other types, such as **float**, are not allowed. The arguments that you pass to a non-type parameter must consist of either an integer constant, or a pointer or reference to a global function or object. Thus, non-type parameters should themselves be thought of as constants, since their values cannot be changed. For example, inside **operator[ ]( )**, the following statement is not allowed.

```
size = 10; // Error
```

Since non-type parameters are treated as constants, they can be used to set the dimension of an array, which is a significant, practical benefit.

As the safe-array example illustrates, the use of non-type parameters greatly expands the utility of template classes. Although the information contained in the non-type argument must be known at compile-time, this restriction is mild compared with the power offered by non-type parameters.

Using Default Arguments with Template Classes

A template class can have a default argument associated with a generic type. For example,

```
template <class X=int> class myclass { //...
```

Here, the type **int** will be used if no other type is specified when an object of type **myclass** is instantiated.

It is also permissible for non-type arguments to take default arguments. The default value is used when no explicit value is specified when the class is instantiated. Default arguments for non-type parameters are specified using the same syntax as default arguments for function parameters.

Here is another version of the safe-array class that uses default arguments for both the type of data and the size of the array.

```cpp
// Demonstrate default template arguments.
#include <iostream>
#include <cstdlib>
using namespace std;

// Here, AType defaults to int and size defaults to 10.
template <class AType=int, int size=10> class atype {
  AType a[size]; // size of array is passed in size
public:
  atype() {
    register int i;
    for(i=0; i<size; i++) a[i] = i;
  }
  AType &operator[](int i);
};

// Provide range checking for atype.
template <class AType, int size>
AType &atype<AType, size>::operator[](int i)
{
  if(i<0 || i> size-1) {
    cout << "\nIndex value of ";
    cout << i << " is out-of-bounds.\n";
    exit(1);
  }
```

```
    return a[i];
}

int main()
{
  atype<int, 100> intarray;   // integer array, size 100
  atype<double> doublearray;  // double array, default size
  atype<> defarray;           // default to int array of size 10

  int i;

  cout << "int array: ";
  for(i=0; i<100; i++) intarray[i] = i;
  for(i=0; i<100; i++) cout << intarray[i] << "  ";
  cout << '\n';

  cout << "double array: ";
  for(i=0; i<10; i++) doublearray[i] = (double) i/3;
  for(i=0; i<10; i++) cout << doublearray[i] << "  ";
  cout << '\n';

  cout << "defarray array: ";
  for(i=0; i<10; i++) defarray[i] = i;
  for(i=0; i<10; i++) cout << defarray[i] << "  ";
  cout << '\n';

  return 0;
}
```

Pay close attention to this line:

```
template <class AType=int, int size=10> class atype {
```

Here, **AType** defaults to type **int**, and **size** defaults to **10**. As the program illustrates, **atype** objects can be created three ways:

■ explicitly specifying both the type and size of the array

■ explicitly specifying the type, but letting the size default to 10

■ letting the type default to **int** and the size default to 10

The use of default arguments—especially default types—adds versatility to your template classes. You can provide a default for the type of data most commonly used while still allowing the user of your classes to specialize them as needed.

Explicit Class Specializations

As with template functions, you can create an explicit specialization of a generic class. To do so, use the **template<>** construct, which works the same as it does for explicit function specializations. For example:

```
// Demonstrate class specialization.
#include <iostream>
using namespace std;

template <class T> class myclass {
  T x;
public:
  myclass(T a) {
    cout << "Inside generic myclass\n";
    x = a;
  }
  T getx() { return x; }
};


// Explicit specialization for int.
template <> class myclass<int> {
  int x;
public:
  myclass(int a) {
    cout << "Inside myclass<int> specialization\n";
    x = a * a;
  }
  int getx() { return x; }
};


int main()
{
  myclass<double> d(10.1);
  cout << "double: " << d.getx() << "\n\n";

  myclass<int> i(5);
```

```
    cout << "int: " << i.getx() << "\n";

    return 0;
}
```

This program displays the following output:

```
Inside generic myclass
double: 10.1

Inside myclass<int> specialization
int: 25
```

In the program, pay close attention to this line:

```
template <> class myclass<int> {
```

It tells the compiler that an explicit integer specialization of **myclass** is being created. This same general syntax is used for any type of class specialization.

Explicit class specialization expands the utility of generic classes because it lets you easily handle one or two special cases while allowing all others to be automatically processed by the compiler. Of course, if you find that you are creating too many specializations, you are probably better off not using a template class in the first place.

The typename and export Keywords

Recently, two keywords were added to C++ that relate specifically to templates: **typename** and **export**. Both play specialized roles in C++ programming. Each is briefly examined.

The **typename** keyword has two uses. First, as mentioned earlier, it can be substituted for the keyword **class** in a template declaration. For example, the **swapargs( )** template function could be specified like this:

```
template <typename X> void swapargs(X &a, X &b)
{
  X temp;

  temp = a;
```

```
    a = b;
    b = temp;
}
```

Here, **typename** specifies the generic type **X**. There is no difference between using **class** and using **typename** in this context.

The second use of **typename** is to inform the compiler that a name used in a template declaration is a type name rather than an object name. For example,

```
typename X::Name someObject;
```

ensures that **X::Name** is treated as a type name.

The **export** keyword can precede a **template** declaration. It allows other files to use a template declared in a different file by specifying only its declaration rather than duplicating its entire definition.

The Power of Templates

Templates help you achieve one of the most elusive goals in programming: the creation of reusable code. Through the use of template classes you can create frameworks that can be applied over and over again to a variety of programming situations. For example, consider the **stack** class. When first shown in Chapter 11, it could only be used to store integer values. Even though the underlying algorithms could be used to store any type of data, the hard-coding of the data type into the **stack** class severely limited its application. However, by making **stack** into a generic class, it can create a stack for any type of data.

Generic functions and classes provide a powerful tool that you can use to amplify your programming efforts. Once you have written and debugged a template class, you have a solid software component that you can use with confidence in a variety of different situations. You are saved from the tedium of creating separate implementations for each data type with which you want the class to work.

While it is true that the template syntax can seem a bit intimidating at first, the rewards are well worth the time it takes to become comfortable with it. Template functions and classes are already becoming commonplace in programming, and this trend is expected to continue. For example, the STL (Standard Template Library) defined by C++ is, as its name implies, built upon templates. One last point: although templates add a layer of abstraction, they still ultimately compile down to the same, high-performance object code that you have come to expect from C++.

The Complete Reference

Chapter 19

Exception Handling

This chapter discusses the exception handling subsystem. *Exception handling* allows you to manage run-time errors in an orderly fashion. Using exception handling, your program can automatically invoke an error-handling routine when an error occurs. The principal advantage of exception handling is that it automates much of the error-handling code that previously had to be coded "by hand" in any large program.

Exception Handling Fundamentals

C++ exception handling is built upon three keywords: **try**, **catch**, and **throw**. In the most general terms, program statements that you want to monitor for exceptions are contained in a **try** block. If an exception (i.e., an error) occurs within the **try** block, it is thrown (using **throw**). The exception is caught, using **catch**, and processed. The following discussion elaborates upon this general description.

Code that you want to monitor for exceptions must have been executed from within a **try** block. (Functions called from within a **try** block may also throw an exception.) Exceptions that can be thrown by the monitored code are caught by a **catch** statement, which immediately follows the **try** statement in which the exception was thrown. The general form of **try** and **catch** are shown here.

```
try {
  // try block
}
catch (type1 arg) {
  // catch block
}
catch (type2 arg) {
  // catch block
}
catch (type3 arg) {
  // catch block
}
    .
    .
    .
catch (typeN arg) {
  // catch block
}
```

The **try** can be as short as a few statements within one function or as all-encompassing as enclosing the **main( )** function code within a **try** block (which effectively causes the entire program to be monitored).

When an exception is thrown, it is caught by its corresponding **catch** statement, which processes the exception. There can be more than one **catch** statement associated with a **try**. Which **catch** statement is used is determined by the type of the exception. That is, if the data type specified by a **catch** matches that of the exception, then that **catch** statement is executed (and all others are bypassed). When an exception is caught, *arg* will receive its value. Any type of data may be caught, including classes that you create. If no exception is thrown (that is, no error occurs within the **try** block), then no **catch** statement is executed.

The general form of the **throw** statement is shown here:

throw *exception*;

throw generates the exception specified by *exception*. If this exception is to be caught, then **throw** must be executed either from within a **try** block itself, or from any function called from within the **try** block (directly or indirectly).

If you throw an exception for which there is no applicable **catch** statement, an abnormal program termination may occur. Throwing an unhandled exception causes the standard library function **terminate( )** to be invoked. By default, **terminate( )** calls **abort( )** to stop your program, but you can specify your own termination handler, as described later in this chapter.

Here is a simple example that shows the way C++ exception handling operates.

```
// A simple exception handling example.
#include <iostream>
using namespace std;

int main()
{
  cout << "Start\n";

  try { // start a try block
    cout << "Inside try block\n";
    throw 100; // throw an error
    cout << "This will not execute";
  }
  catch (int i) { // catch an error
    cout << "Caught an exception -- value is: ";
    cout << i << "\n";
  }

  cout << "End";
```

```
      return 0;
}
```

This program displays the following output:

```
Start
Inside try block
Caught an exception -- value is: 100
End
```

Look carefully at this program. As you can see, there is a **try** block containing three statements and a **catch(int i)** statement that processes an integer exception. Within the **try** block, only two of the three statements will execute: the first **cout** statement and the **throw**. Once an exception has been thrown, control passes to the **catch** expression and the **try** block is terminated. That is, **catch** is *not* called. Rather, program execution is transferred to it. (The program's stack is automatically reset as needed to accomplish this.) Thus, the **cout** statement following the **throw** will never execute.

Usually, the code within a **catch** statement attempts to remedy an error by taking appropriate action. If the error can be fixed, execution will continue with the statements following the **catch**. However, often an error cannot be fixed and a **catch** block will terminate the program with a call to **exit( )** or **abort( )**.

As mentioned, the type of the exception must match the type specified in a **catch** statement. For example, in the preceding example, if you change the type in the **catch** statement to **double**, the exception will not be caught and abnormal termination will occur. This change is shown here.

```cpp
// This example will not work.
#include <iostream>
using namespace std;

int main()
{
  cout << "Start\n";

  try { // start a try block
    cout << "Inside try block\n";
    throw 100; // throw an error
    cout << "This will not execute";
  }
  catch (double i) { // won't work for an int exception
    cout << "Caught an exception -- value is: ";
```

```
      cout << i << "\n";
   }

   cout << "End";

   return 0;
}
```

This program produces the following output because the integer exception will not be caught by the **catch(double i)** statement. (Of course, the precise message describing abnormal termination will vary from compiler to compiler.)

```
Start
Inside try block
Abnormal program termination
```

An exception can be thrown from outside the **try** block as long as it is thrown by a function that is called from within **try** block. For example, this is a valid program.

```
/* Throwing an exception from a function outside the
     try block.
*/
#include <iostream>
using namespace std;

void Xtest(int test)
{
  cout << "Inside Xtest, test is: " << test << "\n";
  if(test) throw test;
}

int main()
{
  cout << "Start\n";

  try { // start a try block
    cout << "Inside try block\n";
    Xtest(0);
    Xtest(1);
    Xtest(2);
  }
  catch (int i) { // catch an error
```

```
      cout << "Caught an exception -- value is: ";
      cout << i << "\n";
   }

   cout << "End";

   return 0;
}
```

This program produces the following output:

```
Start
Inside try block
Inside Xtest, test is: 0
Inside Xtest, test is: 1
Caught an exception -- value is: 1
End
```

A **try** block can be localized to a function. When this is the case, each time the function is entered, the exception handling relative to that function is reset. For example, examine this program.

```
#include <iostream>
using namespace std;

// Localize a try/catch to a function.
void Xhandler(int test)
{
   try{
      if(test) throw test;
   }
   catch(int i) {
      cout << "Caught Exception #: " << i << '\n';
   }
}

int main()
{
   cout << "Start\n";

   Xhandler(1);
```

```
    Xhandler(2);
    Xhandler(0);
    Xhandler(3);

    cout << "End";

    return 0;
}
```

This program displays this output:

```
Start
Caught Exception #: 1
Caught Exception #: 2
Caught Exception #: 3
End
```

As you can see, three exceptions are thrown. After each exception, the function returns. When the function is called again, the exception handling is reset.

It is important to understand that the code associated with a **catch** statement will be executed only if it catches an exception. Otherwise, execution simply bypasses the **catch** altogether. (That is, execution never flows into a **catch** statement.) For example, in the following program, no exception is thrown, so the **catch** statement does not execute.

```
#include <iostream>
using namespace std;

int main()
{
  cout << "Start\n";

  try { // start a try block
    cout << "Inside try block\n";
    cout << "Still inside try block\n";
  }
  catch (int i) { // catch an error
    cout << "Caught an exception -- value is: ";
    cout << i << "\n";
  }
```

```
    cout << "End";

    return 0;
}
```

The preceding program produces the following output.

```
Start
Inside try block
Still inside try block
End
```

As you see, the **catch** statement is bypassed by the flow of execution.

Catching Class Types

An exception can be of any type, including class types that you create. Actually, in real-world programs, most exceptions will be class types rather than built-in types. Perhaps the most common reason that you will want to define a class type for an exception is to create an object that describes the error that occurred. This information can be used by the exception handler to help it process the error. The following example demonstrates this.

```cpp
// Catching class type exceptions.
#include <iostream>
#include <cstring>
using namespace std;

class MyException {
public:
  char str_what[80];
  int what;

  MyException() { *str_what = 0; what = 0; }

  MyException(char *s, int e) {
    strcpy(str_what, s);
    what = e;
  }
};
```

```
int main()
{
  int i;

  try {
    cout << "Enter a positive number: ";
    cin >> i;
    if(i<0)
      throw MyException("Not Positive", i);
  }
  catch (MyException e) { // catch an error
    cout << e.str_what << ": ";
    cout << e.what << "\n";
  }

  return 0;
}
```

Here is a sample run:

```
Enter a positive number: -4
Not Positive: -4
```

The program prompts the user for a positive number. If a negative number is entered, an object of the class **MyException** is created that describes the error. Thus, **MyException** encapsulates information about the error. This information is then used by the exception handler. In general, you will want to create exception classes that will encapsulate information about an error to enable the exception handler to respond effectively.

Using Multiple catch Statements

As stated, you can have more than one **catch** associated with a **try**. In fact, it is common to do so. However, each **catch** must catch a different type of exception. For example, this program catches both integers and strings.

```
#include <iostream>
using namespace std;

// Different types of exceptions can be caught.
```

```
void Xhandler(int test)
{
  try{
    if(test) throw test;
    else throw "Value is zero";
  }
  catch(int i) {
    cout << "Caught Exception #: " << i << '\n';
  }
  catch(const char *str) {
    cout << "Caught a string: ";
    cout << str << '\n';
  }
}

int main()
{
  cout << "Start\n";

  Xhandler(1);
  Xhandler(2);
  Xhandler(0);
  Xhandler(3);

  cout << "End";

  return 0;
}
```

This program produces the following output:

```
Start
Caught Exception #: 1
Caught Exception #: 2
Caught a string: Value is zero
Caught Exception #: 3
End
```

As you can see, each **catch** statement responds only to its own type.

In general, **catch** expressions are checked in the order in which they occur in a program. Only a matching statement is executed. All other **catch** blocks are ignored.

Handling Derived-Class Exceptions

You need to be careful how you order your **catch** statements when trying to catch exception types that involve base and derived classes because a **catch** clause for a base class will also match any class derived from that base. Thus, if you want to catch exceptions of both a base class type and a derived class type, put the derived class first in the **catch** sequence. If you don't do this, the base class **catch** will also catch all derived classes. For example, consider the following program.

```cpp
// Catching derived classes.
#include <iostream>
using namespace std;

class B {
};

class D: public B {
};

int main()
{
  D derived;

  try {
    throw derived;
  }
  catch(B b) {
    cout << "Caught a base class.\n";
  }
  catch(D d) {
    cout << "This won't execute.\n";
  }

  return 0;
}
```

Here, because **derived** is an object that has **B** as a base class, it will be caught by the first **catch** clause and the second clause will never execute. Some compilers will flag this condition with a warning message. Others may issue an error. Either way, to fix this condition, reverse the order of the **catch** clauses.

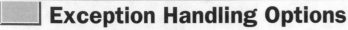

Exception Handling Options

There are several additional features and nuances to C++ exception handling that make it easier and more convenient to use. These attributes are discussed here.

Catching All Exceptions

In some circumstances you will want an exception handler to catch all exceptions instead of just a certain type. This is easy to accomplish. Simply use this form of **catch**.

```
catch(...) {
  // process all exceptions
}
```

Here, the ellipsis matches any type of data. The following program illustrates **catch(...)**.

```cpp
// This example catches all exceptions.
#include <iostream>
using namespace std;

void Xhandler(int test)
{
  try{
    if(test==0) throw test; // throw int
    if(test==1) throw 'a'; // throw char
    if(test==2) throw 123.23; // throw double
  }
  catch(...) { // catch all exceptions
    cout << "Caught One!\n";
  }
}

int main()
{
  cout << "Start\n";

  Xhandler(0);
  Xhandler(1);
  Xhandler(2);

  cout << "End";
```

```
    return 0;
}
```

This program displays the following output.

```
Start
Caught One!
Caught One!
Caught One!
End
```

As you can see, all three **throw**s were caught using the one **catch** statement.

One very good use for **catch(...)** is as the last **catch** of a cluster of catches. In this capacity it provides a useful default or "catch all" statement. For example, this slightly different version of the preceding program explicity catches integer exceptions but relies upon **catch(...)** to catch all others.

```
// This example uses catch(...) as a default.
#include <iostream>
using namespace std;

void Xhandler(int test)
{
  try{
    if(test==0) throw test; // throw int
    if(test==1) throw 'a'; // throw char
    if(test==2) throw 123.23; // throw double
  }
  catch(int i) { // catch an int exception
    cout << "Caught an integer\n";
  }
  catch(...) { // catch all other exceptions
    cout << "Caught One!\n";
  }
}

int main()
{
  cout << "Start\n";
```

C++

```
    Xhandler(0);
    Xhandler(1);
    Xhandler(2);

    cout << "End";

    return 0;
}
```

The output produced by this program is shown here.

```
Start
Caught an integer
Caught One!
Caught One!
End
```

As this example suggests, using **catch(...)** as a default is a good way to catch all exceptions that you don't want to handle explicitly. Also, by catching all exceptions, you prevent an unhandled exception from causing an abnormal program termination.

Restricting Exceptions

You can restrict the type of exceptions that a function can throw outside of itself. In fact, you can also prevent a function from throwing any exceptions whatsoever. To accomplish these restrictions, you must add a **throw** clause to a function definition. The general form of this is shown here:

ret-type func-name(*arg-list*) throw(*type-list*)
{
  // ...
}

Here, only those data types contained in the comma-separated *type-list* may be thrown by the function. Throwing any other type of expression will cause abnormal program termination. If you don't want a function to be able to throw *any* exceptions, then use an empty list.

Attempting to throw an exception that is not supported by a function will cause the standard library function **unexpected( )** to be called. By default, this causes **abort( )** to be called, which causes abnormal program termination. However, you can specify your own unexpected handler if you like, as described later in this chapter.

The following program shows how to restrict the types of exceptions that can be thrown from a function.

```
// Restricting function throw types.
#include <iostream>
using namespace std;

// This function can only throw ints, chars, and doubles.
void Xhandler(int test) throw(int, char, double)
{
  if(test==0) throw test; // throw int
  if(test==1) throw 'a'; // throw char
  if(test==2) throw 123.23; // throw double
}

int main()
{
  cout << "start\n";

  try{
    Xhandler(0); // also, try passing 1 and 2 to Xhandler()
  }
  catch(int i) {
    cout << "Caught an integer\n";
  }
  catch(char c) {
    cout << "Caught char\n";
  }
  catch(double d) {
    cout << "Caught double\n";
  }

  cout << "end";

  return 0;
}
```

In this program, the function **Xhandler( )** may only throw integer, character, and **double** exceptions. If it attempts to throw any other type of exception, an abnormal program termination will occur. (That is, **unexpected( )** will be called.) To see an example of this, remove **int** from the list and retry the program.

It is important to understand that a function can be restricted only in what types of exceptions it throws back to the **try** block that called it. That is, a **try** block *within* a function may throw any type of exception so long as it is caught *within* that function. The restriction applies only when throwing an exception outside of the function.

The following change to **Xhandler( )** prevents it from throwing any exceptions.

```
// This function can throw NO exceptions!
void Xhandler(int test) throw()
{
  /* The following statements no longer work.  Instead,
     they will cause an abnormal program termination. */
  if(test==0) throw test;
  if(test==1) throw 'a';
  if(test==2) throw 123.23;
}
```

Rethrowing an Exception

If you wish to rethrow an expression from within an exception handler, you may do so by calling **throw**, by itself, with no exception. This causes the current exception to be passed on to an outer **try/catch** sequence. The most likely reason for doing so is to allow multiple handlers access to the exception. For example, perhaps one exception handler manages one aspect of an exception and a second handler copes with another. An exception can only be rethrown from within a **catch** block (or from any function called from within that block). When you rethrow an exception, it will not be recaught by the same **catch** statement. It will propagate outward to the next **catch** statement. The following program illustrates rethrowing an exception, in this case a **char *** exception.

```
// Example of "rethrowing" an exception.
#include <iostream>
using namespace std;

void Xhandler()
{
  try {
    throw "hello"; // throw a char *
  }
  catch(const char *) { // catch a char *
    cout << "Caught char * inside Xhandler\n";
    throw ; // rethrow char * out of function
  }
}
```

```
int main()
{
  cout << "Start\n";

  try{
    Xhandler();
  }
  catch(const char *) {
    cout << "Caught char * inside main\n";
  }

  cout << "End";

  return 0;
}
```

This program displays this output:

```
Start
Caught char * inside Xhandler
Caught char * inside main
End
```

Understanding terminate( ) and unexpected( )

As mentioned earlier, **terminate( )** and **unexpected( )** are called when something goes wrong during the exception handling process. These functions are supplied by the Standard C++ library. Their prototypes are shown here:

> void terminate( );
> void unexpected( );

These functions require the header **<exception>**.

The **terminate( )** function is called whenever the exception handling subsystem fails to find a matching **catch** statement for an exception. It is also called if your program attempts to rethrow an exception when no exception was originally thrown. The **terminate( )** function is also called under various other, more obscure circumstances. For example, such a circumstance could occur when, in the process of unwinding the stack because of an exception, a destructor for an object being destroyed throws an exception. In general, **terminate( )** is the handler of last resort when no other handlers for an exception are available. By default, **terminate( )** calls **abort( )**.

The **unexpected( )** function is called when a function attempts to throw an exception that is not allowed by its **throw** list. By default, **unexpected( )** calls **terminate( )**.

Setting the Terminate and Unexpected Handlers

The **terminate( )** and **unexpected( )** functions simply call other functions to actually handle an error. As just explained, by default **terminate( )** calls **abort( )**, and **unexpected( )** calls **terminate( )**. Thus, by default, both functions halt program execution when an exception handling error occurs. However, you can change the functions that are called by **terminate( )** and **unexpected( )**. Doing so allows your program to take full control of the exception handling subsystem.

To change the terminate handler, use **set_terminate( )**, shown here:

terminate_handler set_terminate(terminate_handler *newhandler*) throw( );

Here, *newhandler* is a pointer to the new terminate handler. The function returns a pointer to the old terminate handler. The new terminate handler must be of type **terminate_handler**, which is defined like this:

typedef void (*terminate_handler) ( );

The only thing that your terminate handler must do is stop program execution. It must not return to the program or resume it in any way.

To change the unexpected handler, use **set_unexpected( )**, shown here:

unexpected_handler set_unexpected(unexpected_handler *newhandler*) throw( );

Here, *newhandler* is a pointer to the new unexpected handler. The function returns a pointer to the old unexpected handler. The new unexpected handler must be of type **unexpected_handler**, which is defined like this:

typedef void (*unexpected_handler) ( );

This handler may itself throw an exception, stop the program, or call **terminate( )**. However, it must not return to the program.

Both **set_terminate( )** and **set_unexpected( )** require the header **<exception>**. Here is an example that defines its own **terminate( )** handler.

```
// Set a new terminate handler.
#include <iostream>
```

```
#include <cstdlib>
#include <exception>
using namespace std;

void my_Thandler() {
  cout << "Inside new terminate handler\n";
  abort();
}

int main()
{
  // set a new terminate handler
  set_terminate(my_Thandler);

  try {
    cout << "Inside try block\n";
    throw 100; // throw an error
  }
  catch (double i) { // won't catch an int exception
    // ...
  }

  return 0;
}
```

The output from this program is shown here.

```
Inside try block
Inside new terminate handler
abnormal program termination
```

The uncaught_exception( ) Function

The C++ exception handling subsystem supplies one other function that you may find useful: **uncaught_exception( )**. Its prototype is shown here:

bool uncaught_exception( );

This function returns **true** if an exception has been thrown but not yet caught. Once caught, the function returns **false**.

The exception and bad_exception Classes

When a function supplied by the C++ standard library throws an exception, it will be an object derived from the base class **exception**. An object of the class **bad_exception** can be thrown by the unexpected handler. These classes require the header **<exception>**.

Applying Exception Handling

Exception handling is designed to provide a structured means by which your program can handle abnormal events. This implies that the error handler must do something rational when an error occurs. For example, consider the following simple program. It inputs two numbers and divides the first by the second. It uses exception handling to manage a divide-by-zero error.

```cpp
#include <iostream>
using namespace std;

void divide(double a, double b);

int main()
{
  double i, j;

  do {
    cout << "Enter numerator (0 to stop): ";
    cin >> i;
    cout << "Enter denominator: ";
    cin >> j;
    divide(i, j);
  } while(i != 0);

  return 0;
}

void divide(double a, double b)
{
  try {
    if(!b) throw b; // check for divide-by-zero
    cout << "Result: " << a/b << endl;
  }
  catch (double b) {
    cout << "Can't divide by zero.\n";
```

```
    }
  }
```

While the preceding program is a very simple example, it does illustrate the essential nature of exception handling. Since division by zero is illegal, the program cannot continue if a zero is entered for the second number. In this case, the exception is handled by not performing the division (which would have caused abnormal program termination) and notifying the user of the error. The program then reprompts the user for two more numbers. Thus, the error has been handled in an orderly fashion and the user may continue on with the program. The same basic concepts will apply to more complex applications of exception handling.

Exception handling is especially useful for exiting from a deeply nested set of routines when a catastrophic error occurs. In this regard, C++'s exception handling is designed to replace the rather clumsy C-based **setjmp( )** and **longjmp( )** functions.

Remember, the key point about using exception handling is to provide an orderly way of handling errors. This means rectifying the situation, if possible.

The Complete Reference

C++

Chapter 20

The C++ I/O System Basics

C++ supports two complete I/O systems: the one inherited from C and the object-oriented I/O system defined by C++ (hereafter called simply the C++ I/O system). The C-based I/O system was discussed in Part One. Here we will begin to examine the C++ I/O system. Like C-based I/O, C++'s I/O system is fully integrated. The different aspects of C++'s I/O system, such as console I/O and disk I/O, are actually just different perspectives on the same mechanism. This chapter discusses the foundations of the C++ I/O system. Although the examples in this chapter use "console" I/O, the information is applicable to other devices, including disk files (discussed in Chapter 21).

Since the I/O system inherited from C is extremely rich, flexible, and powerful, you might be wondering why C++ defines yet another system. The answer is that C's I/O system knows nothing about objects. Therefore, for C++ to provide complete support for object-oriented programming, it was necessary to create an I/O system that could operate on user-defined objects. In addition to support for objects, there are several benefits to using C++'s I/O system even in programs that don't make extensive (or any) use of user-defined objects. Frankly, for all new code, you should use the C++ I/O system. The C I/O is supported by C++ only for compatibility.

This chapter explains how to format data, how to overload the << and >> I/O operators so they can be used with classes that you create, and how to create special I/O functions called manipulators that can make your programs more efficient.

Old vs. Modern C++ I/O

There are currently two versions of the C++ object-oriented I/O library in use: the older one that is based upon the original specifications for C++ and the newer one defined by Standard C++. The old I/O library is supported by the header file **<iostream.h>**. The new I/O library is supported by the header **<iostream>**. For the most part the two libraries appear the same to the programmer. This is because the new I/O library is, in essence, simply an updated and improved version of the old one. In fact, the vast majority of differences between the two occur beneath the surface, in the way that the libraries are implemented—not in how they are used.

From the programmer's perspective, there are two main differences between the old and new C++ I/O libraries. First, the new I/O library contains a few additional features and defines some new data types. Thus, the new I/O library is essentially a superset of the old one. Nearly all programs originally written for the old library will compile without substantive changes when the new library is used. Second, the old-style I/O library was in the global namespace. The new-style library is in the **std** namespace. (Recall that the **std** namespace is used by all of the Standard C++ libraries.) Since the old-style I/O library is now obsolete, this book describes only the new I/O library, but most of the information is applicable to the old I/O library as well.

C++ Streams

Like the C-based I/O system, the C++ I/O system operates through streams. Streams were discussed in detail in Chapter 9; that discussion will not be repeated here. However, to summarize: A *stream* is a logical device that either produces or consumes information. A stream is linked to a physical device by the I/O system. All streams behave in the same way even though the actual physical devices they are connected to may differ substantially. Because all streams behave the same, the same I/O functions can operate on virtually any type of physical device. For example, you can use the same function that writes to a file to write to the printer or to the screen. The advantage to this approach is that you need learn only one I/O system.

The C++ Stream Classes

As mentioned, Standard C++ provides support for its I/O system in **<iostream>**. In this header, a rather complicated set of class hierarchies is defined that supports I/O operations. The I/O classes begin with a system of template classes. As explained in Chapter 18, a template class defines the form of a class without fully specifying the data upon which it will operate. Once a template class has been defined, specific instances of it can be created. As it relates to the I/O library, Standard C++ creates two specializations of the I/O template classes: one for 8-bit characters and another for wide characters. This book will use only the 8-bit character classes since they are by far the most common. But the same techniques apply to both.

The C++ I/O system is built upon two related but different template class hierarchies. The first is derived from the low-level I/O class called **basic_streambuf**. This class supplies the basic, low-level input and output operations, and provides the underlying support for the entire C++ I/O system. Unless you are doing advanced I/O programming, you will not need to use **basic_streambuf** directly. The class hierarchy that you will most commonly be working with is derived from **basic_ios**. This is a high-level I/O class that provides formatting, error checking, and status information related to stream I/O. (A base class for **basic_ios** is called **ios_base**, which defines several nontemplate traits used by **basic_ios**.) **basic_ios** is used as a base for several derived classes, including **basic_istream**, **basic_ostream**, and **basic_iostream**. These classes are used to create streams capable of input, output, and input/output, respectively.

As explained, the I/O library creates two specializations of the template class hierarchies just described: one for 8-bit characters and one for wide characters. Here is a list of the mapping of template class names to their character and wide-character versions.

Template Class	Character-based Class	Wide-Character-based Class
basic_streambuf	streambuf	wstreambuf
basic_ios	ios	wios
basic_istream	istream	wistream
basic_ostream	ostream	wostream
basic_iostream	iostream	wiostream
basic_fstream	fstream	wfstream
basic_ifstream	ifstream	wifstream
basic_ofstream	ofstream	wofstream

The character-based names will be used throughout the remainder of this book, since they are the names that you will normally use in your programs. They are also the same names that were used by the old I/O library. This is why the old and the new I/O library are compatible at the source code level.

One last point: The **ios** class contains many member functions and variables that control or monitor the fundamental operation of a stream. It will be referred to frequently. Just remember that if you include **<iostream>** in your program, you will have access to this important class.

C++'s Predefined Streams

When a C++ program begins execution, four built-in streams are automatically opened. They are:

Stream	Meaning	Default Device
cin	Standard input	Keyboard
cout	Standard output	Screen
cerr	Standard error output	Screen
clog	Buffered version of cerr	Screen

Streams **cin**, **cout**, and **cerr** correspond to C's **stdin**, **stdout**, and **stderr**.

By default, the standard streams are used to communicate with the console. However, in environments that support I/O redirection (such as DOS, Unix, OS/2, and Windows), the standard streams can be redirected to other devices or files. For the sake of simplicity, the examples in this chapter assume that no I/O redirection has occurred.

Standard C++ also defines these four additional streams: **win**, **wout**, **werr**, and **wlog**. These are wide-character versions of the standard streams. Wide characters are of type **wchar_t** and are generally 16-bit quantities. Wide characters are used to hold the large character sets associated with some human languages.

Formatted I/O

The C++ I/O system allows you to format I/O operations. For example, you can set a field width, specify a number base, or determine how many digits after the decimal point will be displayed. There are two related but conceptually different ways that you can format data. First, you can directly access members of the **ios** class. Specifically, you can set various format status flags defined inside the **ios** class or call various **ios** member functions. Second, you can use special functions called *manipulators* that can be included as part of an I/O expression.

We will begin the discussion of formatted I/O by using the **ios** member functions and flags.

Formatting Using the ios Members

Each stream has associated with it a set of format flags that control the way information is formatted. The **ios** class declares a bitmask enumeration called **fmtflags** in which the following values are defined. (Technically, these values are defined within **ios_base**, which, as explained earlier, is a base class for **ios**.)

adjustfield	basefield	boolalpha	dec
fixed	floatfield	hex	internal
left	oct	right	scientific
showbase	showpoint	showpos	skipws
unitbuf	uppercase		

These values are used to set or clear the format flags. If you are using an older compiler, it may not define the **fmtflags** enumeration type. In this case, the format flags will be encoded into a long integer.

When the **skipws** flag is set, leading white-space characters (spaces, tabs, and newlines) are discarded when performing input on a stream. When **skipws** is cleared, white-space characters are not discarded.

When the **left** flag is set, output is left justified. When **right** is set, output is right justified. When the **internal** flag is set, a numeric value is padded to fill a field by inserting spaces between any sign or base character. If none of these flags are set, output is right justified by default.

By default, numeric values are output in decimal. However, it is possible to change the number base. Setting the **oct** flag causes output to be displayed in octal. Setting the **hex** flag causes output to be displayed in hexadecimal. To return output to decimal, set the **dec** flag.

Setting **showbase** causes the base of numeric values to be shown. For example, if the conversion base is hexadecimal, the value 1F will be displayed as 0x1F.

By default, when scientific notation is displayed, the **e** is in lowercase. Also, when a hexadecimal value is displayed, the **x** is in lowercase. When **uppercase** is set, these characters are displayed in uppercase.

Setting **showpos** causes a leading plus sign to be displayed before positive values.

Setting **showpoint** causes a decimal point and trailing zeros to be displayed for all floating-point output—whether needed or not.

By setting the **scientific** flag, floating-point numeric values are displayed using scientific notation. When **fixed** is set, floating-point values are displayed using normal notation. When neither flag is set, the compiler chooses an appropriate method.

When **unitbuf** is set, the buffer is flushed after each insertion operation.

When **boolalpha** is set, Booleans can be input or output using the keywords **true** and **false**.

Since it is common to refer to the **oct**, **dec**, and **hex** fields, they can be collectively referred to as **basefield**. Similarly, the **left**, **right**, and **internal** fields can be referred to as **adjustfield**. Finally, the **scientific** and **fixed** fields can be referenced as **floatfield**.

Setting the Format Flags

To set a flag, use the **setf( )** function. This function is a member of **ios**. Its most common form is shown here:

fmtflags setf(fmtflags *flags*);

This function returns the previous settings of the format flags and turns on those flags specified by *flags*. For example, to turn on the **showpos** flag, you can use this statement:

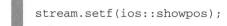

```
stream.setf(ios::showpos);
```

Here, *stream* is the stream you wish to affect. Notice the use of **ios::** to qualify **showpos**. Since **showpos** is an enumerated constant defined by the **ios** class, it must be qualified by **ios** when it is used.

The following program displays the value 100 with the **showpos** and **showpoint** flags turned on.

```
#include <iostream>
using namespace std;

int main()
{
  cout.setf(ios::showpoint);
  cout.setf(ios::showpos);

  cout << 100.0; // displays +100.000

  return 0;
}
```

It is important to understand that **setf( )** is a member function of the **ios** class and affects streams created by that class. Therefore, any call to **setf( )** is done relative to a specific stream. There is no concept of calling **setf( )** by itself. Put differently, there is no concept in C++ of global format status. Each stream maintains its own format status information individually.

Although there is nothing technically wrong with the preceding program, there is a more efficient way to write it. Instead of making multiple calls to **setf( )**, you can simply OR together the values of the flags you want set. For example, this single call accomplishes the same thing:

```
// You can OR together two or more flags,
cout.setf(ios::showpoint | ios::showpos);
```

 *Because the format flags are defined within the **ios** class, you must access their values by using **ios** and the scope resolution operator. For example, **showbase** by itself will not be recognized. You must specify **ios::showbase**.*

Clearing Format Flags

The complement of **setf( )** is **unsetf( )**. This member function of **ios** is used to clear one or more format flags. Its general form is

void unsetf(fmtflags *flags*);

The flags specified by *flags* are cleared. (All other flags are unaffected.)

The following program illustrates **unsetf( )**. It first sets both the **uppercase** and **scientific** flags. It then outputs 100.12 in scientific notation. In this case, the "E" used in the scientific notation is in uppercase. Next, it clears the **uppercase** flag and again outputs 100.12 in scientific notation, using a lowercase "e."

```
#include <iostream>
using namespace std;

int main()
{
  cout.setf(ios::uppercase | ios::scientific);

  cout << 100.12;   // displays 1.001200E+02

  cout.unsetf(ios::uppercase); // clear uppercase

  cout << " \n" << 100.12; // displays 1.001200e+02

  return 0;
}
```

An Overloaded Form of setf( )

There is an overloaded form of **setf( )** that takes this general form:

fmtflags setf(fmtflags *flags1*, fmtflags *flags2*);

In this version, only the flags specified by *flags2* are affected. They are first cleared and then set according to the flags specified by *flags1*. Note that even if *flags1* contains other flags, only those specified by *flags2* will be affected. The previous flags setting is returned. For example,

```
#include <iostream>
using namespace std;

int main( )
{
  cout.setf(ios::showpoint | ios::showpos, ios::showpoint);

  cout << 100.0; // displays 100.000, not +100.000

  return 0;
}
```

Here, **showpoint** is set, but not **showpos**, since it is not specified in the second parameter.

Perhaps the most common use of the two-parameter form of **setf( )** is when setting the number base, justification, and format flags. As explained, references to the **oct**, **dec**, and **hex** fields can collectively be referred to as **basefield**. Similarly, the **left**, **right**, and **internal** fields can be referred to as **adjustfield**. Finally, the **scientific** and **fixed** fields can be referenced as **floatfield**. Since the flags that comprise these groupings are mutually exclusive, you may need to turn off one flag when setting another. For example, the following program sets output to hexadecimal. To output in hexadecimal, some implementations require that the other number base flags be turned off in addition to turning on the **hex** flag. This is most easily accomplished using the two-parameter form of **setf( )**.

```
#include <iostream>
using namespace std;

int main()
{
  cout.setf(ios::hex, ios::basefield);

  cout << 100; // this displays 64

  return 0;
}
```

Here, the **basefield** flags (i.,e., **dec**, **oct**, and **hex**) are first cleared and then the **hex** flag is set.

Remember, only the flags specified in *flags2* can be affected by flags specified by *flags1*. For example, in this program, the first attempt to set the **showpos** flag fails.

```
// This program will not work.
#include <iostream>
using namespace std;

int main()
{
  cout.setf(ios::showpos, ios::hex); // error, showpos not set

  cout << 100 << '\n'; // displays 100, not +100

  cout.setf(ios::showpos, ios::showpos); // this is correct
```

```
    cout << 100; // now displays +100

    return 0;
}
```

Keep in mind that most of the time you will want to use **unsetf( )** to clear flags and the single parameter version of **setf( )** (described earlier) to set flags. The **setf(fmtflags, fmtflags)** version of **setf( )** is most often used in specialized situations, such as setting the number base. Another good use may involve a situation in which you are using a flag template that specifies the state of all format flags but wish to alter only one or two. In this case, you could specify the template in *flags1* and use *flags2* to specify which of those flags will be affected.

Examining the Formatting Flags

There will be times when you only want to know the current format settings but not alter any. To accomplish this goal, **ios** includes the member function **flags( )**, which simply returns the current setting of each format flag. Its prototype is shown here:

   fmtflags flags( );

The following program uses **flags( )** to display the setting of the format flags relative to **cout**. Pay special attention to the **showflags( )** function. You might find it useful in programs you write.

```
#include <iostream>
using namespace std;

void showflags() ;

int main()
{
  // show default condition of format flags
  showflags();

  cout.setf(ios::right | ios::showpoint | ios::fixed);

  showflags();

  return 0;
}
```

```
// This function displays the status of the format flags.
void showflags()
{
  ios::fmtflags f;
  long i;

  f = (long) cout.flags(); // get flag settings

  // check each flag
  for(i=0x4000; i; i = i >> 1)
    if(i & f) cout << "1 ";
    else cout << "0 ";

  cout << " \n";
}
```

Sample output from the program is shown here. (The precise output will vary from compiler to compiler.)

```
0 0 0 0 0 1 0 0 0 0 0 0 0 0 1
0 1 0 0 0 1 0 1 0 0 1 0 0 0 1
```

Setting All Flags

The **flags( )** function has a second form that allows you to set all format flags associated with a stream. The prototype for this version of **flags( )** is shown here:

fmtflags flags(fmtflags *f*);

When you use this version, the bit pattern found in *f* is used to set the format flags associated with the stream. Thus, all format flags are affected. The function returns the previous settings.

The next program illustrates this version of **flags( )**. It first constructs a flag mask that turns on **showpos**, **showbase**, **oct**, and **right**. All other flags are off. It then uses **flags( )** to set the format flags associated with **cout** to these settings. The function **showflags( )** verifies that the flags are set as indicated. (It is the same function used in the previous program.)

```
#include <iostream>
using namespace std;
```

```
void showflags();

int main()
{
  // show default condition of format flags
  showflags();

  // showpos, showbase, oct, right are on, others off
  ios::fmtflags f = ios::showpos | ios::showbase | ios::oct | ios::right;
  cout.flags(f);   // set all flags

  showflags();

  return 0;
}
```

Using width( ), precision( ), and fill( )

In addition to the formatting flags, there are three member functions defined by **ios** that set these format parameters: the field width, the precision, and the fill character. The functions that do these things are **width( )**, **precision( )**, and **fill( )**, respectively. Each is examined in turn.

By default, when a value is output, it occupies only as much space as the number of characters it takes to display it. However, you can specify a minimum field width by using the **width( )** function. Its prototype is shown here:

streamsize width(streamsize w);

Here, w becomes the field width, and the previous field width is returned. In some implementations, the field width must be set before each output. If it isn't, the default field width is used. The **streamsize** type is defined as some form of integer by the compiler.

After you set a minimum field width, when a value uses less than the specified width, the field will be padded with the current fill character (space, by default) to reach the field width. If the size of the value exceeds the minimum field width, the field will be overrun. No values are truncated.

When outputting floating-point values, you can determine the number of digits of precision by using the **precision( )** function. Its prototype is shown here:

streamsize precision(streamsize p);

Here, the precision is set to *p*, and the old value is returned. The default precision is 6. In some implementations, the precision must be set before each floating-point output. If it is not, then the default precision will be used.

By default, when a field needs to be filled, it is filled with spaces. You can specify the fill character by using the **fill( )** function. Its prototype is

char fill(char *ch*);

After a call to **fill( )**, *ch* becomes the new fill character, and the old one is returned.

Here is a program that illustrates these functions:

```cpp
#include <iostream>
using namespace std;

int main()
{
  cout.precision(4) ;
  cout.width(10);

  cout << 10.12345 << "\n";  // displays 10.12

  cout.fill('*');

  cout.width(10);
  cout << 10.12345 << "\n"; // displays *****10.12

  // field width applies to strings, too
  cout.width(10);
  cout << "Hi!" << "\n"; // displays *******Hi!
  cout.width(10);
  cout.setf(ios::left); // left justify
  cout << 10.12345; // displays 10.12*****

  return 0;
}
```

This program's output is shown here:

```
    10.12
*****10.12
*******Hi!
10.12*****
```

There are overloaded forms of **width( )**, **precision( )**, and **fill( )** that obtain but do not change the current setting. These forms are shown here:

```
char fill( );
streamsize width( );
streamsize precision( );
```

Using Manipulators to Format I/O

The second way you can alter the format parameters of a stream is through the use of special functions called *manipulators* that can be included in an I/O expression. The standard manipulators are shown in Table 20-1. As you can see by examining the table, many of the I/O manipulators parallel member functions of the **ios** class. Many of the manipulators were added recently to C++ and will not be supported by older compilers.

Manipulator	Purpose	Input/Output
boolalpha	Turns on **boolapha** flag.	Input/Output
dec	Turns on **dec** flag.	Input/Output
endl	Output a newline character and flush the stream.	Output
ends	Output a null.	Output
fixed	Turns on **fixed** flag.	Output
flush	Flush a stream.	Output
hex	Turns on **hex** flag.	Input/Output
internal	Turns on **internal** flag.	Output
left	Turns on **left** flag.	Output
nobooalpha	Turns off **boolalpha** flag.	Input/Output
noshowbase	Turns off **showbase** flag.	Output
noshowpoint	Turns off **showpoint** flag.	Output
noshowpos	Turns off **showpos** flag.	Output

Table 20-1. *The C++ Manipulators*

Manipulator	Purpose	Input/Output
noskipws	Turns off **skipws** flag.	Input
nounitbuf	Turns off **unitbuf** flag.	Output
nouppercase	Turns off **uppercase** flag.	Output
oct	Turns on **oct** flag.	Input/Output
resetiosflags (fmtflags *f*)	Turn off the flags specified in *f*.	Input/Output
right	Turns on **right** flag.	Output
scientific	Turns on **scientific** flag.	Output
setbase(int *base*)	Set the number base to *base*.	Input/Output
setfill(int *ch*)	Set the fill character to *ch*.	Output
setiosflags(fmtflags *f*)	Turn on the flags specified in *f*.	Input/output
setprecision (int *p*)	Set the number of digits of precision.	Output
setw(int *w*)	Set the field width to *w*.	Output
showbase	Turns on **showbase** flag.	Output
showpoint	Turns on **showpoint** flag.	Output
showpos	Turns on **showpos** flag.	Output
skipws	Turns on **skipws** flag.	Input
unitbuf	Turns on **unitbuf** flag.	Output
uppercase	Turns on **uppercase** flag.	Output
ws	Skip leading white space.	Input

Table 20-1. *The C++ Manipulators* (continued)

To access manipulators that take parameters (such as **setw( )**), you must include **<iomanip>** in your program.

Here is an example that uses some manipulators:

```
#include <iostream>
#include <iomanip>
using namespace std;

int main()
{
  cout << hex << 100 << endl;

  cout << setfill('?') << setw(10) << 2343.0;

  return 0;
}
```

This displays

```
64
??????2343
```

Notice how the manipulators occur within a larger I/O expression. Also notice that when a manipulator does not take an argument, such as **endl( )** in the example, it is not followed by parentheses. This is because it is the address of the function that is passed to the overloaded **<<** operator.

As a comparison, here is a functionally equivalent version of the preceding program that uses **ios** member functions to achieve the same results:

```
#include <iostream>
#include <iomanip>
using namespace std;

int main()
{
  cout.setf(ios::hex, ios::basefield);
  cout << 100 << "\n";  // 100 in hex

  cout.fill('?');
  cout.width(10);
  cout << 2343.0;

  return 0;
}
```

As the examples suggest, the main advantage of using manipulators instead of the **ios** member functions is that they often allow more compact code to be written.

You can use the **setiosflags( )** manipulator to directly set the various format flags related to a stream. For example, this program uses **setiosflags( )** to set the **showbase** and **showpos** flags:

```cpp
#include <iostream>
#include <iomanip>
using namespace std;

int main()
{
  cout << setiosflags(ios::showpos);
  cout << setiosflags(ios::showbase);
  cout << 123 << " " << hex << 123;

  return 0;
}
```

The manipulator **setiosflags( )** performs the same function as the member function **setf( )**.

One of the more interesting manipulators is **boolalpha**. It allows true and false values to be input and output using the words "true" and "false" rather than numbers. For example,

```cpp
#include <iostream>
using namespace std;

int main()
{
  bool b;

  b = true;
  cout << b << " " << boolalpha << b << endl;

  cout << "Enter a Boolean value: ";
  cin >> boolalpha >> b;
  cout << "Here is what you entered:  " << b;

  return 0;
}
```

C++

Here is a sample run.

```
1 true
Enter a Boolean value: false
Here is what you entered:  false
```

Overloading << and >>

As you know, the << and the >> operators are overloaded in C++ to perform I/O operations on C++'s built-in types. You can also overload these operators so that they perform I/O operations on types that you create.

In the language of C++, the << output operator is referred to as the *insertion operator* because it inserts characters into a stream. Likewise, the >> input operator is called the *extraction operator* because it extracts characters from a stream. The functions that overload the insertion and extraction operators are generally called *inserters* and *extractors*, respectively.

Creating Your Own Inserters

It is quite simple to create an inserter for a class that you create. All inserter functions have this general form:

ostream &operator<<(ostream &*stream, class_type obj*)
{
  // body of inserter
  return *stream*;
}

Notice that the function returns a reference to a stream of type **ostream**. (Remember, **ostream** is a class derived from **ios** that supports output.) Further, the first parameter to the function is a reference to the output stream. The second parameter is the object being inserted. (The second parameter may also be a reference to the object being inserted.) The last thing the inserter must do before exiting is return *stream*. This allows the inserter to be used in a larger I/O expression.

Within an inserter function, you may put any type of procedures or operations that you want. That is, precisely what an inserter does is completely up to you. However, for the inserter to be in keeping with good programming practices, you should limit its operations to outputting information to a stream. For example, having an inserter compute pi to 30 decimal places as a side effect to an insertion operation is probably not a very good idea!

To demonstrate a custom inserter, one will be created for objects of type **phonebook**, shown here.

```
class phonebook {
public:
```

```
    char name[80];
    int areacode;
    int prefix;
    int num;
    phonebook(char *n, int a, int p, int nm)
    {
      strcpy(name, n);
      areacode = a;
      prefix = p;
      num = nm;
    }
};
```

This class holds a person's name and telephone number. Here is one way to create an inserter function for objects of type **phonebook**.

```
// Display name and phone number
ostream &operator<<(ostream &stream, phonebook o)
{
  stream << o.name << " ";
  stream << "(" << o.areacode << ") ";
  stream << o.prefix << "-" << o.num << "\n";

  return stream; // must return stream
}
```

Here is a short program that illustrates the **phonebook** inserter function:

```
#include <iostream>
#include <cstring>
using namespace std;

class phonebook {
public:
  char name[80];
  int areacode;
  int prefix;
  int num;
  phonebook(char *n, int a, int p, int nm)
  {
    strcpy(name, n);
    areacode = a;
    prefix = p;
    num = nm;
```

```
    }
};

// Display name and phone number.
ostream &operator<<(ostream &stream, phonebook o)
{
    stream << o.name << " ";
    stream << "(" << o.areacode << ") ";
    stream << o.prefix << "-" << o.num << "\n";

    return stream; // must return stream
}

int main()
{
    phonebook a("Ted", 111, 555, 1234);
    phonebook b("Alice", 312, 555, 5768);
    phonebook c("Tom", 212, 555, 9991);

    cout << a << b << c;

    return 0;
}
```

The program produces this output:

```
Ted (111) 555-1234
Alice (312) 555-5768
Tom (212) 555-9991
```

In the preceding program, notice that the **phonebook** inserter is not a member of **phonebook**. Although this may seem weird at first, the reason is easy to understand. When an operator function of any type is a member of a class, the left operand (passed implicitly through **this**) is the object that generates the call to the operator function. Further, this object is an *object of the class* for which the operator function is a member. There is no way to change this. If an overloaded operator function is a member of a class, the left operand must be an object of that class. However, when you overload inserters, the left operand is a *stream* and the right operand is an object of the class. Therefore, overloaded inserters cannot be members of the class for which they are overloaded. The variables **name**, **areacode**, **prefix**, and **num** are public in the preceding program so that they can be accessed by the inserter.

The fact that inserters cannot be members of the class for which they are defined seems to be a serious flaw in C++. Since overloaded inserters are not members, how can they access the private elements of a class? In the foregoing program, all members were made public. However, encapsulation is an essential component of object-oriented programming. Requiring that all data that will be output be public conflicts with this principle. Fortunately, there is a solution to this dilemma: Make the inserter a **friend** of the class. This preserves the requirement that the first argument to the overloaded inserter be a stream and still grants the function access to the private members of the class for which it is overloaded. Here is the same program modified to make the inserter into a **friend** function:

```cpp
#include <iostream>
#include <cstring>
using namespace std;

class phonebook {
  // now private
  char name[80];
  int areacode;
  int prefix;
  int num;
public:
  phonebook(char *n, int a, int p, int nm)
  {
    strcpy(name, n);
    areacode = a;
    prefix = p;
    num = nm;
  }
  friend ostream &operator<<(ostream &stream, phonebook o);
};

// Display name and phone number.
ostream &operator<<(ostream &stream, phonebook o)
{
  stream << o.name << " ";
  stream << "(" << o.areacode << ") ";
  stream << o.prefix << "-" << o.num << "\n";

  return stream; // must return stream
}
```

```
int main()
{
  phonebook a("Ted", 111, 555, 1234);
  phonebook b("Alice", 312, 555, 5768);
  phonebook c("Tom", 212, 555, 9991);

  cout << a << b << c;

  return 0;
}
```

When you define the body of an inserter function, remember to keep it as general as possible. For example, the inserter shown in the preceding example can be used with any stream because the body of the function directs its output to **stream**, which is the stream that invoked the inserter. While it would not be technically wrong to have written

```
stream << o.name << " ";
```

as

```
cout << o.name << " ";
```

this would have the effect of hard-coding **cout** as the output stream. The original version will work with any stream, including those linked to disk files. Although in some situations, especially where special output devices are involved, you may want to hard-code the output stream, in most cases you will not. In general, the more flexible your inserters are, the more valuable they are.

Note   *The inserter for the **phonebook** class works fine unless the value of **num** is something like 0034, in which case the preceding zeroes will not be displayed. To fix this, you can either make **num** into a string or you can set the fill character to zero and use the **width( )** format function to generate the leading zeroes. The solution is left to the reader as an exercise.*

Before moving on to extractors, let's look at one more example of an inserter function. An inserter need not be limited to handling only text. An inserter can be used to output data in any form that makes sense. For example, an inserter for some class that is part of a CAD system may output plotter instructions. Another inserter might generate graphics images. An inserter for a Windows-based program could display a dialog box. To sample the flavor of outputting things other than text, examine the following program, which draws boxes on the screen. (Because C++ does not define a graphics library, the program uses characters to draw a box, but feel free to substitute graphics if your system supports them.)

```cpp
#include <iostream>
using namespace std;

class box {
  int x, y;
public:
  box(int i, int j) { x=i; y=j; }
  friend ostream &operator<<(ostream &stream, box o);
};

// Output a box.
ostream &operator<<(ostream &stream, box o)
{
  register int i, j;

  for(i=0; i<o.x; i++)
    stream << "*";

  stream << "\n";

  for(j=1; j<o.y-1; j++) {
    for(i=0; i<o.x; i++)
      if(i==0 || i==o.x-1) stream << "*";
      else stream << " ";
    stream << "\n";
  }

  for(i=0; i<o.x; i++)
    stream << "*";
  stream << "\n";

  return stream;
}

int main()
{
  box a(14, 6), b(30, 7), c(40, 5);
```

C++

```
cout << "Here are some boxes:\n";
cout << a << b << c;

return 0;
}
```

The program displays the following:

```
Here are some boxes:
* * * * * * * * * * * * *
*                       *
*                       *
*                       *
*                       *
* * * * * * * * * * * * *
* * * * * * * * * * * * * * * * * * * * * * * * * * * *
*                                   *
*                                   *
*                                   *
*                                   *
*                                   *
* * * * * * * * * * * * * * * * * * * * * * * * * * * *
* * * * * * * * * * * * * * * * * * * * * * * * * * * * * * * * * * * *
*                                           *
*                                           *
*                                           *
* * * * * * * * * * * * * * * * * * * * * * * * * * * * * * * * * * * *
```

Creating Your Own Extractors

Extractors are the complement of inserters. The general form of an extractor function is

```
istream &operator>>(istream &stream, class_type &obj)
{
  // body of extractor
  return stream;
}
```

Extractors return a reference to a stream of type **istream**, which is an input stream. The first parameter must also be a reference to a stream of type **istream**. Notice that the second parameter must be a reference to an object of the class for which the extractor is overloaded. This is so the object can be modified by the input (extraction) operation.

Continuing with the **phonebook** class, here is one way to write an extraction function:

```
istream &operator>>(istream &stream, phonebook &o)
{
  cout << "Enter name: ";
  stream >> o.name;
  cout << "Enter area code: ";
  stream >> o.areacode;
  cout << "Enter prefix: ";
  stream >> o.prefix;
  cout << "Enter number: ";
  stream >> o.num;
  cout << "\n";

  return stream;
}
```

Notice that although this is an input function, it performs output by prompting the user. The point is that although the main purpose of an extractor is input, it can perform any operations necessary to achieve that end. However, as with inserters, it is best to keep the actions performed by an extractor directly related to input. If you don't, you run the risk of losing much in terms of structure and clarity.

Here is a program that illustrates the **phonebook** extractor:

```
#include <iostream>
#include <cstring>
using namespace std;

class phonebook {
  char name[80];
  int areacode;
  int prefix;
  int num;
public:
  phonebook() { };
  phonebook(char *n, int a, int p, int nm)
  {
    strcpy(name, n);
    areacode = a;
    prefix = p;
```

```
      num = nm;
   }
   friend ostream &operator<<(ostream &stream, phonebook o);
   friend istream &operator>>(istream &stream, phonebook &o);
};

// Display name and phone number.
ostream &operator<<(ostream &stream, phonebook o)
{
  stream << o.name << " ";
  stream << "(" << o.areacode << ") ";
  stream << o.prefix << "-" << o.num << "\n";

  return stream; // must return stream
}

// Input name and telephone number.
istream &operator>>(istream &stream, phonebook &o)
{
  cout << "Enter name: ";
  stream >> o.name;
  cout << "Enter area code: ";
  stream >> o.areacode;
  cout << "Enter prefix: ";
  stream >> o.prefix;
  cout << "Enter number: ";
  stream >> o.num;
  cout << "\n";

  return stream;
}

int main()
{
  phonebook a;

  cin >> a;

  cout << a;

  return 0;
}
```

Actually, the extractor for **phonebook** is less than perfect because the **cout** statements are needed only if the input stream is connected to an interactive device such as the console (that is, when the input stream is **cin**). If the extractor is used on a stream connected to a disk file, for example, then the **cout** statements would not be applicable. For fun, you might want to try suppressing the **cout** statements except when the input stream refers to **cin**. For example, you might use **if** statements such as the one shown here.

```
if(stream == cin) cout << "Enter name: ";
```

Now, the prompt will take place only when the output device is most likely the screen.

Creating Your Own Manipulator Functions

In addition to overloading the insertion and extraction operators, you can further customize C++'s I/O system by creating your own manipulator functions. Custom manipulators are important for two main reasons. First, you can consolidate a sequence of several separate I/O operations into one manipulator. For example, it is not uncommon to have situations in which the same sequence of I/O operations occurs frequently within a program. In these cases you can use a custom manipulator to perform these actions, thus simplifying your source code and preventing accidental errors. A custom manipulator can also be important when you need to perform I/O operations on a nonstandard device. For example, you might use a manipulator to send control codes to a special type of printer or to an optical recognition system.

Custom manipulators are a feature of C++ that supports OOP, but also can benefit programs that aren't object oriented. As you will see, custom manipulators can help make any I/O-intensive program clearer and more efficient.

As you know, there are two basic types of manipulators: those that operate on input streams and those that operate on output streams. In addition to these two broad categories, there is a secondary division: those manipulators that take an argument and those that don't. Frankly, the procedures necessary to create a parameterized manipulator vary widely from compiler to compiler, and even between two different versions of the same compiler. For this reason, you must consult the documentation to your compiler for instructions on creating parameterized manipulators. However, the creation of parameterless manipulators is straightforward and the same for all compilers. It is described here.

All parameterless manipulator output functions have this skeleton:

ostream &*manip-name*(ostream &*stream*)
{
  // *your code here*
  return *stream*;
}

Here, *manip-name* is the name of the manipulator. Notice that a reference to a stream of type **ostream** is returned. This is necessary if a manipulator is used as part of a larger I/O expression. It is important to note that even though the manipulator has as its single argument a reference to the stream upon which it is operating, no argument is used when the manipulator is inserted in an output operation.

As a simple first example, the following program creates a manipulator called **sethex( )**, which turns on the **showbase** flag and sets output to hexadecimal.

```cpp
#include <iostream>
#include <iomanip>
using namespace std;

// A simple output manipulator.
ostream &sethex(ostream &stream)
{
  stream.setf(ios::showbase);
  stream.setf(ios::hex, ios::basefield);

  return stream;
}

int main()
{
  cout << 256 << " " << sethex << 256;

  return 0;
}
```

This program displays **256 0x100**. As you can see, **sethex** is used as part of an I/O expression in the same way as any of the built-in manipulators.

Custom manipulators need not be complex to be useful. For example, the simple manipulators **la( )** and **ra( )** display a left and right arrow for emphasis, as shown here:

```cpp
#include <iostream>
#include <iomanip>
using namespace std;

// Right Arrow
ostream &ra(ostream &stream)
{
  stream << "-------> ";
  return stream;
```

```
}

// Left Arrow
ostream &la(ostream &stream)
{
  stream << " <-------";
  return stream;
}

int main()
{
  cout << "High balance " << ra << 1233.23 << "\n";
  cout << "Over draft " << ra << 567.66 << la;

  return 0;
}
```

This program displays:

```
High balance -------> 1233.23
Over draft -------> 567.66 <-------
```

If used frequently, these simple manipulators save you from some tedious typing.

Using an output manipulator is particularly useful for sending special codes to a device. For example, a printer may be able to accept various codes that change the type size or font, or that position the print head in a special location. If these adjustments are going to be made frequently, they are perfect candidates for a manipulator.

All parameterless input manipulator functions have this skeleton:

istream &*manip-name*(istream &*stream*)
{
  // *your code here*
  return *stream*;
}

An input manipulator receives a reference to the stream for which it was invoked. This stream must be returned by the manipulator.

The following program creates the **getpass( )** input manipulator, which rings the bell and then prompts for a password:

```
#include <iostream>
#include <cstring>
```

```
using namespace std;

// A simple input manipulator.
istream &getpass(istream &stream)
{
  cout << '\a';  // sound bell
  cout << "Enter password: ";

  return stream;
}

int main()
{
  char pw[80];

  do {
    cin >> getpass >> pw;
  } while (strcmp(pw, "password"));

  cout << "Logon complete\n";

  return 0;
}
```

Remember that it is crucial that your manipulator return **stream**. If it does not, your manipulator cannot be used in a series of input or output operations.

The Complete Reference

C++

Chapter 21

C++ File I/O

lthough C++ I/O forms an integrated system, file I/O is sufficiently specialized
that it is generally thought of as a special case, subject to its own constraints and
quirks. In part, this is because the most common file is a disk file, and disk files
have capabilities and features that most other devices don't. Keep in mind, however,
that disk file I/O is simply a special case of the general I/O system and that most of the
material discussed in this chapter also applies to streams connected to other types of
devices.

\<fstream\> and the File Classes

To perform file I/O, you must include the header **\<fstream\>** in your program. It
defines several classes, including **ifstream**, **ofstream**, and **fstream**. These classes are
derived from **istream**, **ostream**, and **iostream**, respectively. Remember, **istream**,
ostream, and **iostream** are derived from **ios**, so **ifstream**, **ofstream**, and **fstream** also
have access to all operations defined by **ios** (discussed in the preceding chapter).
Another class used by the file system is **filebuf**, which provides low-level facilities to
manage a file stream. Usually, you don't use **filebuf** directly, but it is part of the other
file classes.

Opening and Closing a File

In C++, you open a file by linking it to a stream. Before you can open a file, you must
first obtain a stream. There are three types of streams: input, output, and input/output.
To create an input stream, you must declare the stream to be of class **ifstream**. To create
an output stream, you must declare it as class **ofstream**. Streams that will be performing
both input and output operations must be declared as class **fstream**. For example, this
fragment creates one input stream, one output stream, and one stream capable of both
input and output:

```
ifstream in;  // input
ofstream out; // output
fstream io;   // input and output
```

Once you have created a stream, one way to associate it with a file is by using **open( )**.
This function is a member of each of the three stream classes. The prototype for each is
shown here:

void ifstream::open(const char *filename, ios::openmode mode = ios::in);
void ofstream::open(const char *filename, ios::openmode mode = ios::out | ios::trunc);
void fstream::open(const char *filename, ios::openmode mode = ios::in | ios::out);

Here, *filename* is the name of the file; it can include a path specifier. The value of *mode* determines how the file is opened. It must be one or more of the following values defined by **openmode**, which is an enumeration defined by **ios** (through its base class **ios_base**).

> ios::app
> ios::ate
> ios::binary
> ios::in
> ios::out
> ios::trunc

You can combine two or more of these values by ORing them together.

Including **ios::app** causes all output to that file to be appended to the end. This value can be used only with files capable of output. Including **ios::ate** causes a seek to the end of the file to occur when the file is opened. Although **ios::ate** causes an initial seek to end-of-file, I/O operations can still occur anywhere within the file.

The **ios::in** value specifies that the file is capable of input. The **ios::out** value specifies that the file is capable of output.

The **ios::binary** value causes a file to be opened in binary mode. By default, all files are opened in text mode. In text mode, various character translations may take place, such as carriage return/linefeed sequences being converted into newlines. However, when a file is opened in binary mode, no such character translations will occur. Understand that any file, whether it contains formatted text or raw data, can be opened in either binary or text mode. The only difference is whether character translations take place.

The **ios::trunc** value causes the contents of a preexisting file by the same name to be destroyed, and the file is truncated to zero length. When creating an output stream using **ofstream**, any preexisting file by that name is automatically truncated.

The following fragment opens a normal output file.

```
ofstream out;
out.open("test", ios::out);
```

However, you will seldom see **open( )** called as shown, because the *mode* parameter provides default values for each type of stream. As their prototypes show, for **ifstream**, *mode* defaults to **ios::in**; for **ofstream**, it is **ios::out | ios::trunc**; and for **fstream**, it is **ios::in | ios::out**. Therefore, the preceding statement will usually look like this:

```
out.open("test"); // defaults to output and normal file
```

Note *Depending on your compiler, the mode parameter for **fstream::open( )** may not default to **in | out**. Therefore, you might need to specify this explicitly.*

If **open( )** fails, the stream will evaluate to false when used in a Boolean expression. Therefore, before using a file, you should test to make sure that the open operation succeeded. You can do so by using a statement like this:

```
if(!mystream) {
  cout << "Cannot open file.\n";
  // handle error
}
```

Although it is entirely proper to open a file by using the **open( )** function, most of the time you will not do so because the **ifstream**, **ofstream**, and **fstream** classes have constructors that automatically open the file. The constructors have the same parameters and defaults as the **open( )** function. Therefore, you will most commonly see a file opened as shown here:

```
ifstream mystream("myfile"); // open file for input
```

As stated, if for some reason the file cannot be opened, the value of the associated stream variable will evaluate to false. Therefore, whether you use a constructor to open the file or an explicit call to **open( )**, you will want to confirm that the file has actually been opened by testing the value of the stream.

You can also check to see if you have successfully opened a file by using the **is_open( )** function, which is a member of **fstream**, **ifstream**, and **ofstream**. It has this prototype:

bool is_open( );

It returns true if the stream is linked to an open file and false otherwise. For example, the following checks if **mystream** is currently open:

```
if(!mystream.is_open()) {
  cout << "File is not open.\n";
  // ...
```

To close a file, use the member function **close( )**. For example, to close the file linked to a stream called **mystream**, use this statement:

```
mystream.close();
```

The **close( )** function takes no parameters and returns no value.

Reading and Writing Text Files

It is very easy to read from or write to a text file. Simply use the << and >> operators the same way you do when performing console I/O, except that instead of using **cin** and **cout**, substitute a stream that is linked to a file. For example, this program creates a short inventory file that contains each item's name and its cost:

```cpp
#include <iostream>
#include <fstream>
using namespace std;

int main()
{
  ofstream out("INVNTRY"); // output, normal file

  if(!out) {
    cout << "Cannot open INVENTORY file.\n";
    return 1;
  }

  out << "Radios " << 39.95 << endl;
  out << "Toasters " << 19.95 << endl;
  out << "Mixers " << 24.80 << endl;

  out.close();
  return 0;
}
```

The following program reads the inventory file created by the previous program and displays its contents on the screen:

```cpp
#include <iostream>
#include <fstream>
using namespace std;

int main()
{
  ifstream in("INVNTRY"); // input

  if(!in) {
    cout << "Cannot open INVENTORY file.\n";
    return 1;
```

```
    }

    char item[20];
    float cost;

    in >> item >>  cost;
    cout << item << " " << cost << "\n";
    in >> item >> cost;
    cout << item << " " << cost << "\n";
    in >> item >> cost;
    cout << item << " " << cost << "\n";

    in.close();
    return 0;
}
```

In a way, reading and writing files by using >> and << is like using the C-based functions **fprintf( )** and **fscanf( )**. All information is stored in the file in the same format as it would be displayed on the screen.

Following is another example of disk I/O. This program reads strings entered at the keyboard and writes them to disk. The program stops when the user enters an exclamation point. To use the program, specify the name of the output file on the command line.

```
#include <iostream>
#include <fstream>
using namespace std;

int main(int argc, char *argv[])
{
  if(argc!=2) {
    cout << "Usage: output <filename>\n";
    return 1;
  }

  ofstream out(argv[1]); // output, normal file

  if(!out) {
    cout << "Cannot open output file.\n";
    return 1;
  }
```

```
char str[80];
cout << "Write strings to disk. Enter ! to stop.\n";

do {
  cout << ": ";
  cin >> str;
  out << str << endl;
} while (*str != '!');

out.close();
return 0;
}
```

When reading text files using the >> operator, keep in mind that certain character translations will occur. For example, white-space characters are omitted. If you want to prevent any character translations, you must open a file for binary access and use the functions discussed in the next section.

When inputting, if end-of-file is encountered, the stream linked to that file will evaluate as false. (The next section illustrates this fact.)

Unformatted and Binary I/O

While reading and writing formatted text files is very easy, it is not always the most efficient way to handle files. Also, there will be times when you need to store unformatted (raw) binary data, not text. The functions that allow you to do this are described here.

When performing binary operations on a file, be sure to open it using the **ios::binary** mode specifier. Although the unformatted file functions will work on files opened for text mode, some character translations may occur. Character translations negate the purpose of binary file operations.

Characters vs. Bytes

Before beginning our examination of unformatted I/O, it is important to clarify an important concept. For many years, I/O in C and C++ was thought of as *byte oriented*. This is because a **char** is equivalent to a byte and the only types of streams available were **char** streams. However, with the advent of wide characters (of type **wchar_t**) and their attendant streams, we can no longer say that C++ I/O is byte oriented. Instead, we must say that it is *character oriented*. Of course, **char** streams are still byte oriented and we can continue to think in terms of bytes, especially when operating on nontextual data. But the equivalency between a byte and a character can no longer be taken for granted.

As explained in Chapter 20, all of the streams used in this book are **char** streams since they are by far the most common. They also make unformatted file handling easier because a **char** stream establishes a one-to-one correspondence between bytes and characters, which is a benefit when reading or writing blocks of binary data.

put( ) and get( )

One way that you may read and write unformatted data is by using the member functions **get( )** and **put( )**. These functions operate on characters. That is, **get( )** will read a character and **put( )** will write a character. Of course, if you have opened the file for binary operations and are operating on a **char** (rather than a **wchar_t** stream), then these functions read and write bytes of data.

The **get( )** function has many forms, but the most commonly used version is shown here along with **put( )**:

istream &get(char &ch);
ostream &put(char ch);

The **get( )** function reads a single character from the invoking stream and puts that value in ch. It returns a reference to the stream. The **put( )** function writes ch to the stream and returns a reference to the stream.

The following program displays the contents of any file, whether it contains text or binary data, on the screen. It uses the **get( )** function.

```
#include <iostream>
#include <fstream>
using namespace std;

int main(int argc, char *argv[])
{
  char ch;

  if(argc!=2) {
    cout << "Usage: PR <filename>\n";
    return 1;
  }

  ifstream in(argv[1], ios::in | ios::binary);
  if(!in) {
    cout << "Cannot open file.";
```

```
      return 1;
    }

  while(in) { // in will be false when eof is reached
    in.get(ch);
    if(in) cout << ch;
  }

  return 0;
}
```

As stated in the preceding section, when the end-of-file is reached, the stream associated with the file becomes false. Therefore, when **in** reaches the end of the file, it will be false, causing the **while** loop to stop.

There is actually a more compact way to code the loop that reads and displays a file, as shown here:

```
while(in.get(ch))
  cout << ch;
```

This works because **get( )** returns a reference to the stream **in**, and **in** will be false when the end of the file is encountered.

The next program uses **put( )** to write all characters from zero to 255 to a file called CHARS. As you probably know, the ASCII characters occupy only about half the available values that can be held by a **char**. The other values are generally called the *extended character set* and include such things as foreign language and mathematical symbols. (Not all systems support the extended character set, but most do.)

```
#include <iostream>
#include <fstream>
using namespace std;

int main()
{
  int i;
  ofstream out("CHARS", ios::out | ios::binary);

  if(!out) {
    cout << "Cannot open output file.\n";
    return 1;
  }
```

```
      // write all characters to disk
      for(i=0; i<256; i++) out.put((char) i);

      out.close();
      return 0;
    }
```

You might find it interesting to examine the contents of the CHARS file to see what extended characters your computer has available.

read( ) and write( )

Another way to read and write blocks of binary data is to use C++'s **read( )** and **write( )** functions. Their prototypes are

istream &read(char *buf*, streamsize *num*);
ostream &write(const char *buf*, streamsize *num*);

The **read( )** function reads *num* characters from the invoking stream and puts them in the buffer pointed to by *buf*. The **write( )** function writes *num* characters to the invoking stream from the buffer pointed to by *buf*. As mentioned in the preceding chapter, **streamsize** is a type defined by the C++ library as some form of integer. It is capable of holding the largest number of characters that can be transferred in any one I/O operation.

The next program writes a structure to disk and then reads it back in:

```
#include <iostream>
#include <fstream>
#include <cstring>
using namespace std;

struct status {
  char name[80];
  double balance;
  unsigned long account_num;
};

int main()
{
  struct status acc;
```

```
        strcpy(acc.name, "Ralph Trantor");
        acc.balance = 1123.23;
        acc.account_num = 34235678;

        // write data
        ofstream outbal("balance", ios::out | ios::binary);
        if(!outbal) {
          cout << "Cannot open file.\n";
          return 1;
        }

        outbal.write((char *) &acc, sizeof(struct status));
        outbal.close();

        // now, read back;
        ifstream inbal("balance", ios::in | ios::binary);
        if(!inbal) {
          cout << "Cannot open file.\n";
          return 1;
        }

        inbal.read((char *) &acc, sizeof(struct status));

        cout << acc.name << endl;
        cout << "Account # " << acc.account_num;
        cout.precision(2);
        cout.setf(ios::fixed);
        cout << endl << "Balance: $" << acc.balance;

        inbal.close();
        return 0;
      }
```

As you can see, only a single call to **read( )** or **write( )** is necessary to read or write the entire structure. Each individual field need not be read or written separately. As this example illustrates, the buffer can be any type of object.

Note   *The type casts inside the calls to **read( )** and **write( )** are necessary when operating on a buffer that is not defined as a character array. Because of C++'s strong type checking, a pointer of one type will not automatically be converted into a pointer of another type.*

If the end of the file is reached before *num* characters have been read, then **read( )** simply stops, and the buffer contains as many characters as were available. You can find out how many characters have been read by using another member function, called **gcount( )**, which has this prototype:

streamsize gcount();

It returns the number of characters read by the last binary input operation. The following program shows another example of **read( )** and **write( )** and illustrates the use of **gcount( )**:

```
#include <iostream>
#include <fstream>
using namespace std;

int main()
{
  double fnum[4] = {99.75, -34.4, 1776.0, 200.1};
  int i;

  ofstream out("numbers", ios::out | ios::binary);
  if(!out) {
    cout << "Cannot open file.";
    return 1;
   }

  out.write((char *) &fnum, sizeof fnum);

  out.close();

  for(i=0; i<4; i++) // clear array
    fnum[i] = 0.0;

  ifstream in("numbers", ios::in | ios::binary);
  in.read((char *) &fnum, sizeof fnum);

  // see how many bytes have been read
  cout << in.gcount() << " bytes read\n";

  for(i=0; i<4; i++) // show values read from file
  cout << fnum[i] << " ";
```

```
    in.close();

    return 0;
}
```

The preceding program writes an array of floating-point values to disk and then reads them back. After the call to **read( )**, **gcount( )** is used to determine how many bytes were just read.

More get( ) Functions

In addition to the form shown earlier, the **get( )** function is overloaded in several different ways. The prototypes for the three most commonly used overloaded forms are shown here:

istream &get(char *buf, streamsize num);
istream &get(char *buf, streamsize num, char delim);
int get( );

The first form reads characters into the array pointed to by buf until either num-1 characters have been read, a newline is found, or the end of the file has been encountered. The array pointed to by buf will be null terminated by **get( )**. If the newline character is encountered in the input stream, it is *not* extracted. Instead, it remains in the stream until the next input operation.

The second form reads characters into the array pointed to by buf until either num-1 characters have been read, the character specified by delim has been found, or the end of the file has been encountered. The array pointed to by buf will be null terminated by **get( )**. If the delimiter character is encountered in the input stream, it is *not* extracted. Instead, it remains in the stream until the next input operation.

The third overloaded form of **get( )** returns the next character from the stream. It returns **EOF** if the end of the file is encountered. This form of **get( )** is similar to C's **getc( )** function.

getline( )

Another function that performs input is **getline( )**. It is a member of each input stream class. Its prototypes are shown here:

istream &getline(char *buf, streamsize num);
istream &getline(char *buf, streamsize num, char delim);

The first form reads characters into the array pointed to by *buf* until either *num*–1 characters have been read, a newline character has been found, or the end of the file has been encountered. The array pointed to by *buf* will be null terminated by **getline( )**. If the newline character is encountered in the input stream, it is extracted, but is not put into *buf*.

The second form reads characters into the array pointed to by *buf* until either *num*–1 characters have been read, the character specified by *delim* has been found, or the end of the file has been encountered. The array pointed to by *buf* will be null terminated by **getline( )**. If the delimiter character is encountered in the input stream, it is extracted, but is not put into *buf*.

As you can see, the two versions of **getline( )** are virtually identical to the **get(buf, num)** and **get(buf, num, delim)** versions of **get( )**. Both read characters from input and put them into the array pointed to by *buf* until either *num*–1 characters have been read or until the delimiter character is encountered. The difference is that **getline( )** reads and removes the delimiter from the input stream; **get( )** does not.

Here is a program that demonstrates the **getline( )** function. It reads the contents of a text file one line at a time and displays it on the screen.

```
// Read and display a text file line by line.

#include <iostream>
#include <fstream>
using namespace std;

int main(int argc, char *argv[])
{
  if(argc!=2) {
    cout << "Usage: Display <filename>\n";
    return 1;
  }

  ifstream in(argv[1]); // input

  if(!in) {
    cout << "Cannot open input file.\n";
    return 1;
  }

  char str[255];
```

```
  while(in) {
    in.getline(str, 255);  // delim defaults to '\n'
    if(in) cout << str << endl;
  }

  in.close();

  return 0;
}
```

Detecting EOF

You can detect when the end of the file is reached by using the member function **eof( )**, which has this prototype:

    bool eof( );

It returns true when the end of the file has been reached; otherwise it returns false.

The following program uses **eof( )** to display the contents of a file in both hexadecimal and ASCII.

```
/* Display contents of specified file
   in both ASCII and in hex.
*/
#include <iostream>
#include <fstream>
#include <cctype>
#include <iomanip>
using namespace std;

int main(int argc, char *argv[])
{
  if(argc!=2) {
    cout << "Usage: Display <filename>\n";
    return 1;
  }
```

```cpp
  ifstream in(argv[1], ios::in | ios::binary);

  if(!in) {
    cout << "Cannot open input file.\n";
    return 1;
  }

  register int i, j;
  int count = 0;
  char c[16];

  cout.setf(ios::uppercase);
  while(!in.eof()) {
    for(i=0; i<16 && !in.eof(); i++) {
      in.get(c[i]);
    }
    if(i<16) i--; // get rid of eof

    for(j=0; j<i; j++)
      cout << setw(3) << hex << (int) c[j];
    for(; j<16; j++) cout << "   ";

    cout << "\t";
    for(j=0; j<i; j++)
      if(isprint(c[j])) cout << c[j];
      else cout << ".";

    cout << endl;

    count++;
    if(count==16) {
      count = 0;
      cout << "Press ENTER to continue: ";
      cin.get();
      cout << endl;
    }
  }

  in.close();

  return 0;
}
```

When this program is used to display itself, the first screen looks like this:

```
2F 2A 20 44 69 73 70 6C 61 79 20 63 6F 6E 74 65      /* Display conte
6E 74 73 20 6F 66 20 73 70 65 63 69 66 69 65 64      nts of specified
20 66 69 6C 65  D  A 20 20 20 69 6E 20 62 6F 74      file..   in bot
68 20 41 53 43 49 49 20 61 6E 64 20 69 6E 20 68      h ASCII and in h
65 78 2E  D  A 2A 2F  D  A 23 69 6E 63 6C 75 64      ex...*/..#includ
65 20 3C 69 6F 73 74 72 65 61 6D 3E  D  A 23 69      e <iostream>..#i
6E 63 6C 75 64 65 20 3C 66 73 74 72 65 61 6D 3E      nclude <fstream>
 D  A 23 69 6E 63 6C 75 64 65 20 3C 63 63 74 79      ..#include <ccty
70 65 3E  D  A 23 69 6E 63 6C 75 64 65 20 3C 69      pe>..#include <i
6F 6D 61 6E 69 70 3E  D  A 75 73 69 6E 67 20 6E      omanip>..using n
61 6D 65 73 70 61 63 65 20 73 74 64 3B  D  A  D      amespace std;...
 A 69 6E 74 20 6D 61 69 6E 28 69 6E 74 20 61 72      .int main(int ar
67 63 2C 20 63 68 61 72 20 2A 61 72 67 76 5B 5D      gc, char *argv[]
29  D  A 7B  D  A 20 20 69 66 28 61 72 67 63 21      )..{..  if(argc!
3D 32 29 20 7B  D  A 20 20 20 20 63 6F 75 74 20      =2) {..    cout
3C 3C 20 22 55 73 61 67 65 3A 20 44 69 73 70 6C      << "Usage: Displ
Press ENTER to continue:
```

The ignore( ) Function

You can use the **ignore( )** member function to read and discard characters from the input stream. It has this prototype:

istream &ignore(streamsize *num*=1, int_type *delim*=EOF);

It reads and discards characters until either *num* characters have been ignored (1 by default) or the character specified by *delim* is encountered (**EOF** by default). If the delimiting character is encountered, it is not removed from the input stream. Here, **int_type** is defined as some form of integer.

The next program reads a file called TEST. It ignores characters until either a space is encountered or 10 characters have been read. It then displays the rest of the file.

```
#include <iostream>
#include <fstream>
using namespace std;

int main()
{
  ifstream in("test");
```

```
if(!in) {
  cout << "Cannot open file.\n";
  return 1;
}

/* Ignore up to 10 characters or until first
   space is found. */
in.ignore(10, ' ');
char c;
while(in) {
  in.get(c);
  if(in) cout << c;
}

in.close();
return 0;
}
```

peek( ) and putback( )

You can obtain the next character in the input stream without removing it from that stream by using **peek( )**. It has this prototype:

   int_type peek( );

It returns the next character in the stream or **EOF** if the end of the file is encountered. (**int_type** is defined as some form of integer.)

   You can return the last character read from a stream to that stream by using **putback( )**. Its prototype is

   istream &putback(char *c*);

where *c* is the last character read.

flush( )

When output is performed, data is not necessarily immediately written to the physical device linked to the stream. Instead, information is stored in an internal buffer until the buffer is full. Only then are the contents of that buffer written to disk. However, you can force the information to be physically written to disk before the buffer is full by calling **flush( )**. Its prototype is

ostream &flush( );

Calls to **flush( )** might be warranted when a program is going to be used in adverse environments (for example, in situations where power outages occur frequently).

> **Note** *Closing a file or terminating a program also flushes all buffers.*

Random Access

In C++'s I/O system, you perform random access by using the **seekg( )** and **seekp( )** functions. Their most common forms are

istream &seekg(off_type *offset*, seekdir *origin*);
ostream &seekp(off_type *offset*, seekdir *origin*);

Here, **off_type** is an integer type defined by **ios** that is capable of containing the largest valid value that *offset* can have. **seekdir** is an enumeration defined by **ios** that determines how the seek will take place.

The C++ I/O system manages two pointers associated with a file. One is the *get pointer*, which specifies where in the file the next input operation will occur. The other is the *put pointer*, which specifies where in the file the next output operation will occur. Each time an input or output operation takes place, the appropriate pointer is automatically sequentially advanced. However, using the **seekg( )** and **seekp( )** functions allows you to access the file in a nonsequential fashion.

The **seekg( )** function moves the associated file's current get pointer *offset* number of characters from the specified *origin*, which must be one of these three values:

ios::beg	Beginning-of-file
ios::cur	Current location
ios::end	End-of-file

The **seekp( )** function moves the associated file's current put pointer *offset* number of characters from the specified *origin*, which must be one of the values just shown.

Generally, random-access I/O should be performed only on those files opened for binary operations. The character translations that may occur on text files could cause a position request to be out of sync with the actual contents of the file.

The following program demonstrates the **seekp( )** function. It allows you to change a specific character in a file. Specify a filename on the command line, followed by the number of the character in the file you want to change, followed by the new character. Notice that the file is opened for read/write operations.

```
#include <iostream>
#include <fstream>
#include <cstdlib>
using namespace std;

int main(int argc, char *argv[])
{
  if(argc!=4) {
    cout << "Usage: CHANGE <filename> <character> <char>\n";
    return 1;
  }

  fstream out(argv[1], ios::in | ios::out | ios::binary);
  if(!out) {
    cout << "Cannot open file.";
    return 1;
  }

  out.seekp(atoi(argv[2]), ios::beg);

  out.put(*argv[3]);
  out.close();

  return 0;
}
```

For example, to use this program to change the twelfth character of a file called TEST to a Z, use this command line:

```
change test 12 Z
```

The next program uses **seekg( )**. It displays the contents of a file beginning with the location you specify on the command line.

```
#include <iostream>
#include <fstream>
```

```
#include <cstdlib>
using namespace std;

int main(int argc, char *argv[])
{
  char ch;

  if(argc!=3) {
    cout << "Usage: SHOW <filename> <starting location>\n";
    return 1;
  }

  ifstream in(argv[1], ios::in | ios::binary);
  if(!in) {
    cout << "Cannot open file.";
    return 1;
  }

  in.seekg(atoi(argv[2]), ios::beg);

  while(in.get(ch))
    cout << ch;

  return 0;
}
```

The following program uses both **seekp( )** and **seekg( )** to reverse the first *<num>* characters in a file.

```
#include <iostream>
#include <fstream>
#include <cstdlib>
using namespace std;

int main(int argc, char *argv[])
{
  if(argc!=3) {
    cout << "Usage: Reverse <filename> <num>\n";
    return 1;
  }
```

```
fstream inout(argv[1], ios::in | ios::out | ios::binary);

if(!inout) {
  cout << "Cannot open input file.\n";
  return 1;
}

long e, i, j;
char c1, c2;
e = atol(argv[2]);

for(i=0, j=e; i<j; i++, j--) {
  inout.seekg(i, ios::beg);
  inout.get(c1);
  inout.seekg(j, ios::beg);
  inout.get(c2);

  inout.seekp(i, ios::beg);
  inout.put(c2);
  inout.seekp(j, ios::beg);
  inout.put(c1);
}

inout.close();
return 0;
}
```

To use the program, specify the name of the file that you want to reverse, followed by the number of characters to reverse. For example, to reverse the first 10 characters of a file called TEST, use this command line:

```
reverse test 10
```

If the file had contained this:

```
This is a test.
```

it will contain the following after the program executes:

```
a si sihTtest.
```

Obtaining the Current File Position

You can determine the current position of each file pointer by using these functions:

    pos_type tellg( );
    pos_type tellp( );

Here, **pos_type** is a type defined by **ios** that is capable of holding the largest value that either function can return. You can use the values returned by **tellg( )** and **tellp( )** as arguments to the following forms of **seekg( )** and **seekp( )**, respectively.

    istream &seekg(pos_type *pos)*;
    ostream &seekp(pos_type *pos)*;

These functions allow you to save the current file location, perform other file operations, and then reset the file location to its previously saved location.

I/O Status

The C++ I/O system maintains status information about the outcome of each I/O operation. The current state of the I/O system is held in an object of type **iostate**, which is an enumeration defined by **ios** that includes the following members.

Name	Meaning
ios::goodbit	No error bits set
ios::eofbit	1 when end-of-file is encountered; 0 otherwise
ios::failbit	1 when a (possibly) nonfatal I/O error has occurred; 0 otherwise
ios::badbit	1 when a fatal I/O error has occurred; 0 otherwise

There are two ways in which you can obtain I/O status information. First, you can call the **rdstate( )** function. It has this prototype:

    iostate rdstate( );

It returns the current status of the error flags. As you can probably guess from looking at the preceding list of flags, **rdstate( )** returns **goodbit** when no error has occurred. Otherwise, an error flag is turned on.

The following program illustrates **rdstate( )**. It displays the contents of a text file. If an error occurs, the program reports it, using **checkstatus( )**.

```cpp
#include <iostream>
#include <fstream>
using namespace std;

void checkstatus(ifstream &in);

int main(int argc, char *argv[])
{
  if(argc!=2) {
    cout << "Usage: Display <filename>\n";
    return 1;
  }

  ifstream in(argv[1]);

  if(!in) {
    cout << "Cannot open input file.\n";
    return 1;
  }

  char c;
  while(in.get(c)) {
    if(in) cout << c;
    checkstatus(in);
  }

  checkstatus(in);   // check final status
  in.close();
  return 0;
}

void checkstatus(ifstream &in)
{
  ios::iostate i;

  i = in.rdstate();

  if(i & ios::eofbit)
    cout << "EOF encountered\n";
```

```
    else if(i & ios::failbit)
      cout << "Non-Fatal I/O error\n";
    else if(i & ios::badbit)
      cout << "Fatal I/O error\n";
}
```

This program will always report one "error." After the **while** loop ends, the final call to **checkstatus( )** reports, as expected, that an **EOF** has been encountered. You might find the **checkstatus( )** function useful in programs that you write.

The other way that you can determine if an error has occurred is by using one or more of these functions:

bool bad( );
bool eof( );
bool fail( );
bool good( );

The **bad( )** function returns true if **badbit** is set. The **eof( )** function was discussed earlier. The **fail( )** returns true if **failbit** is set. The **good( )** function returns true if there are no errors. Otherwise, it returns false.

Once an error has occurred, it may need to be cleared before your program continues. To do this, use the **clear( )** function, which has this prototype:

void clear(iostate *flags*=ios::goodbit);

If *flags* is **goodbit** (as it is by default), all error flags are cleared. Otherwise, set *flags* as you desire.

Customized I/O and Files

In Chapter 20 you learned how to overload the insertion and extraction operators relative to your own classes. In that chapter, only console I/O was performed, but because all C++ streams are the same, you can use the same overloaded inserter or extractor function to perform I/O on the console or a file with no changes whatsoever. As an example, the following program reworks the phone book example in Chapter 20 so that it stores a list on disk. The program is very simple: It allows you to add names to the list or to display the list on the screen. It uses custom inserters and extractors to input and output the telephone numbers. You might find it interesting to enhance the program so that it will find a specific number or delete unwanted numbers.

```cpp
#include <iostream>
#include <fstream>
#include <cstring>
using namespace std;

class phonebook {
  char name[80];
  char areacode[4];
  char prefix[4];
  char num[5];
public:
  phonebook() { };
  phonebook(char *n, char *a, char *p, char *nm)
  {
    strcpy(name, n);
    strcpy(areacode, a);
    strcpy(prefix, p);
    strcpy(num, nm);
  }
  friend ostream &operator<<(ostream &stream, phonebook o);
  friend istream &operator>>(istream &stream, phonebook &o);
};

// Display name and phone number.
ostream &operator<<(ostream &stream, phonebook o)
{
  stream << o.name << " ";
  stream << "(" << o.areacode << ") ";
  stream << o.prefix << "-";
  stream << o.num << "\n";
  return stream; // must return stream
}

// Input name and telephone number.
istream &operator>>(istream &stream, phonebook &o)
{
  cout << "Enter name: ";
  stream >> o.name;
  cout << "Enter area code: ";
  stream >> o.areacode;
  cout << "Enter prefix: ";
  stream >> o.prefix;
  cout << "Enter number: ";
```

```cpp
    stream >> o.num;
    cout << "\n";
    return stream;
}

int main()
{
  phonebook a;
  char c;

  fstream pb("phone", ios::in | ios::out | ios::app);

  if(!pb) {
    cout << "Cannot open phone book file.\n";
    return 1;
  }

  for(;;) {
    do {
      cout << "1. Enter numbers\n";
      cout << "2. Display numbers\n";
      cout << "3. Quit\n";
      cout << "\nEnter a choice: ";
      cin >> c;
    } while(c<'1' || c>'3');

    switch(c) {
      case '1':
        cin >> a;
        cout << "Entry is: ";
        cout << a;  // show on screen
        pb << a;  // write to disk
        break;
      case '2':
        char ch;
        pb.seekg(0, ios::beg);
        while(!pb.eof()) {
          pb.get(ch);
          if(!pb.eof()) cout << ch;
        }
        pb.clear();  // reset eof
        cout << endl;
```

```
          break;
        case '3':
          pb.close();
          return 0;
      }
    }
}
```

Notice that the overloaded << operator can be used to write to a disk file or to the screen without any changes. This is one of the most important and useful features of C++'s approach to I/O.

Chapter 22

Run-Time Type ID and the Casting Operators

tandard C++ contains two features that help support modern, object-oriented
programming: run-time type identification (RTTI for short) and a set of four
additional casting operators. Neither of these were part of the original specification
for C++, but both were added to provide enhanced support for run-time polymorphism.
RTTI allows you to identify the type of an object during the execution of your program.
The casting operators give you safer, more controlled ways to cast. Since one of the
casting operators, **dynamic_cast**, relates directly to RTTI, it makes sense to discuss them
in the same chapter.

Run-Time Type Identification (RTTI)

Run-time type information may be new to you because it is not found in nonpolymorphic languages, such as C. In nonpolymorphic languages there is no need for
run-time type information because the type of each object is known at compile time
(i.e., when the program is written). However, in polymorphic languages such as C++,
there can be situations in which the type of an object is unknown at compile time because
the precise nature of that object is not determined until the program is executed. As
explained in Chapter 17, C++ implements polymorphism through the use of class
hierarchies, virtual functions, and base-class pointers. Since base-class pointers may be
used to point to objects of the base class or *any object derived from that base*, it is not always
possible to know in advance what type of object will be pointed to by a base pointer at
any given moment in time. This determination must be made at run time, using run-time
type identification.

To obtain an object's type, use **typeid**. You must include the header **<typeinfo>** in
order to use **typeid**. Its most commonly used form is shown here:

typeid(*object*)

Here, *object* is the object whose type you will be obtaining. It may be of any type,
including the built-in types and class types that you create. **typeid** returns a reference
to an object of type **type_info** that describes the type of *object*.

The **type_info** class defines the following public members:

bool operator==(const type_info &*ob*);
bool operator!=(const type_info &*ob*);
bool before(const type_info &*ob*);
const char *name( );

The overloaded **==** and **!=** provide for the comparison of types. The **before( )**
function returns true if the invoking object is before the object used as a parameter
in collation order. (This function is mostly for internal use only. Its return value has

nothing to do with inheritance or class hierarchies.) The **name( )** function returns
a pointer to the name of the type.

Here is a simple example that uses **typeid**.

```
// A simple example that uses typeid.
#include <iostream>
#include <typeinfo>
using namespace std;

class myclass1 {
  // ...
};

class myclass2 {
  // ...
};

int main()
{
  int i, j;
  float f;
  char *p;
  myclass1 ob1;
  myclass2 ob2;

  cout << "The type of i is: " << typeid(i).name();
  cout << endl;
  cout << "The type of f is: " << typeid(f).name();
  cout << endl;
  cout << "The type of p is: " << typeid(p).name();
  cout << endl;

  cout << "The type of ob1 is: " << typeid(ob1).name();
  cout << endl;
  cout << "The type of ob2 is: " << typeid(ob2).name();
  cout << "\n\n";

  if(typeid(i) == typeid(j))
    cout << "The types of i and j are the same\n";

  if(typeid(i) != typeid(f))
    cout << "The types of i and f are not the same\n";
```

C++

```
  if(typeid(ob1) != typeid(ob2))
    cout << "ob1 and ob2 are of differing types\n";

  return 0;
}
```

The output produced by this program is shown here:

```
The type of i is: int
The type of f is: float
The type of p is: char *
The type of ob1 is: class myclass1
The type of ob2 is: class myclass2

The types of i and j are the same
The types of i and f are not the same
ob1 and ob2 are of differing types
```

The most important use of **typeid** occurs when it is applied through a pointer of a polymorphic base class. In this case, it will automatically return the type of the actual object being pointed to, which may be a base-class object or an object derived from that base. (Remember, a base-class pointer can point to objects of the base class or of any class derived from that base.) Thus, using **typeid**, you can determine at run time the type of the object that is being pointed to by a base-class pointer. The following program demonstrates this principle.

```
// An example that uses typeid on a polymorphic class hierarchy.
#include <iostream>
#include <typeinfo>
using namespace std;

class Mammal {
public:
  virtual bool lays_eggs() { return false; } // Mammal is polymorphic
  // ...
};

class Cat: public Mammal {
public:
  // ...
```

```
};

class Platypus: public Mammal {
public:
  bool lays_eggs() { return true; }
  // ...
};

int main()
{
  Mammal *p, AnyMammal;
  Cat cat;
  Platypus platypus;

  p = &AnyMammal;
  cout << "p is pointing to an object of type ";
  cout << typeid(*p).name() << endl;

  p = &cat;
  cout << "p is pointing to an object of type ";
  cout << typeid(*p).name() << endl;

  p = &platypus;
  cout << "p is pointing to an object of type ";
  cout << typeid(*p).name() << endl;

  return 0;
}
```

The output produced by this program is shown here:

```
p is pointing to an object of type class Mammal
p is pointing to an object of type class Cat
p is pointing to an object of type class Platypus
```

As explained, when **typeid** is applied to a base-class pointer of a polymorphic type, the type of object pointed to will be determined at run time, as shown by the output produced by the program.

In all cases, when **typeid** is applied to a pointer of a nonpolymorphic class hierarchy, then the base type of the pointer is obtained. That is, no determination of what that pointer is actually pointing to is made. For example, comment out the **virtual** keyword before the function **lays_eggs( )** in **Mammal** and then compile and run the program. You will see the following output.

```
p is pointing to an object of type class Mammal
p is pointing to an object of type class Mammal
p is pointing to an object of type class Mammal
```

Since **Mammal** is no longer a polymorphic class, the type of each object will be **Mammal** because that is the type of the pointer.

Since **typeid** is commonly applied to a dereferenced pointer (i.e., one to which the * operator has been applied), a special exception has been created to handle the situation in which the pointer being dereferenced is null. In this case, **typeid** throws **bad_typeid**.

References to an object of a polymorphic class hierarchy work the same as pointers. When **typeid** is applied to a reference to an object of a polymorphic class, it will return the type of the object actually being referred to, which may be of a derived type. The circumstance where you will most often make use of this feature is when objects are passed to functions by reference. For example, in the following program, the function **WhatMammal( )** declares a reference parameter to objects of type **Mammal**. This means that **WhatMammal( )** can be passed references to objects of type **Mammal** or any class derived from **Mammal**. When the **typeid** operator is applied to this parameter, it returns the actual type of the object being passed.

```cpp
// Use a reference with typeid.
#include <iostream>
#include <typeinfo>
using namespace std;

class Mammal {
public:
  virtual bool lays_eggs() { return false; } // Mammal is polymorphic
  // ...
};

class Cat: public Mammal {
public:
  // ...
};

class Platypus: public Mammal {
public:
```

```
  bool lays_eggs() { return true; }
  // ...
};

 // Demonstrate typeid with a reference parameter.
void WhatMammal(Mammal &ob)
{
  cout << "ob is referencing an object of type ";
  cout << typeid(ob).name() << endl;
}

int main()
{
  Mammal AnyMammal;
  Cat cat;
  Platypus platypus;

  WhatMammal(AnyMammal);
  WhatMammal(cat);
  WhatMammal(platypus);

  return 0;
}
```

The output produced by this program is shown here:

```
ob is referencing an object of type class Mammal
ob is referencing an object of type class Cat
ob is referencing an object of type class Platypus
```

There is a second form of **typeid** that takes a type name as its argument. This form is shown here:

typeid(*type-name*)

For example, the following statement is perfectly acceptable:

```
cout << typeid(int).name();
```

The main use of this form of **typeid** is to obtain a **type_info** object that describes the specified type so that it can be used in a type comparison statement. For example, this form of **WhatMammal( )** reports that cats don't like water:

```
void WhatMammal(Mammal &ob)
{
  cout << "ob is referencing an object of type ";
  cout << typeid(ob).name() << endl;
  if(typeid(ob) == typeid(Cat))
    cout << "Cats don't like water.\n";
}
```

A Simple Application of Run-Time Type ID

The following program hints at the power of RTTI. In the program, the function called **factory( )** creates instances of various types of objects derived from the class **Mammal**. (A function that produces objects is sometimes called an *object factory*.) The specific type of object created is determined by the outcome of a call to **rand( )**, C++'s random number generator. Thus, there is no way to know in advance what type of object will be generated. The program creates 10 objects and counts the number of each type of mammal. Since any type of mammal may be generated by a call to **factory( )**, the program relies upon **typeid** to determine which type of object has actually been made.

```
// Demonstrating run-time type id.
#include <iostream>
using namespace std;

class Mammal {
public:
  virtual bool lays_eggs() { return false; } // Mammal is polymorphic
  // ...
};

class Cat: public Mammal {
public:
  // ...
};

class Platypus: public Mammal {
public:
  bool lays_eggs() { return true; }
  // ...
```

```
};

class Dog: public Mammal {
public:
 // ...
};

// A factory for objects derived from Mammal.
Mammal *factory()
{
  switch(rand() % 3 ) {
    case 0: return new Dog;
    case 1: return new Cat;
    case 2: return new Platypus;
  }
  return 0;
}

int main()
{
  Mammal *ptr; // pointer to base class
  int i;
  int c=0, d=0, p=0;

  // generate and count objects
  for(i=0; i<10; i++) {
    ptr = factory(); // generate an object

    cout << "Object is " << typeid(*ptr).name();
    cout << endl;

    // count it
    if(typeid(*ptr) == typeid(Dog)) d++;
    if(typeid(*ptr) == typeid(Cat)) c++;
    if(typeid(*ptr) == typeid(Platypus)) p++;
  }

  cout << endl;
  cout << "Animals generated:\n";
  cout << "  Dogs: " << d << endl;
  cout << "  Cats: " << c << endl;
```

```
    cout << "  Platypuses: " << p << endl;

    return 0;
}
```

Sample output is shown here.

```
Object is class Platypus
Object is class Platypus
Object is class Cat
Object is class Cat
Object is class Platypus
Object is class Cat
Object is class Dog
Object is class Dog
Object is class Cat
Object is class Platypus

Animals generated:
  Dogs: 2
  Cats: 4
  Platypuses: 4
```

typeid Can Be Applied to Template Classes

The **typeid** operator can be applied to template classes. The type of an object that is an instance of a template class is in part determined by what data is used for its generic data when the object is instantiated. Two instances of the same template class that are created using different data are therefore different types. Here is a simple example:

```
// Using typeid with templates.
#include <iostream>
using namespace std;

template <class T> class myclass {
  T a;
public:
  myclass(T i) { a = i; }
  // ...
};
```

```
int main()
{
  myclass<int> o1(10), o2(9);
  myclass<double> o3(7.2);

  cout << "Type of o1 is ";
  cout << typeid(o1).name() << endl;

  cout << "Type of o2 is ";
  cout << typeid(o2).name() << endl;

  cout << "Type of o3 is ";
  cout << typeid(o3).name() << endl;

  cout << endl;

  if(typeid(o1) == typeid(o2))
    cout << "o1 and o2 are the same type\n";

  if(typeid(o1) == typeid(o3))
    cout << "Error\n";
  else
    cout << "o1 and o3 are different types\n";

  return 0;
}
```

The output produced by this program is shown here.

```
Type of o1 is class myclass<int>
Type of o2 is class myclass<int>
Type of o3 is class myclass<double>

o1 and o2 are the same type
o1 and o3 are different types
```

As you can see, even though two objects are of the same template class type, if their parameterized data does not match, they are not equivalent types. In the program, **o1** is of type **myclass<int>** and **o3** is of type **myclass<double>**. Thus, they are of different types.

Run-time type identification is not something that every program will use. However, when you are working with polymorphic types, it allows you to know what type of object is being operated upon in any given situation.

The Casting Operators

C++ defines five casting operators. The first is the traditional-style cast inherited from C. The remaining four were added a few years ago. They are **dynamic_cast**, **const_cast**, **reinterpret_cast**, and **static_cast**. These operators give you additional control over how casting takes place.

dynamic_cast

Perhaps the most important of the new casting operators is **dynamic_cast**. The **dynamic_cast** performs a run-time cast that verifies the validity of a cast. If the cast is invalid at the time **dynamic_cast** is executed, then the cast fails. The general form of **dynamic_cast** is shown here:

> dynamic_cast<*target-type*> (*expr*)

Here, *target-type* specifies the target type of the cast, and *expr* is the expression being cast into the new type. The target type must be a pointer or reference type, and the expression being cast must evaluate to a pointer or reference. Thus, **dynamic_cast** may be used to cast one type of pointer into another or one type of reference into another.

The purpose of **dynamic_cast** is to perform casts on polymorphic types. For example, given two polymorphic classes B and D, with D derived from B, a **dynamic_cast** can always cast a D* pointer into a B* pointer. This is because a base pointer can always point to a derived object. But a **dynamic_cast** can cast a B* pointer into a D* pointer only if the object being pointed to *actually is* a D object. In general, **dynamic_cast** will succeed if the pointer (or reference) being cast is a pointer (or reference) to either an object of the target type or an object derived from the target type. Otherwise, the cast will fail.If the cast fails, then **dynamic_cast** evaluates to null if the cast involves pointers. If a **dynamic_cast** on reference types fails, a **bad_cast** exception is thrown.

Here is a simple example. Assume that **Base** is a polymorphic class and that **Derived** is derived from **Base**.

```
Base *bp, b_ob;
Derived *dp, d_ob;

bp = &d_ob; // base pointer points to Derived object
```

```
dp = dynamic_cast<Derived *> (bp); // cast to derived pointer OK
if(dp) cout << "Cast OK";
```

Here, the cast from the base pointer **bp** to the derived pointer **dp** works because **bp** is actually pointing to a **Derived** object. Thus, this fragment displays **Cast OK**. But in the next fragment, the cast fails because **bp** is pointing to a **Base** object and it is illegal to cast a base object into a derived object.

```
bp = &b_ob; // base pointer points to Base object
dp = dynamic_cast<Derived *> (bp); // error
if(!dp) cout << "Cast Fails";
```

Because the cast fails, this fragment displays **Cast Fails**.

The following program demonstrates the various situations that **dynamic_cast** can handle.

```
// Demonstrate dynamic_cast.
#include <iostream>
using namespace std;

class Base {
public:
  virtual void f() { cout << "Inside Base\n"; }
  // ...
};

class Derived : public Base {
public:
  void f() { cout << "Inside Derived\n"; }
};

int main()
{
  Base *bp, b_ob;
  Derived *dp, d_ob;

  dp = dynamic_cast<Derived *> (&d_ob);
  if(dp) {
    cout << "Cast from Derived * to Derived * OK.\n";
    dp->f();
  } else
```

```
      cout << "Error\n";

  cout << endl;

  bp = dynamic_cast<Base *> (&d_ob);
  if(bp) {
    cout << "Cast from Derived * to Base * OK.\n";
    bp->f();
  } else
    cout << "Error\n";

  cout << endl;

  bp = dynamic_cast<Base *> (&b_ob);
  if(bp) {
    cout << "Cast from Base * to Base * OK.\n";
    bp->f();
  } else
    cout << "Error\n";

  cout << endl;

  dp = dynamic_cast<Derived *> (&b_ob);
  if(dp)
    cout << "Error\n";
  else
    cout << "Cast from Base * to Derived * not OK.\n";

  cout << endl;

  bp = &d_ob; // bp points to Derived object
  dp = dynamic_cast<Derived *> (bp);
  if(dp) {
    cout << "Casting bp to a Derived * OK\n" <<
      "because bp is really pointing\n" <<
      "to a Derived object.\n";
    dp->f();
  } else
    cout << "Error\n";

  cout << endl;
```

```
bp = &b_ob; // bp points to Base object
dp = dynamic_cast<Derived *> (bp);
if(dp)
  cout << "Error";
else {
  cout << "Now casting bp to a Derived *\n" <<
    "is not OK because bp is really \n" <<
    "pointing to a Base object.\n";
}

cout << endl;

dp = &d_ob; // dp points to Derived object
bp = dynamic_cast<Base *> (dp);
if(bp) {
  cout << "Casting dp to a Base * is OK.\n";
  bp->f();
} else
  cout << "Error\n";

return 0;
}
```

The program produces the following output:

```
Cast from Derived * to Derived * OK.
Inside Derived

Cast from Derived * to Base * OK.
Inside Derived

Cast from Base * to Base * OK.
Inside Base

Cast from Base * to Derived * not OK.

Casting bp to a Derived * OK
because bp is really pointing
to a Derived object.
Inside Derived
```

```
Now casting bp to a Derived *
is not OK because bp is really
pointing to a Base object.

Casting dp to a Base * is OK.
Inside Derived
```

Replacing typeid with dynamic_cast

The **dynamic_cast** operator can sometimes be used instead of **typeid** in certain cases. For example, again assume that **Base** is a polymorphic base class for **Derived**. The following fragment will assign **dp** the address of the object pointed to by **bp** if and only if the object really is a **Derived** object.

```
Base *bp;
Derived *dp;
// ...
if(typeid(*bp) == typeid(Derived)) dp = (Derived *) bp;
```

In this case, a traditional-style cast is used to actually perform the cast. This is safe because the **if** statement checks the legality of the cast using **typeid** before the cast actually occurs. However, a better way to accomplish this is to replace the **typeid** operators and **if** statement with this **dynamic_cast**.

```
dp = dynamic_cast<Derived *> (bp);
```

Since **dynamic_cast** succeeds only if the object being cast is either an object of the target type or an object derived from the target type, after this statement executes **dp** will contain either a null or a pointer to an object of type **Derived**. Since **dynamic_cast** succeeds only if the cast is legal, it can simplify the logic in certain situations. The following program illustrates how a **dynamic_cast** can be used to replace **typeid**. It performs the same set of operations twice—first with **typeid**, then using **dynamic_cast**.

```
// Use dynamic_cast to replace typeid.
#include <iostream>
#include <typeinfo>
using namespace std;

class Base {
public:
```

```
    virtual void f() {}
};

class Derived : public Base {
public:
  void derivedOnly() {
    cout << "Is a Derived Object.\n";
  }
};

int main()
{
  Base *bp, b_ob;
  Derived *dp, d_ob;

  // ***********************************
  // use typeid
  // ***********************************
  bp = &b_ob;
  if(typeid(*bp) == typeid(Derived)) {
    dp = (Derived *) bp;
    dp->derivedOnly();
  }
  else
    cout << "Cast from Base to Derived failed.\n";

  bp = &d_ob;
  if(typeid(*bp) == typeid(Derived)) {
    dp = (Derived *) bp;
    dp->derivedOnly();
  }
  else
    cout << "Error, cast should work!\n";

  // ***********************************
  // use dynamic_cast
  // ***********************************
  bp = &b_ob;
  dp = dynamic_cast<Derived *> (bp);
  if(dp) dp->derivedOnly();
  else
    cout << "Cast from Base to Derived failed.\n";
```

```
    bp = &d_ob;
    dp = dynamic_cast<Derived *> (bp);
    if(dp) dp->derivedOnly();
    else
      cout << "Error, cast should work!\n";

    return 0;
}
```

As you can see, the use of **dynamic_cast** simplifies the logic required to cast a base pointer into a derived pointer. The output from the program is shown here:

```
Cast from Base to Derived failed.
Is a Derived Object.
Cast from Base to Derived failed.
Is a Derived Object.
```

Using dynamic_cast with Template Classes

The **dynamic_cast** operator can also be used with template classes. For example,

```
// Demonstrate dynamic_cast on template classes.
#include <iostream>
using namespace std;

template <class T> class Num {
protected:
  T val;
public:
  Num(T x) { val = x; }
  virtual T getval() { return val; }
  // ...
};

template <class T> class SqrNum : public Num<T> {
public:
  SqrNum(T x) : Num<T>(x) { }
  T getval() { return val * val; }
};
```

```
int main()
{
  Num<int> *bp, numInt_ob(2);
  SqrNum<int> *dp, sqrInt_ob(3);
  Num<double> numDouble_ob(3.3);

  bp = dynamic_cast<Num<int> *> (&sqrInt_ob);
  if(bp) {
    cout << "Cast from SqrNum<int>* to Num<int>* OK.\n";
    cout << "Value is " << bp->getval() << endl;
  } else
    cout << "Error\n";

  cout << endl;

  dp = dynamic_cast<SqrNum<int> *> (&numInt_ob);
  if(dp)
    cout << "Error\n";
  else {
    cout << "Cast from Num<int>* to SqrNum<int>* not OK.\n";
    cout << "Can't cast a pointer to a base object into\n";
    cout << "a pointer to a derived object.\n";
  }
  cout << endl;

  bp = dynamic_cast<Num<int> *> (&numDouble_ob);
  if(bp)
    cout << "Error\n";
  else
    cout << "Can't cast from Num<double>* to Num<int>*.\n";
    cout << "These are two different types.\n";

  return 0;
}
```

The output from this program is shown here:

```
Cast from SqrNum<int>* to Num<int>* OK.
Value is 9

Cast from Num<int>* to SqrNum<int>* not OK.
```

```
Can't cast a pointer to a base object into
a pointer to a derived object.

Can't cast from Num<double>* to Num<int>*.
These are two different types.
```

A key point illustrated by this example is that it is not possible to use **dynamic_cast** to cast a pointer to one type of template instantiation into a pointer to another type of instance. Remember, the precise type of an object of a template class is determined by the type of data used to create an instance of the template. Thus, **Num<double>** and **Num<int>** are two different types.

const_cast

The **const_cast** operator is used to explicitly override **const** and/or **volatile** in a cast. The target type must be the same as the source type except for the alteration of its **const** or **volatile** attributes. The most common use of **const_cast** is to remove **const**-ness. The general form of **const_cast** is shown here.

const_cast<*type*> (*expr*)

Here, *type* specifies the target type of the cast, and *expr* is the expression being cast into the new type.

The following program demonstrates **const_cast**.

```
// Demonstrate const_cast.
#include <iostream>
using namespace std;

void sqrval(const int *val)
{
  int *p;

  // cast away const-ness.
  p = const_cast<int *> (val);

  *p = *val * *val; // now, modify object through v
}

int main()
```

```
{
  int x = 10;

  cout << "x before call: " << x << endl;
  sqrval(&x);
  cout << "x after call: " << x << endl;

  return 0;
}
```

The output produced by this program is shown here:

```
x before call: 10
x after call: 100
```

As you can see, **x** was modified by **sqrval( )** even though the parameter to **sqrval( )** was specified as a **const** pointer.

const_cast can also be used to cast away **const**-ness from a **const** reference. For example, here is the preceding program reworked so that the value being squared is passed as a **const** reference.

```
// Use const_cast on a const reference.
#include <iostream>
using namespace std;

void sqrval(const int &val)
{
  // cast away const on val
  const_cast<int &> (val) = val * val;
}

int main()
{
  int x = 10;

  cout << "x before call: " << x << endl;
  sqrval(x);
  cout << "x after call: " << x << endl;

  return 0;
}
```

This program produces the same output as before. Again, it works only because the **const_cast** temporarily removes the **const** attribute from **val**, allowing it to be used to assign a new value to the calling argument (in this case, **x**).

It must be stressed that the use of **const_cast** to cast way **const**-ness is a potentially dangerous feature. Use it with care.

One other point: Only **const_cast** can cast away **const**-ness. That is, neither **dynamic_cast, static_cast** nor **reinterpret_cast** can alter the **const**-ness of an object.

static_cast

The **static_cast** operator performs a nonpolymorphic cast. It can be used for any standard conversion. No run-time checks are performed. Its general form is

static_cast<*type*> (*expr*)

Here, *type* specifies the target type of the cast, and *expr* is the expression being cast into the new type.

The **static_cast** operator is essentially a substitute for the original cast operator. It simply performs a nonpolymorphic cast. For example, the following casts an **int** value into a **double**.

```
// Use static_cast.
#include <iostream>
using namespace std;

int main()
{
  int i;

  for(i=0; i<10; i++)
    cout << static_cast<double> (i) / 3 << " ";

  return 0;
}
```

reinterpret_cast

The **reinterpret_cast** operator converts one type into a fundamentally different type. For example, it can change a pointer into an integer and an integer into a pointer. It can also be used for casting inherently incompatible pointer types. Its general form is

reinterpret_cast<*type*> (*expr*)

Here, *type* specifies the target type of the cast, and *expr* is the expression being cast into the new type.

The following program demonstrates the use of **reinterpret_cast**:

```
// An example that uses reinterpret_cast.
#include <iostream>
using namespace std;

int main()
{
  int i;
  char *p = "This is a string";

  i = reinterpret_cast<int> (p); // cast pointer to integer

  cout << i;

  return 0;
}
```

Here, **reinterpret_cast** converts the pointer **p** into an integer. This conversion represents a fundamental type change and is a good use of **reinterpret_cast**.

C++

Chapter 23

Namespaces, Conversion Functions, and Other Advanced Topics

This chapter describes namespaces and several other advanced features, including conversion functions, explicit constructors, **const** and **volatile** member functions, the **asm** keyword, and linkage specifications. It ends with a discussion of C++'s array-based I/O and a summary of the differences between C and C++.

Namespaces

Namespaces were briefly introduced earlier in this book. They are a relatively recent addition to C++. Their purpose is to localize the names of identifiers to avoid name collisions. The C++ programming environment has seen an explosion of variable, function, and class names. Prior to the invention of namespaces, all of these names competed for slots in the global namespace and many conflicts arose. For example, if your program defined a function called **abs( )**, it could (depending upon its parameter list) override the standard library function **abs( )** because both names would be stored in the global namespace. Name collisions were compounded when two or more third-party libraries were used by the same program. In this case, it was possible—even likely—that a name defined by one library would conflict with the same name defined by the other library. The situation can be particularly troublesome for class names. For example, if your program defines a class call **ThreeDCircle** and a library used by your program defines a class by the same name, a conflict will arise.

The creation of the **namespace** keyword was a response to these problems. Because it localizes the visibility of names declared within it, a namespace allows the same name to be used in different contexts without conflicts arising. Perhaps the most noticeable beneficiary of **namespace** is the C++ standard library. Prior to **namespace**, the entire C++ library was defined within the global namespace (which was, of course, the only namespace). Since the addition of **namespace**, the C++ library is now defined within its own namespace, called **std**, which reduces the chance of name collisions. You can also create your own namespaces within your program to localize the visibility of any names that you think may cause conflicts. This is especially important if you are creating class or function libraries.

Namespace Fundamentals

The **namespace** keyword allows you to partition the global namespace by creating a declarative region. In essence, a **namespace** defines a scope. The general form of **namespace** is shown here:

```
namespace name {
  // declarations
}
```

Anything defined within a **namespace** statement is within the scope of that namespace.

Here is an example of a **namespace**. It localizes the names used to implement a simple countdown counter class. In the namespace are defined the **counter** class, which implements the counter, and the variables **upperbound** and **lowerbound**, which contain the upper and lower bounds that apply to all counters.

```
namespace CounterNameSpace {
  int upperbound;
  int lowerbound;

  class counter {
     int count;
   public:
     counter(int n) {
       if(n <= upperbound) count = n;
       else count = upperbound;
     }

     void reset(int n) {
       if(n <= upperbound) count = n;
     }

     int run() {
       if(count > lowerbound) return count--;
       else return lowerbound;
     }
  };
}
```

Here, **upperbound**, **lowerbound**, and the class **counter** are part of the scope defined by the **CounterNameSpace** namespace.

Inside a namespace, identifiers declared within that namespace can be referred to directly, without any namespace qualification. For example, within **CounterNameSpace**, the **run( )** function can refer directly to **lowerbound** in the statement

```
if(count > lowerbound) return count--;
```

However, since **namespace** defines a scope, you need to use the scope resolution operator to refer to objects declared within a namespace from outside that namespace.

For example, to assign the value 10 to **upperbound** from code outside
CounterNameSpace, you must use this statement:

```
CounterNameSpace::upperbound = 10;
```

Or to declare an object of type **counter** from outside **CounterNameSpace**, you will use
a statement like this:

```
CounterNameSpace::counter ob;
```

In general, to access a member of a namespace from outside its namespace, precede
the member's name with the name of the namespace followed by the scope resolution
operator.

Here is a program that demonstrates the use of **CounterNameSpace**.

```cpp
// Demonstrate a namespace.
#include <iostream>
using namespace std;

namespace CounterNameSpace {
  int upperbound;
  int lowerbound;

  class counter {
    int count;
  public:
    counter(int n) {
      if(n <= upperbound) count = n;
      else count = upperbound;
    }

    void reset(int n) {
      if(n <= upperbound) count = n;
    }

    int run() {
      if(count > lowerbound) return count--;
      else return lowerbound;
    }
```

```
    };
}

int main()
{
  CounterNameSpace::upperbound = 100;
  CounterNameSpace::lowerbound = 0;

  CounterNameSpace::counter ob1(10);
  int i;

  do {
    i = ob1.run();
    cout << i << " ";
  } while(i > CounterNameSpace::lowerbound);
  cout << endl;

  CounterNameSpace::counter ob2(20);

  do {
    i = ob2.run();
    cout << i << " ";
  } while(i > CounterNameSpace::lowerbound);
  cout << endl;

  ob2.reset(100);
  CounterNameSpace::lowerbound = 90;
  do {
    i = ob2.run();
    cout << i << " ";
  } while(i > CounterNameSpace::lowerbound);

  return 0;
}
```

Notice that the declaration of a **counter** object and the references to **upperbound** and **lowerbound** are qualified by **CounterNameSpace**. However, once an object of type **counter** has been declared, it is not necessary to further qualify it or any of its members. Thus, **ob1.run( )** can be called directly; the namespace has already been resolved.

using

As you can imagine, if your program includes frequent references to the members of a namespace, having to specify the namespace and the scope resolution operator each time you need to refer to one quickly becomes a tedious chore. The **using** statement was invented to alleviate this problem. The **using** statement has these two general forms:

using namespace *name;*
using *name::member;*

In the first form, *name* specifies the name of the namespace you want to access. All of the members defined within the specified namespace are brought into view (i.e., they become part of the current namespace) and may be used without qualification. In the second form, only a specific member of the namespace is made visible. For example, assuming **CounterNameSpace** as shown above, the following **using** statements and assignments are valid.

```
using CounterNameSpace::lowerbound; // only lowerbound is visible
lowerbound = 10; // OK because lowerbound is visible

using namespace CounterNameSpace; // all members are visible
upperbound = 100; // OK because all members are now visible
```

The following program illustrates **using** by reworking the counter example from the previous section.

```
// Demonstrate using.
#include <iostream>
using namespace std;

namespace CounterNameSpace {
  int upperbound;
  int lowerbound;

  class counter {
    int count;
  public:
    counter(int n) {
      if(n <= upperbound) count = n;
      else count = upperbound;
    }
```

```
      void reset(int n) {
        if(n <= upperbound) count = n;
      }

      int run() {
        if(count > lowerbound) return count--;
        else return lowerbound;
      }
  };
}

int main()
{
  // use only upperbound from CounterNameSpace
  using CounterNameSpace::upperbound;

  // now, no qualification needed to set upperbound
  upperbound = 100;

  // qualification still needed for lowerbound, etc.
  CounterNameSpace::lowerbound = 0;

  CounterNameSpace::counter ob1(10);
  int i;

  do {
    i = ob1.run();
    cout << i << " ";
  } while(i > CounterNameSpace::lowerbound);
  cout << endl;

  // now, use entire CounterNameSpace
  using namespace CounterNameSpace;

  counter ob2(20);

  do {
    i = ob2.run();
    cout << i << " ";
  } while(i > lowerbound);
  cout << endl;

  ob2.reset(100);
```

```
  lowerbound = 90;
  do {
    i = ob2.run();
    cout << i << " ";
  } while(i > lowerbound);

  return 0;
}
```

The program illustrates one other important point: using one namespace does not override another. When you bring a namespace into view, it simply adds its names to whatever other namespaces are currently in effect. Thus, by the end of the program, both **std** and **CounterNameSpace** have been added to the global namespace.

Unnamed Namespaces

There is a special type of namespace, called an *unnamed namespace,* that allows you to create identifiers that are unique within a file. Unnamed namespaces are also called *anonymous namespaces.* They have this general form:

namespace {
   // declarations
}

Unnamed namespaces allow you to establish unique identifiers that are known only within the scope of a single file. That is, within the file that contains the unnamed namespace, the members of that namespace may be used directly, without qualification. But outside the file, the identifiers are unknown.

Unnamed namespaces eliminate the need for certain uses of the **static** storage class modifier. As explained in Chapter 2, one way to restrict the scope of a global name to the file in which it is declared is to use **static**. For example, consider the following two files that are part of the same program.

File One

```
static int k;
void f1() {
  k = 99; // OK
}
```

File Two

```
extern int k;
void f2() {
  k = 10; // error
}
```

Because **k** is defined in File One, it may be used in File One. In File Two, **k** is specified as **extern**, which means that its name and type are known but that **k** itself is not actually defined. When these two files are linked, the attempt to use **k** within File Two results in an error because there is no definition for **k**. By preceding **k** with **static** in File One, its scope is restricted to that file and it is not available to File Two.

While the use of **static** global declarations is still allowed in C++, a better way to accomplish the same effect is to use an unnamed namespace. For example:

File One

```
namespace {
  int k;
}
void f1() {
  k = 99; // OK
}
```

File Two

```
extern int k;
void f2() {
  k = 10; // error
}
```

Here, **k** is also restricted to File One. The use of the unnamed namespace rather than **static** is recommended for new code.

Some Namespace Options

There may be more than one namespace declaration of the same name. This allows a namespace to be split over several files or even separated within the same file. For example:

```
#include <iostream>
using namespace std;

namespace NS {
  int i;
}

// ...

namespace NS {
  int j;
}

int main()
{
  NS::i = NS::j = 10;

  // refer to NS specifically
```

```
   cout << NS::i * NS::j << "\n";

   // use NS namespace
   using namespace NS;

   cout << i * j;

   return 0;
}
```

This program produces the following output:

```
100
100
```

Here, **NS** is split into two pieces. However, the contents of each piece are still within the same namespace, that is, **NS**.

A namespace must be declared outside of all other scopes. This means that you cannot declare namespaces that are localized to a function, for example. There is, however, one exception: a namespace can be nested within another. Consider this program:

```
#include <iostream>
using namespace std;

namespace NS1 {
  int i;
  namespace NS2 { // a nested namespace
    int j;
  }
}

int main()
{
  NS1::i = 19;
  // NS2::j = 10; Error, NS2 is not in view
  NS1::NS2::j = 10; // this is right

  cout << NS1::i << " "<<  NS1::NS2::j << "\n";

  // use NS1
```

```
  using namespace NS1;

  /* Now that NS1 is in view, NS2 can be used to
     refer to j. */
  cout << i * NS2::j;

  return 0;
}
```

This program produces the following output:

```
19 10
190
```

Here, the namespace **NS2** is nested within **NS1**. Thus, when the program begins, to refer to **j**, you must qualify it with both the **NS1** and **NS2** namespaces. **NS2** by itself is insufficient. After the statement

```
using namespace NS1;
```

executes, you can refer directly to **NS2** since the **using** statement brings **NS1** into view.

Typically, you will not need to create namespaces for most small to medium-sized programs. However, if you will be creating libraries of reusable code or it you want to ensure the widest portability, then consider wrapping your code within a namespace.

The std Namespace

Standard C++ defines its entire library in its own namespace called **std**. This is the reason that most of the programs in this book include the following statement:

```
using namespace std;
```

This causes the **std** namespace to be brought into the current namespace, which gives you direct access to the names of the functions and classes defined within the library without having to qualify each one with **std::**.

Of course, you can explicitly qualify each name with **std::** if you like. For example, the following program does not bring the library into the global namespace.

```
// Use explicit std:: qualification.
```

```
#include <iostream>

int main()
{
  int val;

  std::cout << "Enter a number: ";

  std::cin >> val;

  std::cout << "This is your number: ";
  std::cout << std::hex << val;

  return 0;
}
```

Here, **cout**, **cin**, and the manipulator **hex** are explicitly qualified by their namespace. That is, to write to standard output, you must specify **std::cout**; to read from standard input, you must use **std::cin**; and the hex manipulator must be referred to as **std::hex**.

You may not want to bring the standard C++ library into the global namespace if your program will be making only limited use of it. However, if your program contains hundreds of references to library names, then including **std** in the current namespace is far easier than qualifying each name individually.

If you are using only a few names from the standard library, it may make more sense to specify a **using** statement for each individually. The advantage to this approach is that you can still use those names without an **std::** qualification, but you will not be bringing the entire standard library into the global namespace. For example:

```
// Bring only a few names into the global namespace.
#include <iostream>

// gain access to cout, cin, and hex
using std::cout;
using std::cin;
using std::hex;

int main()
{
  int val;
```

```
    cout << "Enter a number: ";

    cin >> val;
    cout << "This is your number: ";
    cout << hex << val;
    return 0;
}
```

Here, **cin**, **cout**, and **hex** may be used directly, but the rest of the **std** namespace has not been brought into view.

As explained, the original C++ library was defined in the global namespace. If you will be converting older C++ programs, then you will need to either include a **using namespace std** statement or qualify each reference to a library member with **std::**. This is especially important if you are replacing old .**H** header files with the new-style headers. Remember, the old .**H** headers put their contents into the global namespace; the new-style headers put their contents into the **std** namespace.

Creating Conversion Functions

In some situations, you will want to use an object of a class in an expression involving other types of data. Sometimes, overloaded operator functions can provide the means of doing this. However, in other cases, what you want is a simple type conversion from the class type to the target type. To handle these cases, C++ allows you to create custom *conversion functions*. A conversion function converts your class into a type compatible with that of the rest of the expression. The general format of a type conversion function is

  operator *type*( ) { return *value*; }

Here, *type* is the target type that you are converting your class to, and *value* is the value of the class after conversion. Conversion functions return data of type *type*, and no other return type specifier is allowed. Also, no parameters may be included. A conversion function must be a member of the class for which it is defined. Conversion functions are inherited and they may be virtual.

The following illustration of a conversion function uses the **stack** class first developed in Chapter 11. Suppose that you want to be able to use objects of type **stack** within an integer expression. Further, suppose that the value of a **stack** object used in an integer expression is the number of values currently on the stack. (You might want to do something like this if, for example, you are using **stack** objects in a simulation and are monitoring how quickly the stacks fill up.) One way to approach this is to convert an object of type **stack** into an integer that represents the number of items on the stack. To accomplish this, you use a conversion function that looks like this:

```
operator int() { return tos; }
```

Here is a program that illustrates how the conversion function works:

```cpp
#include <iostream>
using namespace std;

const int SIZE=100;

// this creates the class stack
class stack {
  int stck[SIZE];
  int tos;
public:
  stack() { tos=0; }
  void push(int i);
  int pop(void);
  operator int() { return tos; } // conversion of stack to int
};

void stack::push(int i)
{
  if(tos==SIZE) {
    cout << "Stack is full.\n";
    return;
  }
  stck[tos] = i;
  tos++;
}

int stack::pop()
{
  if(tos==0) {
    cout << "Stack underflow.\n";
    return 0;
  }
```

```
    tos--;
    return stck[tos];
}

int main()
{
  stack stck;
  int i, j;

  for(i=0; i<20; i++)  stck.push(i);

  j = stck; // convert to integer

  cout << j << " items on stack.\n";

  cout << SIZE - stck << " spaces open.\n";
  return 0;
}
```

This program displays this output:

```
20 items on stack.
80 spaces open.
```

As the program illustrates, when a **stack** object is used in an integer expression, such as **j = stck**, the conversion function is applied to the object. In this specific case, the conversion function returns the value 20. Also, when **stck** is subtracted from **SIZE**, the conversion function is also called.

Here is another example of a conversion function. This program creates a class called **pwr( )** that stores and computes the outcome of some number raised to some power. It stores the result as a **double**. By supplying a conversion function to type **double** and returning the result, you can use objects of type **pwr** in expressions involving other **double** values.

```
#include <iostream>
using namespace std;

class pwr {
  double b;
  int e;
  double val;
```

```cpp
public:
  pwr(double base, int exp);
  pwr operator+(pwr o) {
    double base;
    int exp;
    base = b + o.b;
    exp = e + o.e;

    pwr temp(base, exp);
    return temp;
  }
  operator double() { return val; } // convert to double
};

pwr::pwr(double base, int exp)
{
  b = base;
  e = exp;
  val = 1;
  if(exp==0) return;
  for( ; exp>0; exp--) val = val * b;
}

int main()
{
  pwr x(4.0, 2);
  double a;

  a = x; // convert to double
  cout << x + 100.2; // convert x to double and add 100.2
  cout << "\n";

  pwr y(3.3, 3), z(0, 0);

  z = x + y;   // no conversion
  a = z;   // convert to double
  cout << a;

  return 0;
}
```

The output from the program is shown here.

```
116.2
20730.7
```

As you can see, when **x** is used in the expression **x + 100.2**, the conversion function is used to produce the **double** value. Notice also that in the expression **x + y**, no conversion is applied because the expression involves only objects of type **pwr**.

As you can infer from the foregoing examples, there are many situations in which it is beneficial to create a conversion function for a class. Often, conversion functions provide a more natural syntax to be used when class objects are mixed with the built-in types. Specifically, in the case of the **pwr** class, the availability of the conversion to **double** makes using objects of that class in "normal" mathematical expressions both easier to program and easier to understand.

You can create different conversion functions to meet different needs. You could define another that converts to **long**, for example. Each will be applied automatically as determined by the type of each expression.

const Member Functions and mutable

Class member functions may be declared as **const**, which causes **this** to be treated as a **const** pointer. Thus, that function cannot modify the object that invokes it. Also, a **const** object may not invoke a non-**const** member function. However, a **const** member function can be called by either **const** or non-**const** objects.

To specify a member function as **const**, use the form shown in the following example.

```
class X {
  int some_var;
public:
  int f1() const; // const member function
};
```

As you can see, the **const** follows the function's parameter declaration.

The purpose of declaring a member function as **const** is to prevent it from modifying the object that invokes it. For example, consider the following program.

```
/*
    Demonstrate const member functions.
```

```
     This program won't compile.
*/
#include <iostream>
using namespace std;

class Demo {
  int i;
public:
  int geti() const {
    return i; // ok
  }

  void seti(int x) const {
    i = x; // error!
  }
};

int main()
{
  Demo ob;

  ob.seti(1900);
  cout << ob.geti();

  return 0;
}
```

This program will not compile because **seti( )** is declared as **const**. This means that it is not allowed to modify the invoking object. Since it attempts to change **i**, the program is in error. In contrast, since **geti( )** does not attempt to modify **i**, it is perfectly acceptable.

Sometimes there will be one or more members of a class that you want a **const** function to be able to modify even though you don't want the function to be able to modify any of its other members. You can accomplish this through the use of **mutable**. It overrides **const**ness. That is, a **mutable** member can be modified by a **const** member function. For example:

```
// Demonstrate mutable.
#include <iostream>
using namespace std;

class Demo {
```

```
    mutable int i;
    int j;
public:
    int geti() const {
      return i; // ok
    }

    void seti(int x) const {
      i = x; // now, OK.
    }

/* The following function won't compile.
    void setj(int x) const {
      j = x; // Still Wrong!
    }
*/
};

int main()
{
  Demo ob;

  ob.seti(1900);
  cout << ob.geti();

  return 0;
}
```

Here, **i** is specified as **mutable**, so it may be changed by the **seti( )** function. However, **j** is not **mutable** and **setj( )** is unable to modify its value.

Volatile Member Functions

Class member functions may be declared as **volatile**, which causes **this** to be treated as a **volatile** pointer. To specify a member function as **volatile**, use the form shown in the following example:

```
class X {
public:
  void f2(int a) volatile; // volatile member function
};
```

Explicit Constructors

As explained in Chapter 12, any time you have a constructor that requires only one argument, you can use either *ob(x)* or *ob = x* to initialize an object. The reason for this is that whenever you create a constructor that takes one argument, you are also implicitly creating a conversion from the type of that argument to the type of the class. But there may be times when you do not want this automatic conversion to take place. For this purpose, C++ defines the keyword **explicit**. To understand its effects, consider the following program.

```
#include <iostream>
using namespace std;

class myclass {
  int a;
public:
  myclass(int x) { a = x; }
  int geta() { return a; }
};

int main()
{
  myclass ob = 4; // automatically converted into myclass(4)

  cout << ob.geta();

  return 0;
}
```

Here, the constructor for **myclass** takes one parameter. Pay special attention to how **ob** is declared in **main( )**. The statement

```
myclass ob = 4; // automatically converted into myclass(4)
```

is automatically converted into a call to the **myclass** constructor with 4 being the argument. That is, the preceding statement is handled by the compiler as if it were written like this:

```
myclass ob(4);
```

If you do not want this implicit conversion to be made, you can prevent it by using **explicit**. The **explicit** specifier applies only to constructors. A constructor specified as **explicit** will only be used when an initialization uses the normal constructor syntax. It will not perform any automatic conversion. For example, by declaring the **myclass** constructor as **explicit**, the automatic conversion will not be supplied. Here is **myclass( )** declared as **explicit**.

```
#include <iostream>
using namespace std;

class myclass {
  int a;
public:
  explicit myclass(int x) { a = x; }
  int geta() { return a; }
};
```

Now, only constructors of the form

```
myclass ob(4);
```

will be allowed and a statement like

```
myclass ob = 4; // now in error
```

will be invalid.

The Member Initialization Syntax

Example code throughout the preceding chapters has initialized member variables inside the constructor for their class. For example, the following program contains the **MyClass** class, which has two integer data members called **numA** and **numB**. These member variables are initialized inside **MyClass'** constructor.

```
#include <iostream>
using namespace std;
```

```
class MyClass {
  int numA;
  int numB;
public:
  /* Initialize numA and numB inside the MyClass constructor
     using normal syntax. */
  MyClass(int x, int y) {
    numA = x;
    numB = y;
  }

  int getNumA() { return numA; }
  int getNumB() { return numB; }
};

int main()
{
  MyClass ob1(7, 9), ob2(5, 2);

  cout << "Values in ob1 are " << ob1.getNumB() <<
          " and " << ob1.getNumA() << endl;

  cout << "Values in ob2 are " << ob2.getNumB() <<
          " and " << ob2.getNumA() << endl;

  return 0;
}
```

Assigning initial values to member variables **numA** and **numB** inside the constructor, as **MyClass( )** does, is the usual approach, and is the way that member initialization is accomplished for many, many classes. However, this approach won't work in all cases. For example, if **numA** and **numB** were specified as **const**, like this

```
class MyClass {
  const int numA; // const member
  const int numB; // const member
```

then they could not be given values by the **MyClass** constructor because **const** variables must be initialized and cannot be assigned values after the fact. Similar problems arise when using reference members, which must be initialized, and when using class members that don't have default constructors. To solve these types of problems, C++ supports an alternative member initialization syntax, which is used to give a class member an initial value when an object of the class is created.

The member initialization syntax is similar to that used to call a base class constructor. Here is the general form:

constructor(arg-list) : *member1(initializer)*,
                   member2(initializer),
                   // ...
                   memberN(initializer)
{
  // body of constructor
}

The members that you want to initialize are specified before the body of the constructor, separated from the constructor's name and argument list by a colon. You can mix calls to base class constructors with member initializations in the same list.

Here is **MyClass** rewritten so that **numA** and **numB** are **const** members that are given values using the member initialization syntax.

```cpp
#include <iostream>
using namespace std;

class MyClass {
  const int numA; // const member
  const int numB; // const member
public:
  // Initialize numA and numB using initialization syntax.
  MyClass(int x, int y) : numA(x), numB(y) { }

  int getNumA() { return numA; }
  int getNumB() { return numB; }
};

int main()
{
  MyClass ob1(7, 9), ob2(5, 2);

  cout << "Values in ob1 are " << ob1.getNumB() <<
          " and " << ob1.getNumA() << endl;

  cout << "Values in ob2 are " << ob2.getNumB() <<
          " and " << ob2.getNumA() << endl;

  return 0;
}
```

Notice how **numA** and **numB** are initialized by this statement:

```
MyClass(int x, int y) : numA(x), numB(y) { }
```

Here, **numA** is initialized with the value passed in **x**, and **numB** is initialized with the value passed in **y**. Even though **numA** and **numB** are now **const**, they can be given initial values when a **MyClass** object is created because the member initialization syntax is used.

The member initialization syntax is especially useful when you have a member that is of a class type for which there is no default constructor. To understand why, consider this slightly different version of **MyClass** that attempts to store the two integer values in an object of type **IntPair**. Because **IntPair** has no default constructor, this program is in error and won't compile.

```cpp
// This program is in error and won't compile.
#include <iostream>
using namespace std;

class IntPair {
public:
  int a;
  int b;

  IntPair(int i, int j) : a(i), b(j) { }
};

class MyClass {
  IntPair nums; // Error: no default constructor for IntPair!
public:
  // This won't work!
  MyClass(int x, int y) {
    nums.a = x;
    nums.b = y;
  }

  int getNumA() { return nums.a; }
  int getNumB() { return nums.b; }
};

int main()
{
  MyClass ob1(7, 9), ob2(5, 2);
```

```
    cout << "Values in ob1 are " << ob1.getNumB() <<
            " and " << ob1.getNumA() << endl;

    cout << "Values in ob2 are " << ob2.getNumB() <<
            " and " << ob2.getNumA() << endl;

    return 0;
}
```

The reason that the program won't compile is that **IntPair** has only one constructor and it requires two arguments. However, **nums** is declared inside **MyClass** without any parameters and the values of **a** and **b** are set inside **MyClass'** constructor. This causes an error because it implies that a default (i.e., parameterless) constructor is available to initially create an **IntPair** object, which is not the case.

To fix this problem, you could add a default constructor to **IntPair**. However, this only works if you have access to the source code for the class, which might not always be the case. A better solution is to use the member initialization syntax, as shown in this correct version of the program.

```
// This program is now correct.
#include <iostream>
using namespace std;

class IntPair {
public:
  int a;
  int b;

  IntPair(int i, int j) : a(i), b(j) { }
};

class MyClass {
  IntPair nums; // now OK
public:
  // Initialize nums object using initialization syntax.
  MyClass(int x, int y) : nums(x,y) { }

  int getNumA() { return nums.a; }
  int getNumB() { return nums.b; }
};

int main()
```

```
{
  MyClass ob1(7, 9), ob2(5, 2);

  cout << "Values in ob1 are " << ob1.getNumB() <<
          " and " << ob1.getNumA() << endl;

  cout << "Values in ob2 are " << ob2.getNumB() <<
          " and " << ob2.getNumA() << endl;

  return 0;
}
```

Here, **nums** is given an initial value when a **MyClass** object is created. Thus, no default constructor is required.

One last point: Class members are constructed and initialized in the order in which they are declared in a class, not in the order in which their initializers occur.

Using the asm Keyword

While C++ is a comprehensive and powerful programming language, there are a few highly specialized situations that it cannot handle. (For example, there is no C++ statement that disables interrupts.) To accommodate special situations, C++ provides a "trap door" that allows you to drop into assembly code at any time, bypassing the C++ compiler entirely. This "trap door" is the **asm** statement. Using **asm**, you can embed assembly language directly into your C++ program. This assembly code is compiled without any modification, and it becomes part of your program's code at the point at which the **asm** statement occurs.

The general form of the **asm** keyword is shown here:

asm ("*op-code*");

where *op-code* is the assembly language instruction that will be embedded in your program. However, several compilers also allow the following forms of **asm**:

asm *instruction* ;
asm *instruction newline*
asm {
    instruction sequence
}

Here, *instruction* is any valid assembly language instruction. Because of the implementation- specific nature of **asm**, you must check the documentation that came with your compiler for details.

At the time of this writing, Microsoft's Visual C++ uses _ _**asm** for embedding assembly code. It is otherwise similar to **asm**.

Here is a simple (and fairly "safe") example that uses the **asm** keyword:

```
#include <iostream>
using namespace std;

int main()
{
  asm int 5; // generate intertupt 5

  return 0;
}
```

When run under DOS, this program generates an INT 5 instruction, which invokes the print-screen function.

Caution   *A thorough working knowledge of assembly language programming is required for using the **asm** statement. If you are not proficient with assembly language, it is best to avoid using **asm** because very nasty errors may result.*

Linkage Specification

In C++ you can specify how a function is linked into your program. By default, functions are linked as C++ functions. However, by using a *linkage specification,* you can cause a function to be linked for a different type of language. The general form of a linkage specifier is

    extern "*language*" *function-prototype*

where *language* denotes the desired language. All C++ compilers support both C and C++ linkage. Some will also allow linkage specifiers for Fortran, Pascal, or BASIC. (You will need to check the documentation for your compiler.)

This program causes **myCfunc( )** to be linked as a C function.

```
#include <iostream>
using namespace std;
```

```
extern "C" void myCfunc();

int main()
{
  myCfunc();

  return 0;
}

// This will link as a C function.
void myCfunc()
{
  cout << "This links as a C function.\n";
}
```

Note *The **extern** keyword is a necessary part of the linkage specification. Further, the linkage specification must be global; it cannot be used inside of a function.*

You can specify more than one function at a time using this form of the linkage specification:

```
extern "language" {
  prototypes
}
```

Array-Based I/O

In addition to console and file I/O, C++'s stream-based I/O system allows *array-based I/O*. Array-based I/O uses a character array as either the input device, the output device, or both. Array-based I/O is performed through normal C++ streams. In fact, everything you already know about C++ I/O is applicable to array-based I/O. The only thing that makes array-based I/O unique is that the device linked to the stream is an array of characters. Streams that are linked to character arrays are commonly referred to as **char *** streams. To use array-based I/O in your programs, you must include **<strstream>**.

Note *The character-based stream classes described in this section are deprecated by Standard C++. This means that they are still valid, but not recommended for new code. This brief discussion is included for the benefit of readers working on older code.*

The Array-Based Classes

The array-based I/O classes are **istrstream**, **ostrstream**, and **strstream**. These classes are used to create input, output, and input/output streams, respectively. Further, the **istrstream** class is derived from **istream**, the **ostrstream** class is derived from **ostream**, and **strstream** has **iostream** as a base class. Therefore, all array-based classes are indirectly derived from **ios** and have access to the same member functions that the "normal" I/O classes do.

Creating an Array-Based Output Stream

To perform output to an array, you must link that array to a stream using this **ostrstream** constructor:

ostrstream *ostr*(char **buf*, streamsize *size*, openmode *mode*=ios::out);

Here, *buf* is a pointer to the array that will be used to collect characters written to the stream *ostr*. The size of the array is passed in the *size* parameter. By default, the stream is opened for normal output, but you can OR various other options with it to create the mode that you need. For example, you might include **ios::app** to cause output to be written at the end of any information already contained in the array. For most purposes, *mode* will be allowed to default.

Once you have opened an array-based output stream, all output to that stream is put into the array. However, no output will be written outside the bounds of the array. Attempting to do so will result in an error.

Here is a simple program that demonstrates an array-based output stream.

```
#include <strstream>
#include <iostream>
using namespace std;

int main()
{
  char str[80];

  ostrstream outs(str, sizeof(str));

  outs << "C++ array-based I/O. ";
  outs << 1024 << hex << " ";
  outs.setf(ios::showbase);
  outs << 100 << ' ' << 99.789 << ends;
```

C++

```
   cout << str;  // display string on console

   return 0;
}
```

This program displays the following:

```
C++ array-based I/O. 1024 0x64 99.789
```

Keep in mind that **outs** is a stream like any other stream; it has the same capabilities as any other type of stream that you have seen earlier. The only difference is that the device that it is linked to is a character array. Because **outs** is a stream, manipulators like **hex** and **ends** are perfectly valid. **ostream** member functions, such as **setf( )**, are also available for use.

This program manually null terminates the array by using the **ends** manipulator. Whether the array will be automatically null terminated or not depends on the implementation, so it is best to perform null termination manually if it is important to your application.

You can determine how many characters are in the output array by calling the **pcount( )** member function. It has this prototype:

streamsize pcount( );

The number returned by **pcount( )** also includes the null terminator, if it exists.

The following program demonstrates **pcount( )**. It reports that **outs** contains 18 characters: 17 characters plus the null terminator.

```
#include <strstream>
#include <iostream>
using namespace std;

int main()
{
  char str[80];

  ostrstream outs(str, sizeof(str));

  outs << "abcdefg ";
  outs << 27 << " "  << 890.23;
  outs << ends;  // null terminate
```

C++

```
    cout << outs.pcount(); // display how many chars in outs

    cout << " " << str;

    return 0;
}
```

Using an Array as Input

To link an input stream to an array, use this **istrstream** constructor:

   istrstream *istr*(const char **buf*);

Here, *buf* is a pointer to the array that will be used as a source of characters each time input is performed on the stream *istr*. The contents of the array pointed to by *buf* must be null terminated. However, the null terminator is never read from the array.

Here is a sample program that uses a string as input.

```
#include <iostream>
#include <strstream>
using namespace std;

int main()
{
  char s[] = "10 Hello 0x75 42.73 OK";

  istrstream ins(s);

  int i;
  char str[80];
  float f;

  // reading: 10 Hello
  ins >> i;
  ins >> str;
  cout << i << " " << str << endl;

  // reading 0x75 42.73 OK
  ins >> hex >> i;
```

```
    ins >> f;
    ins >> str;

    cout << hex << i << " " << f << " " << str;

    return 0;
}
```

If you want only part of a string to be used for input, use this form of the **istrstream** constructor:

istrstream *istr*(const char **buf*, streamsize *size*);

Here, only the first *size* elements of the array pointed to by *buf* will be used. This string need not be null terminated, since it is the value of *size* that determines the size of the string.

Streams linked to memory behave just like those linked to other devices. For example, the following program demonstrates how the contents of any text array can be read. When the end of the array (same as end-of-file) is reached, **ins** will be false.

```
/* This program shows how to read the contents of any
   array that contains text. */
#include <iostream>
#include <strstream>
using namespace std;

int main()
{
  char s[] = "10.23 this is a test <<>><<?!\n";

  istrstream ins(s);

  char ch;

  /* This will read and display the contents
     of any text array. */

  ins.unsetf(ios::skipws); // don't skip spaces
  while (ins) { // false when end of array is reached
    ins >> ch;
    cout << ch;
```

```
  }

  return 0;
}
```

Input/Output Array-Based Streams

To create an array-based stream that can perform both input and output, use this **strstream** constructor function:

strstream *iostr*(char **buf*, streamsize *size*, openmode *mode* = ios::in | ios::out);

Here, *buf* points to the string that will be used for I/O operations. The value of *size* specifies the size of the array. The value of *mode* determines how the stream *iostr* operates. For normal input/output operations, *mode* will be **ios::in | ios::out**. For input, the array must be null terminated.

Here is a program that uses an array to perform both input and output.

```
// Perform both input and output.
#include <iostream>
#include <strstream>
using namespace std;

int main()
{
  char iostr[80];

  strstream strio(iostr, sizeof(iostr), ios::in | ios::out);

  int a, b;
  char str[80];

  strio << "10 20 testing ";
  strio >> a >> b >> str;
  cout << a << " " << b << " " << str << endl;

  return 0;
}
```

This program first writes **10 20 testing** to the array and then reads it back in again.

Using Dynamic Arrays

In the preceding examples, when you linked a stream to an output array, the array and its size were passed to the **ostrstream** constructor. This approach is fine as long as you know the maximum number of characters that you will be outputting to the array. However, what if you don't know how large the output array needs to be? The solution to this problem is to use a second form of the **ostrstream** constructor, shown here:

    ostrstream( );

When this constructor is used, **ostrstream** creates and maintains a dynamically allocated array, which automatically grows in length to accommodate the output that it must store.

To access the dynamically allocated array, you must use a second function, called **str( )**, which has this prototype:

    char *str( );

This function "freezes" the array and returns a pointer to it. You use the pointer returned by **str( )** to access the dynamic array as a string. Once a dynamic array is frozen, it cannot be used for output again unless its is unfrozen (see below). Therefore, you will not want to freeze the array until you are through outputting characters to it.

Here is a program that uses a dynamic output array.

```
#include <strstream>
#include <iostream>
using namespace std;

int main()
{
  char *p;

  ostrstream outs;  // dynamically allocate array

  outs << "C++ array-based I/O ";
  outs << -10 << hex << " ";
  outs.setf(ios::showbase);
  outs << 100 << ends;

  p = outs.str(); // Freeze dynamic buffer and return
                  // pointer to it.

  cout << p;
```

```
    return 0;
}
```

You can also use dynamic I/O arrays with the **strstream** class, which can perform both input and output on an array.

It is possible to freeze or unfreeze a dynamic array by calling the **freeze( )** function. Its prototype is shown here:

void freeze(bool *action* = true);

If *action* is true, the array is frozen. If *action* is false, the array is unfrozen.

Using Binary I/O with Array-Based Streams

Remember that array-based I/O has all of the functionality and capability of "normal" I/O. Therefore, arrays linked to array-based streams can also contain binary information. When reading binary information, you may need to use the **eof( )** function to determine when the end of the array has been reached. For example, the following program shows how to read the contents of any array—binary or text—using the function **get( )**.

```cpp
#include <iostream>
#include <strstream>
using namespace std;

int main()
{
  char *p = "this is a test\1\2\3\4\5\6\7";

  istrstream ins(p);

  char ch;

  // read and display binary info
  while (!ins.eof()) {
    ins.get(ch);
    cout << hex << (int) ch << ' ';

  }
  return 0;
}
```

In this example, the values formed by \1\2\3, and so on are nonprinting values.

C++

To output binary characters, use the **put( )** function. If you need to read buffers of binary data, you can use the **read( )** member function. To write buffers of binary data, use the **write( )** function.

Summarizing the Differences Between C and C++

For the most part, Standard C++ is a superset of Standard C, and virtually all C programs are also C++ programs. However, a few differences do exist, and these have been discussed throughout Parts One and Two of this book. The most important are summarized here.

In C++, local variables can be declared anywhere within a block. In C, they must be declared at the start of a block, before any "action" statements occur. (C99 has removed this restriction.)

In C, a function declared like

```
int f();
```

says *nothing* about any parameters to that function. That is, when there is nothing specified between the parentheses following the function's name, in C this means that nothing is being stated, one way or the other, about any parameters to that function. It might have parameters, or it might not. However, in C++, a function declaration like this means that the function does *not* have parameters. That is, in C++, these two declarations are equivalent:

```
int f();

int f(void);
```

In C++, **void** in a parameter list is optional. Many C++ programmers include **void** as a means of making it completely clear to anyone reading the program that a function does not have any parameters, but this is technically unnecessary.

In C++, all functions must be prototyped. This is an option in C (although good programming practice suggests full prototyping be used in a C program).

A small but potentially important difference between C and C++ is that in C, a character constant is automatically elevated to an integer. In C++, it is not.

In C, it is not an error to declare a global variable several times, even though this is bad programming practice. In C++, it is an error.

In C, an identifier will have at least 31 significant characters. In C++, all characters are significant. However, from a practical point of view, extremely long identifiers are unwieldy and seldom needed.

In C, although it is unusual, you can call **main( )** from within your program. This is not allowed by C++.

In C, you cannot take the address of a **register** variable. In C++, this is allowed.

In C, if no type specifier is present in some types of declaration statements, the type **int** is assumed. This "default-to-int" rule no longer applies to C++. (C99 also drops the "default-to-int" rule.)

C++

Chapter 24

Introducing the Standard Template Library

This chapter explores what is considered by many to be the most important feature added to C++ in recent years: the *standard template library* (*STL*). The inclusion of the STL was one of the major efforts that took place during the standardization of C++. It provides general-purpose, templatized classes and functions that implement many popular and commonly used algorithms and data structures, including, for example, support for vectors, lists, queues, and stacks. It also defines various routines that access them. Because the STL is constructed from template classes, the algorithms and data structures can be applied to nearly any type of data.

The STL is a complex piece of software engineering that uses some of C++'s most sophisticated features. To understand and use the STL, you must have a complete understanding of the C++ language, including pointers, references, and templates. Frankly, the template syntax that describes the STL can seem quite intimidating—although it looks more complicated than it actually is. While there is nothing in this chapter that is any more difficult than the material in the rest of this book, don't be surprised or dismayed if you find the STL confusing at first. Just be patient, study the examples, and don't let the unfamiliar syntax override the STL's basic simplicity.

The purpose of this chapter is to present an overview of the STL, including its design philosophy, organization, constituents, and the programming techniques needed to use it. Because the STL is a large library, it is not possible to discuss all of its features here. However, a complete reference to the STL is provided in Part Four.

This chapter also describes one of C++'s most important classes: **string**. The **string** class defines a string data type that allows you to work with character strings much as you do other data types: using operators. The **string** class is closely related to the STL.

An Overview of the STL

Although the standard template library is large and its syntax can be intimidating, it is actually quite easy to use once you understand how it is constructed and what elements it employs. Therefore, before looking at any code examples, an overview of the STL is warranted.

At the core of the standard template library are three foundational items: *containers*, *algorithms*, and *iterators*. These items work in conjunction with one another to provide off-the-shelf solutions to a variety of programming problems.

Containers

Containers are objects that hold other objects, and there are several different types. For example, the **vector** class defines a dynamic array, **deque** creates a double-ended queue, and **list** provides a linear list. These containers are called *sequence containers* because in STL terminology, a sequence is a linear list. In addition to the basic containers, the STL also defines *associative containers*, which allow efficient retrieval of values based on keys. For example, a **map** provides access to values with unique keys. Thus, a **map** stores a key/value pair and allows a value to be retrieved given its key.

Each container class defines a set of functions that may be applied to the container. For example, a list container includes functions that insert, delete, and merge elements. A stack includes functions that push and pop values.

Algorithms

Algorithms act on containers. They provide the means by which you will manipulate the contents of containers. Their capabilities include initialization, sorting, searching, and transforming the contents of containers. Many algorithms operate on a *range* of elements within a container.

Iterators

Iterators are objects that act, more or less, like pointers. They give you the ability to cycle through the contents of a container in much the same way that you would use a pointer to cycle through an array. There are five types of iterators:

Iterator	Access Allowed
Random Access	Store and retrieve values. Elements may be accessed randomly.
Bidirectional	Store and retrieve values. Forward and backward moving.
Forward	Store and retrieve values. Forward moving only.
Input	Retrieve, but not store values. Forward moving only.
Output	Store, but not retrieve values. Forward moving only.

In general, an iterator that has greater access capabilities can be used in place of one that has lesser capabilities. For example, a forward iterator can be used in place of an input iterator.

Iterators are handled just like pointers. You can increment and decrement them. You can apply the * operator to them. Iterators are declared using the **iterator** type defined by the various containers.

The STL also supports *reverse iterators*. Reverse iterators are either bidirectional or random-access iterators that move through a sequence in the reverse direction. Thus, if a reverse iterator points to the end of a sequence, incrementing that iterator will cause it to point to one element before the end.

When referring to the various iterator types in template descriptions, this book will use the following terms:

Term	Represents
BiIter	Bidirectional iterator
ForIter	Forward iterator
InIter	Input iterator
OutIter	Output iterator
RandIter	Random access iterator

Other STL Elements

In addition to containers, algorithms, and iterators, the STL relies upon several other standard components for support. Chief among these are allocators, predicates, comparison functions, and function objects.

Each container has defined for it an *allocator*. Allocators manage memory allocation for a container. The default allocator is an object of class **allocator**, but you can define your own allocators if needed by specialized applications. For most uses, the default allocator is sufficient.

Several of the algorithms and containers use a special type of function called a *predicate*. There are two variations of predicates: unary and binary. A *unary* predicate takes one argument, while a *binary* predicate has two. These functions return true/false results. But the precise conditions that make them return true or false are defined by you. For the rest of this chapter, when a unary predicate function is required, it will be notated using the type **UnPred**. When a binary predicate is required, the type **BinPred** will be used. In a binary predicate, the arguments are always in the order of *first,second*. For both unary and binary predicates, the arguments will contain values of the type of objects being stored by the container.

Some algorithms and classes use a special type of binary predicate that compares two elements. Comparison functions return true if their first argument is less than their second. Comparison functions will be notated using the type **Comp**.

In addition to the headers required by the various STL classes, the C++ standard library includes the **<utility>** and **<functional>** headers, which provide support for the STL. For example, the template class **pair**, which can hold a pair of values, is defined in **<utility>**. We will make use of **pair** later in this chapter.

The templates in **<functional>** help you construct objects that define **operator( )**. These are called *function objects* and they may be used in place of function pointers in many places. There are several predefined function objects declared within **<functional>**. They are shown here:

plus	minus	multiplies	divides	modulus
negate	equal_to	not_equal_to	greater	greater_equal
less	less_equal	logical_and	logical_or	logical_not

Perhaps the most widely used function object is **less,** which determines when one object is less than another. Function objects can be used in place of actual function pointers in the STL algorithms described later. Using function objects rather than function pointers allows the STL to generate more efficient code.

Two other entities that populate the STL are *binders* and *negators*. A binder binds an argument to a function object. A negator returns the complement of a predicate.

One final term to know is *adaptor*. In STL terms, an adaptor transforms one thing into another. For example, the container **queue** (which creates a standard queue) is an adaptor for the **deque** container.

The Container Classes

As explained, containers are the STL objects that actually store data. The containers defined by the STL are shown in Table 24-1. Also shown are the headers necessary to use each container. The **string** class, which manages character strings, is also a container, but it is discussed later in this chapter.

Container	Description	Required Header
bitset	A set of bits.	<bitset>
deque	A double-ended queue.	<deque>
list	A linear list.	<list>
map	Stores key/value pairs in which each key is associated with only one value.	<map>
multimap	Stores key/value pairs in which one key may be associated with two or more values.	<map>
multiset	A set in which each element is not necessarily unique.	<set>
priority_queue	A priority queue.	<queue>
queue	A queue.	<queue>
set	A set in which each element is unique.	<set>
stack	A stack.	<stack>
vector	A dynamic array.	<vector>

Table 24-1.   *The Containers Defined by the STL*

Since the names of the generic placeholder types in a template class declaration are arbitrary, the container classes declare **typedef**ed versions of these types. This makes the type names concrete. Some of the most common **typedef** names are shown here:

size_type	Some type of integer
reference	A reference to an element
const_reference	A **const** reference to an element
iterator	An iterator
const_iterator	A **const** iterator
reverse_iterator	A reverse iterator
const_reverse_iterator	A **const** reverse iterator
value_type	The type of a value stored in a container
allocator_type	The type of the allocator
key_type	The type of a key
key_compare	The type of a function that compares two keys
value_compare	The type of a function that compares two values

General Theory of Operation

Although the internal operation of the STL is highly sophisticated, to use the STL is actually quite easy. First, you must decide on the type of container that you wish to use. Each offers certain benefits and trade-offs. For example, a **vector** is very good when a random-access, array-like object is required and not too many insertions or deletions are needed. A **list** offers low-cost insertion and deletion but trades away speed. A **map** provides an associative container, but of course incurs additional overhead.

Once you have chosen a container, you will use its member functions to add elements to the container, access or modify those elements, and delete elements. Except for **bitset**, a container will automatically grow as needed when elements are added to it and shrink when elements are removed.

Elements can be added to and removed from a container a number of different ways. For example, both the sequence containers (**vector**, **list**, and **deque**) and the associative containers (**map**, **multimap**, **set**, and **multiset**) provide a member function called **insert( )**, which inserts elements into a container, and **erase( )**, which removes elements from a container. The sequence containers also provide **push_back( )** and **pop_back( )**, which add an element to or remove an element from the end, respectively. These functions are probably the most common way that individual elements are added to or removed from a sequence container. The **list** and **deque** containers also include **push_front( )** and **pop_front( )**, which add and remove elements from the start of the container.

One of the most common ways to access the elements within a container is through an iterator. The sequence and the associative containers provide the member functions **begin( )** and **end( )**, which return iterators to the start and end of the container, respectively. These iterators are very useful when accessing the contents of a container. For example, to cycle through a container, you can obtain an iterator to its beginning using **begin( )** and then increment that iterator until its value is equal to **end( )**.

The associative containers provide the function **find( )**, which is used to locate an element in an associative container given its key. Since associative containers link a key with its value, **find( )** is how most elements in such a container are located.

Since a **vector** is a dynamic array, it also supports the standard array-indexing syntax for accessing its elements.

Once you have a container that holds information, it can be manipulated using one or more algorithms. The algorithms not only allow you to alter the contents of a container in some prescribed fashion, but they also let you transform one type of sequence into another.

In the following sections, you will learn to apply these general techniques to three representative containers: **vector**, **list**, and **map**. Once you understand how these containers work, you will have no trouble using the others.

Vectors

Perhaps the most general-purpose of the containers is **vector**. The **vector** class supports a dynamic array. This is an array that can grow as needed. As you know, in C++ the size of an array is fixed at compile time. While this is by far the most efficient way to implement arrays, it is also the most restrictive because the size of the array cannot be adjusted at run time to accommodate changing program conditions. A vector solves this problem by allocating memory as needed. Although a vector is dynamic, you can still use the standard array subscript notation to access its elements.

The template specification for **vector** is shown here:

template <class T, class Allocator = allocator<T> > class vector

Here, **T** is the type of data being stored and **Allocator** specifies the allocator, which defaults to the standard allocator. **vector** has the following constructors:

```
explicit vector(const Allocator &a = Allocator( ) );
explicit vector(size_type num, const T &val = T ( ),
          const Allocator &a = Allocator( ));
vector(const vector<T, Allocator> &ob);
template <class InIter> vector(InIter start, InIter end,
          const Allocator &a = Allocator( ));
```

The first form constructs an empty vector. The second form constructs a vector that has *num* elements with the value *val*. The value of *val* may be allowed to default. The third form constructs a vector that contains the same elements as *ob*. The fourth form constructs a vector that contains the elements in the range specified by the iterators *start* and *end*.

For maximum flexibility and portability, any object that will be stored in a **vector** should define a default constructor. It should also define the < and == operations. Some compilers may require that other comparison operators be defined. (Since implementations vary, consult your compiler's documentation for precise information.) All of the built-in types automatically satisfy these requirements.

Although the template syntax looks rather complex, there is nothing difficult about declaring a vector. Here are some examples:

```
vector<int> iv;           // create zero-length int vector
vector<char> cv(5);       // create 5-element char vector
vector<char> cv(5, 'x');  // initialize a 5-element char vector
vector<int> iv2(iv);      // create int vector from an int vector
```

The following comparison operators are defined for **vector**:

==, <, <=, !=, >, >=

The subscripting operator [ ] is also defined for **vector**. This allows you to access the elements of a vector using standard array subscripting notation.

Several of the member functions defined by **vector** are shown in Table 24-2. (Remember, Part Four contains a complete reference to the STL classes.) Some of the most commonly used member functions are **size( )**, **begin( )**, **end( )**, **push_back( )**, **insert( )**, and **erase( )**. The **size( )** function returns the current size of the vector. This function is quite useful because it allows you to determine the size of a vector at run time. Remember, vectors will increase in size as needed, so the size of a vector must be determined during execution, not during compilation.

The **begin( )** function returns an iterator to the start of the vector. The **end( )** function returns an iterator to the end of the vector. As explained, iterators are similar to pointers, and it is through the use of the **begin( )** and **end( )** functions that you obtain an iterator to the beginning and end of a vector.

The **push_back( )** function puts a value onto the end of the vector. If necessary, the vector is increased in length to accommodate the new element. You can also add elements to the middle using **insert( )**. A vector can also be initialized. In any event, once a vector contains elements, you can use array subscripting to access or modify those elements. You can remove elements from a vector using **erase( )**.

Member	Description
reference back( ); const_reference back( ) const;	Returns a reference to the last element in the vector.
iterator begin( ); const_iterator begin( ) const;	Returns an iterator to the first element in the vector.
void clear( );	Removes all elements from the vector.
bool empty( ) const;	Returns true if the invoking vector is empty and false otherwise.
iterator end( ); const_iterator end( ) const;	Returns an iterator to the end of the vector.
iterator erase(iterator *i*);	Removes the element pointed to by *i*. Returns an iterator to the element after the one removed.
iterator erase(iterator *start*, iterator *end*);	Removes the elements in the range *start* to *end*. Returns an iterator to the element after the last element removed.
reference front( ); const_reference front( ) const;	Returns a reference to the first element in the vector.
iterator insert(iterator *i*, const T &*val*);	Inserts *val* immediately before the element specified by *i*. An iterator to the element is returned.
void insert(iterator *i*, size_type *num*, const T & *val*)	Inserts *num* copies of *val* immediately before the element specified by *i*.

template <class InIter>
  void insert(iterator *i*, InIter *start*,
        InIter *end*);
	Inserts the sequence defined by *start* and *end* immediately before the element specified by *i*.

reference operator[ ](size_type *i*) const; const_reference operator[ ](size_type *i*) const;	Returns a reference to the element specified by *i*.
void pop_back( );	Removes the last element in the vector.
void push_back(const T &*val*);	Adds an element with the value specified by *val* to the end of the vector.
size_type size( ) const;	Returns the number of elements currently in the vector.

Table 24-2.   *Some Commonly Used Member Functions Defined by* ***vector***

Here is a short example that illustrates the basic operation of a vector.

```cpp
// Demonstrate a vector.
#include <iostream>
#include <vector>
#include <cctype>
using namespace std;

int main()
{
  vector<char> v(10); // create a vector of length 10
  unsigned int i;

  // display original size of v
  cout << "Size = " << v.size() << endl;

  // assign the elements of the vector some values
  for(i=0; i<10; i++) v[i] = i + 'a';

  // display contents of vector
  cout << "Current Contents:\n";
  for(i=0; i<v.size(); i++) cout << v[i] << " ";
  cout << "\n\n";

  cout << "Expanding vector\n";
  /* put more values onto the end of the vector,
     it will grow as needed */
  for(i=0; i<10; i++) v.push_back(i + 10 + 'a');

  // display current size of v
  cout << "Size now = " << v.size() << endl;

  // display contents of vector
  cout << "Current contents:\n";
  for(i=0; i<v.size(); i++) cout << v[i] << " ";
  cout << "\n\n";

  // change contents of vector
  for(i=0; i<v.size(); i++) v[i] = toupper(v[i]);
  cout << "Modified Contents:\n";
  for(i=0; i<v.size(); i++) cout << v[i] << " ";
  cout << endl;
```

```
   return 0;
}
```

The output of this program is shown here:

```
Size = 10
Current Contents:
a b c d e f g h i j

Expanding vector
Size now = 20
Current contents:
a b c d e f g h i j k l m n o p q r s t

Modified Contents:
A B C D E F G H I J K L M N O P Q R S T
```

Let's look at this program carefully. In **main( )**, a character vector called **v** is created with an initial capacity of 10. That is, **v** initially contains 10 elements. This is confirmed by calling the **size( )** member function. Next, these 10 elements are initialized to the characters a through j and the contents of **v** are displayed. Notice that the standard array subscripting notation is employed. Next, 10 more elements are added to the end of **v** using the **push_back( )** function. This causes **v** to grow in order to accommodate the new elements. As the output shows, its size after these additions is 20. Finally, the values of **v**'s elements are altered using standard subscripting notation.

There is one other point of interest in this program. Notice that the loops that display the contents of **v** use as their target value **v.size( )**. One of the advantages that vectors have over arrays is that it is possible to find the current size of a vector. As you can imagine, this can be quite useful in a variety of situations.

Accessing a Vector Through an Iterator

As you know, arrays and pointers are tightly linked in C++. An array can be accessed either through subscripting or through a pointer. The parallel to this in the STL is the link between vectors and iterators. You can access the members of a vector using subscripting or through the use of an iterator. The following example shows how.

```
// Access the elements of a vector through an iterator.
#include <iostream>
#include <vector>
#include <cctype>
```

```cpp
using namespace std;

int main()
{
  vector<char> v(10); // create a vector of length 10
  vector<char>::iterator p; // create an iterator
  int i;

  // assign elements in vector a value
  p = v.begin();
  i = 0;
  while(p != v.end()) {
    *p = i + 'a';
    p++;
    i++;
  }

  // display contents of vector
  cout << "Original contents:\n";
  p = v.begin();
  while(p != v.end()) {
    cout << *p << " ";
    p++;
  }
  cout << "\n\n";

  // change contents of vector
  p = v.begin();
  while(p != v.end()) {
    *p = toupper(*p);
    p++;
  }

  // display contents of vector
  cout << "Modified Contents:\n";
  p = v.begin();
  while(p != v.end()) {
    cout << *p << " ";
    p++;
  }
  cout << endl;
```

```
    return 0;
}
```

The output from this program is

```
Original contents:
a b c d e f g h i j

Modified Contents:
A B C D E F G H I J
```

In the program, notice how the iterator **p** is declared. The type **iterator** is defined by the container classes. Thus, to obtain an iterator for a particular container, you will use a declaration similar to that shown in the example: simply qualify **iterator** with the name of the container. In the program, **p** is initialized to point to the start of the vector by using the **begin( )** member function. This function returns an iterator to the start of the vector. This iterator can then be used to access the vector an element at a time by incrementing it as needed. This process is directly parallel to the way a pointer can be used to access the elements of an array. To determine when the end of the vector has been reached, the **end( )** member function is employed. This function returns an iterator to the location that is one past the last element in the vector. Thus, when **p** equals **v.end( )**, the end of the vector has been reached.

Inserting and Deleting Elements in a Vector

In addition to putting new values on the end of a vector, you can insert elements into the middle using the **insert( )** function. You can also remove elements using **erase( )**. The following program demonstrates **insert( )** and **erase( )**.

```
// Demonstrate insert and erase.
#include <iostream>
#include <vector>
using namespace std;

int main()
{
  vector<char> v(10);
  vector<char> v2;
  char str[] = "<Vector>";
  unsigned int i;
```

```
// initialize v
for(i=0; i<10; i++) v[i] = i + 'a';

// copy characters in str into v2
for(i=0; str[i]; i++) v2.push_back(str[i]);

// display original contents of vector
cout << "Original contents of v:\n";
for(i=0; i<v.size(); i++) cout << v[i] << " ";
cout << "\n\n";

vector<char>::iterator p = v.begin();
p += 2; // point to 3rd element

// insert 10 X's into v
v.insert(p, 10, 'X');

// display contents after insertion
cout << "Size after inserting X's = " << v.size() << endl;
cout << "Contents after insert:\n";
for(i=0; i<v.size(); i++) cout << v[i] << " ";
cout << "\n\n";

// remove those elements
p = v.begin();
p += 2; // point to 3rd element
v.erase(p, p+10); // remove next 10 elements

// display contents after deletion
cout << "Size after erase = " << v.size() << endl;
cout << "Contents after erase:\n";
for(i=0; i<v.size(); i++) cout << v[i] << " ";
cout << "\n\n";

// Insert v2 into v
v.insert(p, v2.begin(), v2.end());
cout << "Size after v2's insertion = ";
cout << v.size() << endl;
cout << "Contents after insert:\n";
for(i=0; i<v.size(); i++) cout << v[i] << " ";
cout << endl;
```

```
    return 0;
}
```

This program produces the following output:

```
Original contents of v:
a b c d e f g h i j

Size after inserting X's = 20
Contents after insert:
a b X X X X X X X X X X c d e f g h i j

Size after erase = 10
Contents after erase:
a b c d e f g h i j

Size after v2's insertion = 18
Contents after insert:
a b < V e c t o r > c d e f g h i j
```

This program demonstrates two forms of **insert( )**. The first time it is used, it inserts 10 X's into **v**. The second time, it inserts the contents of a second vector, **v2**, into **v**. This second use is the most interesting. It takes three iterator arguments. The first specifies the point at which the insertion will occur within the invoking container. The last two point to the beginning and ending of the sequence to be inserted.

Storing Class Objects in a Vector

Although the preceding examples have only stored objects of the built-in types in a vector, **vector**s are not limited to this. They can store any type of objects, including those of classes that you create. Here is an example that uses a **vector** to store objects that hold the daily temperature highs for a week. Notice that **DailyTemp** defines the default constructor and that overloaded versions of < and == are provided. Remember, depending upon how your compiler implements the STL, these (or other) comparison operators may need to be defined.

```
// Store a class object in a vector.
#include <iostream>
#include <vector>
#include <cstdlib>
using namespace std;
```

```cpp
class DailyTemp {
  int temp;
public:
  DailyTemp() { temp = 0; }
  DailyTemp(int x) { temp = x; }

  DailyTemp &operator=(int x) {
    temp = x; return *this;
  }

  double get_temp() { return temp; }
};

bool operator<(DailyTemp a, DailyTemp b)
{
  return a.get_temp() < b.get_temp();
}

bool operator==(DailyTemp a, DailyTemp b)
{
  return a.get_temp() == b.get_temp();
}

int main()
{
  vector<DailyTemp> v;
  unsigned int i;

  for(i=0; i<7; i++)
    v.push_back(DailyTemp(60 + rand()%30));

  cout << "Fahrenheit temperatures:\n";
  for(i=0; i<v.size(); i++)
    cout << v[i].get_temp() << " ";

  cout << endl;

  // convert from Fahrenheit to Centigrade
  for(i=0; i<v.size(); i++)
    v[i] = (int)(v[i].get_temp()-32) * 5/9 ;

  cout << "Centigrade temperatures:\n";
  for(i=0; i<v.size(); i++)
```

```
    cout << v[i].get_temp() << " ";

  return 0;
}
```

Sample output from this program is shown here:

```
Fahrenheit temperatures:
71 77 64 70 89 64 78
Centigrade temperatures:
21 25 17 21 31 17 25
```

Vectors offer great power, safety, and flexibility, but they are less efficient than normal arrays. Thus, for most programming tasks, normal arrays will still be your first choice. But watch for situations in which the benefits of using a **vector** outweigh its costs.

Lists

The **list** class supports a bidirectional, linear list. Unlike a vector, which supports random access, a list can be accessed sequentially only. Since lists are bidirectional, they may be accessed front to back or back to front.

A **list** has this template specification:

template <class T, class Allocator = allocator<T> > class list

Here, **T** is the type of data stored in the list. The allocator is specified by **Allocator**, which defaults to the standard allocator. It has the following constructors:

explicit list(const Allocator &*a* = Allocator( ));
explicit list(size_type *num*, const T &*val* = T ( ),
           const Allocator &*a* = Allocator( ));
list(const list<T, Allocator> &*ob*);
template <class InIter>list(InIter *start*, InIter *end*,
           const Allocator &*a* = Allocator( ));

The first form constructs an empty list. The second form constructs a list that has *num* elements with the value *val*, which can be allowed to default. The third form constructs a list that contains the same elements as *ob*. The fourth form constructs a list that contains the elements in the range specified by the iterators *start* and *end*.

The following comparison operators are defined for **list**:

==, <, <=, !=, >, >=

Some of the commonly used **list** member functions are shown in Table 24-3. Like vectors, elements may be put into a list by using the **push_back( )** function. You can put elements on the front of the list by using **push_front( )**. An element can also be

Member	Description
reference back( ); const_reference back( ) const;	Returns a reference to the last element in the list.
iterator begin( ); const_iterator begin( ) const;	Returns an iterator to the first element in the list.
void clear( );	Removes all elements from the list.
bool empty( ) const;	Returns true if the invoking list is empty and false otherwise.
iterator end( ); const_iterator end( ) const;	Returns an iterator to the end of the list.
iterator erase(iterator *i*);	Removes the element pointed to by *i*. Returns an iterator to the element after the one removed.
iterator erase(iterator *start*, iterator *end*);	Removes the elements in the range *start* to *end*. Returns an iterator to the element after the last element removed.
reference front( ); const_reference front( ) const;	Returns a reference to the first element in the list.
iterator insert(iterator *i*, const T &*val*);	Inserts *val* immediately before the element specified by *i*. An iterator to the element is returned.
void insert(iterator *i*, size_type *num*, const T &*val*)	Inserts *num* copies of *val* immediately before the element specified by *i*.

template <class InIter>
    void insert(iterator *i*,
        InIter *start*, InIter *end*);
	Inserts the sequence defined by *start* and *end* immediately before the element specified by *i*.

Table 24-3. *Some Commonly Used **list** Member Functions*

Member	Description

void merge(list<T, Allocator> &*ob*);
template <class Comp>
   void merge(list<T, Allocator> &*ob*,
          Comp *cmpfn*);
	Merges the ordered list contained in *ob* with the ordered invoking list. The result is ordered. After the merge, the list contained in *ob* is empty. In the second form, a comparison function can be specified that determines when one element is less than another.

void pop_back( );	Removes the last element in the list.
void pop_front( );	Removes the first element in the list.
void push_back(const T &*val*);	Adds an element with the value specified by *val* to the end of the list.
void push_front(const T &*val*);	Adds an element with the value specified by *val* to the front of the list.
void remove(const T &*val*);	Removes elements with the value *val* from the list.
void reverse( );	Reverses the invoking list.
size_type size( ) const;	Returns the number of elements currently in the list.

void sort( );
template <class Comp>
  void sort(Comp *cmpfn*);
	Sorts the list. The second form sorts the list using the comparison function *cmpfn* to determine when one element is less than another.

void splice(iterator *i*, list<T, Allocator> &*ob*);	The contents of *ob* are inserted into the invoking list at the location pointed to by *i*. After the operation, *ob* is empty.

void splice(iterator *i*,
       list<T, Allocator> &*ob*,
       iterator *el*);
	The element pointed to by *el* is removed from the list *ob* and stored in the invoking list at the location pointed to by *i*.

void splice(iterator *i*,
       list<T, Allocator> &*ob*,
       iterator *start*, iterator *end*);
	The range defined by *start* and *end* is removed from *ob* and stored in the invoking list beginning at the location pointed to by *i*.

Table 24-3. *Some Commonly Used **list** Member Functions* (continued)

inserted into the middle of a list by using **insert( )**. Two lists may be joined using **splice( )**. One list may be merged into another using **merge( )**.

For maximum flexibility and portability, any object that will be held in a list should define a default constructor. It should also define the < operator, and possibly other comparison operators. The precise requirements for an object that will be stored in a list vary from compiler to compiler, so you will need to check your compiler's documentation.

Here is a simple example of a **list**.

```
// List basics.
#include <iostream>
#include <list>
using namespace std;

int main()
{
  list<int> lst; // create an empty list
  int i;

  for(i=0; i<10; i++) lst.push_back(i);

  cout << "Size = " << lst.size() << endl;

  cout << "Contents: ";
  list<int>::iterator p = lst.begin();
  while(p != lst.end()) {
    cout << *p << " ";
    p++;
  }
  cout << "\n\n";

  // change contents of list
  p = lst.begin();
  while(p != lst.end()) {
    *p = *p + 100;
    p++;
  }

  cout << "Contents modified: ";
  p = lst.begin();
  while(p != lst.end()) {
    cout << *p << " ";
```

```
    p++;
  }

  return 0;
}
```

The output produced by this program is shown here:

```
Size = 10
Contents: 0 1 2 3 4 5 6 7 8 9

Contents modified: 100 101 102 103 104 105 106 107 108 109
```

This program creates a list of integers. First, an empty **list** object is created. Next, 10 integers are put into the list. This is accomplished using the **push_back( )** function, which puts each new value on the end of the existing list. Next, the size of the list and the list itself is displayed. The list is displayed via an iterator, using the following code:

```
list<int>::iterator p = lst.begin();
while(p != lst.end()) {
  cout << *p << " ";
  p++;
}
```

Here, the iterator **p** is initialized to point to the start of the list. Each time through the loop, **p** is incremented, causing it to point to the next element. The loop ends when **p** points to the end of the list. This code is essentially the same as was used to cycle through a vector using an iterator. Loops like this are common in STL code, and the fact that the same constructs can be used to access different types of containers is part of the power of the STL.

Understanding end( )

Now is a good time to emphasize a somewhat unexpected attribute of the **end( )** container function. **end( )** does not return a pointer to the last element in a container. Instead, it returns a pointer *one past* the last element. Thus, the last element in a container is pointed to by **end( ) - 1**. This feature allows us to write very efficient algorithms that cycle through all of the elements of a container, including the last one, using an iterator. When the iterator has the same value as the one returned by **end( )**, we know that all elements have been accessed. However, you must keep this feature in mind since it may seem a bit counterintuitive. For example, consider the following program, which displays a list forward and backward.

```
// Understanding end().
#include <iostream>
#include <list>
using namespace std;

int main()
{
  list<int> lst; // create an empty list
  int i;

  for(i=0; i<10; i++) lst.push_back(i);

  cout << "List printed forwards:\n";
  list<int>::iterator p = lst.begin();
  while(p != lst.end()) {
    cout << *p << " ";
    p++;
  }
  cout << "\n\n";

  cout << "List printed backwards:\n";
  p = lst.end();
  while(p != lst.begin()) {
    p--; // decrement pointer before using
    cout << *p << " ";
  }

  return 0;
}
```

The output produced by this program is shown here:

```
List printed forwards:
0 1 2 3 4 5 6 7 8 9

List printed backwards:
9 8 7 6 5 4 3 2 1 0
```

The code that displays the list in the forward direction is the same as we have been using. But pay special attention to the code that displays the list in reverse order. The iterator **p** is initially set to the end of the list through the use of the **end( )** function. Since **end( )** returns an iterator to an object that is one past the last object actually stored in the list, **p** must be decremented before it is used. This is why **p** is decremented before the **cout** statement inside the loop, rather than after. Remember: **end( )** does not return a pointer to the last object in the list; it returns a pointer that is one past the last value in the list.

push_front( ) vs. push_back( )

You can build a list by adding elements to either the end or the start of the list. So far, we have been adding elements to the end by using **push_back( )**. To add elements to the start, use **push_front( )**. For example,

```
/* Demonstrating the difference between
   push_back() and push_front(). */
#include <iostream>
#include <list>
using namespace std;

int main()
{
  list<int> lst1, lst2;
  int i;

  for(i=0; i<10; i++) lst1.push_back(i);
  for(i=0; i<10; i++) lst2.push_front(i);

  list<int>::iterator p;

  cout << "Contents of lst1:\n";
  p = lst1.begin();
  while(p != lst1.end()) {
    cout << *p << " ";
    p++;
  }
  cout << "\n\n";

  cout << "Contents of lst2:\n";
  p = lst2.begin();
  while(p != lst2.end()) {
    cout << *p << " ";
    p++;
  }
```

```
  return 0;
}
```

The output produced by this program is shown here:

```
Contents of lst1:
0 1 2 3 4 5 6 7 8 9

Contents of lst2:
9 8 7 6 5 4 3 2 1 0
```

Since **lst2** is built by putting elements onto its front, the resulting list is in the reverse order of **lst1**, which is built by putting elements onto its end.

Sort a List

A list may be sorted by calling the **sort( )** member function. The following program creates a list of random integers and then puts the list into sorted order.

```cpp
// Sort a list.
#include <iostream>
#include <list>
#include <cstdlib>
using namespace std;

int main()
{
  list<int> lst;
  int i;

  // create a list of random integers
  for(i=0; i<10; i++)
    lst.push_back(rand());

  cout << "Original contents:\n";
  list<int>::iterator p = lst.begin();
  while(p != lst.end()) {
    cout << *p << " ";
    p++;
  }
```

```
  cout << endl << endl;

  // sort the list
  lst.sort();

  cout << "Sorted contents:\n";
  p = lst.begin();
  while(p != lst.end()) {
    cout << *p << " ";
    p++;
  }

  return 0;
}
```

Here is sample output produced by the program:

```
Original contents:
41 18467 6334 26500 19169 15724 11478 29358 26962 24464

Sorted contents:
41 6334 11478 15724 18467 19169 24464 26500 26962 29358
```

Merging One List with Another

One ordered list may be merged with another. The result is an ordered list that contains the contents of the two original lists. The new list is left in the invoking list, and the second list is left empty. The next example merges two lists. The first contains the even numbers between 0 and 9. The second contains the odd numbers. These lists are then merged to produce the sequence 0 1 2 3 4 5 6 7 8 9.

```
// Merge two lists.
#include <iostream>
#include <list>
using namespace std;

int main()
{
  list<int> lst1, lst2;
  int i;
```

C++

```
    for(i=0; i<10; i+=2) lst1.push_back(i);
    for(i=1; i<11; i+=2) lst2.push_back(i);

    cout << "Contents of lst1:\n";
    list<int>::iterator p = lst1.begin();
    while(p != lst1.end()) {
      cout << *p << " ";
      p++;
    }
    cout << endl << endl;

    cout << "Contents of lst2:\n";
    p = lst2.begin();
    while(p != lst2.end()) {
      cout << *p << " ";
      p++;
    }
    cout << endl << endl;

    // now, merge the two lists
    lst1.merge(lst2);
    if(lst2.empty())
      cout << "lst2 is now empty\n";

    cout << "Contents of lst1 after merge:\n";
    p = lst1.begin();
    while(p != lst1.end()) {
      cout << *p << " ";
      p++;
    }

    return 0;
}
```

The output produced by this program is shown here:

```
Contents of lst1:
0 2 4 6 8

Contents of lst2:
1 3 5 7 9
```

```
lst2 is now empty
Contents of lst1 after merge:
0 1 2 3 4 5 6 7 8 9
```

One other thing to notice about this example is the use of the **empty( )** function. It returns true if the invoking container is empty. Since **merge( )** removes all of the elements from the list being merged, it will be empty after the merge is completed, as the program output confirms.

Storing Class Objects in a List

Here is an example that uses a list to store objects of type **myclass**. Notice that the <, >, !=, and == are overloaded for objects of type **myclass**. (For some compilers, you will not need to define all of these. For other compilers, you may need to define additional operators.) The STL uses these functions to determine the ordering and equality of objects in a container. Even though a list is not an ordered container, it still needs a way to compare elements when searching, sorting, or merging.

```cpp
// Store class objects in a list.
#include <iostream>
#include <list>
#include <cstring>
using namespace std;

class myclass {
  int a, b;
  int sum;
public:
  myclass() { a = b = 0; }
  myclass(int i, int j) {
    a = i;
    b = j;
    sum = a + b;
  }
  int getsum() { return sum; }

  friend bool operator<(const myclass &o1,
                        const myclass &o2);
  friend bool operator>(const myclass &o1,
                        const myclass &o2);
  friend bool operator==(const myclass &o1,
```

```
                             const myclass &o2);
    friend bool operator!=(const myclass &o1,
                             const myclass &o2);
};

bool operator<(const myclass &o1, const myclass &o2)
{
  return o1.sum < o2.sum;
}

bool operator>(const myclass &o1, const myclass &o2)
{
  return o1.sum > o2.sum;
}

bool operator==(const myclass &o1, const myclass &o2)
{
  return o1.sum == o2.sum;
}

bool operator!=(const myclass &o1, const myclass &o2)
{
  return o1.sum != o2.sum;
}

int main()
{
  int i;

  // create first list
  list<myclass> lst1;
  for(i=0; i<10; i++) lst1.push_back(myclass(i, i));

  cout << "First list: ";
  list<myclass>::iterator p = lst1.begin();
  while(p != lst1.end()) {
    cout << p->getsum() << " ";
    p++;
```

```
    }
    cout << endl;

    // create a second list
    list<myclass> lst2;
    for(i=0; i<10; i++) lst2.push_back(myclass(i*2, i*3));

    cout << "Second list: ";
    p = lst2.begin();
    while(p != lst2.end()) {
      cout << p->getsum() << " ";
      p++;
    }
    cout << endl;

    // now, merget lst1 and lst2
    lst1.merge(lst2);

    // display merged list
    cout << "Merged list: ";
    p = lst1.begin();
    while(p != lst1.end()) {
      cout << p->getsum() << " ";
      p++;
    }

    return 0;
}
```

The program creates two lists of **myclass** objects and displays the contents of each list. It then merges the two lists and displays the result. The output from this program is shown here:

```
First list: 0 2 4 6 8 10 12 14 16 18
Second list: 0 5 10 15 20 25 30 35 40 45
Merged list: 0 0 2 4 5 6 8 10 10 12 14 15 16 18 20 25 30 35 40 45
```

Maps

The **map** class supports an associative container in which unique keys are mapped with values. In essence, a key is simply a name that you give to a value. Once a value has been stored, you can retrieve it by using its key. Thus, in its most general sense, a map is a list of key/value pairs. The power of a map is that you can look up a value given its key. For example, you could define a map that uses a person's name as its key and stores that person's telephone number as its value. Associative containers are becoming more popular in programming.

As mentioned, a map can hold only unique keys. Duplicate keys are not allowed. To create a map that allows nonunique keys, use **multimap**.

The **map** container has the following template specification:

> template <class Key, class T, class Comp = less<Key>,
>   class Allocator = allocator<pair<const key, T> > class map

Here, **Key** is the data type of the keys, **T** is the data type of the values being stored (mapped), and **Comp** is a function that compares two keys. This defaults to the standard **less( )** utility function object. **Allocator** is the allocator (which defaults to **allocator**) .

A **map** has the following constructors:

> explicit map(const Comp &*cmpfn* = Comp( ),
>   const Allocator &*a* = Allocator( ));
> map(const map<Key, T, Comp, Allocator> &*ob*);
> template <class InIter> map(InIter *start*, InIter *end*,
>   const Comp &*cmpfn* = Comp( ), const Allocator &*a* = Allocator( ));

The first form constructs an empty map. The second form constructs a map that contains the same elements as *ob*. The third form constructs a map that contains the elements in the range specified by the iterators *start* and *end*. The function specified by *cmpfn*, if present, determines the ordering of the map.

In general, any object used as a key should define a default constructor and overload the < operator and any other necessary comparison operators. The specific requirements vary from compiler to compiler.

The following comparison operators are defined for **map**.

> ==, <, <=, !=, >, >=

Several of the **map** member functions are shown in Table 24-4. In the descriptions, **key_type** is the type of the key, and **value_type** represents **pair<Key, T>**.

Member	Description
iterator begin( ); const_iterator begin( ) const;	Returns an iterator to the first element in the map.
void clear( );	Removes all elements from the map.
size_type count(const key_type &k) const;	Returns the number of times k occurs in the map (1 or zero).
bool empty( ) const;	Returns true if the invoking map is empty and false otherwise.
iterator end( ); const_iterator end( ) const;	Returns an iterator to the end of the list.
void erase(iterator i);	Removes the element pointed to by i.
void erase(iterator start, iterator end);	Removes the elements in the range start to end.
size_type erase(const key_type &k)	Removes from the map elements that have keys with the value k.
iterator find(const key_type &k); const_iterator find(const key_type &k) const;	Returns an iterator to the specified key. If the key is not found, then an iterator to the end of the map is returned.
iterator insert(iterator i, const value_type &val);	Inserts val at or after the element specified by i. An iterator to the element is returned.
template <class InIter> void insert(InIter start, InIter end)	Inserts a range of elements.
pair<iterator, bool> insert(const value_type &val);	Inserts val into the invoking map. An iterator to the element is returned. The element is inserted only if it does not already exist. If the element was inserted, pair<iterator, true> is returned. Otherwise, pair<iterator, false> is returned.

Table 24-4.   *Several Commonly Used **map** Member Functions*

Member	Description
mapped_type & operator[ ](const key_type &i)	Returns a reference to the element specified by i. If this element does not exist, it is inserted.
size_type size( ) const;	Returns the number of elements currently in the list.

Table 24-4.   *Several Commonly Used* ***map*** *Member Functions* (continued)

Key/value pairs are stored in a map as objects of type **pair**, which has this template specification.

```
template <class Ktype, class Vtype> struct pair {
  typedef Ktype first_type; // type of key
  typedef Vtype second_type; // type of value
  Ktype first; // contains the key
  Vtype second; // contains the value

  // constructors
  pair();
  pair(const Ktype &k, const Vtype &v);
  template<class A, class B> pair(const<A, B> &ob);
}
```

As the comments suggest, the value in **first** contains the key and the value in **second** contains the value associated with that key.

You can construct a pair using either one of **pair**'s constructors or by using **make_pair( )**, which constructs a **pair** object based upon the types of the data used as parameters. **make_pair( )** is a generic function that has this prototype.

template <class *Ktype*, class *Vtype*>
    pair<*Ktype*, *Vtype*> make_pair(const *Ktype* &k, const *Vtype* &v);

As you can see, it returns a pair object consisting of values of the types specified by *Ktype* and *Vtype*. The advantage of **make_pair( )** is that the types of the objects being stored are determined automatically by the compiler rather than being explicitly specified by you.

The following program illustrates the basics of using a map. It stores key/value pairs that show the mapping between the uppercase letters and their ASCII character codes. Thus, the key is a character and the value is an integer. The key/value pairs stored are

A   65
B   66
C   67

and so on. Once the pairs have been stored, you are prompted for a key (i.e., a letter between A and Z), and the ASCII code for that letter is displayed.

```cpp
// A simple map demonstration.
#include <iostream>
#include <map>
using namespace std;

int main()
{
  map<char, int> m;
  int i;

  // put pairs into map
  for(i=0; i<26; i++) {
    m.insert(pair<char, int>('A'+i, 65+i));
  }

  char ch;
  cout << "Enter key: ";
  cin >> ch;

  map<char, int>::iterator p;

  // find value given key
  p = m.find(ch);
  if(p != m.end())
    cout << "Its ASCII value is  " << p->second;
  else
    cout << "Key not in map.\n";
```

```
    return 0;
}
```

Notice the use of the **pair** template class to construct the key/value pairs. The data types specified by **pair** must match those of the **map** into which the pairs are being inserted.

Once the map has been initialized with keys and values, you can search for a value given its key by using the **find( )** function. **find( )** returns an iterator to the matching element or to the end of the map if the key is not found. When a match is found, the value associated with the key is contained in the **second** member of **pair**.

In the preceding example, key/value pairs were constructed explicitly, using **pair<char, int>**. While there is nothing wrong with this approach, it is often easier to use **make_pair( )**, which constructs a pair object based upon the types of the data used as parameters. For example, assuming the previous program, this line of code will also insert key/value pairs into **m**.

```
    m.insert(make_pair((char)('A'+i), 65+i));
```

Here, the cast to **char** is needed to override the automatic conversion to **int** when **i** is added to 'A.' Otherwise, the type determination is automatic.

Storing Class Objects in a Map

As with all of the containers, you can use a map to store objects of types that you create. For example, the next program creates a simple phone directory. That is, it creates a map of names with their numbers. To do this, it creates two classes called **name** and **number**. Since a map maintains a sorted list of keys, the program also defines the < operator for objects of type **name**. In general, you must define the < operator for any classes that you will use as the key. (Some compilers may require that additional comparison operators be defined.)

```
// Use a map to create a phone directory.
#include <iostream>
#include <map>
#include <cstring>
using namespace std;

class name {
  char str[40];
public:
  name() { strcpy(str, ""); }
```

```
    name(char *s) { strcpy(str, s); }
    char *get() { return str; }

};

// Must define less than relative to name objects.
bool operator<(name a, name b)
{
    return strcmp(a.get(), b.get()) < 0;
}

class phoneNum {
  char str[80];
public:
  phoneNum() { strcmp(str, ""); }
  phoneNum(char *s) { strcpy(str, s); }
  char *get() { return str; }
};


int main()
{
  map<name, phoneNum> directory;

 // put names and numbers into map
  directory.insert(pair<name, phoneNum>(name("Tom"),
                    phoneNum("555-4533")));
  directory.insert(pair<name, phoneNum>(name("Chris"),
                    phoneNum("555-9678")));
  directory.insert(pair<name, phoneNum>(name("John"),
               phoneNum("555-8195")));
  directory.insert(pair<name, phoneNum>(name("Rachel"),
                    phoneNum("555-0809")));

  // given a name, find number
  char str[80];
  cout << "Enter name: ";
  cin >> str;

  map<name, phoneNum>::iterator p;

  p = directory.find(name(str));
```

C++

```
   if(p != directory.end())
     cout << "Phone number: " <<  p->second.get();
   else
     cout << "Name not in directory.\n";

   return 0;
}
```

Here is a sample run:

```
Enter name: Rachel
Phone number: 555-0809.
```

In the program, each entry in the map is a character array that holds a null- terminated string. Later in this chapter, you will see an easier way to write this program that uses the standard **string** type.

Algorithms

As explained, algorithms act on containers. Although each container provides support for its own basic operations, the standard algorithms provide more extended or complex actions. They also allow you to work with two different types of containers at the same time. To have access to the STL algorithms, you must include **<algorithm>** in your program.

The STL defines a large number of algorithms, which are summarized in Table 24-5. All of the algorithms are template functions. This means that they can be applied to any type of container. All of the algorithms in the STL are covered in Part Four. The following sections demonstrate a representative sample.

Counting

One of the most basic operations that you can perform on a sequence is to count its contents. To do this, you can use either **count( )** or **count_if( )**. Their general forms are shown here:

> template <class InIter, class T>
>   ptrdiff_t count(InIter *start*, InIter *end*, const T &*val*);
> template <class InIter, class UnPred>
>   ptrdiff_t count_if(InIter *start*, InIter *end*, UnPred *pfn*);

The type **ptrdiff_t** is defined as some form of integer.

Algorithm	Purpose
adjacent_find	Searches for adjacent matching elements within a sequence and returns an iterator to the first match.
binary_search	Performs a binary search on an ordered sequence.
copy	Copies a sequence.
copy_backward	Same as **copy( )** except that it moves the elements from the end of the sequence first.
count	Returns the number of elements in the sequence.
count_if	Returns the number of elements in the sequence that satisfy some predicate.
equal	Determines if two ranges are the same.
equal_range	Returns a range in which an element can be inserted into a sequence without disrupting the ordering of the sequence.
fill and fill_n	Fills a range with the specified value.
find	Searches a range for a value and returns an iterator to the first occurrence of the element.
find_end	Searches a range for a subsequence. It returns an iterator to the end of the subsequence within the range.
find_first_of	Finds the first element within a sequence that matches an element within a range.
find_if	Searches a range for an element for which a user-defined unary predicate returns true.
for_each	Applies a function to a range of elements.
generate and generate_n	Assign elements in a range the values returned by a generator function.
includes	Determines if one sequence includes all of the elements in another sequence.
inplace_merge	Merges a range with another range. Both ranges must be sorted in increasing order. The resulting sequence is sorted.
iter_swap	Exchanges the values pointed to by its two iterator arguments.
lexicographical_compare	Alphabetically compares one sequence with another.

Table 24-5.   *The STL Algorithms*

C++

Algorithm	Purpose
lower_bound	Finds the first point in the sequence that is not less than a specified value.
make_heap	Constructs a heap from a sequence.
max	Returns the maximum of two values.
max_element	Returns an iterator to the maximum element within a range.
merge	Merges two ordered sequences, placing the result into a third sequence.
min	Returns the minimum of two values.
min_element	Returns an iterator to the minimum element within a range.
mismatch	Finds first mismatch between the elements in two sequences. Iterators to the two elements are returned.
next_permutation	Constructs next permutation of a sequence.
nth_element	Arranges a sequence such that all elements less than a specified element E come before that element and all elements greater than E come after it.
partial_sort	Sorts a range.
partial_sort_copy	Sorts a range and then copies as many elements as will fit into a resulting sequence.
partition	Arranges a sequence such that all elements for which a predicate returns true come before those for which the predicate returns false.
pop_heap	Exchanges the first and last −1 elements and then rebuilds the heap.
prev_permutation	Constructs previous permutation of a sequence.
push_heap	Pushes an element onto the end of a heap.
random_shuffle	Randomizes a sequence.
remove, remove_if, remove_copy, and remove_copy_if	Removes elements from a specified range.
replace, replace_copy, replace_if, and replace_copy_if	Replaces elements within a range.

Table 24-5. *The STL Algorithms* (continued)

Algorithm	Purpose
reverse and reverse_copy	Reverses the order of a range.
rotate and rotate_copy	Left-rotates the elements in a range.
search	Searches for subsequence within a sequence.
search_n	Searches for a sequence of a specified number of similar elements.
set_difference	Produces a sequence that contains the difference between two ordered sets.
set_intersection	Produces a sequence that contains the intersection of the two ordered sets.
set_symmetric_difference	Produces a sequence that contains the symmetric difference between the two ordered sets.
set_union	Produces a sequence that contains the union of the two ordered sets.
sort	Sorts a range.
sort_heap	Sorts a heap within a specified range.
stable_partition	Arranges a sequence such that all elements for which a predicate returns true come before those for which the predicate returns false. The partitioning is stable. This means that the relative ordering of the sequence is preserved.
stable_sort	Sorts a range. The sort is stable. This means that equal elements are not rearranged.
swap	Exchanges two values.
swap_ranges	Exchanges elements in a range.
transform	Applies a function to a range of elements and stores the outcome in a new sequence.
unique and unique_copy	Eliminates duplicate elements from a range.
upper_bound	Finds the last point in a sequence that is not greater than some value.

Table 24-5. *The STL Algorithms* (continued)

C++

The **count( )** algorithm returns the number of elements in the sequence beginning at *start* and ending at *end* that match *val*. The **count_if( )** algorithm returns the number of elements in the sequence beginning at *start* and ending at *end* for which the unary predicate *pfn* returns true.

The following program demonstrates **count( )**.

```
// Demonstrate count().
#include <iostream>
#include <vector>
#include <cstdlib>
#include <algorithm>
using namespace std;

int main()
{
  vector<bool> v;
  unsigned int i;

  for(i=0; i < 10; i++) {
   if(rand() % 2) v.push_back(true);
   else v.push_back(false);
  }

  cout << "Sequence:\n";
  for(i=0; i<v.size(); i++)
    cout << boolalpha << v[i] << " ";
  cout << endl;

  i = count(v.begin(), v.end(), true);
  cout << i << " elements are true.\n";

  return 0;
}
```

This program displays the following output:

```
Sequence:
true true false false true false false false false false
3 elements are true.
```

The program begins by creating a vector comprised of randomly generated true and false values. Next, **count( )** is used to count the number of **true** values.

This next program demonstrates **count_if( )**. It creates a vector containing the numbers 1 through 19. It then counts those that are evenly divisible by 3. To do this, it creates a unary predicate called **dividesBy3( )**, which returns **true** if its argument is evenly divisible by 3.

```cpp
// Demonstrate count_if().
#include <iostream>
#include <vector>
#include <algorithm>
using namespace std;

/* This is a unary predicate that determines
   if number is divisible by 3. */
bool dividesBy3(int i)
{
  if((i%3) == 0) return true;

  return false;
}

int main()
{
  vector<int> v;
  int i;

  for(i=1; i < 20; i++) v.push_back(i);

  cout << "Sequence:\n";
  for(i=0; i<v.size(); i++)
    cout << v[i] << " ";
  cout << endl;

  i = count_if(v.begin(), v.end(), dividesBy3);
  cout << i << " numbers are divisible by 3.\n";

  return 0;
}
```

This program produces the following output.

```
Sequence:
1 2 3 4 5 6 7 8 9 10 11 12 13 14 15 16 17 18 19
6 numbers are divisible by 3.
```

Notice how the unary predicate **dividesBy3( )** is coded. All unary predicates receive as a parameter an object that is of the same type as that stored in the container upon which the predicate is operating. The predicate must then return a **true** or **false** result based upon this object.

Removing and Replacing Elements

Sometimes it is useful to generate a new sequence that consists of only certain items from an original sequence. One algorithm that does this is **remove_copy( )**. Its general form is shown here:

> template <class InIter, class OutIter, class T>
> OutIter remove_copy(InIter *start*, InIter *end*,
>   OutIter *result*, const T &*val*);

The **remove_copy( )** algorithm copies elements from the specified range, removing those that are equal to *val*. It puts the result into the sequence pointed to by *result* and returns an iterator to the end of the result. The output container must be large enough to hold the result.

To replace one element in a sequence with another when a copy is made, use **replace_copy( )**. Its general form is shown here:

> template <class InIter, class OutIter, class T>
> OutIter replace_copy(InIter *start*, InIter *end*,
>   OutIter *result*, const T &*old*, const T &*new*);

The **replace_copy( )** algorithm copies elements from the specified range, replacing elements equal to *old* with *new*. It puts the result into the sequence pointed to by *result* and returns an iterator to the end of the result. The output container must be large enough to hold the result.

The following program demonstrates **remove_copy( )** and **replace_copy( )**. It creates a sequence of characters. It then removes all of the spaces from the sequence. Next, it replaces all spaces with colons.

```
// Demonstrate remove_copy and replace_copy.
#include <iostream>
#include <vector>
#include <algorithm>
```

```
using namespace std;

int main()
{
  char str[] = "The STL is power programming.";
  vector<char> v, v2(30);
  unsigned int i;

  for(i=0; str[i]; i++) v.push_back(str[i]);

  // **** demonstrate remove_copy ****
  cout << "Input sequence:\n";
  for(i=0; i<v.size(); i++) cout << v[i];
  cout << endl;

  // remove all spaces
  remove_copy(v.begin(), v.end(), v2.begin(), ' ');

  cout << "Result after removing spaces:\n";
  for(i=0; i<v2.size(); i++) cout << v2[i];
  cout << endl << endl;

  // **** now, demonstrate replace_copy ****
  cout << "Input sequence:\n";
  for(i=0; i<v.size(); i++) cout << v[i];
  cout << endl;

  // replace spaces with colons
  replace_copy(v.begin(), v.end(), v2.begin(), ' ', ':');


  cout << "Result after replacing spaces with colons:\n";
  for(i=0; i<v2.size(); i++) cout << v2[i];
  cout << endl << endl;

  return 0;
}
```

The output produced by this program is shown here.

```
Input sequence:
The STL is power programming.
Result after removing spaces:
TheSTLispowerprogramming.

Input sequence:
The STL is power programming.
Result after replacing spaces with colons:
The:STL:is:power:programming.
```

Reversing a Sequence

An often useful algorithm is **reverse( )**, which reverses a sequence. Its general form is

template <class BiIter> void reverse(BiIter *start*, BiIter *end*);

The **reverse( )** algorithm reverses the order of the range specified by *start* and *end*.
The following program demonstrates **reverse( )**.

```cpp
// Demonstrate reverse.
#include <iostream>
#include <vector>
#include <algorithm>
using namespace std;

int main()
{
  vector<int> v;
  unsigned int i;

  for(i=0; i<10; i++) v.push_back(i);

  cout << "Initial: ";
  for(i=0; i<v.size(); i++) cout << v[i] << " ";
  cout << endl;

  reverse(v.begin(), v.end());

  cout << "Reversed: ";
  for(i=0; i<v.size(); i++) cout << v[i] << " ";

  return 0;
}
```

The output from this program is shown here:

```
Initial:  0 1 2 3 4 5 6 7 8 9
Reversed: 9 8 7 6 5 4 3 2 1 0
```

Transforming a Sequence

One of the more interesting algorithms is **transform( )** because it modifies each element in a range according to a function that you provide. The **transform( )** algorithm has these two general forms:

template <class InIter, class OutIter, class Func)
    OutIter transform(InIter *start*, InIter *end*, OutIter *result*, Func *unaryfunc*);
template <class InIter1, class InIter2, class OutIter, class Func)
    OutIter transform(InIter1 *start1*, InIter1 *end1*, InIter2 *start2*,
                    OutIter *result*, Func *binaryfunc*);

The **transform( )** algorithm applies a function to a range of elements and stores the outcome in *result*. In the first form, the range is specified by *start* and *end*. The function to be applied is specified *unaryfunc*. This function receives the value of an element in its parameter, and it must return its transformation. In the second form, the transformation is applied using a binary operator function that receives the value of an element from the sequence to be transformed in its first parameter and an element from the second sequence as its second parameter. Both versions return an iterator to the end of the resulting sequence.

The following program uses a simple transformation function called **reciprocal( )** to transform the contents of a list of numbers into their reciprocals. Notice that the resulting sequence is stored in the same list that provided the original sequence.

```cpp
// An example of the transform algorithm.
#include <iostream>
#include <list>
#include <algorithm>
using namespace std;

// A simple transformation function.
double reciprocal(double i) {
  return 1.0/i; // return reciprocal
}

int main()
```

```
{
    list<double> vals;
    int i;

    // put values into list
    for(i=1; i<10; i++) vals.push_back((double)i);

    cout << "Original contents of vals:\n";
    list<double>::iterator p = vals.begin();
    while(p != vals.end()) {
      cout << *p << " ";
      p++;
    }

    cout << endl;

    // transform vals
    p = transform(vals.begin(), vals.end(),
                  vals.begin(), reciprocal);

    cout << "Transformed contents of vals:\n";
    p = vals.begin();
    while(p != vals.end()) {
      cout << *p << " ";
      p++;
    }

    return 0;
}
```

The output produced by the program is shown here:

```
Original contents of vals:
1 2 3 4 5 6 7 8 9
Transformed contents of vals:
1 0.5 0.333333 0.25 0.2 0.166667 0.142857 0.125 0.111111
```

As you can see, each element in **vals** has been transformed into its reciprocal.

Using Function Objects

As explained at the start of this chapter, the STL supports (and extensively utilizes) function objects. Recall that function objects are simply classes that define **operator( )**. The STL provides many built-in function objects, such as **less**, **minus**, etc. It also allows you to define your own function objects. Frankly, it is beyond the scope of this book to fully describe all of the issues surrounding the creation and use of function objects. Fortunately, as the preceding examples have shown, you can make significant use of the STL without ever creating a function object. However, since function objects are a main ingredient of the STL, it is important to have a general understanding.

Unary and Binary Function Objects

Just as there are unary and binary predicates, there are unary and binary function objects. A unary function object requires one argument; a binary function object requires two. You must use the type of object required. For example, if an algorithm is expecting a binary function object, you must pass it a binary function object.

Using the Built-in Function Objects

The STL provides a rich assortment of built-in function objects. The binary function objects are shown here:

plus	minus	multiplies	divides	modulus
equal_to	not_equal_to	greater	greater_equal	less
less_equal	logical_and	logical_or		

Here are the unary function objects:

logical_not   negate

The function objects perform the operations specified by their names. The only one that may not be self-evident is **negate( )**, which reverses the sign of its argument.

The built-in function objects are template classes that overload **operator( )**, which returns the result of the specified operation on whatever type of data you select. For example, to invoke the binary function object **plus( )** for **float** data, use this syntax:

```
plus<float>()
```

The built-in function objects use the header **<functional>**.

Let's begin with a simple example. The following program uses the **transform( )** algorithm (described in the preceding section) and the **negate( )** function object to reverse the sign of a list of values.

```cpp
// Use a unary function object.
#include <iostream>
#include <list>
#include <functional>
#include <algorithm>
using namespace std;

int main()
{
  list<double> vals;
  int i;

  // put values into list
  for(i=1; i<10; i++) vals.push_back((double)i);

  cout << "Original contents of vals:\n";
  list<double>::iterator p = vals.begin();
  while(p != vals.end()) {
    cout << *p << " ";
    p++;
  }
  cout << endl;

  // use the negate function object
  p = transform(vals.begin(), vals.end(),
              vals.begin(),
              negate<double>()); // call function object

  cout << "Negated contents of vals:\n";
  p = vals.begin();
  while(p != vals.end()) {
    cout << *p << " ";
    p++;
  }

  return 0;
}
```

This program produces the following output:

```
Original contents of vals:
1 2 3 4 5 6 7 8 9
Negated contents of vals:
-1 -2 -3 -4 -5 -6 -7 -8 -9
```

In the program, notice how **negate( )** is invoked. Since **vals** is a list of **double** values, **negate( )** is called using **negate<double>( )**. The **transform( )** algorithm automatically calls **negate( )** for each element in the sequence. Thus, the single parameter to **negate( )** receives as its argument an element from the sequence.

The next program demonstrates the use of the binary function object **divides( )**. It creates two lists of double values and has one divide the other. This program uses the binary form of the **transform( )** algorithm.

```cpp
// Use a binary function object.
#include <iostream>
#include <list>
#include <functional>
#include <algorithm>
using namespace std;

int main()
{
  list<double> vals;
  list<double> divisors;
  int i;

  // put values into list
  for(i=10; i<100; i+=10) vals.push_back((double)i);
  for(i=1; i<10; i++) divisors.push_back(3.0);

  cout << "Original contents of vals:\n";
  list<double>::iterator p = vals.begin();
  while(p != vals.end()) {
    cout << *p << " ";
    p++;
  }

  cout << endl;

  // transform vals
```

```
    p = transform(vals.begin(), vals.end(),
              divisors.begin(), vals.begin(),
              divides<double>()); // call function object

  cout << "Divided contents of vals:\n";
  p = vals.begin();
  while(p != vals.end()) {
    cout << *p << " ";
    p++;
  }

  return 0;
}
```

The output from this program is shown here:

```
Original contents of vals:
10 20 30 40 50 60 70 80 90
Divided contents of vals:
3.33333 6.66667 10 13.3333 16.6667 20 23.3333 26.6667 30
```

In this case, the binary function object **divides( )** divides the elements from the first sequence by their corresponding elements from the second sequence. Thus, **divides( )** receives arguments in this order:

divides(*first*, *second*)

This order can be generalized. Whenever a binary function object is used, its arguments are ordered *first*, *second*.

Creating a Function Object

In addition to using the built-in function objects, you can create your own. To do so, you will simply create a class that overloads the **operator( )** function. However, for the greatest flexibility, you will want to use one of the following classes defined by the STL as a base class for your function objects.

```
template <class Argument, class Result> struct unary_function {
  typedef Argument argument_type;
  typedef Result result_type;
};
```

```
template <class Argument1, class Argument2, class Result>
struct binary_function {
  typedef Argument1 first_argument_type;
  typedef Argument2 second_argument_type;
  typedef Result result_type;
};
```

These template classes provide concrete type names for the generic data types used by the function object. Although they are technically a convenience, they are almost always used when creating function objects.

The following program demonstrates a custom function object. It converts the **reciprocal( )** function (used to demonstrate the **transform( )** algorithm earlier) into a function object.

```
// Create a reciprocal function object.
#include <iostream>
#include <list>
#include <functional>
#include <algorithm>
using namespace std;

// A simple function object.
class reciprocal: unary_function<double, double> {
public:
  result_type operator()(argument_type i)
  {
    return (result_type) 1.0/i; // return reciprocal
  }
};

int main()
{
  list<double> vals;
  int i;

  // put values into list
  for(i=1; i<10; i++) vals.push_back((double)i);

  cout << "Original contents of vals:\n";
  list<double>::iterator p = vals.begin();
  while(p != vals.end()) {
```

```
      cout << *p << " ";
      p++;
    }
    cout << endl;

    // use reciprocal function object
    p = transform(vals.begin(), vals.end(),
                  vals.begin(),
                  reciprocal()); // call function object

    cout << "Transformed contents of vals:\n";
    p = vals.begin();
    while(p != vals.end()) {
      cout << *p << " ";
      p++;
    }

    return 0;
}
```

Notice two important aspects of **reciprocal( )**. First, it inherits the base class **unary_function**. This gives it access to the **argument_type** and **result_type** types. Second, it defines **operator( )** such that it returns the reciprocal of its argument. In general, to create a function object, simply inherit the proper base class and overload **operator( )** as required. It really is that easy.

Using Binders

When using a binary function object, it is possible to bind a value to one of the arguments. This can be useful in many situations. For example, you may wish to remove all elements from a sequence that are greater than some value, such as 8. To do this, you need some way to bind 8 to the right-hand operand of the function object **greater( )**. That is, you want **greater( )** to perform the comparison

val > 8

for each element of the sequence. The STL provides a mechanism, called *binders*, that accomplishes this.

There are two binders: **bind2nd( )** and **bind1st( )**. They take these general forms:

bind1st(*binfunc_obj, value*)
bind2nd(*binfunc_obj, value*)

Here, *binfunc_obj* is a binary function object. **bind1st( )** returns a unary function object that has *binfunc_obj*'s left-hand operand bound to *value*. **bind2nd( )** returns a unary function object that has *binfunc_obj*'s right-hand operand bound to *value*. The **bind2nd( )** binder is by far the most commonly used. In either case, the outcome of a binder is a unary function object that is bound to the value specified.

To demonstrate the use of a binder, we will use the **remove_if( )** algorithm. It removes elements from a sequence based upon the outcome of a predicate. It has this prototype:

```
template <class ForIter, class UnPred>
    ForIter remove_if(ForIter start, ForIter end, UnPred func);
```

The algorithm removes elements from the sequence defined by *start* and *end* if the unary predicate defined by *func* is true. The algorithm returns a pointer to the new end of the sequence which reflects the deletion of the elements.

The following program removes all values from a sequence that are greater than the value 8. Since the predicate required by **remove_if( )** is unary, we cannot simply use the **greater( )** function object as-is because **greater( )** is a binary object. Instead, we must bind the value 8 to the second argument of **greater( )** using the **bind2nd( )** binder, as shown in the program.

```
// Demonstrate bind2nd().
#include <iostream>
#include <list>
#include <functional>
#include <algorithm>
using namespace std;

int main()
{
  list<int> lst;
  list<int>::iterator p, endp;

  int i;

  for(i=1; i < 20; i++) lst.push_back(i);

  cout << "Original sequence:\n";
  p = lst.begin();
  while(p != lst.end()) {
    cout << *p << " ";
    p++;
```

```
   }
   cout << endl;

   endp = remove_if(lst.begin(), lst.end(),
                    bind2nd(greater<int>(), 8));

   cout << "Resulting sequence:\n";
   p = lst.begin();
   while(p != endp) {
     cout << *p << " ";
     p++;
   }

   return 0;
 }
```

The output produced by the program is shown here:

```
Original sequence:
1 2 3 4 5 6 7 8 9 10 11 12 13 14 15 16 17 18 19
Resulting sequence:
1 2 3 4 5 6 7 8
```

You might want to experiment with this program, trying different function objects and binding different values. As you will discover, binders expand the power of the STL in very significant ways.

One last point: There is an object related to a binder called a *negator*. The negators are **not1( )** and **not2( )**. They return the negation (i.e., the complement of) whatever predicate they modify. They have these general forms:

not1(*unary_predicate*)
not2(*binary_predicate*)

For example, if you substitute the line

```
   endp = remove_if(lst.begin(), lst.end(),
                    not1(bind2nd(greater<int>(), 8)));
```

into the preceding program, it will remove all elements from **lst** that are not greater than 8.

The string Class

As you know, C++ does not support a built-in string type per se. It does, however, provide for two ways of handling strings. First, you may use the traditional, null-terminated character array with which you are already familiar. This is sometimes referred to as a *C string*. The second way is as a class object of type **string**; this is the approach examined here.

Actually, the **string** class is a specialization of a more general template class called **basic_string**. In fact, there are two specializations of **basic_string**: **string**, which supports 8-bit character strings, and **wstring**, which supports wide-character strings. Since 8-bit characters are by far the most commonly used in normal programming, **string** is the version of **basic_string** examined here.

Before looking at the **string** class, it is important to understand why it is part of the C++ library. Standard classes have not been casually added to C++. In fact, a significant amount of thought and debate has accompanied each new addition. Given that C++ already contains some support for strings as null-terminated character arrays, it may at first seem that the inclusion of the **string** class is an exception to this rule. However, this is actually far from the truth. Here is why: Null-terminated strings cannot be manipulated by any of the standard C++ operators. Nor can they take part in normal C++ expressions. For example, consider this fragment:

```
char s1[80], s2[80], s3[80];

s1 = "Alpha"; // can't do
s2 = "Beta"; // can't do
s3 = s1 + s2; // error, not allowed
```

As the comments show, in C++ it is not possible to use the assignment operator to give a character array a new value (except during initialization), nor is it possible to use the + operator to concatenate two strings. These operations must be written using library functions, as shown here:

```
strcpy(s1, "Alpha");
strcpy(s2, "Beta");
strcpy(s3, s1);
strcat(s3, s2);
```

Since null-terminated character arrays are not technically data types in their own right, the C++ operators cannot be applied to them. This makes even the most rudimentary string operations clumsy. More than anything else, it is the inability to operate on null-terminated strings using the standard C++ operators that has driven the development of a standard string class. Remember, when you define a class in C++, you are defining a new data type that can be fully integrated into the C++ environment. This, of course, means that the operators can be overloaded relative to the new class. Therefore, by adding a standard string class, it becomes possible to manage strings in the same way as any other type of data: through the use of operators.

There is, however, one other reason for the standard string class: safety. In the hands of an inexperienced or careless programmer, it is very easy to overrun the end of an array that holds a null-terminated string. For example, consider the standard string copy function **strcpy( )**. This function contains no provision for checking the boundary of the target array. If the source array contains more characters than the target array can hold, then a program error or system crash is possible (likely). As you will see, the standard **string** class prevents such errors.

In the final analysis, there are three reasons for the inclusion of the standard **string** class: consistency (a string now defines a data type), convenience (you may use the standard C++ operators), and safety (array boundaries will not be overrun). Keep in mind that there is no reason that you should abandon normal, null-terminated strings altogether. They are still the most efficient way in which to implement strings. However, when speed is not an overriding concern, using the new **string** class gives you access to a safe and fully integrated way to manage strings.

Although not traditionally thought of as part of the STL, **string** is another container class defined by C++. This means that it supports the algorithms described in the previous section. However, strings have additional capabilities. To have access to the **string** class, you must include **<string>** in your program.

The **string** class is very large, with many constructors and member functions. Also, many member functions have multiple overloaded forms. For this reason, it is not possible to look at the entire contents of **string** in this chapter. Instead, we will examine several of its most commonly used features. Once you have a general understanding of how **string** works, you can easily explore the rest of it on your own.

The **string** class supports several constructors. The prototypes for three of its most commonly used ones are shown here:

```
string( );
string(const char *str);
string(const string &str);
```

The first form creates an empty **string** object. The second creates a **string** object from the null-terminated string pointed to by *str*. This form provides a conversion from null-terminated strings to **string** objects. The third form creates a **string** from another **string**.

A number of operators that apply to strings are defined for **string** objects, including:

Operator	Meaning
=	Assignment
+	Concatenation
+=	Concatenation assignment
==	Equality
!=	Inequality
<	Less than
<=	Less than or equal
>	Greater than
>=	Greater than or equal
[ ]	Subscripting
<<	Output
>>	Input

These operators allow the use of **string** objects in normal expressions and eliminate the need for calls to functions such as **strcpy( )** or **strcat( )**, for example. In general, you can mix **string** objects with normal, null-terminated strings in expressions. For example, a **string** object can be assigned a null-terminated string.

The + operator can be used to concatenate a string object with another string object or a string object with a C-style string. That is, the following variations are supported:

string + string
string + C-string
C-string + string

The + operator can also be used to concatenate a character onto the end of a string.

The **string** class defines the constant **npos**, which is −1. This constant represents the length of the longest possible string.

The C++ string classes make string handling extraordinarily easy. For example, using **string** objects you can use the assignment operator to assign a quoted string to a **string**, the + operator to concatenate strings, and the comparison operators to compare strings. The following program illustrates these operations.

```cpp
// A short string demonstration.
#include <iostream>
#include <string>
using namespace std;

int main()
{
  string str1("Alpha");
  string str2("Beta");
  string str3("Omega");
  string str4;

  // assign a string
  str4 = str1;
  cout << str1 << "\n" << str3 << "\n";

  // concatenate two strings
  str4 = str1 + str2;
  cout << str4 << "\n";

  // concatenate a string with a C-string
  str4 = str1 + " to " + str3;
  cout << str4 << "\n";

  // compare strings
  if(str3 > str1) cout << "str3 > str1\n";
  if(str3 == str1+str2)
    cout << "str3 == str1+str2\n";

  /* A string object can also be
     assigned a normal string. */
  str1 = "This is a null-terminated string.\n";
  cout << str1;

  // create a string object using another string object
  string str5(str1);
  cout << str5;

  // input a string
  cout << "Enter a string: ";
  cin >> str5;
  cout << str5;
```

```
    return 0;
}
```

This program produces the following output:

```
Alpha
Omega
AlphaBeta
Alpha to Omega
str3 > str1
This is a null-terminated string.
This is a null-terminated string.
Enter a string: STL
STL
```

Notice the ease with which the string handling is accomplished. For example, the + is used to concatenate strings and the > is used to compare two strings. To accomplish these operations using C-style, null-terminated strings, less convenient calls to the **strcat( )** and **strcmp( )** functions would be required. Because C++ **string** objects can be freely mixed with C-style null-terminated strings, there is no disadvantage to using them in your program—and there are considerable benefits to be gained.

There is one other thing to notice in the preceding program: the size of the strings is not specified. **string** objects are automatically sized to hold the string that they are given. Thus, when assigning or concatenating strings, the target string will grow as needed to accommodate the size of the new string. It is not possible to overrun the end of the string. This dynamic aspect of **string** objects is one of the ways that they are better than standard null-terminated strings (which *are* subject to boundary overruns).

Some string Member Functions

Although most simple string operations can be accomplished using the string operators, more complex or subtle ones are accomplished using **string** member functions. While **string** has far too many member functions to discuss them all, we will examine several of the most common.

Basic String Manipulations

To assign one string to another, use the **assign( )** function. Two of its forms are shown here.

```
string &assign(const string &strob, size_type start, size_type num);
string &assign(const char *str, size_type num);
```

In the first form, *num* characters from *strob* beginning at the index specified by *start* will be assigned to the invoking object. In the second form, the first *num* characters of the null-terminated string *str* are assigned to the invoking object. In each case, a reference to the invoking object is returned. Of course, it is much easier to use the = to assign one entire string to another. You will need to use the **assign( )** function only when assigning a partial string.

You can append part of one string to another using the **append( )** member function. Two of its forms are shown here:

```
string &append(const string &strob, size_type start, size_type num);
string &append(const char *str, size_type num);
```

Here, *num* characters from *strob* beginning at the index specified by *start* will be appended to the invoking object. In the second form, the first *num* characters of the null-terminated string *str* are appended to the invoking object. In each case, a reference to the invoking object is returned. Of course, it is much easier to use the + to append one entire string to another. You will need to use the **append( )** function only when appending a partial string.

You can insert or replace characters within a string using **insert( )** and **replace( )**. The prototypes for their most common forms are shown here:

```
string &insert(size_type start, const string &strob);
string &insert(size_type start, const string &strob,
                size_type insStart, size_type num);
string &replace(size_type start, size_type num, const string &strob);
string &replace(size_type start, size_type orgNum, const string &strob,
                size_type replaceStart, size_type replaceNum);
```

The first form of **insert( )** inserts *strob* into the invoking string at the index specified by *start*. The second form of **insert( )** function inserts *num* characters from *strob* beginning at *insStart* into the invoking string at the index specified by *start*.

Beginning at *start*, the first form of **replace( )** replaces *num* characters from the invoking string, with *strob*. The second form replaces *orgNum* characters, beginning at s*tart*, in the invoking string with the *replaceNum* characters from the string specified by *strob* beginning at *replaceStart*. In both cases, a reference to the invoking object is returned.

You can remove characters from a string using **erase( )**. One of its forms is shown here:

string &erase(size_type *start* = 0, size_type *num* = npos);

It removes *num* characters from the invoking string beginning at *start*. A reference to the invoking string is returned.

The following program demonstrates the **insert( )**, **erase( )**, and **replace( )** functions.

```
// Demonstrate insert(), erase(), and replace().
#include <iostream>
#include <string>
using namespace std;

int main()
{
  string str1("String handling C++ style.");
  string str2("STL Power");

  cout << "Initial strings:\n";
  cout << "str1: " << str1 << endl;
  cout << "str2: " << str2 << "\n\n";

  // demonstrate insert()
  cout << "Insert str2 into str1:\n";
  str1.insert(6, str2);
  cout << str1 << "\n\n";

  // demonstrate erase()
  cout << "Remove 9 characters from str1:\n";
  str1.erase(6, 9);
  cout << str1 <<"\n\n";

  // demonstrate replace
  cout << "Replace 8 characters in str1 with str2:\n";
  str1.replace(7, 8, str2);
  cout << str1 << endl;

  return 0;
}
```

The output produced by this program is shown here.

```
Initial strings:
str1: String handling C++ style.
str2: STL Power

Insert str2 into str1:
StringSTL Power handling C++ style.

Remove 9 characters from str1:
String handling C++ style.

Replace 8 characters in str1 with str2:
String STL Power C++ style.
```

Searching a String

The **string** class provides several member functions that search a string, including **find( )** and **rfind( )**. Here are the prototypes for the most common versions of these functions:

size_type find(const string &*strob*, size_type *start*=0) const;
size_type rfind(const string &*strob*, size_type *start*=npos) const;

Beginning at *start*, **find( )** searches the invoking string for the first occurrence of the string contained in *strob*. If found, **find( )** returns the index at which the match occurs within the invoking string. If no match is found, then **npos** is returned. **rfind( )** is the opposite of **find( )**. Beginning at *start*, it searches the invoking string in the reverse direction for the first occurrence of the string contained in *strob* (i.e, it finds the last occurrence of *strob* within the invoking string). If found, **rfind( )** returns the index at which the match occurs within the invoking string. If no match is found, **npos** is returned.

Here is a short example that uses **find( )** and **rfind( )**.

```
#include <iostream>
#include <string>
using namespace std;

int main()
{
  int i;
  string s1 =
    "Quick of Mind, Strong of Body, Pure of Heart";
  string s2;
```

```
  i = s1.find("Quick");
  if(i!=string::npos) {
    cout << "Match found at " << i << endl;
    cout << "Remaining string is:\n";
    s2.assign(s1, i, s1.size());
    cout << s2;
  }
  cout << "\n\n";

  i = s1.find("Strong");
  if(i!=string::npos) {
    cout << "Match found at " << i << endl;
    cout << "Remaining string is:\n";
    s2.assign(s1, i, s1.size());
    cout << s2;
  }
  cout << "\n\n";

  i = s1.find("Pure");
  if(i!=string::npos) {
    cout << "Match found at " << i << endl;
    cout << "Remaining string is:\n";
    s2.assign(s1, i, s1.size());
    cout << s2;
  }
  cout << "\n\n";

  // find list "of"
  i = s1.rfind("of");
  if(i!=string::npos) {
    cout << "Match found at " << i << endl;
    cout << "Remaining string is:\n";
    s2.assign(s1, i, s1.size());
    cout << s2;
  }

  return 0;
}
```

The output produced by this program is shown here.

```
Match found at 0
Remaining string is:
Quick of Mind, Strong of Body, Pure of Heart

Match found at 15
Remaining string is:
Strong of Body, Pure of Heart

Match found at 31
Remaining string is:
Pure of Heart

Match found at 36
Remaining string is:
of Heart
```

Comparing Strings

To compare the entire contents of one string object to another, you will normally use the overloaded relational operators described earlier. However, if you want to compare a portion of one string to another, you will need to use the **compare( )** member function, shown here:

    int compare(size_type *start*, size_type *num*, const string &*strob*) const;

Here, *num* characters in *strob*, beginning at *start*, will be compared against the invoking string. If the invoking string is less than *strob*, **compare( )** will return less than zero. If the invoking string is greater than *strob*, it will return greater than zero. If *strob* is equal to the invoking string, **compare( )** will return zero.

Obtaining a Null-Terminated String

Although **string** objects are useful in their own right, there will be times when you will need to obtain a null-terminated character-array version of the string. For example, you might use a **string** object to construct a filename. However, when opening a file, you will need to specify a pointer to a standard, null-terminated string. To solve this problem, the member function **c_str( )** is provided. Its prototype is shown here:

    const char *c_str( ) const;

This function returns a pointer to a null-terminated version of the string contained in the invoking **string** object. The null-terminated string must not be altered. It is also not guaranteed to be valid after any other operations have taken place on the **string** object.

Strings Are Containers

The **string** class meets all of the basic requirements necessary to be a container. Thus, it supports the common container functions, such as **begin( )**, **end( )**, and **size( )**. It also supports iterators. Therefore, a **string** object can also be manipulated by the STL algorithms. Here is a simple example:

```
// Strings as containers.
#include <iostream>
#include <string>
#include <algorithm>
using namespace std;

int main()
{
  string str1("Strings handling is easy in C++");
  string::iterator p;
  unsigned int i;

  // use size()
  for(i=0; i<str1.size(); i++)
    cout << str1[i];
  cout << endl;

  // use iterator
  p = str1.begin();
  while(p != str1.end())
    cout << *p++;
  cout << endl;

  // use the count() algorithm
  i = count(str1.begin(), str1.end(), 'i');
  cout << "There are " << i << " i's in str1\n";

  // use transform() to upper case the string
  transform(str1.begin(), str1.end(), str1.begin(),
            toupper);
  p = str1.begin();
  while(p != str1.end())
    cout << *p++;
  cout << endl;
```

```
    return 0;
}
```

Output from the program is shown here:

```
Strings handling is easy in C++
Strings handling is easy in C++
There are 4 i's in str1
STRINGS HANDLING IS EASY IN C++
```

Putting Strings into Other Containers

Even though **string** is a container, objects of type string are commonly held in other STL containers, such as maps or lists. For example, here is a better way to write the telephone directory program shown earlier. It uses a map of **string** objects, rather than null-terminated strings, to hold the names and telephone numbers.

```cpp
// Use a map of strings to create a phone directory.
#include <iostream>
#include <map>
#include <string>
using namespace std;

int main()
{
  map<string, string> directory;

  directory.insert(pair<string, string>("Tom", "555-4533"));
  directory.insert(pair<string, string>("Chris", "555-9678"));
  directory.insert(pair<string, string>("John", "555-8195"));
  directory.insert(pair<string, string>("Rachel", "555-0809"));

  string s;
  cout << "Enter name: ";
  cin >> s;

  map<string, string>::iterator p;

  p = directory.find(s);
  if(p != directory.end())
    cout << "Phone number: " << p->second;
```

```
    else
      cout << "Name not in directory.\n";

    return 0;
}
```

Final Thoughts on the STL

The STL is an important, integral part of the C++ language. Many programming tasks can (and will) be framed in terms of it. The STL combines power with flexibility, and while its syntax is a bit complex, its ease of use is remarkable. No C++ programmer can afford to neglect the STL because it will play an important role in the way future programs are written.

The
Complete
Reference

Part III

The Standard Function Library

C++ defines two types of libraries. The first is the standard function
library. This library consists of general-purpose, stand-alone functions
that are not part of any class. The function library is inherited from C.
The second library is the object-oriented class library. Part Three of the
book provides a reference to the standard function library. Part Four
describes the class library.

The standard function library is divided into the following categories:

■ I/O
■ String and character handling
■ Mathematical
■ Time, date, and localization
■ Dynamic allocation
■ Miscellaneous
■ Wide-character functions

The last category was added to Standard C in 1995 and was subsequently incorporated into C++. It provides wide-character (**wchar_t**) equivalents to several of the library functions. Frankly, the use of the wide-character library has been very limited, and C++ provides a better way of handling wide-character environments, but it is briefly described in Chapter 31 for completeness.

C99 added some new elements to the C function library. Several of these additions, such as support for complex arithmetic and type-generic macros for the mathematical functions, duplicate functionality already found in C++. Some provide new features that might be incorporated into C++ in the future. In all cases, the library elements added by C99 are incompatible with C++. Thus, the additions made to the Standard C library by C99 are not discussed in this book.

One last point: All compilers supply more functions than are defined by Standard C/C++. These additional functions typically provide for operating-system interfacing and other environment-dependent operations. You will want to check your compiler's documentation.

The
Complete
Reference

Chapter 25

The C-Based
I/O Functions

699

This chapter describes the C-based I/O functions. These functions are also supported by Standard C++. While you will usually want to use C++'s object-oriented I/O system for new code, there is no fundamental reason that you cannot use the C I/O functions in a C++ program when you deem it appropriate. The functions in this chapter were first specified by the ANSI C standard, and they are commonly referred to collectively as the ANSI C I/O system.

The header associated with the C-based I/O functions is called **<cstdio>**. (A C program must use the header file **stdio.h**.) This header defines several macros and types used by the file system. The most important type is **FILE**, which is used to declare a file pointer. Two other types are **size_t** and **fpos_t**. The **size_t** type (usually some form of unsigned integer) defines an object that is capable of holding the size of the largest file allowed by the operating environment. The **fpos_t** type defines an object that can hold all information needed to uniquely specify every position within a file. The most commonly used macro defined by the headers is **EOF**, which is the value that indicates end-of-file.

Many of the I/O functions set the built-in global integer variable **errno** when an error occurs. Your program can check this variable when an error occurs to obtain more information about the error. The values that **errno** may take are implementation dependent.

For an overview of the C-based I/O system, see Chapters 8 and 9 in Part One.

 *This chapter describes the character-based I/O functions. These are the functions that were originally defined for Standard C and C++ and are, by far, the most widely used. In 1995, several wide-character (**wchar_t**) functions were added, and they are briefly described in Chapter 31.*

clearerr

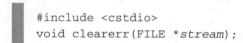

```
#include <cstdio>
void clearerr(FILE *stream);
```

The **clearerr( )** function resets (i.e., sets to zero) the error flag associated with the stream pointed to by *stream*. The end-of-file indicator is also reset.

The error flags for each stream are initially set to zero by a successful call to **fopen( )**.

File errors can occur for a wide variety of reasons, many of which are system dependent. The exact nature of the error can be determined by calling **perror( )**, which displays what error has occurred (see **perror( )**).

Related functions are **feof( )**, **ferror( )**, and **perror( )**.

fclose

```
#include <cstdio>
int fclose(FILE *stream);
```

The **fclose( )** function closes the file associated with *stream* and flushes its buffer. After an **fclose( )**, *stream* is no longer connected with the file, and any automatically allocated buffers are deallocated.

If **fclose( )** is successful, zero is returned; otherwise **EOF** is returned. Trying to close a file that has already been closed is an error. Removing the storage media before closing a file will also generate an error, as will lack of sufficient free disk space.

Related functions are **fopen( )**, **freopen( )**, and **fflush( )**.

feof

```
#include <cstdio>
int feof(FILE *stream);
```

The **feof( )** function checks the file position indicator to determine if the end of the file associated with *stream* has been reached. A nonzero value is returned if the file position indicator is at end-of-file; zero is returned otherwise.

Once the end of the file has been reached, subsequent read operations will return **EOF** until either **rewind( )** is called or the file position indicator is moved using **fseek( )**.

The **feof( )** function is particularly useful when working with binary files because the end-of-file marker is also a valid binary integer. Explicit calls must be made to **feof( )** rather than simply testing the return value of **getc( )**, for example, to determine when the end of a binary file has been reached.

Related functions are **clearerr( )**, **ferror( )**, **perror( )**, **putc( )**, and **getc( )**.

ferror

```
#include <cstdio>
int ferror(FILE *stream);
```

The **ferror( )** function checks for a file error on the given *stream*. A return value of zero indicates that no error has occurred, while a nonzero value means an error.

To determine the exact nature of the error, use the **perror( )** function.
Related functions are **clearerr( )**, **feof( )**, and **perror( )**.

fflush

```
#include <cstdio>
int fflush(FILE *stream);
```

If *stream* is associated with a file opened for writing, a call to **fflush( )** causes the
contents of the output buffer to be physically written to the file. The file remains open.

A return value of zero indicates success; **EOF** indicates that a write error has
occurred.

All buffers are automatically flushed upon normal termination of the program or
when they are full. Also, closing a file flushes its buffer.

Related functions are **fclose( )**, **fopen( )**, **fread( )**, **fwrite( )**, **getc( )**, and **putc( )**.

fgetc

```
#include <cstdio>
int fgetc(FILE *stream);
```

The **fgetc( )** function returns the next character from the input *stream* from the
current position and increments the file position indicator. The character is read as
an **unsigned char** that is converted to an integer.

If the end of the file is reached, **fgetc( )** returns **EOF**. However, since **EOF** is a valid
integer value, when working with binary files you must use **feof( )** to check for the end
of the file. If **fgetc( )** encounters an error, **EOF** is also returned. If working with binary
files, you must use **ferror( )** to check for file errors.

Related functions are **fputc( )**, **getc( )**, **putc( )**, and **fopen( )**.

fgetpos

```
#include <cstdio>
int fgetpos(FILE *stream, fpos_t *position);
```

The **fgetpos( )** function stores the current value of the file position indicator in the object pointed to by *position*. The object pointed to by *position* must be of type **fpos_t**. The value stored there is useful only in a subsequent call to **fsetpos( )**.

If an error occurs, **fgetpos( )** returns nonzero; otherwise it returns zero.

Related functions are **fsetpos( )**, **fseek( )**, and **ftell( )**.

fgets

```
#include <cstdio>
char *fgets(char *str, int num, FILE *stream);
```

The **fgets( )** function reads up to *num*-1 characters from *stream* and places them into the character array pointed to by *str*. Characters are read until either a newline or an **EOF** is received or until the specified limit is reached. After the characters have been read, a null is placed in the array immediately after the last character read. A newline character will be retained and will be part of the array pointed to by *str*.

If successful, **fgets( )** returns *str*; a null pointer is returned upon failure. If a read error occurs, the contents of the array pointed to by *str* are indeterminate. Because a null pointer will be returned when either an error has occurred or when the end of the file is reached, you should use **feof( )** or **ferror( )** to determine what has actually happened.

Related functions are **fputs( )**, **fgetc( )**, **gets( )**, and **puts( )**.

fopen

```
#include <cstdio>
FILE *fopen(const char *fname, const char *mode);
```

The **fopen( )** function opens a file whose name is pointed to by *fname* and returns the stream that is associated with it. The type of operations that will be allowed on the file are defined by the value of *mode*. The legal values for *mode* are shown in Table 25-1. The filename must be a string of characters comprising a valid filename as defined by the operating system and may include a path specification if the environment supports it.

If **fopen( )** is successful in opening the specified file, a **FILE** pointer is returned. If the file cannot be opened, a null pointer is returned.

THE STANDARD FUNCTION LIBRARY

Mode	Meaning
"r"	Open text file for reading.
"w"	Create a text file for writing.
"a"	Append to text file.
"rb"	Open binary file for reading.
"wb"	Create binary file for writing.
"ab"	Append to a binary file.
"r+"	Open text file for read/write.
"w+"	Create text file for read/write.
"a+"	Open text file for read/write.
"rb+" or "r+b"	Open binary file for read/write.
"wb+" or "w+b"	Create binary file for read/write.
"ab+" or "a+b"	Open binary file for read/write.

Table 25-1.   *The Legal Values for the mode Parameter of **fopen( )***

As the table shows, a file may be opened in either text or binary mode. In text mode, some character translations may occur. For example, newlines may be converted into carriage return/linefeed sequences. No such translations occur on binary files.

The correct method of opening a file is illustrated by this code fragment:

```
FILE *fp;

if ((fp = fopen("test", "w"))==NULL) {
  printf("Cannot open file.\n");
  exit(1);
}
```

This method detects any error in opening a file, such as a write-protected or a full disk, before attempting to write to it.

If you use **fopen( )** to open a file for output, any preexisting file by that name will be erased and a new file started. If no file by that name exists, one will be created.

Opening a file for read operations requires that the file exists. If it does not exist, an error will be returned. If you want to add to the end of the file, you must use mode "a." If the file does not exist, it will be created.

When accessing a file opened for read/write operations, you cannot follow an output operation with an input operation without an intervening call to either **fflush( )**, **fseek( )**, **fsetpos( )**, or **rewind( )**. Also, you cannot follow an input operation with an output operation without an intervening call to one of the previously mentioned functions, except when the end of the file is reached during input. That is, output can directly follow input at the end of the file.

Related functions are **fclose( )**, **fread( )**, **fwrite( )**, **putc( )**, and **getc( )**.

fprintf

```
#include <cstdio>
int fprintf(FILE *stream, const char *format, ...);
```

The **fprintf( )** function outputs the values of the arguments that comprise the argument list as specified in the *format* string to the stream pointed to by *stream*. The return value is the number of characters actually printed. If an error occurs, a negative number is returned.

There may be from zero to several arguments, with the maximum number being system dependent.

The operations of the format control string and commands are identical to those in **printf( )**; see **printf( )** for a complete description.

Related functions are **printf( )** and **fscanf( )**.

fputc

```
#include <cstdio>
int fputc(int ch, FILE *stream);
```

The **fputc( )** function writes the character *ch* to the specified stream at the current file position and then advances the file position indicator. Even though *ch* is declared to be an **int** for historical reasons, it is converted by **fputc( )** into an **unsigned char**. Because all character arguments are elevated to integers at the time of the call, you will generally see character values used as arguments. If an integer were used, the high-order byte(s) would simply be discarded.

The value returned by **fputc( )** is the value of the character written. If an error occurs, **EOF** is returned. For files opened for binary operations, an **EOF** may be a valid character, and the function **ferror( )** will need to be used to determine whether an error has actually occurred.

Related functions are **fgetc( )**, **fopen( )**, **fprintf( )**, **fread( )**, and **fwrite( )**.

fputs

```
#include <cstdio>
int fputs(const char *str, FILE *stream);
```

The **fputs( )** function writes the contents of the string pointed to by *str* to the specified stream. The null terminator is not written.

The **fputs( )** function returns nonnegative on success and **EOF** on failure.

If the stream is opened in text mode, certain character translations may take place. This means that there may not be a one-to-one mapping of the string onto the file. However, if the stream is opened in binary mode, no character translations will occur, and a one-to-one mapping between the string and the file will exist.

Related functions are **fgets( )**, **gets( )**, **puts( )**, **fprintf( )**, and **fscanf( )**.

fread

```
#include <cstdio>
size_t fread(void *buf, size_t size, size_t count,
             FILE *stream);
```

The **fread( )** function reads *count* number of objects, each object being *size* bytes in length, from the stream pointed to by *stream* and places them in the array pointed to by *buf*. The file position indicator is advanced by the number of characters read.

The **fread( )** function returns the number of items actually read. If fewer items are read than are requested in the call, either an error has occurred or the end of the file has been reached. You must use **feof( )** or **ferror( )** to determine what has taken place.

If the stream is opened for text operations, certain character translations, such as carriage return/linefeed sequences being transformed into newlines, may occur.

Related functions are **fwrite( )**, **fopen( )**, **fscanf( )**, **fgetc( )**, and **getc( )**.

freopen

```
#include <cstdio>
FILE *freopen(const char *fname, const char *mode,
              FILE *stream);
```

The **freopen( )** function associates an existing stream with a different file. The new file's name is pointed to by *fname*, the access mode is pointed to by *mode*, and the stream to be reassigned is pointed to by *stream*. The string *mode* uses the same format as **fopen( )**; a complete discussion is found in the **fopen( )** description.

When called, **freopen( )** first tries to close a file that may currently be associated with *stream*. However, if the attempt to close the file fails, the **freopen( )** function still continues to open the other file.

The **freopen( )** function returns a pointer to *stream* on success and a null pointer otherwise.

The main use of **freopen( )** is to redirect the system defined streams **stdin**, **stdout**, and **stderr** to some other file.

Related functions are **fopen( )** and **fclose( )**.

fscanf

```
#include <cstdio>
int fscanf(FILE *stream, const char *format, ...);
```

The **fscanf( )** function works exactly like the **scanf( )** function, except that it reads the information from the stream specified by *stream* instead of **stdin**. See **scanf( )** for details.

The **fscanf( )** function returns the number of arguments actually assigned values. This number does not include skipped fields. A return value of **EOF** means that a failure occurred before the first assignment was made.

Related functions are **scanf( )** and **fprintf( )**.

fseek

```
#include <cstdio>
int fseek(FILE *stream, long offset, int origin);
```

The **fseek( )** function sets the file position indicator associated with stream according to the values of *offset* and *origin*. Its purpose is to support random-access I/O operations. The *offset* is the number of bytes from *origin* to seek to. The values for *origin* must be one of these macros (defined in **<cstdio>**).

Name	Meaning
SEEK_SET	Seek from start of file
SEEK_CUR	Seek from current location
SEEK_END	Seek from end of file

A return value of zero means that **fseek( )** succeeded. A nonzero value indicates failure.

You may use **fseek( )** to move the position indicator anywhere in the file, even beyond the end. However, it is an error to attempt to set the position indicator before the beginning of the file.

The **fseek( )** function clears the end-of-file flag associated with the specified stream. Furthermore, it nullifies any prior **ungetc( )** on the same stream (see **ungetc( )**).

Related functions are **ftell( )**, **rewind( )**, **fopen( )**, **fgetpos( )**, and **fsetpos( )**.

fsetpos

```
#include <cstdio>
int fsetpos(FILE *stream, const fpos_t *position);
```

The **fsetpos( )** function moves the file position indicator to the point specified by the object pointed to by *position*. This value must have been previously obtained through a call to **fgetpos( )**. After **fsetpos( )** is executed, the end-of-file indicator is reset. Also, any previous call to **ungetc( )** is nullified.

If **fsetpos( )** fails, it returns nonzero. If it is successful, it returns zero.

Related functions are **fgetpos( )**, **fseek( )**, and **ftell( )**.

ftell

```
#include <cstdio>
long ftell(FILE *stream);
```

The **ftell( )** function returns the current value of the file position indicator for the specified *stream*. In the case of binary streams, the value is the number of bytes the indicator is from the beginning of the file. For text streams, the return value may not be meaningful except as an argument to **fseek( )** because of possible character translations, such as carriage return/linefeeds being substituted for newlines, which affect the apparent size of the file.

The **ftell( )** function returns −1 when an error occurs.

Related functions are **fseek( )** and **fgetpos( )**.

fwrite

```
#include <cstdio>
size_t fwrite(const void *buf, size_t size,
              size_t count, FILE *stream);
```

The **fwrite( )** function writes *count* number of objects, each object being *size* bytes in length, to the stream pointed to by *stream* from the character array pointed to by *buf*. The file position indicator is advanced by the number of characters written.

The **fwrite( )** function returns the number of items actually written, which, if the function is successful, will equal the number requested. If fewer items are written than are requested, an error has occurred.

Related functions are **fread( )**, **fscanf( )**, **getc( )**, and **fgetc( )**.

getc

```
#include <cstdio>
int getc(FILE *stream);
```

The **getc( )** function returns the next character from the input stream and increments the file position indicator. The character is read as an **unsigned char** that is converted to an integer.

If the end of the file is reached, **getc( )** returns **EOF**. However, since **EOF** is a valid integer value, when working with binary files you must use **feof( )** to check for the end-of-file character. If **getc( )** encounters an error, **EOF** is also returned. If working with binary files, you must use **ferror( )** to check for file errors.

The functions **getc( )** and **fgetc( )** are identical, and in most implementations **getc( )** is simply defined as the macro shown here.

```
#define getc(fp) fgetc(fp)
```

This causes the **fgetc( )** function to be substituted for the **getc( )** macro.

Related functions are **fputc( )**, **fgetc( )**, **putc( )**, and **fopen( )**.

getchar

```
#include <cstdio>
int getchar(void);
```

The **getchar( )** function returns the next character from **stdin**. The character is read as an **unsigned char** that is converted to an integer.

If the end of the file is reached, **getchar( )** returns **EOF**. If **getchar( )** encounters an error, **EOF** is also returned.

The **getchar( )** function is often implemented as a macro.

Related functions are **fputc( )**, **fgetc( )**, **putc( )**, and **fopen( )**.

gets

```
#include <cstdio>
char *gets(char *str);
```

The **gets( )** function reads characters from **stdin** and places them into the character array pointed to by *str*. Characters are read until a newline or an **EOF** is received. The newline character is not made part of the string; instead, it is translated into a null to terminate the string.

If successful, **gets( )** returns *str*; a null pointer is returned upon failure. If a read error occurs, the contents of the array pointed to by *str* are indeterminate. Because a null pointer will be returned when either an error has occurred or when the end of the file is reached, you should use **feof( )** or **ferror( )** to determine what has actually happened.

There is no way to limit the number of characters that **gets( )** will read, and it is possible for the array pointed to by *str* to be overrun. Thus, **gets( )** is inherently dangerous.

Related functions are **fputs( )**, **fgetc( )**, **fgets( )**, and **puts( )**.

perror

```
#include <cstdio>
void perror(const char *str);
```

The **perror( )** function maps the value of the global variable **errno** onto a string and writes that string to **stderr**. If the value of *str* is not null, it is written first, followed by a colon, and then the implementation-defined error message.

printf

```
#include <cstdio>
int printf(const char *format, ...);
```

The **printf( )** function writes to **stdout** the arguments that comprise the argument list as specified by the string pointed to by *format*.

The string pointed to by *format* consists of two types of items. The first type is made up of characters that will be printed on the screen. The second type contains format specifiers that define the way the arguments are displayed. A format specifier begins with a percent sign and is followed by the format code. There must be exactly the same number of arguments as there are format specifiers, and the format specifiers and the arguments are matched in order. For example, the following **printf( )** call displays "Hi c 10 there!".

```
printf("Hi %c %d %s", 'c', 10, "there!");
```

If there are insufficient arguments to match the format specifiers, the output is undefined. If there are more arguments than format specifiers, the remaining arguments are discarded. The format specifiers are shown in Table 25-2.

The **printf( )** function returns the number of characters actually printed. A negative return value indicates that an error has taken place.

The format codes may have modifiers that specify the field width, precision, and a left-justification flag. An integer placed between the % sign and the format code acts as a *minimum field-width specifier*. This pads the output with spaces or 0's to ensure that it is at least a certain minimum length. If the string or number is greater than that minimum, it will be printed in full, even if it overruns the minimum. The default padding is done with spaces. If you wish to pad with 0's, place a 0 before the field-width specifier. For example, **%05d** will pad a number of less than five digits with 0's so that its total length is 5.

The exact meaning of the *precision modifier* depends on the format code being modified. To add a precision modifier, place a decimal point followed by the precision after the field-width specifier. For **e**, **E**, and **f** formats, the precision modifier determines

Code	Format
%c	Character
%d	Signed decimal integers
%i	Signed decimal integers
%e	Scientific notation (lowercase e)
%E	Scientific notation (uppercase E)
%f	Decimal floating point
%g	Uses %e or %f, whichever is shorter (if %e, uses lowercase e)
%G	Uses %E or %f, whichever is shorter (if %E, uses uppercase E)
%o	Unsigned octal
%s	String of characters
%u	Unsigned decimal integers
%x	Unsigned hexadecimal (lowercase letters)
%X	Unsigned hexadecimal (uppercase letters)
%p	Displays a pointer
%n	The associated argument is a pointer to an integer into which is placed the number of characters written so far
%%	Prints a % sign

Table 25-2.   *The **printf( )** Format Specifiers*

the number of decimal places printed. For example, **%10.4f** will display a number at least 10 characters wide with four decimal places. When the precision modifier is applied to the **g** or **G** format code, it determines the maximum number of significant digits displayed. When applied to integers, the precision modifier specifies the minimum number of digits that will be displayed. Leading zeros are added, if necessary.

When the precision modifier is applied to strings, the number following the period specifies the maximum field length. For example, **%5.7s** will display a string that will be at least five characters long and will not exceed seven. If the string is longer than the maximum field width, the characters will be truncated off the end.

By default, all output is *right-justified*: if the field width is larger than the data printed, the data will be placed on the right edge of the field. You can force the information to be left-justified by placing a minus sign directly after the %. For example, %–**10.2f** will left-justify a floating-point number with two decimal places in a 10-character field.

There are two format modifiers that allow **printf( )** to display short and long integers. These modifiers may be applied to the **d**, **i**, **o**, **u**, and **x** type specifiers. The **l** modifier tells **printf( )** that a long data type follows. For example, %**ld** means that a long integer is to be displayed. The **h** modifier tells **printf( )** to display a short integer. Therefore, %**hu** indicates that the data is of type short unsigned integer.

If you are using a modern compiler that supports the wide-character features added in 1995, then you may use the **l** modifier with the **c** specifier to indicate a wide-character of type **wchar_t**. You may also use the **l** modifier with the **s** format command to indicate a wide-character string.

An **L** modifier may prefix the floating-point commands of **e**, **f**, and **g** and indicates that a **long double** follows.

The %**n** command causes the number of characters that have been written at the time the %**n** is encountered to be placed in an integer variable whose pointer is specified in the argument list. For example, this code fragment displays the number 14 after the line "This is a test":

```
int i;

printf("This is a test%n", &i);
printf("%d", i);
```

You can apply the **l** or **h** modifer to the **n** specifier to indicate that the corresponding argument points to a long or short integer, respectively.

The **#** has a special meaning when used with some **printf( )** format codes. Preceding a **g**, **G**, **f**, **e**, or **E** code with a **#** ensures that the decimal point will be present, even if there are no decimal digits. If you precede the **x** or **X** format code with a **#**, the hexadecimal number will be printed with a **0x** prefix. If you precede the **o** format with a **#**, the octal value will be printed with a **0** prefix. The **#** cannot be applied to any other format specifiers.

The minimum field-width and precision specifiers may be provided by arguments to **printf( )** instead of by constants. To accomplish this, use an * as a placeholder. When the format string is scanned, **printf( )** will match each * to an argument in the order in which they occur.

Related functions are **scanf( )** and **fprintf( )**.

putc

```
#include <cstdio>
int putc(int ch, FILE *stream);
```

The **putc( )** function writes the character contained in the least significant byte of *ch* to the output stream pointed to by *stream*. Because character arguments are elevated to integer at the time of the call, you may use character values as arguments to **putc( )**.

The **putc( )** function returns the character written on success or **EOF** if an error occurs. If the output stream has been opened in binary mode, **EOF** is a valid value for *ch*. This means that you must use **ferror( )** to determine if an error has occurred.

Related functions are **fgetc( )**, **fputc( )**, **getchar( )**, and **putchar( )**.

putchar

```
#include <cstdio>
int putchar(int ch);
```

The **putchar( )** function writes the character contained in the least significant byte of *ch* to **stdout**. It is functionally equivalent to **putc(ch, stdout)**. Because character arguments are elevated to integer at the time of the call, you may use character values as arguments to **putchar( )**.

The **putchar( )** function returns the character written on success or **EOF** if an error occurs.

A related function is **putc( )**.

puts

```
#include <cstdio>
int puts(const char *str);
```

The **puts( )** function writes the string pointed to by *str* to the standard output device. The null terminator is translated to a newline.

The **puts( )** function returns a nonnegative value if successful and an **EOF** upon failure.

Related functions are **putc( )**, **gets( )**, and **printf( )**.

remove

```
#include <cstdio>
int remove(const char *fname);
```

The **remove( )** function erases the file specified by *fname*. It returns zero if the file was successfully deleted and nonzero if an error occurred.

A related function is **rename( )**.

rename

```
#include <cstdio>
int rename(const char *oldfname, const char *newfname);
```

The **rename( )** function changes the name of the file specified by *oldfname* to *newfname*. The *newfname* must not match any existing directory entry.

The **rename( )** function returns zero if successful and nonzero if an error has occurred.

A related function is **remove( )**.

rewind

```
#include <cstdio>
void rewind(FILE *stream);
```

The **rewind( )** function moves the file position indicator to the start of the specified stream. It also clears the end-of-file and error flags associated with *stream*. It has no return value.

A related function is **fseek( )**.

scanf

```
#include <cstdio>
int scanf(const char *format, ...);
```

THE STANDARD
FUNCTION LIBRARY

The **scanf( )** function is a general-purpose input routine that reads the stream **stdin** and stores the information in the variables pointed to in its argument list. It can read all the built-in data types and automatically convert them into the proper internal format.

The control string pointed to by *format* consists of three classifications of characters:

Format specifiers
White-space characters
Non–white-space characters

The input format specifiers begin with a % sign and tell **scanf( )** what type of data is to be read next. The format specifiers are listed in Table 25-3. For example, **%s** reads a string while **%d** reads an integer. The format string is read left to right and the format specifiers are matched, in order, with the arguments that comprise the argument list.

Code	Meaning
%c	Reads a single character.
%d	Reads a decimal integer.
%i	Reads an integer.
%e	Reads a floating-point number.
%f	Reads a floating-point number.
%g	Reads a floating-point number.
%o	Reads an octal number.
%s	Reads a string.
%x	Reads a hexadecimal number.
%p	Reads a pointer.
%n	Receives an integer value equal to the number of characters read so far.
%u	Reads an unsigned integer.
%[ ]	Scans for a set of characters.
%%	Reads a percent sign.

Table 25-3. *The scanf( ) Format Specifiers*

To read a long integer, put an **l** (*ell*) in front of the format specifier. To read a short integer, put an **h** in front of the format specifier. These modifiers can be used with the **d**, **i**, **o**, **u**, and **x** format codes.

By default, the **f**, **e**, and **g** specifiers instruct **scanf( )** to assign data to a **float**. If you put an **l** (*ell*) in front of one of these specifiers, **scanf( )** assigns the data to a **double**. Using an **L** tells **scanf( )** that the variable receiving the data is a **long double**.

If you are using a modern compiler that supports wide-character features added in 1995, you may use the **l** modifier with the **c** format code to indicate a pointer to a wide character of type **wchar_t**. You may also use the **l** modifier with the **s** format code to indicate a pointer to a wide-character string. The **l** may also be used to modify a scanset to indicate wide characters.

A white-space character in the format string causes **scanf( )** to skip over one or more white-space characters in the input stream. A white-space character is either a space, a tab character, or a newline. In essence, one white-space character in the control string will cause **scanf( )** to read, but not store, any number (including zero) of white-space characters up to the first non–white-space character.

A non–white-space character in the format string causes **scanf( )** to read and discard a matching character. For example, **%d,%d** causes **scanf( )** to first read an integer, then read and discard a comma, and finally read another integer. If the specified character is not found, **scanf( )** will terminate.

All the variables used to receive values through **scanf( )** must be passed by their addresses. This means that all arguments must be pointers.

The input data items must be separated by spaces, tabs, or newlines. Punctuation such as commas, semicolons, and the like do not count as separators. This means that

```
scanf("%d%d", &r, &c);
```

will accept an input of **10 20** but fail with **10,20**.

An * placed after the % and before the format code will read data of the specified type but suppress its assignment. Thus, the command

```
scanf("%d%*c%d", &x, &y);
```

given the input **10/20**, will place the value 10 into **x**, discard the divide sign, and give **y** the value 20.

The format commands can specify a maximum field-length modifier. This is an integer number placed between the % and the format code that limits the number of characters read for any field. For example, if you wish to read no more than 20 characters into **address**, you would write the following.

```
scanf("%20s", address);
```

If the input stream were greater than 20 characters, a subsequent call to input would begin where this call left off. Input for a field may terminate before the maximum field length is reached if a white space is encountered. In this case, **scanf( )** moves on to the next field.

Although spaces, tabs, and newlines are used as field separators, when reading a single character, these are read like any other character. For example, with an input stream of **x y**,

```
scanf("%c%c%c", &a, &b, &c);
```

will return with the character x in **a**, a space in **b** and the character y in **c**.

Beware: Any other characters in the control string—including spaces, tabs, and newlines—will be used to match and discard characters from the input stream. Any character that matches is discarded. For example, given the input stream **10t20**,

```
scanf("%dt%d", &x, &y);
```

will place 10 into **x** and 20 into **y**. The **t** is discarded because of the **t** in the control string.

Another feature of **scanf( )** is called a *scanset*. A scanset defines a set of characters that will be read by **scanf( )** and assigned to the corresponding character array. A scanset is defined by putting the characters you want to scan for inside square brackets. The beginning square bracket must be prefixed by a percent sign. For example, this scanset tells **scanf( )** to read only the characters A, B, and C:

```
%[ABC]
```

When a scanset is used, **scanf( )** continues to read characters and put them into the corresponding character array until a character that is not in the scanset is encountered. The corresponding variable must be a pointer to a character array. Upon return from **scanf( )**, the array will contain a null-terminated string comprised of the characters read.

You can specify an inverted set if the first character in the set is a ^. When the ^ is present, it instructs **scanf( )** to accept any character that *is not* defined by the scanset.

For many implementations, you can specify a range using a hyphen. For example, this tells **scanf( )** to accept the characters A through Z.

```
%[A-Z]
```

One important point to remember is that the scanset is case sensitive. Therefore, if you want to scan for both upper- and lowercase letters, they must be specified individually.

The **scanf( )** function returns a number equal to the number of fields that were successfully assigned values. This number will not include fields that were read but not assigned because the * modifier was used to suppress the assignment. **EOF** is returned if an error occurs before the first field is assigned.

Related functions are **printf( )** and **fscanf( )**.

setbuf

```
#include <cstdio>
void setbuf(FILE *stream, char *buf);
```

The **setbuf( )** function is used either to specify the buffer that *stream* will use or, if called with *buf* set to null, to turn off buffering. If a programmer-defined buffer is to be specified, it must be **BUFSIZ** characters long. **BUFSIZ** is defined in **<cstdio>**.

The **setbuf( )** function returns no value.

Related functions are **fopen( )**, **fclose( )**, and **setvbuf( )**.

setvbuf

```
#include <cstdio>
int setvbuf(FILE *stream, char *buf, int mode, size_t size);
```

The **setvbuf( )** function allows the programmer to specify the buffer, its size, and its mode for the specified stream. The character array pointed to by *buf* is used as the stream buffer for I/O operations. The size of the buffer is set by *size*, and *mode* determines how buffering will be handled. If *buf* is null, **setvbuf( )** will allocate its own buffer.

The legal values of *mode* are **_IOFBF**, **_IONBF**, and **_IOLBF**. These are defined in **<cstdio>**. When *mode* is set to **_IOFBF**, full buffering will take place. If *mode* is **_IOLBF**, the stream will be line buffered, which means that the buffer will be flushed each time a newline character is written for output streams; for input streams, input is buffered until a newline character is read. If mode is **_IONBF**, no buffering takes place.

THE STANDARD FUNCTION LIBRARY

The **setvbuf( )** function returns zero on success, nonzero on failure.
A related function is **setbuf( )**.

sprintf

```
#include <cstdio>
int sprintf(char *buf, const char *format, ...);
```

The **sprintf( )** function is identical to **printf( )** except that the output is put into the array pointed to by *buf* instead of being written to the console. See **printf( )** for details.
The return value is equal to the number of characters actually placed into the array.
Related functions are **printf( )** and **fsprintf( )**.

sscanf

```
#include <cstdio>
int sscanf(const char *buf, const char *format, ...);
```

The **sscanf( )** function is identical to **scanf( )** except that data is read from the array pointed to by *buf* rather than **stdin**. See **scanf( )** for details.
The return value is equal to the number of variables that were actually assigned values. This number does not include fields that were skipped through the use of the * format command modifier. A value of zero means that no fields were assigned, and **EOF** indicates that an error occurred prior to the first assignment.
Related functions are **scanf( )** and **fscanf( )**.

tmpfile

```
#include <cstdio>
FILE *tmpfile(void);
```

The **tmpfile( )** function opens a temporary file for update and returns a pointer to the stream. The function automatically uses a unique filename to avoid conflicts with existing files.
The **tmpfile( )** function returns a null pointer on failure; otherwise it returns a pointer to the stream.

The temporary file created by **tmpfile( )** is automatically removed when the file is closed or when the program terminates.

A related function is **tmpnam( )**.

tmpnam

```
#include <cstdio>
char *tmpnam(char *name);
```

The **tmpnam( )** function generates a unique filename and stores it in the array pointed to by *name*. This array must be at least **L_tmpnam** characters long. (**L_tmpnam** is defined in **<cstdio>**.) The main purpose of **tmpnam( )** is to generate a temporary filename that is different from any other file in the current disk directory.

The function may be called up to **TMP_MAX** times. **TMP_MAX** is defined in **<cstdio>**, and it will be at least 25. Each time **tmpnam( )** is called, it will generate a new temporary filename.

A pointer to *name* is returned on success; otherwise a null pointer is returned. If *name* is null, the temporary filename is held in a static array owned by **tmpnam( )**, and a pointer to this array is returned. This array is overwritten by a subsequent call.

A related function is **tmpfile( )**.

ungetc

```
#include <cstdio>
int ungetc(int ch, FILE *stream);
```

The **ungetc( )** function returns the character specified by the low-order byte of *ch* to the input stream *stream*. This character will then be obtained by the next read operation on *stream*. A call to **fflush( )**, **fseek( )**, or **rewind( )** undoes an **ungetc( )** operation and discards the character.

A one-character pushback is guaranteed; however, some implementations will accept more.

You may not unget an **EOF**.

A call to **ungetc( )** clears the end-of-file flag associated with the specified stream. The value of the file position indicator for a text stream is undefined until all pushed-back characters are read, in which case it will be the same as it was prior to the first **ungetc( )** call. For binary streams, each **ungetc( )** call decrements the file position indicator.

The return value is equal to *ch* on success and **EOF** on failure.

THE STANDARD FUNCTION LIBRARY

A related function is **getc( )**.

vprintf, vfprintf, and vsprintf

```
#include <cstdarg>
#include <cstdio>
int vprintf(char *format, va_list arg_ptr);
int vfprintf(FILE *stream, const char *format,
             va_list arg_ptr);
int vsprintf(char *buf, const char *format,
             va_list arg_ptr);
```

The functions **vprintf( )**, **vfprintf( )**, and **vsprintf( )** are functionally equivalent to **printf( )**, **fprintf( )**, and **sprintf( )**, respectively, except that the argument list has been replaced by a pointer to a list of arguments. This pointer must be of type **va_list**, which is defined in the header **<cstdarg>** (or the C header file **stdarg.h**).

Related functions are **va_arg( )**, **va_start( )**, and **va_end( )**.

Chapter 26

The String and
Character Functions

T he standard function library has a rich and varied set of string and character handling functions. The string functions operate on null-terminated arrays of characters and require the header **<cstring>**. The character functions use the header **<cctype>**. C programs must use the header files **string.h** and **ctype.h**.

Because C/C++ has no bounds checking on array operations, it is the programmer's responsibility to prevent an array overflow. Neglecting to do so may cause your program to crash.

In C/C++, a *printable character* is one that can be displayed on a terminal. These are usually the characters between a space (0x20) and tilde (0xFE). *Control characters* have values between (0) and (0x1F) as well as DEL (0x7F).

For historical reasons, the parameters to the character functions are integers, but only the low-order byte is used; the character functions automatically convert their arguments to **unsigned char**. However, you are free to call these functions with character arguments because characters are automatically elevated to integers at the time of the call.

The header **<cstring>** defines the **size_t** type, which is essentially the same as **unsigned**.

This chapter describes only those functions that operate on characters of type **char**. These are the functions originally defined by Standard C and C++, and they are by far the most widely used and supported. Wide-character functions that operate on characters of type **wchar_t** are discussed in Chapter 31.

isalnum

```
#include <cctype>
int isalnum(int ch);
```

The **isalnum( )** function returns nonzero if its argument is either a letter of the alphabet or a digit. If the character is not alphanumeric, zero is returned.

Related functions are **isalpha( )**, **iscntrl( )**, **isdigit( )**, **isgraph( )**, **isprint( )**, **ispunct( )**, and **isspace( )**.

isalpha

```
#include <cctype>
int isalpha(int ch);
```

The **isalpha( )** function returns nonzero if *ch* is a letter of the alphabet; otherwise zero is returned. What constitutes a letter of the alphabet may vary from language to language. For English, these are the upper- and lowercase letters A through Z.

Related functions are **isalnum( )**, **iscntrl( )**, **isdigit( )**, **isgraph( )**, **isprint( )**, **ispunct( )**, and **isspace( )**.

iscntrl

```
#include <cctype>
int iscntrl(int ch);
```

The **iscntrl( )** function returns nonzero if *ch* is between zero and 0x1F or is equal to 0x7F (DEL); otherwise zero is returned.

Related functions are **isalnum( )**, **isalpha( )**, **isdigit( )**, **isgraph( )**, **isprint( )**, **ispunct( )**, and **isspace( )**.

isdigit

```
#include <cctype>
int isdigit(int ch);
```

The **isdigit( )** function returns nonzero if *ch* is a digit, that is, 0 through 9. Otherwise zero is returned.

Related functions are **isalnum( )**, **isalpha( )**, **iscntrl( )**, **isgraph( )**, **isprint( )**, **ispunct( )**, and **isspace( )**.

isgraph

```
#include <cctype>
int isgraph(int ch);
```

The **isgraph( )** function returns nonzero if *ch* is any printable character other than a space; otherwise zero is returned. These are characters generally in the range 0x21 through 0x7E.

Related functions are **isalnum( )**, **isalpha( )**, **iscntrl( )**, **isdigit( )**, **isprint( )**, **ispunct( )**, and **isspace( )**.

islower

```
#include <cctype>
int islower(int ch);
```

THE STANDARD
FUNCTION LIBRARY

The **islower( )** function returns nonzero if *ch* is a lowercase letter; otherwise zero is returned.

A related function is **isupper( )**.

isprint

```
#include <cctype>
int isprint(int ch);
```

The **isprint( )** function returns nonzero if *ch* is a printable character, including a space; otherwise zero is returned. Printable characters are often in the range 0x20 through 0x7E.

Related functions are **isalnum( )**, **isalpha( )**, **iscntrl( )**, **isdigit( )**, **isgraph( )**, **ispunct( )**, and **isspace( )**.

ispunct

```
#include <cctype>
int ispunct(int ch);
```

The **ispunct( )** function returns nonzero if *ch* is a punctuation character; otherwise zero is returned. The term "punctuation," as defined by this function, includes all printing characters that are neither alphanumeric nor a space.

Related functions are **isalnum( )**, **isalpha( )**, **iscntrl( )**, **isdigit( )**, **isgraph( )**, and **isspace( )**.

isspace

```
#include <cctype>
int isspace(int ch);
```

The **isspace( )** function returns nonzero if *ch* is either a space, horizontal tab, vertical tab, formfeed, carriage return, or newline character; otherwise zero is returned.

Related functions are **isalnum( )**, **isalpha( )**, **iscntrl( )**, **isdigit( )**, **isgraph( )**, and **ispunct( )**.

isupper

```
#include <cctype>
int isupper(int ch);
```

The **isupper( )** function returns nonzero if *ch* is an uppercase letter; otherwise zero is returned.

A related function is **islower( )**.

isxdigit

```
#include <cctype>
int isxdigit(int ch);
```

The **isxdigit( )** function returns nonzero if *ch* is a hexadecimal digit; otherwise zero is returned. A hexadecimal digit will be in one of these ranges: A–F, a–f, or 0–9.

Related functions are **isalnum( )**, **isalpha( )**, **iscntrl( )**, **isdigit( )**, **isgraph( )**, **ispunct( )**, and **isspace( )**.

memchr

```
#include <cstring>
void *memchr(const void *buffer, int ch, size_t count);
```

The **memchr( )** function searches the array pointed to by *buffer* for the first occurrence of *ch* in the first *count* characters.

The **memchr( )** function returns a pointer to the first occurrence of *ch* in *buffer*, or it returns a null pointer if *ch* is not found.

Related functions are **memcpy( )** and **isspace( )**.

memcmp

```
#include <cstring>
int memcmp(const void *buf1, const void *buf2, size_t count);
```

The **memcmp( )** function compares the first *count* characters of the arrays pointed to by *buf1* and *buf2*.

The **memcmp( )** function returns an integer that is interpreted as indicated here:

Value	Meaning
Less than zero	*buf1* is less than *buf2*.
Zero	*buf1* is equal to *buf2*.
Greater than zero	*buf1* is greater than *buf2*.

Related functions are **memchr( )**, **memcpy( )**, and **strcmp( )**.

memcpy

```
#include <cstring>
void *memcpy(void *to, const void *from, size_t count);
```

The **memcpy( )** function copies *count* characters from the array pointed to by *from* into the array pointed to by *to*. If the arrays overlap, the behavior of **memcopy( )** is undefined.

The **memcpy( )** function returns a pointer to *to*.

A related function is **memmove( )**.

memmove

```
#include <cstring>
void *memmove(void *to, const void *from, size_t count);
```

The **memmove( )** function copies *count* characters from the array pointed to by *from* into the array pointed to by *to*. If the arrays overlap, the copy will take place correctly, placing the correct contents into *to* but leaving *from* modified.

The **memmove( )** function returns a pointer to *to*.

A related function is **memcpy( )**.

memset

```
#include <cstring>
void *memset(void *buf, int ch, size_t count);
```

The **memset( )** function copies the low-order byte of *ch* into the first *count* characters of the array pointed to by *buf.* It returns *buf.*

The most common use of **memset( )** is to initialize a region of memory to some known value.

Related functions are **memcmp( )**, **memcpy( )**, and **memmove( )**.

strcat

```
#include <cstring>
char *strcat(char *str1, const char *str2);
```

The **strcat( )** function concatenates a copy of *str2* to *str1* and terminates *str1* with a null. The null terminator originally ending *str1* is overwritten by the first character of *str2*. The string *str2* is untouched by the operation. If the arrays overlap, the behavior of **strcat( )** is undefined.

The **strcat( )** function returns *str1*.

Remember, no bounds checking takes place, so it is the programmer's responsibility to ensure that *str1* is large enough to hold both its original contents and also those of *str2*.

Related functions are **strchr( )**, **strcmp( )**, and **strcpy( )**.

strchr

```
#include <cstring>
char *strchr(const char *str, int ch);
```

The **strchr( )** function returns a pointer to the first occurrence of the low-order byte of *ch* in the string pointed to by *str*. If no match is found, a null pointer is returned.

Related functions are **strpbrk( )**, **strspn( )**, **strstr( )**, and **strtok( )**.

strcmp

```
#include <cstring>
int strcmp(const char *str1, const char *str2);
```

The **strcmp( )** function lexicographically compares two strings and returns an integer based on the outcome as shown here:

Value	Meaning
Less than zero	*str1* is less than *str2*.
Zero	*str1* is equal to *str2*.
Greater than zero	*str1* is greater than *str2*.

Related functions are **strchr( )**, **strcpy( )**, and **strcmp( )**.

strcoll

```
#include <cstring>
int strcoll(const char *str1, const char *str2);
```

The **strcoll( )** function compares the string pointed to by *str1* with the one pointed to by *str2*. The comparison is performed in accordance to the locale specified using the **setlocale( )** function (see **setlocale** for details).

The **strcoll( )** function returns an integer that is interpreted as indicated here:

Value	Meaning
Less than zero	*str1* is less than *str2*.
Zero	*str1* is equal to *str2*.
Greater than zero	*str1* is greater than *str2*.

Related functions are **memcmp( )** and **strcmp( )**.

strcpy

```
#include <cstring>
char *strcpy(char *str1, const char *str2);
```

The **strcpy( )** function copies the contents of *str2* into *str1*. *str2* must be a pointer to a null-terminated string. The **strcpy( )** function returns a pointer to *str1*.

If *str1* and *str2* overlap, the behavior of **strcpy( )** is undefined.

Related functions are **memcpy( )**, **strchr( )**, **strcmp( )**, and **strncmp( )**.

strcspn

```
#include <cstring>
size_t strcspn(const char *str1, const char *str2);
```

The **strcspn( )** function returns the length of the initial substring of the string pointed to by *str1* that is made up of only those characters not contained in the string pointed to by *str2*. Stated differently, **strcspn( )** returns the index of the first character in the string pointed to by *str1* that matches any of the characters in the string pointed to by *str2*.

Related functions are **strrchr( )**, **strpbrk( )**, **strstr( )**, and **strtok( )**.

strerror

```
#include <cstring>
char *strerror(int errnum);
```

The **strerror( )** function returns a pointer to an implementation-defined string associated with the value of *errnum*. Under no circumstances should you modify the string.

strlen

```
#include <cstring>
size_t strlen(const char *str);
```

The **strlen( )** function returns the length of the null-terminated string pointed to by *str*. The null terminator is not counted.

Related functions are **memcpy( )**, **strchr( )**, **strcmp( )**, and **strncmp( )**.

strncat

```
#include <cstring>
char *strncat(char *str1, const char *str2, size_t count);
```

The **strncat( )** function concatenates not more than *count* characters of the string pointed to by *str2* to the string pointed to by *str1* and terminates *str1* with a null. The null terminator originally ending *str1* is overwritten by the first character of *str2*. The string *str2* is untouched by the operation. If the strings overlap, the behavior is undefined.

The **strncat( )** function returns *str1*.

Remember that no bounds checking takes place, so it is the programmer's responsibility to ensure that *str1* is large enough to hold both its original contents and also those of *str2*.

Related functions are **strcat( )**, **strnchr( )**, **strncmp( )**, and **strncpy( )**.

strncmp

```
#include <cstring>
int strncmp(const char *str1, const char *str2, size_t count);
```

The **strncmp( )** function lexicographically compares not more than *count* characters from the two null-terminated strings and returns an integer based on the outcome, as shown here:

Value	Meaning
Less than zero	*str1* is less than *str2*.
Zero	*str1* is equal to *str2*.
Greater than zero	*str1* is greater than *str2*.

If there are less than *count* characters in either string, the comparison ends when the first null is encountered.

Related functions are **strcmp( )**, **strnchr( )**, and **strncpy( )**.

strncpy

```
#include <cstring>
char *strncpy(char *str1, const char *str2, size_t count);
```

The **strncpy( )** function copies up to *count* characters from the string pointed to by *str2* into the string pointed to by *str1*. *str2* must be a pointer to a null-terminated string.

If *str1* and *str2* overlap, the behavior of **strncpy( )** is undefined.

If the string pointed to by *str2* has less than *count* characters, nulls will be appended to the end of *str1* until *count* characters have been copied.

Alternatively, if the string pointed to by *str2* is longer than *count* characters, the resultant string pointed to by *str1* will not be null terminated.

The **strncpy( )** function returns a pointer to *str1*.

Related functions are **memcpy( )**, **strchr( )**, **strncat( )**, and **strncmp( )**.

strpbrk

```
#include <cstring>
char *strpbrk(const char *str1, const char *str2);
```

The **strpbrk( )** function returns a pointer to the first character in the string pointed to by *str1* that matches any character in the string pointed to by *str2*. The null terminators are not included. If there are no matches, a null pointer is returned.

Related functions are **strspn( )**, **strrchr( )**, **strstr( )**, and **strtok( )**.

strrchr

```
#include <cstring>
char *strrchr(const char *str, int ch);
```

The **strrchr( )** function returns a pointer to the last occurrence of the low-order byte of *ch* in the string pointed to by *str*. If no match is found, a null pointer is returned.

Related functions are **strpbrk( )**, **strspn( )**, **strstr( )**, and **strtok( )**.

strspn

```
#include <cstring>
size_t strspn(const char *str1, const char *str2);
```

The **strspn( )** function returns the length of the initial substring of the string pointed to by *str1* that is made up of only those characters contained in the string pointed to by *str2*. Stated differently, **strspn( )** returns the index of the first character in the string pointed to by *str1* that does not match any of the characters in the string pointed to by *str2*.

Related functions are **strpbrk( )**, **strrchr( )**, **strstr( )**, and **strtok( )**.

strstr

```
#include <cstring>
char *strstr(const char *str1, const char *str2);
```

The **strstr( )** function returns a pointer to the first occurrence in the string pointed to by *str1* of the string pointed to by *str2*. It returns a null pointer if no match is found.

Related functions are **strchr( )**, **strcspn( )**, **strpbrk( )**, **strspn( )**, **strtok( )**, and **strrchr( )**.

strtok

```
#include <cstring>
char *strtok(char *str1, const char *str2);
```

The **strtok( )** function returns a pointer to the next token in the string pointed to by *str1*. The characters making up the string pointed to by *str2* are the delimiters that determine the token. A null pointer is returned when there is no token to return.

To tokenize a string, the first call to **strtok( )** must have *str1* point to the string being tokenized. Subsequent calls must use a null pointer for *str1*. In this way, the entire string can be reduced to its tokens.

It is possible to use a different set of delimiters for each call to **strtok( )**.

Related functions are **strchr( )**, **strcspn( )**, **strpbrk( )**, **strrchr( )**, and **strspn( )**.

strxfrm

```
#include <cstring>
size_t strxfrm(char *str1, const char *str2, size_t count);
```

The **strxfrm( )** function transforms the string pointed to by *str2* so that it can be used by the **strcmp( )** function and puts the result into the string pointed to by *str1*. After the transformation, the outcome of a **strcmp( )** using *str1* and a **strcoll( )** using the original string pointed to by *str2* will be the same. Not more than *count* characters are written to the array pointed to by *str1*.

The **strxfrm( )** function returns the length of the transformed string.

A related function is **strcoll( )**.

tolower

```
#include <cctype>
int tolower(int ch);
```

The **tolower( )** function returns the lowercase equivalent of *ch* if *ch* is a letter; otherwise *ch* is returned unchanged.

A related function is **toupper( )**.

toupper

```
#include <cctype>
int toupper(int ch);
```

The **toupper( )** function returns the uppercase equivalent of *ch* if *ch* is a letter; otherwise *ch* is returned unchanged.

A related function is **tolower( )**.

Chapter 27

The Mathematical
Functions

The standard function library contains several mathematical functions, which fall into the following categories:

- Trigonometric functions
- Hyperbolic functions
- Exponential and logarithmic functions
- Miscellaneous functions

All the math functions require the header **<cmath>.** (C programs must use the header file **math.h.**) In addition to declaring the math functions, this header defines the macro called **HUGE_VAL**. The macros **EDOM** and **ERANGE** are also used by the math functions. These macros are defined in the header **<cerrno>** (or the file **errno.h**). If an argument to a math function is not in the domain for which it is defined, an implementation-defined value is returned, and the built-in global integer variable **errno** is set equal to **EDOM**. If a routine produces a result that is too large to be represented, an overflow occurs. This causes the routine to return **HUGE_VAL**, and **errno** is set to **ERANGE**, indicating a range error. If an underflow happens, the function returns zero and sets **errno** to **ERANGE**.

All angles are in radians.

Originally, the mathematical functions were specified as operating on values of type **double**, but Standard C++ added overloaded versions to explicitly accommodate values of type **float** and **long double**. The operation of the functions is otherwise unchanged.

acos

```
#include <cmath>
float acos(float arg);
double acos(double arg);
long double acos(long double arg);
```

The **acos( )** function returns the arc cosine of *arg*. The argument to **acos( )** must be in the range –1 to 1; otherwise a domain error will occur.

Related functions are **asin( )**, **atan( )**, **atan2( )**, **sin( )**, **cos( )**, **tan( )**, **sinh( )**, **cosh( )**, and **tanh( )**.

asin

```
#include <cmath>
float asin(float arg);
```

```
double asin(double arg);
long double asin(long double arg);
```

The **asin( )** function returns the arc sine of *arg*. The argument to **asin( )** must be in the range –1 to 1; otherwise a domain error will occur.

Related functions are **acos( )**, **atan( )**, **atan2( )**, **sin( )**, **cos( )**, **tan( )**, **sinh( )**, **cosh( )**, and **tanh( )**.

atan

```
#include <cmath>
float atan(float arg);
double atan(double arg);
long double atan(long double arg);
```

The **atan( )** function returns the arc tangent of *arg*.

Related functions are **asin( )**, **acos( )**, **atan2( )**, **tan( )**, **cos( )**, **sin( )**, **sinh( )**, **cosh( )**, and **tanh( )**.

atan2

```
#include <cmath>
float atan2(float y, float x);
double atan2(double y, double x);
long double atan2(long double y, long double x);
```

The **atan2( )** function returns the arc tangent of *y/x*. It uses the signs of its arguments to compute the quadrant of the return value.

Related functions are **asin( )**, **acos( )**, **atan( )**, **tan( )**, **cos( )**, **sin( )**, **sinh( )**, **cosh( )**, and **tanh( )**.

ceil

```
#include <cmath>
float ceil(float num);
double ceil(double num);
long double ceil(long double num);
```

The **ceil( )** function returns the smallest integer (represented as a floating-point value) not less than *num*. For example, given 1.02, **ceil( )** would return 2.0. Given –1.02, **ceil( )** would return –1.

Related functions are **floor( )** and **fmod( )**.

cos

```
#include <cmath>
float cos(float arg);
double cos(double arg);
long double cos(long double arg);
```

The **cos( )** function returns the cosine of *arg*. The value of *arg* must be in radians.

Related functions are **asin( )**, **acos( )**, **atan2( )**, **atan( )**, **tan( )**, **sin( )**, **sinh( )**, **cos( )**, and **tanh( )**.

cosh

```
#include <cmath>
float cosh(float arg);
double cosh(double arg);
long double cosh(long double arg);
```

The **cosh( )** function returns the hyperbolic cosine of *arg*.

Related functions are **asin( )**, **acos( )**, **atan2( )**, **atan( )**, **tan( )**, **sin( )**, **cosh( )**, and **tanh( )**.

exp

```
#include <cmath>
float exp(float arg);
double exp(double arg);
long double exp(long double arg);
```

The **exp( )** function returns the natural logarithm base *e* raised to the *arg* power. A related function is **log( )**.

fabs

```
#include <cmath>
float fabs(float num);
double fabs(double num);
long double fabs(long double num);
```

The **fabs( )** function returns the absolute value of *num*.
A related function is **abs( )**.

floor

```
#include <cmath>
float floor(float num);
double floor(double num);
long double floor(long double num);
```

The **floor( )** function returns the largest integer (represented as a floating-point value) not greater than *num*. For example, given 1.02, **floor( )** would return 1.0. Given –1.02, **floor( )** would return –2.0.
Related functions are **fceil( )** and **fmod( )**.

fmod

```
#include <cmath>
float fmod(float x, float y);
double fmod(double x, double y);
long double fmod(long double x, long double y);
```

The **fmod( )** function returns the remainder of *x/y*.
Related functions are **ceil( )**, **floor( )**, and **fabs( )**.

frexp

```
#include <cmath>
float frexp(float num, int *exp);
```

```
double frexp(double num, int *exp);
long double frexp(long double num, int *exp);
```

The **frexp( )** function decomposes the number *num* into a mantissa in the range 0.5 to less than 1, and an integer exponent such that $num = mantissa * 2^{exp}$. The mantissa is returned by the function, and the exponent is stored in the variable pointed to by *exp*.

A related function is **ldexp( )**.

ldexp

```
#include <cmath>
float ldexp(float num, int exp);
double ldexp(double num, int exp);
long double ldexp(long double num, int exp);
```

The **ldexp( )** returns the value of $num * 2^{exp}$. If overflow occurs, **HUGE_VAL** is returned.

Related functions are **frexp( )** and **modf( )**.

log

```
#include <cmath>
float log(float num);
double log(double num);
long double log(long double num);
```

The **log( )** function returns the natural logarithm for *num*. A domain error occurs if *num* is negative, and a range error occurs if the argument is zero.

A related function is **log10( )**.

log10

```
#include <cmath>
float log10(float num);
double log10(double num);
long double log10(long double num);
```

The **log10( )** function returns the base 10 logarithm for *num*. A domain error occurs if *num* is negative, and a range error occurs if the argument is zero.

A related function is **log( )**.

modf

```
#include <cmath>
float modf(float num, float *i);
double modf(double num, double *i);
long double modf(long double num, long double *i);
```

The **modf( )** function decomposes *num* into its integer and fractional parts. It returns the fractional portion and places the integer part in the variable pointed to by *i*.

Related functions are **frexp( )** and **ldexp( )**.

pow

```
#include <cmath>
float pow(float base, float exp);
float pow(float base, int exp);
double pow(double base, double exp);
double pow(double base, int exp);
long double pow(long double base, long double exp);
long double pow(long double base, int exp);
```

The **pow( )** function returns *base* raised to the *exp* power ($base^{exp}$). A domain error may occur if *base* is zero and *exp* is less than or equal to zero. It will also happen if *base* is negative and *exp* is not an integer. An overflow produces a range error.

Related functions are **exp( )**, **log( )**, and **sqrt( )**.

sin

```
#include <cmath>
float sin(float arg);
double sin(double arg);
long double sin(long double arg);
```

The **sin( )** function returns the sine of *arg*. The value of *arg* must be in radians.

THE STANDARD FUNCTION LIBRARY

Related functions are **asin( )**, **acos( )**, **atan2( )**, **atan( )**, **tan( )**, **cos( )**, **sinh( )**, **cosh( )**, and **tanh( )**.

sinh

```
#include <cmath>
float sinh(float arg);
double sinh(double arg);
long double sinh(long double arg);
```

The **sinh( )** function returns the hyperbolic sine of *arg*.

Related functions are **asin( )**, **acos( )**, **atan2( )**, **atan( )**, **tan( )**, **cos( )**, **tanh( )**, **cosh( )**, and **sin( )**.

sqrt

```
#include <cmath>
float sqrt(float num);
double sqrt(double num);
long double sqrt(long double num);
```

The **sqrt( )** function returns the square root of *num*. If it is called with a negative argument, a domain error will occur.

Related functions are **exp( )**, **log( )**, and **pow( )**.

tan

```
#include <cmath>
float tan(float arg);
double tan(double arg);
long double tan(long double arg);
```

The **tan( )** function returns the tangent of *arg*. The value of *arg* must be in radians.

Related functions are **acos( )**, **asin( )**, **atan( )**, **atan2( )**, **cos( )**, **sin( )**, **sinh( )**, **cosh( )**, and **tanh( )**.

tanh

```
#include <cmath>
float tanh(float arg);
double tanh(double arg);
long double tanh(long double arg);
```

The **tanh( )** function returns the hyperbolic tangent of *arg*.

Related functions are **acos( )**, **asin( )**, **atan( )**, **atan2( )**, **cos( )**, **sin( )**, **cosh( )**, **sinh( )**, and **tan( )**.

The Complete Reference

C++

Chapter 28

Time, Date, and Localization Functions

The standard function library defines several functions that deal with the date and time. It also defines functions that handle the geopolitical information associated with a program. These functions are described here.

The time and date functions require the header **<ctime>**. (A C program must use the header file **time.h**.) This header defines three time-related types: **clock_t**, **time_t**, and **tm**. The types **clock_t** and **time_t** are capable of representing the system time and date as some sort of integer. This is called the *calendar time*. The structure type **tm** holds the date and time broken down into its elements. The **tm** structure is defined as shown here:

```
struct tm {
  int tm_sec;   /* seconds, 0-61 */
  int tm_min;   /* minutes, 0-59 */
  int tm_hour;  /* hours, 0-23 */
  int tm_mday;  /* day of the month, 1-31 */
  int tm_mon;   /* months since Jan, 0-11 */
  int tm_year;  /* years from 1900 */
  int tm_wday;  /* days since Sunday, 0-6 */
  int tm_yday;  /* days since Jan 1, 0-365 */
  int tm_isdst  /* Daylight Saving Time
                   indicator */
}
```

The value of **tm_isdst** will be positive if daylight saving time is in effect, zero if it is not in effect, and negative if there is no information available. This form of the time and date is called the *broken-down time*.

In addition, **<ctime>** defines the macro **CLOCKS_PER_SEC**, which is the number of system clock ticks per second.

The geopolitical environmental functions require the header **<clocale>**. (A C program must use the header file **locale.h**.)

asctime

```
#include <ctime>
char *asctime(const struct tm *ptr);
```

The **asctime( )** function returns a pointer to a string that contains the information stored in the structure pointed to by *ptr* converted into the following form:

day month date hours:minutes:seconds year\n\0

For example:

```
Fri Apr 15 12:05:34 2005
```

The structure pointer passed to **asctime( )** is usually obtained from either **localtime( )** or **gmtime( )**.

The buffer used by **asctime( )** to hold the formatted output string is a statically allocated character array and is overwritten each time the function is called. If you wish to save the contents of the string, you must copy it elsewhere.

Related functions are **localtime( )**, **gmtime( )**, **time( )**, and **ctime( )**.

clock

```
#include <ctime>
clock_t clock(void);
```

The **clock( )** function returns a value that approximates the amount of time the calling program has been running. To transform this value into seconds, divide it by **CLOCKS_PER_SEC**. A value of –1 is returned if the time is not available.

Related functions are **time( )**, **asctime( )**, and **ctime( )**.

ctime

```
#include <ctime>
char *ctime(const time_t *time);
```

The **ctime( )** function returns a pointer to a string of the form

day month year hours:minutes:seconds year\n\0

given a pointer to the calendar time. The calendar time is often obtained through a call to **time( )**.

The buffer used by **ctime( )** to hold the formatted output string is a statically allocated character array and is overwritten each time the function is called. If you wish to save the contents of the string, it is necessary to copy it elsewhere.

Related functions are **localtime( )**, **gmtime( )**, **time( )**, and **asctime( )**.

difftime

```
#include <ctime>
double difftime(time_t time2, time_t time1);
```

The **difftime( )** function returns the difference, in seconds, between *time1* and *time2*. That is, *time2 –time1.*

Related functions are **localtime( )**, **gmtime( )**, **time( )**, **asctime( )**.

gmtime

```
#include <ctime>
struct tm *gmtime(const time_t *time);
```

The **gmtime( )** function returns a pointer to the broken-down form of *time* in the form of a **tm** structure. The time is represented in Coordinated Universal Time (UTC), which is essentially Greenwich mean time. The *time* value is usually obtained through a call to **time( )**. If the system does not support UTC, **NULL** is returned.

The structure used by **gmtime( )** to hold the broken-down time is statically allocated and is overwritten each time the function is called. If you wish to save the contents of the structure, you must copy it elsewhere.

Related functions are **localtime( )**, **time( )**, and **asctime( )**.

localeconv

```
#include <clocale>
struct lconv *localeconv(void);
```

The **localeconv( )** function returns a pointer to a structure of type **lconv**, which contains various geopolitical environmental information relating to the way numbers are formatted. The **lconv** structure is organized as shown here:

```
struct lconv {
  char *decimal_point;      /* decimal point character
                               for nonmonetary values */
  char *thousands_sep;      /* thousands separator
                               for nonmonetary values */
  char *grouping;           /* specifies grouping for
```

```
                            nonmonetary values */
  char *int_curr_symbol;    /* international currency symbol */
  char *currency_symbol;    /* local currency symbol */
  char *mon_decimal_point;  /* decimal point character for
                               monetary values */
  char *mon_thousands_sep;  /* thousands separator for
                               monetary values */
  char *mon_grouping;       /* specifies grouping for
                               monetary values */
  char *positive_sign;      /* positive value indicator for
                               monetary values */
  char *negative_sign;      /* negative value indicator for
                               monetary values */
  char int_frac_digits;     /* number of digits displayed to the
                               right of the decimal point for
                               monetary values displayed using
                               international format */
  char frac_digits;         /* number of digits displayed to the
                               right of the decimal point for
                               monetary values displayed using
                               local format */
  char p_cs_precedes;       /* 1 if currency symbol precedes
                               positive value, 0 if currency
                               symbol follows value */
  char p_sep_by_space;      /* 1 if currency symbol is
                               separated from value by a space,
                               0 otherwise */
  char n_cs_precedes;       /* 1 if currency symbol precedes
                               a negative value, 0 if currency
                               symbol follows value */
  char n_sep_by_space;      /* 1 if currency symbol is
                               separated from a negative
                               value by a space, 0 if
                               currency symbol follows value */
  char p_sign_posn;         /* indicates position of
                               positive value symbol */
  char n_sign_posn;         /* indicates position of
                               negative value symbol */
}
```

The **localeconv( )** function returns a pointer to the **lconv** structure. You must not alter the contents of this structure. Refer to your compiler's documentation for implementation-specific information relating to the **lconv** structure.

A related function is **setlocale( )**.

localtime

```
#include <ctime>
struct tm *localtime(const time_t *time);
```

The **localtime( )** function returns a pointer to the broken-down form of *time* in the form of a **tm** structure. The time is represented in local time. The *time* value is usually obtained through a call to **time( )**.

The structure used by **localtime( )** to hold the broken-down time is statically allocated and is overwritten each time the function is called. If you wish to save the contents of the structure, you must copy it elsewhere.

Related functions are **gmtime( )**, **time( )**, and **asctime( )**.

mktime

```
#include <ctime>
time_t mktime(struct tm *time);
```

The **mktime( )** function returns the calendar-time equivalent of the broken-down time found in the structure pointed to by *time*. The elements **tm_wday** and **tm_yday** are set by the function, so they need not be defined at the time of the call.

If **mktime( )** cannot represent the information as a valid calendar time, –1 is returned.

Related functions are **time( )**, **gmtime( )**, **asctime( )**, and **ctime( )**.

setlocale

```
#include <clocale>
char *setlocale(int type, const char *locale);
```

The **setlocale( )** function allows certain parameters that are sensitive to the geopolitical environment of a program's execution to be queried or set. If *locale* is null, **setlocale( )** returns a pointer to the current localization string. Otherwise, **setlocale( )** attempts to use the string specified by *locale* to set the locale parameters as specified by *type*. Refer to your compiler's documentation for the localization strings that it supports.

At the time of the call, *type* must be one of the following macros:

LC_ALL
LC_COLLATE
LC_CTYPE
LC_MONETARY
LC_NUMERIC
LC_TIME

LC_ALL refers to all localization categories. **LC_COLLATE** affects the operation of the **strcoll( )** function. **LC_CTYPE** alters the way the character functions work. **LC_MONETARY** determines the monetary format. **LC_NUMERIC** changes the decimal-point character for formatted input/output functions. Finally, **LC_TIME** determines the behavior of the **strftime( )** function.

The **setlocale( )** function returns a pointer to a string associated with the *type* parameter.

Related functions are **localeconv( )**, **time( )**, **strcoll( )**, and **strftime( )**.

strftime

```
#include <ctime>
size_t strftime(char *str, size_t maxsize, const char *fmt,
               const struct tm *time);
```

The **strftime( )** function places time and date information, along with other information, into the string pointed to by *str* according to the format commands found in the string pointed to by *fmt* and using the broken-down time *time*. A maximum of *maxsize* characters will be placed into *str*.

The **strftime( )** function works a little like **sprintf( )** in that it recognizes a set of format commands that begin with the percent sign (%) and places its formatted output into a string. The format commands are used to specify the exact way various time and date information is represented in *str*. Any other characters found in the format string are placed into *str* unchanged. The time and date displayed are in local time. The format commands are shown in the table below. Notice that many of the commands are case sensitive.

The **strftime( )** function returns the number of characters placed in the string pointed to by *str* or zero if an error occurs.

Command	Replaced By
%a	Abbreviated weekday name
%A	Full weekday name

Command	Replaced By
%b	Abbreviated month name
%B	Full month name
%c	Standard date and time string
%d	Day of month as a decimal (1-31)
%H	Hour (0-23)
%I	Hour (1-12)
%j	Day of year as a decimal (1-366)
%m	Month as decimal (1-12)
%M	Minute as decimal (0-59)
%p	Locale's equivalent of AM or PM
%S	Second as decimal (0-60)
%U	Week of year, Sunday being first day (0-53)
%w	Weekday as a decimal (0-6, Sunday being 0)
%W	Week of year, Monday being first day (0-53)
%x	Standard date string
%X	Standard time string
%y	Year in decimal without century (0-99)
%Y	Year including century as decimal
%Z	Time zone name
%%	The percent sign

Related functions are **time( )**, **localtime( )**, and **gmtime( )**.

time

```
#include <ctime>
time_t time(time_t *time);
```

The **time( )** function returns the current calendar time of the system. If the system has no time, –1 is returned.

The **time( )** function can be called either with a null pointer or with a pointer to a variable of type **time_t**. If the latter is used, the variable will also be assigned the calendar time.

Related functions are **localtime( )**, **gmtime( )**, **strftime( )**, and **ctime( )**.

Chapter 29

The Dynamic
Allocation Functions

757

This chapter describes the dynamic allocation functions, which were inherited from the C language. At their core are the functions **malloc( )** and **free( )**. Each time **malloc( )** is called, a portion of the remaining free memory is allocated. Each time **free( )** is called, memory is returned to the system. The region of free memory from which memory is allocated is called the *heap*. The prototypes for the dynamic allocation functions are in **<cstdlib>**. A C program must use the header file **stdlib.h**.

All C++ compilers will include at least these four dynamic allocation functions: **calloc( )**, **malloc( )**, **free( )**, **realloc( )**. However, your compiler will almost certainly contain several variants on these functions to accommodate various options and environmental differences. You will want to refer to your compiler's documentation.

While C++ supports the dynamic allocation functions described here, you will typically not use them in a C++ program. The reason for this is that C++ provides the dynamic allocation operators **new** and **delete**. There are several advantages to using the dynamic allocation operators. First, **new** automatically allocates the correct amount of memory for the type of data being allocated. Second, it returns the correct type of pointer to that memory. Third, both **new** and **delete** can be overloaded. Since **new** and **delete** have advantages over the C-based dynamic allocation functions, their use is recommended for C++ programs.

calloc

```
#include <cstdlib>
void *calloc(size_t num, size_t size);
```

The **calloc( )** function allocates memory the size of which is equal to *num * size*. That is, **calloc( )** allocates sufficient memory for an array of *num* objects of size *size*.

The **calloc( )** function returns a pointer to the first byte of the allocated region. If there is not enough memory to satisfy the request, a null pointer is returned. It is always important to verify that the return value is not null before attempting to use it.

Related functions are **free( )**, **malloc( )**, and **realloc( )**.

free

```
#include <cstdlib>
void free(void *ptr);
```

The **free( )** function returns the memory pointed to by *ptr* to the heap. This makes the memory available for future allocation.

It is imperative that **free( )** only be called with a pointer that was previously allocated using one of the dynamic allocation system's functions (either **malloc( )** or **calloc( )**).

Using an invalid pointer in the call most likely will destroy the memory management mechanism and cause a system crash.

Related functions are **calloc( )**, **malloc( )**, and **realloc( )**.

malloc

```
#include <cstdlib>
void *malloc(size_t size);
```

The **malloc( )** function returns a pointer to the first byte of a region of memory of size *size* that has been allocated from the heap. If there is insufficient memory in the heap to satisfy the request, **malloc( )** returns a null pointer. It is always important to verify that the return value is not null before attempting to use it. Attempting to use a null pointer will usually result in a system crash.

Related functions are **free( )**, **realloc( )**, and **calloc( )**.

realloc

```
#include <cstdlib>
void *realloc(void *ptr, size_t size);
```

The **realloc( )** function changes the size of the previously allocated memory pointed to by *ptr* to that specified by *size.* The value of *size* may be greater or less than the original. A pointer to the memory block is returned because it may be necessary for **realloc( )** to move the block in order to increase its size. If this occurs, the contents of the old block are copied into the new block—no information is lost.

If *ptr* is null, **realloc( )** simply allocates *size* bytes of memory and returns a pointer to it. If *size* is zero, the memory pointed to by *ptr* is freed.

If there is not enough free memory in the heap to allocate *size* bytes, a null pointer is returned, and the original block is left unchanged.

Related functions are **free( )**, **malloc( )**, and **calloc( )**.

Chapter 30

Utility Functions

The standard function library defines several utility functions that provide various commonly used services. They include a number of conversions, variable-length argument processing, sorting and searching, and random number generation. Many of the functions covered here require the use of the header **<cstdlib>**. (A C program must use the header file **stdlib.h**.) In this header are defined **div_t** and **ldiv_t**, which are the types of values returned by **div( )** and **ldiv( )**, respectively. Also defined is the type **size_t**, which is the unsigned value returned by **sizeof**. The following macros are defined:

Macro	Meaning
MB_CUR_MAX	Maximun length (in bytes) of a multibyte character.
NULL	A null pointer.
RAND_MAX	The maximum value that can be returned by the **rand( )** function.
EXIT_FAILURE	The value returned to the calling process if program termination is unsuccessful.
EXIT_SUCCESS	The value returned to the calling process if program termination is successful.

If a function requires a different header than **<cstdlib>**, that function description will discuss it.

abort

```
#include <cstdlib>
void abort(void);
```

The **abort( )** function causes immediate abnormal termination of a program. Generally, no files are flushed. In environments that support it, **abort( )** will return an implementation-defined value to the calling process (usually the operating system) indicating failure.

Related functions are **exit( )** and **atexit( )**.

abs

```
#include <cstdlib>
int abs(int num);
long abs(long num);
double abs(double num);
```

The **abs( )** function returns the absolute value of *num*. The **long** version of **abs( )** is the same as **labs( )**. The **double** version of **abs( )** is the same as **fabs( )**.

A related function is **labs( )**.

assert

```
#include <cassert>
void assert(int exp);
```

The **assert( )** macro, defined in its header **<cassert>**, writes error information to **stderr** and then aborts program execution if the expression *exp* evaluates to zero. Otherwise, **assert( )** does nothing. Although the exact output is implementation defined, many compilers use a message similar to this:

Assertion failed: *<expression>*, file *<file>*, line *<linenum>*

The **assert( )** macro is generally used to help verify that a program is operating correctly, with the expression being devised in such a way that it evaluates to true only when no errors have taken place.

It is not necessary to remove the **assert( )** statements from the source code once a program is debugged because if the macro **NDEBUG** is defined (as anything), the **assert( )** macros will be ignored.

A related function is **abort( )**.

atexit

```
#include <cstdlib>
int atexit(void (*func)(void));
```

The **atexit( )** function causes the function pointed to by *func* to be called upon normal program termination. The **atexit( )** function returns zero if the function is successfully registered as a termination function, nonzero otherwise.

At least 32 termination functions may be established, and they will be called in the reverse order of their establishment.

Related functions are **exit( )** and **abort( )**.

atof

```
#include <cstdlib>
double atof(const char *str);
```

THE STANDARD
FUNCTION LIBRARY

The **atof( )** function converts the string pointed to by *str* into a **double** value. The string must contain a valid floating-point number. If this is not the case, the returned value is undefined.

The number may be terminated by any character that cannot be part of a valid floating-point number. This includes white space, punctuation (other than periods), and characters other than E or e. This means that if **atof( )** is called with "100.00HELLO", the value 100.00 will be returned.

Related functions are **atoi( )** and **atol( )**.

atoi

```
#include <cstdlib>
int atoi(const char *str);
```

The **atoi( )** function converts the string pointed to by *str* into an **int** value. The string must contain a valid integer number. If this is not the case, the returned value is undefined; however, most implementations will return zero.

The number may be terminated by any character that cannot be part of an integer number. This includes white space, punctuation, and characters. This means that if **atoi( )** is called with "123.23", the integer value 123 will be returned, and the ".23" is ignored.

Related functions are **atof( )** and **atol( )**.

atol

```
#include <cstdlib>
long atol(const char *str);
```

The **atol( )** function converts the string pointed to by *str* into a **long** value. The string must contain a valid long integer number. If this is not the case, the returned value is undefined; however, most implementations will return zero.

The number may be terminated by any character that cannot be part of an integer number. This includes white space, punctuation, and characters. This means that if **atol( )** is called with "123.23", the long integer value 123L will be returned, and the ".23" is ignored.

Related functions are **atof( )** and **atoi( )**.

bsearch

```
#include <cstdlib>
void *bsearch(const void *key, const void *buf,
```

```
                        size_t num, size_t size,
                        int (*compare)(const void *, const void *));
```

The **bsearch( )** function performs a binary search on the sorted array pointed to by *buf* and returns a pointer to the first member that matches the key pointed to by *key*. The number of elements in the array is specified by *num*, and the size (in bytes) of each element is described by *size*.

The function pointed to by *compare* is used to compare an element of the array with the key. The form of the *compare* function must be as follows:

int *func_name*(const void **arg1*, const void **arg2*);

It must return values as described in the following table:

Comparison	Value Returned
arg1 is less than *arg2*	Less than zero
arg1 is equal to *arg2*	Zero
arg1 is greater than *arg2*	Greater than zero

The array must be sorted in ascending order with the lowest address containing the lowest element.

If the array does not contain the key, a null pointer is returned.

A related function is **qsort( )**.

div

```
#include <cstdlib>
div_t div(int numerator, int denominator);
ldiv_t div(long numerator, long denominator);
```

The **int** version of **div( )** returns the quotient and the remainder of the operation *numerator / denominator* in a structure of type **div_t**. The **long** version of **div( )** returns the quotient and remainder in a structure of type **ldiv_t**. The **long** version of **div( )** provides the same capabilities as the **ldiv( )** function.

The structure type **div_t** will have at least these two fields:

```
int quot; /* quotient */
int rem;  /* remainder */
```

The structure type **ldiv_t** will have at least these two fields:

```
long quot; /* quotient */
long rem;  /* remainder */
```

A related function is **ldiv( )**.

exit

```
#include <cstdlib>
void exit(int exit_code);
```

The **exit( )** function causes immediate, normal termination of a program.

The value of *exit_code* is passed to the calling process, usually the operating system, if the environment supports it. By convention, if the value of *exit_code* is zero, or **EXIT_SUCCESS**, normal program termination is assumed. A nonzero value, or **EXIT_FAILURE**, is used to indicate an implementation-defined error.

Related functions are **atexit( )** and **abort( )**.

getenv

```
#include <cstdlib>
char *getenv(const char *name);
```

The **getenv( )** function returns a pointer to environmental information associated with the string pointed to by *name* in the implementation-defined environmental information table. The string returned must never be changed by the program.

The environment of a program may include such things as path names and devices online. The exact nature of this data is implementation defined. You will need to refer to your compiler's documentation for details.

If a call is made to **getenv( )** with an argument that does not match any of the environment data, a null pointer is returned.

A related function is **system( )**.

labs

```
#include <cstdlib>
long labs(long num);
```

The **labs( )** function returns the absolute value of *num*.

A related function is **abs( )**.

ldiv

```
#include <cstdlib>
ldiv_t ldiv(long numerator, long denominator);
```

The **ldiv( )** function returns the quotient and the remainder of the operation *numerator / denominator*.

The structure type **ldiv_t** will have at least these two fields:

```
long quot; /* quotient */
long rem;  /* remainder */
```

A related function is **div( )**.

longjmp

```
#include <csetjmp>
void longjmp(jmp_buf envbuf, int status);
```

The **longjmp( )** function causes program execution to resume at the point of the last call to **setjmp( )**. These two functions provide a means of jumping between functions. Notice that the header **<csetjmp>** is required.

The **longjmp( )** function operates by resetting the stack to the state as described in *envbuf*, which must have been set by a prior call to **setjmp( )**. This causes program execution to resume at the statement following the **setjmp( )** invocation. That is, the computer is "tricked" into thinking that it never left the function that called **setjmp( )**. (As a somewhat graphic explanation, the **longjmp( )** function "warps" across time and (memory) space to a previous point in your program without having to perform the normal function return process.)

The buffer *evnbuf* is of type **jmp_buf**, which is defined in the header **<csetjmp>**. The buffer must have been set through a call to **setjmp( )** prior to calling **longjmp( )**.

The value of *status* becomes the return value of **setjmp( )** and may be interrogated to determine where the long jump came from. The only value that is not allowed is zero.

By far the most common use of **longjmp( )** is to return from a deeply nested set of routines when an error occurs.

A related function is **setjmp( )**.

mblen

```
#include <cstdlib>
int mblen(const char *str, size_t size);
```

The **mblen( )** function returns the length (in bytes) of a multibyte character pointed to by *str*. Only the first *size* number of characters are examined. It returns –1 on error.

If *str* is null, then **mblen( )** returns non-zero if multibyte characters have state-dependent encodings. If they do not, zero is returned.

Related functions are **mbtowc( ) and wctomb( )**.

mbstowcs

```
#include <cstdlib>
size_t mbstowcs(wchar_t *out, const char *in, size_t size);
```

The **mbstowcs( )** function converts the multibyte string pointed to by *in* into a wide character string and puts that result in the array pointed to by *out*. Only *size* number of bytes will be stored in *out*.

The **mbstowcs( )** function returns the number of multibyte characters that are converted. If an error occurs, the function returns –1.

Related functions are **wcstombs( )**, **mbtowc( )**.

mbtowc

```
#include <cstdlib>
int mbtowc(wchar_t *out, const char *in, size_t size);
```

The **mbtowc( )** function converts the multibyte character in the array pointed to by *in* into its wide character equivalent and puts that result in the object pointed to by *out*. Only *size* number of characters will be examined.

This function returns the number of bytes that are put into *out*. –1 is returned if an error occurs. If *in* is null, then **mbtowc( )** returns non-zero if multibyte characters have state-dependent encodings. If they do not, zero is returned.

Related functions are **mblen( )**, **wctomb( )**.

qsort

```
#include <cstdlib>
void qsort(void *buf, size_t num, size_t size,
          int (*compare) (const void *, const void *));
```

The **qsort( )** function sorts the array pointed to by *buf* using a Quicksort (developed by C.A.R. Hoare). The Quicksort is the best general-purpose sorting algorithm. Upon termination, the array will be sorted. The number of elements in the array is specified by *num*, and the size (in bytes) of each element is described by *size*.

The function pointed to by *compare* is used to compare an element of the array with the key. The form of the *compare* function must be as follows:

int *func_name*(const void **arg1,* const void **arg2*);

It must return values as described here:

Comparison	Value Returned
arg1 is less than *arg2*	Less than zero
arg1 is equal to *arg2*	Zero
arg1 is greater than *arg2*	Greater than zero

The array is sorted into ascending order with the lowest address containing the lowest element.

A related function is **bsearch( )**.

raise

```
#include <csignal>
int raise(int signal);
```

The **raise( )** function sends the signal specified by *signal* to the executing program. It returns zero if successful, and nonzero otherwise. It uses the header **<csignal>**.

The following signals are defined by Standard C++. Of course, your compiler is free to provide additional signals.

Macro	Meaning
SIGABRT	Termination error
SIGFPE	Floating-point error
SIGILL	Bad instruction

Macro	Meaning
SIGINT	User pressed CTRL-C
SIGSEGV	Illegal memory access
SIGTERM	Terminate program

A related function is **signal( )**.

rand

```
#include <cstdlib>
int rand(void);
```

The **rand( )** function generates a sequence of pseudorandom numbers. Each time it is called, an integer between zero and **RAND_MAX** is returned.

A related function is **srand( )**.

setjmp

```
#include <csetjmp>
int setjmp(jmp_buf envbuf);
```

The **setjmp( )** function saves the contents of the system stack in the buffer *envbuf* for later use by **longjmp( )**. It uses the header **<csetjmp>**.

The **setjmp( )** function returns zero upon invocation. However, **longjmp( )** passes an argument to **setjmp( )** when it executes, and it is this value (always nonzero) that will appear to be the value of **setjmp( )** after a call to **longjmp( )** has occurred.

See **longjmp** for additional information.

A related function is **longjmp( )**.

signal

```
#include <csignal>
void (*signal(int signal, void (*func)(int))) (int);
```

The **signal( )** function registers the function pointed to by *func* as a handler for the signal specified by *signal*. That is, the function pointed to by *func* will be called when *signal* is received by your program.

The value of *func* may be the address of a signal handler function or one of the following macros, defined in **<csignal>**:

Macro	Meaning
SIG_DFL	Use default signal handling
SIG_IGN	Ignore the signal

If a function address is used, the specified handler will be executed when its signal is received.

On success, **signal( )** returns the address of the previously defined function for the specified signal. On error, **SIG_ERR** (defined in **<csignal>**) is returned.

A related function is **raise( )**.

srand

```
#include <cstdlib>
void srand(unsigned seed);
```

The **srand( )** function is used to set a starting point for the sequence generated by **rand( )**. (The **rand( )** function returns pseudorandom numbers.)

srand( ) is generally used to allow multiple program runs to use different sequences of pseudorandom numbers by specifying different starting points. Conversely, you can also use **srand( )** to generate the same pseudorandom sequence over and over again by calling it with the same seed before obtaining each sequence.

A related function is **rand( )**.

strtod

```
#include <cstdlib>
double strtod(const char *start, char **end);
```

The **strtod( )** function converts the string representation of a number stored in the string pointed to by *start* into a **double** and returns the result.

The **strtod( )** function works as follows. First, any white space in the string pointed to by *start* is stripped. Next, each character that comprises the number is read. Any character that cannot be part of a floating-point number will cause this process to stop. This includes white space, punctuation (other than periods), and characters other than E or e. Finally, *end* is set to point to the remainder, if any, of the original string. This means that if **strtod( )** is called with "100.00 Pliers", the value 100.00 will be returned, and *end* will point to the space that precedes "Pliers".

If no conversion takes place, zero is returned. If overflow occurs, **strtod( )** returns either **HUGE_VAL** or **–HUGE_VAL** (indicating positive or negative overflow), and the global variable **errno** is set to **ERANGE**, indicating a range error. If underflow occurs, then zero is returned and the global variable **errno** is set to **ERANGE**.

A related function is **atof( )**.

strtol

```
#include <cstdlib>
long strtol(const char *start, char **end,
            int radix);
```

The **strtol( )** function converts the string representation of a number stored in the string pointed to by *start* into a **long** and returns the result. The base of the number is determined by *radix*. If *radix* is zero, the base is determined by rules that govern constant specification. If *radix* is other than zero, it must be in the range 2 through 36.

The **strtol( )** function works as follows. First, any white space in the string pointed to by *start* is stripped. Next, each character that comprises the number is read. Any character that cannot be part of a long integer number will cause this process to stop. This includes white space, punctuation, and characters. Finally, *end* is set to point to the remainder, if any, of the original string. This means that if **strtol( )** is called with "100 Pliers", the value 100L will be returned, and *end* will point to the space that precedes "Pliers".

If the result cannot be represented by a long integer, **strtol( )** returns either **LONG_MAX** or **LONG_MIN** and the global **errno** is set to **ERANGE**, indicating a range error. If no conversion takes place, zero is returned.

A related function is **atol( )**.

strtoul

```
#include <cstdlib>
unsigned long strtoul(const char *start, char **end,
                      int radix);
```

The **strtoul( )** function converts the string representation of a number stored in the string pointed to by *start* into an **unsigned long** and returns the result. The base of the number is determined by *radix*. If *radix* is zero, the base is determined by rules that govern constant specification. If the radix is specified, it must be in the range 2 through 36.

The **strtoul( )** function works as follows. First, any white space in the string pointed to by *start* is stripped. Next, each character that comprises the number is read. Any character that cannot be part of an unsigned long integer number will cause this process to stop. This includes white space, punctuation, and characters. Finally, *end* is set to point to the remainder, if any, of the original string. This means that if **strtoul( )** is called with " 100 Pliers", the value 100L will be returned, and *end* will point to the space that precedes "Pliers".

If the result cannot be represented by an unsigned long integer, **strtoul( )** returns **ULONG_MAX** and the global variable **errno** is set to **ERANGE**, indicating a range error. If no conversion takes place, zero is returned.

A related function is **strtol( )**.

system

```
#include <cstdlib>
int system(const char *str);
```

The **system( )** function passes the string pointed to by *str* as a command to the command processor of the operating system.

If **system( )** is called with a null pointer, it will return nonzero if a command processor is present, and zero otherwise. (Some C++ code will be executed in dedicated systems that do not have operating systems and command processors, so you may not be able to assume that a command processor is present.) The return value of **system( )** is implementation defined. However, generally it will return zero if the command was successfully executed, and nonzero otherwise.

A related function is **exit( )**.

va_arg, va_start, and va_end

```
#include <cstdarg>
type va_arg(va_list argptr, type);
void va_end(va_list argptr);
void va_start(va_list argptr, last_parm);
```

The **va_arg( )**, **va_start( )**, and **va_end( )** macros work together to allow a variable number of arguments to be passed to a function. The most common example of a function that takes a variable number of arguments is **printf( )**. The type **va_list** is defined by **<cstdarg>**.

The general procedure for creating a function that can take a variable number of arguments is as follows. The function must have at least one known parameter, but may have more, prior to the variable parameter list. The rightmost known parameter is called the *last_parm*. The name of *last_parm* is used as the second parameter in a call to **va_start( )**. Before any of the variable-length parameters can be accessed, the argument pointer *argptr* must be initialized through a call to **va_start( )**. After that, parameters are returned via calls to **va_arg( )**, with *type* being the type of the next parameter. Finally, once all the parameters have been read and prior to returning from the function, a call to **va_end( )** must be made to ensure that the stack is properly restored. If **va_end( )** is not called, a program crash is very likely.

A related function is **vprintf( )**.

wcstombs

```
#include <cstdlib>
size_t wcstombs(char *out, const wchar_t *in, size_t size);
```

The **wcstombs( )** converts the wide-character array pointed to by *in* into its multibyte equivalent and puts the result in the array pointed to by *out*. Only the first *size* bytes of *in* are converted. Conversion stops before that if the null terminator is encountered.

If successful, **wcstombs( )** returns the number of bytes converted. On failure, –1 is returned.

Related functions are **wctomb( )** and **mbstowcs( )**.

wctomb

```
#include <cstdlib>
int wctomb(char *out,  wchar_t in);
```

The **wctomb( )** converts the wide character in *in* into its multibyte equivalent and puts the result in the object pointed to by *out*. The array pointed to by *out* must be at least **MB_CUR_MAX** characters long.

If successful, **wctomb( )** returns the number of bytes contained in the multibyte character. On failure, –1 is returned.

If *out* is null, then **wctomb( )** returns nonzero if the multibyte character has state-dependent encodings and zero if it does not.

Related functions are **wcstombs( )** and **mbtowc( )**.

Chapter 31

The Wide-Character Functions

In 1995, a number of wide-character functions were added to Standard C and subsequently adopted by Standard C++. The wide-character functions operate on characters of type **wchar_t**, which are 16 bits. For the most part these functions parallel their **char** equivalents. For example, the function **iswspace( )** is the wide-character version of **isspace( )**. In general, the wide-character functions use the same names as their **char** equivalents, except that a "w" is added.

The wide-character functions use two headers: **<cwchar>** and **<cwctype>**. The C header files **wchar.h** and **wctype.h** are also supported.

The header **<cwctype>** defines the types **wint_t**, **wctrans_t**, and **wctype_t**. Many of the wide-character functions receive a wide character as a parameter. The type of this parameter is **wint_t**. It is capable of holding a wide character. The use of the **wint_t** type in the wide-character functions parallels the use of **int** in the **char**-based functions. **wctrans_t** and **wctype_t** are the types of objects used to represent a character mapping (i.e., character translation) and the classification of a character, respectively. The wide-character EOF mark is defined as **WEOF**.

In addition to defining **win_t**, the header **<cwchar>** defines the types **wchar_t**, **size_t**, and **mbstate_t**. The **wchar_t** type creates a wide character object, and **size_t** is the type of value returned by **sizeof**. The **mbstate_t** type describes an object that holds the state of a multibyte-to-wide-character conversion. The **<cwchar>** header also defines the macros **NULL**, **WEOF**, **WCHAR_MAX**, and **WCHAR_MIN**. The last two define the maximum and minimum value that can be held in an object of type **wchar_t**.

Although the standard function library's support for wide characters is quite extensive, these functions are not frequently used. One reason for this is that the Standard C++ I/O system and class libraries provide both normal and wide-character support through the use of template classes. Also, interest in wide-character-compliant programs has been less than expected. Of course, this situation may change.

Since most of the wide-character functions simply parallel their **char** equivalents and are not frequently used by most C++ programmers, only a brief description of these functions is provided.

The Wide-Character Classification Functions

The header **<cwctype>** provides the prototypes for the wide-character functions that support character classification. These functions categorize wide characters as to their type or convert the case of a character. Table 31-1 lists these functions along with their **char** equivalents, which are described in Chapter 26.

In addition to the functions shown in Table 31-1, **<cwctype>** defines the following ones, which provide an open-ended means of classifying characters.

```
wctype_t wctype(const char *attr);
int iswctype(wint_t ch, wctype_t attr_ob);
```

Function	char Equivalent
int iswalnum(wint_t *ch*)	isalnum( )
int iswalpha(wint_t *ch*)	isalpha( )
int iswcntrl(wint_t *ch*)	iscntrl( )
int iswdigit(wint_t *ch*)	isdigit( )
int iswgraph(wint_t *ch*)	isgraph( )
int iswlower(wint_t *ch*)	islower( )
int iswprint(wint_t *ch*)	isprint( )
int iswpunct(wint_t *c*)	ispunct( )
int iswspace(wint_t *ch*)	isspace( )
int iswupper(wint_t *ch*)	isupper( )
int iswxdigit(wint_t *ch*)	isxdigit( )
wint_t tolower(wint_t *ch*)	tolower( )
wint_t toupper(wint_t *ch*)	toupper( )

Table 31-1. *The Wide-Character Classification Functions*

The function **wctype( )** returns a value that can be passed to the *attr_ob* parameter to **iswctype( )**. The string pointed to by *attr* specifies a property that a character must have. The value in *attr_ob* is used to determine if *ch* is a character that has that property. If it does, **iswctype( )** returns nonzero. Otherwise, it returns zero. The following property strings are defined for all execution environments.

alnum	alpha	cntrl	digit
graph	lower	print	punct
space	upper	xdigit	

The following program demonstrates the **wctype( )** and **iswctype( )** functions.

```
#include <iostream>
#include <cwctype>
using namespace std;
```

```
int main()
{
  wctype_t x;

  x = wctype("space");

  if(iswctype(L' ', x))
    cout << "Is a space.\n";

  return 0;
}
```

This program displays "Is a space."

The functions **wctrans( )** and **towctrans( )** are also defined in **<cwctype>**. They are shown here:

wctrans_t wctrans(const char *_mapping_);
wint_t towctrans(wint_t _ch_, wctrans_t _mapping_ob_);

The function **wctrans( )** returns a value that can be passed to the _mapping_ob_ parameter to **towctrans( )**. Here, the string pointed to by _mapping_ specifies a mapping of one character to another. This value can then be used by **iswctrans( )** to map _ch_. The mapped value is returned. The following mapping strings are supported in all execution environments.

  tolower   toupper

Here is a short example that demonstrates **wctrans( )** and **towctrans( )**.

```
#include <iostream>
#include <cwctype>
using namespace std;

int main()
{
  wctrans_t x;

  x = wctrans("tolower");
```

```
    wchar_t ch = towctrans(L'W', x);
    cout << (char) ch;

    return 0;
}
```

This program displays a lowercase "w".

The Wide-Character I/O Functions

Several of the I/O functions described in Chapter 25 have wide-character implementations. These functions are shown in Table 31-2. The wide-character I/O functions use the header **<cwchar>**. Notice that **swprintf( )** and **vswprintf( )** require an additional parameter not needed by their **char** equivalents.

In addition to those shown in the table, the following wide-character I/O function has been added:

   int fwide(FILE *stream, int how);

If *how* is positive, **fwide( )** makes *stream* a wide-character stream. If *how* is negative, **fwide( )** makes stream into a **char** stream. If *how* is zero, the stream is unaffected. If the stream has already been oriented to either wide or normal characters, it will not be changed. The function returns positive if the stream uses wide characters, negative if the stream uses **char**s, and zero if the stream has not yet been oriented. A stream's orientation is also determined by its first use.

The Wide-Character String Functions

There are wide-character versions of the string manipulation functions described in Chapter 26. These are shown in Table 31-3. They use the header **<cwchar>**. Note that **wcstok( )** requires an additional parameter not used by its **char** equivalent.

Wide-Character String Conversion Functions

The functions shown in Table 31-4 provide wide-character versions of the standard numeric and time conversion functions. These functions use the header **<cwchar>**.

Function	char Equivalent
win_t fgetwc(FILE *stream)	fgetc( )
wchar_t *fgetws(wchar_t *str, int num, FILE *stream)	fgets( )
wint_t fputwc(wchar_t ch, FILE *stream)	fputc( )
int fputws(const wchar_t *str, FILE *stream)	fputs( )
int fwprintf(FILE *stream, const wchar_t fmt, ...)	fprintf( )
int fwscanf(FILE *stream, const wchar_t fmt, ...)	fscanf( )
wint_t getwc(FILE *stream)	getc( )
wint_t getwchar( )	getchar( )
wint_t putwc(wchar_t ch, FILE *stream)	putc( )
wint_t putwchar(wchar_t ch)	putchar( )
int swprintf(wchar_t *str, size_t num, const wchar_t *fmt, ...)	sprintf( ) Note the addition of the parameter num, which limits the number of characters written to str.
int swscanf(const wchar_t *str, const wchar_t *fmt, ...)	sscanf( )
wint_t ungetwc(wint_t ch, FILE *stream)	ungetc( )
int vfwprintf(FILE *stream, const wchar_t fmt, va_list arg)	vfprintf( )
int vswprintf(wchar_t *str, size_t num, const wchar_t *fmt, va_list arg)	vsprintf( ) Note the addition of the parameter num, which limits the number of characters written to str.
int vwprintf(const wchar_t *fmt, va_list arg)	vprintf( )
int wprintf(const wchar_t *fmt, ...)	printf( )
int wscanf(const wchar_t *fmt, ...)	scanf( )

Table 31-2.   *The Wide-Character I/O Functions*

Function	char Equivalent
wchar_t *wcscat(wchar_t *str1, const wchar_t *str2)	strcat( )
wchar_t *wcschr(const wchar_t *str, wchar_t ch)	strchr( )
int wcscmp(const wchar_t *str1, const wchar_t *str2)	strcmp( )
int wcscoll(const wchar_t *str1, const wchar_t *str2)	strcoll( )
size_t wcscspn(const wchar_t *str1, const wchar_t *str2)	strcspn( )
wchar_t *wcscpy(wchar_t *str1, const wchar_t *str2)	strcpy( )
size_t wcslen(const wchar_t *str)	strlen( )
wchar_t *wcsncpy(wchar_t *str1, const wchar_t str2, size_t num)	strncpy( )
wchar_t *wcsncat(wchar_t *str1, const wchar_t str2, size_t num)	strncat( )
int wcsncmp(const wchar_t *str1, const wchar_t *str2, size_t num)	strncmp( )
wchar_t *wcspbrk(const wchar_t *str1, const wchar_t *str2)	strpbrk( )
wchar_t *wcsrchr(const wchar_t *str, wchar_t ch)	strrchr( )
size_t wcsspn(const wchar_t *str1, const wchar_t str2)	strspn( )
wchar_t *wcstok(wchar_t *str1, const wchar_t *str2, wchar_t **endptr)	strtok( ) Here, *endptr* is a pointer that holds information necessary to continue the tokenizing process.
wchar_t *wcsstr(const wchar_t *str1, const wchar_t *str2)	strstr( )
size_t wcsxfrm(wchar_t *str1, const wchar_t *str2, size_t num)	strxfrm( )

Table 31-3. *The Wide-Character String Functions*

Function	char Equivalent

size_t wcsftime(wchar_t *str, size_t max,
            const wchar_t *fmt,
            const struct tm *ptr)
	strftime( )

double wcstod(const wchar_t *start, wchar_t **end);	strtod( )
long wcstol(const wchar_t *start, wchar_t **end, int radix)	strtol( )
unsigned long wcstoul(const wchar_t *start, wchar_t **end, int radix)	strtoul( )

Table 31-4.   *The Wide-Character Conversion Functions*

Wide-Character Array Functions

The standard character array-manipulation functions, such as **memcpy( )**, also have
wide-character equivalents. They are shown in Table 31-5. These functions use the
header **<cwchar>**.

Function	char Equivalent
wchar_t *wmemchr(const wchar_t *str, wchar_t ch, size_t num)	memchr( )
int wmemcmp(const wchar_t *str1, const wchar_t *str2, size_t num)	memcmp( )

wchar_t *wmemcpy(wchar_t *str1,
            const wchar_t *str2,
            size_t num)
	memcpy( )

wchar_t *wmemmove(wchar_t *str1,
            const wchar_t *str2,
            size_t num)
	memmove( )

wchar_t *wmemset(wchar_t *str, wchar_t ch, size_t num)	memset( )

Table 31-5.   *The Wide-Character Array Functions*

Multibyte/Wide-Character Conversion Functions

The Standard C++ function library supplies various functions that support conversions between multibyte and wide characters. These functions, shown in Table 31-6, use the header **<cwchar>**. Many of them are *restartable* versions of the normal multibyte functions. The restartable version utilizes the state information passed to it in a parameter of type **mbstate_t**. If this parameter is null, the function will provide its own **mbstate_t** object.

Function	Description
win_t btowc(int *ch*)	Converts *ch* into its wide-character equivalent and returns the result. Returns **WEOF** on error or if *ch* is not a one-byte, multibyte character.
size_t mbrlen(const char **str*, size_t *num*, mbstate_t **state*)	Restartable version of **mblen( )** as described by *state*. Returns a positive value that indicates the length of the next multibyte character. Zero is returned if the next character is null. A negative value is returned if an error occurs.
size_t mbrtowc(wchar_t **out*, const char **in*, size_t *num*, mbstate_t **state*)	Restartable version of **mbtowc( )** as described by *state*. Returns a positive value that indicates the length of the next multibyte character. Zero is returned if the next character is null. A negative value is returned if an error occurs. If an error occurs, the macro **EILSEQ** is assigned to **errno**.
int mbsinit(const mbstate_t **state*)	Returns true if *state* represents an initial conversion state.
size_t mbsrtowcs(wchar_t **out*, const char ***in*, size_t *num*, mbstate_t *state*)	Restartable version of **mbstowcs( )** as described by *state*. Also, **mbsrtowcs( )** differs from **mbstowcs( )** in that *in* is an indirect pointer to the source array. If an error occurs, the macro **EILSEQ** is assigned to **errno**.

Table 31-6. *Wide-Character/Multibyte Conversion Functions*

Function	Description
size_t wcrtomb(char *out, wchar_t ch, mbstate_t *state)	Restartable version of **wctomb( )** as described by *state*. If an error occurs, the macro **EILSEQ** is assigned to **errno**.
size_t wcsrtombs(char *out, const wchar_t **in, size_t num, mbstate_t *state)	Restartable version of **wcstombs( )** as described by *state*. Also, **wcsrtombs( )** differs from **wcstombs( )** in that *in* is an indirect pointer to the source array. If an error occurs, the macro **EILSEQ** is assigned to **errno**.
int wctob(wint_t ch)	Converts *ch* into its one-byte, multibyte equivalent. It returns **EOF** on failure.

Table 31-6.   *Wide-Character/Multibyte Conversion Functions* (continued*)*

The Complete Reference

C++

Part IV

The Standard C++ Class Library

Standard C++ defines an extensive set of classes that provide support for a number of common activities, including I/O, strings, and numeric processing. The class library is in addition to the function library described in Part Three. The class library forms a major portion of the C++ language and defines much of its character. Despite its size, the class library is easy to master because it is organized around object-oriented principles.

The Standard C++ library is quite large and an in-depth description of all of its classes, features, attributes, and implementation details is beyond the scope of this book. (A full description of the class library would easily fill a large book!) However, while most of the class library is for general use, some of it is intended mostly for compiler developers, or those programmers implementing extensions or enhancements. Therefore, this section describes only those parts of the class library that are typically used in an application. If you will be using the library for specialized work, you will need to acquire a copy of the C++ standard, which contains the technical description of the class library.

Chapter 32

The Standard C++ I/O Classes

This chapter describes the Standard C++ I/O class library. As explained in Part Two, there are currently two versions of C++'s I/O library in common use. The first is the old-style library, which is not defined by Standard C++. The second is the modern, templatized Standard C++ I/O system. Since the modern I/O library is essentially a superset of the old-style one, its is the only one described here. However, much of the information still applies to the older version.

> **Note** *For an overview of C++ I/O, see Chapters 20 and 21.*

The I/O Classes

The Standard C++ I/O system is constructed from a rather complex system of template classes. These classes are shown here.

Class	Purpose
basic_ios	Provides general-purpose I/O operations
basic_streambuf	Low-level support for I/O
basic_istream	Support for input operations
basic_ostream	Support for output operations
basic_iostream	Support for input/output operations
basic_filebuf	Low-level support for file I/O
basic_ifstream	Support for file input
basic_ofstream	Support for file output
basic_fstream	Support for file input/output
basic_stringbuf	Low-level support for string-based I/O
basic_istringstream	Support for string-based input
basic_ostringstream	Support for string-based output
basic_stringstream	Support for string-based input/output

Also part of the I/O class hierarchy is the non-template class **ios_base**. It provides definitions for various elements of the I/O system.

The C++ I/O system is built upon two related but different template class hierarchies. The first is derived from the low-level I/O class called **basic_streambuf**. This class supplies the basic, low-level input and output operations, and provides the underlying support for the entire C++ I/O system. The classes **basic_filebuf** and **basic_stringbuf** are derived from **basic_streambuf**. Unless you are doing advanced I/O programming, you will not need to use **basic_streambuf** or its subclasses directly.

The class hierarchy that you will most commonly be working with is derived from **basic_ios**. This is a high-level I/O class that provides formatting, error-checking, and status information related to stream I/O. **basic_ios** is used as a base for several derived classes, including **basic_istream**, **basic_ostream**, and **basic_iostream**. These classes are used to create streams capable of input, output, and input/output, respectively. Specifically, from **basic_istream** are derived the classes **basic_ifstream** and **basic_istringstream**, from **basic_ostream** are derived **basic_ofstream** and **basic_ostringstream**, and from **basic_iostream** are derived **basic_fstream** and **basic_stringstream**. A base class for **basic_ios** is **ios_base**. Thus, any class derived from **basic_ios** has access to the members of **ios_base**.

The I/O classes are parameterized for the type of characters that they act upon and for the traits associated with those characters. For example, here is the template specification for **basic_ios**:

```
template <class CharType, class Attr = char_traits<CharType> >
  class basic_ios: public ios_base
```

Here, **CharType** specifies the type of character (such as **char** or **wchar_t**) and **Attr** specifies a type that describes its attributes. The generic type **char_traits** is a utility class that defines the attributes associated with a character.

As explained in Chapter 20, the I/O library creates two specializations of the template class hierarchies just described: one for 8-bit characters and one for wide characters. Here is a complete list of the mapping of template class names to their character and wide-character versions.

Template Class	Character-Based Class	Wide-Character-Based Class
basic_ios	ios	wios
basic_istream	istream	wistream
basic_ostream	ostream	wostream
basic_iostream	iostream	wiostream

Template Class	Character-Based Class	Wide-Character-Based Class
basic_ifstream	ifstream	wifstream
basic_ofstream	ofstream	wofstream
basic_fstream	fstream	wfstream
basic_istringstream	istringstream	wistringstream
basic_ostringstream	ostringstream	wostringstream
basic_stringstream	stringstream	wstringstream
basic_streambuf	streambuf	wstreambuf
basic_filebuf	filebuf	wfilebuf
basic_stringbuf	stringbuf	wstringbuf

Since the vast majority of programmers will be using character-based I/O, those are the names used by this chapter. Thus, when referring to the I/O classes, we will simply use their character-based names rather than their internal, template names. For instance, this chapter will use the name **ios** rather than **basic_ios**, **istream** rather than **basic_istream**, and **fstream** rather than **basic_fstream**. Remember, parallel classes exist for wide-character streams and they work in the same way as those described here.

The I/O Headers

The Standard C++ I/O system relies upon several headers. They are shown here.

Header	For
<fstream>	File I/O
<iomanip>	Parameterized I/O manipulators
<ios>	Basic I/O support
<iosfwd>	Forward declarations used by the I/O system
<iostream>	General I/O
<istream>	Basic input support
<ostream>	Basic output support

Header	For
<sstream>	String-based streams
<streambuf>	Low-level I/O support

Several of these headers are used internally by the I/O system. In general, your program will only include **<iostream>**, **<fstream>**, **<sstream>**, or **<iomanip>**.

The Format Flags and I/O Manipulators

Each stream has associated with it a set of format flags that control the way information is formatted. The **ios_base** class declares a bitmask enumeration called **fmtflags** in which the following values are defined.

adjustfield	basefield	boolalpha	dec
fixed	floatfield	hex	internal
left	oct	right	scientific
showbase	showpoint	showpos	skipws
unitbuf	uppercase		

These values are used to set or clear the format flags, using functions such as **setf( )** and **unsetf( )**. A detailed description of these flags is found in Chapter 20.

In addition to setting or clearing the format flags directly, you may alter the format parameters of a stream through the use of special functions called manipulators, which can be included in an I/O expression. The standard manipulators are shown in the following table:

Manipulator	Purpose	Input/Output
boolalpha	Turns on **boolapha** flag.	Input/Output
dec	Turns on **dec** flag.	Input/Output
endl	Output a newline character and flush the stream.	Output
ends	Output a null.	Output
fixed	Turns on **fixed** flag.	Output
flush	Flush a stream.	Output
hex	Turns on **hex** flag.	Input/Output

Manipulator	Purpose	Input/Output
internal	Turns on **internal** flag.	Output
left	Turns on **left** flag.	Output
noboolalpha	Turns off **boolalpha** flag.	Input/Output
noshowbase	Turns off **showbase** flag.	Output
noshowpoint	Turns off **showpoint** flag.	Output
noshowpos	Turns off **showpos** flag.	Output
noskipws	Turns off **skipws** flag.	Input
nounitbuf	Turns off **unitbuf** flag.	Output
nouppercase	Turns off **uppercase** flag.	Output
oct	Turns on **oct** flag.	Input/Output
resetiosflags (fmtflags *f*)	Turn off the flags specified in *f*.	Input/Output
right	Turns on **right** flag.	Output
scientific	Turns on **scientific** flag.	Output
setbase(int *base*)	Set the number base to *base*.	Input/Output
setfill(int *ch*)	Set the fill character to *ch*.	Output
setiosflags(fmtflags *f*)	Turn on the flags specified in *f*.	Input/output
setprecision (int *p*)	Set the number of digits of precision.	Output
setw(int *w*)	Set the field width to *w*.	Output
showbase	Turns on **showbase** flag.	Output
showpoint	Turns on **showpoint** flag.	Output
showpos	Turns on **showpos** flag.	Output
skipws	Turns on **skipws** flag.	Input
unitbuf	Turns on **unitbuf** flag.	Output
uppercase	Turns on **uppercase** flag.	Output
ws	Skip leading white space.	Input

To use a manipulator that takes a parameter, you must include **<iomanip>**.

Several Data Types

In addition to the **fmtflags** type just described, the Standard C++ I/O system defines several other types.

The streamsize and streamoff Types

An object of type **streamsize** is capable of holding the largest number of bytes that will be transferred in any one I/O operation. It is typically some form of integer. An object of type **streamoff** is capable of holding a value that indicates an offset position within a stream. It is typically some form of integer. These types are defined in the header **<ios>**, which is automatically included by the I/O system.

The streampos and wstreampos Types

An object of type **streampos** is capable of holding a value that represents a position within a **char** stream. The **wstreampos** type is capable of holding a value that represents a position with a **wchar_t** stream. These are defined in **<iosfwd>**, which is automatically included by the I/O system.

The pos_type and off_type Types

The types **pos_type** and **off_type** create objects (typically integers) that are capable of holding a value that represents the position and an offset, respectively, within a stream. These types are defined by **ios** (and other classes) and are essentially the same as **streamoff** and **streampos** (or their wide-character equivalents).

The openmode Type

The type **openmode** is defined by **ios_base** and describes how a file will be opened. It will be one or more of these values.

app	Append to end of file.
ate	Seek to end of file on creation.
binary	Open file for binary operations.
in	Open file for input.
out	Open file for output.
trunc	Erase previously existing file.

You can combine two or more of these values by ORing them together.

The iostate Type

The current status of an I/O stream is described by an object of type **iostate**, which is an enumeration defined by **ios_base** that includes these members.

Name	Meaning
goodbit	No errors occurred.
eofbit	End-of-file is encountered.
failbit	A nonfatal I/O error has occurred.
badbit	A fatal I/O error has occurred.

The seekdir Type

The **seekdir** type describes how a random-access file operation will take place. It is defined within **ios_base**. Its valid values are shown here.

beg	Beginning-of-file
cur	Current location
end	End-of-file

The failure Class

In **ios_base** is defined the exception type **failure**. It serves as a base class for the types of exceptions that can be thrown by the I/O system. It inherits **exception** (the standard exception class). The **failure** class has the following constructor:

    explicit failure(const string &str);

Here, *str* is a message that describes the error. This message can be obtained from a **failure** object by calling its **what( )** function, shown here:

    virtual const char *what( ) const throw( );

Overload << and >> Operators

The following classes overload the << and/or >> operators relative to all of the built-in data types.

basic_istream
basic_ostream
basic_iostream

Any classes derived from these classes inherit these operators.

The General-Purpose I/O Functions

The remainder of this chapter describes the general-purpose I/O functions supplied by Standard C++. As explained, the Standard C++ I/O system is built upon an intricate hierarchy of template classes. Many of the members of the low-level classes are not used for application programming. Thus, they are not described here.

bad

```
#include <iostream>
bool bad() const;
```

The **bad( )** function is a member of **ios.**
The **bad( )** function returns **true** if a fatal I/O error has occurred in the associated stream; otherwise, **false** is returned.
A related function is **good( )**.

clear

```
#include <iostream>
void clear(iostate flags = goodbit);
```

The **clear( )** function is a member of **ios.**
The **clear( )** function clears the status flags associated with a stream. If *flags* is **goodbit** (as it is by default), then all error flags are cleared (reset to zero). Otherwise, the status flags will be set to whatever value is specified in *flags*.
A related function is **rdstate( )**.

eof

```
#include <iostream>
bool eof() const;
```

The **eof( )** function is a member of **ios.**

The **eof( )** function returns **true** when the end of the associated input file has been encountered; otherwise it returns **false.**

Related functions are **bad( )**, **fail( )**, **good( )**, **rdstate( )**, and **clear( )**.

exceptions

```
#include <iostream>
iostate exceptions() const;
void exceptions(iostate flags);
```

The **exceptions( )** function is a member of **ios.**

The first form returns an **iostate** object that indicates which flags cause an exception. The second form sets these values.

A related function is **rdstate( )**.

fail

```
#include <iostream>
bool fail() const;
```

The **fail( )** function is a member of **ios.**

The **fail( )** function returns **true** if an I/O error has occurred in the associated stream. Otherwise, it returns **false.**

Related functions are **good( )**, **eof( )**, **bad( )**, **clear( )**, and **rdstate( )**.

fill

```
#include <iostream>
char fill() const;
char fill(char ch);
```

The **fill( )** function is a member of **ios.**

By default, when a field needs to be filled, it is filled with spaces. However, you can specify the fill character using the **fill( )** function and specifying the new fill character in *ch*. The old fill character is returned.

To obtain the current fill character, use the first form of **fill( )**, which returns the current fill character.

Related functions are **precision( )** and **width( )**.

flags

```
#include <iostream>
fmtflags flags() const;
fmtflags flags(fmtflags f);
```

The **flags( )** function is a member of **ios** (inherited from **ios_base**).

The first form of **flags( )** simply returns the current format flags settings of the associated stream.

The second form of **flags( )** sets all format flags associated with a stream as specified by *f*. When you use this version, the bit pattern found in *f* is copied into the format flags associated with the stream. This version also returns the previous settings.

Related functions are **unsetf( )** and **setf( )**.

flush

```
#include <iostream>
ostream &flush();
```

The **flush( )** function is a member of **ostream**.

The **flush( )** function causes the buffer connected to the associated output stream to be physically written to the device. The function returns a reference to its associated stream.

Related functions are **put( )** and **write( )**.

fstream, ifstream, and ofstream

```
#include <fstream>
fstream();
explicit fstream(const char *filename,
                 ios::openmode mode = ios::in | ios::out);
ifstream();
explicit ifstream(const char *filename, ios::openmode mode=ios::in);

ofstream();
explicit ofstream(const char *filename,
                  ios::openmode mode=ios::out);
```

The **fstream( )**, **ifstream( )**, and **ofstream( )** functions are the constructors of the **fstream**, **ifstream**, and **ofstream** classes, respectively.

The versions of **fstream( )**, **ifstream( )**, and **ofstream( )** that take no parameters create a stream that is not associated with any file. This stream can then be linked to a file using **open( )**.

The versions of **fstream( )**, **ifstream( )**, and **ofstream( )** that take a filename for their first parameters are the most commonly used in application programs. Although it is entirely proper to open a file using the **open( )** function, most of the time you will not do so because these **ifstream**, **ofstream**, and **fstream** constructors automatically open the file when the stream is created. The constructors have the same parameters and defaults as the **open( )** function. (See **open** for details.) For instance, this is the most common way you will see a file opened:

```
ifstream mystream("myfile");
```

If for some reason the file cannot be opened, the value of the associated stream variable will be **false**. Therefore, whether you use a constructor to open the file or an explicit call to **open( )**, you will want to confirm that the file has actually been opened by testing the value of the stream.

Related functions are **close( )** and **open( )**.

gcount

```
#include <iostream>
streamsize gcount() const;
```

The **gcount( )** function is a member of **istream**.

The **gcount( )** function returns the number of characters read by the last input operation.

Related functions are **get( )**, **getline( )**, and **read( )**.

get

```
#include <iostream>
int get();
istream &get(char &ch):
istream &get(char *buf, streamsize num);
istream &get(char *buf, streamsize num, char delim);
istream &get(streambuf &buf);
istream &get(streambuf &buf, char delim);
```

The **get( )** function is a member of **istream**.

In general, **get( )** reads characters from an input stream. The parameterless form of **get( )** reads a single character from the associated stream and returns that value.

get(char &*ch*) reads a character from the associated stream and puts that value in *ch*. It returns a reference to the stream.

get(char **buf**, **streamsize *num*)** reads characters into the array pointed to by *buf* until either *num*−1 characters have been read, a newline is found, or the end of the file has been encountered. The array pointed to by *buf* will be null terminated by **get( )**. If the newline character is encountered in the input stream, it is *not* extracted. Instead, it remains in the stream until the next input operation. This function returns a reference to the stream.

get(char **buf**, **streamsize *num*, **char *delim*)** reads characters into the array pointed to by *buf* until either *num*−1 characters have been read, the character specified by *delim* has been found, or the end of the file has been encountered. The array pointed to by *buf* will be null terminated by **get( )**. If the delimiter character is encountered in the input stream, it is *not* extracted. Instead, it remains in the stream until the next input operation. This function returns a reference to the stream.

get(streambuf &*buf*) reads characters from the input stream into the **streambuf** object. Characters are read until a newline is found or the end of the file is encountered. It returns a reference to the stream. If the newline character is encountered in the input stream, it is not extracted.

get(streambuf &*buf*, **char *delim*) reads characters from the input stream into the **streambuf** object. Characters are read until the character specified by *delim* is found or the end of the file is encountered. It returns a reference to the stream. If the delimiter character is encountered in the input stream, it is not extracted.

Related functions are **put( )**, **read( )**, and **getline( )**.

getline

```
#include <iostream>
istream &getline(char *buf, streamsize num);
istream &getline(char *buf, streamsize num, char delim);
```

The **getline( )** function is a member of **istream**.

getline(char **buf**, **streamsize *num*)** reads characters into the array pointed to by *buf* until either *num*−1 characters have been read, a newline character has been found, or the end of the file has been encountered. The array pointed to by *buf* will be null terminated by **getline( )**. If the newline character is encountered in the input stream, it is extracted but is not put into *buf*. This function returns a reference to the stream.

getline(char **buf**, **streamsize *num*, **char *delim*)** reads characters into the array pointed to by *buf* until either *num*−1 characters have been read, the character specified by *delim* has been found, or the end of the file has been encountered. The array pointed to by *buf* will be null terminated by **getline( )**. If the delimiter character is encountered in the input stream, it is extracted but is not put into *buf*. This function returns a reference to the stream.

Related functions are **get( )** and **read( )**.

good

```
#include <iostream>
bool good() const;
```

The **good( )** function is a member of **ios**.

The **good( )** function returns **true** if no I/O errors have occurred in the associated stream; otherwise, it returns **false**.

Related functions are **bad( )**, **fail( )**, **eof( )**, **clear( )**, and **rdstate( )**.

ignore

```
#include <iostream>
istream &ignore(streamsize num = 1, int delim = EOF);
```

The **ignore( )** function is a member of **istream**.

You can use the **ignore( )** member function to read and discard characters from the input stream. It reads and discards characters until either *num* characters have been ignored (1 by default) or until the character specified by *delim* is encountered (**EOF** by default). If the delimiting character is encountered, it is removed from the input stream. The function returns a reference to the stream.

Related functions are **get( )** and **getline( )**.

open

```
#include <fstream>
void fstream::open(const char *filename,
                   ios::openmode mode = ios::in | ios:: out);
void ifstream::open(const char *filename,
                    ios::openmode mode = ios::in);
void ofstream::open(const char *filename,
                    ios::openmode mode = ios:: out | ios::trunc);
```

The **open( )** function is a member of **fstream**, **ifstream**, and **ofstream**.

A file is associated with a stream by using the **open( )** function. Here, *filename* is the name of the file, which may include a path specifier. The value of *mode* determines how the file is opened. It must be one (or more) of these values:

ios::app
ios::ate
ios::binary
ios::in
ios::out
ios::trunc

You can combine two or more of these values by ORing them together.

Including **ios::app** causes all output to that file to be appended to the end. This value can only be used with files capable of output. Including **ios::ate** causes a seek to the end of the file to occur when the file is opened. Although **ios::ate** causes a seek to the end-of-file, I/O operations can still occur anywhere within the file.

The **ios::binary** value causes the file to be opened for binary I/O operations. By default, files are opened in text mode.

The **ios::in** value specifies that the file is capable of input. The **ios::out** value specifies that the file is capable of output. However, creating an **ifstream** stream implies input, and creating an **ofstream** stream implies output, and opening a file using **fstream** implies both input and output.

The **ios::trunc** value causes the contents of a preexisting file by the same name to be destroyed, and the file is truncated to zero length.

In all cases, if **open( )** fails, the stream will be **false**. Therefore, before using a file, you should test to make sure that the open operation succeeded.

Related functions are **close( )**, **fstream( )**, **ifstream( )**, and **ofstream( )**.

peek

```
#include <iostream>
int peek();
```

The **peek( )** function is a member of **istream**.

The **peek( )** function returns the next character in the stream or **EOF** if the end of the file is encountered. It does not, under any circumstances, remove the character from the stream.

A related function is **get( )**.

precision

```
#include <iostream>
streamsize precision() const;
streamsize precision(streamsize p);
```

The **precision( )** function is a member of **ios** (inherited from **ios_base**).

By default, six digits of precision are displayed when floating-point values are output. However, using the second form of **precision( )**, you can set this number to the value specified in *p*. The original value is returned.

The first version of **precision( )** returns the current value.

Related functions are **width( )** and **fill( )**.

put

```
#include <iostream>
ostream &put(char ch);
```

The **put( )** function is a member of **ostream**.

The **put( )** function writes *ch* to the associated output stream. It returns a reference to the stream.

Related functions are **write( )** and **get( )**.

putback

```
#include <iostream>
istream &putback(char ch);
```

The **putback( )** function is a member of **istream**.

The **putback( )** function returns *ch* to the associated input stream.

A related function is **peek( )**.

rdstate

```
#include <iostream>
iostate rdstate() const;
```

The **rdstate( )** function is a member of **ios**.

The **rdstate( )** function returns the status of the associated stream. The C++ I/O system maintains status information about the outcome of each I/O operation relative to each active stream. The current state of a stream is held in an object of type **iostate**, in which the following flags are defined:

Name	Meaning
goodbit	No errors occurred.
eofbit	End-of-file is encountered.
failbit	A nonfatal I/O error has occurred.
badbit	A fatal I/O error has occurred.

These flags are enumerated inside **ios** (via **ios_base**).

rdstate( ) returns **goodbit** when no error has occurred; otherwise, an error bit has been set.

Related functions are **eof( )**, **good( )**, **bad( )**, **clear( )**, **setstate( )**, and **fail( )**.

read

```
#include <iostream>
istream &read(char *buf, streamsize num);
```

The **read( )** function is a member of **istream**.

The **read( )** function reads *num* bytes from the associated input stream and puts them in the buffer pointed to by *buf*. If the end of the file is reached before *num* characters have been read, **read( )** simply stops, sets **failbit**, and the buffer contains as many characters as were available. (See **gcount( )**.) **read( )** returns a reference to the stream.

Related functions are **gcount( )**, **readsome( )**, **get( )**, **getline( )**, and **write( )**.

readsome

```
#include <iostream>
streamsize readsome(char *buf, streamsize num);
```

The **readsome( )** function is a member of **istream**.

The **readsome( )** function reads *num* bytes from the associated input stream and puts them in the buffer pointed to by *buf*. If the stream contains less than *num* characters, that number of characters are read. **readsome( )** returns the number of characters read. The difference between **read( )** and **readsome( )** is that **readsome( )** does not set the **failbit** if there are less than *num* characters available.

Related functions are **gcount( )**, **read( )**, and **write( )**.

seekg and seekp

```
#include <iostream>
istream &seekg(off_type offset, ios::seekdir origin)
istream &seekg(pos_type position);

ostream &seekp(off_type offset, ios::seekdir origin);
ostream &seekp(pos_type position);
```

The **seekg( )** function is a member of **istream**, and the **seekp( )** function is a member of **ostream**.

In C++'s I/O system, you perform random access using the **seekg( )** and **seekp( )** functions. To this end, the C++ I/O system manages two pointers associated with a file. One is the *get pointer*, which specifies where in the file the next input operation will occur. The other is the *put pointer*, which specifies where in the file the next output operation will occur. Each time an input or an output operation takes place, the appropriate pointer is automatically sequentially advanced. However, using the **seekg( )** and **seekp( )** functions, it is possible to access the file in a nonsequential fashion.

The two-parameter version of **seekg( )** moves the get pointer *offset* number of bytes from the location specified by *origin*. The two-parameter version of **seekp( )** moves the put pointer *offset* number of bytes from the location specified by *origin*. The *offset* parameter is of type **off_type**, which is capable of containing the largest valid value that *offset* can have.

The *origin* parameter is of type **seekdir** and is an enumeration that has these values:

ios::beg	Seek from beginning
ios::cur	Seek from current position
ios::end	Seek from end

The single-parameter versions of **seekg( )** and **seekp( )** move the file pointers to the location specified by *position*. This value must have been previously obtained using a call to either **tellg( )** or **tellp( )**, respectively. **pos_type** is a type that is capable of containing the largest valid value that *position* can have. These functions return a reference to the associated stream.

Related functions are **tellg( )** and **tellp( )**.

setf

```
#include <iostream>
fmtflags setf(fmtflags flags);
fmtflags setf(fmtflags flags1, fmtflags flags2);
```

The **setf( )** function is a member of **ios** (inherited from **ios_base**).

The **setf( )** function sets the format flags associated with a stream. See the discussion of format flags earlier in this section.

The first version of **setf( )** turns on the format flags specified by *flags*. (All other flags are unaffected.) For example, to turn on the **showpos** flag for **cout**, you can use this statement:

```
cout.setf(ios::showpos);
```

When you want to set more than one flag, you can OR together the values of the flags you want set.

It is important to understand that a call to **setf( )** is done relative to a specific stream. There is no concept of calling **setf( )** by itself. Put differently, there is no concept in C++ of global format status. Each stream maintains its own format status information individually.

The second version of **setf( )** affects only the flags that are set in *flags2*. The corresponding flags are first reset and then set according to the flags specified by *flags1*. Even if *flags1* contains other set flags, only those specified by *flags2* will be affected.

Both versions of **setf( )** return the previous settings of the format flags associated with the stream.

Related functions are **unsetf( )** and **flags( )**.

setstate

```
#include <iostream>
void setstate(iostate flags) const;
```

The **setstate( )** function is a member of **ios**.

The **setstate( )** function sets the status of the associated stream as described by *flags*. See **rdstate( )** for further details.

Related functions are **clear( )** and **rdstate( )**.

str

```
#include <sstream>
string str() const;
void str(string &s)
```

The **str( )** function is a member of **stringstream**, **istringstream**, and **ostringstream**.

The first form of the **str( )** function returns a **string** object that contains the current contents of the string-based stream.

The second form frees the string currently contained in the string stream and substitutes the string referred to by *s*.

Related functions are **get( )** and **put( )**.

stringstream, istringstream, ostringstream

```
#include <sstream>
explicit stringstream(ios::openmode mode = ios::in | ios::out);
explicit stringstream(const string &str,
                      ios::openmode mode = ios::in | ios::out);
explicit istringstream(ios::openmode mode=ios::in);
explicit istringstream(const string str, ios::openmode mode=ios::in);
explicit ostringstream(ios::openmode mode=ios::out);
explicit ostringstream(const string str, ios::openmode
                mode=ios::out);
```

The **stringstream( )**, **istringstream( )**, and **ostringstream( )** functions are the constructors of the **stringstream**, **istringstream**, and **ostringstream** classes, respectively. These construct streams that are tied to strings.

The versions of **stringstream( )**, **istringstream( )**, and **ostringstream( )** that specify only the **openmode** parameter create empty streams. The versions that take a **string** parameter initialize the string stream.

Here is an example that demonstrates the use of a string stream.

```
// Demonstrate string streams.
#include <iostream>
#include <sstream>
using namespace std;
```

```
int main()
{
  stringstream s("This is initial string.");

  // get string
  string str = s.str();
  cout << str << endl;

  // output to string stream
  s << "Numbers: " << 10 << " " << 123.2;

  int i;
  double d;
  s >> str >> i >> d;
  cout << str << " " << i << " " << d;

  return 0;
}
```

The output produced by this program is shown here:

```
This is initial string.
Numbers: 10 123.2
```

A related function is **str( )**.

sync_with_stdio

```
#include <iostream>
bool sync_with_stdio(bool sync = true );
```

The **sync_with_stdio( )** function is a member of **ios** (inherited from **ios_base**).
Calling **sync_with_stdio( )** allows the standard C-like I/O system to be safely used
concurrently with the C++ class-based I/O system. To turn off **stdio** synchronization,
pass **false** to **sync_with_stdio( )**. The previous setting is returned: **true** for synchronized;
false for no synchronization. By default, the standard streams are synchronized. This
function is reliable only if called prior to any other I/O operations.

tellg and tellp

```
#include <iostream>
pos_type tellg();
pos_type tellp():
```

The **tellg( )** function is a member of **istream**, and **tellp( )** is a member of **ostream**.

The C++ I/O system manages two pointers associated with a file. One is the *get pointer*, which specifies where in the file the next input operation will occur. The other is the *put pointer*, which specifies where in the file the next output operation will occur. Each time an input or an output operation takes place, the appropriate pointer is automatically sequentially advanced. You can determine the current position of the get pointer using **tellg( )** and of the put pointer using **tellp( )**.

pos_type is a type that is capable of holding the largest value that either function can return.

The values returned by **tellg( )** and **tellp( )** can be used as parameters to **seekg( )** and **seekp( )**, respectively.

Related functions are **seekg( )** and **seekp( )**.

unsetf

```
#include <iostream>
void unsetf(fmtflags flags);
```

The **unsetf( )** function is a member of **ios** (inherited from **ios_base**).
The **unsetf( )** function is used to clear one or more format flags.
The flags specified by *flags* are cleared. (All other flags are unaffected.)
Related functions are **setf( )** and **flags( )**.

width

```
#include <iostream>
streamsize width() const;
streamsize width(streamsize w);
```

The **width( )** function is a member of **ios** (inherited from **ios_base**).

To obtain the current field width, use the first form of **width( )**. It returns the current field width. To set the field width, use the second form. Here, *w* becomes the field width, and the previous field width is returned.

Related functions are **precision( )** and **fill( )**.

write

```
#include <iostream>
ostream &write(const char *buf, streamsize num);
```

The **write( )** function is a member of **ostream**.

The **write( )** function writes *num* bytes to the associated output stream from the buffer pointed to by *buf*. It returns a reference to the stream.

Related functions are **read( )** and **put( )**.

Chapter 33

The STL Container Classes

This chapter describes the classes that implement the containers defined by the standard template library (STL). Containers are the part of the STL that provide storage for other objects. In addition to supplying the memory necessary to store objects, they define the mechanisms by which the objects in the container may be accessed. Thus, containers are high-level storage devices.

Note   *For an overview and tutorial to the STL, refer to Chapter 24.*

In the container descriptions, the following conventions will be observed. When referring to the various iterator types generically, this book will use the terms listed here.

Term	Represents
BiIter	Bidirectional iterator
ForIter	Forward iterator
InIter	Input iterator
OutIter	Output iterator
RandIter	Random access iterator

When a unary predicate function is required, it will be notated using the type **UnPred**. When a binary predicate is required, the type **BinPred** will be used. In a binary predicate, the arguments are always in the order of *first,second* relative to the function that calls the predicate. For both unary and binary predicates, the arguments will contain values of the type of objects being stored by the container.

Comparison functions will be notated using the type **Comp**.

One other point: In the descriptions that follow, when an iterator is said to point to the end of a container, this means that the iterator points just beyond the last object in the container.

The Container Classes

The containers defined by the STL are shown here.

Container	Description	Required Header
bitset	A set of bits.	<bitset>
deque	A double-ended queue.	<deque>
list	A linear list.	<list>

Container	Description	Required Header
map	Stores key/value pairs in which each key is associated with only one value.	<map>
multimap	Stores key/value pairs in which one key may be associated with two or more values.	<map>
multiset	A set in which each element is not necessarily unique.	<set>
priority_queue	A priority queue.	<queue>
queue	A queue.	<queue>
set	A set in which each element is unique.	<set>
stack	A stack.	<stack>
vector	A dynamic array.	<vector>

Each of the containers is summarized in the following sections. Since the containers are implemented using template classes, various placeholder data types are used. In the descriptions, the generic type **T** represents the type of data stored by a container.

Since the names of the placeholder types in a template class are arbitrary, the container classes declare **typedef**ed versions of these types. This makes the type names concrete. Here are the **typedef** names used by the container classes.

size_type	Some integral type roughly equivalent to **size_t**.
reference	A reference to an element.
const_reference	A **const** reference to an element.
difference_type	Can represent the difference between two addresses.
iterator	An iterator.
const_iterator	A **const** iterator.
reverse_iterator	A reverse iterator.
const_reverse_iterator	A **const** reverse iterator.

value_type	The type of a value stored in a container. (Often the same as the generic type T.)
allocator_type	The type of the allocator.
key_type	The type of a key.
key_compare	The type of a function that compares two keys.
mapped_type	The type of value stored in a map. (Same as the generic type T.)
value_compare	The type of a function that compares two values.
pointer	The type of a pointer.
const_pointer	The type of a **const** pointer.
container_type	The type of a container.

bitset

The **bitset** class supports operations on a set of bits. Its template specification is

    template <size_t N> class bitset;

Here, N specifies the length of the bitset, in bits. It has the following constructors:

    bitset( );

    bitset(unsigned long *bits*);

    explicit bitset(const string &*s*, size_t *i* = 0, size_t *num* = npos);

The first form constructs an empty bitset. The second form constructs a bitset that has its bits set according to those specified in *bits*. The third form constructs a bitset using the string *s*, beginning at *i*. The string must contain only 1's and 0's. Only *num* or *s*.**size**( )-*i* values are used, whichever is less. The constant **npos** is a value that is sufficiently large to describe the maximum length of *s*.

The output operators **<<** and **>>** are defined for **bitset**.

bitset contains the following member functions.

Member	Description
bool any( ) const;	Returns true if any bit in the invoking bitset is 1; otherwise returns false.
size_t count( ) const;	Returns the number of 1 bits.
bitset<N> &flip( );	Reverses the state of all bits in the invoking bitset and returns ***this.**
bitset<N> &flip(size_t *i*);	Reverses the bit in position *i* in the invoking bitset and returns ***this**.
bool none( ) const;	Returns true if no bits are set in the invoking bitset.
bool operator !=(const bitset<N> &*op2*) const;	Returns true if the invoking bitset differs from the one specified by right-hand operator, *op2*.
bool operator ==(const bitset<N> &*op2*) const;	Returns true if the invoking bitset is the same as the one specified by right-hand operator, *op2*.
bitset<N> &operator &=(const bitset<N> &*op2*);	ANDs each bit in the invoking bitset with the corresponding bit in *op2* and leaves the result in the invoking bitset. It returns ***this**.
bitset<N> &operator ^=(const bitset<N> &*op2*);	XORs each bit in the invoking bitset with the corresponding bit in *op2* and leaves the result in the invoking bitset. It returns ***this**.
bitset<N> &operator |=(const bitset<N> &*op2*);	ORs each bit in the invoking bitset with the corresponding bit in *op2* and leaves the result in the invoking bitset. It returns ***this**.
bitset<N> &operator ~( ) const;	Reverses the state of all bits in the invoking bitset and returns the result.
bitset<N> &operator <<=(size_t *num*);	Left-shifts each bit in the invoking bitset *num* positions and leaves the result in the invoking bitset. It returns ***this**.
bitset<N> &operator >>=(size_t *num*);	Right-shifts each bit in the invoking bitset *num* positions and leaves the result in the invoking bitset. It returns ***this**.

Member	Description
reference operator [ ](size_t *i*);	Returns a reference to bit *i* in the invoking bitset.
bitset<N> &reset( );	Clears all bits in the invoking bitset and returns ***this**.
bitset<N> &reset(size_t *i*);	Clears the bit in position *i* in the invoking bitset and returns ***this**.
bitset<N> &set( );	Sets all bits in the invoking bitset and returns ***this**.
bitset<N> &set(size_t *i*, int *val* = 1);	Sets the bit in position *i* to the value specified by *val* in the invoking bitset and returns ***this**. Any nonzero value for *val* is assumed to be 1.
size_t size( ) const;	Returns the number of bits that the bitset can hold.
bool test(size_t *i*) const;	Returns the state of the bit in position *i*.
string to_string( ) const;	Returns a string that contains a representation of the bit pattern in the invoking bitset.
unsigned long to_ulong( ) const;	Converts the invoking bitset into an unsigned long integer.

deque

The **deque** class supports a double-ended queue. Its template specification is

    template <class T, class Allocator = allocator<T> > class deque

Here, **T** is the type of data stored in the **deque**. It has the following constructors:

    explicit deque(const Allocator &*a* = Allocator( ));

    explicit deque(size_type *num*, const T &*val* = T ( ),
        const Allocator &*a* = Allocator( ));

    deque(const deque<T, Allocator> &*ob*);

template <class InIter> deque(InIter *start*, InIter *end*,
    const Allocator &*a* = Allocator( ));

The first form constructs an empty deque. The second form constructs a deque that has
num elements with the value *val*. The third form constructs a deque that contains the
same elements as *ob*. The fourth form constructs a deque that contains the elements in
the range specified by *start* and *end*.

The following comparison operators are defined for **deque**:

==, <, <=, !=, >, >=

deque contains the following member functions.

Member	Description
template <class InIter> void assign(InIter *start*, InIter *end*);	Assigns the deque the sequence defined by *start* and *end*.
void assign(size_type *num*, const T &*val*);	Assigns the deque *num* elements of value *val*.
reference at(size_type *i*); const_reference at(size_type *i*) const;	Returns a reference to the element specified by *i*.
reference back( ); const_reference back( ) const;	Returns a reference to the last element in the deque.
iterator begin( ); const_iterator begin( ) const;	Returns an iterator to the first element in the deque.
void clear( );	Removes all elements from the deque.
bool empty( ) const;	Returns true if the invoking deque is empty and false otherwise.
const_iterator end( ) const; iterator end( );	Returns an iterator to the end of the deque.
iterator erase(iterator *i*);	Removes the element pointed to by *i*. Returns an iterator to the element after the one removed.
iterator erase(iterator *start*, iterator *end*);	Removes the elements in the range *start* to *end*. Returns an iterator to the element after the last element removed.
reference front( ); const_reference front( ) const;	Returns a reference to the first element in the deque.

Member	Description
allocator_type get_allocator( ) const;	Returns deque's allocator.
iterator insert(iterator *i*, const T &*val*);	Inserts *val* immediately before the element specified by *i*. An iterator to the element is returned.
void insert(iterator *i*, size_type *num*, const T &*val*);	Inserts *num* copies of *val* immediately before the element specified by *i*.
template <class InIter> void insert(iterator *i*, InIter *start*, InIter *end*);	Inserts the sequence defined by *start* and *end* immediately before the element specified by *i*.
size_type max_size( ) const;	Returns the maximum number of elements that the deque can hold.
reference operator[ ](size_type *i*); const_reference operator[ ](size_type *i*) const;	Returns a reference to the *i*th element.
void pop_back( );	Removes the last element in the deque.
void pop_front( );	Removes the first element in the deque.
void push_back(const T &*val*);	Adds an element with the value specified by *val* to the end of the deque.
void push_front(const T &*val*);	Adds an element with the value specified by *val* to the front of the deque.
reverse_iterator rbegin( ); const_reverse_iterator rbegin( ) const;	Returns a reverse iterator to the end of the deque.
reverse_iterator rend( ); const_reverse_iterator rend( ) const;	Returns a reverse iterator to the start of the deque.
void resize(size_type *num*, T *val* = T ( ));	Changes the size of the deque to that specified by *num*. If the deque must be lengthened, then elements with the value specified by *val* are added to the end.
size_type size( ) const;	Returns the number of elements currently in the deque.
void swap(deque<T, Allocator> &*ob*);	Exchanges the elements stored in the invoking deque with those in *ob*.

list

The **list** class supports a list. Its template specification is

    template <class T, class Allocator = allocator<T> > class list

Here, **T** is the type of data stored in the list. It has the following constructors:

    explicit list(const Allocator &*a* = Allocator( ));

    explicit list(size_type *num*, const T &*val* = T ( ),
                   const Allocator &*a* = Allocator( ));

    list(const list<T, Allocator> &*ob*);

    template <class InIter>list(InIter *start*, InIter *end*,
                   const Allocator &*a* = Allocator( ));

The first form constructs an empty list. The second form constructs a list that has *num* elements with the value *val*. The third form constructs a list that contains the same elements as *ob*. The fourth form constructs a list that contains the elements in the range specified by *start* and *end*.

The following comparison operators are defined for **list**:

    ==, <, <=, !=, >, >=

list contains the following member functions.

Member	Description
template <class InIter> void assign(InIter *start*, InIter *end*);	Assigns the list the sequence defined by *start* and *end*.
void assign(size_type *num*, const T &*val*);	Assigns the list *num* elements of value *val*.
reference back( ); const_reference back( ) const;	Returns a reference to the last element in the list.
iterator begin( ); const_iterator begin( ) const;	Returns an iterator to the first element in the list.

Member	Description
void clear( );	Removes all elements from the list.
bool empty( ) const;	Returns true if the invoking list is empty and false otherwise.
iterator end( ); const_iterator end( ) const;	Returns an iterator to the end of the list.
iterator erase(iterator *i*);	Removes the element pointed to by *i*. Returns an iterator to the element after the one removed.
iterator erase(iterator *start*, iterator *end*);	Removes the elements in the range *start* to *end*. Returns an iterator to the element after the last element removed.
reference front( ); const_reference front( ) const;	Returns a reference to the first element in the list.
allocator_type get_allocator( ) const;	Returns list's allocator.
iterator insert(iterator *i*, const T &*val* = T( ));	Inserts *val* immediately before the element specified by *i*. An iterator to the element is returned.
void insert(iterator *i*, size_type *num*, const T & *val*);	Inserts *num* copies of *val* immediately before the element specified by *i*.

template <class InIter>
   void insert(iterator *i*,
        InIter *start*, InIter *end*);
	Inserts the sequence defined by *start* and *end* immediately before the element specified by *i*.

size_type max_size( ) const;	Returns the maximum number of elements that the list can hold.

void merge(list<T, Allocator> &*ob*);
template <class Comp>
   void merge(<list<T, Allocator> &*ob*,
        Comp *cmpfn*);
	Merges the ordered list contained in *ob* with the ordered invoking list. The result is ordered. After the merge, the list contained in *ob* is empty. In the second form, a comparison function can be specified that determines when one element is less than another.

void pop_back( );	Removes the last element in the list.
void pop_front( );	Removes the first element in the list.

Member	Description
void push_back(const T &*val*);	Adds an element with the value specified by *val* to the end of the list.
void push_front(const T &*val*);	Adds an element with the value specified by *val* to the front of the list.
reverse_iterator rbegin( ); const_reverse_iterator rbegin( ) const;	Returns a reverse iterator to the end of the list.
void remove(const T &*val*);	Removes elements with the value *val* from the list.
template <class UnPred> void remove_if(UnPred *pr*);	Removes elements for which the unary predicate *pr* is true.
reverse_iterator rend( ); const_reverse_iterator rend( ) const;	Returns a reverse iterator to the start of the list.
void resize(size_type *num*, T *val* = T ( ));	Changes the size of the list to that specified by *num*. If the list must be lengthened, then elements with the value specified by *val* are added to the end.
void reverse( );	Reverses the invoking list.
size_type size( ) const;	Returns the number of elements currently in the list.

void sort( );
 template <class Comp>
    void sort(Comp *cmpfn*);
	Sorts the list. The second form sorts the list using the comparison function *cmpfn* to determine when one element is less than another.

void splice(iterator *i*, list<T, Allocator> &*ob*);	The contents of *ob* are inserted into the invoking list at the location pointed to by *i*. After the operation, *ob* is empty.

void splice(iterator *i*,
        list<T, Allocator> &*ob*,
        iterator *el*);
	The element pointed to by *el* is removed from the list *ob* and stored in the invoking list at the location pointed to by *i*.

void splice(iterator *i*,
        list<T, Allocator> &ob,
        iterator *start*, iterator *end*);
	The range defined by *start* and *end* is removed from *ob* and stored in the invoking list beginning at the location pointed to by *i*.

Member	Description
void swap(list<T, Allocator> &*ob*);	Exchanges the elements stored in the invoking list with those in *ob*.

void unique( );
 template <class BinPred>
   void unique(BinPred *pr*);
	Removes duplicate elements from the invoking list. The second form uses *pr* to determine uniqueness.

map

The **map** class supports an associative container in which unique keys are mapped with values. Its template specification is shown here:

    template <class Key, class T, class Comp = less<Key>,
            class Allocator = allocator<pair<const Key, T > > > class map

Here, **Key** is the data type of the keys, **T** is the data type of the values being stored (mapped), and **Comp** is a function that compares two keys. It has the following constructors:

    explicit map(const Comp &*cmpfn* = Comp( ),
            const Allocator &*a* = Allocator( ));

    map(const map<Key, T, Comp, Allocator> &*ob*);

    template <class InIter> map(InIter *start*, InIter *end*,
            const Comp &*cmpfn* = Comp( ),
            const Allocator &*a* = Allocator( ));

The first form constructs an empty map. The second form constructs a map that contains the same elements as *ob*. The third form constructs a map that contains the elements in the range specified by *start* and *end*. The function specified by *cmpfn*, if present, determines the ordering of the map.

The following comparison operators are defined for **map**.

    ==, <, <=, !=, >, >=

The member functions contained by **map** are shown here. In the descriptions, **key_type** is the type of the key, and **value_type** represents **pair<Key, T>**.

Member	Description
iterator begin( ); const_iterator begin( ) const;	Returns an iterator to the first element in the map.
void clear( );	Removes all elements from the map.
size_type count(const key_type &k) const;	Returns the number of times k occurs in the map (1 or zero).
bool empty( ) const;	Returns true if the invoking map is empty and false otherwise.
iterator end( ); const_iterator end( ) const;	Returns an iterator to the end of the map.

pair<iterator, iterator>
   equal_range(const key_type &k);
pair<const_iterator, const_iterator>
   equal_range(const key_type &k) const;
	Returns a pair of iterators that point to the first and last elements in the map that contain the specified key.

void erase(iterator i);	Removes the element pointed to by i.
void erase(iterator *start*, iterator *end*);	Removes the elements in the range *start* to *end*.
size_type erase(const key_type &k);	Removes from the map elements that have keys with the value k.
iterator find(const key_type &k); const_iterator find(const key_type &k) const;	Returns an iterator to the specified key. If the key is not found, then an iterator to the end of the map is returned.
allocator_type get_allocator( ) const;	Returns map's allocator.
iterator insert(iterator i, const value_type &*val*);	Inserts *val* at or after the element specified by i. An iterator to the element is returned.
template <class InIter> void insert(InIter *start*, InIter *end*);	Inserts a range of elements.
pair<iterator, bool> insert(const value_type &*val*);	Inserts *val* into the invoking map. An iterator to the element is returned. The element is only inserted if it does not already exist. If the element was inserted, **pair<iterator, true>** is returned. Otherwise, **pair<iterator, false>** is returned.

Member	Description
key_compare key_comp( ) const;	Returns the function object that compares keys.
iterator lower_bound(const key_type &k); const_iterator lower_bound(const key_type &k) const;	Returns an iterator to the first element in the map with the key equal to or greater than k.
size_type max_size( ) const;	Returns the maximum number of elements that the map can hold.
mapped_type & operator[ ] (const key_type &i);	Returns a reference to the element specified by i. If this element does not exist, it is inserted.
reverse_iterator rbegin( ); const_reverse_iterator rbegin( ) const;	Returns a reverse iterator to the end of the map.
reverse_iterator rend( ); const_reverse_iterator rend( ) const;	Returns a reverse iterator to the start of the map.
size_type size( ) const;	Returns the number of elements currently in the map.
void swap(map<Key, T, Comp, Allocator> &ob);	Exchanges the elements stored in the invoking map with those in ob.
iterator upper_bound(const key_type &k); const_iterator upper_bound(const key_type &k) const;	Returns an iterator to the first element in the map with the key greater than k.
value_compare value_comp( ) const;	Returns the function object that compares values.

multimap

The **multimap** class supports an associative container in which possibly nonunique keys are mapped with values. Its template specification is shown here:

template <class Key, class T, class Comp = less<Key>,
       class Allocator = allocator<pair<const Key, T > > > class multimap

Here, **Key** is the data type of the keys, **T** is the data type of the values being stored (mapped), and **Comp** is a function that compares two keys. It has the following constructors:

explicit multimap(const Comp &*cmpfn* = Comp( ),
   const Allocator &*a* = Allocator( ));

multimap(const multimap<Key, T, Comp, Allocator> &*ob*);

template <class InIter> multimap(InIter *start*, InIter *end*,
   const Comp &*cmpfn* = Comp( ),
   const Allocator &*a* = Allocator( ));

The first form constructs an empty multimap. The second form constructs a multimap that contains the same elements as *ob*. The third form constructs a multimap that contains the elements in the range specified by *start* and *end*. The function specified by *cmpfn*, if present, determines the ordering of the multimap.

The following comparison operators are defined by **multimap**:

==, <, <=, !=, >, >=

The member functions contained by **multimap** are shown here. In the descriptions, **key_type** is the type of the key, **T** is the value, and **value_type** represents **pair<Key, T>**.

Member	Description
iterator begin( ); const_iterator begin( ) const;	Returns an iterator to the first element in the multimap.
void clear( );	Removes all elements from the multimap.
size_type count(const key_type &*k*) const;	Returns the number of times *k* occurs in the multimap.
bool empty( ) const;	Returns true if the invoking multimap is empty and false otherwise.
iterator end( ); const_iterator end( ) const;	Returns an iterator to the end of the list.

pair<iterator, iterator>
 equal_range(const key_type &*k*);
 pair<const_iterator, const_iterator>
 equal_range(const key_type &*k*) const;
	Returns a pair of iterators that point to the first and last elements in the multimap that contain the specified key.

void erase(iterator *i*);	Removes the element pointed to by *i*.
void erase(iterator *start*, iterator *end*);	Removes the elements in the range *start* to *end*.

Member	Description
size_type erase(const key_type &k);	Removes from the multimap elements that have keys with the value k.
iterator find(const key_type &k); const_iterator find(const key_type &k) const;	Returns an iterator to the specified key. If the key is not found, then an iterator to the end of the multimap is returned.
allocator_type get_allocator( ) const;	Returns multimap's allocator.
iterator insert(iterator i, const value_type &val);	Inserts val at or after the element specified by i. An iterator to the element is returned.
template <class InIter> void insert(InIter start, InIter end);	Inserts a range of elements.
iterator insert(const value_type &val);	Inserts val into the invoking multimap.
key_compare key_comp( ) const;	Returns the function object that compares keys.

iterator lower_bound(const key_type &k);
 const_iterator
   lower_bound(const key_type &k) const;
	Returns an iterator to the first element in the multimap with the key equal to or greater than k.

size_type max_size( ) const;	Returns the maximum number of elements that the multimap can hold.
reverse_iterator rbegin( ); const_reverse_iterator rbegin( ) const;	Returns a reverse iterator to the end of the multimap.
reverse_iterator rend( ); const_reverse_iterator rend( ) const;	Returns a reverse iterator to the start of the multimap.
size_type size( ) const;	Returns the number of elements currently in the multimap.
void swap(multimap<Key, T, Comp, Allocator> &ob);	Exchanges the elements stored in the invoking multimap with those in ob.

iterator upper_bound(const key_type &k);
 const_iterator
   upper_bound(const key_type &k) const;
	Returns an iterator to the first element in the multimap with the key greater than k.

value_compare value_comp( ) const;	Returns the function object that compares values.

multiset

The **multiset** class supports a set containing possibly nonunique keys. Its template specification is shown here:

template <class Key, class Comp = less<Key>,
        class Allocator = allocator<Key> > class multiset

Here, **Key** is the data of the keys and **Comp** is a function that compares two keys. It has the following constructors:

explicit multiset(const Comp &*cmpfn* = Comp( ),
        const Allocator &*a* = Allocator( ));

multiset(const multiset<Key, Comp, Allocator> &*ob*);

template <class InIter> multiset(InIter *start*, InIter *end*,
        const Comp &*cmpfn* = Comp( ),
        const Allocator &*a* = Allocator( ));

The first form constructs an empty multiset. The second form constructs a multiset that contains the same elements as *ob*. The third form constructs a multiset that contains the elements in the range specified by *start* and *end*. The function specified by *cmpfn*, if present, determines the ordering of the set.

The following comparison operators are defined for **multiset**.

==, <, <=, !=, >, >=

The member functions contained by **multiset** are shown here. In the descriptions, both **key_type** and **value_type** are **typedef**s for **Key**.

Member	Description
iterator begin( ); const_iterator begin( ) const;	Returns an iterator to the first element in the multiset.
void clear( );	Removes all elements from the multiset.
size_type count(const key_type &*k*) const;	Returns the number of times *k* occurs in the multiset.
bool empty( ) const;	Returns true if the invoking multiset is empty and false otherwise.

Member	Description
iterator end( ); const_iterator end( ) const;	Returns an iterator to the end of the multiset.
pair<iterator, iterator> equal_range(const key_type &*k*) const;	Returns a pair of iterators that point to the first and last elements in the multiset that contain the specified key.
void erase(iterator *i*);	Removes the element pointed to by *i*.
void erase(iterator *start*, iterator *end*);	Removes the elements in the range *start* to *end*.
size_type erase(const key_type &*k*);	Removes from the multiset elements that have keys with the value *k*.
iterator find(const key_type &*k*) const;	Returns an iterator to the specified key. If the key is not found, then an iterator to the end of the multiset is returned.
allocator_type get_allocator( ) const;	Returns multiset's allocator.
iterator insert(iterator *i*, const value_type &*val*);	Inserts *val* at or after the element specified by *i*. An iterator to the element is returned.
template <class InIter> void insert(InIter *start*, InIter *end*);	Inserts a range of elements.
iterator insert(const value_type &*val*);	Inserts *val* into the invoking multiset. An iterator to the element is returned.
key_compare key_comp( ) const;	Returns the function object that compares keys.
iterator lower_bound(const key_type &*k*) const;	Returns an iterator to the first element in the multiset with the key equal to or greater than *k*.
size_type max_size( ) const;	Returns the maximum number of elements that the multiset can hold.
reverse_iterator rbegin( ); const_reverse_iterator rbegin( ) const;	Returns a reverse iterator to the end of the multiset.
reverse_iterator rend( ); const_reverse_iterator rend( ) const;	Returns a reverse iterator to the start of the multiset.

Member	Description
size_type size( ) const;	Returns the number of elements currently in the multiset.
void swap(multiset<Key, Comp, Allocator> &*ob*);	Exchanges the elements stored in the invoking multiset with those in *ob*.
iterator upper_bound(const key_type &*k*) const;	Returns an iterator to the first element in the multiset with the key greater than *k*.
value_compare value_comp( ) const;	Returns the function object that compares values.

queue

The **queue** class supports a single-ended queue. Its template specification is shown here:

template <class T, class Container = deque<T> > class queue

Here, **T** is the type of data being stored and **Container** is the type of container used to hold the queue. It has the following constructor:

explicit queue(const Container &*cnt* = Container( ));

The **queue( )** constructor creates an empty queue. By default it uses a **deque** as a container, but a **queue** can only be accessed in a first-in, first-out manner. You can also use a **list** as a container for a queue. The container is held in a protected object called **c** of type **Container**.

The following comparison operators are defined for **queue**:

==, <, <=, !=, >, >=

queue contains the following member functions.

Member	Description
value_type &back( ); const value_type &back( ) const;	Returns a reference to the last element in the queue.
bool empty( ) const;	Returns true if the invoking queue is empty and false otherwise.

Member	Description
value_type &front( ); const value_type &front( ) const;	Returns a reference to the first element in the queue.
void pop( );	Removes the first element in the queue.
void push(const value_type &*val*);	Adds an element with the value specified by *val* to the end of the queue.
size_type size( ) const;	Returns the number of elements currently in the queue.

priority_queue

The **priority_queue** class supports a single-ended priority queue. Its template specification is shown here:

```
template <class T, class Container = vector<T>,
        class Comp = less<Container::value_type> >
        class priority_queue
```

Here, **T** is the type of data being stored. **Container** is the type of container used to hold the queue, and **Comp** specifies the comparison function that determines when one member for the priority queue is lower in priority than another. It has the following constructors:

```
explicit priority_queue(const Comp &cmpfn = Comp( ),
        Container &cnt = Container( ));
```

```
template <class InIter> priority_queue(InIter start, InIter end,
        const Comp &cmpfn = Comp( ),
        Container &cnt = Container( ));
```

The first **priority_queue( )** constructor creates an empty priority queue. The second creates a priority queue that contains the elements specified by the range *start* and *end*. By default it uses a **vector** as a container. You can also use a **deque** as a container for a priority queue. The container is held in a protected object called **c** of type **Container**. **priority_queue** contains the following member functions.

Member	Description
bool empty( ) const;	Returns true if the invoking priority queue is empty and false otherwise.
void pop( );	Removes the first element in the priority queue.
void push(const T &*val*);	Adds an element to the priority queue.
size_type size( ) const;	Returns the number of elements current in the priority queue.
const value_type &top( ) const;	Returns a reference to the element with the highest priority. The element is not removed.

set

The **set** class supports a set containing unique keys. Its template specification is shown here:

    template <class Key, class Comp = less<Key>,
            class Allocator = allocator<Key> > class set

Here, **Key** is the data of the keys and **Comp** is a function that compares two keys. It has the following constructors:

    explicit set(const Comp &*cmpfn* = Comp( ),
            const Allocator &*a* = Allocator( ));

    set(const set<Key, Comp, Allocator> &*ob*);

    template <class InIter> set(InIter *start*, InIter *end*,
            const Comp &*cmpfn* = Comp( ),
            const Allocator &*a* = Allocator( ));

The first form constructs an empty set. The second form constructs a set that contains the same elements as *ob*. The third form constructs a set that contains the elements in the range specified by *start* and *end*. The function specified by *cmpfn*, if present, determines the ordering of the set.

The following comparison operators are defined for **set**:

    ==, <, <=, !=, >, >=

The member functions contained by **set** are shown here.

Member	Description
iterator begin( ); const_iterator begin( ) const;	Returns an iterator to the first element in the set.
void clear( );	Removes all elements from the set.
size_type count(const key_type &k) const;	Returns the number of times k occurs in the set.
bool empty( ) const;	Returns true if the invoking set is empty and false otherwise.
const_iterator end( ) const; iterator end( );	Returns an iterator to the end of the set.
pair<iterator, iterator> equal_range(const key_type &k) const;	Returns a pair of iterators that point to the first and last elements in the set that contain the specified key.
void erase(iterator i);	Removes the element pointed to by i.
void erase(iterator start, iterator end);	Removes the elements in the range start to end.
size_type erase(const key_type &k);	Removes from the set elements that have keys with the value k. The number of elements removed is returned.
iterator find(const key_type &k) const;	Returns an iterator to the specified key. If the key is not found, then an iterator to the end of the set is returned.
allocator_type get_allocator( ) const;	Returns set's allocator.
iterator insert(iterator i, const value_type &val);	Inserts val at or after the element specified by i. Duplicate elements are not inserted. An iterator to the element is returned.
template <class InIter> void insert(InIter start, InIter end);	Inserts a range of elements. Duplicate elements are not inserted.

Member	Description
pair<iterator, bool> insert(const value_type &*val*);	Inserts *val* into the invoking set. An iterator to the element is returned. The element is inserted only if it does not already exist. If the element was inserted, **pair<iterator, true>** is returned. Otherwise, **pair<iterator, false>** is returned.
iterator lower_bound(const key_type &*k*) const;	Returns an iterator to the first element in the set with the key equal to or greater than *k*.
key_compare key_comp( ) const;	Returns the function object that compares keys.
size_type max_size( ) const;	Returns the maximum number of elements that the set can hold.
reverse_iterator rbegin( ); const_reverse_iterator rbegin( ) const;	Returns a reverse iterator to the end of the set.
reverse_iterator rend( ); const_reverse_iterator rend( ) const;	Returns a reverse iterator to the start of the set.
size_type size( ) const;	Returns the number of elements currently in the set.
void swap(set<Key, Comp,Allocator> &*ob*);	Exchanges the elements stored in the invoking set with those in *ob*.
iterator upper_bound(const key_type &*k*) const;	Returns an iterator to the first element in the set with the key greater than *k*.
value_compare value_comp( ) const;	Returns the function object that compares values.

stack

The **stack** class supports a stack. Its template specification is shown here:

    template <class T, class Container = deque<T> > class stack

Here, **T** is the type of data being stored and **Container** is the type of container used to hold the stack. It has the following constructor:

explicit stack(const Container &*cnt* = Container( ));

The **stack( )** constructor creates an empty stack. By default it uses a **deque** as a container, but a **stack** can only be accessed in a last-in, first-out manner. You may also use a **vector** or **list** as a container for a stack. The container is held in a protected member called **c** of type **Container**.

The following comparison operators are defined for **stack**:

==, <, <=, !=, >, >=

stack contains the following member functions.

Member	Description
bool empty( ) const;	Returns true if the invoking stack is empty and false otherwise.
void pop( );	Removes the top of the stack, which is technically the last element in the container.
void push(const value_type &*val*);	Pushes an element onto the end of the stack. The last element in the container represents the top of the stack.
size_type size( ) const;	Returns the number of elements currently in the stack.
value_type &top( ); cont value_type &top( ) const;	Returns a reference to the top of the stack, which is the last element in the container. The element is not removed.

vector

The **vector** class supports a dynamic array. Its template specification is shown here.

template <class T, class Allocator = allocator<T> > class vector

Here, **T** is the type of data being stored and **Allocator** specifies the allocator. It has the following constructors.

explicit vector(const Allocator &*a* = Allocator( ));

explicit vector(size_type *num*, const T &*val* = T ( ),
        const Allocator &*a* = Allocator( ));

vector(const vector<T, Allocator> &*ob*);

template <class InIter> vector(InIter *start*, InIter *end*,
        const Allocator &a = Allocator( ));

The first form constructs an empty vector. The second form constructs a vector that has
num elements with the value *val*. The third form constructs a vector that contains the
same elements as *ob*. The fourth form constructs a vector that contains the elements in
the range specified by *start* and *end*.

The following comparison operators are defined for **vector**:

==, <, <=, !=, >, >=

vector contains the following member functions.

Member	Description
template <class InIter> void assign(InIter *start*, InIter *end*);	Assigns the vector the sequence defined by *start* and *end*.
void assign(size_type *num*, const T &*val*);	Assigns the vector *num* elements of value *val*.
reference at(size_type *i*); const_reference at(size_type *i*) const;	Returns a reference to an element specified by *i*.
reference back( ); const_reference back( ) const;	Returns a reference to the last element in the vector.
iterator begin( ); const_iterator begin( ) const;	Returns an iterator to the first element in the vector.
size_type capacity( ) const;	Returns the current capacity of the vector. This is the number of elements it can hold before it will need to allocate more memory.
void clear( );	Removes all elements from the vector.
bool empty( ) const;	Returns true if the invoking vector is empty and false otherwise.

THE STANDARD C++
CLASS LIBRARY

Member	Description
iterator end( ); const_iterator end( ) const;	Returns an iterator to the end of the vector.
iterator erase(iterator *i*);	Removes the element pointed to by *i*. Returns an iterator to the element after the one removed.
iterator erase(iterator *start*, iterator *end*);	Removes the elements in the range *start* to *end*. Returns an iterator to the element after the last element removed.
reference front( ); const_reference front( ) const;	Returns a reference to the first element in the vector.
allocator_type get_allocator( ) const;	Returns vector's allocator.
iterator insert(iterator *i*, const T &*val*);	Inserts *val* immediately before the element specified by *i*. An iterator to the element is returned.
void insert(iterator *i*, size_type *num*, const T & *val*);	Inserts *num* copies of *val* immediately before the element specified by *i*.

template <class InIter>
   void insert(iterator *i*, InIter *start*,
           InIter *end*);
	Inserts the sequence defined by *start* and *end* immediately before the element specified by *i*.

size_type max_size( ) const;	Returns the maximum number of elements that the vector can hold.
reference operator[ ](size_type *i*) const; const_reference operator[ ](size_type *i*) const;	Returns a reference to the element specified by *i*.
void pop_back( );	Removes the last element in the vector.
void push_back(const T &*val*);	Adds an element with the value specified by *val* to the end of the vector.
reverse_iterator rbegin( ); const_reverse_iterator rbegin( ) const;	Returns a reverse iterator to the end of the vector.
reverse_iterator rend( ); const_reverse_iterator rend( ) const;	Returns a reverse iterator to the start of the vector.

Member	Description
void reserve(size_type *num*);	Sets the capacity of the vector so that it is equal to at least *num*.
void resize(size_type *num*, T val = T ( ));	Changes the size of the vector to that specified by *num*. If the vector must be lengthened, then elements with the value specified by *val* are added to the end.
size_type size( ) const;	Returns the number of elements currently in the vector.
void swap(vector<T, Allocator> &*ob*);	Exchanges the elements stored in the invoking vector with those in *ob*.

The STL also contains a specialization of **vector** for Boolean values. It includes all of the functionality of **vector** and adds these two members.

void flip( );	Reverses all bits in the vector.
static void swap(reference *i*, reference *j*);	Exchanges the bits specified by *i* and *j*.

The
Complete
Reference

Chapter 34

The STL Algorithms

The algorithms defined by the standard template library are described here. These algorithms operate on containers through iterators. All of the algorithms are template functions. Here are descriptions of the generic type names used by the algorithms.

Generic Name	Represents
BiIter	Bidirectional iterator
ForIter	Forward iterator
InIter	Input iterator
OutIter	Output iterator
RandIter	Random access iterator
T	Some type of data
Size	Some type of integer
Func	Some type of function
Generator	A function that generates objects
BinPred	Binary predicate
UnPred	Unary predicate
Comp	Comparison function

adjacent_find

```
template <class ForIter>
  ForIter adjacent_find(ForIter start, ForIter end);
template <class ForIter, class BinPred>
  ForIter adjacent_find(ForIter start, ForIter end, BinPred pfn);
```

The **adjacent_find( )** algorithm searches for adjacent matching elements within a sequence specified by *start* and *end* and returns an iterator to the first element. If no adjacent pair is found, *end* is returned. The first version looks for equivalent elements. The second version lets you specify your own method for determining matching elements.

binary_search

```
template <class ForIter, class T>
  bool binary_search(ForIter start, ForIter end, const T &val);
```

```
template <class ForIter, class T, class Comp>
  bool binary_search(ForIter start, ForIter end, const T &val,
                     Comp cmpfn);
```

The **binary_search( )** algorithm performs a binary search on an ordered sequence beginning at *start* and ending with *end* for the value specified by *val*. It returns true if *val* is found and false otherwise. The first version compares the elements in the specified sequence for equality. The second version allows you to specify your own comparison function.

copy

```
template <class InIter, class OutIter>
  OutIter copy(InIter start, InIter end, OutIter result);
```

The **copy( )** algorithm copies a sequence beginning at *start* and ending with *end*, putting the result into the sequence pointed to by *result*. It returns an iterator to the end of the resulting sequence. The range to be copied must not overlap with *result*.

copy_backward

```
template <class BiIter1, class BiIter2>
  BiIter2 copy_backward(BiIter1 start, BiIter1 end, BiIter2 result);
```

The **copy_backward( )** algorithm is the same as **copy( )** except that it moves the elements from the end of the sequence first.

count

```
template <class InIter, class T>
  ptrdiff_t count(InIter start, InIter end, const T &val);
```

The **count( )** algorithm returns the number of elements in the sequence beginning at *start* and ending at *end* that match *val*.

count_if

```
template <class InIter, class UnPred>
  ptrdiff_t count_if(InIter start, InIter end, UnPred pfn);
```

The **count_if( )** algorithm returns the number of elements in the sequence beginning at *start* and ending at *end* for which the unary predicate *pfn* returns true. The type **ptrdiff_t** is defined as some form of integer.

equal

```
template <class InIter1, class InIter2>
  bool equal(InIter1 start1, InIter1 end1, InIter2 start2);
template <class InIter1, class InIter2, class BinPred>
  bool equal(InIter1 start1, InIter1 end1, InIter2 start2,
            BinPred pfn);
```

The **equal( )** algorithm determines if two ranges are the same. The range determined by *start1* and *end1* is tested against the sequence pointed to by *start2*. If the ranges are the same, true is returned. Otherwise, false is returned.

The second form allows you to specify a binary predicate that determines when two elements are equal.

equal_range

```
template <class ForIter, class T>
  pair<ForIter, ForIter> equal_range(ForIter start, ForIter end,
                                     const T &val);
template <class ForIter, class T, class Comp>
  pair<ForIter, ForIter> equal_range(ForIter start, ForIter end,
                                     const T &val, Comp cmpfn);
```

The **equal_range( )** algorithm returns a range in which an element can be inserted into a sequence without disrupting the ordering of the sequence. The region in which to search for such a range is specified by *start* and *end*. The value is passed in *val*. To specify your own search criteria, specify the comparison function *cmpfn*.

The template class **pair** is a utility class that can hold a pair of objects in its **first** and **second** members.

fill and fill_n

```
template <class ForIter, class T>
  void fill(ForIter start, ForIter end, const T &val);
template <class OutIter, class Size, class T>
  void fill_n(OutIter start, Size num, const T &val);
```

The **fill( )** and **fill_n( )** algorithms fill a range with the value specified by *val*. For **fill( )** the range is specified by *start* and *end*. For **fill_n( )**, the range begins at *start* and runs for *num* elements.

find

```
template <class InIter, class T>
  InIter find(InIter start, InIter end, const T &val);
```

The **find( )** algorithm searches the range *start* to *end* for the value specified by *val*. It returns an iterator to the first occurrence of the element or to *end* if the value is not in the sequence.

find_end

```
template <class ForIter1, class ForIter2>
  ForIter1 find_end(ForIter1 start1, ForIter1 end1,
                    ForIter2 start2, ForIter2 end2);
template <class ForIter1, class ForIter2, class BinPred>
  ForIter1 find_end(ForIter1 start1, ForIter1 end1,
                    ForIter2 start2, ForIter2 end2, BinPred pfn);
```

The **find_end( )** algorithm finds the last subsequence defined by *start2* and *end2* within the range *start1* and *end1*. If the sequence is found, an iterator to the first element in the sequence is returned. Otherwise, the iterator *end1* is returned.

The second form allows you to specify a binary predicate that determines when elements match.

find_first_of

```
template <class ForIter1, class ForIter2>
  ForIter1 find_first_of(ForIter1 start1, ForIter1 end1,
```

```
                               ForIter2 start2, ForIter2 end2);
template <class ForIter1, class ForIter2, class BinPred>
  ForIter1 find_first_of(ForIter1 start1, ForIter1 end1,
                         ForIter2 start2, ForIter2 end2,
                         BinPred pfn);
```

The **find_first_of( )** algorithm finds the first element within the sequence defined by *start1* and *end1* that matches an element within the range *start1* and *end1*. If no matching element is found, the iterator *end1* is returned.

The second form allows you to specify a binary predicate that determines when elements match.

find_if

```
template <class InIter, class UnPred>
  InIter find_if(InIter start, InIter end, UnPred pfn);
```

The **find_if( )** algorithm searches the range *start* to *end* for an element for which the unary predicate *pfn* returns true. It returns an iterator to the first occurrence of the element or to *end* if the value is not in the sequence.

for_each

```
template<class InIter, class Func>
  Func for_each(InIter start, InIter end, Func fn);
```

The **for_each( )** algorithm applies the function *fn* to the range of elements specified by *start* and *end*. It returns *fn*.

generate and generate_n

```
template <class ForIter, class Generator>
  void generate(ForIter start, ForIter end, Generator fngen);
template <class ForIter, class Size, class Generator>
  void generate_n(OutIter start, Size num, Generator fngen);
```

The algorithms **generate( )** and **generate_n( )** assign to elements in a range the values returned by a generator function. For **generate( )**, the range being assigned is specified by *start* and *end*. For **generate_n( )**, the range begins at *start* and runs for *num* elements. The generator function is passed in *fngen*. It has no parameters.

includes

```
template <class InIter1, class InIter2>
  bool includes(InIter1 start1, InIter1 end1,
                InIter2 start2, InIter2 end2);
template <class InIter1, class InIter2, class Comp>
  bool includes(InIter1 start1, InIter1 end1,
                InIter2 start2, InIter2 end2, Comp cmpfn);
```

The **includes( )** algorithm determines if the sequence defined by *start1* and *end1* includes all of the elements in the sequence defined by *start2* and *end2*. It returns true if the elements are all found and false otherwise.

The second form allows you to specify a comparison function that determines when one element is less than another.

inplace_merge

```
template <class BiIter>
  void inplace_merge(BiIter start, BiIter mid, BiIter end);
template <class BiIter, class Comp>
  void inplace_merge(BiIter start, BiIter mid, BiIter end, Comp cmpfn);
```

Within a single sequence, the **inplace_merge( )** algorithm merges the range defined by *start* and *mid* with the range defined by *mid* and *end*. Both ranges must be sorted in increasing order. After executing, the resulting sequence is sorted in increasing order.

The second form allows you to specify a comparison function that determines when one element is less than another.

iter_swap

```
template <class ForIter1, class ForIter2>
  void iter_swap(ForIter1 i, ForIter2 j)
```

The **iter_swap( )** algorithm exchanges the values pointed to by its two iterator arguments.

lexicographical_compare

```
template <class InIter1, class InIter2>
  bool lexicographical_compare(InIter1 start1, InIter1 end1,
                                 InIter2 start2, InIter2 end2);
template <class InIter1, class InIter2, class Comp>
  bool lexicographical_compare(InIter1 start1, InIter1 end1,
                                 InIter2 start2, InIter2 end2,
                                 Comp cmpfn);
```

The **lexicographical_compare( )** algorithm alphabetically compares the sequence defined by *start1* and *end1* with the sequence defined by *start2* and *end2*. It returns true if the first sequence is lexicographically less than the second (that is, if the first sequence would come before the second using dictionary order).

The second form allows you to specify a comparison function that determines when one element is less than another.

lower_bound

```
template <class ForIter, class T>
  ForIter lower_bound(ForIter start, ForIter end, const T &val);
template <class ForIter, class T, class Comp>
  ForIter lower_bound(ForIter start, ForIter end, const T &val,
                        Comp cmpfn);
```

The **lower_bound( )** algorithm finds the first point in the sequence defined by *start* and *end* that is not less than *val*. It returns an iterator to this point.

The second form allows you to specify a comparison function that determines when one element is less than another.

make_heap

```
template <class RandIter>
  void make_heap(RandIter start, RandIter end);
template <class RandIter, class Comp>
  void make_heap(RandIter start, RandIter end, Comp cmpfn);
```

The **make_heap( )** algorithm constructs a heap from the sequence defined by *start* and *end*.

The second form allows you to specify a comparison function that determines when one element is less than another.

max

```
template <class T>
  const T &max(const T &i, const T &j);
template <class T, class Comp>
  const T &max(const T &i, const T &j, Comp cmpfn);
```

The **max( )** algorithm returns the maximum of two values.

The second form allows you to specify a comparison function that determines when one element is less than another.

max_element

```
template <class ForIter>
  ForIter max_element(ForIter start, ForIter last);
template <class ForIter, class Comp>
  ForIter max_element(ForIter start, ForIter last, Comp cmpfn);
```

The **max_element( )** algorithm returns an iterator to the maximum element within the range *start* and *last*.

The second form allows you to specify a comparison function that determines when one element is less than another.

merge

```
template <class InIter1, class InIter2, class OutIter>
  OutIter merge(InIter1 start1, InIter1 end1,
               InIter2 start2, InIter2 end2,
               OutIter result);
template <class InIter1, class InIter2, class OutIter, class Comp>
  OutIter merge(InIter1 start1, InIter1 end1,
               InIter2 start2, InIter2 end2,
               OutIter result, Comp cmpfn);
```

The **merge( )** algorithm merges two ordered sequences, placing the result into a third sequence. The sequences to be merged are defined by *start1, end1* and *start2, end2*.

The result is put into the sequence pointed to by *result*. An iterator to the end of the resulting sequence is returned.

The second form allows you to specify a comparison function that determines when one element is less than another.

min

```
template <class T>
  const T &min(const T &i, const T &j);
template <class T, class Comp>
  const T &min(const T &i, const T &j, Comp cmpfn);
```

The **min( )** algorithm returns the minimum of two values.

The second form allows you to specify a comparison function that determines when one element is less than another.

min_element

```
template <class ForIter>
  ForIter min_element(ForIter start, ForIter last);
template <class ForIter, class Comp>
  ForIter min_element(ForIter start, ForIter last, Comp cmpfn);
```

The **min_element( )** algorithm returns an iterator to the minimum element within the range *start* and *last*.

The second form allows you to specify a comparison function that determines when one element is less than another.

mismatch

```
template <class InIter1, class InIter2>
  pair<InIter1, InIter2> mismatch(InIter1 start1, InIter1 end1,
                                  InIter2 start2);
template <class InIter1, class InIter2, class BinPred>
  pair<InIter1, InIter2> mismatch(InIter1 start1, InIter1 end1,
                                  InIter2 start2, BinPred pfn);
```

The **mismatch( )** algorithm finds the first mismatch between the elements in two sequences. Iterators to the two elements are returned. If no mismatch is found, iterators to the end of the sequence are returned.

The second form allows you to specify a binary predicate that determines when one element is equal to another.

The **pair** template class contains two data members called **first** and **second** that hold the pair of values.

next_permutation

```
template <class BiIter>
  bool next_permutation(BiIter start, BiIter end);
template <class BiIter, class Comp>
  bool next_permutation(BiIter start, BiIter end, Comp cmfn);
```

The **next_permutation( )** algorithm constructs the next permutation of a sequence. The permutations are generated assuming a sorted sequence: from low to high represents the first permutation. If the next permutation does not exist, **next_permutation( )** sorts the sequence as its first permutation and returns false. Otherwise, it returns true.

The second form allows you to specify a comparison function that determines when one element is less than another.

nth_element

```
template <class RandIter>
  void nth_element(RandIter start, RandIter element, RandIter end);
template <class RandIter, class Comp>
  void nth_element(RandIter start, RandIter element,
                   RandIter end, Comp cmpfn);
```

The **nth_element( )** algorithm arranges the sequence specified by *start* and *end* such that all elements less than *element* come before that element and all elements greater than *element* come after it.

The second form allows you to specify a comparison function that determines when one element is greater than another.

partial_sort

```
template <class RandIter>
  void partial_sort(RandIter start, RandIter mid, RandIter end);
template <class RandIter, class Comp>
  void partial_sort(RandIter start, RandIter mid,
                    RandIter end, Comp cmpfn);
```

The **partial_sort( )** algorithm sorts the range *start* to *end*. However, after execution, only elements in the range *start* to *mid* will be in sorted order.

The second form allows you to specify a comparison function that determines when one element is less than another.

partial_sort_copy

```
template <class InIter, class RandIter>
  RandIter partial_sort_copy(InIter start, InIter end,
                             RandIter res_start, RandIter res_end);
template <class InIter, class RandIter, class Comp>
  RandIter partial_sort_copy(InIter start, InIter end,
                             RandIter res_start, RandIter res_end,
                             Comp cmpfn);
```

The **partial_sort_copy( )** algorithm sorts the range *start* to *end* and then copies as many elements as will fit into the resulting sequence defined by *res_start* and *res_end*. It returns an iterator to one past the last element copied into the resulting sequence.

The second form allows you to specify a comparison function that determines when one element is less than another.

partition

```
template <class BiIter, class UnPred>
  BiIter partition(BiIter start, BiIter end, UnPred pfn);
```

The **partition( )** algorithm arranges the sequence defined by *start* and *end* such that all elements for which the predicate specified by *pfn* returns true come before those for which the predicate returns false. It returns an iterator to the beginning of the elements for which the predicate is false.

pop_heap

```
template <class RandIter>
  void pop_heap(RandIter start, RandIter end);
template <class RandIter, class Comp>
  void pop_heap(RandIter start, RandIter end, Comp cmpfn);
```

The **pop_heap( )** algorithm exchanges the *first* and *last*–1 elements and then rebuilds the heap.

The second form allows you to specify a comparison function that determines when one element is less than another.

prev_permutation

```
template <class BiIter>
  bool prev_permutation(BiIter start, BiIter end);
template <class BiIter, class Comp>
  bool prev_permutation(BiIter start, BiIter end, Comp cmpfn);
```

The **prev_permutation( )** algorithm constructs the previous permutation of a sequence. The permutations are generated assuming a sorted sequence: from low to high represents the first permutation. If the next permutation does not exist, **prev_permutation( )** sorts the sequence as its final permutation and returns false. Otherwise, it returns true.

The second form allows you to specify a comparison function that determines when one element is less than another.

push_heap

```
template <class RandIter>
  void push_heap(RandIter start, RandIter end);
template <class RandIter, class Comp>
  void push_heap(RandIter start, RandIter end, Comp cmpfn);
```

The **push_heap( )** algorithm pushes an element onto the end of a heap. The range specified by *start* and *end* is assumed to represent a valid heap.

The second form allows you to specify a comparison function that determines when one element is less than another.

random_shuffle

```
template <class RandIter>
  void random_shuffle(RandIter start, RandIter end);
template <class RandIter, class Generator>
  void random_shuffle(RandIter start, RandIter end, Generator rand_gen);
```

The **random_shuffle( )** algorithm randomizes the sequence defined by *start* and *end*.

The second form specifies a custom random number generator. This function must have the following general form:

rand_gen(*num*);

It must return a random number between zero and *num*.

remove, remove_if, remove_copy, and remove_copy_if

```
template <class ForIter, class T>
  ForIter remove(ForIter start, ForIter end, const T &val);
template <class ForIter, class UnPred>
  ForIter remove_if(ForIter start, ForIter end,  UnPred pfn);
template <class InIter, class OutIter, class T>
  OutIter remove_copy(InIter start, InIter end,
                         OutIter result, const T &val);
template <class InIter, class OutIter, class UnPred>
  OutIter remove_copy_if(InIter start, InIter end,
                         OutIter result, UnPred pfn);
```

The **remove( )** algorithm removes elements from the specified range that are equal to *val*. It returns an iterator to the end of the remaining elements.

The **remove_if( )** algorithm removes elements from the specified range for which the predicate *pfn* is true. It returns an iterator to the end of the remaining elements.

The **remove_copy( )** algorithm copies elements from the specified range that are equal to *val* and puts the result into the sequence pointed to by *result*. It returns an iterator to the end of the result.

The **remove_copy_if( )** algorithm copies elements from the specified range for which the predicate *pfn* is true and puts the result into the sequence pointed to by *result*. It returns an iterator to the end of the result.

replace, replace_copy, replace_if, and replace_copy_if

```
template <class ForIter, class T>
  void replace(ForIter start, ForIter end,
             const T &old, const T &new);
template <class ForIter, class UnPred, class T>
  void replace_if(ForIter start, ForIter end,
                 UnPred pfn, const T &new);
template <class InIter, class OutIter, class T>
```

```
OutIter replace_copy(InIter start, InIter end, OutIter result,
                     const T &old, const T &new);
template <class InIter, class OutIter, class UnPred, class T>
  OutIter replace_copy_if(InIter start, InIter end, OutIter result,
                          UnPred pfn, const T &new);
```

Within the specified range, the **replace( )** algorithm replaces elements with the value *old* with elements that have the value *new*.

Within the specified range, the **replace_if( )** algorithm replaces those elements for which the predicate *pfn* is true with elements that have the value *new*.

Within the specified range, the **replace_copy( )** algorithm copies elements to *result*. In the process it replaces elements that have the value *old* with elements that have the value *new*. The original range is unchanged. An iterator to the end of *result* is returned.

Within the specified range, the **replace_copy_if( )** algorithm copies elements to *result*. In the process it replaces elements for which the predicate *pfn* returns true with elements that have the value *new*. The original range is unchanged. An iterator to the end of *result* is returned.

reverse and reverse_copy

```
template <class BiIter>
  void reverse(BiIter start, BiIter end);
template <class BiIter, class OutIter>
  OutIter reverse_copy(BiIter start, BiIter end, OutIter result);
```

The **reverse( )** algorithm reverses the order of the range specified by *start* and *end*.

The **reverse_copy( )** algorithm copies in reverse order the range specified by *start* and *end* and stores the result in *result*. It returns an iterator to the end of *result*.

rotate and rotate_copy

```
template <class ForIter>
  void rotate(ForIter start, ForIter mid, ForIter end);
template <class ForIter, class OutIter>
  OutIter rotate_copy(ForIter start, ForIter mid, ForIter end,
                      OutIter result);
```

The **rotate( )** algorithm left-rotates the elements in the range specified by *start* and *end* so that the element specified by *mid* becomes the new first element.

THE STANDARD C++ CLASS LIBRARY

The **rotate_copy( )** algorithm copies the range specified by *start* and *end,* storing the result in *result.* In the process it left-rotates the elements so that the element specified by *mid* becomes the new first element. It returns an iterator to the end of *result.*

search

```
template <class ForIter1, class ForIter2>
  ForIter1 search(ForIter1 start1, ForIter1 end1,
                  ForIter2 start2, ForIter2 end2);
template <class ForIter1, class ForIter2, class BinPred>
  ForIter1 search(ForIter1 start1, ForIter1 end1,
                  ForIter2 start2, ForIter2 end2, BinPred pfn);
```

The **search( )** algorithm searches for a subsequence within a sequence. The sequence being searched is defined by *start1* and *end1.* The subsequence being searched is specified by *start2* and *end2.* If the subsequence is found, an iterator to its beginning is returned. Otherwise, *end1* is returned.

The second form allows you to specify a binary predicate that determines when one element is equal to another.

search_n

```
template <class ForIter, class Size, class T>
  ForIter search_n(ForIter start, ForIter end,
                   Size num, const T &val);
template <class ForIter, class Size, class T, class BinPred>
  ForIter search_n(ForIter start, ForIter end,
                   Size num, const T &val, BinPred pfn);
```

The **search_n( )** algorithm searches for a sequence of *num* elements equal to *val* within a sequence. The sequence being searched is defined by *start1* and *end1.* If the subsequence is found, an iterator to its beginning is returned. Otherwise, *end* is returned.

The second form allows you to specify a binary predicate that determines when one element is equal to another.

set_difference

```
template <class InIter1, class InIter2, class OutIter>
  OutIter set_difference(InIter1 start1, InIter1 end1,
```

```
            InIter2 start2, InIter2 end2, OutIter result);
template <class InIter1, class InIter2, class OutIter, class Comp>
  OutIter set_difference(InIter1 start1, InIter1 end1,
            InIter2 start2, InIter2 end2,
            OutIter result, Comp cmpfn);
```

The **set_difference( )** algorithm produces a sequence that contains the difference between the two ordered sets defined by *start1, end1* and *start2, end2*. That is, the set defined by *start2, end2* is subtracted from the set defined by *start1, end1*. The result is ordered and put into *result*. It returns an iterator to the end of the result.

The second form allows you to specify a comparison function that determines when one element is less than another.

set_intersection

```
template <class InIter1, class InIter2, class OutIter>
  OutIter set_intersection(InIter1 start1, InIter1 end1,
            InIter2 start2, InIter2 end2, OutIter result);
template <class InIter1, class InIter2, class OutIter, class Comp>
  OutIter set_intersection(InIter1 start1, InIter1 end1,
            InIter2 start2, InIter2 end2,
            OutIter result, Comp cmpfn);
```

The **set_intersection( )** algorithm produces a sequence that contains the intersection of the two ordered sets defined by *start1, end1* and *start2, end2*. These are the elements common to both sets. The result is ordered and put into *result*. It returns an iterator to the end of the result.

The second form allows you to specify a comparison function that determines when one element is less than another.

set_symmetric_difference

```
template <class InIter1, class InIter2, class OutIter>
  OutIter set_symmetric_difference(InIter1 start1, InIter1 end1,
            InIter2 start2, InIter2 end2, OutIter result);
template <class InIter1, class InIter2, class OutIter, class Comp>
  OutIter set_symmetric_difference(InIter1 start1, InIter1 end1,
            InIter2 start2, InIter2 end2, OutIter result,
            Comp cmpfn);
```

THE STANDARD C++
CLASS LIBRARY

The **set_symmetric_difference( )** algorithm produces a sequence that contains the symmetric difference between the two ordered sets defined by *start1*, *end1* and *start2*, *end2*. That is, the resultant set contains only those elements that are not common to both sets. The result is ordered and put into *result*. It returns an iterator to the end of the result.

The second form allows you to specify a comparison function that determines when one element is less than another.

set_union

```
template <class InIter1, class InIter2, class OutIter>
  OutIter set_union(InIter1 start1, InIter1 end1,
            InIter2 start2, InIter2 end2, OutIter result);
template <class InIter1, class InIter2, class OutIter, class Comp>
  OutIter set_union(InIter1 start1, InIter1 end1,
            InIter2 start2, InIter2 end2, OutIter result,
            Comp cmpfn);
```

The **set_union( )** algorithm produces a sequence that contains the union of the two ordered sets defined by *start1*, *end1* and *start2*, *end2*. Thus, the resultant set contains those elements that are in both sets. The result is ordered and put into *result*. It returns an iterator to the end of the result.

The second form allows you to specify a comparison function that determines when one element is less than another.

sort

```
template <class RandIter>
  void sort(RandIter start, RandIter end);
template <class RandIter, classComp>
  void sort(RandIter start, RandIter end, Comp cmpfn);
```

The **sort( )** algorithm sorts the range specified by *start* and *end*.

The second form allows you to specify a comparison function that determines when one element is less than another.

sort_heap

```
template <class RandIter>
  void sort_heap(RandIter start, RandIter end);
```

```
template <class RandIter, class Comp>
  void sort_heap(RandIter start, RandIter end, Comp cmpfn);
```

The **sort_heap( )** algorithm sorts a heap within the range specified by *start* and *end*. The second form allows you to specify a comparison function that determines when one element is less than another.

stable_partition

```
template <class BiIter, class UnPred>
  BiIter stable_partition(BiIter start, BiIter end, UnPred pfn);
```

The **stable_partition( )** algorithm arranges the sequence defined by *start* and *end* such that all elements for which the predicate specified by *pfn* returns true come before those for which the predicate returns false. The partitioning is stable. This means that the relative ordering of the sequence is preserved. It returns an iterator to the beginning of the elements for which the predicate is false.

stable_sort

```
template <class RandIter>
  void stable_sort(RandIter start, RandIter end);
template <class RandIter, class Comp>
  void stable_sort(RandIter start, RandIter end, Comp cmpfn);
```

The **sort( )** algorithm sorts the range specified by *start* and *end*. The sort is stable. This means that equal elements are not rearranged.

The second form allows you to specify a comparison function that determines when one element is less than another.

swap

```
template <class T>
  void swap(T &i, T &j);
```

The **swap( )** algorithm exchanges the values referred to by *i* and *j*.

swap_ranges

```
template <class ForIter1, class ForIter2>
  ForIter2 swap_ranges(ForIter1 start1, ForIter1 end1,
                       ForIter2 start2);
```

The **swap_ranges( )** algorithm exchanges elements in the range specified by *start1* and *end1* with elements in the sequence beginning at *start2*. It returns an iterator to the end of the sequence specified by *start2*.

transform

```
template <class InIter, class OutIter, class Func>
  OutIter transform(InIter start, InIter end,
                    OutIter result, Func unaryfunc);
template <class InIter1, class InIter2, class OutIter, class Func>
  OutIter transform(InIter1 start1, InIter1 end1,
                    InIter2 start2, OutIter result,
                    Func binaryfunc);
```

The **transform( )** algorithm applies a function to a range of elements and stores the outcome in *result*. In the first form, the range is specified by *start* and *end*. The function to be applied is specified by *unaryfunc*. This function receives the value of an element in its parameter and it must return its transformation.

In the second form, the transformation is applied using a binary operator function that receives the value of an element from the sequence to be transformed in its first parameter and an element from the second sequence as its second parameter.

Both versions return an iterator to the end of the resulting sequence.

unique and unique_copy

```
template <class ForIter>
  ForIter unique(ForIter start, ForIter end);
template <class ForIter, class BinPred>
  ForIter unique(ForIter start, ForIter end, BinPred pfn);
template <class ForIter, class OutIter>
  OutIter unique_copy(ForIter start, ForIter end, OutIter result);
template <class ForIter, class OutIter, class BinPred>
  OutIter unique_copy(ForIter start, ForIter end, OutIter result,
                      BinPred pfn);
```

The **unique( )** algorithm eliminates duplicate elements from the specified range. The second form allows you to specify a binary predicate that determines when one element is equal to another. **unique( )** returns an iterator to the end of the range.

The **unique_copy( )** algorithm copies the range specified by *start1* and *end1*, eliminating duplicate elements in the process. The outcome is put into *result*. The second form allows you to specify a binary predicate that determines when one element is equal to another. **unique_copy( )** returns an iterator to the end of the range.

upper_bound

```
template <class ForIter, class T>
  ForIter upper_bound(ForIter start, ForIter end, const T &val);
template <class ForIter, class T, class Comp>
  ForIter upper_bound(ForIter start, ForIter end, const T &val,
                      Comp cmpfn);
```

The **upper_bound( )** algorithm finds the last point in the sequence defined by *start* and *end* that is not greater than *val*. It returns an iterator to this point.

The second form allows you to specify a comparison function that determines when one element is less than another.

Chapter 35

STL Iterators, Allocators, and Function Objects

This chapter describes the classes and functions that support iterators, allocators, and function objects. These components are part of the standard template library. They may also be used for other purposes.

Iterators

While containers and algorithms form the foundation of the standard template library, iterators are the glue that holds it together. An *iterator* is a generalization (or perhaps more precisely, an abstraction) of a pointer. Iterators are handled in your program like pointers, and they implement the standard pointer operators. They give you the ability to cycle through the contents of a container in much the same way that you would use a pointer to cycle through an array.

Standard C++ defines a set of classes and functions that support iterators. However, for the vast majority of STL-based programming tasks, you will not use these classes directly. Instead, you will use the iterators provided by the various containers in the STL, manipulating them like you would any other pointer. The preceding notwithstanding, it is still valuable to have a general understanding of the iterator classes and their contents. For example, it is possible to create your own iterators that accommodate special situations. Also, developers of third-party libraries will find the iterator classes useful.

Iterators use the header **<iterator>**.

The Basic Iterator Types

There are five types of iterators:

Iterator	Access Allowed
Random Access	Store and retrieve values. Elements may be accessed randomly.
Bidirectional	Store and retrieve values. Forward and backward moving.
Forward	Store and retrieve values. Forward moving only.
Input	Retrieve but not store values. Forward moving only.
Output	Store but not retrieve values. Forward moving only.

In general, an iterator that has greater access capabilities can be used in place of one that has lesser capabilities. For example, a forward iterator can be used in place of an input iterator.

The STL also supports *reverse iterators*. Reverse iterators are either bidirectional or random-access iterators that move through a sequence in the reverse direction. Thus, if a reverse iterator points to the end of a sequence, incrementing that iterator will cause it to point one element before the end.

Stream-based iterators are available that allow you to operate on streams through iterators. Finally, insert iterator classes are provided that simplify the insertion of elements into a container.

All iterators must support the pointer operations allowed by their type. For example, an input iterator class must support –>, ++, *, ==, and !=. Further, the * operator cannot be used to assign a value. By contrast, a random-access iterator must support –>, +, ++, –, – –, *, <, >, <=, >=, –=, +=, ==, !=, and [ ]. Also, the * must allow assignment.

The Low-Level Iterator Classes

The **<iterator>** header defines several classes that provide support for and aid in the implementation of iterators. As explained in Chapter 24, each of the STL containers defines its own iterator type, which is **typedef**ed as **iterator**. Thus, when using the standard STL containers, you will not usually interact directly with the low-level iterator classes themselves. But you can use the classes described here to derive your own iterators.

Several of the iterator classes make use of the **ptrdiff_t** type. This type is capable of representing the difference between two pointers.

iterator

The **iterator** class is a base for iterators. It is shown here:

```
template <class Cat, class T, class Dist = ptrdiff_t,
  class Pointer = T *, class Ref = T &>
struct iterator {
  typedef T value_type;
  typedef Dist difference_type;
  typedef Pointer pointer;
  typedef Ref reference;
  typedef Cat iterator_category;
};
```

Here, **difference_type** is a type that can hold the difference between two addresses, **value_type** is the type of value operated upon, **pointer** is the type of a pointer to a value, **reference** is the type of a reference to a value, and **iterator_category** describes the type of the iterator (such as input, random-access, etc.).

The following category classes are provided.

```
struct input_iterator_tag {};
struct output_iterator_tag {};
```

THE STANDARD C++
CLASS LIBRARY

```
struct forward_iterator_tag: public input_iterator_tag {};
struct bidirectional_iterator_tag: public forward_iterator_tag {};
struct random_access_iterator_tag: public
        bidirectional_iterator_tag {};
```

iterator_traits

The class **iterator_traits** provides a convenient means of exposing the various types
defined by an iterator. It is defined like this:

```
template<class Iterator> struct iterator_traits {
   typedef Iterator::difference_type difference_type;
   typedef Iterator::value_type value_type;
   typedef Iterator::pointer pointer;
   typedef Iterator::reference reference;
   typedef Iterator::iterator_category iterator_category;
}
```

The Predefined Iterators

The **<iterator>** header contains several predefined iterators that may be used directly
by your program or to help create other iterators. These iterators are shown in Table 35-1.
Notice that there are four iterators that operate on streams. The main purpose for the
stream iterators is to allow streams to be manipulated by algorithms. Also notice the
insert iterators. When these iterators are used in an assignment statement, they insert
elements into a sequence rather than overwriting existing elements.

Each of the predefined iterators is examined here.

insert_iterator

The **insert_iterator** class supports output iterators that insert objects into a container. Its
template definition is shown here:

> template <class Cont> class insert_iterator:
>   public iterator<output_iterator_tag, void, void, void, void>

Here, **Cont** is the type of container that the iterator operates upon. **insert_iterator** has
the following constructor:

> insert_iterator(Cont &*cnt*, typename Cont::iterator *itr*);

Here, *cnt* is the container being operated upon and *itr* is an iterator into the container
that will be used to initialize the **insert_iterator**.

Class	Description
insert_iterator	An output iterator that inserts anywhere in the container.
back_insert_iterator	An output iterator that inserts at the end of a container.
front_insert_iterator	An output iterator that inserts at the front of a container.
reverse_iterator	A reverse, bidirectional, or random-access iterator.
istream_iterator	An input stream iterator.
istreambuf_iterator	An input streambuf iterator.
ostream_iterator	An output stream iterator.
ostreambuf_iterator	An output streambuf iterator.

Table 35-1. *The Predefined Iterator Classes*

insert_iterator defines the following operators: =, *, ++. A pointer to the container is stored in a protected variable called **container**. The container's iterator is stored in a protected variable called **iter**.

Also defined is the function **inserter( )**, which creates an **insert_iterator**. It is shown here:

```
template <class Cont, class Iterator> insert_iterator<Cont>
    inserter(Cont &cnt, Iterator itr);
```

Insert iterators insert into, rather than overwrite, the contents of a container. To fully understand the effects of an insert iterator, consider the following program. It first creates a small vector of integers, and then uses an **insert_iterator** to insert new elements into the vector rather than overwriting existing elements.

```
// Demonstrate insert_iterator.
#include <iostream>
#include <iterator>
#include <vector>
using namespace std;

int main()
{
  vector<int> v;
```

THE STANDARD C++
CLASS LIBRARY

```
vector<int>::iterator itr;
int i;

for(i=0; i<5; i++)
  v.push_back(i);

cout << "Original array: ";
itr = v.begin();
while(itr != v.end())
  cout << *itr++ << " ";
cout << endl;

itr = v.begin();
itr += 2; // point to element 2

// create insert_iterator to element 2
insert_iterator<vector<int> > i_itr(v, itr);

// insert rather than overwrite
*i_itr++ = 100;
*i_itr++ = 200;

cout << "Array after insertion: ";
itr = v.begin();
while(itr != v.end())
  cout << *itr++ << " ";

return 0;
}
```

The output from the program is shown here:

```
Original array: 0 1 2 3 4
Array after insertion: 0 1 100 200 2 3 4
```

In the program, had the assignments of 100 and 200 been done using a standard iterator, the original elements in the array would have been overwritten. The same basic process applies to **back_insert_iterator** and **front_insert_iterator** as well.

back_insert_iterator

The **back_insert_iterator** class supports output iterators that insert objects on the end of a container using **push_back( )**. Its template definition is shown here:

```
template <class Cont> class back_insert_iterator:
    public iterator<output_iterator_tag, void, void, void, void>
```

Here, **Cont** is the type of container that the iterator operates upon. **back_insert_iterator** has the following constructor:

```
explicit back_insert_iterator(Cont &cnt);
```

Here, *cnt* is the container being operated upon. All insertions will occur at the end.

back_insert_iterator defines the following operators: =, *, ++. A pointer to the container is stored in a protected variable called **container**.

Also defined is the function **back_inserter( )**, which creates a **back_insert_iterator**. It is shown here:

```
template <class Cont> back_insert_iterator<Cont> back_inserter(Cont &cnt);
```

front_insert_iterator

The **front_insert_iterator** class supports output iterators that insert objects on the front of a container using **push_front( )**. Its template definition is shown here:

```
template <class Cont> class front_insert_iterator:
    public iterator<output_iterator_tag, void, void, void, void>
```

Here, **Cont** is the type of container that the iterator operates upon. **front_insert_iterator** has the following constructor:

```
explicit front_insert_iterator(Cont &cnt);
```

Here, *cnt* is the container being operated upon. All insertions will occur at the front.

front_insert_iterator defines the following operators: =, *, ++. A pointer to the container is stored in a protected variable called **container**.

Also defined is the function **front_inserter( )**, which creates a **front_insert_iterator**. It is shown here:

```
template <class Cont> front_insert_iterator<Cont> inserter(Cont &cnt);
```

reverse_iterator

The **reverse_iterator** class supports reverse iterator operations. A reverse iterator operates the opposite of a normal iterator. For example, **++** causes a reverse iterator to back up. Its template definition is shown here:

```
template <class Iter> class reverse_iterator:
    public iterator<iterator_traits<Iter>::iterator_category,
                iterator_traits<Iter>::value_type,
                iterator_traits<Iter>::difference_type,
                iterator_traits<Iter>::pointer,
                iterator_traits<Iter>::reference>
```

Here, **Iter** is either a random-access iterator or a bidirectional iterator. **reverse_iterator** has the following constructors:

```
reverse_iterator( );
explicit reverse_iterator(Iter itr);
```

Here, *itr* is an iterator that specifies the starting location.

If **Iter** is a random-access iterator, then the following operators are available: **–>, +, ++, –, – –, *, <, >, <=, >=, –=, +=, ==, !=,** and **[ ]** . If **Iter** is a bidirectional iterator, then only **–>, ++, – –, *, ==,** and **!=** are available.

The **reverse_iterator** class defines a protected member called **current**, which is an iterator to the current location.

The function **base( )** is also defined by **reverse_iterator**. Its prototype is shown here:

```
Iter base( ) const;
```

It returns an iterator to the current location.

istream_iterator

The **istream_iterator** class supports input iterator operations on a stream. Its template definition is shown here:

```
template <class T, class CharType, class Attr = char_traits<CharType>,
        class Dist = ptrdiff_t> class istream_iterator:
    public iterator<input_iterator_tag, T, Dist, const T *, const T &>
```

Here, **T** is the type of data being transferred, and **CharType** is the character type (**char** or **wchar_t**) that the stream is operating upon. **Dist** is a type capable of holding the difference between two addresses. **istream_iterator** has the following constructors:

istream_iterator( );
istream_iterator(istream_type &*stream*);
istream_iterator(const istream_iterator<T, CharType, Attr, Dist> &*ob*);

The first constructor creates an iterator to an empty stream. The second creates an iterator to the stream specified by *stream*. The type **istream_type** is a **typedef** that specifies the type of the input stream. The third form creates a copy of an **istream_iterator** object.

The **istream_iterator** class defines the following operators: **–>**, *****, **++**. The operators **==** and **!=** are also defined for objects of type **istream_iterator**.

Here is a short program that demonstrates **istream_iterator**. It reads and displays characters from **cin** until a period is received.

```
// Use istream_iterator
#include <iostream>
#include <iterator>
using namespace std;

int main()
{
  istream_iterator<char> in_it(cin);

  do {
    cout << *in_it++;
  } while (*in_it != '.');

  return 0;
}
```

istreambuf_iterator

The **istreambuf_iterator** class supports character input iterator operations on a stream. Its template definition is shown here:

template <class CharType, class Attr = char_traits<CharType> >
class istreambuf_iterator:
    public iterator<input_iterator_tag, CharType, typename Attr::off_type,
                    CharType *, CharType &>

Here, **CharType** is the character type (**char** or **wchar_t**) that the stream is operating upon. **istreambuf_iterator** has the following constructors:

istreambuf_iterator( ) throw( );
istreambuf_iterator(istream_type &*stream*) throw( );
istreambuf_iterator(streambuf_type **streambuf*) throw( );

The first constructor creates an iterator to an empty stream. The second creates an iterator to the stream specified by *stream*. The type **istream_type** is a **typedef** that specifies the type of the input stream. The third form creates an iterator using the stream buffer specified by *streambuf*.

The **istreambuf_iterator** class defines the following operators: *****, **++**. The operators **==** and **!=** are also defined for objects of type **istreambuf_iterator**.

istreambuf_iterator defines the member function **equal( )**, which is shown here:

    bool equal(istreambuf_iterator<CharType, Attr> &*ob*);

Its operation is a bit counterintuitive. It returns **true** if the invoking iterator and *ob* both point to the end of the stream. It also returns **true** if both iterators do not point to the end of the stream. There is no requirement that what they point to be the same. It returns **false** otherwise. The **==** and **!=** operators work in the same fashion.

ostream_iterator

The **ostream_iterator** class supports output iterator operations on a stream. Its template definition is shown here:

    template <class T, class CharType, class Attr = char_traits<CharType> >
    class ostream_iterator:
        public iterator<output_iterator_tag, void, void, void, void>

Here, **T** is the type of data being transferred, **CharType** is the character type (**char** or **wchar_t**) that the stream is operating upon. **ostream_iterator** has the following constructors:

    ostream_iterator(ostream_type &*stream*);
    ostream_iterator(ostream_type &*stream*, const CharType **delim*);
    ostream_iterator(const ostream_iterator<T, CharType, Attr> &*ob*);

The first creates an iterator to the stream specified by *stream*. The type **ostream_type** is a **typedef** that specifies the type of the output stream. The second form creates an iterator to the stream specified by *stream* and uses the delimiters specified by *delim*. The delimiters are written to the stream after every output operation. The third form creates a copy of an **ostream_iterator** object.

The **ostream_iterator** class defines the following operators: **=**, *****, **++**.

Here is a short program that demonstrates **ostream_iterator**.

```
// Use ostream_iterator
#include <iostream>
#include <iterator>
using namespace std;

int main()
{
  ostream_iterator<char> out_it(cout);

  *out_it = 'X';
  out_it++;
  *out_it = 'Y';
  out_it++;
  *out_it = ' ';

  char str[] = "C++ Iterators are powerful.\n";
  char *p = str;

  while(*p) *out_it++ = *p++;

  ostream_iterator<double> out_double_it(cout);
  *out_double_it = 187.23;
  out_double_it++;
  *out_double_it = -102.7;

  return 0;
}
```

The output from this program is shown here:

```
XY C++ Iterators are powerful.
187.23-102.7
```

ostreambuf_iterator

The **ostreambuf_iterator** class supports character output iterator operations on a stream. Its template definition is shown here:

template <class CharType, class Attr = char_traits<CharType> >
class ostreambuf_iterator:
    public iterator<output_iterator_tag, void, void, void, void>

Here, **CharType** is the character type (**char** or **wchar_t**) that the stream is operating upon. **ostreambuf_iterator** has the following constructors:

> ostreambuf_iterator(ostream_type &*stream*) throw( );
> ostreambuf_iterator(streambuf_type **streambuf) throw( );

The first creates an iterator to the stream specified by *stream*. The type **ostream_type** is a **typedef** that specifies the type of the input stream. The second form creates an iterator using the stream buffer specified by *streambuf*. The type **streambuf_type** is a **typedef** that specifies the type of the stream buffer.

The **ostreambuf_iterator** class defines the following operators: =, *, ++. The member function **failed( )** is also defined as shown here:

> bool failed( ) const throw( );

It returns **false** if no failure has occurred and **true** otherwise.

Two Iterator Functions

There are two special functions defined for iterators: **advance( )** and **distance( )**. They are shown here:

> template <class InIter, class Dist> void advance(InIter &*itr*, Dist *d*);
> template <class InIter> ptrdiff_t distance(InIter *start*, InIter *end*);

The **advance( )** function increments *itr* by the amount specified by *d*. The **distance( )** function returns the number of elements between *start* and *end*.

The reason for these two functions is that only random-access iterators allow a value to be added to or subtracted from an iterator. The **advance( )** and **distance( )** functions overcome this restriction. It must be noted, however, that some iterators will not be able to implement these functions efficiently.

Function Objects

Function objects are classes that define **operator( )**. The STL defines several built-in function objects that your programs may use. You can also define your own function objects. Support for function objects is in the **<functional>** header. Also defined in **<functional>** are several entities that support function objects. These are binders, negators, and adaptors. Each is described here.

| Note | *Refer to Chapter 24 for an overview of function objects.* |

Function Objects

Function objects come in two varieties: binary and unary. The built-in binary function objects are shown here:

plus	minus	multiplies	divides	modulus
equal_to	not_equal_to	greater	greater_equal	less
less_equal	logical_and	logical_or		

Here are the built-in unary function objects.

logical_not   negate

The general form for invoking a function object is shown here:

func_ob<type>( )

For example,

```
less<int>()
```

invokes **less( )** relative to operands of type **int**.

A base class for all binary function objects is **binary_function**, shown here:

```
template <class Argument1, class Argument2, class Result>
struct binary_function {
  typedef Argument1 first_argument_type;
  typedef Argument2 second_argument_type;
  typedef Result result_type;
};
```

The base class for all unary functions is **unary_function**, shown here:

```
template <class Argument, class Result> struct unary_function {
  typedef Argument argument_type;
  typedef Result result_type;
};
```

These template classes provide concrete type names for the generic data types used by the function object. Although they are technically a convenience, they are almost always used when creating function objects.

The template specifications for all binary function objects are similar, and the template specifications for all unary function objects are similar. Here are examples of each:

```
template <class T> struct plus : binary_function<T, T, T>
{
  T operator() (const T &arg1, const T&arg2) const;
};

template <class T> struct negate : unary_function<T, T>
{
  T operator() (const T &arg) const;
};
```

Each **operator( )** function returns the specified result.

Binders

Binders bind a value to an argument of a binary function object, producing a unary function object. There are two binders: **bind2nd( )** and **bind1st( )**. Here is how they are defined:

template <class BinFunc, class T>
      binder1st<BinFunc> bind1st(const BinFunc &*op*, const T &*value*);
template <class BinFunc, class T>
      binder2nd<BinFunc> bind2nd(const BinFunc &*op*, const T &*value*);

Here, *op* is a binary function object, such as **less( )** or **greater( )**, that provides the desired operation, and *value* is the value being bound. **bind1st( )** returns a unary function object that has *op*'s left-hand operand bound to *value*. **bind2nd( )** returns a unary function object that has *op*'s right-hand operand bound to *value*. The **bind2nd( )** binder is by far the most commonly used. In either case, the outcome of a binder is a unary function object that is bound to the value specified.

The **binder1st** and **binder2nd** classes are shown here:

```
template <class BinFunc> class binder1st:
  public unary_function(typename BinFunc::second_argument_type,
                        typename BinFunc::result_type>
{
protected:
  BinFunc op;
  typename BinFunc::first_argument_type value;
public:
```

```
   binder1st(const BinFunc &op,
             const typename BinFunc::first_argument_type &v);
   result_type operator()(const argument_type &v) const;
};


template <class BinFunc> class binder2nd:
   public unary_function(typename BinFunc::first_argument_type,
                         typename BinFunc::result_type>
{
protected:
   BinFunc op;
   typename BinFunc::second_argument_type value;
public:
   binder2nd(const BinFunc &op,
             const typename BinFunc::second_argument_type &v);
   result_type operator()(const argument_type &v) const;
};
```

Here, *BinFunc* is the type of a binary function object. Notice that both classes inherit **unary_function**. This is why the resulting object of **bind1st( )** and **bind2nd( )** can be used anywhere that a unary function can be.

Negators

Negators return predicates that yield the opposite of whatever predicate they modify. The negators are **not1( )** and **not2( )**. They are defined like this:

template <class UnPred> unary_negate<UnPred> not1(const UnPred &*pred*);
template <class BinPred> binary_negate<BinPred> not2(const BinPred &pred);

The classes are shown here:

```
template <class UnPred> class unary_negate:
   public unary_function<typename UnPred::argument_type, bool>
{
public:
   explicit unary_negate(const UnPred &pred);
   bool operator()(const argument_type &v) const;
};


template <class BinPred> class binary_negate:
```

```
        public binary_function<typename BinPred::first_argument_type,
                               typename BinPred::second_argument_type,
                               bool>
{
public:
  explicit binary_negate(const BinPred &pred);
  bool operator()(const first_argument_type &v1,
                  const second_argument_type &v2) const;

};
```

In both classes, **operator( )** returns the negation of the predicate specified by *pred*.

Adaptors

The header **<functional>** defines several classes called *adaptors* that allow you to adapt a function pointer to a form that can be used by the STL. For example, you can use an adaptor to allow a function such as **strcmp( )** to be used as a predicate. Adaptors also exist for member pointers.

The Pointer-to-Function Adaptors

The pointer-to-function adaptors are shown here:

```
template <class Argument, class Result>
  pointer_to_unary_function<Argument, Result>
    ptr_fun(Result (*func)(Argument));
template <class Argument1, class Argument2, class Result>
  pointer_to_binary_function<Argument1, Argument2, Result>
    ptr_fun(Result (*func)(Argument1, Argument2));
```

Here, **ptr_fun( )** returns either an object of type **pointer_to_unary_function** or **pointer_to_binary_function**. These classes are shown here:

```
template <class Argument, class Result>
class pointer_to_unary_function:
  public unary_function<Argument, Result>
{
public:
  explicit pointer_to_unary_function(Result (*func)(Argument));
  Result operator()(Argument arg) const;
};
```

```
template <class Argument1, class Argument2, class Result>
class pointer_to_binary_function:
  public binary_function<Argument1, Argument2, Result>
{
public:
  explicit pointer_to_binary_function(
           Result (*func)(Argument1, Argument2));
  Result operator()(Argument1 arg1, Argument2 arg2) const;
};
```

For unary functions, **operator( )** returns

   func(*arg*).

For binary functions, **operator( )** returns

   func(*arg1*, *arg2*);

The type of the result of the operation is specified by the **Result** generic type.

The Pointer-to-Member Function Adaptors

The pointer-to-member function adaptors are shown here:

   template<class Result, class T>
       mem_fun_t<Result, T> mem_fun(Result (T::*func)( ));
   template<class Result, class T, class Argument>
       mem_fun1_t<Result, T, Argument>
          mem_fun1(Result (T::*func)(Argument));

Here, **mem_fun( )** returns an object of type **mem_fun_t,** and **mem_fun1( )** returns an object of type **mem_fun1_t**. These classes are shown here:

```
template <class Result, class T> class mem_fun_t:
  public unary_function<T *, Result> {
public:
  explicit mem_fun_t(Result (T::*func)());
  Result operator() (T *func) const;
```

```
};

template <class Result, class T,
          class Argument> class mem_fun1_t:
  public binary_function<T *, Argument, Result> {
public:
  explicit mem_fun1_t(Result (T::*func)(Argument));
  Result operator() (T *func, Argument arg) const;
};
```

Here, the **mem_fun_t** constructor calls the member function specified as its parameter. The **mem_fun1_t** constructor calls the member function specified as its first parameter, passing a value of type **Argument** as its second parameter.

There are parallel classes and functions for using references to members. The general form of the functions is shown here:

template<class Result, class T>
    mem_fun_ref_t<Result, T> mem_fun_ref(Result (T::*func)( ));

template<class Result, class T, class Argument>
    mem_fun1_ref_t<Result, T, Argument>
      mem_fun1_ref(Result (T::*func)(Argument));

The classes are shown here:

```
template <class Result, class T> class mem_fun_ref_t:
  public unary_function<T, Result>
{
public:
  explicit mem_fun_ref_t(Result (T::*func)());
  Result operator()(T &func) const;
};

template <class Result, class T, class Argument>
  class mem_fun1_ref_t:
    public binary_function<T, Result, Argument>
{
public:
  explicit mem_fun1_ref_t(Result (T::*func)(Argument));
  Result operator()(T &func, Argument arg) const;
};
```

Allocators

An allocator manages memory allocation for a container. Since the STL defines a default allocator that is automatically used by the containers, most programmers will never need to know the details about allocators or create their own. However, these details are useful if you are creating your own library classes, etc.

All allocators must satisfy several requirements. First, they must define the following types:

const_pointer	A **const** pointer to an object of type **value_type**.
const_reference	A **const** reference to an object of type **value_type**.
difference_type	Can represent the difference between two addresses.
pointer	A pointer to an object of type **value_type**.
reference	A reference to an object of type **value_type**.
size_type	Capable of holding the size of the largest possible object that can be allocated.
value_type	The type of object being allocated.

Second, they must provide the following functions.

address	Returns a pointer given a reference.
allocate	Allocates memory.
deallocate	Frees memory.
max_size	Returns the maximum number of objects that can be allocated.
construct	Constructs an object.
destroy	Destroys an object.

The operations **==** and **!=** must also be defined.

The default allocator is **allocator**, and it is defined within the header **<memory>**. Its template specification is shown here:

template <class T> class allocator

Here, **T** is the type of objects that **allocator** will be allocating. **allocator** defines the following constructors:

allocator( ) throw( );
allocator(const allocator<T> &*ob*) throw( );

The first creates a new allocator. The second creates a copy of *ob*.

The operators == and != are defined for **allocator**. The member functions defined by **allocator** are shown in Table 35-2.

One last point: A specialization of **allocator** for **void *** pointers is also defined.

Function	Description
pointer address(reference *ob*) const; const_pointer address(const_reference *ob*) const;	Returns the address of *ob*.
pointer allocate(size_type *num*, allocator<void>::const_pointer *h* = 0);	Returns a pointer to allocated memory that is large enough to hold *num* objects of type T. The value of *h* is a hint to the function that can be used to help satisfy the request or ignored.
void construct(pointer *ptr*, const_reference *val*);	Constructs an object of type T with the value specified by *val* at *ptr*.
void deallocate(pointer *ptr*, size_type *num*);	Deallocates *num* objects of type T starting at *ptr*. The value of *ptr* must have been obtained from **allocate( )**.
void destroy(pointer *ptr*);	Destroys the object at *ptr*. Its destructor is automatically called.
size_type max_size( ) const throw( );	Returns the maximum number of objects of type T that can be allocated.

Table 35-2. *Member Functions of **allocator***

The Complete Reference

C++

Chapter 36

The String Class

This chapter describes the Standard C++ string class. C++ supports character strings two ways. The first is as a null-terminated character array. This is sometimes referred to as a *C string*. The second way is as a class object of type **basic_string**. There are two specializations of **basic_string**: **string**, which supports **char** strings, and **wstring**, which supports **wchar_t** (wide character) strings. Most often, you will use string objects of type **string**.

The **basic_string** class is essentially a container. This means that iterators and the STL algorithms can operate on strings. However, strings have additional capabilities.

A class used by **basic_string** is **char_traits**, which defines several attributes of the characters that comprise a string. It is important to understand that while the most common strings are made up of either **char** or **wchar_t** characters, **basic_string** can operate on any object that can be used to represent a text character. Both **basic_string** and **char_traits** are described here.

> **Note** *For an overview of using the string class, refer to Chapter 24.*

The basic_string Class

The template specification for **basic_string** is

> template <class CharType, class Attr = char_traits<CharType>,
>   class Allocator = allocator<T> > class basic_string

Here, **CharType** is the type of character being used, **Attr** is the class that describes the character's traits, and **Allocator** specifies the allocator. **basic_string** has the following constructors:

> explicit basic_string(const Allocator &*a* = Allocator( ));
> basic_string(size_type *len*, CharType *ch* ,
>   const Allocator &*a* = Allocator( ));
> basic_string(const CharType **str*, const Allocator &*a* = Allocator( ));
> basic_string(const CharType **str*, size_type *len*,
>   const Allocator &*a* = Allocator( ));
> basic_string(const basic_string &*str*, size_type *indx* = 0,
>   size_type *len*=npos, const Allocator &*a* = Allocator( ));
> template <class InIter> basic_string(InIter *start*, InIter *end*,
>   const Allocator &*a* = Allocator( ));

The first form constructs an empty string. The second form constructs a string that has *len* characters of value *ch*. The third form constructs a string that contains the same elements as *str*. The fourth form constructs a string that contains a substring of *str* that begins at zero and is *len* characters long. The fifth form constructs a string from another

basic_string using the substring that begins at *indx* that is *len* characters long. The sixth form constructs a string that contains the elements in the range specified by *start* and *end*.

The following comparison operators are defined for **basic_string**:

==, <, <=, !=, >, >=

Also defined is the + operator, which yields the result of concatenating one string with another, and the I/O operators << and >>, which can be used to input and output strings.

The + operator can be used to concatenate a string object with another string object or a string object with a C-style string. That is, the following variations are supported:

string + string
string + C-string
C-string + string

The + operator can also be used to concatenate a character onto the end of a string.

The **basic_string** class defines the constant **npos**, which is –1. This constant represents the length of the longest possible string.

In the descriptions, the generic type **CharType** represents the type of character stored by a string. Since the names of the placeholder types in a template class are arbitrary, **basic_string** declares **typedef**ed versions of these types. This makes the type names concrete. The types defined by **basic_string** are shown here:

size_type	Some integral type loosely equivalent to **size_t**.
reference	A reference to a character within a string.
const_reference	A **const** reference to a character within a string.
iterator	An iterator.
const_iterator	A **const** iterator.
reverse_iterator	A reverse iterator.
const_reverse_iterator	A **const** reverse iterator.
value_type	The type of character stored in a string.
allocator_type	The type of the allocator.
pointer	A pointer to a character within a string.
const_pointer	A **const** pointer to a character within a string.
traits_type	A **typedef** for **char_traits<CharType>**
difference_type	A type that can store the difference between two addresses.

The member functions defined by **basic_string** are shown in Table 36-1. Since the vast majority of programmers will be using **char** strings (and to keep the descriptions easy-to-understand), the table uses the type **string**, but the functions also apply to objects of type **wstring** (or any other type of **basic_string**).

Member	Description
string &append(const string &*str*);	Appends *str* onto the end of the invoking string. Returns ***this**.
string &append(const string &*str*, size_type *indx*, size_type *len*);	Appends a substring of *str* onto the end of the invoking string. The substring being appended begins at *indx* and runs for *len* characters. Returns ***this**.
string &append(const CharType **str*);	Appends *str* onto the end of the invoking string. Returns ***this**.
string &append(const CharType **str*, size_type *num*);	Appends the first *num* characters from *str* onto the end of the invoking string. Returns ***this**.
string &append(size_type *len*, CharType *ch*);	Appends *len* characters specified by *ch* onto the end of the invoking string. Returns ***this**.
template<class InIter> string &append(InIter *start*, InIter *end*);	Appends the sequence specified by *start* and *end* onto the end of the invoking string. Returns ***this**.
string &assign(const string &*str*);	Assigns *str* to the invoking string. Returns ***this**.
string &assign(const string &*str*, size_type *indx*, size_type *len*);	Assigns a substring of *str* to the invoking string. The substring being assigned begins at *indx* and runs for *len* characters. Returns ***this**.
string &assign(const CharType **str*);	Assigns *str* to the invoking string. Returns ***this**.

Table 36-1.   *The String Member Functions*

Member	Description
string &assign(const CharType *str, size_type len);	Assigns the first len characters from str to the invoking string. Returns ***this**.
string &assign(size_type len, CharType ch);	Assigns len characters specified by ch to the end of the invoking string. Returns ***this**.
template<class InIter> string &assign(InIter start, InIter end);	Assigns the sequence specified by start and end to the invoking string. Returns ***this**.
reference at(size_type indx); const_reference at(size_type indx) const;	Returns a reference to the character specified by indx.
iterator begin( ); const_iterator begin( ) const;	Returns an iterator to the first element in the string.
const CharType *c_str( ) const;	Returns a pointer to a C-style (i.e., null-terminated) version of the invoking string.
size_type capacity( ) const;	Returns the current capacity of the string. This is the number of characters it can hold before it will need to allocate more memory.
int compare(const string &str) const;	Compares str to the invoking string. It returns one of the following: Less than zero if ***this** < str Zero if ***this** == str Greater than zero if ***this** > str
int compare(size_type indx, size_type len, const string &str) const;	Compares str to a substring within the invoking string. The substring begins at indx and is len characters long. It returns one of the following: Less than zero if ***this** < str Zero if ***this** == str Greater than zero if ***this** > str

Table 36-1. *The String Member Functions* (continued)

Member	Description
int compare(size_type *indx*, size_type *len*, const string &*str*, size_type *indx2*, size_type *len2*) const;	Compares a substring of *str* to a substring within the invoking string. The substring in the invoking string begins at *indx* and is *len* characters long. The substring in *str* begins at *indx2* and is *len2* characters long. It returns one of the following: Less than zero if ***this** < *str* Zero if ***this** == *str* Greater than zero if ***this** > *str*
int compare(const CharType **str*) const;	Compares *str* to the invoking string. It returns one of the following: Less than zero if ***this** < *str* Zero if ***this** == *str* Greater than zero if ***this** > *str*
int compare(size_type *indx*, size_type *len*, const CharType **str*, size_type *len2* = npos) const;	Compares a substring of *str* to a substring within the invoking string. The substring in the invoking string begins at *indx* and is *len* characters long. The substring in *str* begins at zero and is *len2* characters long. It returns one of the following: Less than zero if ***this** < *str* Zero if ***this** == *str* Greater than zero if ***this** > *str*
size_type copy(CharType **str*, size_type *len*, size_type *indx* = 0) const;	Beginning at *indx*, copies *len* characters from the invoking string into the character array pointed to by *str*. Returns the number of characters copied.
const CharType *data( ) const;	Returns a pointer to the first character in the invoking string.
bool empty( ) const;	Returns **true** if the invoking string is empty and **false** otherwise.

Table 36-1.   *The String Member Functions* (continued)

Member	Description
iterator end( ); const_iterator end( ) const;	Returns an iterator to the end of the string.
iterator erase(iterator *i*);	Removes character pointed to by *i*. Returns an iterator to the character after the one removed.
iterator erase(iterator *start*, iterator *end*);	Removes characters in the range *start* to *end*. Returns an iterator to the character after the last character removed.
string &erase(size_type *indx* = 0, size_type *len* = npos);	Beginning at *indx*, removes *len* characters from the invoking string. Returns ***this**.
size_type find(const string &*str*, size_type *indx* = 0) const;	Returns the index of the first occurrence of *str* within the invoking string. The search begins at index *indx*. **npos** is returned if no match is found.
size_type find(const CharType **str*, size_type *indx* = 0) const;	Returns the index of the first occurrence of *str* within the invoking string. The search begins at index *indx*. **npos** is returned if no match is found.

size_type find(const CharType **str*,
        size_type *indx*,
        size_type *len*) const;
	Returns the index of the first occurrence of the first *len* characters of *str* within the invoking string. The search begins at index *indx*. **npos** is returned if no match is found.

size_type find(CharType *ch*, size_type *indx* = 0) const;	Returns the index of the first occurrence of *ch* within the invoking string. The search begins at index *indx*. **npos** is returned if no match is found.

Table 36-1. *The String Member Functions* (continued)

Member	Description
size_type find_first_of(const string &*str*, size_type *indx* = 0) const;	Returns the index of the first character within the invoking string that matches any character in *str*. The search begins at index *indx*. **npos** is returned if no match is found.
size_type find_first_of(const CharType **str*, size_type *indx* = 0) const;	Returns the index of the first character within the invoking string that matches any character in *str*. The search begins at index *indx*. **npos** is returned if no match is found.
size_type find_first_of(const CharType **str*, size_type *indx*, size_type *len*) const;	Returns the index of the first character within the invoking string that matches any character in the first *len* characters of *str*. The search begins at index *indx*. **npos** is returned if no match is found.
size_type find_first_of(CharType *ch*, size_type *indx* = 0) const;	Returns the index of the first occurrence of *ch* within the invoking string. The search begins at index *indx*. **npos** is returned if no match is found.
size_type find_first_not_of(const string &*str*, size_type *indx* = 0) const;	Returns the index of the first character within the invoking string that does not match any character in *str*. The search begins at index *indx*. **npos** is returned if no mismatch is found.
size_type find_first_not_of(const CharType **str*, size_type *indx* = 0) const;	Returns the index of the first character within the invoking string that does not match any character in *str*. The search begins at index *indx*. **npos** is returned if no mismatch is found.

Table 36-1.   *The String Member Functions* (continued)

Member	Description

size_type find_first_not_of(
    const CharType *str,
    size_type indx,
    size_type len) const;
	Returns the index of the first character within the invoking string that does not match any character in the first len characters of str. The search begins at index indx. **npos** is returned if no mismatch is found.

size_type find_first_not_of(
    CharType ch,
    size_type indx = 0) const;
	Returns the index of the first character within the invoking string that does not match ch. The search begins at index indx. **npos** is returned if no mismatch is found.

size_type find_last_of(const string &str, size_type indx = npos) const;	Returns the index of the last character within the invoking string that matches any character in str. The search ends at index indx. **npos** is returned if no match is found.
size_type find_last_of(const CharType *str, size_type indx = npos) const;	Returns the index of the last character within the invoking string that matches any character in str. The search ends at index indx. **npos** is returned if no match is found.

size_type find_last_of(const CharType *str,
    size_type indx,
    size_type len) const;
	Returns the index of the last character within the invoking string that matches any character in the first len characters of str. The search ends at index indx. **npos** is returned if no match is found.

size_type find_last_of(CharType ch, size_type indx = npos) const;	Returns the index of the last occurrence of ch within the invoking string. The search ends at index indx. **npos** is returned if no match is found.

Table 36-1. *The String Member Functions* (continued)

Member	Description
size_type find_last_not_of(const string &*str*, size_type *indx* = npos) const;	Returns the index of the last character within the invoking string that does not match any character in *str*. The search ends at index *indx*. **npos** is returned if no mismatch is found.
size_type find_last_not_of(const CharType *str*, size_type *indx* = npos) const;	Returns the index of the last character within the invoking string that does not match any character in *str*. The search ends at index *indx*. **npos** is returned if no mismatch is found.
size_type find_last_not_of(const CharType *str*, size_type *indx*, size_type *len*) const;	Returns the index of the last character within the invoking string that does not match any character in the first *len* characters of *str*. The search ends at index *indx*. **npos** is returned if no mismatch is found.
size_type find_last_not_of(CharType *ch*, size_type *indx* = npos) const;	Returns the index of the last character within the invoking string that does not match *ch*. The search ends at index *indx*. **npos** is returned if no mismatch is found.
allocator_type get_allocator( ) const;	Returns the string's allocator.
iterator insert(iterator *i*, const CharType &*ch*);	Inserts *ch* immediately before the character specified by *i*. An iterator to the character is returned.
string &insert(size_type *indx*, const string &*str*);	Inserts *str* into the invoking string at the index specified by *indx*. Returns ***this**.
string &insert(size_type *indx1*, const string &*str*, size_type *indx2*, size_type *len*);	Inserts a substring of *str* into the invoking string at the index specified by *indx1*. The substring begins at *indx2* and is *len* characters long. Returns ***this**.

Table 36-1. *The String Member Functions* (continued)

Member	Description
string &insert(size_type *indx*, const CharType *str*);	Inserts *str* into the invoking string at the index specified by *indx*. Returns ***this**.

string &insert(size_type *indx*,
            const CharType *str*,
            size_type *len*);
	Inserts the first *len* characters of *str* into the invoking string at the index specified by *indx*. Returns ***this**.

string &insert(size_type *indx*,
            size_type *len*,
            CharType *ch*);
	Inserts *len* characters of value *ch* into the invoking string at the index specified by *indx*. Returns ***this**.

void insert(iterator *i*, size_type *len*, const CharType &*ch*)	Inserts *len* copies of *ch* immediately before the element specified by *i*.

template <class InIter>
  void insert(iterator *i*, InIter *start*,
            InIter *end*);
	Inserts the sequence defined by *start* and *end* immediately before the element specified by *i*.

size_type length( ) const;	Returns the number of characters in the string.
size_type max_size( ) const;	Returns the maximum number of characters that the string can hold.
reference operator[ ](size_type *indx*) const; const_reference operator[ ](size_type *indx*) const;	Returns a reference to the character specified by *indx*.

string &operator=(const string &*str*);
string &operator=(const CharType *str*);
string &operator=(CharType *ch*);
	Assigns the specified string or character to the invoking string. Returns ***this**.

string &operator+=(const string &*str*);
string &operator+=(const CharType *str*);
string &operator+=(CharType *ch*);
	Appends the specified string or character onto the end of the invoking string. Returns ***this**.

void push_back (const CharType *ch*)	Adds *ch* to the end of the invoking string.
reverse_iterator rbegin( ); const_reverse_iterator rbegin( ) const;	Returns a reverse iterator to the end of the string.
reverse_iterator rend( ); const_reverse_iterator rend( ) const;	Returns a reverse iterator to the start of the string.

Table 36-1.   *The String Member Functions* (continued)

Member	Description
string &replace(size_type *indx*, size_type *len*, const string &*str*);	Replaces up to *len* characters in the invoking string, beginning at *indx* with the string in *str*. Returns ***this**.
string &replace(size_type *indx1*, size_type *len1*, const string &*str*, size_type *indx2*, size_type *len2*);	Replaces up to *len1* characters in the invoking string beginning at *indx1* with the *len2* characters from the string in *str* that begins at *indx2*. Returns ***this**.
string &replace(size_type *indx*, size_type *len*, const CharType **str*);	Replaces up to *len* characters in the invoking string, beginning at *indx* with the string in *str*. Returns ***this**.
string &replace(size_type *indx*, size_type *len1*, const CharType **str*, size_type *len2*);	Replaces up to *len1* characters in the invoking string beginning at *indx* with the *len2* characters from the string in *str*. Returns ***this**.
string &replace(size_type *indx*, size_type *len1*, size_type *len2*, CharType *ch*);	Replaces up to *len1* characters in the invoking string beginning at *indx* with *len2* characters specified by *ch*. Returns ***this**.
string &replace(iterator *start*, iterator *end*, const string &*str*);	Replaces the range specified by *start* and *end* with *str*. Returns ***this**.
string &replace(iterator *start*, iterator *end*, const CharType **str*);	Replaces the range specified by *start* and *end* with *str*. Returns ***this**.
string &replace(iterator *start*, iterator *end*, const CharType **str*, size_type *len*);	Replaces the range specified by *start* and *end* with the first *len* characters from *str*. Returns ***this**.
string &replace(iterator *start*, interator *end*, size_type *len*, CharType *ch*);	Replaces the range specified by *start* and *end* with the *len* characters specified by *ch*. Returns ***this**.

Table 36-1.   *The String Member Functions* (continued)

Member	Description

template <class InIter>
  string &replace(iterator *start1*,
               interator *end1*,
               InIter *start2*,
               InIter *end2*);
	Replaces the range specified by *start1* and *end1* with the characters specified by *start2* and *end2*. Returns ***this**.

void reserve(size_type *num* = 0);	Sets the capacity of the string so that it is equal to at least *num*.
void resize(size_type *num*) void resize(size_type *num*, CharType *ch*);	Changes the size of the string to that specified by *num*. If the string must be lengthened, then elements with the value specified by *ch* are added to the end.
size_type rfind(const string &*str*, size_type *indx* = npos) const;	Returns the index of the last occurrence of *str* within the invoking string. The search ends at index *indx*. **npos** is returned if no match is found.
size_type rfind(const CharType **str*, size_type *indx* = npos) const;	Returns the index of the last occurrence of *str* within the invoking string. The search ends at index *indx*. **npos** is returned if no match is found.

size_type rfind(const CharType **str*,
        size_type *indx*,
        size_type *len*) const;
	Returns the index of the last occurrence of the first *len* characters of *str* within the invoking string. The search ends at index *indx*. **npos** is returned if no match is found.

size_type rfind(CharType *ch*, size_type *indx* = npos) const;	Returns the index of the last occurrence of *ch* within the invoking string. The search ends at index *indx*. **npos** is returned if no match is found.
size_type size( ) const;	Returns the number of characters currently in the string.

Table 36-1.   *The String Member Functions* (continued)

Member	Description
string substr(size_type *indx* = 0, size_type *len* = npos) const;	Returns a substring of *len* characters beginning at *indx* within the invoking string.
void swap(string &*str*)	Exchanges the characters stored in the invoking string with those in *ob*.

Table 36-1.   *The String Member Functions* (continued)

The char_traits Class

The class **char_traits** describes several attributes associated with a character. Its template specification is shown here:

        template<class CharType> struct char_traits

Here, **CharType** specifies the type of the character.

The C++ library provides two specializations of **char_traits**: one for **char** characters and one for **wchar_t** characters. The **char_traits** class defines the following five data types:

char_type	The type of the character. This is a **typedef** for **CharType**.
int_type	An integer type that can hold a character of type **char_type** or the EOF character.
off_type	An integer type that can represent an offset in a stream.
pos_type	An integer type that can represent a position in a stream.
state_type	An object type that stores the conversion state. (Applies to multibyte characters.)

The member functions of **char_traits** are shown in Table 36-2.

Member	Description
static void assign(char_type &*ch1*, const char_type &*ch2*);	Assigns *ch2* to *ch1*.
static char_type *assign(char_type **str*, size_t *num*, char_type *ch2*);	Assigns *ch2* to the first *num* characters in *str*. Returns *str*.
static int compare(const char_type **str1*, const char_type **str2*, size_t *num*);	Compares *num* characters in *str1* to those in *str2*. Returns zero if the strings are same. Otherwise, returns less than zero if *str1* is less than *str2* or greater than zero if *str1* is greater than *str2*.
static char_type *copy(char_type **to*, const char_type **from*, size_t *num*);	Copies *num* characters from *from* to *to*. Returns *to*.
static int_type eof( );	Returns the end-of-file character.
static bool eq(const char_type &*ch1*, const char_type &*ch2*);	Compares *ch1* to *ch2* and returns **true** if the characters are the same and **false** otherwise.
static bool eq_int_type(const int_type &*ch1*, const int_type &*ch2*);	Returns **true** if *ch1* equals *ch2* and **false** otherwise.
static const char_type *find(const char_type **str*, size_t *num*, const char_type **ch*);	Returns a pointer to the first occurrence of *ch* in *str*. Only the first *num* characters are examined. Returns a null pointer on failure.
static size_t length(const char_type **str*);	Returns the length of *str*.
static bool lt(const char_type &*ch1*, const char_type &*ch2*);	Returns **true** if *ch1* is less than *ch2* and **false** otherwise.

Table 36-2. *The **char_traits** Member Functions*

THE STANDARD C++
CLASS LIBRARY

Member	Description
static char_type *move(char_type *to, const char_type *from, size_t num);	Copies num characters from from to to. Returns to.
static int_type not_eof(const int_type &ch);	If ch is not the EOF character, then ch is returned. Otherwise, the EOF character is returned.
static char_type to_char_type(const int_type &ch);	Converts ch into a **char_type** and returns the result.
static int_type to_int_type(const char_type &ch);	Converts ch into an **int_type** and returns the result.

Table 36-2. *The **char_traits** Member Functions* (continued)

Chapter 37

The Numeric Classes

One of the features added during the standardization of C++ is the numeric class library. These classes aid in the development of numerical programs. Several of the member functions of these classes parallel the stand-alone functions inherited from the C library. The difference is that many of the numeric functions described here operate on objects of type **valarray**, which is essentially an array of values, or on objects of type **complex**, which represent complex numbers. By including the numeric classes, Standard C++ has expanded the scope of programming tasks to which it can be conveniently applied.

The complex Class

The header **<complex>** defines the **complex** class, which represents complex numbers. It also defines a series of functions and operators that operate on objects of type **complex**.

The template specification for **complex** is shown here:

> template <class T> class complex

Here, **T** specifies the type used to store the components of a complex number. There are three predefined specializations of **complex**:

> class complex<float>
> class complex<double>
> class complex<long double>

The **complex** class has the following constructors:

> complex(const T &*real* = T( ), const T &*imaginary* = T( ));
> complex(const complex &*ob*);
> template <class T1> complex(const complex<T1> &*ob*);

The first constructs a **complex** object with a real component of *real* and an imaginary component of *imaginary*. These values default to zero if not specified. The second creates a copy of *ob*. The third creates a **complex** object from *ob*.

The following operations are defined for **complex** objects:

+	–	*	/
–=	+=	/=	*=
=	==	!=	

The nonassignment operators are overloaded three ways. Once for operations involving a **complex** object on the left and a scalar object on the right, again for operations involving a scalar on the left and a **complex** object on the right, and finally for operations involving two **complex** objects. For example, the following types of operations are allowed:

```
complex_ob + scalar
scalar + complex_ob
complex_ob + complex_ob
```

Operations involving scalar quantities affect only the real component.

Two member functions are defined for **complex**: **real( )** and **imag( )**. They are shown here:

```
T real( ) const;
T imag( ) const;
```

The **real( )** function returns the real component of the invoking object, and **imag( )** returns the imaginary component. The functions shown in Table 37-1 are also defined for **complex** objects.

Here is a sample program that demonstrates **complex**.

```
// Demonstrate complex.
#include <iostream>
#include <complex>
using namespace std;

int main()
{
  complex<double> cmpx1(1, 0);
  complex<double> cmpx2(1, 1);

  cout << cmpx1 << " " << cmpx2 << endl;

  complex<double> cmpx3 = cmpx1 + cmpx2;
  cout << cmpx3 << endl;

  cmpx3 += 10;
  cout << cmpx3 << endl;

  return 0;
}
```

Its output is shown here:

```
(1,0)  (1,1)
(2,1)
(12,1)
```

Function	Description
template <class T> T abs(const complex<T> &ob);	Returns the absolute value of ob.
template <class T> T arg(const complex<T> &ob);	Returns the phase angle of ob.
template <class T> complex<T> conj(const complex<T> &ob);	Returns the conjugate of ob.
template <class T> complex<T> cos(const complex<T> &ob);	Returns the cosine of ob.

template <class T>
  complex<T>
    cosh(const complex<T> &ob);
	Returns the hyperbolic cosine of ob.

template <class T>
  complex<T>
    exp(const complex<T> &ob);
	Returns the e^{ob}.

template <class T> T imag(const complex<T> &ob);	Returns the imaginary component of ob.

template <class T>
  complex<T>
    log(const complex<T> &ob);
	Returns the natural logarithm of ob.

template <class T>
  complex<T>
    log10(const complex<T> &ob);
	Returns the base 10 logarithm of ob.

template <class T> T norm(const complex<T> &ob);	Returns the magnitude of ob squared.

Table 37-1.   *Functions Defined for **complex***

Function	Description

template <class T>
  complex<T>
    polar(const T &*v*, const T &*theta*=0);
	Returns a complex number that has the magnitude specified by *v* and a phase angle of *theta*.

template <class T>
  complex<T>
    pow(const complex<T> &*b*, int *e*);
	Returns b^e.

template <class T>
  complex<T>
    pow(const complex<T> &*b*,
        const T &*e*);
	Returns b^e.

template <class T>
  complex<T>
    pow(const complex<T> &*b*,
        const complex<T> &*e*);
	Returns b^e.

template <class T>
  complex<T>
    pow(const T &*b*,
        const complex<T> &*e*);
	Returns b^e.

template <class T> T real(const complex<T> &*ob*);	Returns the real component of *ob*.
template <class T> complex<T> sin(const complex<T> &*ob*);	Returns the sine of *ob*.

template <class T>
  complex<T>
    sinh(const complex<T> &*ob*);
	Returns the hyperbolic sine of *ob*.

template <class T>
  complex<T>
    sqrt(const complex<T> &*ob*);
	Returns the square root of *ob*.

template <class T>
  complex<T>
    tan(const complex<T> &*ob*);
	Returns the tangent of *ob*.

template <class T>
  complex<T>
    tanh(const complex<T> &*ob*);
	Returns the hyperbolic tangent of *ob*.

Table 37-1.   *Functions Defined for **complex*** (continued)

The valarray Class

The header **<valarray>** defines a number of classes that support numeric arrays. The main class is **valarray**, and it defines a one-dimensional array of values. There are a wide variety of member operators and functions defined for it as well as a large number of nonmember functions. While the description of **valarray** that is given here will be sufficient for most programmers, those especially interested in numeric processing will want to study **valarray** in greater detail. One other point: Although **valarray** is very large, most of its operations are intuitive.

The **valarray** class has this template specification:

    template <class T> class valarray

It defines the following constructors:

    valarray( );
    explicit valarray (size_t *num*);
    valarray(const T &*v*, size_t *num*);
    valarray(const T **ptr*, size_t *num*);
    valarray(const valarray<T> &*ob*);
    valarray(const slice_array<T> &*ob*);
    valarray(const gslice_array<T> &*ob*);
    valarray(const mask_array<T> &*ob*);
    valarray(const indirect_array<T> &*ob*);

Here, the first constructor creates an empty object. The second creates a **valarray** of length *num*. The third creates a **valarray** of length *num* initialized to *v*. The fourth creates a **valarray** of length *num* and initializes it with the elements pointed to by *ptr*. The fifth form creates a copy of *ob*. The next four constructors create a **valarray** from one of **valarray**'s helper classes.

The following operators are defined for **valarray**:

+	–	*	/
–=	+=	/=	*=
=	==	!=	<<
>>	<<=	>>=	^
^=	%	%=	~
!	|	|=	&
&=	[ ]		

Chapter 37: The Numeric Classes 903

These operators have several overloaded forms that are described in the accompanying tables.

The member functions and operators defined by **valarray** are shown in Table 37-2. The nonmember operator functions defined for **valarray** are shown in Table 37-3. The transcendental functions defined for **valarray** are shown in Table 37-4.

Function	Description
valarray<T> apply(T *func*(T)) const; valarray<T> apply(T *func*(const T &*ob*)) const;	Applies *func( )* to the invoking array and returns an array containing the result.
valarray<T> cshift(int *num*) const;	Left-rotates the invoking array *num* places. (That is, it performs a circular shift left.) Returns an array containing the result.
T max( ) const;	Returns the maximum value in the invoking array.
T min( ) const	Returns the minimum value in the invoking array.
valarray<T> &operator=(const valarray<T> &*ob*);	Assigns the elements in *ob* to the corresponding elements in the invoking array. Returns a reference to the invoking array.
valarray<T> &operator=(const T &*v*);	Assigns each element in the invoking array the value *v*. Returns a reference to the invoking array.
valarray<T> &operator=(const slice_array<T> &*ob*);	Assigns a subset. Returns a reference to the invoking array.
valarray<T> &operator=(const gslice_array<T> &*ob*);	Assigns a subset. Returns a reference to the invoking array.
valarray<T> &operator=(const mask_array<T> &*ob*);	Assigns a subset. Returns a reference to the invoking array.

Table 37-2. *The Member Functions of **valarray***

THE STANDARD C++ CLASS LIBRARY

Function	Description
valarray<T> &operator=(const indirect_array<T> &*ob*);	Assigns a subset. Returns a reference to the invoking array.
valarray<T> operator+( ) const;	Unary plus applied to each element in the invoking array. Returns the resulting array.
valarray<T> operator–( ) const;	Unary minus applied to each element in the invoking array. Returns the resulting array.
valarray<T> operator~( ) const;	Unary bitwise NOT applied to each element in the invoking array. Returns the resulting array.
valarray<T> operator!( ) const;	Unary logical NOT applied to each element in the invoking array. Returns the resulting array.
valarray<T> &operator+=(const T &*v*) const;	Adds *v* to each element in the invoking array. Returns a reference to the invoking array.
valarray<T> &operator–=(const T &*v*) const;	Subtracts *v* from each element in the invoking array. Returns a reference to the invoking array.
valarray<T> &operator/=(const T &*v*) const;	Divides each element in the invoking array by *v*. Returns a reference to the invoking array.
valarray<T> &operator*=(const T &*v*) const;	Multiplies each element in the invoking array by *v*. Returns a reference to the invoking array.
valarray<T> &operator%=(const T &*v*) const;	Assigns each element in the invoking array the remainder of a division by *v*. Returns a reference to the invoking array.

Table 37-2.   *The Member Functions of **valarray** (continued)*

Function	Description
valarray<T> &operator^=(const T &v) const;	XORs v with each element in the invoking array. Returns a reference to the invoking array.
valarray<T> &operator&=(const T &v) const;	ANDs v with each element in the invoking array. Returns a reference to the invoking array.
valarray<T> &operator | =(const T &v) const;	ORs v to each element in the invoking array. Returns a reference to the invoking array.
valarray<T> &operator<<=(const T &v) const;	Left-shifts each element in the invoking array v places. Returns a reference to the invoking array.
valarray<T> &operator>>=(const T &v) const;	Right-shifts each element in the invoking array v places. Returns a reference to the invoking array.
valarray<T> &operator+=(const valarray<T> &ob) const;	Corresponding elements of the invoking array and ob are added together. Returns a reference to the invoking array.
valarray<T> &operator−=(const valarray<T> &ob) const;	The elements in ob are subtracted from their corresponding elements in the invoking array. Returns a reference to the invoking array.
valarray<T> &operator/=(const valarray<T> &ob) const;	The elements in the invoking array are divided by their corresponding elements in ob. Returns a reference to the invoking array.
valarray<T> &operator*=(const valarray<T> &ob) const;	Corresponding elements of the invoking array and ob are multiplied together. Returns a reference to the invoking array.

Table 37-2. *The Member Functions of* **valarray** (continued)

Function	Description
valarray<T> &operator%=(const valarray<T> &*ob*) const;	The elements in the invoking array are divided by their corresponding elements in *ob* and the remainder is stored. Returns a reference to the invoking array.
valarray<T> &operator^=(const valarray<T> &*ob*) const;	The XOR operator is applied to corresponding elements in *ob* and the invoking array. Returns a reference to the invoking array.
valarray<T> &operator&=(const valarray<T> &*ob*) const;	The AND operator is applied to corresponding elements in *ob* and the invoking array. Returns a reference to the invoking array.
valarray<T> &operator	=(const valarray<T> &*ob*) const;	The OR operator is applied to corresponding elements in *ob* and the invoking array. Returns a reference to the invoking array.
valarray<T> &operator<<=(const valarray<T> &*ob*) const;	Elements in the invoking array are left-shifted by the number of places specified in the corresponding elements in *ob*. Returns a reference to the invoking array.
valarray<T> &operator>>=(const valarray<T> &*ob*) const;	Elements in invoking array are right-shifted by the number of places specified in the corresponding elements in *ob*. Returns a reference to the invoking array.

Table 37-2.   *The Member Functions of **valarray*** (continued)

Function	Description
T &operator[ ] (size_t *indx*) ;	Returns a reference to the element at the specified index.
T operator[ ] (size_t *indx*) const;	Returns the value at the specified index.
slice_array<T> operator[ ](slice *ob*);	Returns the specified subset.
valarray<T> operator[ ](slice *ob*) const;	Returns the specified subset.
gslice_array<T> operator[ ](const gslice &*ob*);	Returns the specified subset.
valarray<T> operator[ ](const gslice &*ob*) const;	Returns the specified subset.
mask_array<T> operator[ ](valarray<bool> &*ob*);	Returns the specified subset.
valarray<T> operator[ ](valarray<bool> &*ob*) const;	Returns the specified subset.
indirect_array<T> operator[ ](const valarray<size_t> &*ob*);	Returns the specified subset.
valarray<T> operator[ ](const valarray<size_t> &*ob*) const;	Returns the specified subset.
void resize(size_t *num*, T *v* = T( ));	Resizes the invoking array. If elements must be added, they are assigned the value of *v*.
size_t size( ) const;	Returns the size (i.e., the number of elements) of the invoking array.
valarray<T> shift(int *num*) const;	Shifts the invoking array left *num* places. Returns an array containing the result.
T sum( ) const;	Returns the sum of the values stored in the invoking array.

Table 37-2. *The Member Functions of **valarray*** (continued)

Function	Description
template <class T> valarray<T> operator+(const valarray<T> *ob*, const T &*v*);	Adds *v* to each element of *ob*. Returns an array containing the result.
template <class T> valarray<T> operator+(const T &*v*, const valarray<T> *ob);*	Adds *v* to each element of *ob*. Returns an array containing the result.
template <class T> valarray<T> operator+(const valarray<T> *ob1*, const valarray<T> &*ob2*);	Adds each element in *ob1* to its corresponding element in *ob2*. Returns an array containing the result.
template <class T> valarray<T> operator−(const valarray<T> *ob*, const T &*v*);	Subtracts *v* from each element of *ob*. Returns an array containing the result.
template <class T> valarray<T> operator−(const T &*v*, const valarray<T> *ob);*	Subtracts each element of *ob* from *v*. Returns an array containing the result.
template <class T> valarray<T> operator−(const valarray<T> *ob1*, const valarray<T> &*ob2*);	Subtracts each element in *ob2* from its corresponding element in *ob1*. Returns an array containing the result.
template <class T> valarray<T> operator*(const valarray<T> *ob*, const T &*v*);	Multiplies each element in *ob* by *v*. Returns an array containing the result.
template <class T> valarray<T> operator*(const T &*v*, const valarray<T> *ob);*	Multiplies each element in *ob* by *v*. Returns an array containing the result.
template <class T> valarray<T> operator*(const valarray<T> *ob1*, const valarray<T> &*ob2*);	Multiplies corresponding elements in *ob1* by those in *ob2*. Returns an array containing the result.

Table 37-3. *The Nonmember Operator Functions Defined for **valarray***

Function	Description

template <class T> valarray<T>
    operator/(const valarray<T> *ob*,
            const T &*v*);
	Divides each element in *ob* by *v*. Returns an array containing the result.

template <class T> valarray<T>
    operator/(const T &*v*,
            const valarray<T> *ob)*;
	Divides *v* by each element in *ob*. Returns an array containing the result.

template <class T> valarray<T>
    operator/(const valarray<T> *ob1*,
            const valarray<T> &*ob2*);
	Divides each element in *ob1* by its corresponding element in *ob2*. Returns an array containing the result.

template <class T> valarray<T>
    operator%(const valarray<T> *ob*,
            const T &*v*);
	Obtains the remainder that results from dividing each element in *ob* by *v*. Returns an array containing the result.

template <class T> valarray<T>
    operator%(const T &*v*,
            const valarray<T> *ob)*;
	Obtains the remainder that results from dividing *v* by each element in *ob*. Returns an array containing the result.

template <class T> valarray<T>
    operator%(const valarray<T> *ob1*,
            const valarray<T> &*ob2*);
	Obtains the remainder that results from dividing each element in *ob1* by its corresponding element in *ob2*. Returns an array containing the result.

template <class T> valarray<T>
    operator^(const valarray<T> *ob*,
            const T &*v*);
	XORs each element in *ob* with *v*. Returns an array containing the result.

template <class T> valarray<T>
    operator^(const T &*v*,
            const valarray<T> *ob)*;
	XORs each element in *ob* with *v*. Returns an array containing the result.

Table 37-3.   *The Nonmember Operator Functions Defined for **valarray** (continued)*

Function	Description

template \<class T\> valarray\<T\>
    operator^(const valarray\<T\> *ob1*,
        const valarray\<T\> &*ob2*);
	XORs each element in *ob1* with its corresponding element in *ob2*. Returns an array containing the result.

template \<class T\> valarray\<T\>
    operator&(const valarray\<T\> *ob*,
        const T &*v*);
	ANDs each element in *ob* with *v*. Returns an array containing the result.

template \<class T\> valarray\<T\>
    operator&(const T &*v*,
        const valarray\<T\> *ob)*;
	ANDs each element in *ob* with *v*. Returns an array containing the result.

template \<class T\> valarray\<T\>
    operator&(const valarray\<T\> *ob1*,
        const valarray\<T\> &*ob2*);
	ANDs each element in *ob1* with its corresponding element in *ob2*. Returns an array containing the result.

template \<class T\> valarray\<T\>
    operator | (const valarray\<T\> *ob*,
        const T &*v*);
	ORs each element in *ob* with *v*. Returns an array containing the result.

template \<class T\> valarray\<T\>
    operator | (const T &*v*,
        const valarray\<T\> *ob)*;
	ORs each element in *ob* with *v*. Returns an array containing the result.

template \<class T\> valarray\<T\>
    operator | (const valarray\<T\> *ob1*,
        const valarray\<T\> &*ob2*);
	ORs each element in *ob1* with its corresponding element in *ob2*. Returns an array containing the result.

template \<class T\> valarray\<T\>
    operator\<\<(const valarray\<T\> *ob*,
        const T &*v*);
	Left-shifts each element in *ob* by the number of places specified by *v*. Returns an array containing the result.

Table 37-3.   *The Nonmember Operator Functions Defined for **valarray** (continued)*

Function	Description

`template <class T> valarray<T>`
`    operator<<(const T &v,`
`        const valarray<T> ob);`
	Left-shifts *v* the number of places specified by the elements in *ob*. Returns an array containing the result.

`template <class T> valarray<T>`
`    operator<<(const valarray<T> ob1,`
`        const valarray<T> &ob2);`
	Left-shifts each element in *ob1* the number of places specified by its corresponding element in *ob2*. Returns an array containing the result.

`template <class T> valarray<T>`
`    operator>>(const valarray<T> ob,`
`        const T &v);`
	Right-shifts each element in *ob* the number of places specified by *v*. Returns an array containing the result.

`template <class T> valarray<T>`
`    operator>>(const T &v,`
`        const valarray<T> ob);`
	Right-shifts *v* the number of places specified by the elements in *ob*. Returns an array containing the result.

`template <class T> valarray<T>`
`    operator>>(const valarray<T> ob1,`
`        const valarray<T> &ob2);`
	Right-shifts each element in *ob1* the number of places specified by its corresponding element in *ob2*. Returns an array containing the result.

`template <class T> valarray<bool>`
`    operator==(const valarray<T> ob,`
`        const T &v);`
	For every i, performs *ob*[i] == *v*. Returns a Boolean array containing the result.

`template <class T> valarray<bool>`
`    operator==(const T &v,`
`        const valarray<T> ob);`
	For every i, performs *v* == *ob*[i]. Returns a Boolean array containing the result.

`template <class T> valarray<bool>`
`    operator==(const valarray<T> ob1,`
`        const valarray<T> &ob2);`
	For every i, performs *ob1*[i] == *ob2*[i]. Returns a Boolean array containing the result.

Table 37-3. *The Nonmember Operator Functions Defined for **valarray** (continued)*

Function	Description

template <class T> valarray<bool>
  operator!=(const valarray<T> *ob*,
    const T &*v*);
	For every i, performs *ob*[i] != *v*.
	Returns a Boolean array
	containing the result.

template <class T> valarray<bool>
  operator!=(const T &*v*,
    const valarray<T> *ob)*;
	For every i, performs *v* != *ob*[i].
	Returns a Boolean array
	containing the result.

template <class T> valarray<bool>
  operator!=(const valarray<T> *ob1*,
    const valarray<T> &*ob2*);
	For every i, performs *ob1*[i] !=
	ob2[i]. Returns a Boolean array
	containing the result.

template <class T> valarray<bool>
  operator<(const valarray<T> *ob*,
    const T &*v*);
	For every i, performs *ob*[i] < *v*.
	Returns a Boolean array
	containing the result.

template <class T> valarray<bool>
  operator<(const T &*v*,
    const valarray<T> *ob)*;
	For every i, performs *v* < *ob*[i].
	Returns a Boolean array
	containing the result.

template <class T> valarray<bool>
  operator<(const valarray<T> *ob1*,
    const valarray<T> &*ob2*);
	For every i, performs *ob1*[i] <
	ob2[i]. Returns a Boolean array
	containing the result.

template <class T> valarray<bool>
  operator<=(const valarray<T> *ob*,
    const T &*v*);
	For every i, performs *ob*[i] <= *v*.
	Returns a Boolean array
	containing the result.

template <class T> valarray<bool>
  operator<=(const T &*v*,
    const valarray<T> *ob)*;
	For every i, performs *v* <= *ob*[i].
	Returns a Boolean array
	containing the result.

template <class T> valarray<bool>
  operator<=(const valarray<T> *ob1*,
    const valarray<T> &*ob2*);
	For every i, performs *ob1*[i] <=
	ob2[i]. Returns a Boolean array
	containing the result.

template <class T> valarray<bool>
  operator>(const valarray<T> *ob*,
    const T &*v*);
	For every i, performs *ob*[i] > *v*.
	Returns a Boolean array
	containing the result.

Table 37-3.   *The Nonmember Operator Functions Defined for **valarray** (continued)*

Function	Description
template <class T> valarray<bool> operator>(const T &*v*, const valarray<T> *ob)*;	For every i, performs *v* > *ob*[i]. Returns a Boolean array containing the result.
template <class T> valarray<bool> operator>(const valarray<T> *ob1*, const valarray<T> &*ob2*);	For every i, performs *ob1*[i] > *ob2*[i]. Returns a Boolean array containing the result.
template <class T> valarray<bool> operator>=(const valarray<T> *ob*, const T &*v*);	For every i, performs *ob*[i] >= *v*. Returns a Boolean array containing the result.
template <class T> valarray<bool> operator>=(const T &*v*, const valarray<T> *ob)*;	For every i, performs *v* >= *ob*[i]. Returns a Boolean array containing the result.
template <class T> valarray<bool> operator>=(const valarray<T> *ob1*, const valarray<T> &*ob2*);	For every i, performs *ob1*[i] >= *ob2*[i]. Returns a Boolean array containing the result.
template <class T> valarray<bool> operator&&(const valarray<T> *ob*, const T &*v*);	For every i, performs *ob*[i] && *v*. Returns a Boolean array containing the result.
template <class T> valarray<bool> operator&&(const T &*v*, const valarray<T> *ob)*;	For every i, performs *v* && *ob*[i]. Returns a Boolean array containing the result.
template <class T> valarray<bool> operator&&(const valarray<T> *ob1*, const valarray<T> &*ob2*);	For every i, performs *ob1*[i] && *ob2*[i]. Returns a Boolean array containing the result.
template <class T> valarray<bool> operator||(const valarray<T> *ob*, const T &*v*);	For every i, performs *ob*[i] || *v*. Returns a Boolean array containing the result.
template <class T> valarray<bool> operator||(const T &*v*, const valarray<T> *ob)*;	For every i, performs *v* || *ob*[i]. Returns a Boolean array containing the result.
template <class T> valarray<bool> operator||(const valarray<T> *ob1*, const valarray<T> &*ob2*);	For every i, performs *ob1*[i] || *ob2*[i]. Returns a Boolean array containing the result.

Table 37-3. *The Nonmember Operator Functions Defined for **valarray*** (continued)

Function	Description
template<class T> valarray<T> abs(const valarray<T> &*ob*);	Obtains the absolute value of each element in *ob* and returns an array containing the result.
template<class T> valarray<T> acos(const valarray<T> &*ob*);	Obtains the arc cosine of each element in *ob* and returns an array containing the result.
template<class T> valarray<T> asin(const valarray<T> &*ob*);	Obtains the arc sine of each element in *ob* and returns an array containing the result.
template<class T> valarray<T> atan(const valarray<T> &*ob*);	Obtains the arc tangent of each element in *ob* and returns an array containing the result.

template<class T> valarray<T>
    atan2(const valarray<T> &*ob1*,
        const valarray<T> &*ob2*);
	For all i, obtains the arc tangent of *ob1*[i] / *ob2*[i] and returns an array containing the result.

template<class T> valarray<T> atan2(const T &*v*, const valarray<T> &*ob*);	For all i, obtains the arc tangent of *v* / *ob1*[i] and returns an array containing the result.
template<class T> valarray<T> atan2(const valarray<T> &*ob*, const T &*v*);	For all i, obtains the arc tangent of *ob1*[i] / *v* and returns an array containing the result.
template<class T> valarray<T> cos(const valarray<T> &*ob*);	Obtains the cosine of each element in *ob* and returns an array containing the result.
template<class T> valarray<T> cosh(const valarray<T> &*ob*);	Obtains the hyperbolic cosine of each element in *ob* and returns an array containing the result.
template<class T> valarray<T> exp(const valarray<T> &*ob*);	Computes exponential function for each element in *ob* and returns an array containing the result.

Table 37-4.   *Transcendental Functions Defined for **valarray***

Function	Description
template<class T> valarray<T> log(const valarray<T> &ob);	Obtains the natural logarithm of each element in *ob* and returns an array containing the result.
template<class T> valarray<T> log10(const valarray<T> &ob);	Obtains the common logarithm of each element in *ob* and returns an array containing the result.

template<class T> valarray<T>
  pow(const valarray<T> &ob1,
     const valarray<T> &ob2);
	For all i, computes $ob1[i]^{ob2[i]}$ and returns an array containing the result.

template<class T> valarray<T> pow(const T &v, const valarray<T> &ob);	For all i, computes $v^{ob[i]}$ and returns an array containing the result.
template<class T> valarray<T> pow(const valarray<T> &ob, const T &v);	For all i, computes $ob1[i]^{v}$ and returns an array containing the result.
template<class T> valarray<T> sin(const valarray<T> &ob);	Obtains the sine of each element in *ob* and returns an array containing the result.
template<class T> valarray<T> sinh(const valarray<T> &ob);	Obtains the hyperbolic sine of each element in *ob* and returns an array containing the result.
template<class T> valarray<T> sqrt(const valarray<T> &ob);	Obtains the square root of each element in *ob* and returns an array containing the result.
template<class T> valarray<T> tan(const valarray<T> &ob);	Obtains the tangent of each element in *ob* and returns an array containing the result.
template<class T> valarray<T> tanh(const valarray<T> &ob);	Obtains the hyperbolic tangent of each element in *ob* and returns an array containing the result.

Table 37-4. *Transcendental Functions Defined for **valarray** (continued)*

The following program demonstrates a few of the many capabilities of **valarray**.

```cpp
// Demonstrate valarray
#include <iostream>
#include <valarray>
#include <cmath>
using namespace std;

int main()
{
  valarray<int> v(10);
  int i;

  for(i=0; i<10; i++) v[i] = i;

  cout << "Original contents: ";
  for(i=0; i<10; i++)
    cout << v[i] << " ";
  cout << endl;

  v = v.cshift(3);

  cout << "Shifted contents: ";
  for(i=0; i<10; i++)
    cout << v[i] << " ";
  cout << endl;

  valarray<bool> vb = v < 5;
  cout << "Those elements less than 5: ";
  for(i=0; i<10; i++)
    cout << vb[i] << " ";
  cout << endl << endl;

  valarray<double> fv(5);
  for(i=0; i<5; i++) fv[i] = (double) i;

  cout << "Original contents: ";
  for(i=0; i<5; i++)
    cout << fv[i] << " ";
  cout << endl;
```

```
    fv = sqrt(fv);

    cout << "Square roots: ";
    for(i=0; i<5; i++)
      cout << fv[i] << " ";
    cout << endl;

    fv = fv + fv;
    cout << "Double the square roots: ";
    for(i=0; i<5; i++)
      cout << fv[i] << " ";
    cout << endl;

    fv = fv - 10.0;
    cout << "After subtracting 10 from each element:\n";
    for(i=0; i<5; i++)
      cout << fv[i] << " ";
    cout << endl;

    return 0;
}
```

Its output is shown here:

```
Original contents: 0 1 2 3 4 5 6 7 8 9
Shifted contents: 3 4 5 6 7 8 9 0 1 2
Those elements less than 5: 1 1 0 0 0 0 0 1 1 1

Original contents: 0 1 2 3 4
Square roots: 0 1 1.41421 1.73205 2
Double the square roots: 0 2 2.82843 3.4641 4
After subtracting 10 from each element:
-10 -8 -7.17157 -6.5359 -6
```

The slice and gslice Classes

The **<valarray>** header defines two utility classes called **slice** and **gslice**. These classes encapsulate a slice (i.e., a portion) from an array. These classes are used with the subset forms of **valarray**'s operator[ ].

The **slice** class is shown here:

```
class slice {
public:
  slice();
  slice(size_t start, size_t len, size_t interval);
  size_t start() const;
  size_t size() const;
  size_t stride();
};
```

The first constructor creates an empty slice. The second constructor creates a slice that specifies the starting element, the number of elements, and the interval between elements (that is, the *stride*). The member functions return these values.

Here is a program that demonstrates **slice**.

```
// Demonstrate slice
#include <iostream>
#include <valarray>
using namespace std;

int main()
{
  valarray<int> v(10), result;
  unsigned int i;

  for(i=0; i<10; i++) v[i] = i;

  cout << "Contents of v: ";
  for(i=0; i<10; i++)
    cout << v[i] << " ";
  cout << endl;

  result = v[slice(0,5,2)];

  cout << "Contents of result: ";
  for(i=0; i<result.size(); i++)
    cout << result[i] << " ";

  return 0;
}
```

The output from the program is shown here:

```
Contents of v: 0 1 2 3 4 5 6 7 8 9
Contents of result: 0 2 4 6 8
```

As you can see, the resulting array consists of 5 elements of **v**, beginning at 0, that are 2 apart.

The **gslice** class is shown here:

```
class gslice {
public:
  gslice();
  gslice()(size_t start, const valarray<size_t> &lens,
          const valarray<size_t> &intervals);
  size_t start() const;
  valarray<size_t> size() const;
  valarray<size_t> stride() const;
};
```

The first constructor creates an empty slice. The second constructor creates a slice that specifies the starting element, an array that specifies the number of elements, and an array that specifies the intervals between elements (that is, the *strides*). The number of lengths and intervals must be the same. The member functions return these parameters. This class is used to create multidimensional arrays from a **valarray** (which is always one-dimensional).

The following program demonstrates **gslice**.

```
// Demonstrate gslice()
#include <iostream>
#include <valarray>
using namespace std;

int main()
{
  valarray<int> v(12), result;
  valarray<size_t> len(2), interval(2);
  unsigned int i;

  for(i=0; i<12; i++) v[i] = i;

  len[0] = 3; len[1] = 3;
```

```
        interval[0] = 2; interval[1] = 3;

        cout << "Contents of v: ";
        for(i=0; i<12; i++)
          cout << v[i] << " ";
        cout << endl;

        result = v[gslice(0,len,interval)];

        cout << "Contents of result: ";
        for(i=0; i<result.size(); i++)
          cout << result[i] << " ";

        return 0;
      }
```

The output is shown here:

```
Contents of v: 0 1 2 3 4 5 6 7 8 9 10 11
Contents of result: 0 3 6 2 5 8 4 7 10
```

The Helper Classes

The numeric classes rely upon these "helper" classes, which your program will never instantiate directly: **slice_array**, **gslice_array**, **indirect_array**, and **mask_array**.

The Numeric Algorithms

The header **<numeric>** defines four numeric algorithms that can be used to process the contents of containers. Each is examined here.

accumulate

The **accumulate( )** algorithm computes a summation of all of the elements within a specified range and returns the result. Its prototypes are shown here:

> template <class InIter, class T> T accumulate(InIter *start*, InIter *end*, T *v*);
> template <class InIter, class T, class BinFunc>
>   T accumulate(InIter *start*, InIter *end*, T *v*, BinFunc *func*);

Here, **T** is the type of values being operated upon. The first version computes the sum of all elements in the range *start* to *end*. The second version applies *func* to the running total. (That is, *func* specifies how the summation will occur.) The value of *v* provides an initial value to which the running total is added.

Here is an example that demonstrates **accumulate( )**.

```
// Demonstrate accumulate()
#include <iostream>
#include <vector>
#include <numeric>
using namespace std;

int main()
{
  vector<int> v(5);
  int i, total;

  for(i=0; i<5; i++) v[i] = i;

  total = accumulate(v.begin(), v.end(), 0);

  cout << "Summation of v is: " << total;

  return 0;
}
```

The following output is produced:

```
Summation of v is: 10
```

adjacent_difference

The **adjacent_difference( )** algorithm produces a new sequence in which each element is the difference between adjacent elements in the original sequence. (The first element in the result is the same as the original first element.) The prototypes for **adjacent_difference( )** are shown here:

template <class InIter, class OutIter>
   OutIter adjacent_difference(InIter *start*, InIter *end*, OutIter *result*);
template <class InIter, class OutIter, class BinFunc>
   OutIter adjacent_difference(InIter *start*, InIter *end*, OutIter *result*,
                    BinFunc *func*);

Here, *start* and *end* are iterators to the beginning and ending of the original sequence. The resulting sequence is stored in the sequence pointed to by *result*. In the first form, adjacent elements are subtracted, with the element at location *n* being subtracted from the element at location *n+1*. In the second, the binary function *func* is applied to adjacent elements. An iterator to the end of *result* is returned.

Here is an example that uses **adjacent_difference( )**.

```
// Demonstrate adjacent_difference()
#include <iostream>
#include <vector>
#include <numeric>
using namespace std;

int main()
{
  vector<int> v(10), r(10);
  int i;

  for(i=0; i<10; i++) v[i] = i*2;
  cout << "Original sequence: ";
  for(i=0; i<10; i++)
    cout << v[i] << " ";
  cout << endl;

  adjacent_difference(v.begin(), v.end(), r.begin());

  cout << "Resulting sequence: ";
  for(i=0; i<10; i++)
    cout << r[i] << " ";

  return 0;
}
```

The output produced is shown here:

```
Original sequence:  0 2 4 6 8 10 12 14 16 18
Resulting sequence:  0 2 2 2 2 2 2 2 2 2
```

As you can see, the resulting sequence contains the difference between the value of adjacent elements.

inner_product

The **inner_product( )** algorithm produces a summation of the product of corresponding elements in two sequences and returns the result. It has these prototypes:

```
template <class InIter1, class InIter2, class T>
    T inner_product(InIter1 start1, InIter1 end1, InIter2 start2, T v);
template <class InIter1, class InIter2, class T, class BinFunc1, class BinFunc2>
    T inner_product(InIter1 start1, InIter1 end1, InIter2 start2, T v,
                    BinFunc1 func2, BinFunc2 func2);
```

Here, *start1* and *end1* are iterators to the beginning and end of the first sequence. The iterator *start2* is an iterator to the beginning of the second sequence. The value *v* provides an initial value to which the running total is added. In the second form, *func1* specifies a binary function that determines how the running total is computed, and *func2* specifies a binary function that determines how the two sequences are multiplied together.

Here is a program that demonstrates **inner_product( )**.

```cpp
// Demonstrate inner_product()
#include <iostream>
#include <vector>
#include <numeric>
using namespace std;

int main()
{
  vector<int> v1(5), v2(5);
  int i, total;

  for(i=0; i<5; i++) v1[i] = i;
  for(i=0; i<5; i++) v2[i] = i+2;

  total = inner_product(v1.begin(), v1.end(),
                        v2.begin(), 0);

  cout << "Inner product is: " << total;

  return 0;
}
```

Here is the output:

Inner product is: 50

partial_sum

The **partial_sum( )** algorithm sums a sequence of values, putting the current total into each successive element of a new sequence as it goes. (That is, it creates a sequence that is a running total of the original sequence.) The first element in the result is the same as the first element in the original sequence. The prototypes for **partial_sum( )** are shown here:

> template <class InIter, class OutIter>
>   OutIter partial_sum(InIter *start*, InIter *end*, OutIter *result*);
> template <class InIter, class OutIter, class BinFunc>
>   OutIter partial_sum(InIter *start*, InIter *end*, OutIter *result*,
>   BinFunc *func*);

Here, *start* and *end* are iterators to the beginning and end of the original sequence. The iterator *result* is an iterator to the beginning of the resulting sequence. In the second form, *func* specifies a binary function that determines how the running total is computed. An iterator to the end of *result* is returned.

Here is an example of **partial_sum( )**.

```cpp
// Demonstrate partial_sum()
#include <iostream>
#include <vector>
#include <numeric>
using namespace std;

int main()
{
  vector<int> v(5), r(5);
  int i;

  for(i=0; i<5; i++) v[i] = i;
  cout << "Original sequence: ";
  for(i=0; i<5; i++)
    cout << v[i] << " ";
  cout << endl;

  partial_sum(v.begin(), v.end(), r.begin());

  cout << "Resulting sequence: ";
  for(i=0; i<5; i++)
    cout << r[i] << " ";

  return 0;
}
```

Here is its output:

```
Original sequence: 0 1 2 3 4
Resulting sequence: 0 1 3 6 10
```

Chapter 38

Exception Handling and Miscellaneous Classes

This chapter describes the exception handling classes. It also describes the **auto_ptr** and **pair** classes, and gives a brief introduction to the localization library.

Exceptions

The Standard C++ library defines two headers that relate to exceptions: **<exception>** and **<stdexcept>**. Exceptions are used to report error conditions. Each header is examined here.

<exception>

The **<exception>** header defines classes, types, and functions that relate to exception handling. The classes defined by **<exception>** are shown here.

```
class exception {
public:
  exception() throw();
  exception(const bad_exception &ob) throw();
  virtual ~exception() throw();

  exception &operator=(const exception &ob) throw();
  virtual const char *what(() const throw();
};

class bad_exception: public exception {
public:
  bad_exception() throw();
  bad_exception(const bad_exception &ob) throw();
  virtual ~bad_exception() throw();

  bad_exception &operator=(const bad_exception &ob) throw();
  virtual const char *what(() const throw();
};
```

The **exception** class is a base for all exceptions defined by the C++ standard library. The **bad_exception** class is the type of exception thrown by the **unexpected( )** function. In each, the member function **what( )** returns a pointer to a null-terminated string that describes the exception.

Several important classes are derived from **exception**. The first is **bad_alloc**, thrown when the **new** operator fails. Next is **bad_typeid**. It is thrown when an illegal **typeid** expression is executed. Finally, **bad_cast** is thrown when an invalid dynamic cast is attempted. These classes contain the same members as **exception**.

The types defined by **<exception>** are:

Type	Meaning
terminate_handler	void (*terminate_handler) ( );
unexpected_handler	void (*unexpected_handler) ( );

The functions declared in **<exception>** are shown in Table 38-1.

<stdexcept>

The header **<stdexcept>** defines several standard exceptions that may be thrown by C++ library functions and/or its run-time system. There are two general types of exceptions defined by **<stdexcept>**: logic errors and run-time errors. Logic errors occur because of mistakes made by the programmer. Run-time errors occur because of mistakes in library functions or the run-time system, and are beyond programmer control.

Function	Description
terminate_handler set_terminate(terminate_handler *fn*) throw( );	Sets the function specified by *fn* as the terminate handler. A pointer to the old terminate handler is returned.
unexpected_handler set_unexpected(unexpected_handler *fn*) throw( );	Sets the function specified by *fn* as the unexpected handler. A pointer to the old unexpected handler is returned.
void terminate( );	Calls the terminate handler when a fatal exception is unhandled. Calls **abort( )** by default.
bool uncaught_exception( );	Returns true if an exception is uncaught.
void unexpected( );	Calls the unexpected exception handler when a function throws a disallowed exception. By default, **terminate( )** is called.

Table 38-1. *The Functions Defined Within* **<exception>**

The standard exceptions defined by C++ caused by logic errors are derived from the base class **logic_error**. These exceptions are shown here.

Exception	Meaning
domain_error	Domain error occurred.
invalid_argument	Invalid argument used in function call.
length_error	An attempt was made to create an object that was too large.
out_of_range	An argument to a function was not in the required range.

The following run-time exceptions are derived from the base class **runtime_error**.

Exception	Meaning
overflow_error	Arithmetic overflow occurred.
range_error	An internal range error occurred.
underflow_error	An underflow occurred.

auto_ptr

A very interesting class is **auto_ptr**, which is declared in the header **<memory>**. An **auto_ptr** is a pointer that owns the object to which it points. Ownership of this object can be transferred to another **auto_ptr**, but some **auto_ptr** always owns the object. The key purpose of this scheme is to ensure that dynamically allocated objects are properly destroyed in all circumstances (that is, that the object's destructor is always properly executed). For example, when one **auto_ptr** object is assigned to another, only the target of the assignment will own the object. When the pointers are destroyed, the object will only be destroyed once, when the pointer holding ownership is destroyed. One benefit of this approach is that dynamically allocated objects can be destroyed when an exception is handled.

The template specification for **auto_ptr** is shown here:

    template <class T> class auto_ptr

Here, **T** specifies the type of pointer stored by the **auto_ptr**.

Here are the constructors for **auto_ptr**:

    explicit auto_ptr(T *ptr = 0) throw( );

auto_ptr(auto_ptr &*ob*) throw( );

template <class T2> auto_ptr(auto_ptr<T2> &*ob*) throw( );

The first constructor creates an **auto_ptr** to the object specified by *ptr*. The second constructor creates a copy of the **auto_ptr** specified by *ob* and transfers ownership to the new object. The third converts *ob* to type T (if possible) and transfers ownership.

The **auto_ptr** class defines the =, *, and –> operators. Here are two of its member functions:

T *get( ) const throw( );

T *release( ) const throw( );

The **get( )** function returns a pointer to the stored object. The **release( )** function removes ownership of the stored object from the invoking **auto_ptr** and returns a pointer to the object. After a call to **release( )**, the pointed-to object is not automatically destroyed when the **auto_ptr** object goes out-of-scope.

Here is a short program that demonstrates the use of **auto_ptr**.

```
// Demonstrate an auto_ptr.
#include <iostream>
#include <memory>
using namespace std;

class X {
public:
  X() { cout << "constructing\n"; }
  ~X() { cout << "destructing\n"; }
  void f() { cout << "Inside f()\n"; }
};

int main()
{
  auto_ptr<X> p1(new X), p2;

  p2 = p1; // transfer ownership
  p2->f();

  // can assign to a normal pointer
  X *ptr = p2.get();
```

```
    ptr->f();

    return 0;
}
```

The output produced by this program is shown here:

```
constructing
Inside f()
Inside f()
destructing
```

Notice that **X**'s member function **f( )** can be called either through an **auto_ptr** or through the "normal" pointer returned by **get( )**.

The pair Class

The **pair** class is used to house pairs of objects, such as might be stored in an associative container. It has this template specification:

```
template <class Ktype, class Vtype> struct pair {
  typedef Ktype first_type;
  typedef Vtype second_type;
  Ktype first;
  Vtype second;

  // constructors
  pair();
  pair(const Ktype &k, const Vtype &v);
  template<class A, class B> pair(const<A, B> &ob);
}
```

The value in **first** typically contains a key, and the value in **second** typically contains the value associated with that key.

The following operators are defined for **pair**: **==, !=, <, <=, >,** and **>=**.

You can construct a pair using either one of **pair**'s constructors or by using **make_pair( )**, which constructs a pair object based upon the types of the data used as parameters. **make_pair( )** is a generic function that has this prototype:

template <class *Ktype*, class *Vtype*>
pair<*Ktype*, *Vtype*> make_pair(const *Ktype* &*k*, const *Vtype* &*v*);

As you can see, it returns a pair object consisting of values of the types specified by *Ktype* and *Vtype*. The advantage of **make_pair( )** is that the types of the objects being stored are determined automatically by the compiler rather than being explicitly specified by you.

The **pair** class and the **make_pair( )** function require the header **<utility>**.

Localization

Standard C++ provides an extensive localization class library. These classes allow an application to set or obtain information about the geopolitical environment in which it is executing. Thus, it defines such things as the format of currency, time and date, and collation order. It also provides for character classification. The localization library uses the header **<locale>**. It operates through a series of classes that define facets (bits of information associated with a locale). All facets are derived from the class **facet**, which is a nested class inside the **locale** class.

Frankly, the localization library is extraordinarily large and complex. A description of its features is beyond the scope of this book. While most programmers will not make direct use of the localization library, if you are involved in the preparation of internationalized programs, you will want to explore its features.

Other Classes of Interest

Here are a few other classes defined by the Standard C++ library that may be of interest.

Class	Description
type_info	Used in conjunction with the **typeid** operator and fully described in Chapter 22. Uses the header **<typeinfo>**.
numeric_limts	Encapsulates various numeric limits. Uses the header **<limits>**.
raw_storage_iterator	Encapsulates allocation of uninitialized memory. Uses the header **<memory>**.

The Complete Reference

Part V

Applying C++

Part Five of this book provides two sample C++ applications. The purpose of this section is twofold. First, the examples help illustrate the benefits of object-oriented programming. Second, they show how C++ can be applied to solve two very different types of programming problems.

Chapter 39

Integrating
New Classes:
A Custom String Class

This chapter designs and implements a small string class. As you know, Standard C++ provides a full-featured, powerful string class called **basic_string**. The purpose of this chapter is not to develop an alternative to this class, but rather to give you insight into how any new data type can be easily added and integrated into the C++ environment. The creation of a string class is the quintessential example of this process. In the past, many programmers honed their object-oriented skills developing their own personal string classes. In this chapter, we will do the same.

While the example string class developed in this chapter is much simpler than the one supplied by Standard C++, it does have one advantage: it gives you full control over how strings are implemented and manipulated. You may find this useful in certain situations. It is also just plain fun to play with!

The StrType Class

Our string class is loosely modeled on the one provided by the standard library. Of course, it is not as large or as sophisticated. The string class defined here will meet the following requirements:

- Strings may be assigned by using the assignment operator.
- Both string objects and quoted strings may be assigned to string objects.
- Concatenation of two string objects is accomplished with the + operator.
- Substring deletion is performed using the – operator.
- String comparisons are performed with the relational operators.
- String objects may be initialized by using either a quoted string or another string object.
- Strings must be able to be of arbitrary and variable lengths. This implies that storage for each string is dynamically allocated.
- A method of converting string objects to null-terminated strings will be provided.

Although our string class will, in general, be less powerful than the standard string class, it does include one feature not defined by **basic_string**: substring deletion via the – operator.

The class that will manage strings is called **StrType**. Its declaration is shown here:

```
class StrType {
  char *p;
  int size;
public:
  StrType();
```

```cpp
    StrType(char *str);
    StrType(const StrType &o); // copy constructor

    ~StrType() { delete [] p; }

    friend ostream &operator<<(ostream &stream, StrType &o);
    friend istream &operator>>(istream &stream, StrType &o);

    StrType operator=(StrType &o); // assign a StrType object
    StrType operator=(char *s); // assign a quoted string

    StrType operator+(StrType &o); // concatenate a StrType object
    StrType operator+(char *s); // concatenate a quoted string
    friend StrType operator+(char *s, StrType &o); /*  concatenate
                a quoted string with a StrType object */

    StrType operator-(StrType &o); // subtract a substring
    StrType operator-(char *s); // subtract a quoted substring

    // relational operations between StrType objects
    int operator==(StrType &o) { return !strcmp(p, o.p); }
    int operator!=(StrType &o) { return strcmp(p, o.p); }
    int operator<(StrType &o) { return strcmp(p, o.p) < 0; }
    int operator>(StrType &o) { return strcmp(p, o.p) > 0; }
    int operator<=(StrType &o) { return strcmp(p, o.p) <= 0; }
    int operator>=(StrType &o) { return strcmp(p, o.p) >= 0; }

    // operations between StrType objects and quoted strings
    int operator==(char *s) { return !strcmp(p, s); }
    int operator!=(char *s) { return strcmp(p, s); }
    int operator<(char *s) { return strcmp(p, s) < 0; }
    int operator>(char *s) { return strcmp(p, s) > 0; }
    int operator<=(char *s) { return strcmp(p, s) <= 0; }
    int operator>=(char *s) { return strcmp(p, s) >= 0; }

    int strsize() { return strlen(p); } // return size of string
    void makestr(char *s) { strcpy(s, p); } // make quoted string

    operator char *() { return p; } // conversion to char *
};
```

The private part of **StrType** contains only two items: **p** and **size**. When a string object is created, memory to hold the string is dynamically allocated by using **new**, and a pointer to that memory is put in **p**. The string pointed to by **p** will be a normal, null-terminated character array. Although it is not technically necessary, the size of the string is held in **size**. Because the string pointed to by **p** is a null-terminated string, it would be possible to compute the size of the string each time it is needed. However, as you will see, this value is used so often by the **StrType** member functions that the repeated calls to **strlen( )** cannot be justified.

The next several sections detail how the **StrType** class works.

The Constructors and Destructors

A **StrType** object may be declared in three different ways: without any initialization, with a quoted string as an initializer, or with a **StrType** object as an initializer. The constructors that support these three operations are shown here:

```
// No explicit initialization.
StrType::StrType() {
  size = 1; // make room for null terminator
  try {
    p = new char[size];
  } catch (bad_alloc xa) {
    cout << "Allocation error\n";
    exit(1);
  }
  strcpy(p, "");
}


// Initialize using a quoted string.
StrType::StrType(char *str) {
  size = strlen(str) + 1; // make room for null terminator
  try {
    p = new char[size];
  } catch (bad_alloc xa) {
    cout << "Allocation error\n";
    exit(1);
  }
  strcpy(p, str);
}


// Initialize using a StrType object.
StrType::StrType(const StrType &o) {
```

```
  size = o.size;
  try {
    p = new char[size];
  } catch (bad_alloc xa) {
    cout << "Allocation error\n";
    exit(1);
  }
  strcpy(p, o.p);
}
```

When a **StrType** object is created with no initializer, it is assigned a null-string. Although the string could have been left undefined, knowing that all **StrType** objects contain a valid, null-terminated string simplifies several other member functions.

When a **StrType** object is initialized by a quoted string, first the size of the string is determined. This value is stored in **size**. Then, sufficient memory is allocated by **new** and the initializing string is copied into the memory pointed to by **p**.

When a **StrType** object is used to initialize another, the process is similar to using a quoted string. The only difference is that the size of the string is known and does not have to be computed. This version of the **StrType** constructor is also the class' copy constructor. This constructor will be invoked whenever one **StrType** object is used to initialize another. This means that it is called when temporary objects are created and when objects of type **StrType** are passed to functions. (See Chapter 14 for a discussion of copy constructors.)

Given the three preceding constructors, the following declarations are allowed:

```
StrType x("my string"); // use quoted string
StrType y(x); // use another object
StrType z; // no explicit initialization
```

The **StrType** destructor simply frees the memory pointed to by **p**.

I/O on Strings

Because it is common to input or output strings, the **StrType** class overloads the **<<** and **>>** operators, as shown here:

```
// Output a string.
ostream &operator<<(ostream &stream, StrType &o)
{
  stream << o.p;
```

```
    return stream;
}

// Input a string.
istream &operator>>(istream &stream, StrType &o)
{
  char t[255]; // arbitrary size - change if necessary
  int len;

  stream.getline(t, 255);
  len = strlen(t) + 1;

  if(len > o.size) {
    delete [] o.p;
    try {
      o.p = new char[len];
    } catch (bad_alloc xa) {
      cout << "Allocation error\n";
      exit(1);
    }
    o.size = len;
  }
  strcpy(o.p, t);
  return stream;
}
```

As you can see, output is very simple. However, notice that the parameter **o** is passed by reference. Since **StrType** objects may be quite large, passing one by reference is more efficient than passing one by value. For this reason, all **StrType** parameters are passed by reference. (Any function you create that takes **StrType** parameters should probably do the same.)

Inputting a **string** proves to be a little more difficult than outputting one. First, the string is read using the **getline( )** function. The length of the largest string that can be input is limited to 254 plus the null terminator. As the comments indicate, you can change this if you like. Characters are read until a newline is encountered. Once the string has been read, if the size of the new string exceeds that of the one currently held by **o**, that memory is released and a larger amount is allocated. The new string is then copied into it.

The Assignment Functions

You can assign a **StrType** object a string in two ways. First, you can assign another **StrType** object to it. Second, you can assign it a quoted string. The two overloaded **operator=( )** functions that accomplish these operations are shown here:

```
// Assign a StrType object to a StrType object.
StrType StrType::operator=(StrType &o)
{
  StrType temp(o.p);

  if(o.size > size) {
    delete [] p; // free old memory
    try {
      p = new char[o.size];
    } catch (bad_alloc xa) {
      cout << "Allocation error\n";
      exit(1);
    }
    size = o.size;
  }

  strcpy(p, o.p);
  strcpy(temp.p, o.p);

  return temp;
}

// Assign a quoted string to a StrType object.
StrType StrType::operator=(char *s)
{
  int len = strlen(s) + 1;
  if(size < len) {
    delete [] p;
    try {
      p = new char[len];
    } catch (bad_alloc xa) {
      cout << "Allocation error\n";
      exit(1);
```

```
        }
      size = len;
    }
    strcpy(p, s);
    return *this;
}
```

These two functions work by first checking to see if the memory currently pointed to by **p** of the target **StrType** object is sufficiently large to hold what will be copied to it. If not, the old memory is released and new memory is allocated. Then the string is copied into the object and the result is returned. These functions allow the following types of assignments:

```
StrType x("test"), y;

y = x; // StrType object to StrType object

x = "new string for x"; // quoted string to StrType object
```

Each assignment function returns the value assigned (that is, the right-hand value) so that multiple assignments like this can be supported:

```
StrType x, y, z;

x = y = z = "test";
```

Concatenation

Concatenation of two strings is accomplished by using the **+** operator. The **StrType** class allows for the following three distinct concatenation situations:

- Concatenation of a **StrType** object with another **StrType** object
- Concatenation of a **StrType** object with a quoted string
- Concatenation of a quoted string with a **StrType** object

When used in these situations, the **+** operator produces as its outcome a **StrType** object that is the concatenation of its two operands. It does not actually modify either operand.

The overloaded **operator+( )** functions are shown here:

```
// Concatenate two StrType objects.
StrType StrType::operator+(StrType &o)
{
  int len;
  StrType temp;

  delete [] temp.p;
  len = strlen(o.p) + strlen(p) + 1;
  temp.size = len;
  try {
    temp.p = new char[len];
  } catch (bad_alloc xa) {
    cout << "Allocation error\n";
    exit(1);
  }
  strcpy(temp.p, p);

  strcat(temp.p, o.p);

  return temp;
}

// Concatenate a StrType object and a quoted string.
StrType StrType::operator+(char *s)
{
  int len;
  StrType temp;

  delete [] temp.p;

  len = strlen(s) + strlen(p) + 1;
  temp.size = len;
  try {
    temp.p = new char[len];
  } catch (bad_alloc xa) {
    cout << "Allocation error\n";
```

```
      exit(1);
    }
    strcpy(temp.p, p);

    strcat(temp.p, s);

    return temp;
}


// Concatenate a quoted string and a StrType object.
StrType operator+(char *s, StrType &o)
{
    int len;
    StrType temp;

    delete [] temp.p;

    len = strlen(s) + strlen(o.p) + 1;
    temp.size = len;
    try {
      temp.p = new char[len];
    } catch (bad_alloc xa) {
      cout << "Allocation error\n";
      exit(1);
    }
    strcpy(temp.p, s);

    strcat(temp.p, o.p);

    return temp;
}
```

All three functions work basically in the same way. First, a temporary **StrType** object called **temp** is created. This object will contain the outcome of the concatenation, and it is the object returned by the functions. Next, the memory pointed to by **temp.p** is freed. The reason for this is that when **temp** is created, only 1 byte of memory is allocated (as a placeholder) because there is no explicit initialization. Next, enough memory is allocated to hold the concatenation of the two strings. Finally, the two strings are copied into the memory pointed to by **temp.p**, and **temp** is returned.

Substring Subtraction

A useful string function not found in **basic_string** is *substring subtraction*. As implemented by the **StrType** class, substring subtraction removes all occurrences of a specified substring from another string. Substring subtraction is accomplished by using the – operator.

The **StrType** class supports two cases of substring subtraction. One allows a **StrType** object to be subtracted from another **StrType** object. The other allows a quoted string to be removed from a **StrType** object. The two **operator–( )** functions are shown here:

```
// Subtract a substring from a string using StrType objects.
StrType StrType::operator-(StrType &substr)
{
  StrType temp(p);
  char *s1;
  int i, j;

  s1 = p;
  for(i=0; *s1; i++) {
    if(*s1!=*substr.p) { // if not first letter of substring
      temp.p[i] = *s1;   // then copy into temp
      s1++;
    }
    else {
      for(j=0; substr.p[j]==s1[j] && substr.p[j]; j++) ;
      if(!substr.p[j]) { // is substring, so remove it
        s1 += j;
        i--;
      }
      else { // is not substring, continue copying
        temp.p[i] = *s1;
        s1++;
      }
    }
  }
  temp.p[i] = '\0';
  return temp;
}

// Subtract quoted string from a StrType object.
StrType StrType::operator-(char *substr)
{
  StrType temp(p);
```

```
    char *s1;
    int i, j;

    s1 = p;
    for(i=0; *s1; i++) {
      if(*s1!=*substr) { // if not first letter of substring
        temp.p[i] = *s1; // then copy into temp
        s1++;
      }
      else {
        for(j=0; substr[j]==s1[j] && substr[j]; j++) ;
        if(!substr[j]) { // is substring, so remove it
          s1 += j;
          i--;
        }
        else { // is not substring, continue copying
          temp.p[i] = *s1;
          s1++;
        }
      }
    }
    temp.p[i] = '\0';
    return temp;
}
```

These functions work by copying the contents of the left-hand operand into **temp**, removing any occurrences of the substring specified by the right-hand operand during the process. The resulting **StrType** object is returned. Understand that neither operand is modified by the process.

The **StrType** class allows substring subtractions like these:

```
StrType x("I like C++"), y("like");
StrType z;

z = x - y; // z will contain "I C++"

z = x - "C++"; // z will contain "I like "

// multiple occurrences are removed
z = "ABCDABCD";
x = z -"A"; // x contains "BCDBCD"
```

The Relational Operators

The **StrType** class supports the full range of relational operations to be applied to strings. The overloaded relational operators are defined within the **StrType** class declaration. They are repeated here for your convenience:

```
// relational operations between StrType objects
int operator==(StrType &o) { return !strcmp(p, o.p); }
int operator!=(StrType &o) { return strcmp(p, o.p); }
int operator<(StrType &o) { return strcmp(p, o.p) < 0; }
int operator>(StrType &o) { return strcmp(p, o.p) > 0; }
int operator<=(StrType &o) { return strcmp(p, o.p) <= 0; }
int operator>=(StrType &o) { return strcmp(p, o.p) >= 0; }


// operations between StrType objects and quoted strings
int operator==(char *s) { return !strcmp(p, s); }
int operator!=(char *s) { return strcmp(p, s); }
int operator<(char *s) { return strcmp(p, s) < 0; }
int operator>(char *s) { return strcmp(p, s) > 0; }
int operator<=(char *s) { return strcmp(p, s) <= 0; }
int operator>=(char *s) { return strcmp(p, s) >= 0; }
```

The relational operations are very straightforward; you should have no trouble understanding their implementation. However, keep in mind that the **StrType** class implements comparisons between two **StrType** objects or comparisons that have a **StrType** object as the left operand and a quoted string as the right operand. If you want to be able to put the quoted string on the left and a **StrType** object on the right, you will need to add additional relational functions.

Given the overloaded relational operator functions defined by **StrType**, the following types of string comparisons are allowed:

```
StrType x("one"), y("two"), z("three");

if(x < y) cout << "x less than y";

if(z=="three")  cout << "z equals three";

y = "o";
z = "ne";
if(x==(y+z)) cout << "x equals y+z";
```

Miscellaneous String Functions

The **StrType** class defines three functions that make **StrType** objects integrate more completely with the C++ programming environment. They are **strsize( )**, **makestr( )**, and the conversion function **operator char *( )**. These functions are defined within the **StrType** declaration and are shown here:

```
int strsize() { return strlen(p); } // return size of string
void makestr(char *s) { strcpy(s, p); } // make quoted string
operator char *(){ return p; } // conversion to char *
```

The first two functions are easy to understand. As you can see, the **strsize( )** function returns the length of the string pointed to by **p**. Since the length of the string might be different than the value stored in the **size** variable (because of an assignment of a shorter string, for example), the length is computed by calling **strlen( )**. The **makestr( )** function copies into a character array the string pointed to by **p**. This function is useful when you want to obtain a null-terminated string given a **StrType** object.

The conversion function **operator char *( )** returns **p**, which is, of course, a pointer to the string contained within the object. This function allows a **StrType** object to be used anywhere that a null-terminated string can be used. For example, this is valid code:

```
StrType x("Hello");
char s[20];

// copy a string object using the strcpy() function
strcpy(s, x); // automatic conversion to char *
```

Recall that a conversion function is automatically executed when an object is involved in an expression for which the conversion is defined. In this case, because the prototype for the **strcpy( )** function tells the compiler that its second argument is of type **char ***, the conversion from **StrType** to **char *** is automatically performed, causing a pointer to the string contained within **x** to be returned. This pointer is then used by **strcpy( )** to copy the string into **s**. Because of the conversion function, you can use an **StrType** object in place of a null-terminated string as an argument to any function that takes an argument of type **char ***.

Note
> *The conversion to **char** * does circumvent encapsulation, because once a function has a pointer to the object's string, it is possible for that function to modify the string directly, bypassing the **StrType** member functions and without that object's knowledge. For this reason, you must use the conversion to **char** * with care. You can prevent the underlying string from being modified by having the conversion to **char** * return a **const** pointer. With this approach, encapsulation is preserved. You might want to try this change on your own.*

The Entire StrType Class

Here is a listing of the entire **StrType** class along with a short **main( )** function that demonstrates its features:

```
#include <iostream>
#include <new>
#include <cstring>
#include <cstdlib>
using namespace std;

class StrType {
  char *p;
  int size;
public:
  StrType();
  StrType(char *str);
  StrType(const StrType &o); // copy constructor

  ~StrType() { delete [] p; }

  friend ostream &operator<<(ostream &stream, StrType &o);
  friend istream &operator>>(istream &stream, StrType &o);

  StrType operator=(StrType &o); // assign a StrType object
  StrType operator=(char *s); // assign a quoted string

  StrType operator+(StrType &o); // concatenate a StrType object
  StrType operator+(char *s); // concatenate a quoted string
  friend StrType operator+(char *s, StrType &o); /*  concatenate
                  a quoted string with a StrType object */
```

```
   StrType operator-(StrType &o); // subtract a substring
   StrType operator-(char *s); // subtract a quoted substring

   // relational operations between StrType objects
   int operator==(StrType &o) { return !strcmp(p, o.p); }
   int operator!=(StrType &o) { return strcmp(p, o.p); }
   int operator<(StrType &o) { return strcmp(p, o.p) < 0; }
   int operator>(StrType &o) { return strcmp(p, o.p) > 0; }
   int operator<=(StrType &o) { return strcmp(p, o.p) <= 0; }
   int operator>=(StrType &o) { return strcmp(p, o.p) >= 0; }

   // operations between StrType objects and quoted strings
   int operator==(char *s) { return !strcmp(p, s); }
   int operator!=(char *s) { return strcmp(p, s); }
   int operator<(char *s) { return strcmp(p, s) < 0; }
   int operator>(char *s) { return strcmp(p, s) > 0; }
   int operator<=(char *s) { return strcmp(p, s) <= 0; }
   int operator>=(char *s) { return strcmp(p, s) >= 0; }

   int strsize() { return strlen(p); } // return size of string
   void makestr(char *s) { strcpy(s, p); } // null-terminated string
   operator char *() { return p; } // conversion to char *
};

// No explicit initialization.
StrType::StrType() {
  size = 1; // make room for null terminator
  try {
    p = new char[size];
  } catch (bad_alloc xa) {
    cout << "Allocation error\n";
    exit(1);
  }
  strcpy(p, "");
}

// Initialize using a quoted string.
StrType::StrType(char *str) {
  size = strlen(str) + 1; // make room for null terminator
  try {
    p = new char[size];
  } catch (bad_alloc xa) {
```

```
      cout << "Allocation error\n";
      exit(1);
   }
   strcpy(p, str);
}

// Initialize using a StrType object.
StrType::StrType(const StrType &o) {
   size = o.size;
   try {
      p = new char[size];
   } catch (bad_alloc xa) {
      cout << "Allocation error\n";
      exit(1);
   }
   strcpy(p, o.p);
}

// Output a string.
ostream &operator<<(ostream &stream, StrType &o)
{
   stream << o.p;
   return stream;
}

// Input a string.
istream &operator>>(istream &stream, StrType &o)
{
   char t[255]; // arbitrary size - change if necessary
   int len;

   stream.getline(t, 255);
   len = strlen(t) + 1;

   if(len > o.size) {
      delete [] o.p;
      try {
         o.p = new char[len];
      } catch (bad_alloc xa) {
         cout << "Allocation error\n";
         exit(1);
      }
```

```
    o.size = len;
  }
  strcpy(o.p, t);
  return stream;
}

// Assign a StrType object to a StrType object.
StrType StrType::operator=(StrType &o)
{
  StrType temp(o.p);

  if(o.size > size) {
    delete [] p; // free old memory
    try {
      p = new char[o.size];
    } catch (bad_alloc xa) {
      cout << "Allocation error\n";
      exit(1);
    }
    size = o.size;
  }

  strcpy(p, o.p);
  strcpy(temp.p, o.p);

  return temp;
}

// Assign a quoted string to a StrType object.
StrType StrType::operator=(char *s)
{
  int len = strlen(s) + 1;
  if(size < len) {
    delete [] p;
    try {
      p = new char[len];
    } catch (bad_alloc xa) {
      cout << "Allocation error\n";
      exit(1);
    }
    size = len;
  }
```

```
    strcpy(p, s);
    return *this;
}

// Concatenate two StrType objects.
StrType StrType::operator+(StrType &o)
{
  int len;
  StrType temp;

  delete [] temp.p;
  len = strlen(o.p) + strlen(p) + 1;
  temp.size = len;
  try {
    temp.p = new char[len];
  } catch (bad_alloc xa) {
    cout << "Allocation error\n";
    exit(1);
  }
  strcpy(temp.p, p);

  strcat(temp.p, o.p);

  return temp;
}

// Concatenate a StrType object and a quoted string.
StrType StrType::operator+(char *s)
{
  int len;
  StrType temp;

  delete [] temp.p;

  len = strlen(s) + strlen(p) + 1;
  temp.size = len;
  try {
    temp.p = new char[len];
  } catch (bad_alloc xa) {
    cout << "Allocation error\n";
    exit(1);
  }
```

```
    strcpy(temp.p, p);

    strcat(temp.p, s);

    return temp;
}

// Concatenate a quoted string and a StrType object.
StrType operator+(char *s, StrType &o)
{
    int len;
    StrType temp;

    delete [] temp.p;

    len = strlen(s) + strlen(o.p) + 1;
    temp.size = len;
    try {
        temp.p = new char[len];
    } catch (bad_alloc xa) {
        cout << "Allocation error\n";
        exit(1);
    }
    strcpy(temp.p, s);

    strcat(temp.p, o.p);

    return temp;
}

// Subtract a substring from a string using StrType objects.
StrType StrType::operator-(StrType &substr)
{
    StrType temp(p);
    char *s1;
    int i, j;

    s1 = p;
    for(i=0; *s1; i++) {
        if(*s1!=*substr.p) { // if not first letter of substring
            temp.p[i] = *s1;   // then copy into temp
            s1++;
```

```
    }
    else {
      for(j=0; substr.p[j]==s1[j] && substr.p[j]; j++) ;
      if(!substr.p[j]) { // is substring, so remove it
        s1 += j;
        i--;
      }
      else { // is not substring, continue copying
        temp.p[i] = *s1;
        s1++;
      }
    }
  }
  temp.p[i] = '\0';
  return temp;
}


// Subtract quoted string from a StrType object.
StrType StrType::operator-(char *substr)
{
  StrType temp(p);
  char *s1;
  int i, j;

  s1 = p;
  for(i=0; *s1; i++) {
    if(*s1!=*substr) { // if not first letter of substring
      temp.p[i] = *s1; // then copy into temp
      s1++;
    }
    else {
      for(j=0; substr[j]==s1[j] && substr[j]; j++) ;
      if(!substr[j]) { // is substring, so remove it
        s1 += j;
        i--;
      }
      else { // is not substring, continue copying
        temp.p[i] = *s1;
        s1++;
      }
    }
  }
```

```cpp
    temp.p[i] = '\0';
    return temp;
}

int main()
{
  StrType s1("A sample session using string objects.\n");
  StrType s2(s1);
  StrType s3;
  char s[80];

  cout << s1 << s2;

  s3 = s1;
  cout << s1;

  s3.makestr(s);
  cout << "Convert to a string: " << s;

  s2 = "This is a new string.";
  cout << s2 << endl;

  StrType s4(" So is this.");
  s1 = s2+s4;
  cout << s1 << endl;

  if(s2==s3) cout << "Strings are equal.\n";
  if(s2!=s3) cout << "Strings are not equal.\n";
  if(s1<s4) cout << "s1 less than s4\n";
  if(s1>s4) cout << "s1 greater than s4\n";
  if(s1<=s4) cout << "s1 less than or equals s4\n";
  if(s1>=s4) cout << "s1 greater than or equals s4\n";

  if(s2 > "ABC") cout << "s2 greater than ABC\n\n";

  s1 = "one two three one two three\n";
  s2 = "two";
  cout << "Initial string: " << s1;
  cout << "String after subtracting two: ";
  s3 = s1 - s2;
  cout << s3;
```

```
cout << endl;
s4 = "Hi there!";
s3 = s4 + " C++ strings are fun\n";
cout << s3;
s3 = s3 - "Hi there!";
s3 = "Aren't" + s3;
cout << s3;

s1 = s3 - "are ";
cout << s1;
s3 = s1;

cout << "Enter a string: ";
cin >> s1;
cout << s1 << endl;
cout << "s1 is " << s1.strsize() << " characters long.\n";

puts(s1); // convert to char *

s1 = s2 = s3;
cout << s1 << s2 << s3;

s1 = s2 = s3 = "Bye ";
cout << s1 << s2 << s3;

return 0;
}
```

The preceding program produces this output:

```
A sample session using string objects.
A sample session using string objects.
A sample session using string objects.
Convert to a string: A sample session using string objects.
This is a new string.
This is a new string. So is this.
Strings are not equal.
s1 greater than s4
s1 greater than or equals s4
s2 greater than ABC
```

```
Initial string: one two three one two three
String after subtracting two: one   three one   three

Hi there! C++ strings are fun
Aren't C++ strings are fun
Aren't C++ strings fun
Enter a string: I like C++
s1 is 10 characters long.
I like C++
Aren't C++ strings fun
Aren't C++ strings fun
Aren't C++ strings fun
Bye Bye Bye
```

This output assumes that the string "I like C++" was entered by the user when prompted for input.

To have easy access to the **StrType** class, remove the **main( )** function and put the rest of the preceding listing into a file called STR.H. Then, just include this header file with any program in which you want to use **StrType**.

Using the StrType Class

To conclude this chapter, two short examples are given that illustrate the **StrType** class. As you will see, because of the operators defined for it and because of its conversion function to **char ***, **StrType** is fully integrated into the C++ programming environment. That is, it can be used like any other type defined by Standard C++.

The first example creates a simple thesaurus by using **StrType** objects. It first creates a two-dimensional array of **StrType** objects. Within each pair of strings, the first contains the key word, which may be looked up. The second string contains a list of alternative or related words. The program prompts for a word, and if the word is in the thesaurus, alternatives are displayed. This program is very simple, but notice how clean and clear the string handling is because of the use of the **StrType** class and its operators. (Remember, the header file STR.H contains the **StrType** class.)

```
#include "str.h"
#include <iostream>
using namespace std;

StrType thesaurus[][2] = {
  "book", "volume, tome",
```

```
    "store", "merchant, shop, warehouse",
    "pistol", "gun, handgun, firearm",
    "run", "jog, trot, race",
    "think", "muse, contemplate, reflect",
    "compute", "analyze, work out, solve",
    "", ""
};

int main()
{
  StrType x;

  cout << "Enter word: ";
  cin >> x;

  int i;
  for(i=0; thesaurus[i][0]!=""; i++)
    if(thesaurus[i][0]==x) cout << thesaurus[i][1];

  return 0;
}
```

The next example uses a **StrType** object to check if there is an executable version of a program, given its filename. To use the program, specify the filename without an extension on the command line. The program then repeatedly tries to find an executable file by that name by adding an extension, trying to open that file, and reporting the results. (If the file does not exist, it cannot be opened.) After each extension is tried, the extension is subtracted from the filename and a new extension is added. Again, the **StrType** class and its operators make the string manipulations clean and easy to follow.

```
#include "str.h"
#include <iostream>
#include <fstream>
using namespace std;

// executable file extensions
char ext[3][4] = {
  "EXE",
  "COM",
  "BAT"
};
```

```
int main(int argc, char *argv[])
{
  StrType fname;
  int i;

  if(argc!=2) {
    cout << "Usage: fname\n";
    return 1;
  }

  fname = argv[1];

  fname = fname + "."; // add period
  for(i=0; i<3; i++) {
    fname = fname + ext[i]; // add extension
    cout << "Trying " << fname << " ";
    ifstream f(fname);
    if(f) {
      cout << "- Exists\n";
      f.close();
    }
    else cout << "- Not found\n";
    fname = fname - ext[i]; // subtract extension
  }

  return 0;
}
```

For example, if this program is called ISEXEC, and assuming that TEST.EXE exists, the command line **ISEXEC TEST** produces this output:

```
Trying TEST.EXE - Exists
Trying TEST.COM - Not found
Trying TEST.BAT - Not found
```

One thing to notice about the program is that an **StrType** object is used by the **ifstream** constructor. This works because the conversion function **char *( )** is automatically invoked. As this situation illustrates, by the careful application of C++ features, you can achieve significant integration between C++'s standard types and types that you create.

Creating and Integrating New Types in General

As the **StrType** class has demonstrated, it is actually quite easy to create and integrate a new data type into the C++ environment. To do so, just follow these steps.

1. Overload all appropriate operators, including the I/O operators.

2. Define all appropriate conversion functions.

3. Provide constructors that allow objects to be easily created in a variety of situations.

Part of the power of C++ is its extensibility. Don't be afraid to take advantage of it.

A Challenge

Here is an interesting challenge that you might enjoy. Try implementing **StrType** using the STL. That is, use a container to store the characters that comprise a string. Use iterators to operate on the strings, and use the algorithms to perform the various string manipulations.

Chapter 40

Parsing Expressions

While Standard C++ is quite extensive, there are still a few things that it does not provide. In this chapter we will examine one of them: the *expression parser*. An expression parser is used to evaluate an algebraic expression, such as (10 – 8) * 3. Expression parsers are quite useful and are applicable to a wide range of applications. They are also one of programming's more elusive entities. For various reasons, the procedures used to create an expression parser are not widely taught or disseminated. Indeed, many otherwise accomplished programmers are mystified by the process of expression parsing.

Expression parsing is actually very straightforward, and in many ways easier than other programming tasks. The reason for this is that the task is well defined and works according to the strict rules of algebra. This chapter will develop what is commonly referred to as a *recursive-descent parser* and all the necessary support routines that enable you to evaluate numeric expressions. Three versions of the parser will be created. The first two are nongeneric versions. The final one is generic and may be applied to any numeric type. However, before any parser can be developed, a brief overview of expressions and parsing is necessary.

Expressions

Since an expression parser evaluates an algebraic expression, it is important to understand what the constituent parts of an expression are. Although expressions can be made up of all types of information, this chapter deals only with numeric expressions. For our purposes, numeric expressions are composed of the following items:

- Numbers
- The operators +, –, /, *, ^, %, =
- Parentheses
- Variables

For our parser, the operator ^ indicates exponentiation (not the XOR as it does in C++), and = is the assignment operator. These items can be combined in expressions according to the rules of algebra. Here are some examples:

10 – 8

(100 – 5) * 14 / 6

a + b – c

10^5

a = 10 – b

Assume this precedence for each operator:

highest   + − (unary)

                 ^

                 * / %

                 + −

lowest   =

Operators of equal precedence evaluate from left to right.

In the examples in this chapter, all variables are single letters (in other words, 26 variables, **A** through **Z**, are available). The variables are not case sensitive (**a** and **A** are treated as the same variable). For the first version of the parser, all numeric values are elevated to **double**, although you could easily write the routines to handle other types of values. Finally, to keep the logic clear and easy to understand, only a minimal amount of error checking is included.

Parsing Expressions: The Problem

If you have not thought much about the problem of expression parsing, you might assume that it is a simple task. However, to better understand the problem, try to evaluate this sample expression:

10 − 2 * 3

You know that this expression is equal to the value 4. Although you could easily create a program that would compute that *specific* expression, the question is how to create a program that gives the correct answer for any *arbitrary* expression. At first you might think of a routine something like this:

```
a = get first operand
while(operands present) {
    op = get operator
    b = get second operand
    a = a op b
}
```

This routine gets the first operand, the operator, and the second operand to perform the first operation and then gets the next operator and operand to perform the next operation, and so on. However, if you use this basic approach, the expression 10 – 2 * 3 evaluates to 24 (that is, 8 * 3) instead of 4 because this procedure neglects the precedence of the operators. You cannot just take the operands and operators in order from left to right because the rules of algebra dictate that multiplication must be done before subtraction. Some beginners think that this problem can be easily overcome, and sometimes, in very restricted cases, it can. But the problem only gets worse when you add parentheses, exponentiation, variables, unary operators, and the like.

Although there are a few ways to write a routine that evaluates expressions, the one developed here is the one most easily written by a person. It is also the most common. The method used here is called a *recursive-descent parser*, and in the course of this chapter you will see how it got its name. (Some of the other methods used to write parsers employ complex tables that must be generated by another computer program. These are sometimes called *table-driven parsers*.)

Parsing an Expression

There are a number of ways to parse and evaluate an expression. For use with a recursive-descent parser, think of expressions as *recursive data structures*—that is, expressions that are defined in terms of themselves. If, for the moment, we assume that expressions can only use +, –, *, /, and parentheses, all expressions can be defined with the following rules:

expression –> term [+ term] [– term]

term –> factor [* factor] [/ factor]

factor –> variable, number, or (expression)

The square brackets designate an optional element, and the –> means *produces*. In fact, the rules are usually called the *production rules* of the expression. Therefore, you could say: "Term produces factor times factor or factor divided by factor" for the definition of *term*. Notice that the precedence of the operators is implicit in the way an expression is defined.

The expression

10 + 5 * B

has two terms: 10, and 5 * B. The second term contains two factors: 5 and B. These factors consist of one number and one variable.

On the other hand, the expression

14 * (7 − C)

has two factors: 14 and (7−C). The factors consist of one number and one parenthesized expression. The parenthesized expression contains two terms: one number and one variable.

This process forms the basis for a recursive-descent parser, which is a set of mutually recursive functions that work in a chainlike fashion and implement the production rules. At each appropriate step, the parser performs the specified operations in the algebraically correct sequence. To see how the production rules are used to parse an expression, let's work through an example using this expression:

9/3 − (100 + 56)

Here is the sequence that you will follow:

1. Get the first term, 9/3.

2. Get each factor and divide the integers. The resulting value is 3.

3. Get the second term, (100 + 56). At this point, start recursively analyzing the second subexpression.

4. Get each term and add. The resulting value is 156.

5. Return from the recursive call, and subtract 156 from 3. The answer is −153.

If you are a little confused at this point, don't feel bad. This is a fairly complex concept that takes some getting used to. There are two basic things to remember about this recursive view of expressions. First, the precedence of the operators is implicit in the way the production rules are defined. Second, this method of parsing and evaluating expressions is very similar to the way humans evaluate mathematical expressions.

The remainder of this chapter develops three parsers. The first will parse and evaluate floating-point expressions of type **double** that consist only of constant values. Next, this parser is enhanced to support the use of variables. Finally, in the third version, the parser is implemented as a template class that can be used to parse expressions of any type.

The Parser Class

The expression parser is built upon the **parser** class. The first version of **parser** is shown here. Subsequent versions of the parser build upon it.

```cpp
class parser {
  char *exp_ptr;  // points to the expression
  char token[80]; // holds current token
  char tok_type;  // holds token's type

  void eval_exp2(double &result);
  void eval_exp3(double &result);
  void eval_exp4(double &result);
  void eval_exp5(double &result);
  void eval_exp6(double &result);
  void atom(double &result);
  void get_token();
  void serror(int error);
  int isdelim(char c);
public:
  parser();
  double eval_exp(char *exp);
};
```

The **parser** class contains three private member variables. The expression to be evaluated is contained in a null-terminated string pointed to by **exp_ptr**. Thus, the parser evaluates expressions that are contained in standard ASCII strings. For example, the following strings contain expressions that the parser can evaluate:

"10 – 5"

"2 * 3.3 / (3.1416 * 3.3)"

When the parser begins execution, **exp_ptr** must point to the first character in the expression string. As the parser executes, it works its way through the string until the null-terminator is encountered.

The meaning of the other two member variables, **token** and **tok_type**, are described in the next section.

The entry point to the parser is through **eval_exp( )**, which must be called with a pointer to the expression to be analyzed. The functions **eval_exp2( )** through **eval_exp6( )** along with **atom( )** form the recursive-descent parser. They implement an enhanced set of the expression production rules discussed earlier. In subsequent versions of the parser, a function called **eval_exp1( )** will also be added.

The **serror( )** handles syntax errors in the expression. The functions **get_token( )** and **isdelim( )** are used to dissect the expression into its component parts, as described in the next section.

Dissecting an Expression

In order to evaluate expressions, you need to be able to break an expression into its components. Since this operation is fundamental to parsing, let's look at it before examining the parser itself.

Each component of an expression is called a *token*. For example, the expression

A * B − (W + 10)

contains the tokens A, *, B, −, (, W, +, 10, and). Each token represents an indivisible unit of the expression. In general, you need a function that sequentially returns each token in the expression individually. The function must also be able to skip over spaces and tabs and detect the end of the expression. The function that we will use to perform this task is called **get_token( )**, which is a member function of the **parser** class.

Besides the token, itself, you will also need to know what type of token is being returned. For the parser developed in this chapter, you need only three types: **VARIABLE**, **NUMBER**, and **DELIMITER**. (**DELIMITER** is used for both operators and parentheses.)

The **get_token( )** function is shown here. It obtains the next token from the expression pointed to by **exp_ptr** and puts it into the member variable **token**. It puts the type of the token into the member variable **tok_type**.

```
// Obtains the next token.
void parser::get_token()
{
  register char *temp;

  tok_type = 0;
  temp = token;
  *temp = '\0';

  if(!*exp_ptr) return; // at end of expression

  while(isspace(*exp_ptr)) ++exp_ptr; // skip over white space

  if(strchr("+-*/%^=()", *exp_ptr)){
    tok_type = DELIMITER;
```

```
    // advance to next char
    *temp++ = *exp_ptr++;
  }
  else if(isalpha(*exp_ptr)) {
    while(!isdelim(*exp_ptr)) *temp++ = *exp_ptr++;
    tok_type = VARIABLE;
  }
  else if(isdigit(*exp_ptr)) {
    while(!isdelim(*exp_ptr)) *temp++ = *exp_ptr++;
    tok_type = NUMBER;
  }

  *temp = '\0';
}


// Return true if c is a delimiter.
int parser::isdelim(char c)
{
  if(strchr(" +-/*%^=()", c) || c==9 || c=='\r' || c==0)
    return 1;
  return 0;
}
```

Look closely at the preceding functions. After the first few initializations, **get_token( )** checks to see if the null terminating the expression has been found. It does so by checking the character pointed to by **exp_ptr**. Since **exp_ptr** is a pointer to the expression being analyzed, if it points to a null, the end of the expression has been reached. If there are still more tokens to retrieve from the expression, **get_token( )** first skips over any leading spaces. Once the spaces have been skipped, **exp_ptr** is pointing to either a number, a variable, an operator, or if trailing spaces end the expression, a null. If the next character is an operator, it is returned as a string in **token**, and **DELIMITER** is placed in **tok_type**. If the next character is a letter instead, it is assumed to be one of the variables. It is returned as a string in **token**, and **tok_type** is assigned the value **VARIABLE**. If the next character is a digit, the entire number is read and placed in its string form in **token** and its type is **NUMBER**. Finally, if the next character is none of the preceding, it is assumed that the end of the expression has been reached. In this case, **token** is null, which signals the end of the expression.

As stated earlier, to keep the code in this function clean, a certain amount of error checking has been omitted and some assumptions have been made. For example, any unrecognized character may end an expression. Also, in this version, variables may be of any length, but only the first letter is significant. You can add more error checking and other details as your specific application dictates.

To better understand the tokenization process, study what it returns for each token and type in the following expression:

A + 100 – (B * C) /2

Token	Token type
A	VARIABLE
+	DELIMITER
100	NUMBER
–	DELIMITER
(	DELIMITER
B	VARIABLE
*	DELIMITER
C	VARIABLE
)	DELIMITER
/	DELIMITER
2	NUMBER
null	null

Remember that **token** always holds a null-terminated string, even if it contains just a single character.

A Simple Expression Parser

Here is the first version of the parser. It can evaluate expressions that consist solely of constants, operators, and parentheses. It cannot accept expressions that contain variables.

```
/* This module contains the recursive descent
   parser that does not use variables.
*/

#include <iostream>
#include <cstdlib>
#include <cctype>
#include <cstring>
```

```cpp
using namespace std;

enum types { DELIMITER = 1, VARIABLE, NUMBER};

class parser {
  char *exp_ptr;  // points to the expression
  char token[80]; // holds current token
  char tok_type;  // holds token's type

  void eval_exp2(double &result);
  void eval_exp3(double &result);
  void eval_exp4(double &result);
  void eval_exp5(double &result);
  void eval_exp6(double &result);
  void atom(double &result);
  void get_token();
  void serror(int error);
  int isdelim(char c);
public:
  parser();
  double eval_exp(char *exp);
};

// Parser constructor.
parser::parser()
{
  exp_ptr = NULL;
}

// Parser entry point.
double parser::eval_exp(char *exp)
{
  double result;

  exp_ptr = exp;

  get_token();
  if(!*token) {
    serror(2); // no expression present
    return 0.0;
  }
  eval_exp2(result);
```

```
    if(*token) serror(0); // last token must be null
    return result;
}

// Add or subtract two terms.
void parser::eval_exp2(double &result)
{
  register char op;
  double temp;

  eval_exp3(result);
  while((op = *token) == '+' || op == '-') {
    get_token();
    eval_exp3(temp);
    switch(op) {
      case '-':
        result = result - temp;
        break;
      case '+':
        result = result + temp;
        break;
    }
  }
}

// Multiply or divide two factors.
void parser::eval_exp3(double &result)
{
  register char op;
  double temp;

  eval_exp4(result);
  while((op = *token) == '*' || op == '/' || op == '%') {
    get_token();
    eval_exp4(temp);
    switch(op) {
      case '*':
        result = result * temp;
        break;
      case '/':
        result = result / temp;
        break;
```

```
      case '%':
        result = (int) result % (int) temp;
        break;
    }
  }
}

// Process an exponent.
void parser::eval_exp4(double &result)
{
  double temp, ex;
  register int t;

  eval_exp5(result);
  if(*token== '^') {
    get_token();
    eval_exp4(temp);
    ex = result;
    if(temp==0.0) {
      result = 1.0;
      return;
    }
    for(t=(int)temp-1; t>0; --t) result = result * (double)ex;
  }
}

// Evaluate a unary + or -.
void parser::eval_exp5(double &result)
{
  register char  op;

  op = 0;
  if((tok_type == DELIMITER) && *token=='+' || *token == '-') {
    op = *token;
    get_token();
  }
  eval_exp6(result);
  if(op=='-') result = -result;
}

// Process a parenthesized expression.
void parser::eval_exp6(double &result)
```

```cpp
{
  if((*token == '(')) {
    get_token();
    eval_exp2(result);
    if(*token != ')')
      serror(1);
    get_token();
  }
  else atom(result);
}

// Get the value of a number.
void parser::atom(double &result)
{
  switch(tok_type) {
    case NUMBER:
      result = atof(token);
      get_token();
      return;
    default:
      serror(0);
  }
}

// Display a syntax error.
void parser::serror(int error)
{
  static char *e[]= {
      "Syntax Error",
      "Unbalanced Parentheses",
      "No expression Present"
  };
  cout << e[error] << endl;
}

// Obtain the next token.
void parser::get_token()
{
  register char *temp;

  tok_type = 0;
  temp = token;
```

APPLYING C++

```
  *temp = '\0';

  if(!*exp_ptr) return; // at end of expression

  while(isspace(*exp_ptr)) ++exp_ptr; // skip over white space

  if(strchr("+-*/%^=()", *exp_ptr)){
    tok_type = DELIMITER;
    // advance to next char
    *temp++ = *exp_ptr++;
  }
  else if(isalpha(*exp_ptr)) {
    while(!isdelim(*exp_ptr)) *temp++ = *exp_ptr++;
    tok_type = VARIABLE;
  }
  else if(isdigit(*exp_ptr)) {
    while(!isdelim(*exp_ptr)) *temp++ = *exp_ptr++;
    tok_type = NUMBER;
  }

  *temp = '\0';
}

// Return true if c is a delimiter.
int parser::isdelim(char c)
{
  if(strchr(" +-/*%^=()", c) || c==9 || c=='\r' || c==0)
    return 1;
  return 0;
}
```

The parser as it is shown can handle the following operators: +, –, *, /, %. In addition, it can handle integer exponentiation (^) and the unary minus. The parser can also deal with parentheses correctly. The actual evaluation of an expression takes place in the mutually recursive functions **eval_exp2( )** through **eval_exp6( )**, plus the **atom( )** function, which returns the value of a number. The comments at the start of each function describe what role it plays in parsing the expression.

The simple **main( )** function that follows demonstrates the use of the parser.

```
int main()
{
```

```
       char expstr[80];

       cout << "Enter a period to stop.\n";

       parser ob; // instantiate a parser

       for(;;) {
         cout << "Enter expression: ";
         cin.getline(expstr, 79);
         if(*expstr=='.') break;
         cout << "Answer is: " << ob.eval_exp(expstr) << "\n\n";
       };

       return 0;
     }
```

Here is a sample run.

```
Enter a period to stop.
Enter expression: 10-2*3
Answer is: 4

Enter expression: (10-2)*3
Answer is: 24

Enter expression: 10/3
Answer is: 3.33333

Enter expression: .
```

Understanding the Parser

To understand exactly how the parser evaluates an expression, work through the
following expression. (Assume that **exp_ptr** points to the start of the expression.)

$$10 - 3 * 2$$

When **eval_exp( )**, the entry point into the parser, is called, it gets the first token. If
the token is null, the function prints the message **No Expression Present** and returns.
However, in this case, the token contains the number **10**. Since the first token is not null,
eval_exp2( ) is called. As a result, **eval_exp2( )** calls **eval_exp3( )**, and **eval_exp3( )** calls

eval_exp4( ), which in turn calls **eval_exp5( )**. Then **eval_exp5( )** checks whether the token is a unary plus or minus, which in this case it is not, so **eval_exp6( )** is called. At this point **eval_exp6( )** either recursively calls **eval_exp2( )** (in the case of a parenthesized expression) or calls **atom( )** to find the value of a number. Since the token is not a left parentheses, **atom( )** is executed and **result** is assigned the value 10. Next, another token is retrieved, and the functions begin to return up the chain. Since the token is now the operator –, the functions return up to **eval_exp2( )**.

What happens next is very important. Because the token is –, it is saved in **op**. The parser then gets the next token, which is **3**, and the descent down the chain begins again. As before, **atom( )** is entered. The value 3 is returned in **result**, and the token * is read. This causes a return back up the chain to **eval_exp3( )**, where the final token 2 is read. At this point, the first arithmetic operation occurs—the multiplication of 2 and 3. The result is returned to **eval_exp2( )**, and the subtraction is performed. The subtraction yields the answer 4. Although the process may at first seem complicated, work through some other examples to verify that this method functions correctly every time.

This parser would be suitable for use by a simple desktop calculator, as is illustrated by the previous program. Before it could be used in a computer language, database, or in a sophisticated calculator, however, it would need the ability to handle variables. This is the subject of the next section.

Adding Variables to the Parser

All programming languages, many calculators, and spreadsheets use variables to store values for later use. Before the parser can be used for such applications, it needs to be expanded to include variables. To accomplish this, you need to add several things to the parser. First, of course, are the variables themselves. As stated earlier, we will use the letters **A** through **Z** for variables. The variables will be stored in an array inside the **parser** class. Each variable uses one array location in a 26-element array of **double**s. Therefore, add the following to the **parser** class:

```
double vars[NUMVARS]; // holds variables' values
```

You will also need to change the **parser** constructor, as shown here.

```
// parser constructor
parser::parser()
{
  int i;

  exp_ptr = NULL;
```

```
    for(i=0; i<NUMVARS; i++) vars[i] = 0.0;
}
```

As you can see, the variables are initialized to 0 as a courtesy to the user.

You will also need a function to look up the value of a given variable. Because the variables are named **A** through **Z**, they can easily be used to index the array **vars** by subtracting the ASCII value for **A** from the variable name. The member function **find_var( )**, shown here, accomplishes this:

```
// Return the value of a variable.
double parser::find_var(char *s)
{
  if(!isalpha(*s)){
    serror(1);
    return 0.0;
  }
  return vars[toupper(*token)-'A'];
}
```

As this function is written, it will actually accept long variable names, but only the first letter is significant. You may modify this to fit your needs.

You must also modify the **atom( )** function to handle both numbers and variables. The new version is shown here:

```
// Get the value of a number or a variable.
void parser::atom(double &result)
{
  switch(tok_type) {
    case VARIABLE:
      result = find_var(token);
      get_token();
      return;
    case NUMBER:
      result = atof(token);
      get_token();
      return;
    default:
      serror(0);
  }
}
```

Technically, these additions are all that is needed for the parser to use variables correctly; however, there is no way for these variables to be assigned a value. Often this is done outside the parser, but you can treat the equal sign as an assignment operator (which is how it is handled in C++) and make it part of the parser. There are various ways to do this. One method is to add another function, called **eval_exp1( )**, to the **parser** class. This function will now begin the recursive-descent chain. This means that it, not **eval_exp2( )**, must be called by **eval_exp( )** to begin parsing the expression. **eval_exp1( )** is shown here:

```cpp
// Process an assignment.
void parser::eval_exp1(double &result)
{
  int slot;
  char ttok_type;
  char temp_token[80];

  if(tok_type==VARIABLE) {
    // save old token
    strcpy(temp_token, token);
    ttok_type = tok_type;

    // compute the index of the variable
    slot = toupper(*token) - 'A';

    get_token();
    if(*token != '=') {
      putback(); // return current token
      // restore old token - not assignment
      strcpy(token, temp_token);
      tok_type = ttok_type;
    }
    else {
      get_token(); // get next part of exp
      eval_exp2(result);
      vars[slot] = result;
      return;
    }
  }

  eval_exp2(result);
}
```

As you can see, the function needs to look ahead to determine whether an assignment is actually being made. This is because a variable name always precedes an assignment, but a variable name alone does not guarantee that an assignment expression follows. That is, the parser will accept A = 100 as an assignment, but is also smart enough to know that A/10 is not. To accomplish this, **eval_exp1( )** reads the next token from the input stream. If it is not an equal sign, the token is returned to the input stream for later use by calling **putback( )**. The **putback( )** function must also be included in the **parser** class. It is shown here:

```
// Return a token to the input stream.
void parser::putback()
{
  char *t;

  t = token;
  for(; *t; t++) exp_ptr--;
}
```

After making all the necessary changes, the parser will now look like this.

```
/* This module contains the recursive descent
   parser that recognizes variables.
*/

#include <iostream>
#include <cstdlib>
#include <cctype>
#include <cstring>
using namespace std;

enum types { DELIMITER = 1, VARIABLE, NUMBER};

const int NUMVARS = 26;

class parser {
  char *exp_ptr;  // points to the expression
  char token[80]; // holds current token
  char tok_type;  // holds token's type
  double vars[NUMVARS]; // holds variables' values

  void eval_exp1(double &result);
  void eval_exp2(double &result);
```

```
        void eval_exp3(double &result);
        void eval_exp4(double &result);
        void eval_exp5(double &result);
        void eval_exp6(double &result);
        void atom(double &result);
        void get_token();
        void putback();
        void serror(int error);
        double find_var(char *s);
        int isdelim(char c);
    public:
        parser();
        double eval_exp(char *exp);
    };

    // Parser constructor.
    parser::parser()
    {
        int i;

        exp_ptr = NULL;

        for(i=0; i<NUMVARS; i++) vars[i] = 0.0;
    }

    // Parser entry point.
    double parser::eval_exp(char *exp)
    {
        double result;

        exp_ptr = exp;

        get_token();
        if(!*token) {
            serror(2); // no expression present
            return 0.0;
        }
        eval_exp1(result);
        if(*token) serror(0); // last token must be null
        return result;
    }
```

```cpp
// Process an assignment.
void parser::eval_exp1(double &result)
{
  int slot;
  char ttok_type;
  char temp_token[80];

  if(tok_type==VARIABLE) {
    // save old token
    strcpy(temp_token, token);
    ttok_type = tok_type;

    // compute the index of the variable
    slot = toupper(*token) - 'A';

    get_token();
    if(*token != '=') {
      putback(); // return current token
      // restore old token - not assignment
      strcpy(token, temp_token);
      tok_type = ttok_type;
    }
    else {
      get_token(); // get next part of exp
      eval_exp2(result);
      vars[slot] = result;
      return;
    }
  }

  eval_exp2(result);
}

// Add or subtract two terms.
void parser::eval_exp2(double &result)
{
  register char op;
  double temp;

  eval_exp3(result);
  while((op = *token) == '+' || op == '-') {
    get_token();
```

```cpp
      eval_exp3(temp);
      switch(op) {
        case '-':
          result = result - temp;
          break;
        case '+':
          result = result + temp;
          break;
      }
    }
}

// Multiply or divide two factors.
void parser::eval_exp3(double &result)
{
  register char op;
  double temp;

  eval_exp4(result);
  while((op = *token) == '*' || op == '/' || op == '%') {
    get_token();
    eval_exp4(temp);
    switch(op) {
      case '*':
        result = result * temp;
        break;
      case '/':
        result = result / temp;
        break;
      case '%':
        result = (int) result % (int) temp;
        break;
    }
  }
}

// Process an exponent.
void parser::eval_exp4(double &result)
{
  double temp, ex;
  register int t;
```

```
    eval_exp5(result);
    if(*token== '^') {
      get_token();
      eval_exp4(temp);
      ex = result;
      if(temp==0.0) {
        result = 1.0;
        return;
      }
      for(t=(int)temp-1; t>0; --t) result = result * (double)ex;
    }
}


// Evaluate a unary + or -.
void parser::eval_exp5(double &result)
{
  register char  op;

  op = 0;
  if((tok_type == DELIMITER) && *token=='+' || *token == '-') {
    op = *token;
    get_token();
  }
  eval_exp6(result);
  if(op=='-') result = -result;
}


// Process a parenthesized expression.
void parser::eval_exp6(double &result)
{
  if((*token == '(')) {
    get_token();
    eval_exp2(result);
    if(*token != ')')
      serror(1);
    get_token();
  }
  else atom(result);
}


// Get the value of a number or a variable.
void parser::atom(double &result)
```

```cpp
{
  switch(tok_type) {
    case VARIABLE:
      result = find_var(token);
      get_token();
      return;
    case NUMBER:
      result = atof(token);
      get_token();
      return;
    default:
      serror(0);
  }
}

// Return a token to the input stream.
void parser::putback()
{
  char *t;

  t = token;
  for(; *t; t++) exp_ptr--;
}

// Display a syntax error.
void parser::serror(int error)
{
  static char *e[]= {
      "Syntax Error",
      "Unbalanced Parentheses",
      "No expression Present"
  };
  cout << e[error] << endl;
}

// Obtain the next token.
void parser::get_token()
{
  register char *temp;

  tok_type = 0;
  temp = token;
```

```
  *temp = '\0';

  if(!*exp_ptr) return; // at end of expression

  while(isspace(*exp_ptr)) ++exp_ptr; // skip over white space

  if(strchr("+-*/%^=()", *exp_ptr)){
    tok_type = DELIMITER;
    // advance to next char
    *temp++ = *exp_ptr++;
  }
  else if(isalpha(*exp_ptr)) {
    while(!isdelim(*exp_ptr)) *temp++ = *exp_ptr++;
    tok_type = VARIABLE;
  }
  else if(isdigit(*exp_ptr)) {
    while(!isdelim(*exp_ptr)) *temp++ = *exp_ptr++;
    tok_type = NUMBER;
  }

  *temp = '\0';
}

// Return true if c is a delimiter.
int parser::isdelim(char c)
{
  if(strchr(" +-/*%^=()", c) || c==9 || c=='\r' || c==0)
    return 1;
  return 0;
}

// Return the value of a variable.
double parser::find_var(char *s)
{
  if(!isalpha(*s)){
    serror(1);
    return 0.0;
  }
  return vars[toupper(*token)-'A'];
}
```

To try the enhanced parser, you may use the same **main( )** function that you used for the simple parser. With the enhanced parser, you can now enter expressions like

A = 10/4

A – B

C = A * (F – 21)

Syntax Checking in a Recursive-Descent Parser

Before moving on to the template version of the parser, let's briefly look at syntax checking. In expression parsing, a syntax error is simply a situation in which the input expression does not conform to the strict rules required by the parser. Most of the time, this is caused by human error, usually typing mistakes. For example, the following expressions are not valid for the parsers in this chapter:

10 ** 8

(10 – 5) * 9)

/8

The first contains two operators in a row, the second has unbalanced parentheses, and the last has a division sign at the start of an expression. None of these conditions is allowed by the parsers. Because syntax errors can cause the parser to give erroneous results, you need to guard against them.

As you studied the code of the parsers, you probably noticed the **serror( )** function, which is called under certain situations. Unlike many other parsers, the recursive-descent method makes syntax checking easy because, for the most part, it occurs in **atom( )**, **find_var( )**, or **eval_exp6( )**, where parentheses are checked. The only problem with the syntax checking as it now stands is that the entire parser is not terminated on syntax error. This can lead to multiple error messages.

The best way to implement the **serror( )** function is to have it execute some sort of reset. For example, all C++ compilers come with a pair of companion functions called **setjmp( )** and **longjmp( )**. These two functions allow a program to branch to a *different* function. Therefore, **serror( )** could execute a **longjmp( )** to some safe point in your program outside the parser.

Depending upon the use you put the parser to, you might also find that C++'s exception handling mechanism (implemented through **try**, **catch**, and **throw**) will be beneficial when handling errors.

If you leave the code the way it is, multiple syntax-error messages may be issued. This can be an annoyance in some situations but a blessing in others because multiple errors may be caught. Generally, however, you will want to enhance the syntax checking before using it in commercial programs.

Building a Generic Parser

The two preceding parsers operated on numeric expressions in which all values were assumed to be of type **double**. While this is fine for applications that use **double** values, it is certainly excessive for applications that use only integer values, for example. Also, by hard-coding the type of values being evaluated, the application of the parser is unnecessarily restricted. Fortunately, by using a class template, it is an easy task to create a generic version of the parser that can work with any type of data for which algebraic-style expressions are defined. Once this has been done, the parser can be used both with built-in types and with numeric types that you create.

Here is the generic version of the expression parser.

```cpp
// A generic parser.

#include <iostream>
#include <cstdlib>
#include <cctype>
#include <cstring>
using namespace std;

enum types { DELIMITER = 1, VARIABLE, NUMBER};

const int NUMVARS = 26;

template <class PType> class parser {
  char *exp_ptr;  // points to the expression
  char token[80]; // holds current token
  char tok_type;  // holds token's type
  PType vars[NUMVARS]; // holds variable's values

  void eval_exp1(PType &result);
  void eval_exp2(PType &result);
  void eval_exp3(PType &result);
  void eval_exp4(PType &result);
  void eval_exp5(PType &result);
  void eval_exp6(PType &result);
  void atom(PType &result);
  void get_token(), putback();
  void serror(int error);
  PType find_var(char *s);
  int isdelim(char c);
public:
```

```
    parser();
    PType eval_exp(char *exp);
};

// Parser constructor.
template <class PType> parser<PType>::parser()
{
    int i;

    exp_ptr = NULL;

    for(i=0; i<NUMVARS; i++) vars[i] = (PType) 0;
}

// Parser entry point.
template <class PType> PType parser<PType>::eval_exp(char *exp)
{
    PType result;

    exp_ptr = exp;

    get_token();
    if(!*token) {
        serror(2); // no expression present
        return (PType) 0;
    }
    eval_exp1(result);
    if(*token) serror(0); // last token must be null
    return result;
}

// Process an assignment.
template <class PType> void parser<PType>::eval_exp1(PType &result)
{
    int slot;
    char ttok_type;
    char temp_token[80];

    if(tok_type==VARIABLE) {
        // save old token
        strcpy(temp_token, token);
        ttok_type = tok_type;
```

```
    // compute the index of the variable
    slot = toupper(*token) - 'A';

    get_token();
    if(*token != '=') {
      putback(); // return current token
      // restore old token - not assignment
      strcpy(token, temp_token);
      tok_type = ttok_type;
    }
    else {
      get_token(); // get next part of exp
      eval_exp2(result);
      vars[slot] = result;
      return;
    }
  }

  eval_exp2(result);
}

// Add or subtract two terms.
template <class PType> void parser<PType>::eval_exp2(PType &result)
{
  register char op;
  PType temp;

  eval_exp3(result);
  while((op = *token) == '+' || op == '-') {
    get_token();
    eval_exp3(temp);
    switch(op) {
      case '-':
        result = result - temp;
        break;
      case '+':
        result = result + temp;
        break;
    }
  }
}
```

```cpp
// Multiply or divide two factors.
template <class PType> void parser<PType>::eval_exp3(PType &result)
{
  register char op;
  PType temp;

  eval_exp4(result);
  while((op = *token) == '*' || op == '/' || op == '%') {
    get_token();
    eval_exp4(temp);
    switch(op) {
      case '*':
        result = result * temp;
        break;
      case '/':
        result = result / temp;
        break;
      case '%':
        result = (int) result % (int) temp;
        break;
    }
  }
}

// Process an exponent.
template <class PType> void parser<PType>::eval_exp4(PType &result)
{
  PType temp, ex;
  register int t;

  eval_exp5(result);
  if(*token== '^') {
    get_token();
    eval_exp4(temp);
    ex = result;
    if(temp==0.0) {
      result = (PType) 1;
      return;
    }
    for(t=(int)temp-1; t>0; --t) result = result * ex;
  }
}
```

```cpp
// Evaluate a unary + or -.
template <class PType> void parser<PType>::eval_exp5(PType &result)
{
  register char  op;

  op = 0;
  if((tok_type == DELIMITER) && *token=='+' || *token == '-') {
    op = *token;
    get_token();
  }
  eval_exp6(result);
  if(op=='-') result = -result;
}


// Process a parenthesized expression.
template <class PType> void parser<PType>::eval_exp6(PType &result)
{
  if((*token == '(')) {
    get_token();
    eval_exp2(result);
    if(*token != ')')
      serror(1);
    get_token();
  }
  else atom(result);
}


// Get the value of a number or a variable.
template <class PType> void parser<PType>::atom(PType &result)
{
  switch(tok_type) {
    case VARIABLE:
      result = find_var(token);
      get_token();
      return;
    case NUMBER:
      result = (PType) atof(token);
      get_token();
      return;
    default:
      serror(0);
  }
```

```cpp
}

// Return a token to the input stream.
template <class PType> void parser<PType>::putback()
{
  char *t;

  t = token;
  for(; *t; t++) exp_ptr--;
}

// Display a syntax error.
template <class PType> void parser<PType>::serror(int error)
{
  static char *e[]= {
      "Syntax Error",
      "Unbalanced Parentheses",
      "No expression Present"
  };
  cout << e[error] << endl;
}

// Obtain the next token.
template <class PType> void parser<PType>::get_token()
{
  register char *temp;

  tok_type = 0;
  temp = token;
  *temp = '\0';

  if(!*exp_ptr) return; // at end of expression

  while(isspace(*exp_ptr)) ++exp_ptr; // skip over white space

  if(strchr("+-*/%^=()", *exp_ptr)){
    tok_type = DELIMITER;
    // advance to next char
    *temp++ = *exp_ptr++;
  }
  else if(isalpha(*exp_ptr)) {
    while(!isdelim(*exp_ptr)) *temp++ = *exp_ptr++;
```

```
    tok_type = VARIABLE;
  }
  else if(isdigit(*exp_ptr)) {
    while(!isdelim(*exp_ptr)) *temp++ = *exp_ptr++;
    tok_type = NUMBER;
  }

  *temp = '\0';
}


// Return true if c is a delimiter.
template <class PType> int parser<PType>::isdelim(char c)
{
  if(strchr(" +-/*%^=()", c) || c==9 || c=='\r' || c==0)
    return 1;
  return 0;
}


// Return the value of a variable.
template <class PType> PType parser<PType>::find_var(char *s)
{
  if(!isalpha(*s)){
    serror(1);
    return (PType) 0;
  }
  return vars[toupper(*token)-'A'];
}
```

As you can see, the type of data now operated upon by the parser is specified by the generic type **PType**. The following **main( )** function demonstrates the generic parser.

```
int main()
{
  char expstr[80];

  // Demonstrate floating-point parser.
  parser<double> ob;

  cout << "Floating-point parser.  ";
  cout << "Enter a period to stop\n";
  for(;;) {
```

```
      cout << "Enter expression: ";
      cin.getline(expstr, 79);
      if(*expstr=='.') break;
      cout << "Answer is: " << ob.eval_exp(expstr) << "\n\n";
    }
    cout << endl;

    // Demonstrate integer-based parser.
    parser<int> Iob;

    cout << "Integer parser.  ";
    cout << "Enter a period to stop\n";
    for(;;) {
      cout << "Enter expression: ";
      cin.getline(expstr, 79);
      if(*expstr=='.') break;
      cout << "Answer is: " << Iob.eval_exp(expstr) << "\n\n";
    }

    return 0;
}
```

Here is a sample run.

```
Floating-point parser.  Enter a period to stop
Enter expression: a=10.1
Answer is: 10.1

Enter expression: b=3.2
Answer is: 3.2

Enter expression: a/b
Answer is: 3.15625

Enter expression: .

Integer parser.  Enter a period to stop
Enter expression: a=10
Answer is: 10

Enter expression: b=3
```

```
Answer is: 3

Enter expression: a/b
Answer is: 3

Enter expression: .
```

As you can see, the floating-point parser uses floating-point values, and the integer parser uses integer values.

Some Things to Try

As mentioned early on in this chapter, only minimal error checking is performed by the parser. You might want to add detailed error reporting. For example, you could highlight the point in the expression at which an error was detected. This would allow the user to find and correct a syntax error.

As the parser now stands it can evaluate only numeric expressions. However, with a few additions, it is possible to enable the parser to evaluate other types of expressions, such as strings, spatial coordinates, or complex numbers. For example, to allow the parser to evaluate string objects, you must make the following changes:

1. Define a new token type called STRING.
2. Enhance **get_token( )** so that it recognizes strings.
3. Add a new case inside **atom( )** that handles STRING type tokens.

After implementing these steps, the parser could handle string expressions like these:

> a = "one"
>
> b = "two"
>
> c = a + b

The result in **c** should be the concatenation of **a** and **b**, or "onetwo".

Here is one good application for the parser: create a simple, pop-up mini-calculator that accepts an expression entered by the user and then displays the result. This would make an excellent addition to nearly any commercial application. If you are programming for Windows, this would be especially easy to do.

Appendix A

The .NET Managed
Extensions to C++

M icrosoft's .NET Framework defines an environment that supports the
development and execution of highly-distributed, component-based applications.
It enables differing computer languages to work together, and provides for
security, program portability, and a common programming model for the Windows
platform. Although the .NET Framework is a relatively recent addition to computing,
it is an environment in which many C++ programmers will likely be working in the
near future.

Microsoft's .NET Framework provides a managed environment that oversees
program execution. A program targeted for the .NET Framework is not compiled into
executable object code. Rather, it is compiled into Microsoft Intermediate Language
(MSIL), which is then executed under the control of the Common Language Runtime
(CLR). Managed execution is the mechanism that supports the key advantages offered
by the .NET Framework.

To take advantage of .NET managed execution, it is necessary for a C++ program
to use a set of nonstandard, extended keywords and preprocessor directives that have
been defined by Microsoft. It is important to understand that these extensions are not
defined by ANSI/ISO standard C++. Thus, code in which they are used is nonportable
to other environments.

It is far beyond the scope of this book to describe the .NET Framework, or the C++
programming techniques necessary to utilize it. (A thorough explanation of the .NET
Framework and how to create C++ code for it would easily fill a large book!) However,
a brief synopsis of the .NET managed extensions to C++ is given here for the benefit of
those programmers working in the .NET environment. A basic understanding of the
.NET Framework is assumed.

The .NET Keyword Extensions

To support the .NET managed execution environment, Microsoft adds the following
keywords to the C++ language:

_ _abstract	_ _box	_ _delegate
_ _event	_ _finally	_ _gc
_ _identifier	_ _interface	_ _nogc
_ _pin	_ _property	_ _sealed
_ _try_cast	_ _typeof	_ _value

Each of these is briefly described in the following sections.

_ _abstract

_ _**abstract** is used in conjunction with _ _**gc** to specify an abstract managed class.
No object of an _ _**abstract** class can be created. A class specified as _ _**abstract** is
not required to contain pure virtual functions.

_ _box

_ _**box** wraps a value within an object. Boxing enables a value type to be used by code that requires an object derived from **System::Object**, which is the base class of all .NET objects.

_ _delegate

_ _**delegate** specifies a delegate, which encapsulates a pointer to a function within a managed class (that is, a class modified by _ _**gc**).

_ _event

_ _**event** specifies a function that represents an event. Only the prototype for the function is specified.

_ _finally

_ _**finally** is an addition to the standard C++ exception handling mechanism. It is used to specify a block of code that will execute when a **try/catch** block is left. It does not matter what conditions cause the **try/catch** block to terminate. In all cases, the _ _**finally** block will be executed.

_ _gc

_ _**gc** specifies a managed class. Here, "gc" stands for "garbage collection" and indicates that objects of the class are automatically garbage collected when they are no longer needed. An object is no longer needed when no references to the object exist. Objects of a _ _**gc** class must be created using **new**. Arrays, pointers, and interfaces can also be specified as _ _**gc**.

_ _identifier

_ _**identifier** allows a C++ keyword to be used as an identifier. This is a special-purpose extension that will not be used by most programs.

_ _interface

_ _**interface** specifies a class that will act as an interface. In an interface, no function can include a body. All functions in an interface are implicitly pure virtual functions. Thus, an interface is essentially an abstract class in which no function has an implementation.

_ _nogc

_ _**nogc** specifies a nonmanaged class. Since this is the type of class created by default, the _ _**nogc** keyword is not usually used.

_ _pin

_ _**pin** is used to specify a pointer that fixes the location in memory of the object to which it points. Thus, an object that is "pinned" will not be moved in memory by the garbage collector. As a result, garbage collection does not invalidate a pointer modified by _ _**pin**.

_ _property

_ _**property** specifies a property, which is a member function that gets or sets the value of a member variable. Properties provide a convenient means to control access to private or protected data.

_ _sealed

_ _**sealed** prevents the class that it modifies from being inherited. It can also be used to specify that a virtual function cannot be overridden.

_ _try_cast

_ _**try_cast** attempts to cast one type of expression into another. If the cast fails, an exception of type **System::InvalidCastException** is thrown.

_ _typeof

_ _**typeof** obtains an object that encapsulates type information for a given type. This object is an instance of **System::Type**.

_ _value

_ _**value** specifies a class that is represented as a value type. A value type holds its own values. This differs from a _ _**gc** type, which must allocate storage through the use of **new**. Value types are not subject to garbage collection.

Preprocessor Extensions

To support .NET, Microsoft defines the **#using** preprocessor directive, which is used to import metadata into your program. Metadata contains type and member information in a form that is independent of a specific computer language. Thus, metadata helps support mixed-language programming. All managed C++ programs must import **<mscorlib.dll>**, which contains the metadata for the .NET Framework.

Microsoft defines two pragmas that relate to the .NET Framework. (Pragmas are used with the **#pragma** preprocessing directive.) The first is, **managed**, which specifies managed code. The second is **unmanaged**, which specifies unmanaged (that is, native) code. These pragmas can be used within a program to selectively create managed and unmanaged code.

The attribute Attribute

Microsoft defines **attribute**, which is the attribute used to declare another attribute.

Compiling Managed C++

At the time of this writing, the only compiler commonly available that can target the .NET Framework is the one supplied by Microsoft's Visual Studio .NET. To compile a managed code program, you must use the **/clr** option, which targets code for the Common Language Runtime.

Appendix B

C++ and the
Robotics Age

I have had a long term interest in robotics, especially robotic control languages. In fact, years ago I designed and implemented industrial robotic control languages for use on small educational robots. Although I no longer work professionally in the area of robotics, it remains an important and engaging special interest of mine. Over the years I have seen the capabilities of robots (and the code that controls them) make major leaps forward. We now stand at the beginning of the robotics age. There are already robots that can mow the lawn and vacuum the floor. They assemble our cars and work in environments dangerous to humans. Battlefield robots are now becoming a reality. Many more robotic applications are on the way. As robots become more commonplace, integrating themselves into the fabric of everyday life, increasing numbers of programmers will find themselves writing robotic control code. And, much of that code will be in C++.

C++ is a natural choice for robotic programming because robots require efficient, high-performance code. This is especially true for the low-level motor control routines, and for such things as vision processing, where speed is quite important. Although some parts of a robotic subsystem, such as a natural language processor, may be written in a language such as C#, the low-level code will almost certainly remain in C++. C++ and robotics go hand-in-hand.

If you are interested in robotics, especially if you are interested in creating your own robot for experimentation, then you might find the robot in Figure B-1 of interest. This is my current test robot. Several things make this robot interesting. First, it contains an

Figure B-1.   *A simple, yet effective experimental robot (Photo by Ken Kaiser)*

on-board microprocessor that provides basic motor control and sensor feedback. Second, it contains an RS-232 transceiver that is used to receive instructions from the main computer and return results. This approach enables a remote computer to provide the intensive processing that is necessary in robotics without adding all that weight to the robot, itself. Third, it contains a video camera that is connected to a wireless video transmitter.

The robot is built on a Hobbico M1 Abrams R/C tank chassis. (I have found that the chassis of R/C model tanks and cars often work well as a robot base.) I removed most of the internals from the tank, including the receiver and speed controls, but I kept the motors. The Hobbico tank is well suited for a robotics platform because it is quite strong, the motors are good, it can carry a lot of weight, and its tank treads don't fall off. Also, by using tank treads, the robot has a zero turning radius and can run on uneven ground. The chassis is about 18 inches long and about 8 inches wide.

Once the chassis was empty, I added the following components. To provide on-board control, I used a BASIC Stamp 2, which is a simple, yet powerful microprocessor manufactured by Parallax. Inc. (www.parallaxinc.com). The RS-232 transceiver is also from Parallax, as is the video camera and transmitter. Both the wireless RS-232 transceiver and the video transmitter have a range of about 300 feet. I also added electronic speed controllers for the tank motors. They are of the type used by high-performance R/C cars. They are controlled by the BASIC Stamp microprocessor.

Here is the way the robot works. The remote computer runs the main robotic control program. This program handles all "heavy-duty" processing, such as vision, guidance, and spatial orientation. It can also learn a series of moves and then replay them. The remote computer transmits motion-control instructions (via the wireless RS-232 link) to the robot. The BASIC Stamp receives those instructions and puts them into action. For example, if a "move forward" command is received, the BASIC Stamp sends the proper signals to the electronic speed controllers connected to the motors. When the robot has completed a command, it returns an acknowledgement code. Thus, communication between the remote computer and the robot is bi-directional, and the successful completion of each command can be confirmed.

Because the main processing for the robot occurs on the remote computer, there are no severe limitations to the amount of processing that I can do. For example, at the time of this writing, the robot can follow an object by using its vision system. This capability requires a fair amount of processing that would be difficult to carry on board.

Recently, I have begun work on a robot arm that will be added to the robot. A prototype of the arm is shown in Figure B-2. Although there are several commercial robot arms available to the experimenter and hobbyist, I decided to create my own because I wanted an arm that would be stronger and able to lift heavier objects than was commonly available. The arm uses a stepper motor mounted at its base to turn a long, threaded screw which opens and closes the gripper. This approach allows precise movement along with considerable strength. The arm is controlled by its own Stamp. Thus, the main robot controller simply hands off arm commands to the second Stamp. This allows fully parallel operation of the robot and the arm, and prevents bogging down the main robot controller.

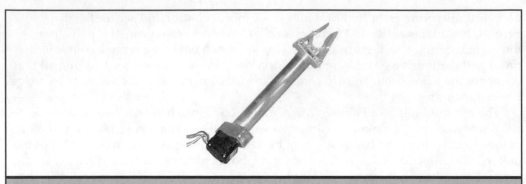

Figure B-2.   *A prototype robot arm (Photo by Ken Kaiser)*

Although the main robotic control code will always remain in C++, I am experimenting with migrating a couple of subsystems, including the RS-232 communication routines, to C#. C# offers a convenient interface to IP data transfers and being able to control the robot from a remote location via the Internet is a tantalizing thought.

Index

INTERNATIONAL CONTACT INFORMATION

AUSTRALIA
McGraw-Hill Book Company Australia Pty. Ltd.
TEL +61-2-9900-1800
FAX +61-2-9878-8881
http://www.mcgraw-hill.com.au
books-it_sydney@mcgraw-hill.com

CANADA
McGraw-Hill Ryerson Ltd.
TEL +905-430-5000
FAX +905-430-5020
http://www.mcgraw-hill.ca

GREECE, MIDDLE EAST, & AFRICA
(Excluding South Africa)
McGraw-Hill Hellas
TEL +30-210-6560-990
TEL +30-210-6560-993
TEL +30-210-6560-994
FAX +30-210-6545-525

MEXICO (Also serving Latin America)
McGraw-Hill Interamericana Editores S.A. de C.V.
TEL +525-117-1583
FAX +525-117-1589
http://www.mcgraw-hill.com.mx
fernando_castellanos@mcgraw-hill.com

SINGAPORE (Serving Asia)
McGraw-Hill Book Company
TEL +65-863-1580
FAX +65-862-3354
http://www.mcgraw-hill.com.sg
mghasia@mcgraw-hill.com

SOUTH AFRICA
McGraw-Hill South Africa
TEL +27-11-622-7512
FAX +27-11-622-9045
robyn_swanepoel@mcgraw-hill.com

SPAIN
McGraw-Hill/Interamericana de España, S.A.U.
TEL +34-91-180-3000
FAX +34-91-372-8513
http://www.mcgraw-hill.es
professional@mcgraw-hill.es

UNITED KINGDOM, NORTHERN,
EASTERN, & CENTRAL EUROPE
McGraw-Hill Education Europe
TEL +44-1-628-502500
FAX +44-1-628-770224
http://www.mcgraw-hill.co.uk
computing_europe@mcgraw-hill.com

ALL OTHER INQUIRIES Contact:
Osborne/McGraw-Hill
TEL +1-510-549-6600
FAX +1-510-883-7600
http://www.osborne.com
omg_international@mcgraw-hill.com